100
Coffee Dishes

100
Coffee Dishes

Susan Locke
and
Heather Lambert

OCTOPUS

Contents

NOTES
Standard spoon measurements are used in all recipes
1 tablespoon = one 15 ml spoon
1 teaspoon = one 5 ml spoon
All spoon measures are level.

Fresh herbs are used unless otherwise stated. If unobtainable, substitute a
bouquet garni of the equivalent dried herbs, or use dried herbs instead but
halve the quantities stated.
Ovens and grills (broilers) should be preheated to the specified temperature
or heat setting.
For all recipes, quantities are given in metric, imperial and American
measures. Follow one set of measures only, because they are not
interchangeable.

First published 1983 by
Octopus Books Limited
59 Grosvenor Street, London W1,
in association with The London Coffee Information Centre, 21 Berners Street,
London W1.

© 1983 Octopus Books Limited

ISBN 0 7064 1957 X

Produced by Mandarin Publishers Ltd
22a Westlands Rd
Quarry Bay, Hong Kong

Printed in Hong Kong

*Frontispiece: Marinated Mushrooms (page 8); Moroccan Chicken (page 20);
Coffee Baked Apples (page 33)*

Introduction

All the delicious recipes in this book have been specially created to show you how versatile coffee can be. There are plenty of super ideas for desserts and cakes, pastries and candies. But coffee is also particularly good in savoury dishes; use it as a marinade for meat or for baking fish and discover the subtle flavour that coffee adds to all kinds of exciting starters and main meals. These recipes are made with delicious freshly-brewed coffee or, in some cases, with instant coffee.

Perfect coffee has a special unique flavour which, once discovered, is never forgotten. It is well worth the little extra trouble required to brew your own perfect cup. There are many excellent methods of brewing coffee all of which produce good coffee. However, there are a few golden rules worth remembering.

Ideally buy freshly roasted beans and grind them at home each time you make some coffee. If this is not possible, have the beans specially ground for you, making sure that the grind is correct for the method you use to brew. To ensure freshness, always buy coffee in small quantities.

The actual flavour and strength of coffee is a matter of personal taste. Experiment with various blends of coffee until you have found a smooth, full-bodied blend that is neither too acid nor too bitter. Above all, be generous with the coffee – a rounded tablespoon per cup is a good guide. Again, it will depend on the grind you require.

All the different methods of brewing produce good coffee. Filter coffee is rapidly becoming one of the most popular methods. Then there is the plunger pot or the expresso pot, again both excellent. The vacuum method and percolator are favourites with many people, while others still insist that the best coffee is made simply in a jug. It really is all a matter of taste.

Whichever coffee-making method you use, there are a number of points to remember. The equipment should be spotlessly clean and the water you use must be fresh cold water. The infusion period should be no more than from three to five minutes. If it is longer, the coffee can become 'over-extracted' which is the bitter taste some people associate with coffee. It is important that coffee should not boil and that it should not be left standing for more than twenty minutes. Drink freshly-brewed coffee as soon as it is ready and give it a stir first. Now that you have discovered these recipes, good coffee need never be wasted again – simply use it to cook any of these exciting dishes.

Coffee is now firmly established as the world's most popular beverage. Like so many of the best things in life, the ideal cup of coffee is as YOU like it!

Starters

Party Terrine

METRIC/IMPERIAL	AMERICAN
350 g/12 oz minced veal	¾ lb ground veal
225 g/8 oz cooked gammon, minced	½ lb ground cooked ham (about 1 cup)
225 g/8 oz chicken livers, chopped	½ lb chicken livers, chopped
150 ml/¼ pint strong black coffee	¾ cup strong black coffee
1 egg, beaten	1 egg, beaten
2 tablespoons single cream	2 tablespoons light cream
2 tablespoons sherry	2 tablespoons sherry
1 tablespoon chopped fresh basil	1 tablespoon chopped fresh basil
1 clove garlic, crushed	1 clove garlic, crushed
salt and freshly ground pepper	salt and freshly ground pepper
Garnish	**Garnish**
parsley sprigs	parsley sprigs
cucumber slices	cucumber slices

Combine the veal, gammon (ham) and chicken livers. Add the remaining ingredients, with salt and pepper to taste, and mix well. Pack into a greased 20 cm/8 inch pâté tin or terrine, or 500 g/1 lb (7 × 3 inch) loaf pan, and cover with foil.

Place the tin in a larger tin containing enough hot water to come halfway up the sides of the pâté tin. Cook in a preheated moderate oven (160°C/325°F, Gas Mark 3) for 1½ hours.

Leave to cool in the tin, then put a weight on top and chill well, preferably overnight. Turn out and garnish with parsley sprigs and cucumber slices. Serve with wholemeal (wholewheat) toast.
Serves 8 to 10

Savoury Coffee Chestnut Loaf

METRIC/IMPERIAL	AMERICAN
Pastry:	**Dough:**
225 g/8 oz plain flour	2 cups all-purpose flour
¼ teaspoon salt	¼ teaspoon salt
100 g/4 oz unsalted butter	½ cup unsalted butter
beaten egg to glaze	beaten egg for glaze
Filling:	**Filling:**
25 g/1 oz butter	2 tablespoons butter
1 onion, chopped	1 onion, chopped
2 cloves garlic, crushed	2 cloves garlic, crushed
1 × 275 g/10 oz can chestnuts, drained and chopped	1 can (10 oz) whole chestnuts, drained and chopped
1 egg	1 egg
1 × 275 g/10 oz can unsweetened chestnut purée	1 can (10 oz) unsweetened chestnut purée
150 ml/¼ pint strong black coffee	¾ cup strong black coffee
salt and pepper	salt and pepper

Sift the flour and salt into a bowl and rub in (cut in) the butter until the mixture resembles breadcrumbs. Mix in enough water to make a firm dough. Chill for 30 minutes.

Melt the butter in a frying pan, add the onion and garlic and fry until softened. Add the chopped chestnuts. Mix together, then remove from the heat and allow to cool. Beat the egg, add the chestnut purée and coffee and mix well together. Combine both chestnut mixtures and season to taste with salt and pepper.

Roll out two-thirds of the dough and line a 23 × 8.5 cm/9 × 3½ inch pâté tin with collapsible sides. Spoon in the chestnut mixture. Roll out the remaining dough and place on top. Brush edges of lid with egg to ensure a good seal. Press down with the end of a knife and decorate with pastry leaves. Brush with egg to glaze.

Cook in a preheated moderate oven (180°C/350°F, Gas Mark 4) for 45 minutes. Leave to cool in the tin before removing the loaf.
Serves 8 to 10

Party Terrine; Savoury Coffee Chestnut Loaf

Marinated Mushrooms

METRIC/IMPERIAL
225 g/8 oz button
  mushrooms,
  trimmed
1 tablespoon lemon
  juice
250 ml/8 fl oz strong
  black coffee
250 ml/8 fl oz
  vegetable oil
120 ml/4 fl oz wine
  vinegar
2 cloves garlic,
  chopped
1 teaspoon brown
  sugar
1 teaspoon coriander
  seeds
salt and freshly
  ground pepper
2 tablespoons
  chopped parsley to
  garnish

AMERICAN
½ lb button
  mushrooms,
  trimmed
1 tablespoon lemon
  juice
1 cup strong black
  coffee
1 cup vegetable oil
½ cup wine vinegar
2 cloves garlic,
  chopped
1 teaspoon brown
  sugar
1 teaspoon coriander
  seeds
salt and freshly
  ground pepper
2 tablespoons
  chopped parsley for
  garnish

Blanch the mushrooms in boiling water, with the lemon juice, for 5 minutes. Drain and leave to cool.

Mix together the remaining ingredients, with salt and pepper to taste. Pour over the cooled mushrooms and leave to marinate for at least 4 hours, or preferably overnight, in the refrigerator. Sprinkle with the parsley before serving.
Serves 6

Iced Coffee Cucumber Soup

METRIC/IMPERIAL
1 cucumber, peeled
1 onion, chopped
600 ml/1 pint milk
150 ml/¼ pint
  medium strength
  black coffee
salt and freshly
  ground pepper
40 g/1½ oz butter
25 g/1 oz plain flour
1 teaspoon chopped
  fresh mint or
  ½ teaspoon dried
  mint
150 ml/¼ pint single
  cream

AMERICAN
1 cucumber, peeled
1 onion, chopped
2½ cups milk
¾ cup medium
  strength black
  coffee
salt and freshly
  ground pepper
3 tablespoons butter
¼ cup all-purpose
  flour
1 teaspoon chopped
  fresh mint or
  ½ teaspoon dried
  mint
¾ cup light cream

Set aside one-third of the cucumber. Chop the remaining cucumber roughly and place in a saucepan with the onion, milk, coffee and salt and pepper to taste. Simmer gently until the vegetables are soft. Cool, then purée the mixture in a blender or food processor, or sieve it, until smooth.

Melt the butter in a clean saucepan, stir in the flour and cook for 2 minutes. Gradually add the puréed cucumber mixture and mint, stirring well. Bring to the boil and simmer for 5 to 6 minutes. Pour into a mixing bowl and allow the soup to cool, then chill well.

Dice the reserved cucumber and spread out on a plate. Sprinkle with a little salt and chill.

When ready to serve, whisk the cream into the soup and pour into individual soup bowls. Drain the excess liquid from the diced cucumber and divide between the bowls.
Serves 4 to 6

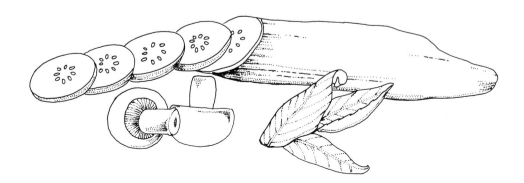

Stuffed Tomatoes

METRIC/IMPERIAL	AMERICAN
6 large tomatoes	6 large tomatoes
25 g/1 oz butter	2 tablespoons butter
1 onion, chopped	1 onion, chopped
1 clove garlic, chopped	1 clove garlic, chopped
50 g/2 oz walnuts, ground	½ cup ground walnuts
50 g/2 oz fresh breadcrumbs	1 cup soft bread crumbs
3 tablespoons strong black coffee	3 tablespoons strong black coffee
1 tablespoon vegetable oil	1 tablespoon vegetable oil
1 tablespoon chopped fresh basil	1 tablespoon chopped fresh basil
salt and freshly ground pepper	salt and freshly ground pepper
25 g/1 oz sesame seeds	2 tablespoons sesame seeds
6 lettuce leaves to serve	6 lettuce leaves to serve

Carefully cut the tops off the tomatoes. Spoon out the seeds and membrane and discard.

Melt the butter in a frying pan, add the onion and garlic and fry until softened. Remove from the heat and mix in the walnuts, breadcrumbs, coffee, oil, basil and salt and pepper to taste. Stuff the tomatoes with the mixture and sprinkle a few sesame seeds on top of each.

Cook in a preheated moderate oven (180°C/350°F, Gas Mark 4) for 30 minutes. Serve each tomato on a lettuce leaf.
Serves 6

Creamy Haddock Pâté

METRIC/IMPERIAL	AMERICAN
450 g/1 lb haddock fillets	1 lb haddock fillets
150 ml/¼ pint strong black coffee	¾ cup strong black coffee
150 ml/¼ pint milk	¾ cup milk
20 g/¾ oz butter	1½ tablespoons butter
20 g/¾ oz flour	3 tablespoons flour
15 g/½ oz gelatine	1 envelope unflavored gelatin
3 tablespoons hot water	3 tablespoons hot water
2 hard-boiled eggs, chopped	2 hard-cooked eggs, chopped
150 ml/¼ pint mayonnaise	¾ cup mayonnaise
150 ml/¼ pint double cream, whipped	¾ cup heavy cream, whipped
pinch of paprika	pinch of paprika
salt and freshly ground pepper	salt and freshly ground pepper
Garnish:	**Garnish:**
6 thin cucumber slices	6 thin cucumber slices
parsley sprigs	parsley sprigs

Place the haddock fillets in a pan and cover with the coffee and milk. Bring slowly to the boil and simmer gently for 5 minutes. Drain the fish, reserving the cooking liquid. Flake the fish, removing any skin and bones.

Melt the butter in another saucepan and stir in the flour. Cook for 1 minute. Gradually add the reserved cooking liquid, stirring well. Simmer gently for 5 minutes or until smooth and thickened. Remove from the heat.

Dissolve the gelatine in the hot water and stir into the hot sauce. Allow to cool, then stir in the eggs, mayonnaise, whipped cream, paprika and salt and pepper to taste. Pour into a 900 ml/1½ pint (1 quart) soufflé dish or 6 individual dishes. Leave to set in the refrigerator. Garnish with cucumber slices and parsley sprigs.
Serves 6

Stuffed Chinese Avocados

METRIC/IMPERIAL	AMERICAN
1 × 200 g/7 oz can tuna fish, drained and flaked	1 can (7 oz) tuna fish, drained and flaked
75 g/3 oz bean sprouts, chopped	1 cup chopped bean sprouts
1 medium carrot, grated	1 medium-size carrot, grated
1 tablespoon chopped parsley	1 tablespoon chopped parsley
1 stick celery, finely chopped	1 stalk celery, finely chopped
1 tablespoon mayonnaise	1 tablespoon mayonnaise
1 tablespoon strong black coffee	1 tablespoon strong black coffee
salt and freshly ground pepper	salt and freshly ground pepper
3 avocados	3 avocados
lemon juice	lemon juice
celery leaves to garnish	celery leaves for garnish

Mix together the tuna fish, bean sprouts, carrot, chopped parsley and celery. Blend together the mayonnaise and coffee and season to taste with salt and pepper. Fold into the tuna mixture. Leave to stand for 30 minutes.

Halve the avocados and remove the stones (seeds). Sprinkle the cut surfaces with a little lemon juice to prevent discoloration. Pile the tuna mixture in the hollows. Garnish with celery leaves and serve with brown bread and butter.

Serves 6

Coffee Nut Beignets

METRIC/IMPERIAL	AMERICAN
25 g/1 oz butter	2 tablespoons butter
150 ml/¼ pint weak black coffee	¾ cup weak black coffee
50 g/2 oz plain flour, sifted	½ cup sifted all-purpose flour
1 egg	1 egg
1 egg yolk	1 egg yolk
75 g/3 oz streaky bacon, derinded, grilled and crumbled	6 slices bacon, fried and crumbled
25 g/1 oz blanched almonds, chopped	¼ cup chopped almonds
1 tablespoon chopped parsley	1 tablespoon chopped parsley
1 teaspoon ground coffee	1 teaspoon ground coffee
salt and freshly ground pepper	salt and freshly ground pepper
oil for deep frying	oil for deep frying
sweet chutney to serve	sweet chutney to serve

Heat the butter and coffee in a saucepan until the butter has melted, then bring to the boil.

Add the flour and beat over low heat until the mixture is smooth and leaves the sides of the pan. Remove from the heat. Beat the egg and egg yolk together and gradually beat into the coffee mixture until well incorporated and the paste is smooth and shiny. Stir in the bacon, almonds, parsley and ground coffee with salt and pepper to taste.

Heat the oil in a deep fat fryer. Drop heaped teaspoonfuls of the mixture into the oil and fry for about 5 minutes or until crisp and golden brown. Drain on kitchen paper towels and serve hot with sweet chutney as an accompaniment.

Serves 4 to 6

Note: Savoury beignets are usually served as an appetizer, but can be served as a canapé for a drinks party.

Stuffed Chinese Avocados;
Coffee Nut Beignets

Stuffed Mushrooms

METRIC/IMPERIAL	AMERICAN
6 large flat mushrooms	6 large flat mushrooms
50 g/2 oz butter	¼ cup butter
1 onion, chopped	1 onion, chopped
2 cloves garlic, chopped	2 cloves garlic, chopped
175 g/6 oz fresh wholemeal breadcrumbs	3 cups soft wholewheat bread crumbs
225 g/8 oz pork sausagemeat	½ lb bulk pork sausagemeat
2 tablespoons chopped parsley	2 tablespoons chopped parsley
2 tablespoons strong black coffee	2 tablespoons strong black coffee
salt and freshly ground pepper	salt and freshly ground pepper

Remove the stalks from the mushrooms and arrange mushrooms in one layer, stalk sides up, on a greased baking sheet.

Melt 25 g/1 oz (2 tablespoons) of the butter in a frying pan, add the onion and garlic and fry until softened. Remove from the heat and add the breadcrumbs, sausagemeat, parsley, coffee and salt and pepper to taste. Mix well. Pile the mixture on top of the mushrooms and dot with the remaining butter.

Cook in a preheated moderate oven (180°C/350°F, Gas Mark 4) for 40 minutes. Serve hot.
Serves 6

Chicken Liver Pâté

METRIC/IMPERIAL	AMERICAN
100 g/4 oz butter	½ cup butter
225 g/8 oz chicken livers, chopped	½ lb chicken livers, chopped
2 cloves garlic, chopped	2 cloves garlic, chopped
100 g/4 oz back bacon, derinded and chopped	¼ lb Canadian bacon, chopped
4 tablespoons strong black coffee	¼ cup strong black coffee
1 tablespoon single cream	1 tablespoon light cream
1 tablespoon sherry	1 tablespoon sherry
salt and freshly ground pepper	salt and freshly ground pepper

Melt 25 g/1 oz (2 tablespoons) of the butter in a frying pan. Add the livers, garlic and bacon and fry until just cooked. The livers should still be slightly pink in the centre. Place in a food processor or blender and add the remaining butter, coffee, cream and sherry. Blend the pâté in a blender for 30 seconds or until smooth. Season to taste with salt and pepper. Spoon into individual ramekins or a pâté dish. Chill in the refrigerator overnight.
Serves 6

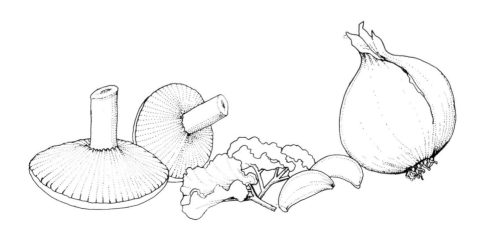

Mocha Mushroom Quiche

METRIC/IMPERIAL	AMERICAN
Pastry:	**Dough:**
225 g/8 oz plain flour	2 cups all-purpose
50 g/2 oz butter	flour
50 g/2 oz lard	¼ cup butter
Filling:	¼ cup shortening
25 g/1 oz butter	**Filling:**
175 g/6 oz	2 tablespoons butter
mushrooms, sliced	1½ cups sliced
5 medium potatoes,	mushrooms
cooked and sliced	5 medium-size
3 spring onions,	potatoes, cooked
chopped	and sliced
5 large eggs, beaten	3 scallions, chopped
250 ml/8 fl oz plain	5 large eggs, beaten
yogurt	1 cup plain yogurt
175 ml/6 fl oz strong	¾ cup strong black
black coffee	coffee
2 tablespoons cream	2 tablespoons cream
salt and freshly	salt and freshly
ground pepper	ground pepper

To make the pastry: sift the flour into a bowl and rub (cut) in the fats until the mixture resembles breadcrumbs. Mix in enough water to make a firm dough. Leave to rest in the refrigerator for 30 minutes.

Melt the butter in a frying pan, add the mushrooms and fry until soft. Add the potatoes and fry, stirring, for 1 minute. Remove from the heat and allow to cool.

Roll out the pastry thinly and line a 23 cm/ 9 inch flan or quiche pan. Spread the mushroom and potato mixture in the pastry case and sprinkle with the spring onions (scallions). Beat the eggs with the yogurt, coffee, cream and salt and pepper to taste. Pour over the vegetables in the pastry case.

Cook in a preheated moderate oven (180°C/ 350°F, Gas Mark 4) for 45 minutes. Serve warm or cold.
Serves 6 to 8

Montego Patties

METRIC/IMPERIAL	AMERICAN
Pastry:	**Dough:**
225 g/8 oz plain flour	2 cups all-purpose
½ teaspoon salt	flour
50 g/2 oz lard	½ teaspoon salt
50 g/2 oz butter	¼ cup shortening
beaten egg to glaze	¼ cup butter
Filling:	beaten egg to glaze
2 tablespoons	**Filling:**
vegetable oil	2 tablespoons
1 onion, sliced	vegetable oil
1 clove garlic,	1 onion, sliced
chopped	1 clove garlic,
225 g/8 oz minced	chopped
beef	½ lb ground beef
120 ml/4 fl oz strong	½ cup strong black
black coffee	coffee
50 g/2 oz fresh brown	1 cup soft brown
breadcrumbs	bread crumbs
1 teaspoon chilli	1 teaspoon chili
powder	powder
1 teaspoon curry	1 teaspoon curry
powder	powder
salt and freshly	salt and freshly
ground pepper	ground pepper

To make the pastry: sift the flour and salt into a bowl and rub (cut) in the fat until the mixture resembles breadcrumbs. Mix in enough water to make a firm dough. Leave to rest in the refrigerator for 30 minutes.

Heat the oil in a frying pan, add the onion and garlic and fry until softened. Add the beef and fry for about 5 minutes, stirring frequently. Remove from the heat and add the coffee, breadcrumbs, chilli powder, curry powder and salt and pepper to taste. Mix well.

Roll out the dough as thinly as possible and cut into 10 cm/4 inch rounds. Brush the edges of the rounds with beaten egg. Place a teaspoon of the meat mixture in the centre of each round, fold over and press the edges together to seal. Brush tops of patties with beaten egg and arrange on a baking sheet.

Cook in a preheated moderate oven (180°C/350°F, Gas Mark 4) for 30 minutes or until golden brown. Serve hot or cold.
Makes 15 to 18

Main
Meals

Sole Véronique à la Café

METRIC/IMPERIAL
12 sole fillets
300 ml/½ pint hot
 medium strength
 black coffee
18 large white grapes,
 halved and pipped
150 ml/¼ pint dry
 white wine
150 ml/¼ pint single
 cream
150 ml/¼ pint milk
25 g/1 oz butter
1 tablespoon plain
 flour
salt and freshly
 ground pepper

AMERICAN
12 sole fillets (6 whole
 fish)
1¼ cups hot medium
 strength black
 coffee
18 large green
 grapes, halved and
 seeded
¾ cup dry white wine
¾ cup light cream
¾ cup milk
2 tablespoons butter
1 tablespoon
 all-purpose flour
salt and freshly
 ground pepper

Roll up each fillet of sole and hold together with a wooden cocktail stick. Place in a shallow baking dish and cover with the hot coffee. Cook in a preheated moderate oven (180°C/350°F, Gas Mark 4) for 20 minutes. Drain the fish rolls, reserving the cooking liquid. Place the fish in a clean gratin dish, removing the cocktail sticks. Add the grapes to the dish. Set aside.

Combine the reserved cooking liquid, wine, cream and milk. Melt the butter in a saucepan and stir in the flour. Cook gently for 1 minute, then add the liquid and bring to the boil, stirring well. Season to taste with salt and pepper. Pour the sauce over the fish and grapes. Put the dish in the oven and heat through for 5 minutes.
Serves 6 to 8

Trout Café

METRIC/IMPERIAL
4 medium trout,
 cleaned
salt and freshly
 ground pepper
900 ml/1½ pints hot
 medium strength
 black coffee
Sauce:
25 g/1 oz butter
1 tablespoon plain
 flour
2 tablespoons single
 cream
150 ml/¼ pint milk

AMERICAN
4 medium-size trout,
 cleaned
salt and freshly
 ground pepper
4 cups medium
 strength black
 coffee
Sauce:
2 tablespoons butter
1 tablespoon
 all-purpose flour
2 tablespoons light
 cream
¾ cup milk

Season the fish with salt and pepper and place in a shallow gratin dish in one layer. Cover with the coffee. Cook in a preheated moderate oven (180°C/350°F, Gas Mark 4) for 30 minutes.

Pour off 300 ml/½ pint (1¼ cups) of the cooking liquid and reserve. Melt the butter in a small saucepan. Stir in the flour and cook for 1 minute. Add the reserved cooking liquid, cream and milk and bring to the boil, stirring well. Serve this sauce with the fish.
Serves 4
Note: For slimmers, serve the trout without the sauce.

Sole Véronique à la Café

Mocha Monkfish

METRIC/IMPERIAL
2 monkfish (weighing
  about 450-750 g/
  1-1½ lb each)
250 ml/8 fl oz milk
50 g/2 oz butter
1 tablespoon plain
  flour
4 tablespoons strong
  black coffee
2 tablespoons single
  cream
salt and freshly
  ground pepper

AMERICAN
2 monkfish or other
  firm-fleshed white
  fish (weighing
  about 1-1½ lb each)
1 cup milk
¼ cup butter
1 tablespoon
  all-purpose flour
¼ cup strong black
  coffee
2 tablespoons light
  cream
salt and freshly
  ground pepper

Remove the backbone from the monkfish. Place the fish in a shallow gratin dish with the milk and dot with half of the butter. Cook in a preheated moderate oven (180°C/350°F, Gas Mark 4) for 30 minutes. Drain the fish, reserving the cooking liquid. Keep the fish hot.

Melt the remaining butter in a saucepan. Stir in the flour and cook for 1 minute. Add the reserved liquid from the fish and stir well. Stir in the coffee, cream and salt and pepper to taste and pour over the fish. Put back in the oven to reheat for 5 minutes, then serve with mashed potatoes and peas.
Serves 4

Boeuf à la Bourguignonne

METRIC/IMPERIAL
2 tablespoons
  vegetable oil
1 kg/2 lb braising
  steak, cubed
2 onions, sliced
2 cloves garlic, sliced
2 carrots, sliced
100 g/4 oz button
  mushrooms
1 tablespoon plain
  flour
450 ml/¾ pint strong
  black coffee
½ bottle of red wine
1 teaspoon dried basil
2 bay leaves
salt and freshly
  ground pepper

AMERICAN
2 tablespoons
  vegetable oil
2 lb flank steak, cubed
2 onions, sliced
2 cloves garlic, sliced
2 carrots, sliced
1 cup button
  mushrooms
1 tablespoon
  all-purpose flour
2 cups strong black
  coffee
½ bottle of red wine
1 teaspoon dried basil
2 bay leaves
salt and freshly
  ground pepper

Heat 1 tablespoon of the oil in a frying pan. Add the steak cubes and fry briskly to brown on all sides. As the cubes are browned, transfer them to an 18 cm/7 inch casserole. Heat the remaining oil in the frying pan and add the onions, garlic and carrots. Fry until softened. Add the vegetables to the casserole with the mushrooms.

Stir the flour into the oil remaining in the frying pan and cook gently for 1 minute. Gradually add the coffee and cook, stirring, for another minute. Strain into the casserole and add the wine and herbs. Season to taste with salt and pepper. Cook in a preheated moderate oven (160°C/325°F, Gas Mark 3) for 2 hours, stirring occasionally. Remove the bay leaves before serving.
Serves 6

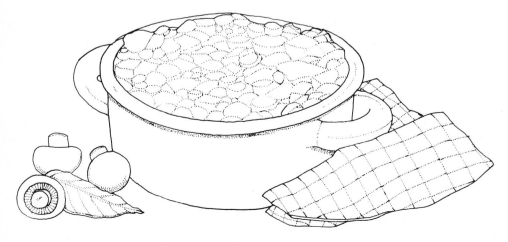

Marinated Kebabs

METRIC/IMPERIAL	AMERICAN
1 kg/2 lb rump steak, cubed	2 lb sirloin or top round steak, cubed
225 g/8 oz button mushrooms	½ lb button mushrooms
2 red peppers, cored, seeded and cut into squares	2 red peppers, seeded and cut into squares
2 medium onions, cut into wedges	2 medium onions, cut into wedges
salt and freshly ground pepper	salt and freshly ground pepper
2 tablespoons vegetable oil	2 tablespoons vegetable oil
Marinade:	**Marinade:**
450 ml/¾ pint strong black coffee	2 cups strong black coffee
450 ml/¾ pint olive oil	2 cups olive oil
450 ml/¾ pint red wine	2 cups red wine
10 coffee beans	10 coffee beans

Thread the steak cubes, mushrooms, pieces of pepper and onions alternately on to skewers. Season all over with salt and pepper. Make up the marinade by combining the coffee, oil, wine and coffee beans. Place the kebabs in a roasting pan and pour over the marinade. Marinate in the refrigerator for 3 to 4 hours.

Drain the kebabs and pat dry with kitchen paper towels. Sprinkle the 2 tablespoons of oil over them and cook under a hot grill (broiler) for about 20 minutes, turning frequently. Serve with a salad.
Serves 6 to 8

Flambé Coffee Steaks

METRIC/IMPERIAL	AMERICAN
4 × 150 g/6 oz sirloin steaks	4 (6 oz) sirloin steaks
50 g/2 oz freshly ground coffee	¼ cup freshly ground coffee
75 g/3 oz butter	6 tablespoons butter
juice of ½ lemon	juice of ½ lemon
4 tablespoons brandy	¼ cup brandy
150 ml/¼ pint single cream	¾ cup light cream
salt and freshly ground pepper	salt and freshly ground pepper

Place the steaks on a board and sprinkle each one on both sides with the ground coffee. Press the coffee into the steaks. Melt the butter with the lemon juice in a heavy frying pan. Add the steaks and fry on both sides until browned and cooked to your liking. The length of frying time will depend on how well done you like your steak to be.

Warm the brandy in a small pan, then pour it over the steaks and ignite. Shake the frying pan gently until the flames die down. Remove the steaks from the pan and keep warm. Stir the cream into the pan juices, season to taste with salt and pepper and pour over the steaks. Serve immediately.
Serves 4

Coffee Crusted Lamb

METRIC/IMPERIAL	AMERICAN
2 best ends of neck of lamb, French trimmed	2 racks of lamb, French-style
100 g/4 oz fresh breadcrumbs	2 cups soft bread crumbs
1 tablespoon fine ground coffee	1 tablespoon fine ground coffee
2 eggs, beaten	2 eggs, beaten
1 tablespoon vegetable oil	1 tablespoon vegetable oil
salt and freshly ground pepper	salt and freshly ground pepper

Divide each best end (rack) of lamb in half to provide four portions. Place in a roasting pan and roast in a preheated moderately hot oven (200°C/400°F, Gas Mark 6) for 25 minutes. (At this point, you can wait until the meat is required or go straight ahead with the recipe.)

Mix together the breadcrumbs, coffee, eggs, oil and salt and pepper to taste. Press on to the fat side of the lamb and cook for a further 10 minutes. (If the lamb is cold at this stage, cook for a further 20 minutes.) Serve hot with roast potatoes.
Serves 4

Lamb Couscous

METRIC/IMPERIAL	AMERICAN
40 g/1½ oz butter	3 tablespoons butter
2 tablespoons vegetable oil	2 tablespoons vegetable oil
750 g/1½ lb best stewing lamb, trimmed and cubed	1½ lb lamb for stew, cubed
3 onions, sliced	3 onions, sliced
1 green pepper, cored, seeded and diced	1 green pepper, seeded and diced
2 tablespoons plain flour	2 tablespoons all-purpose flour
300 ml/½ pint beef stock	1¼ cups beef broth
300 ml/½ pint medium strength black coffee	1¼ cups medium strength black coffee
3 tablespoons clear honey	3 tablespoons honey
1 teaspoon ground cinnamon	1 teaspoon ground cinnamon
pinch of ground saffron	pinch of ground saffron
pinch of ground mace	pinch of ground mace
1 teaspoon chopped fresh mint	1 teaspoon chopped fresh mint
salt and freshly ground pepper	salt and freshly ground pepper
Couscous base:	**Couscous base:**
225 g/8 oz couscous	½ lb couscous
600 ml/1 pint medium strength black coffee	2½ cups medium strength black coffee
25 g/1 oz butter	2 tablespoons butter

Melt the butter with the oil in a large flameproof casserole. Add the lamb cubes and fry until lightly browned all over. Remove the lamb from the pan. Add the onions and green pepper and fry until lightly golden. Stir in the flour and cook for 1 to 2 minutes. Gradually add the stock (broth) and coffee and stir well. Add the honey, cinnamon, saffron, mace and mint, then return the lamb to the pan. Season to taste with salt and pepper. Simmer for 45 minutes or until the meat is tender.

Meanwhile prepare the couscous base. Place the couscous, coffee and butter in a heavy saucepan. Cook over a gentle heat for 15 to 20 minutes, stirring occasionally, until the couscous has absorbed all the liquid.

To serve: pile the couscous on to a serving dish and make a well in the centre. Place the lamb stew in the well and serve any leftover pan juices separately. Garnish with mint.
Serves 6

Coffee Fettuccine

METRIC/IMPERIAL	AMERICAN
225 g/8 oz egg noodles	½ lb egg noodles
salt and freshly ground pepper	salt and freshly ground pepper
4 tablespoons vegetable oil	¼ cup vegetable oil
2 onions, sliced	2 onions, sliced
1 red pepper, cored, seeded and chopped	1 red pepper, seeded and chopped
1 green pepper, cored, seeded and chopped	1 green pepper, seeded and chopped
75 g/3 oz cooked ham, cut into strips	⅓ cup cooked chopped ham
100 g/4 oz button mushrooms, sliced	1 cup sliced button mushrooms
2 tablespoons brandy	2 tablespoons brandy
150 ml/¼ pint medium strength black coffee	¾ cup medium strength black coffee
150 ml/¼ pint double cream	¾ cup heavy cream
grated Parmesan cheese to serve	grated Parmesan cheese to serve

Cook the noodles in boiling salted water, with a few drops of the vegetable oil added, until just tender. Drain and rinse under running hot water to remove any excess starch. Keep hot.

Heat the remaining oil in a frying pan. Add the onions and peppers and fry until golden brown. Add the ham and mushrooms and cook, stirring occasionally, for 5 minutes. Warm the brandy in a small pan, then pour into the frying pan and set alight. Stir gently until the flames subside, then add the coffee and cream. Mix well. Add the noodles to the sauce and toss gently to coat. Season to taste with salt and pepper. Serve immediately, with Parmesan cheese.
Serves 6

Coffee Fettuccine; Coffee Lamb Couscous

Coffee Moussaka

METRIC/IMPERIAL	AMERICAN
2 medium aubergines, sliced	2 medium-size eggplants, sliced
salt and freshly ground pepper	salt and freshly ground pepper
4 tablespoons vegetable oil	¼ cup vegetable oil
2 onions, sliced	2 onions, sliced
2 cloves garlic, sliced	2 cloves garlic, sliced
1 kg/2 lb minced lamb	2 lb ground lamb
1 × 225 g/8 oz can tomatoes, drained	1 can (8 oz) tomatoes, drained
300 ml/½ pint strong black coffee	1¼ cups strong black coffee
Topping:	**Topping:**
600 ml/1 pint milk	2½ cups milk
2 eggs, beaten	2 eggs, beaten
150 ml/¼ pint plain yogurt	¾ cup plain yogurt
¼ teaspoon salt	¼ teaspoon salt

Lay the slices of aubergine (eggplant) on a board and sprinkle with salt. Leave for 10 minutes.

Meanwhile heat half the oil in a frying pan, add the onions and garlic and fry until softened. Add the lamb and fry, stirring frequently, for 5 minutes. If the lamb is very fatty you may have to pour off some of the fat. Add the tomatoes, coffee and salt and pepper to taste. Remove from the heat.

Rinse the salt from the aubergines (eggplants) and pat dry with kitchen paper towels. Heat the remaining oil in a clean frying pan and brown the aubergine (eggplant) slices on both sides. Add more oil to the pan, if necessary. Line a large gratin dish with some of the aubergine (eggplant) slices, then pour in the meat mixture. Place the remaining aubergine (eggplant) slices on top of the meat mixture. Beat together the topping ingredients and pour over the aubergines (eggplants). Cook in a preheated moderate oven (180°C/350°F, Gas Mark 4) for 45 minutes.
Serves 8

Moroccan Chicken

METRIC/IMPERIAL	AMERICAN
6 chicken breast portions	6 chicken breast portions (from 3 chickens)
300 ml/½ pint medium strength black coffee	1¼ cups medium strength black coffee
75 g/3 oz sultanas	½ cup golden raisins
pinch of ground mace	pinch of ground mace
50 g/2 oz butter	¼ cup butter
3 tablespoons clear honey	3 tablespoons honey
50 g/2 oz flaked almonds	½ cup slivered almonds
Sauce:	**Sauce:**
25 g/1 oz butter	2 tablespoons butter
25 g/1 oz plain flour	¼ cup all-purpose flour
150 ml/¼ pint single cream	¾ cup light cream
salt and freshly ground pepper	salt and freshly ground pepper

Arrange the chicken breasts in a shallow dish. Mix together the coffee, sultanas (raisins) and mace and pour over the chicken. Leave to marinate in a cool place for 6 to 8 hours or overnight.

Drain the chicken, reserving the marinade. Use the butter to grease a roasting pan generously and lay the chicken in it. Coat each breast with honey. Cook in a preheated moderate oven (180°C/350°F, Gas Mark 4) for 30 minutes, basting twice with the butter in the pan. Sprinkle over the almonds and cook for a further 10 minutes.

Meanwhile make the sauce. Melt the butter in a pan and stir in the flour. Cook for 1 to 2 minutes, then stir in the reserved marinade. Bring the sauce to the boil, stirring, and simmer for 5 minutes. Remove from the heat and stir in the cream and salt and pepper to taste.

Arrange the chicken on a serving platter. Mix the pan juices into the sauce and pour over the chicken. Serve immediately.
Serves 6

Marinated Venison

METRIC/IMPERIAL	AMERICAN
1 haunch of venison or 1 leg of lamb	1 haunch of venison or 1 leg of lamb
Marinade:	**Marinade:**
600 ml/1 pint strong black coffee	2½ cups strong black coffee
600 ml/1 pint olive oil	2½ cups olive oil
600 ml/1 pint red wine	2½ cups red wine
2 cloves garlic, chopped	2 cloves garlic, chopped
50 g/2 oz coffee beans	¼ cup coffee beans
salt and freshly ground pepper	salt and freshly ground pepper

Place the venison or lamb in a shallow glass dish. Mix together the marinade ingredients, with salt and pepper to taste. Pour the marinade over the meat and leave to stand in a cool place for 24 hours, basting frequently and turning the meat regularly.

Drain the meat and place in a roasting bag or make a 'bag' with foil. Add some of the marinade to the meat. Roast in a preheated moderately hot oven (200°C/400°F, Gas Mark 6) for 2 hours. Baste frequently. Make a gravy with the meat juices and serve with roast potatoes, roast parsnips, cauliflower au gratin and peas.
Serves 6 to 8

Veal with Mushroom Sauce

METRIC/IMPERIAL	AMERICAN
6 × 175 g/6 oz veal escalopes	6 veal cutlets (about 6 oz each)
flour for coating	flour for coating
salt and freshly ground pepper	salt and freshly ground pepper
75 g/3 oz butter	6 tablespoons butter
175 g/6 oz button mushrooms, sliced	1½ cups sliced button mushrooms
1 shallot, finely chopped	1 shallot, finely chopped
1 tablespoon brandy	1 tablespoon brandy
150 ml/¼ pint strong black coffee	¾ cup strong black coffee
300 ml/½ pint single cream	1¼ cups light cream

Place the veal between sheets of greaseproof (parchment or wax) paper and beat until really thin. Season the flour with salt and pepper and use to coat the veal on both sides. Melt the butter in a heavy frying pan. Add the veal and fry gently for 4 minutes on each side. Arrange on a serving dish and keep warm.

Add the mushrooms and shallot to the frying pan and fry gently for 5 minutes. Warm the brandy, then pour over the vegetables and set alight. Stir until the flames subside. Add the coffee and bring to the boil, stirring. Season to taste with salt and pepper. Remove the sauce from the heat and stir in the cream. Pour the sauce over the veal and serve immediately.
Serves 6

Mild Chicken Coffee Curry

METRIC/IMPERIAL	AMERICAN
50 g/2 oz butter	¼ cup butter
1 × 1.5 kg/3½ lb chicken, cut into 8 joints	1 chicken (about 3½ lb), cut up into 8 pieces
2 onions, sliced	2 onions, sliced
2 tablespoons plain flour	2 tablespoons all-purpose flour
1 teaspoon curry paste	1 teaspoon curry paste
300 ml/½ pint medium strength black coffee	1¼ cups medium strength black coffee
150 ml/¼ pint milk	¾ cup milk
juice of ½ lemon	juice of ½ lemon
1 tablespoon peach chutney	1 tablespoon peach chutney
50 g/2 oz unsalted peanuts	½ cup unsalted peanuts
50 g/2 oz currants	⅓ cup currants
hot boiled rice to serve	hot boiled rice to serve

Melt the butter in a frying pan. Add the chicken pieces and brown them all over. Remove and leave on one side. Add the onions to the pan and fry for 6 to 8 minutes or until golden brown. Lower the heat and stir in the flour and curry paste. Cook for 1 to 2 minutes. Gradually stir in the coffee, milk and lemon juice, then add the chutney, peanuts and currants. Bring the mixture to the boil, stirring well. Return the chicken to the pan, cover and simmer gently for 30 to 40 minutes.

Arrange the rice around the edge of a serving dish and put the chicken pieces in the centre. Pour the sauce over and serve immediately, with poppadoms, sliced bananas and various chutneys.
Serves 6

Stuffed Pork Fillets (Tenderloin)

METRIC/IMPERIAL	AMERICAN
2 pork fillets	2 pork tenderloin
25 g/1 oz butter	2 tablespoons butter
1 tablespoon vegetable oil	1 tablespoon vegetable oil
600 ml/1 pint medium strength black coffee	2½ cups medium strength black coffee
2 tablespoons cornflour	2 tablespoons cornstarch
3 tablespoons water	3 tablespoons water
parsley sprigs to garnish	parsley sprigs for garnish
Stuffing:	**Stuffing:**
100 g/4 oz dried apricots, soaked in water overnight, drained and finely chopped	¾ cup finely chopped dried apricots, soaked in water overnight and drained
50 g/2 oz fresh white breadcrumbs	1 cup soft white bread crumbs
4 rashers streaky bacon, derinded, grilled and crumbled	4 slices bacon, fried and crumbled
25 g/1 oz flaked almonds	¼ cup slivered almonds
1 tablespoon chopped parsley	1 tablespoon chopped parsley
grated rind and juice of 1 small orange	grated rind and juice of 1 small orange
1 egg, beaten	1 egg, beaten
salt and freshly ground pepper	salt and freshly ground pepper

Mix together all the stuffing ingredients with salt and pepper to taste. Remove the transparent skin from the pork and any excess fat. Slit each piece of pork open lengthways, cutting to within 1 cm/½ inch of the base, and open out. Spread the stuffing down the centre of one piece of pork and place the other piece of pork on top, cut surface down. Tie together with string, tucking in the ends.

Melt the butter with the oil in a flameproof casserole. Add the pork and fry until light golden brown on all sides. Pour over the coffee, cover the casserole and cook in a preheated moderately hot oven (190°C/375°F, Gas Mark 5) for 40 minutes.

Remove the pork from the casserole and place on a serving platter. Keep hot while making the sauce. Place the casserole over heat on top of the stove and simmer for 5 minutes.

Mix the cornflour (cornstarch) with the water and stir into the liquid. Simmer the sauce, stirring, for a further 2 to 3 minutes, then pour over the pork. Garnish with parsley sprigs.
Serves 6

Coffee Glazed Ham

METRIC/IMPERIAL	AMERICAN
1 smoked gammon joint (about 1.5 kg/ 3 lb), soaked overnight if necessary and drained	1 ham (about 3 lb)
3.6 litres/6 pints plus 2 tablespoons strong black coffee	3½ quarts plus 2 tablespoons strong black coffee
1 tablespoon dry mustard	1 tablespoon dry mustard
4 tablespoons clear honey	¼ cup honey
12 coffee beans	12 coffee beans

Soak the gammon (ham) in 3.6 litres/6 pints (3½ quarts) of the coffee for 3 to 4 hours, turning frequently. Drain. Rinse under cold running water, then place in a large saucepan. Add cold water to cover and the mustard. Bring to the boil and simmer for 1½ hours.

Drain the gammon (ham) and cool slightly, then remove any rind. Score the fat into squares. Place the gammon (ham) on a rack in a roasting pan. Heat the remaining coffee and honey together in a saucepan and brush some of the mixture over the gammon (ham). Cook in a preheated moderately hot oven (200°C/400°F, Gas Mark 6) for 15 to 20 minutes or until glazed and crisp. Baste with the honey mixture two or three times. Serve hot or cold, studded with the coffee beans.
Serves 6 to 8

Coffee Glazed Ham

Coffee Nut Balls

METRIC/IMPERIAL
1 tablespoon
vegetable oil
1 onion, sliced
2 cloves garlic,
crushed
100 g/4 oz mixed
nuts, ground
100 g/4 oz fresh
wholemeal
breadcrumbs
4 tablespoons strong
black coffee
1 egg, beaten
1 teaspoon dried sage
salt and freshly
ground pepper
2 tablespoons sesame
seeds

AMERICAN
1 tablespoon
vegetable oil
1 onion, sliced
2 cloves garlic,
crushed
1 cup ground mixed
nuts
2 cups soft
wholewheat bread
crumbs
¼ cup strong black
coffee
1 egg, beaten
1 teaspoon dried sage
salt and freshly
ground pepper
2 tablespoons sesame
seeds

Heat the oil in a frying pan. Add the onion and garlic and fry until softened. Remove from the heat and add the nuts, breadcrumbs, coffee, egg, sage and salt and pepper to taste. Mix well.

Shape the mixture into small balls and coat in the sesame seeds. Place on a greased baking sheet. Cook in a preheated moderate oven (180°C/350°F, Gas Mark 4) for 40 minutes. Serve with a mixed salad.
Makes 12

Stuffed Peppers

METRIC/IMPERIAL
2 tablespoons
vegetable oil
1 onion, chopped
2 cloves garlic,
chopped
225 g/8 oz minced
beef
225 g/8 oz minced
pork
100 g/4 oz fresh
breadcrumbs
120 ml/4 fl oz strong
black coffee
salt and freshly
ground pepper
8 green peppers

AMERICAN
2 tablespoons
vegetable oil
1 onion, chopped
2 cloves garlic,
chopped
½ lb ground beef
½ lb ground pork
2 cups soft bread
crumbs
½ cup strong black
coffee
salt and freshly
ground pepper
8 green peppers

Heat the oil in a frying pan. Add the onion and garlic and fry until softened. Add the meat and cook gently for 10 minutes, stirring well. Remove from the heat and add the breadcrumbs, coffee and salt and pepper to taste.

Cut the tops off the peppers and remove the seeds and core. Stuff the peppers with the meat mixture and replace the tops. Arrange, standing upright, in a shallow baking dish. Cook in a preheated moderate oven (180°C/350°F, Gas Mark 4) for 50 minutes. Serve with rice and peas.
Serves 4 to 8

Beef and Pork Loaf

METRIC/IMPERIAL
2 tablespoons
  vegetable oil
1 onion, sliced
2 cloves garlic,
  chopped
225 g/8 oz minced
  beef
225 g/8 oz minced
  pork
100 g/4 oz fresh
  brown breadcrumbs
3 tablespoons strong
  black coffee
2 tablespoons red
  wine
2 tablespoons
  chopped parsley
salt and freshly
  ground pepper

AMERICAN
2 tablespoons
  vegetable oil
1 onion, sliced
2 cloves garlic,
  chopped
½ lb ground beef
½ lb ground pork
2 cups soft brown
  breadcrumbs
3 tablespoons strong
  black coffee
2 tablespoons red
  wine
2 tablespoons
  chopped parsley
salt and freshly
  ground pepper

Heat the oil in a frying pan. Add the onion and garlic and fry until softened. Add the meat and fry gently for 5 minutes, stirring well. Remove from the heat and add the breadcrumbs, coffee, wine, parsley and salt and pepper to taste. Pack into a 450 g/1 lb (7 × 3 inch) loaf pan.

Cook in a preheated moderate oven (180°C/ 350°F, Gas Mark 4) for 45 minutes. Serve with a mixed salad.
Serves 6 to 8

Savoury Coffee Peanut Loaf

METRIC/IMPERIAL
175 g/6 oz salted
  peanuts
50 g/2 oz onion,
  chopped
50 g/2 oz celery,
  chopped
50 g/2 oz carrot,
  chopped
50 g/2 oz parsley,
  chopped
175 g/6 oz fresh
  breadcrumbs
4 tablespoons strong
  black coffee
2 large eggs, beaten
1 teaspoon salt

AMERICAN
1½ cups salted
  peanuts
½ cup chopped onion
½ cup chopped celery
½ cup chopped carrot
1 cup chopped
  parsley
3 cups soft bread
  crumbs
¼ cup strong black
  coffee
2 large eggs, beaten
1 teaspoon salt

Place the peanuts, onion, celery, carrot and parsley in a food processor and process together. Pour into a bowl and add the breadcrumbs, coffee, eggs and salt. Mix well together. Pack into a 23 × 8.5 cm/9 × 3½ inch pâté tin with collapsible sides.

Cook in a preheated moderate oven (180°C/ 350°F, Gas Mark 4) for 1 hour. Leave to cool slightly before removing the loaf from the tin. Serve with salad.
Serves 6 to 8

Desserts

Coffee Liqueur Pancakes (Crêpes)

METRIC/IMPERIAL	AMERICAN
100 g/4 oz plain flour	1 cup all-purpose flour
pinch of salt	pinch of salt
1 teaspoon caster sugar	1 teaspoon sugar
250 ml/8 fl oz milk	1 cup milk
4 tablespoons cold strong black coffee	¼ cup cold strong black coffee
1 egg	1 egg
1 egg yolk	1 egg yolk
1 teaspoon vegetable oil	1 teaspoon vegetable oil
oil for frying	oil for frying
To serve:	**To serve:**
15 g/½ oz butter	1 tablespoon butter
grated rind and juice of ½ lemon	grated rind and juice of ½ lemon
2 tablespoons coffee liqueur	2 tablespoons coffee liqueur

Sift the flour, salt and sugar into a bowl. Add the milk, coffee, egg, egg yolk and oil and whisk until the batter is smooth.

Lightly oil a 15 cm/6 inch pancake (crêpe) or frying pan and heat. Pour in a little of the batter and tilt the pan to swirl the batter so that it covers the bottom. Cook for 1 or 2 minutes or until golden brown underneath. Flip or toss the pancake (crêpe) and cook the other side for about 30 seconds. Tip out of the pan and make 11 more pancakes (crêpes) in the same way. Fold each pancake (crêpe) into quarters.

Melt the butter in a large frying pan and arrange the pancakes (crêpes) in the pan. Add the lemon rind and juice and coffee liqueur. Heat gently, basting the pancakes (crêpes) with the liquid, until piping hot. Serve immediately with cream.
Serves 4 to 6

*Coffee Liqueur Pancakes (Crêpes);
Maria Baked Bananas*

Maria Baked Bananas

METRIC/IMPERIAL	AMERICAN
6 bananas	6 bananas
50 g/2 oz brown sugar	⅓ cup brown sugar
120 ml/4 fl oz strong black coffee	½ cup strong black coffee
120 ml/4 fl oz coffee liqueur	½ cup coffee liqueur
single cream to serve	light cream to serve

Peel the bananas and cut in half lengthways. Put in a shallow baking dish and sprinkle with the sugar. Mix the coffee and liqueur together and pour over the bananas. Cook in a preheated very cool oven (120°C/250°F, Gas Mark ½) for 2 hours. Serve with single (light) cream.
Serves 6

Mocha Pears

METRIC/IMPERIAL	AMERICAN
6 small pears	6 small pears
50 g/2 oz plain chocolate	2 squares (1 oz each) semisweet chocolate
3 tablespoons strong black coffee	3 tablespoons strong black coffee
25 g/1 oz butter	2 tablespoons butter
2 egg yolks	2 egg yolks

Peel the pears, leaving the stalk intact. Take a small slice from the bottom of each to make a flat base.

Melt the chocolate in a double boiler or heatproof bowl over a saucepan of hot water, and add the coffee, butter and egg yolks. Stir until thickened. Holding each pear by the stalk, coat with the chocolate mixture. Place on a plate or in individual ramekins and chill until set.
Serves 6

Mocha Crumble Pie

METRIC/IMPERIAL	AMERICAN
Pastry:	**Dough:**
175 g/6 oz plain flour, sifted	1½ cups all-purpose flour, sifted
pinch of salt	pinch of salt
75 g/3 oz butter, cut into pieces	6 tablespoons butter, cut into pieces
Filling:	**Filling:**
1 tablespoon cornflour	1 tablespoon cornstarch
150 ml/¼ pint medium strength black coffee	¾ cup medium strength black coffee
150 ml/¼ pint milk	¾ cup milk
50 g/2 oz caster sugar	¼ cup sugar
1 tablespoon cocoa powder	1 tablespoon cocoa powder
2 egg yolks	2 egg yolks
Topping:	**Topping:**
25 g/1 oz butter	2 tablespoons butter
50 g/2 oz plain flour, sifted	½ cup all-purpose flour, sifted
25 g/1 oz demerara sugar	2½ tablespoons raw brown sugar
25 g/1 oz fresh brown breadcrumbs	½ cup soft brown bread crumbs

To make the pastry: sift the flour and salt into a bowl and rub (cut) in the butter until the mixture resembles breadcrumbs. Mix in enough water to make a light dough. Knead gently, then roll out and line an 18 cm/7 inch fluted flan ring on a baking sheet, or quiche pan. Prick holes in the bottom of the pastry case and line with greaseproof (parchment) paper and dried beans. Bake blind in a preheated moderately hot oven (190°C/375°F, Gas Mark 5) for 20 minutes. Remove the paper and beans and cook for a further 10 minutes or until the pastry is a light golden brown. Leave to cool.

Blend the cornflour (cornstarch) with a little of the coffee until smooth. Mix together the remaining coffee, milk, sugar and cocoa in a saucepan and bring to the boil. Add the cornflour (cornstarch) mixture. Simmer for 2 to 3 minutes, then allow to cool. Beat in the egg yolks and pour the sauce into the pastry case.

For the topping: rub (cut) the butter into the flour, then stir in the sugar and breadcrumbs. Sprinkle over the filling. Cook in a preheated moderately hot oven (190°C/375°F, Gas Mark 5) for 20 minutes. Serve hot or cold, with whipped cream.
Serves 6

Coffee Cheesecake

METRIC/IMPERIAL	AMERICAN
14 digestive biscuits, finely crushed	1¾ cups finely crushed graham crackers
1 teaspoon finely ground coffee	1 teaspoon finely ground coffee
50 g/2 oz unsalted butter, melted	¼ cup unsalted butter, melted
225 g/8 oz cream cheese	½ lb cream cheese
225 g/8 oz cottage cheese, sieved	½ lb cottage cheese, sieved (about 1 cup)
15 g/½ oz gelatine	1 envelope unflavored gelatin
3 tablespoons hot water	3 tablespoons hot water
1 teaspoon vanilla essence	1 teaspoon vanilla
300 ml/½ pint double cream	1¼ cups heavy cream
4 egg whites	4 egg whites
Topping:	**Topping:**
1 × 225 g/8 oz can pineapple rings, drained and syrup reserved	1 can (8 oz) pineapple rings, drained and syrup reserved
2 tablespoons strong black coffee	2 tablespoons strong black coffee
1 teaspoon arrowroot	1 teaspoon arrowroot
2 teaspoons water	2 teaspoons water

Mix together the biscuits (graham crackers), ground coffee and butter. Press over the bottom of a 20 cm/8 inch springform cake pan. Chill while making the filling.

Mix the two cheeses together. Dissolve the gelatine in the hot water and stir into the cheeses with the vanilla. Whip the cream until thick. Beat the egg whites until stiff. Fold the cream and egg whites into the cheese mixture. Pour into the tin on top of the crumb crust and chill until set.

Reserve five or seven pineapple rings, depending on size, and purée the remaining pineapple with the syrup. Heat this mixture in a pan with the coffee. Dissolve the arrowroot in the water and add to the pan. Simmer, stirring, until thickened. Leave to cool.

When the cheesecake filling is set, place the pineapple rings on top and pour over the coffee and pineapple mixture. Leave to cool and set before removing from the pan.
Serves 6 to 8

Coffee and Almond Meringue Cake

METRIC/IMPERIAL	AMERICAN
4 egg whites	4 egg whites
225 g/8 oz caster sugar	1 cup sugar
1 tablespoon instant coffee powder	1 tablespoon instant coffee powder
50 g/2 oz flaked almonds	½ cup sliced almonds
Filling:	**Filling:**
300 ml/½ pint double cream	1¼ cups heavy cream
25 g/1 oz vanilla sugar	2 tablespoons vanilla sugar
1 punnet of raspberries	½ pint fresh raspberries

Beat the egg whites until they form really stiff peaks. Sift together the sugar and coffee and beat 2 tablespoons into the egg whites. Fold in the remaining sugar and coffee together with the almonds.

Spread or pipe the meringue mixture in two 18 cm/7 inch diameter rounds on baking sheets lined with non-stick (parchment) paper. Cook in a preheated moderate oven (160°C/325°F, Gas Mark 3) for 40 to 50 minutes or until golden brown on top and firm on the base. Peel off the paper lining and leave the meringue layers to cool on a wire rack.

Whip the cream with the vanilla sugar until stiff. Spread some over one cold cake layer. Cover with most of the raspberries, then the remaining cream and finally place the second cake layer on top. Decorate with the reserved raspberries and extra whipped cream if liked.
Serves 8

Hot Coffee Soufflé

METRIC/IMPERIAL	AMERICAN
25 g/1 oz butter	2 tablespoons butter
1 tablespoon plain flour	1 tablespoon all-purpose flour
120 ml/4 fl oz hot strong black coffee	½ cup hot strong black coffee
120 ml/4 fl oz hot milk	½ cup hot milk
4 eggs, separated	4 eggs, separated
50 g/2 oz caster sugar	¼ cup sugar
few drops of vanilla essence	few drops of vanilla

Melt the butter in a saucepan and add the flour. Cook gently, stirring, for 1 to 2 minutes. Mix the coffee and milk together and gradually add to the pan. Simmer the sauce, stirring, until thickened. Beat the egg yolks with the sugar and add to the sauce with the vanilla. Remove from the heat and allow to cool.

Beat the egg whites until stiff and gently fold them into the coffee custard. Spoon into a greased 23 cm/9 inch soufflé dish. Place the dish in a pan with hot water to come halfway up the sides of dish. Cook in a preheated moderately hot oven (190°C/375°F, Gas Mark 5) for 30 minutes until well risen. Serve at once.
Serves 6

Coffee and Raspberry Tart

METRIC/IMPERIAL	AMERICAN
Pastry:	**Dough:**
150 g/5 oz plain flour	1¼ cups all-purpose flour
50 g/2 oz caster sugar	¼ cup sugar
25 g/1 oz instant coffee powder	¼ cup instant coffee powder
2 egg yolks	2 egg yolks
75 g/3 oz butter, cut into pieces	6 tablespoons butter, cut into pieces
Filling:	**Filling:**
225 g/8 oz raspberries	½ lb raspberries
175 g/6 oz sugar	¾ cup sugar
Glaze:	**Glaze:**
4 tablespoons redcurrant jelly	¼ cup redcurrant jelly
1 tablespoon strong black coffee	1 tablespoon strong black coffee

Sift the flour, sugar and coffee on to a board or marble slab. Make a well in the centre and drop in the egg yolks and butter. Using the fingertips, work these ingredients together until a stiff dough is formed. Knead the dough gently, then chill for 30 minutes.

Place the raspberries in a pan with sugar and cook gently for 5 to 10 minutes. Cool.

Roll out about three-quarters of the dough and line an 18 cm/7 inch loose-based flan or quiche pan. Fill the pastry case with the raspberries. Roll out the remaining dough and cut into strips. Lay the strips over the raspberries to make a lattice pattern.

Cook in a preheated moderately hot oven (190°C/375°F, Gas Mark 5) for 25 to 30 minutes. Leave to cool. Melt the redcurrant jelly and coffee together in a pan over a low heat and brush this glaze over the top of the tart.
Serves 6

Coffee Gâteau St. Honoré

METRIC/IMPERIAL
Pastry base:
150 g/5 oz plain flour
75 g/3 oz butter, cut
  into pieces
50 g/2 oz caster sugar
2 egg yolks
Choux pastry:
150 ml/¼ pint water
50 g/2 oz butter
65 g/2½ oz plain
  flour, sifted
2 eggs, beaten
Filling:
300 ml/½ pint milk
300 ml/½ pint
  medium strength
  black coffee
2 tablespoons custard
  powder
50 g/2 oz caster sugar
25 g/1 oz toasted
  flaked almonds to
  decorate
Caramel syrup:
150 ml/¼ pint
  medium strength
  black coffee
175 g/6 oz caster
  sugar

AMERICAN
Pastry base:
1¼ cups all-purpose
  flour
6 tablespoons butter,
  cut into pieces
¼ cup sugar
2 egg yolks
Choux pastry:
¾ cup water
¼ cup butter
½ cup plus
  2 tablespoons
  all-purpose flour,
  sifted
2 eggs, beaten
Filling:
1¼ cups milk
1¼ cups medium
  strength black
  coffee
2 tablespoons Bird's
  English dessert mix
¼ cup sugar
¼ cup toasted
  slivered almonds to
  decorate
Caramel syrup:
¾ cup medium
  strength black
  coffee
¾ cup sugar

First make the pastry base. Sift the flour on to a board or marble slab and make a well in the centre. Place the butter, sugar and egg yolks into the well and gradually work them together with the fingertips until a dough is formed. Knead gently, then roll out the dough to a 20 cm/8 inch round. Neaten the edges. Place on a greased baking sheet and leave to rest in the refrigerator or a cool place.

To make the choux pastry: place the water and butter in a saucepan and heat gently until the butter melts. Bring to the boil, then quickly add the flour. Beat over the heat until the mixture is smooth and leaves the side of the pan. Remove from the heat and beat in the eggs, a little at a time. Spoon the choux pastry into a large piping bag fitted with a 1 cm/½ inch nozzle and pipe a circle around the edge of the pastry base. Pipe the remaining choux pastry in small balls on a separate greased baking sheet.

Cook together in a preheated hot oven (220°C/425°F, Gas Mark 7) for 10 minutes, then reduce the heat to moderately hot (190°C/375°F, Gas Mark 5) and cook for a further 20 to 25 minutes or until firm and golden brown. Leave to cool. If, during the baking, the centre of the pastry base becomes too brown, cover it with a circle of greaseproof (parchment) paper.

To make the filling: reserve 6 tablespoons of the milk and coffee and put remaining milk and coffee into a saucepan. Bring to the boil. Blend the custard (dessert) powder and sugar with the reserved milk and coffee. Pour over the hot milk and coffee and mix well. Rinse out the pan, then return the sauce to it and bring back to the boil, stirring to prevent lumps forming. Cook the sauce for 2 to 3 minutes, then allow to cool. Pour into the centre of the choux ring.

For the caramel, place the coffee and sugar in a saucepan and allow the sugar to dissolve over a low heat. Bring to the boil and boil rapidly until a thick syrup is obtained. Dip the choux balls into the syrup and quickly place on top of the choux ring to form a crown. Decorate the centre of the gâteau with the almonds.
Serves 6 to 8

Coffee Cream Caramel

METRIC/IMPERIAL	AMERICAN
75 g/3 oz caster sugar	6 tablespoons sugar
3 tablespoons hot strong black coffee	3 tablespoons hot strong black coffee
600 ml/1 pint milk	2½ cups milk
2 eggs, beaten	2 eggs, beaten
To decorate:	**For decoration:**
whipped cream	whipped cream
grated nutmeg	grated nutmeg

Place 50 g/2 oz (¼ cup) of the sugar in a saucepan and melt over a low heat, stirring constantly with a wooden spoon. When the sugar is pale brown in colour, quickly and carefully stir in 1 tablespoon of the black coffee. Pour into a 600 ml/1 pint (2½ cup) baking dish.

Whisk together the milk, eggs and remaining coffee and sugar and strain into the dish. Place the dish in a roasting pan and add enough hot water to come halfway up the sides of the dish. Cook in a preheated cool oven (150°C/300°F, Gas Mark 2) for 1 hour. Leave to cool.

Turn out on to a serving dish and decorate with whipped cream and grated nutmeg.
Serves 6

Coffee Gâteau St. Honoré

Coffee Bread and Butter Pudding

METRIC/IMPERIAL	AMERICAN
14 slices of bread, crusts removed and halved	14 slices of bread, crusts removed and halved
butter	butter
2 tablespoons sultanas	2 tablespoons golden raisins
120 ml/4 fl oz strong black coffee	½ cup strong black coffee
450 ml/¾ pint milk	2 cups milk
300 ml/½ pint single cream	1¼ cups light cream
2 eggs	2 eggs
2 tablespoons sugar	2 tablespoons sugar
pinch of salt	pinch of salt
½ teaspoon vanilla essence	½ teaspoon vanilla
¼ teaspoon grated nutmeg	¼ teaspoon grated nutmeg

Butter the bread. Make layers of the bread in a shallow baking dish, sprinkling each layer with sultanas (raisins). Place the coffee, milk and cream in a saucepan and bring to just below boiling point. Beat the eggs, sugar, salt and vanilla together and add the milk mixture. Stir well. Pour over the bread and sprinkle with the nutmeg.

Cook in a preheated moderate oven (180°C/350°F, Gas Mark 4) for 45 minutes. Serve hot.
Serves 6

Little Coffee Custards

METRIC/IMPERIAL	AMERICAN
300 ml/½ pint double cream	1¼ cups heavy cream
6 egg yolks	6 egg yolks
50 g/2 oz caster sugar	¼ cup sugar
120 ml/4 fl oz strong black coffee	½ cup strong black coffee
1 teaspoon vanilla essence	1 teaspoon vanilla
50 g/2 oz plain chocolate, grated	2 squares (1 oz each) semisweet or sweet chocolate, grated

Carefully warm the cream in a double boiler or heatproof bowl placed over a saucepan of hot water. Beat the egg yolks and sugar together, then slowly add to the cream. Gradually stir in the coffee and then the vanilla. Stir continuously for about 10 minutes until the custard has thickened and coats the spoon. Pour into 6 individual pots or one large dish. Leave to cool, then chill until set. Serve sprinkled with grated chocolate.
Serves 6

Coffee Pecan Pie

METRIC/IMPERIAL	AMERICAN
175 g/6 oz digestive biscuits, finely crushed	1½ cups finely crushed graham crackers
75 g/3 oz butter, melted	6 tablespoons butter, melted
25 g/1 oz demerara sugar	2½ tablespoons raw brown sugar
75 g/3 oz pecan nut halves	¾ cup pecan halves
225 g/8 oz marshmallows	½ lb marshmallows
300 ml/½ pint medium strength black coffee	1¼ cups medium strength black coffee
15 g/½ oz gelatine	1 envelope unflavored gelatin
3 tablespoons hot water	3 tablespoons hot water
150 ml/¼ pint double cream	¾ cup heavy cream
1 teaspoon ground coffee	1 teaspoon ground coffee

Mix together the biscuits (graham crackers), butter and sugar. Press the mixture over the base and up the sides of an 18 cm/7 inch springform cake pan. Chill while making the filling.

Set aside eight of the nut halves for decoration and chop the remainder. Place the marshmallows and coffee in a heavy saucepan and heat gently, stirring frequently, until the marshmallows have melted. Dissolve the gelatine in the water and stir into the marshmallow mixture. Leave to cool until on the point of setting.

Whip the cream until it forms soft peaks. Fold into the coffee mixture with the chopped nuts. Pour into the crumb crust and chill until set.

When ready to serve, remove from the pan and place on a serving dish. Decorate with the reserved nut halves and a sprinkling of ground coffee.
Serves 6

Coffee Custard Tart

METRIC/IMPERIAL	AMERICAN
100 g/4 oz unsalted butter	½ cup unsalted butter
150 g/5 oz rolled oats	1⅔ cups rolled oats
100 g/4 oz flaked almonds	1 cup slivered almonds
100 g/4 oz brown sugar	⅔ cup brown sugar
Filling:	**Filling:**
3 eggs, beaten	3 eggs, beaten
150 ml/¼ pint single cream	¾ cup light cream
150 ml/¼ pint milk	¾ cup milk
150 ml/¼ pint strong black coffee	¾ cup strong black coffee
2 tablespoons caster sugar	2 tablespoons sugar

Melt the butter in a frying pan. Add the oats, almonds and sugar and fry for 5 minutes, stirring frequently. Press over the bottom and up the sides of a 20 cm/8 inch flan or quiche pan.

Whisk together the eggs, cream, milk, coffee and sugar. Pour into the oat crust. Cook in a preheated moderate oven (180°C/350°F, Gas Mark 4) for 45 minutes. Serve warm or cold.
Serves 6

Coffee Baked Apples

METRIC/IMPERIAL	AMERICAN
4 large cooking apples	4 large tart apples
2 bananas	2 bananas
1 teaspoon lemon juice	1 teaspoon lemon juice
50 g/2 oz ground almonds	½ cup ground almonds
50 g/2 oz sultanas	⅓ cup golden raisins
1 teaspoon ground coffee	1 teaspoon ground coffee
150 ml/¼ pint strong black coffee	¾ cup strong black coffee
1 tablespoon soft brown sugar	1 tablespoon brown sugar

Remove the cores from the apples and make a slit around the middle of each one. Mash the bananas with the lemon juice, then stir in the ground almonds, sultanas (raisins) and ground coffee. Fill the holes in the apples with the mixture and place in a baking dish. Mix the coffee and brown sugar together and pour over the top.

Cook in a preheated moderately hot oven (190°C/375°F, Gas Mark 5) for 30 minutes, basting the apples occasionally with the juices in the dish. Serve hot or cold, with cream.
Serves 4

Coffee Bavarois

METRIC/IMPERIAL	AMERICAN
5 egg yolks	5 egg yolks
100 g/4 oz caster sugar	½ cup sugar
300 ml/½ pint milk	1¼ cups milk
150 ml/¼ pint strong black coffee	¾ cup strong black coffee
20 g/¾ oz gelatine	1½ envelopes unflavored gelatin
4 tablespoons hot water	¼ cup hot water
300 ml/½ pint double cream	1¼ cups heavy cream
To decorate:	**For decoration:**
150 ml/¼ pint double cream, whipped	¾ cup heavy cream, whipped
1 tablespoon ground coffee	1 tablespoon ground coffee

Beat the egg yolks and sugar together until thick and pale yellow in colour. Heat the milk and coffee together until just below boiling point. Gradually pour on to the egg yolks and sugar mixture, stirring constantly. Strain the mixture into a clean, heavy saucepan or double boiler, and heat gently, stirring, until the mixture coats the back of a spoon. Do not allow the mixture to boil or it will curdle.

Dissolve the gelatine in the water. Stir into the custard and pour the mixture into a large bowl. Allow to cool, then chill until on the point of setting.

Whip the cream until it forms soft peaks. Fold into the custard mixture. Pour into a 23 cm/ 9 inch ring mould and return to the refrigerator to set.

When ready to serve, turn out the bavarois on to a serving dish and decorate with rosettes of whipped cream. Sprinkle each rosette with some ground coffee.
Serves 6 to 8

Dried Fruit Compote

METRIC/IMPERIAL	AMERICAN
100 g/4 oz dried apricots	⅔ cup dried apricots
50 g/2 oz dried apple	⅓ cup dried apple
100 g/4 oz prunes	⅔ cup prunes
50 g/2 oz raisins	⅓ cup raisins
50 g/2 oz sultanas	⅓ cup golden raisins
50 g/2 oz currants	⅓ cup currants
600 ml/1 pint strong black coffee	2½ cups strong black coffee

Place all the ingredients in a saucepan and bring to the boil. Simmer for 2 to 3 minutes, then pour into a bowl. Allow to cool, then cover and leave in a cool place for at least 12 hours.
Serves 4 to 6
Note: This dish is delicious served with muesli (granola) for breakfast, or in Coffee Coupelles (page 49). Sugar may be added to taste.

Coffee Parfait

METRIC/IMPERIAL	AMERICAN
100 g/4 oz unsalted butter	½ cup unsalted butter
100 g/4 oz rolled oats	1⅓ cups rolled oats
100 g/4 oz flaked almonds	1 cup sliced almonds
1 teaspoon instant coffee powder	1 teaspoon instant coffee powder
2 teaspoons soft brown sugar	2 teaspoons brown sugar
Filling:	**Filling:**
2 teaspoons lemon juice	2 teaspoons lemon juice
225 g/8 oz cream cheese	½ lb cream cheese
300 ml/½ pint double cream	1¼ cups heavy cream
1 tablespoon sugar	1 tablespoon sugar
450 g/1 lb raspberries	1 lb raspberries

Melt the butter in a saucepan. Add the oats, almonds, coffee and sugar. Cook until golden brown, turning frequently. Spoon into a 20 cm/ 8 inch flan or quiche pan and press over the base and up the sides.

Mix the lemon juice, cream cheese, cream and sugar together until smooth and place on the oat mixture. Pile the raspberries on top and sprinkle with instant coffee powder.
Serves 6 to 8

Little Mocha Pots

METRIC/IMPERIAL	AMERICAN
2 eggs, separated	2 eggs, separated
25 g/1 oz caster sugar	2 tablespoons sugar
100 g/4 oz plain chocolate	4 squares (1 oz each) chocolate
2 teaspoons coffee liqueur	2 teaspoons coffee liqueur
75 ml/3 fl oz cream	⅓ cup cream
2 teaspoons medium ground coffee	2 teaspoons medium ground coffee
1 teaspoon ground walnuts	1 teaspoon ground walnuts

Put the egg yolks and sugar in a large heatproof bowl and place over a pan of gently simmering water. Whisk until the mixture is fluffy. Remove the bowl from the heat and continue whisking until the mixture is cool.

Melt the chocolate with the liqueur and cool. Stir in the cream and fold into the egg mixture. Beat the egg whites until stiff and fold into the chocolate mixture with the ground coffee and walnuts. Divide the mixture between six individual pots and chill until set.
Serves 6

Peach Coffee Kuchen

METRIC/IMPERIAL	AMERICAN
175 g/6 oz self-raising flour	1½ cups self-rising flour
¼ teaspoon salt	¼ teaspoon salt
50 g/2 oz butter	¼ cup butter
50 g/2 oz caster sugar	¼ cup sugar
1 egg, beaten	1 egg, beaten
3 tablespoons milk	3 tablespoons milk
3 tablespoons strong black coffee	3 tablespoons strong black coffee
1 × 425 g/15 oz can peach halves, drained	1 can (16 oz) peach halves, drained

Sift the flour and salt together. Cream the butter with the sugar until light and fluffy. Beat in the egg. Fold in the flour with the milk and coffee. Pour into a greased 23 cm/9 inch flan or quiche pan. Press the peaches into the mixture.

Cook in a preheated moderately hot oven (190°C/375°F, Gas Mark 5) for 30 minutes or until firm and brown. Serve warm or cold.
Serves 6 to 8

Dried Fruit Compote in Coffee Coupelles
(page 49)

Coffee Walnut Mousse

METRIC/IMPERIAL	AMERICAN
175 g/6 oz unsalted butter	¾ cup unsalted butter
175 g/6 oz caster sugar	¾ cup sugar
100 g/4 oz ground walnuts	1 cup ground walnuts
2 eggs, separated	2 eggs, separated
2 tablespoons strong black coffee	2 tablespoons strong black coffee
2 tablespoons coffee liqueur	2 tablespoons coffee liqueur
300 ml/½ pint double cream	1¼ cups heavy cream
To decorate:	**For decoration:**
12 walnut halves	12 walnut halves
whipped cream	whipped cream

Cream the butter and sugar together until light and fluffy. Beat in the walnuts and egg yolks. Add the coffee and liqueur. Whip the cream until thick. Beat the egg whites until stiff. Fold the cream and egg whites into the walnut mixture. Spoon into a serving dish.

Leave the mousse overnight in the refrigerator. Decorate with the walnut halves and whipped cream before serving.
Serves 6

Coffee Jelly (Gelatin) à la Sabayon

METRIC/IMPERIAL	AMERICAN
450 ml/¾ pint strong black coffee	2 cups strong black coffee
450 ml/¾ pint water	2 cups water
25 g/1 oz gelatine	2 envelopes unflavored gelatin
50 g/2 oz caster sugar	¼ cup sugar
Sabayon sauce:	**Sabayon sauce:**
75 g/3 oz unsalted butter	6 tablespoons unsalted butter
225 g/8 oz caster sugar	1 cup sugar
2 eggs, separated	2 eggs, separated
1 tablespoon strong black coffee	1 tablespoon strong black coffee
1 teaspoon coffee liqueur (optional)	1 teaspoon coffee liqueur (optional)

Mix the coffee and water together over a low heat. Dissolve the gelatine in 6 tablespoons of the hot coffee and water mixture, then add to the remainder with the sugar. Stir gently until the sugar has dissolved. Pour into a dampened 900 ml/1½ pint (1 quart) decorative mould. Chill until firm.

To make the sauce: cream the butter and sugar together until light and fluffy. Place in a double boiler or heatproof bowl over a pan of hot water. Beat the egg yolks thoroughly and add to the pan. Cook very gently, stirring vigorously, until the mixture thickens. Do not boil or the mixture will curdle. Stir in the coffee and coffee liqueur, if using. Remove from the heat. Beat the egg whites until they form soft peaks and fold them into the sauce. Serve warm with the unmoulded jelly (gelatin).
Serves 6

Coffee Chestnut Delight

METRIC/IMPERIAL	AMERICAN
100 g/4 oz fresh brown breadcrumbs	2 cups soft brown bread crumbs
1 × 275 g/10 oz can of whole chestnuts, drained and chopped	1 can (10 oz) whole chestnuts, drained and chopped
50 g/2 oz caster sugar	¼ cup sugar
175 ml/6 fl oz strong black coffee	¾ cup strong black coffee
15 g/½ oz gelatine	1 envelope unflavored gelatin
3 tablespoons hot water	3 tablespoons hot water
300 ml/½ pint double cream	1¼ cups heavy cream
15 g/½ oz vanilla sugar	1 tablespoon vanilla sugar
4 egg whites	4 egg whites
pinch of salt	pinch of salt
To decorate:	**For decoration:**
whipped cream	whipped cream
glacé cherries	glacé cherries

Place the breadcrumbs, chestnuts, sugar and coffee in a food processor or blender and purée until smooth. Dissolve the gelatine in the water and stir into the chestnut mixture. Chill until on the point of setting.

Whip the cream with the vanilla sugar until thick. Beat the egg whites with the salt until they form soft peaks. Fold the egg whites and cream into the chestnut mixture. Pour into a large soufflé dish or individual ramekins and chill until set. Serve decorated with whipped cream and glacé cherries.
Serves 10 to 12

Coffee Ice Cream

METRIC/IMPERIAL	AMERICAN
300 ml/½ pint single cream	1¼ cups light cream
150 ml/¼ pint strong black coffee	¾ cup strong black coffee
3 egg yolks	3 egg yolks
100 g/4 oz caster sugar	½ cup sugar
450 ml/¾ pint double cream	2 cups heavy cream

Combine the single (light) cream and coffee in a saucepan and bring to just below boiling point.

Beat the egg yolks and sugar together until thick and pale yellow in colour. Gradually pour the hot coffee mixture into the egg mixture, stirring constantly. Strain into a double boiler or heavy saucepan and stir over a gentle heat until the custard thickens enough to coat the back of the spoon. Do not allow the custard to boil. Pour the custard into a bowl and leave to cool.

Whip the double (heavy) cream until it forms soft peaks. Fold into the custard. Pour into a freezerproof container and freeze for 1 hour. Beat the mixture well, then freeze for a further hour. Beat again, then freeze for at least a further 1 to 2 hours.
Serves 4 to 6

Coffee and Brown Breadcrumb Ice Cream

METRIC/IMPERIAL	AMERICAN
100 g/4 oz soft brown sugar	⅔ cup dark brown sugar
150 ml/¼ pint strong black coffee	¾ cup strong black coffee
25 g/1 oz butter	2 tablespoons butter
2 teaspoons lemon juice	2 teaspoons lemon juice
2 teaspoons arrowroot, dissolved in a little water	2 teaspoons arrowroot, dissolved in a little water
1 × 400 g/14 oz can evaporated milk, chilled overnight	1 can (16 oz) evaporated milk, chilled overnight
50 g/2 oz dry brown breadcrumbs, toasted	⅔ cup dry brown bread crumbs, toasted

Heat the sugar and coffee gently in a pan, stirring until the sugar has dissolved. Add the butter and lemon juice and bring to the boil. Boil for 5 minutes without stirring. Stir in the arrowroot and simmer, stirring, until thickened. Leave to cool.

Whisk the evaporated milk until thick and frothy, then fold into the coffee mixture with the breadcrumbs. Pour into a freezerproof container and freeze for 1 hour. Beat the mixture well, then freeze for a further hour. Beat again, then freeze for another 4 hours.
Serves 4 to 6

Coffee and Vanilla Bombe

METRIC/IMPERIAL	AMERICAN
1 quantity coffee ice cream (see left)	1 quantity coffee ice cream (see left)
4 tablespoons water	¼ cup water
75 g/3 oz caster sugar	6 tablespoons sugar
4 egg yolks	4 egg yolks
450 ml/¾ pint double cream	2 cups heavy cream
3 drops of vanilla essence	3 drops of vanilla
25 g/1 oz ground coffee	¼ cup ground coffee
2 tablespoons coffee liqueur	2 tablespoons coffee liqueur
To decorate:	**For decoration:**
150 ml/¼ pint double cream, whipped	¾ cup heavy cream, whipped
12 coffee beans	12 coffee beans

Remove the coffee ice cream from the freezer and allow to soften for 25 minutes. Completely line a chilled 1.2 litre/2 pint (5 cup) bombe mould with the ice cream and return to the freezer to harden

Put the water and sugar in a heavy saucepan. Heat gently, stirring occasionally, until the sugar has dissolved. Raise the heat and boil rapidly until the thread stage is reached (110°C/230°F) on a sugar thermometer.

Beat the egg yolks, preferably using an electric mixer. Gradually beat in the sugar syrup. Whip the cream until thick and fold into the yolk mixture with the vanilla, ground coffee and liqueur. Spoon into the ice cream lined mould and cover with oiled greaseproof or wax paper and the lid of the bombe mould. Freeze for at least 12 hours.

To serve, turn out the bombe on to a serving plate. Decorate with cream and coffee beans.
Serves 6

Cakes & Pastries

Coffee Palmiers

METRIC/IMPERIAL
225 g/8 oz frozen puff
  pastry, thawed
50 g/2 oz caster sugar
25 g/1 oz instant
  coffee powder

AMERICAN
½ lb frozen patty
  shells, thawed
¼ cup sugar
¼ cup instant coffee
  powder

Roll out the dough to a rectangle about 33 × 15 cm/13 × 6 inches. Brush the surface with water, then sprinkle over half the sugar and half the coffee. Fold in the long sides so that they meet in the middle, then brush the newly exposed surfaces with a little more water. Sprinkle over the remaining sugar and coffee. Fold together the long sides.

Cut the strip into 1 cm/½ inch pieces and lay them on a dampened baking sheet, well apart, and cut side down. Press lightly to flatten. Cook in a preheated hot oven (220°C/425°F, Gas Mark 7) for 10 minutes or until set and just beginning to colour.

Remove the palmiers from the oven and turn with a palette knife. Return to the oven and continue cooking for 5 to 7 minutes or until crisp and golden. Leave to cool on a wire rack.
Makes 26

Coffee Palmiers; Coffee Macaroons; Coffee Butterfly Cakes; Coffee Coconut Pyramids

Coffee Butterfly Cakes

METRIC/IMPERIAL
100 g/4 oz butter,
  softened
100 g/4 oz caster
  sugar
2 eggs, beaten
75 g/3 oz self-raising
  flour
25 g/1 oz instant
  coffee powder
1 tablespoon milk
20 coffee beans to
  decorate
Icing:
50 g/2 oz unsalted
  butter
100 g/4 oz icing sugar
2 tablespoons strong
  black coffee

AMERICAN
½ cup butter,
  softened
½ cup sugar
2 eggs, beaten
¾ cup self-rising flour
¼ cup instant coffee
  powder
1 tablespoon milk
20 coffee beans to
  decorate
Icing:
¼ cup unsalted butter
1 cup confectioners'
  sugar
2 tablespoons strong
  black coffee

Cream the butter and sugar together until light and fluffy. Gradually beat in the eggs. Mix together the flour and coffee and fold into the creamed mixture. Beat in the milk. Divide the mixture between 20 small paper cake cases and arrange them on a baking sheet. Cook in a preheated moderately hot oven (190°C/375°F, Gas Mark 5) for 15 minutes or until risen and light golden brown in colour. Remove from the oven and allow to cool.

Meanwhile make the icing: cream the butter until light and really soft, then gradually beat in the sugar. Beat in the coffee. Cut the tops off the cakes and cut each top in half. Place a blob of icing on each cake, and press in the tops to form 'wings'. Decorate each cake with a whole coffee bean.
Makes 20

Coffee Coconut Pyramids

METRIC/IMPERIAL	AMERICAN
40 g/1½ oz rice flour	6 tablespoons rice flour
100 g/4 oz caster sugar	½ cup sugar
225 g/8 oz desiccated coconut	2⅔ cups shredded coconut
½ teaspoon vanilla essence	½ teaspoon vanilla
1 teaspoon instant coffee powder	1 teaspoon instant coffee powder
3 egg whites	3 egg whites

Mix the rice flour, sugar, coconut, vanilla and coffee together. Whisk the egg whites until little peaks form. Fold the egg whites into the coconut mixture with a metal spoon.

Form the mixture into pyramids in the palm of the hand and place on baking sheets lined with rice paper. Cook in a preheated cool oven (150°C/300°F, Gas Mark 2) for 1 hour or until brown. Leave to cool on the baking sheet, then cut the rice paper around the pyramids.
Makes 12
Illustrated on page 38

Coffee Macaroons

METRIC/IMPERIAL	AMERICAN
100 g/4 oz caster sugar	½ cup sugar
100 g/4 oz ground almonds	1 cup ground almonds
1 teaspoon rice flour	1 teaspoon rice flour
1 teaspoon instant coffee powder	1 teaspoon instant coffee powder
2 egg whites, beaten	2 egg whites, beaten
½ teaspoon vanilla essence	½ teaspoon vanilla
shredded almonds to decorate	shredded almonds to decorate

Mix the sugar, ground almonds, rice flour and coffee together. Beat the egg whites until stiff. Fold into the almond mixture with the vanilla.

Place dessertspoonfuls of the mixture on to a baking sheet lined with rice paper. Decorate with the shredded almonds. Cook in a preheated moderate oven (180°C/350°F, Gas Mark 4) for 20 minutes. Leave to cool on the baking sheet, then cut the rice paper around the biscuits (cookies).
Makes 10
Illustrated on page 38

Coffee Almond Slices

METRIC/IMPERIAL	AMERICAN
225 g/8 oz unsalted butter	1 cup unsalted butter
100 g/4 oz caster sugar	½ cup sugar
350 g/12 oz plain flour, sifted	3 cups all-purpose flour, sifted
1 tablespoon instant coffee powder	1 tablespoon instant coffee powder
7 tablespoons raspberry jam	7 tablespoons raspberry jam
100 g/4 oz flaked almonds	1 cup sliced almonds

Cream the butter and sugar together until light and fluffy. Fold in the flour and coffee and mix together well. Spread the mixture in a greased 33 × 23 cm/13 × 9 inch baking tin. Spread the jam over the top and sprinkle with the almonds.

Cook in a preheated moderate oven (180°C/350°F, Gas Mark 4) for 25 minutes. Leave to cool in the tin for 5 minutes, then cut in half and transfer to wire rack. When cold, cut into slices.
Makes 18

Coffee and Almond Shortbread

METRIC/IMPERIAL	AMERICAN
100 g/4 oz plain flour	1 cup all-purpose flour
50 g/2 oz rice flour	½ cup rice flour
50 g/2 oz caster sugar	¼ cup sugar
1 tablespoon instant coffee powder	1 tablespoon instant coffee powder
100 g/4 oz butter, cut into pieces	½ cup butter, cut into pieces
50 g/2 oz ground almonds	½ cup ground almonds

Sift the flour, rice flour, sugar and coffee into a mixing bowl. Rub (cut) in the butter until the mixture forms a light dough, working in the almonds towards the end. Do not overwork the dough or the shortbread will be heavy when cooked.

Roll out the dough on a lightly floured board or marble slab to about 1 cm/½ inch thickness, and cut it into 2 × 5 cm/¾ × 2 inch fingers. Arrange the fingers on a lightly greased baking sheet. Cook in a preheated moderate oven (180°C/350°F, Gas Mark 4) for 20 to 25 minutes or until pale golden and firm. Cool the biscuits (cookies) on a wire rack.
Makes 12

Coffee Puff Pastry Twists

METRIC/IMPERIAL	AMERICAN
225 g/8 oz frozen puff pastry, thawed	½ lb frozen patty shells, thawed
1 egg white, lightly beaten	1 egg white, lightly beaten
25 g/1 oz caster sugar	2 tablespoons sugar
2 teaspoons instant coffee powder	2 teaspoons instant coffee powder
50 g/2 oz walnuts, chopped	½v cup chopped walnuts
25 g/1 oz icing sugar, sifted	¼ cup confectioners' sugar, sifted

Roll out the dough to a 30 × 20 cm/12 × 8 inch rectangle. Lightly mark in half lengthways. Brush half with the egg white, then sprinkle with the caster sugar, coffee and walnuts. Fold the dough over in half then roll up firmly to seal in the filling. Cut into 1 cm/½ inch lengths and twist each one. Place on a dampened baking sheet.

Cook in a preheated hot oven (230°C/450°F, Gas Mark 8) for 8 to 10 minutes or until the twists are puffed and light golden in colour.

Leave to cool on a wire rack. Serve dusted with the icing (confectioners') sugar.
Makes about 20

Chocolate Mocha Biscuits (Cookies)

METRIC/IMPERIAL	AMERICAN
100 g/4 oz butter	½ cup butter
100 g/4 oz sugar	½ cup sugar
1 egg, beaten	1 egg, beaten
3 drops of vanilla essence	3 drops of vanilla
225 g/8 oz self-raising flour	2 cups self-rising flour
1 teaspoon instant coffee powder	1 teaspoon instant coffee powder
1 tablespoon cocoa powder	1 tablespoon cocoa powder
milk	milk
Icing:	**Icing:**
100 g/4 oz unsalted butter	½ cup unsalted butter
100 g/4 oz icing sugar, sifted	1 cup confectioners' sugar, sifted
2 teaspoons instant coffee powder	2 teaspoons instant coffee powder

Cream the butter and sugar together until light and fluffy. Gradually beat in the egg. Add the vanilla. Sift the flour with the coffee and cocoa and fold into the creamed mixture. If necessary, add a little milk to make a firm dough.

Lightly flour your hands and form the dough into balls about 2.5 cm/1 inch in diameter. Place the balls on a lightly greased baking sheet, leaving 7.5 cm/3 inches between each ball to allow for spreading. Dip a fork in cold water and gently flatten each ball to a thickness of 1 cm/½ inch.

Cook in a preheated moderately hot oven (190°C/375°F, Gas Mark 5) for 10 to 12 minutes. Leave to cool on a wire rack.

To make the icing: cream the butter until light and really soft, then gradually beat in the sugar and coffee. Use the icing to sandwich the cooled biscuits (cookies) together in pairs.
Makes about 12

Old-fashioned Coffee Walnut Cake

METRIC/IMPERIAL	AMERICAN
175 g/6 oz butter	¾ cup butter
175 g/6 oz caster sugar	¾ cup sugar
3 eggs, beaten	3 eggs, beaten
175 g/6 oz self-raising flour, sifted	1½ cups self-rising flour, sifted
2 tablespoons very strong black coffee	2 tablespoons very strong black coffee
8 walnut halves to decorate	8 walnut halves to decorate
Icing:	**Icing:**
100 g/4 oz unsalted butter	½ cup unsalted butter
175 g/6 oz icing sugar, sifted	1½ cups confectioners' sugar, sifted
2 teaspoons instant coffee powder	2 teaspoons instant coffee powder

Cream the butter and sugar together until light and fluffy. Gradually beat in the eggs. Fold the flour gently into the mixture, then add the coffee. Divide the mixture between two greased and floured 18 cm/7 inch sandwich tins (layer cake pans).

Cook in a preheated moderately hot oven (190°C/375°F, Gas Mark 5) for 20 to 25 minutes or until golden brown and firm to the touch. Leave the cakes to cool in the tins for 5 minutes before turning out on to a wire rack.

To make the icing: cream the butter until soft, then beat in the sugar and coffee.

When the cakes are completely cold, sandwich them together with half the icing. Spread the remaining icing over the top. Use a fork to make a pattern on the icing, then decorate the cake with the walnut halves.
Makes one 18 cm/7 inch cake

Old-fashioned Coffee Walnut Cake

Mocha Cake

METRIC/IMPERIAL	AMERICAN
100 g/4 oz cocoa powder	1 cup cocoa powder
1 tablespoon instant coffee powder	1 tablespoon instant coffee powder
450 ml/¾ pint boiling water	2 cups boiling water
225 g/8 oz butter	1 cup butter
225 g/8 oz caster sugar	1 cup sugar
4 large eggs, beaten	4 large eggs, beaten
2 teaspoons vanilla essence	2 teaspoons vanilla
350 g/12 oz self-raising flour, sifted	3 cups self-rising flour, sifted
1 teaspoon baking powder, sifted	1 teaspoon baking powder, sifted
Icing:	**Icing:**
175 g/6 oz plain chocolate	6 squares (1 oz each) semisweet chocolate
1 tablespoon instant coffee powder	1 tablespoon instant coffee powder
175 g/6 oz unsalted butter, melted	¾ cup unsalted butter, melted
225 g/8 oz icing sugar, sifted	2 cups confectioners' sugar, sifted
Filling:	**Filling:**
300 ml/½ pint double cream	1¼ cups heavy cream
25 g/1 oz vanilla sugar	2 tablespoons vanilla sugar

Dissolve the cocoa and coffee in the boiling water; cool. Cream the butter with the sugar until light and fluffy. Slowly beat in the eggs and the vanilla. Fold in the flour and baking powder alternately with the cocoa mixture.

Divide the mixture between three greased 23 cm/9 inch round deep cake pans and smooth the tops. Cook in a preheated moderate oven (180°C/350°F, Gas Mark 4) for 30 minutes. Leave to cool in the tins for a few minutes, then carefully turn out on to a wire rack and leave to cool completely.

Break up the chocolate and place in a pan with the coffee and butter. Heat gently, stirring, until the chocolate and butter have melted. Cool slightly, then beat in the sugar to make a firm icing.

Whip the cream with the vanilla sugar until stiff. Use to sandwich together the cake layers, then smooth the chocolate icing over the top.
Makes one 23 cm/9 inch cake

Mocha Genoese Gâteau

METRIC/IMPERIAL	AMERICAN
4 eggs	4 eggs
115 g/4½ oz caster sugar	½ cup plus 1 tablespoon sugar
100 g/4 oz plain flour, sifted	1 cup all-purpose flour, sifted
40 g/1½ oz butter, melted and cooled	3 tablespoons butter, melted and cooled
100 g/4 oz blanched almonds, chopped and toasted	1 cup chopped toasted almonds
Icing:	**Icing:**
65 g/2½ oz sugar	5 tablespoons sugar
150 ml/¼ pint water	¾ cup water
2 egg yolks, beaten	2 egg yolks, beaten
150 g/5 oz unsalted butter, slightly softened	10 tablespoons unsalted butter, slightly softened
50 g/2 oz chocolate, melted and cooled	2 squares (1 oz each) chocolate, melted and cooled
2 tablespoons very strong black coffee	2 tablespoons very strong black coffee

Place the eggs and sugar in a heatproof bowl over a pan of hot water and whisk until thick and mousse-like. Remove the bowl from the heat and continue whisking until cool. (If using an electric mixer, no heat is needed.) Gently fold in the flour and butter until all is well incorporated. Pour the cake mixture into a greased 20 cm/8 inch round deep cake tin.

Cook in a preheated moderate oven (180°C/350°F, Gas Mark 4) for 35 to 40 minutes or until the cake is firm and begins to shrink from sides of tin. Cool the cake on a wire rack.

Meanwhile make the icing. Place the sugar and water in a saucepan and heat, stirring to dissolve the sugar. Raise the heat and boil to the large thread stage (110°C/230°F) on a sugar thermometer. Cool a little, then pour the sugar syrup very slowly on to the egg yolks, beating well all the time. When cool, thick and fluffy, gradually beat in the butter. Divide the icing in half. Flavour one half with the melted chocolate, and the other half with the coffee.

Split the cooled cake into two layers and sandwich together with a little of the chocolate icing. Spread the sides of the cake with a little of the coffee icing, and coat with the almonds. Put the remaining icings into two piping bags fitted with rose nozzles (tubes). Pipe two opposite quarters of the top of the cake with rosettes of one flavour, and the remaining two quarters with the second flavour.
Makes one 20 cm/8 inch cake

Coffee Cashew Cake

METRIC/IMPERIAL	AMERICAN
100 g/4 oz unsalted butter	½ cup unsalted butter
100 g/4 oz caster sugar	½ cup sugar
2 eggs, beaten	2 eggs, beaten
225 g/8 oz plain flour, sifted	2 cups all-purpose flour, sifted
2 teaspoons baking powder, sifted	2 teaspoons baking powder, sifted
100 g/4 oz cashew nuts, 12 left whole and the remainder ground	¼ lb cashew nuts, 12 left whole and the remainder ground (about ¾ cup ground)
4 tablespoons strong black coffee	¼ cup strong black coffee
½ teaspoon ground cinnamon	½ teaspoon ground cinnamon
½ teaspoon salt	½ teaspoon salt
Filling:	**Filling:**
50 g/2 oz butter	¼ cup butter
50 g/2 oz icing sugar	½ cup confectioners' sugar
1 teaspoon instant coffee powder	1 teaspoon instant coffee powder

Cream the butter and sugar together until light and fluffy. Slowly beat in the eggs. Fold in the flour, baking powder and ground cashew nuts, then add the coffee, cinnamon and salt and mix well. Divide the mixture between two greased 19 cm/7½ inch sandwich tins (layer cake pans). Decorate the top of one with the whole cashew nuts.

Cook in a preheated moderate oven (180°C/350°F, Gas Mark 4) for 30 minutes. Turn out on to a wire rack and leave to cool.

To make the filling: cream the butter until really light and soft, then beat in the sugar. Beat in the coffee. Use to sandwich the two cake layers together, placing the layer decorated with whole cashew nuts on top.

Serves 6 to 8

Coffee 'Hedgehog' Cake

METRIC/IMPERIAL	AMERICAN
100 g/4 oz unsalted butter	½ cup unsalted butter
100 g/4 oz caster sugar	½ cup sugar
100 g/4 oz ground almonds	1 cup ground almonds
4 eggs, beaten	4 eggs, beaten
225 g/8 oz self-raising flour, sifted	2 cups self-rising flour, sifted
2 teaspoons baking powder	2 teaspoons baking powder
120 ml/4 fl oz strong black coffee	½ cup strong black coffee
100 g/4 oz flaked almonds, toasted	1 cup toasted sliced almonds
Icing:	**Icing:**
75 g/3 oz unsalted butter	6 tablespoons unsalted butter
75 g/3 oz icing sugar, sifted	¾ cup confectioners' sugar, sifted
2 teaspoons instant coffee powder	2 teaspoons instant coffee powder

Cream the butter with the sugar until light and fluffy. Beat in the ground almonds and the eggs. Fold in the flour, baking powder and coffee. Pour into a greased 23 cm/9 inch round deep cake tin.

Cook in a preheated moderate oven (180°C/350°F, Gas Mark 4) for 45 minutes or until a knife inserted in the centre comes out clean. Leave to cool on a wire rack.

For the icing, cream the butter until soft, then beat in the sugar and coffee. Use to ice the cake. Stick the almonds into the icing to resemble the hedgehog's quills.

Makes one 23 cm/9 inch cake

Mille Feuilles

METRIC/IMPERIAL	AMERICAN
1 × 225 g/8 oz packet frozen puff pastry, thawed	½ lb frozen patty shells, thawed
Filling:	**Filling:**
300 ml/½ pint milk	1¼ cups milk
300 ml/½ pint strong black coffee	1¼ cups strong black coffee
5 drops of vanilla essence	5 drops of vanilla
150 g/5 oz caster sugar	⅔ cup sugar
6 egg yolks	6 egg yolks
20 g/¾ oz plain flour	3 tablespoons all-purpose flour
20 g/¾ oz cornflour	3 tablespoons cornstarch
Glacé icing:	**Glacé icing:**
100 g/4 oz icing sugar	1 cup confectioners' sugar
about 1 tablespoon water	about 1 tablespoon water
Coffee icing:	**Coffee icing:**
50 g/2 oz icing sugar	½ cup confectioners' sugar
2 tablespoons strong black coffee	2 tablespoons strong black coffee

Roll out the dough to a rectangle about 23 × 30 cm/9 × 12 inches. Trim the edges and cut in half lengthways. Place the two strips of dough on a dampened baking sheet and cook in a preheated hot oven (220°C/425°F, Gas Mark 7) for 25 to 30 minutes or until well risen and golden brown. Transfer to a wire rack and leave to cool.

Meanwhile make the filling. Bring the milk and coffee to the boil in a heavy saucepan together with the vanilla and 50 g/2 oz (¼ cup) of the sugar, stirring until the sugar has dissolved. Put the egg yolks and remaining sugar in a large mixing bowl and whisk together until the mixture becomes thick and pale in colour. Gradually whisk in the flour and cornflour (cornstarch), making sure that there are no lumps. Slowly whisk in the hot milk and coffee mixture. Rinse out the saucepan and pour in the mixture. Place the pan back on the heat and stir until the custard thickens. Pour the custard into a bowl and allow to cool.

Split each pastry rectangle in half horizontally and sandwich together with the custard.

To make the glacé icing, sift the sugar into a bowl and gradually beat in enough water to make a smooth, thick icing. Make up the coffee icing by the same method.

Place the coffee icing in a piping bag fitted with a size 2 writing nozzle (tube). Spread the top of the mille feuilles with the white glacé icing and immediately pipe lines of coffee icing across the top, 1 cm/½ inch apart. Pull a wet skewer across the lines in alternate directions at 2.5 cm/1 inch intervals. Leave to set before serving.
Serves 6 to 8

Coffee Galettes

METRIC/IMPERIAL	AMERICAN
65 g/2½ oz butter	5 tablespoons butter
90 g/3½ oz caster sugar	7 tablespoons sugar
75 g/3 oz blanched almonds, chopped	¾ cup chopped almonds
75 g/3 oz chopped mixed candied peel	½ cup chopped mixed candied fruit peel
40 g/1½ oz plain flour, sifted	6 tablespoons all-purpose flour, sifted
2 teaspoons strong black coffee	2 teaspoons strong black coffee

Cream the butter and sugar together until light and fluffy. Stir in the almonds and candied peel, then gently fold in the flour and coffee. Place the mixture in small spoonfuls 5 cm/2 inches apart on a lightly greased baking sheet. Flatten each gently with a wet fork.

Cook in a preheated hot oven (220°C/425°F, Gas Mark 7) for 5 to 7 minutes. Remove the biscuits (cookies) immediately from the baking sheet and leave to cool on a wire rack.
Makes 12
Note: These biscuits make a delicious accompaniment to ice creams.

Mille Feuilles

Coffee Ginger Biscuits (Cookies)

METRIC/IMPERIAL	AMERICAN
100 g/4 oz butter	½ cup butter
100 g/4 oz caster sugar	½ cup sugar
3 tablespoons clear honey	3 tablespoons honey
4 tablespoons strong black coffee	¼ cup strong black coffee
1 teaspoon ground ginger	1 teaspoon ground ginger
½ teaspoon mixed spice	½ teaspoon apple pie spice
½ teaspoon ground cinnamon	½ teaspoon ground cinnamon
1 teaspoon bicarbonate of soda	1 teaspoon baking soda
375 g/13 oz plain flour	3¼ cups all-purpose flour

Melt the butter in a small saucepan with the sugar, honey and coffee. Stir well. Remove from the heat and allow to cool. Stir in the spices and soda.

Sift the flour into a bowl and make a well in the centre. Pour the cooled coffee mixture into the well and mix with the flour. Knead until smooth. Divide the dough in half and shape into two 'sausages'. Leave to rest in the refrigerator for at least 3 hours, or preferably overnight.

Cut into 5 mm/¼ inch thick slices and place on a greased baking sheet. Cook in a preheated moderate oven (180°C/350°F, Gas Mark 4) for 10 minutes. Leave to cool on a wire rack.
Makes 50 to 60

Coffee Snaps

METRIC/IMPERIAL	AMERICAN
50 g/2 oz golden syrup	2½ tablespoons light corn syrup
50 g/2 oz butter	¼ cup butter
150 g/5 oz caster sugar	⅔ cup sugar
1 teaspoon instant coffee powder	1 teaspoon instant coffee powder
50 g/2 oz plain flour, sifted	½ cup all-purpose flour, sifted
½ teaspoon grated lemon rind	½ teaspoon grated lemon rind
½ teaspoon lemon juice	½ teaspoon lemon juice
Filling:	**Filling:**
300 ml/½ pint double cream	1¼ cups heavy cream
1 teaspoon very strong black coffee	1 teaspoon very strong black coffee
1 teaspoon caster sugar	1 teaspoon sugar

Place the syrup, butter, sugar and instant coffee in a saucepan and stir over a gentle heat until all the ingredients have melted or dissolved. Remove from the heat. Fold in the flour and lemon rind and juice. Drop three small spoonfuls of the mixture on to a greased baking sheet, leaving plenty of room for the biscuits (cookies) to spread. Cook in a preheated moderate oven (180°C/350°F, Gas Mark 4) for 7 to 10 minutes or until golden in colour.

Gently remove the coffee snaps from the baking sheet, one at a time, with a palette knife and shape them by winding around the handle of a wooden spoon. When set, remove from the spoon and cool on a wire rack.

Cook and shape the remaining biscuits (cookies) in the same way and allow to cool.

To make the filling: whip the cream until it forms soft peaks. Fold in the coffee and sugar. Using a piping bag with a small rose nozzle (tube), pipe the cream filling into the coffee snaps. Serve chilled.
Makes 12
Note: The coffee snaps are easier to remove and shape if using a non-stick baking sheet.

Coffee Hazelnut Meringue Cake

METRIC/IMPERIAL	AMERICAN
6 eggs, separated	6 eggs, separated
175 g/6 oz caster sugar	¾ cup sugar
1 tablespoon instant coffee powder	1 tablespoon instant coffee powder
175 g/6 oz hazelnuts, toasted and ground	1½ cups ground toasted hazelnuts
To finish:	**To finish:**
300 ml/½ pint double cream	1¼ cups heavy cream
2 teaspoons coffee liqueur	2 teaspoons coffee liqueur
2 tablespoons ground coffee	2 tablespoons ground coffee
1 tablespoon icing sugar	1 tablespoon confectioners' sugar

Whisk the egg yolks and sugar together until light and fluffy. Lightly mix in the coffee and nuts. Whisk the egg whites until they form soft peaks. Fold the egg whites into the mixture.

Divide between two greased 20 cm/8 inch sandwich tins (layer cake pans) and smooth over the tops. Cook in a preheated moderate oven (180°C/350°F, Gas Mark 4) for 30 minutes. Leave to cool in the tins for 10 minutes, then turn out on to a wire rack to cool completely.

Whip the cream until thick and fold in the coffee liqueur and 1 tablespoon of the coffee. Use to sandwich the two meringue layers together and place the cake on a serving dish. Decorate with the icing (confectioners') sugar and remaining coffee.
Serves 6 to 8

Coffee Almond Tiles

METRIC/IMPERIAL	AMERICAN
2 egg whites	2 egg whites
65 g/2½ oz caster sugar	5 tablespoons sugar
50 g/2 oz plain flour	½ cup all-purpose flour
1 teaspoon instant coffee powder	1 teaspoon instant coffee powder
50 g/2 oz butter, melted and cooled	¼ cup butter, melted and cooled
25 g/1 oz blanched almonds, chopped	¼ cup finely chopped almonds
1 teaspoon ground coffee	1 teaspoon ground coffee

Whisk the egg whites until frothy, then gradually add the sugar and continue whisking until stiff and glossy. Gently fold in the sifted flour and instant coffee powder, together with the butter and almonds.

Drop three or four spoonfuls of the mixture on to a greased baking sheet. Spread out each into a shallow round and sprinkle with a pinch of ground coffee. Cook in a preheated moderately hot oven (200°C/400°F, Gas Mark 6) for about 5 minutes or until light golden brown around the edges. Carefully remove the biscuits (cookies) from the baking sheet, one at a time, and place on a lightly greased rolling pin, pressing gently with the fingers to make a tile shape. When set, leave to cool on a wire rack.

Bake and shape the remaining biscuits (cookies) in the same way, using a cool baking sheet for each batch.
Makes 10 to 12

Coffee Coupelles

METRIC/IMPERIAL	AMERICAN
2 egg whites	2 egg whites
65 g/2½ oz caster sugar	5 tablespoons sugar
50 g/2 oz plain flour, sifted	½ cup all-purpose flour, sifted
50 g/2 oz butter, melted and cooled	¼ cup butter, melted and cooled
1 tablespoon freshly ground coffee	1 tablespoon freshly ground coffee

Whisk the egg whites until frothy, then gradually add the sugar and continue whisking until stiff and glossy. Fold in the flour and melted butter.

Drop 3 tablespoonfuls of the mixture on to a greased baking sheet and spread each out thinly to a 10 cm/4 inch round. Sprinkle each with a pinch of ground coffee.

Cook in a preheated moderately hot oven (200°C/400°F, Gas Mark 6) for 5 to 7 minutes or until the edges are golden brown. Remove from the baking sheet one at a time and shape into a cup around an inverted ramekin dish. When set, remove from the dish and leave to cool on a wire rack. Cook and shape the remaining biscuits (cookies) in the same way.

To serve, fill with ice cream, fresh fruit or dried fruit compôte (see page 34).
Makes 8 to 10
Illustrated on page 35

Teatime Breads

Coffee Rum Babas

METRIC/IMPERIAL	AMERICAN
100 g/4 oz plain flour	1 cup all-purpose flour
pinch of salt	pinch of salt
15 g/½ oz fresh yeast	½ oz cake compressed yeast
2 tablespoons caster sugar	2 tablespoons sugar
4 tablespoons lukewarm medium strength black coffee	¼ cup lukewarm medium strength black coffee
2 eggs, beaten	2 eggs, beaten
65 g/2½ oz butter, softened	5 tablespoons butter, softened
Rum syrup:	**Rum syrup:**
100 g/4 oz sugar	½ cup sugar
175 ml/6 fl oz medium strength black coffee	¾ cup medium strength black coffee
4 tablespoons rum	¼ cup rum

Sift the flour and salt into a warm mixing bowl. Cream the yeast and sugar together in a small bowl, then mix in the coffee and eggs. Make a well in the centre of the flour and pour in the yeast liquid. Gradually mix all together, using a wooden spoon, to form a smooth batter. Cover the bowl with a clean teatowel and leave to rise in a warm place for 45 minutes or until doubled in bulk.

Beat in the softened butter, then divide the mixture between eight lightly greased 10 cm/ 4 inch rings or crumpet moulds placed on a greased baking sheet. Each mould should be half full. Leave in a warm place until the dough rises to the tops of the rings.

Cook in a preheated moderately hot oven (200°C/400°F, Gas Mark 6) for 15 minutes or until well risen and golden brown.

Coffee Rum Baba; Coffee Fruit Plait (Braid); Coffee and Walnut Loaf

Meanwhile make the syrup. Dissolve the sugar in the coffee, then boil until syrupy. Stir in the rum.

When the babas are cooked, remove them from the rings. Spoon over the syrup, leaving them to soak up any excess. Leave to cool before serving. The babas may be topped with fresh fruit and whipped cream, if liked.
Makes 8

Coffee Fruit Plait (Braid)

METRIC/IMPERIAL	AMERICAN
1 quantity Coffee Milk Bread dough (see page 53)	1 quantity Coffee Milk Bread dough (see page 53)
50 g/2 oz raisins	⅓ cup raisins
50 g/2 oz sultanas	⅓ cup golden raisins
50 g/2 oz currants	⅓ cup currants
25 g/1 oz chopped mixed candied peel	2 tablespoons chopped mixed candied fruit peel
beaten egg to glaze	beaten egg to glaze
poppy seeds to finish	poppy seeds to finish

Make the Coffee Milk Bread dough and knead in the fruits and peel. Leave to rise as instructed in the recipe for Coffee Milk Bread.

Divide the dough into three equal portions and form each into a sausage shape. Join the three pieces together at one end, then plait (braid) them together, turning the ends under. Place the plait (braid) on a greased baking sheet and leave to rise in a warm place for 30 minutes.

Brush the loaf lightly with beaten egg and sprinkle with poppy seeds. Cook in a preheated moderately hot oven (200°C/400°F, Gas Mark 6) for 35 to 40 minutes or until well risen and golden brown. Cool on a wire rack.
Makes 1 loaf

Coffee Savarin

METRIC/IMPERIAL	AMERICAN
250 g/9 oz plain flour	*2¼ cups all-purpose flour*
15 g/½ oz fresh yeast	*½ oz cake compressed yeast*
2 tablespoons lukewarm water	*2 tablespoons lukewarm water*
2 eggs, beaten	*2 eggs, beaten*
1½ tablespoons caster sugar	*1½ tablespoons sugar*
½ teaspoon salt	*½ teaspoon salt*
100 g/4 oz butter, melted and cooled	*½ cup butter, melted and cooled*
Syrup:	**Syrup:**
225 g/8 oz caster sugar	*1 cup sugar*
300 ml/½ pint strong black coffee	*1¼ cups strong black coffee*
2 tablespoons coffee liqueur	*2 tablespoons coffee liqueur*
To decorate:	**For decoration:**
225 g/8 oz seasonal fruits, prepared as necessary and chopped	*½ lb seasonal fruits, prepared as necessary and chopped (about 1 cup)*
150 ml/¼ pint double cream, whipped	*¾ cup heavy cream, whipped*
1 teaspoon ground coffee	*1 teaspoon ground coffee*

Sift the flour into a warm bowl and make a well in the centre. Dissolve the yeast in the water and pour into the well. Sprinkle the liquid with a little of the flour and leave in a warm place until the yeast begins to bubble up. This will take about 20 minutes.

Drop the eggs into the well and add the sugar and salt. Mix to a smooth dough, using the hands, then beat for 10 to 15 minutes, adding a little more water if the dough appears to be too stiff. (This process can be done in an electric mixer, using a dough hook.) Beat in the melted butter. Cover the bowl with a clean teatowel, and leave to rise in a warm place until doubled in bulk.

Stir the mixture gently, then pour into a 900 ml/1½ pint (1 quart) ring mould. Leave to rise again in a warm place until the mixture fills the tin.

Cook in a preheated hot oven (230°C/450°F, Gas Mark 8) for 20 to 25 minutes. If the savarin becomes too brown, lower the heat to moderately hot (200°C/400°F, Gas Mark 6).

While the savarin is cooking, make the syrup. Dissolve the sugar in the coffee, then raise the heat and boil until a light syrup is formed, 104°C/218°F on a sugar thermometer. Stir in the coffee liqueur.

When the savarin is cooked, turn out on to a wire rack set over a baking sheet. Spoon over the hot syrup until the savarin is saturated. Leave to cool.

To serve, place the savarin on a round serving dish and fill the middle with the fruits. Decorate with the whipped cream and sprinkle with the coffee.

Serves 6

Coffee and Walnut Loaf

METRIC/IMPERIAL	AMERICAN
350 g/12 oz plain flour, sifted	*3 cups all-purpose flour, sifted*
1 teaspoon sugar	*1 teaspoon sugar*
1 teaspoon salt	*1 teaspoon salt*
2 tablespoons instant coffee powder	*2 tablespoons instant coffee powder*
7 g/¼ oz dried yeast	*1 package active dry yeast*
175 ml/6 fl oz lukewarm milk	*¾ cup lukewarm milk*
50 g/2 oz butter, melted and cooled	*¼ cup butter, melted and cooled*
50 g/2 oz walnuts, chopped	*½ cup chopped walnuts*

Combine the flour, sugar, salt, coffee and yeast in a warm bowl. Make a well in the centre and pour in the milk and melted butter. Knead well until the dough is a firm springy ball. Leave to rise in a warm place for 2 hours.

Knead the dough lightly for 2 to 3 minutes, then mix in the walnuts. Shape into two round loaves or one large one and place on a greased baking sheet. Leave in a warm place to rise for 45 minutes.

Cook in a preheated moderately hot oven (190°C/375°F, Gas Mark 5) for 45 minutes (55 minutes if making 1 large loaf). Leave to cool on a wire rack.

Makes 1 or 2 loaves

Note: Fresh yeast can also be used in this recipe.

Illustrated on page 50

Coffee Milk Bread

METRIC/IMPERIAL
450 g/1 lb strong
   white plain flour
1 teaspoon salt
40 g/1½ oz butter,
   melted
150 ml/¼ pint
   lukewarm black
   coffee
150 ml/¼ pint
   lukewarm milk
15 g/½ oz fresh yeast
2 teaspoons caster
   sugar
1 egg, beaten

AMERICAN
4 cups strong bread
   flour
1 teaspoon salt
3 tablespoons butter,
   melted
¾ cup lukewarm
   black coffee
¾ cup lukewarm milk
½ oz cake
   compressed yeast
2 teaspoons sugar
1 egg, beaten

Sift the flour and salt into a warm mixing bowl. Mix together the butter, coffee and milk. Cream the yeast and sugar together and add to the liquid with the egg. Make a well in the centre of the flour and pour in the liquid. Beat the flour and the liquid together until they form a dough.

Turn out on to a lightly floured board and knead thoroughly for 8 to 10 minutes. Place the dough in a warm, lightly oiled mixing bowl, cover with a clean teatowel and leave to rise in a warm place until doubled in size.

Turn the risen dough on to a floured board and knead gently for 1 to 2 minutes. Shape the dough into a loaf and place in a 1 kg/2 lb (9 × 5 inch) loaf tin. Place the tin in a large oiled plastic bag and tie loosely. Set aside to rise until doubled in size.

Remove from the bag and cook in a preheated moderately hot oven (200°C/400°F, Gas Mark 6) for 35 to 40 minutes or until well risen and golden brown. When cooked, the bread will sound hollow when tapped on the base. Cool on a wire rack.
Makes one 1 kg/2 lb loaf

Coffee and Treacle (Molasses) Tea Loaf

METRIC/IMPERIAL
750 g/1½ lb
   wholemeal flour
1 teaspoon salt
25 g/1 oz butter
25 g/1 oz fresh yeast
1 tablespoon caster
   sugar
300 ml/½ pint strong
   black coffee
175 ml/6 fl oz milk
3 tablespoons black
   treacle

AMERICAN
6 cups wholewheat
   flour
1 teaspoon salt
2 tablespoons butter
1 oz cake compressed
   yeast
1 tablespoon sugar
1½ cups strong black
   coffee
¾ cup milk
3 tablespoons
   molasses

Mix the flour and salt in a warm mixing bowl and rub (cut) in the butter. Cream the yeast with the sugar. Combine the coffee, milk and treacle (molasses) in a saucepan and heat until lukewarm. Remove from the heat. Dissolve the yeast in the liquid, then make a well in the flour and pour in the yeast liquid. Sprinkle a little of the flour over the liquid in the well, and set aside in a warm place until the yeast begins to bubble up.

Mix the flour and liquid together, then turn the dough on to a floured board. Knead for 5 to 7 minutes, then place in a clean, lightly oiled mixing bowl. Cover with a clean teatowel and leave to rise in a warm place until doubled in size.

Turn the risen dough on to a floured board and knead gently. Divide the dough in half and shape into loaves. Place in two 450 g/1 lb (7 × 3 inch) loaf tins. Place the tins in large oiled plastic bags and tie loosely. Leave the dough to rise in a warm place until doubled in size.

Remove the tins from the bags and cook in a preheated hot oven (220°C/425°F, Gas Mark 7) for 20 minutes. Reduce the heat to moderately hot (200°C/400°F, Gas Mark 6) and cook for a further 15 minutes. When cooked, the bread will sound hollow if tapped on the base. Leave to cool on a wire rack.
Makes two 450 g/1 lb loaves

Coffee Banana Bread

METRIC/IMPERIAL	AMERICAN
225 g/8 oz plain flour	2 cups all-purpose flour
1 teaspoon bicarbonate of soda	1 teaspoon baking soda
½ teaspoon cream of tartar	½ teaspoon cream of tartar
pinch of salt	pinch of salt
100 g/4 oz butter, cut into pieces	½ cup butter, cut into pieces
175 g/6 oz soft brown sugar	1 cup dark brown sugar
1 teaspoon grated orange rind	1 teaspoon grated orange rind
1 teaspoon orange juice	1 teaspoon orange juice
3 tablespoons very strong black coffee	3 tablespoons very strong black coffee
2 bananas, mashed	2 bananas, mashed
2 eggs, beaten	2 eggs, beaten
1 teaspoon ground coffee	1 teaspoon ground coffee

Sift the flour, soda, cream of tartar and salt into a mixing bowl. Rub (cut) in the butter until the mixture resembles fine breadcrumbs. Stir in the sugar.

In a small bowl, mix together the orange rind and juice, black coffee, mashed bananas and eggs. Gently stir this mixture into the flour until well mixed. Turn into a greased 1 kg/2 lb (9 × 5 inch) loaf tin. Sprinkle the top with the ground coffee.

Cook in a preheated moderate oven (180°C/350°F, Gas Mark 4) for 1¼ hours or until a skewer inserted in the centre comes out clean. Cool on a wire rack.
Makes 1 loaf
Note: This tea bread is best made the day before eating. When cold, store in an airtight container, or wrapped in foil.

Coffee, Apple and Date Loaf

METRIC/IMPERIAL	AMERICAN
175 g/6 oz plain flour, sifted	1½ cups all-purpose flour, sifted
175 g/6 oz wholemeal flour	1½ cups wholewheat flour
1 tablespoon baking powder	1 tablespoon baking powder
100 g/4 oz caster sugar	½ cup sugar
1 teaspoon salt	1 teaspoon salt
1 tablespoon instant coffee powder	1 tablespoon instant coffee powder
1 egg, beaten	1 egg, beaten
300 ml/½ pint milk	1¼ cups milk
2 apples, peeled, cored and chopped	2 apples, peeled, cored and chopped
50 g/2 oz dates, stoned and chopped	⅓ cup chopped dates

Combine the flours, baking powder, sugar, salt and coffee. Beat together the egg and milk and add to the flour mixture with the apples and dates. Mix well. Pour into a greased 450 g/1 lb (7 × 3 inch) loaf tin.

Cook in a preheated moderate oven (180°C/350°F, Gas Mark 4) for 1 hour or until a knife inserted in the centre comes out clean. Allow to cool in the tin.
Makes 1 loaf

Coffee, Apple and Date Loaf; Coffee Soda Bread (page 56); Coffee Banana Bread

Coffee Soda Bread

METRIC/IMPERIAL	AMERICAN
225 g/8 oz plain flour, sifted	2 cups all-purpose flour, sifted
225 g/8 oz wholemeal flour	2 cups wholewheat flour
4 teaspoons cream of tartar	4 teaspoons cream of tartar
2 teaspoons bicarbonate of soda	2 teaspoons baking soda
1 teaspoon salt	1 teaspoon salt
50 g/2 oz butter, cut into pieces	¼ cup butter, cut into pieces
150 ml/¼ pint milk	¾ cup milk
150 ml/¼ pint strong black coffee	¾ cup strong black coffee
2 tablespoons golden syrup	2 tablespoons light corn syrup

Mix the flours together in a large mixing bowl, then stir in the cream of tartar, soda and salt. Rub (cut) in the butter. Place the milk, coffee and syrup in a saucepan and heat gently, stirring until all the ingredients are blended. Leave the liquid to cool a little, then stir it into the flour mixture to form a soft dough.

Turn the dough on to a floured board and knead gently for 2 minutes. Shape the dough into a ball and place it on a lightly greased baking sheet. Cut a deep cross in the top.

Cook in a preheated moderately hot oven (200°C/400°F, Gas Mark 6) for 35 to 40 minutes or until well risen and golden brown. Leave to cool on a wire rack.

Makes 1 loaf

Illustrated on page 55

Coffee Carrot Loaf

METRIC/IMPERIAL	AMERICAN
50 g/2 oz butter	¼ cup butter
3 tablespoons clear honey	3 tablespoons honey
4 tablespoons strong black coffee	¼ cup strong black coffee
2 tablespoons brown sugar	2 tablespoons brown sugar
100 g/4 oz carrots, grated	1 cup grated carrots
75 g/3 oz walnut halves, 3 left whole and the remainder chopped	3 oz walnut halves, 3 left whole and the remainder chopped (about ¾ cup chopped)
2 large eggs, beaten	2 large eggs, beaten
175 g/6 oz wholemeal flour	1½ cups wholewheat flour
1 tablespoon baking powder	1 tablespoon baking powder
1 teaspoon ground cinnamon	1 teaspoon ground cinnamon
pinch of salt	pinch of salt

Melt the butter in a saucepan. Add the honey, coffee and sugar. Stir well, then leave on one side to cool.

Mix the carrots and chopped walnuts together. Beat in the eggs and then the coffee mixture. Sift in the flour, baking powder, cinnamon and salt. Mix well, but be careful not to overmix. Pour into a greased 450 g/1 lb (7 × 3 inch) loaf tin. Arrange the whole walnut halves on top.

Cook in a preheated moderate oven (180°C/350°F, Gas Mark 4) for 1 hour or until a knife inserted in the centre comes out clean. Leave to cool on a wire rack.

Makes 1 loaf

Coffee Chestnut Bread

METRIC/IMPERIAL
100 g/4 oz plain flour
100 g/4 oz self-raising
  flour
½ teaspoon baking
  powder
2 tablespoons instant
  coffee powder
50 g/2 oz butter
50 g/2 oz caster sugar
100 g/4 oz canned
  whole chestnuts,
  drained and
  chopped
50 g/2 oz dates,
  stoned and
  chopped
1 egg, beaten
150 ml/¼ pint milk

AMERICAN
1 cup all-purpose
  flour
1 cup self-rising flour
½ teaspoon baking
  powder
2 tablespoons instant
  coffee powder
¼ cup butter
¼ cup sugar
½ cup chopped
  canned chestnuts
⅓ cup chopped dates
1 egg, beaten
¾ cup milk

Sift the flours, baking powder and coffee into a bowl. Rub (cut) in the butter and stir in the sugar. Mix in the chestnuts and dates. Make a well in the centre and add the egg and milk. Combine all the ingredients thoroughly. Place in a greased 450 g/1 lb (7 × 3 inch) loaf tin.

Cook in a preheated moderate oven (180°C/350°F, Gas Mark 4) for 45 minutes. Leave to cool in the tin for 10 minutes, then turn out on to a wire rack to cool completely.
Makes 1 loaf

Oatmeal Muffins

METRIC/IMPERIAL
100 g/4 oz self-raising
  flour, sifted
100 g/4 oz rolled oats
½ teaspoon salt
50 g/2 oz butter
2 tablespoons clear
  honey
120 ml/4 fl oz strong
  black coffee
120 ml/4 fl oz milk
100 g/4 oz blanched
  almonds, chopped

AMERICAN
1 cup self-rising flour,
  sifted
1 cup rolled oats
½ teaspoon salt
¼ cup butter
2 tablespoons honey
½ cup strong black
  coffee
½ cup milk
1 cup chopped
  almonds

Combine the flour, oats and salt in a bowl. Melt the butter with the honey and coffee in a small saucepan and stir in the milk. Heat until almost boiling, but do not allow to boil. Add to the dry ingredients with the almonds and mix well. Place the mixture in greased patty tins (muffin pans).

Cook in a preheated moderately hot oven (200°C/400°F, Gas Mark 6) for 30 minutes. Leave for 5 minutes then turn out on to a cake rack. Serve warm or cold.
Makes 12

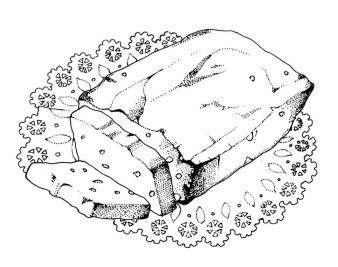

Sweets & Candies

Coffee and Almond Fudge

METRIC/IMPERIAL	AMERICAN
2 × 400 g/14 oz cans condensed milk	2 cans (16 oz each) condensed milk
450 g/1 lb caster sugar	2 cups sugar
100 g/4 oz butter	½ cup butter
100 g/4 oz blanched almonds, chopped	1 cup chopped almonds
50 g/2 oz ground coffee	½ cup ground coffee

Place the condensed milk, sugar and butter in a heavy saucepan. Heat gently, stirring to dissolve the sugar and melt the butter. Bring to the boil, stirring constantly, and boil until the soft ball stage is reached (116°C/240°F on a sugar thermometer). The fudge must be cooked very slowly or it will stick to the bottom of the pan.

Turn the fudge into a large bowl. Beat with a wooden spoon until the fudge begins to thicken. Beat in the almonds and coffee. Continue beating until the mixture is very stiff and 'fudging' around the edge of the bowl.

Spread out evenly in a lightly oiled 28 × 18 cm/ 11 × 7 inch tin. Leave to set, then cut into 2.5 cm/1 inch squares.
Makes 77

Miniature Coffee Meringues; Coffee Peppermint Creams; Coffee Liqueur Truffles; Coffee Almond Balls; Peanut Brittle; Coffee and Almond Fudge; Coffee Coconut Ice

Coffee Peppermint Creams

METRIC/IMPERIAL	AMERICAN
750 g/1½ lb icing sugar	5¼ cups confectioners' sugar
1 egg white	1 egg white
6 drops peppermint essence	6 drops peppermint-flavored extract
1 tablespoon single cream	1 tablespoon light cream
1 tablespoon strong black coffee	1 tablespoon strong black coffee
175 g/6 oz plain chocolate	6 squares (1 oz each) semisweet chocolate

Sift the sugar into a large mixing bowl. Make a well in the centre and put in the egg white, peppermint essence (extract), cream and coffee. Work the ingredients together to a smooth paste. Leave the paste to relax in the refrigerator for 1 hour.

Dust a board with extra icing (confectioners') sugar. Roll out the paste to 5 mm/¼ inch thickness. Cut out rounds with a plain 4 cm/1½ inch cutter. Arrange the rounds on a tray covered with greaseproof (wax) paper and allow to dry out for at least 12 hours, or preferably overnight.

Melt the chocolate and spread a little over the top of each peppermint cream. Allow to set, then place the candies on a wire rack and coat the bottoms with the remaining chocolate. Leave to set before serving.
Makes 25

Coffee Stuffed Dates

METRIC/IMPERIAL	AMERICAN
100 g/4 oz icing sugar	1 cup confectioners' sugar
150 g/5 oz ground almonds	1¼ cups ground almonds
1 tablespoon egg white	1 tablespoon egg white
1 tablespoon strong black coffee	1 tablespoon strong black coffee
30 dates	30 dates
30 coffee beans to decorate	30 coffee beans to decorate

Sift the sugar into a bowl and stir in the ground almonds. Make a well in the centre and add the egg white and coffee. Using a wooden spoon, gradually work in the ground almonds and sugar from the sides until the mixture forms a paste. Turn on to a board, sprinkled with icing (confectioners') sugar and knead gently. Leave the mixture to rest for 1 hour in the refrigerator.

Split open the dates lengthways and remove the stones. Form the coffee marzipan into small fat sausage shapes and use to stuff the dates. Decorate each one with a coffee bean and put into paper sweet (candy) cases.
Makes 30

Coffee Coconut Ice

METRIC/IMPERIAL	AMERICAN
750 g/1½ lb sugar	3 cups sugar
150 ml/¼ pint strong black coffee	¾ cup strong black coffee
300 ml/½ pint water	1¼ cups water
175 g/6 oz powdered glucose	6 oz powdered glucose
225 g/8 oz desiccated coconut	2⅔ cups shredded coconut

Dissolve the sugar in the coffee and water and bring to the boil. Add the glucose and boil to the soft ball stage (116°C/240°F on a sugar thermometer). Work the syrup against the sides of the pan with a wooden spoon until it becomes grainy. Stir in the coconut.

Pour into a lined and oiled 28 × 18 cm/11 × 7 inch tin and leave to set. Cut into 2.5 cm/1 inch squares.
Makes 77

Coffee Liqueur Truffles

METRIC/IMPERIAL	AMERICAN
100 g/4 oz plain chocolate, broken into pieces	4 squares (1 oz each) semisweet chocolate, broken into pieces
3 tablespoons coffee liqueur	3 tablespoons coffee liqueur
100 g/4 oz Madeira cake crumbs	2 cups plain or pound cake crumbs
100 g/4 oz ground almonds	1 cup ground almonds
50 g/2 oz icing sugar, sifted	½ cup confectioners' sugar, sifted
2 tablespoons apricot jam, sieved	2 tablespoons apricot jam, sieved
15 g/½ oz instant coffee powder	1 tablespoon instant coffee powder
50 g/2 oz chocolate vermicelli	½ cup chocolate sprinkles

Put the chocolate and coffee liqueur in a small heatproof bowl and place over a pan of gently simmering water. Heat until the chocolate melts, stirring occasionally. Place the cake crumbs and ground almonds in a bowl and stir in the sugar. Pour in the melted chocolate mixture and stir well to combine. Turn the mixture on to a board sprinkled with icing (confectioners') sugar and knead lightly until smooth. Leave the mixture to rest in the refrigerator for 1 hour.

Shape the mixture into 25 balls and coat each with jam. Mix the coffee and vermicelli (sprinkles) together in a plastic bag. Add the truffles, a few at a time, and shake until each one is coated. Chill until firm, then place in paper sweet (candy) cases.
Makes 25

Miniature Coffee Meringues

METRIC/IMPERIAL	AMERICAN
2 egg whites	2 egg whites
100 g/4 oz caster sugar	½ cup sugar
1 tablespoon instant coffee powder	1 tablespoon instant coffee powder
300 ml/½ pint double cream	1¼ cups heavy cream
2 teaspoons coffee liqueur	2 teaspoons coffee liqueur

Whisk the egg whites until they form really stiff peaks. Mix together the sugar and coffee, and whisk 1 tablespoon into the egg whites. Fold in the remaining sugar and coffee mixture. Spoon the meringue mixture into a piping bag fitted with a small rose nozzle (tube) and pipe miniature meringues, 2.5 cm/1 inch in diameter, on to lined and oiled baking sheets.

Dry out in a preheated cool oven (110°C/225°F, Gas Mark ¼) for 45 minutes. Turn off the oven and leave the meringues inside for a further 15 minutes. Cool on a wire rack.

Whip the cream until thick and flavour with the coffee liqueur. Sandwich the meringues together with the cream just before serving.
Makes 25

Coffee Toffee

METRIC/IMPERIAL	AMERICAN
450 g/1 lb demerara sugar	2⅔ cups raw brown sugar
150 ml/¼ pint strong black coffee	¾ cup strong black coffee
pinch of cream of tartar	pinch of cream of tartar
100 g/4 oz butter, cut into pieces	½ cup butter, cut into pieces

Dissolve the sugar in the coffee over a gentle heat. Add the cream of tartar, then bring to the boil and boil to the hard ball stage (120°C/248°F on a sugar thermometer).

Remove from the heat and beat in the butter a little at a time. Return to the heat and boil to the soft crack stage (140°C/285°F). Pour into an oiled 28 × 18 cm/11 × 7 inch tin and leave to cool slightly. Mark the toffee into squares and cool completely. Break into squares and wrap each in Cellophane (wax) paper, twisting the ends.
Makes 50

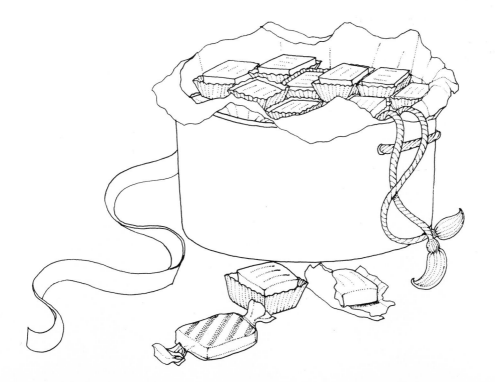

Coffee Almond Balls

METRIC/IMPERIAL	AMERICAN
225 g/8 oz ground almonds	2 cups ground almonds
100 g/4 oz plus 1 teaspoon icing sugar	1 cup plus 1 teaspoon confectioners' sugar
100 g/4 oz caster sugar	½ cup granulated sugar
2 tablespoons very strong black coffee	2 tablespoons very strong black coffee
¼ teaspoon vanilla essence	¼ teaspoon vanilla
1 teaspoon instant coffee powder	1 teaspoon instant coffee powder

Mix together the ground almonds, 100 g/4 oz of the icing sugar (1 cup of the confectioners' sugar), the caster (granulated) sugar, liquid coffee and vanilla. Leave to rest in the refrigerator for 1 hour.

Form the mixture into small balls. Mix the remaining icing (confectioners') sugar with the coffee powder and use to coat the balls.
Makes 12 to 15

Peanut Brittle

METRIC/IMPERIAL	AMERICAN
100 g/4 oz salted peanuts	1 cup salted peanuts
175 g/6 oz sugar	¾ cup sugar
2 tablespoons very hot strong black coffee	2 tablespoons very hot strong black coffee

Spread the peanuts evenly on a small buttered baking sheet. Place the sugar in a saucepan and melt over gentle heat, stirring constantly with a wooden spoon. When the sugar is pale brown in colour, remove from the heat and slowly stir in the hot coffee. Put back on the heat and cook, stirring constantly, for a further 5 minutes.

Pour the sugar mixture over the peanuts and allow to cool and set. Crack into pieces to serve.
Makes about 24 pieces

Coffee and Walnut Fudge

METRIC/IMPERIAL	AMERICAN
450 g/1 lb sugar	2 cups sugar
150 ml/¼ pint milk	¾ cup milk
50 g/2 oz butter	¼ cup butter
2 tablespoons instant coffee powder	2 tablespoons instant coffee powder
1 teaspoon vanilla essence	1 teaspoon vanilla
100 g/4 oz walnuts, chopped	1 cup chopped walnuts

Combine the sugar and milk in a saucepan and leave to stand for 1 hour. Add the butter and stir over a low heat until the sugar has dissolved. Stir in the coffee and vanilla. Bring to the boil and boil until the soft ball stage is reached (116°C/240°F on a sugar thermometer). Cool slightly, then beat vigorously, adding the chopped walnuts. Pour into a greased 28 × 18 cm/11 × 7 inch tin. When cool, cut into 2.5 cm/1 inch squares.
Makes 77

Index

The publishers wish to acknowledge photographer Bryce Attwell and photographic stylist Roisin Nield. Illustrations by Susan Neale.

PDO 83-063

Pages 72–73

75

74

SOUTH AMERICA

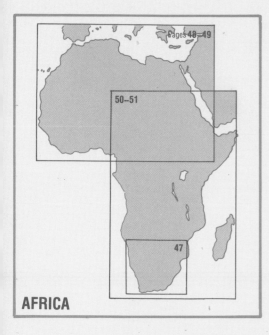

Pages 48–49

50–51

47

AFRICA

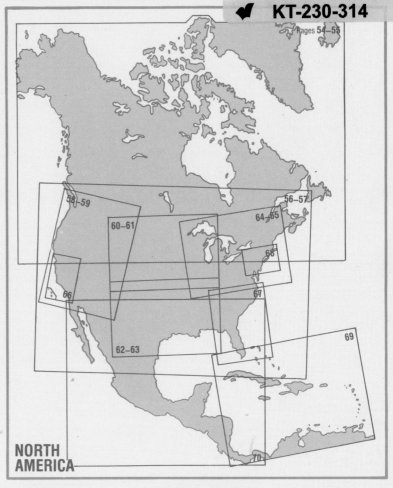

Pages 54–55

58–59

56–57

60–61

64–65

68

66

67

62–63

69

70

NORTH AMERICA

GENERAL MAPS

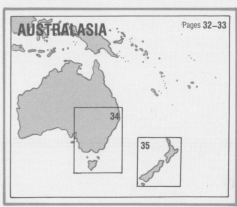

AUSTRALASIA

Pages 32–33

34

35

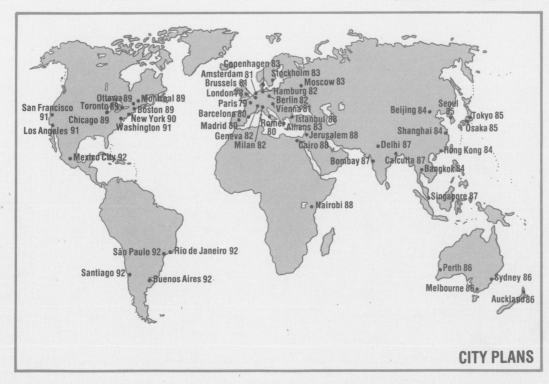

Copenhagen 83
Amsterdam 81
Brussels 81
London 78
Paris 79
Ottawa 89
Montreal 89
Toronto 89
Boston 89
San Francisco 91
Chicago 89
New York 90
Los Angeles 91
Washington 91
Barcelona 80
Madrid 80
Geneva 82
Milan 82
Stockholm 83
Moscow 83
Hamburg 82
Berlin 82
Vienna 81
Istanbul 88
Rome 80
Athens 83
Jerusalem 88
Cairo 88
Beijing 84
Seoul 85
Tokyo 85
Osaka 85
Shanghai 84
Delhi 87
Hong Kong 84
Bombay 87
Calcutta 87
Bangkok 84
Singapore 87
Nairobi 88
São Paulo 92
Rio de Janeiro 92
Santiago 92
Buenos Aires 92
Perth 86
Sydney 86
Melbourne 86
Auckland 86

CITY PLANS

KT-230-314

THE TIMES ATLAS OF THE WORLD

FAMILY EDITION

TIMES BOOKS

A Division of HarperCollinsPublishers

Published in 1995 by
TIMES BOOKS
HarperCollins*Publishers*
77-85 Fulham Palace Road
Hammersmith
London W6 8JB

First edition 1988
Reprinted 1988
Reprinted with revisions 1989, 1990, 1991
Second edition 1992
Reprinted with revisions 1993 (twice)
Third edition 1995

Copyright © Times Books and
Bartholomew 1995

Maps and index prepared by
Bartholomew,
HarperCollins*Publishers*,
Edinburgh

Geographical Dictionary prepared by
Professor B.W. Atkinson

Physical Earth Maps
Duncan Mackay

Design
Ivan Dodd

Printed and bound in Italy by
L.E.G.O. SpA

The Publishers would like to extend
their grateful thanks to the following:

Mrs J. Candy, Geographical Research
    Associates, Maidenhead
Flag information provided and authenticated
    by the Flag Institute, Chester
Mr P.J.M. Geelan, Place-name consultant
Mr Michael Hendrie, Astronomy
    Correspondent, *The Times*, London
Mr H.A.G. Lewis OBE, Geographical
    consultant to *The Times*

British Library Cataloguing in
Publication Data.
A catalogue record for
this book is available
from the British Library.

ISBN 0-7230-0712-8

This, *The Times Atlas of the World, Family Edition,* has been extensively revised since it was first published in 1988. This is the third edition of this popular atlas. It is a reference work for use in the home, office or school, for those who travel the world and those, like Francis Bacon, who journey only "in map and chart".

An index of no fewer than 30,000 entries, keyed to the main map plates will aid those who, whilst familiar with the name of a place, are uncertain of just where it lies on a map.

It is by no means always easy to ascertain the correct title and status of a country as distinct from its everyday name used on maps. The list of states and territories gives in addition to name, title and status, the population and area, the national currency, the major religions and the national flag.

Maps, being an efficient way of storing and displaying information, are used to amplify the list of states and territories and the geographical comparisons of the continents, oceans, lakes and islands. They form the basis of the section on earthquakes, volcanoes, economic minerals, vegetation temperature, rainfall and population.

Maps are also, by nature, illustrative and a 14-page section shows the world's major physical features in the way they appear from space but with the names of the features added.

Amongst the statistical data contained in the Atlas is a listing of the major metropolitan areas with their populations. For the past several decades there has been, throughout the world, an accelerating flow of people from the land to towns and cities and especially the major cities, some of which now contain the bulk of the national population. Growth in air travel has turned those same cities into centres of tourism. Influx of population and the demands of tourism have enhanced the status of the cities. Generous space has, therefore, been allocated to maps of the major cities and their environs.

Geographical names in this Atlas are given in their anglicized (conventional) form where such a form is in current use. Other names are given in their national Roman alphabet or else converted into English by transliteration (letter to letter) or transcription (sound to sound). Because Roman alphabet letters, sometimes modified, are pronounced in a variety of ways a brief guide to pronunciation has been included. The whole is supplemented by a dictionary of geographical terms.

In the names, in the portrayal of international boundaries and in the list of states and territories, the aim has been to show the situation as it pertains in the area at the time of going to press. This must not be taken as an endorsement by the publishers of the status of the territories concerned. The aim throughout has been to show things as they are. In that way the Atlas will best serve the reader to whom, it is hoped, it will bring interest benefit and continuing pleasure.

H.A.G. Lewis, OBE
Geographical Consultant to *The Times*

CONTENTS

3

AFGHANISTAN

STATUS: Islamic State
AREA: 652,225 sq km (251,773 sq miles)
POPULATION: 16,433,000
ANNUAL NATURAL INCREASE: 2.5%
CAPITAL: Kabul
LANGUAGE: Pushtu, Dari
RELIGION: 90% Sunni, 9% Shi'a Muslim,
Hindu, Sikh and Jewish minorities
CURRENCY: Afghani (AFA)
ORGANIZATIONS: Col. Plan, UN

Afghanistan is a mountainous landlocked country in southwest Asia with a climate of extremes. In summer the lowland southwest reaches a temperature of over 40°C (104°F); in winter this may drop to -26°C (-15°F) in the northern mountains. The country is one of the poorest in the world with barely 10 per cent of the land suitable for agriculture. Main crops are wheat, fruit and vegetables. Sheep and goats are the main livestock. Mineral resources are rich but underdeveloped with natural gas, coal and iron ore deposits predominating. The main industrial area was centred on Kabul, but both Kabul and the rural areas have been devastated by civil war.

ÅLAND

STATUS: Self-governing Island Province of Finland
AREA: 1,505 sq km (581 sq miles)
POPULATION: 24,993
CAPITAL: Mariehamn

ALBANIA

STATUS: Republic
AREA: 28,750 sq km (11,100 sq miles)
POPULATION: 3,363,000
ANNUAL NATURAL INCREASE: 1.7%

CAPITAL: Tirana (Tiranë)
LANGUAGE: Albanian (Gheg, Tosk)
RELIGION: 70% Muslim, 20% Greek Orthodox,
10% Roman Catholic
CURRENCY: lek (ALL)
ORGANIZATIONS: UN

Albania is situated on the eastern seaboard of the Adriatic. With the exception of a coastal strip, most of the territory is mountainous and largely unfit for cultivation. The climate is Mediterranean along the coast, but cooler inland. Average temperatures in July reach 25°C (77°F) and there is 1,400 mm (55 inches) of rainfall annually. The country possesses mineral resources, notably chrome which is a major export, and deposits of coal, oil and natural gas. After decades of self-imposed political and economic isolation Albania shook off its own peculiar variant of communism in 1990. Administrative chaos and a massive fall in production ensued resulting in acute food shortages and widespread emigration. The country is one of the poorest in Europe with a backward rural economy and nearly half the labour force unemployed.

ALGERIA

STATUS: Republic
AREA: 2,381,745 sq km (919,355 sq miles)
POPULATION: 26,600,000
ANNUAL NATURAL INCREASE: 2.7%
CAPITAL: Algiers (Alger, El-Djezaïr)
LANGUAGE: 83% Arabic, French, Berber
RELIGION: Muslim
CURRENCY: Algerian dinar (DZD)
ORGANIZATIONS: Arab League, OAU, OPEC, UN

Physically the country is divided between the coastal Atlas mountain ranges of the north and the Sahara to the south. Algeria is mainly hot, with negligible rainfall, but along the Mediterranean coast temperatures are more moderate, with most rain falling during the mild winters. Arable land occupies small areas of the northern valleys and coastal strip, with wheat, barley and vines the leading crops. Sheep, goats and cattle are the most important livestock. Although oil from

the southern deserts dominates the economy, it is now declining and natural gas output has increased dramatically. A virtual civil war has existed between the army and Islamic extremists which has caused the economy to deteriorate.

AMERICAN SAMOA

STATUS: Unincorporated Territory of USA
AREA: 197 sq km (76 sq miles)
POPULATION: 132,726
CAPITAL: Pago Pago

ANDORRA

STATUS: Principality
AREA: 465 sq km (180 sq miles)
POPULATION: 59,000
CAPITAL: Andorra la Vella
LANGUAGE: Catalan, Spanish, French
RELIGION: Roman Catholic majority
CURRENCY: French franc (FRF),
Andorran peseta (ADP)
ORGANIZATIONS: UN

Andorra, a tiny state in the Pyrenees between France and Spain, achieved fuller independence from these countries in 1993. The climate is alpine with a long winter, which lasts for six months, a mild spring and a warm summer. Tourism is the main occupation, with Andorra becoming an important skiing centre during the winter. Tobacco and potatoes are the principal crops, sheep and cattle the main livestock. Other important sources of revenue are the sale of hydro-electricity, stamps, duty-free goods and financial services.

ANGOLA

STATUS: Republic
AREA: 1,246,700 sq km (481,225 sq miles)
POPULATION: 10,770,000
ANNUAL NATURAL INCREASE: 2.9%
CAPITAL: Luanda
LANGUAGE: Portuguese, tribal dialects
RELIGION: mainly traditional beliefs,
Roman Catholic and Protestant minorities
CURRENCY: new kwanza (AOK)
ORGANIZATIONS: OAU, UN

Independent from the Portuguese since 1975 Angola is a large country south of the equator in southwest Africa. Much of the interior is savannah plateaux with average rainfall varying from 250 mm (10 inches) in the south to 1,270 mm (50 inches) in the north. Most of the population is engaged in agriculture producing cassava, maize and coffee. Most consumer products and textiles are imported. Angola possesses vast wealth in the form of diamonds, oil, iron ore, copper and other minerals. Apart from the production of oil which is the biggest export, the economy has collapsed as a result of many years of civil war.

ABBREVIATIONS

The following abbreviations have been used. Codes given in brackets following the name of a currency are those issued by the International Standards Organization.

ANZUS	Australia, New Zealand, United States Security Treaty
ASEAN	Association of Southeast Asian Nations
Caricom	Caribbean Community and Common Market
CACM	Central American Common Market
CIS	Commonwealth of Independent States
Col. Plan	Colombo Plan
Comm.	Commonwealth
CSCE	Council for Security and Co-operation in Europe
ECOWAS	Economic Community of West African States
EEA	European Economic Area
EFTA	European Free Trade Association
EU	European Union
G7	Group of seven industrialized nations:– (Canada, France, Germany, Italy, Japan, UK, USA)
Mercosur	Common Market of the Southern Cone
NAFTA	North American Free Trade Agreement
NATO	North Atlantic Treaty Organization
OAS	Organization of American States
OAU	Organization of African Unity
OECD	Organization for Economic Co-operation and Development
OPEC	Organization of Petroleum Exporting Countries
UN	United Nations
WEU	Western European Union

ANGUILLA

STATUS: UK Dependent Territory
AREA: 115 sq km (60 sq miles)
POPULATION: 8,960
CAPITAL: The Valley

ANTIGUA AND BARBUDA

STATUS: Commonwealth State
AREA: 442 sq km (171 sq miles)
POPULATION: 65,962
ANNUAL NATURAL INCREASE: 1.0%
CAPITAL: St John's (on Antigua)
LANGUAGE: English
RELIGION: Anglican Christian majority
CURRENCY: E Caribbean dollar (XCD)
ORGANIZATIONS: Caricom, Comm., OAS, UN

The country consists of two main islands in the Leeward group in the West Indies. Tourism is the main activity. Local agriculture is being encouraged to reduce food imports and the growth of sea island cotton is making a comeback. The production of rum is the main manufacturing industry; there is also an oil refinery.

ARGENTINA

STATUS: Republic
AREA: 2,766,889 sq km
(1,068,302 sq miles)
POPULATION: 33,101,000
ANNUAL NATURAL INCREASE: 1.3%
CAPITAL: Buenos Aires
LANGUAGE: Spanish
RELIGION: 90% Roman Catholic,
2% Protestant, Jewish minority
CURRENCY: peso (ARP)
ORGANIZATIONS: Mercosur, OAS, UN

Relief is highest in the west in the Andes mountains, where altitudes exceed 6,000 m (19,500 ft). East of the Andes there are fertile plains known as the Pampas. In the northern scrub forests and grasslands of the Chaco hot tropical conditions exist. Central Argentina lies in temperate latitudes, but the southernmost regions are cold, wet and stormy. The economy of Argentina was long dominated by the produce of the rich soils of the Pampas, beef and grain. Agricultural products still account for some 40 per cent of export revenue, with grain crops predominating, despite a decline due to competition and falling world prices. Beef exports also decreased by over 50 per cent between 1970 and 1983, due to strong competition from western Europe. Industry is now the chief export earner. Industrial activity includes petrochemicals, steel, cars, and food and drink processing. There are oil and gas reserves and an abundant supply of hydroelectric power.

ARMENIA

STATUS: Republic
AREA: 30,000 sq km
(11,580 sq miles)
POPULATION: 3,686,000
ANNUAL NATURAL INCREASE: 1.2%
CAPITAL: Yerevan
LANGUAGE: Armenian, Russian
RELIGION: Russian Orthodox,
Armenian Catholic
CURRENCY: dram
ORGANIZATIONS: CIS, UN

Armenia is a country of rugged terrain, with most of the land above 1,000 m (3,300 feet). The climate, much influenced by altitude, has continental tendencies. Rainfall, although occurring throughout the year, is heaviest in summer. Agriculture is dependent upon irrigation and the main crops are vegetables, fruit and tobacco. Conflict over the disputed area of Nagornyy Karabakh, an enclave of Armenian Orthodox Christians within the territory of Azerbaijan, is casting a cloud over the immediate future of the country.

ARUBA

STATUS: Self-governing Island of
Netherlands Realm
AREA: 193 sq km (75 sq miles)
POPULATION: 68,897
CAPITAL: Oranjestad

ASCENSION

STATUS: Island Dependency of St Helena
AREA: 88 sq km (34 sq miles)
POPULATION: 1,117
CAPITAL: Georgetown

ASHMORE AND CARTIER ISLANDS

STATUS: External Territory of Australia
AREA: 3 sq km (1.2 sq miles)
POPULATION: no permanent population

AUSTRALIA

STATUS: Federal Nation
AREA: 7,682,300 sq km (2,965,370 sq miles)
POPULATION: 17,662,000
ANNUAL NATURAL INCREASE: 1.6%
CAPITAL: Canberra
LANGUAGE: English
RELIGION: 75% Christian,
Aboriginal beliefs, Jewish minority
CURRENCY: Australian dollar (AUD)
ORGANIZATIONS: ANZUS, Col. Plan,
Comm., OECD, UN

The Commonwealth of Australia was founded in 1901. The British Monarch, as head of state, is represented by a governor-general. It is the sixth largest country in the world in terms of area. The western half of the country is primarily arid plateaux, ridges and vast deserts. The central-eastern area comprises lowlands of river systems draining into Lake Eyre, while to the east is the Great Dividing Range. Climate varies from cool temperate to tropical monsoon. Rainfall is high only in the northeast, where it exceeds 1,000 mm (39 inches) annually, and decreases markedly from the coast to the interior which is hot and dry. Over 50 per cent of the land area comprises desert and scrub with less than 250 mm (10 inches) of rain a year. The majority of the population live in cities concentrated along the southeast coast. Australia is rich in both agricultural and natural resources. It is the world's leading producer of wool, which together with wheat, meat, sugar and dairy products accounts for over 40 per cent of export revenue. There are vast reserves of coal, oil, natural gas, nickel, iron ore, bauxite and uranium ores. Gold, silver, lead, zinc and copper ores are also exploited. Minerals now account for over 30 per cent of Australia's export revenue. New areas of commerce have been created in eastern Asia, particularly in Japan, to counteract the sharp decline of the traditional European markets. Tourism is becoming a large revenue earner and showed a 200 per cent growth between 1983 and 1988. This has slowed recently, although the Olympics Games, due to be held in Sydney in the year 2000, are expected to attract an additional 1.5 million overseas visitors.

AUSTRALIAN CAPITAL TERRITORY
STATUS: Federal Territory
AREA: 2,432 sq km (939 sq miles)
POPULATION: 299,000
CAPITAL: Canberra

NEW SOUTH WALES
STATUS: State
AREA: 801,430 sq km (309,350 sq miles)
POPULATION: 6,009,000
CAPITAL: Sydney

NORTHERN TERRITORY
STATUS: Territory
AREA: 1,346,200 sq km (519,635 sq miles)
POPULATION: 168,000
CAPITAL: Darwin

QUEENSLAND
STATUS: State
AREA: 1,727,000 sq km (666,620 sq miles)
POPULATION: 3,113,000
CAPITAL: Brisbane

SOUTH AUSTRALIA
STATUS: State
AREA: 984,380 sq km (79,970 sq miles)
POPULATION: 1,462,000
CAPITAL: Adelaide

TASMANIA
STATUS: State
AREA: 68,330 sq km (26,375 sq miles)
POPULATION: 472,000
CAPITAL: Hobart

VICTORIA
STATUS: State
AREA: 227,600 sq km (87,855 sq miles)
POPULATION: 4,462,000
CAPITAL: Melbourne

WESTERN AUSTRALIA
STATUS: State
AREA: 2,525,500 sq km (974,845 sq miles)
POPULATION: 1,678,000
CAPITAL: Perth

AUSTRIA
STATUS: Federal Republic
AREA: 83,855 sq km (32,370 sq miles)
POPULATION: 7,910,000
ANNUAL NATURAL INCREASE: 0.6%
CAPITAL: Vienna (Wien)
LANGUAGE: German
RELIGION: 89% Roman Catholic, 6% Protestant
CURRENCY: schilling (ATS)
ORGANIZATIONS: Council of Europe, EEA, EFTA, OECD, UN

Austria is an alpine, landlocked country in central Europe. The mountainous Alps which cover 75 per cent of the land consist of a series of east-west ranges enclosing lowland basins. The climate is continental with temperatures and rainfall varying with altitude. About 25 per cent of the country, in the north and northeast, is lower foreland or flat land containing most of Austria's fertile farmland. Half is arable and the remainder is mainly for root or fodder crops. Manufacturing and heavy industry, however, account for the majority of export revenues, particularly pig-iron, steel, chemicals and vehicles. Over 70 per cent of the country's power is hydro-electric. Tourism and forestry are also important to the economy.

AZERBAIJAN
STATUS: Republic
AREA: 87,000 sq km (33,580 sq miles)
POPULATION: 7,398,000
ANNUAL NATURAL INCREASE: 1.0%
CAPITAL: Baku
LANGUAGE: 83% Azeri, 6% Armenian, 6% Russian
RELIGION: 83% Muslim, Armenian Apostolic, Orthodox
CURRENCY: manat
ORGANIZATIONS: CIS, UN

Azerbaijan gained independence on the breakup of the USSR in 1991. It is a mountainous country that has a continental climate, greatly influenced by altitude. Arable land accounts for less than 10 per cent of the total area, with raw cotton and tobacco the leading products. Major reserves of oil and gas exist beneath and around the Caspian Sea, which are as of yet fully undeveloped. The country includes two autonomous regions: Nakhichevan, which it is cut off by a strip of intervening Armenian territory and the enclave of Nagornyy Karabakh, over which long standing tensions escalated into conflict in 1992.

AZORES
STATUS: Self-governing Island Region of Portugal
AREA: 2,335 sq km (901 sq miles)
POPULATION: 237,100
CAPITAL: Ponta Delgada

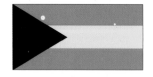

BAHAMAS
STATUS: Commonwealth Nation
AREA: 13,865 sq km (5,350 sq miles)
POPULATION: 262,000
ANNUAL NATURAL INCREASE: 1.9%
CAPITAL: Nassau
LANGUAGE: English
RELIGION: Anglican Christian majority, Baptist and Roman Catholic minorities
CURRENCY: Bahamian dollar (BSD)
ORGANIZATIONS: Caricom, Comm., OAS, UN

About 700 islands and over 2,000 coral sand cays (reefs) constitute the sub-tropical Commonwealth of the Bahamas. The island group extends from the coast of Florida to Cuba and Haiti in the south. Only 29 islands are inhabited. Most of the 1,000 mm (39 inches) of rainfall falls in the summer. The tourist industry is the main source of income and, although fluctuating through recession, still employs over 70 per cent of the working population. Recent economic plans have concentrated on reducing imports by developing fishing and domestic agriculture. Other important sources of income are ship registration (the world's fourth largest open-registry fleet), income generated by offshore finance and banking, and export of rum, salt and cement.

BAHRAIN
STATUS: State
AREA: 661 sq km (225 sq miles)
POPULATION: 539,000
ANNUAL NATURAL INCREASE: 3.2%
CAPITAL: Manama (Al Manāmah)
LANGUAGE: Arabic, English
RELIGION: 60% Shi'a and 40% Sunni Muslim, Christian minority
CURRENCY: Bahraini dinar (BHD)
ORGANIZATIONS: Arab League, UN

The sheikdom is a barren island in the Persian Gulf with less than 80 mm (3 inches) rainfall a year. Summer temperatures average 32°C (89°F). Bahrain was the first country in the Arabian peninsula to strike oil, in 1932. Oil still accounts for 60 per cent of revenue and gas is becoming increasingly important. Lower oil prices and decreased production is now causing the government to diversify the economy with expansion of light and heavy industry and chemical plants, and the subsequent encouragement of trade and foreign investment.

BANGLADESH
STATUS: Republic
AREA: 144,000 sq km (55,585 sq miles)
POPULATION: 118,700,000
ANNUAL NATURAL INCREASE: 2.2%
CAPITAL: Dhaka, (Dhākā, Dacca)
LANGUAGE: Bengali (Bangla), Bihari, Hindi, English
RELIGION: 85% Muslim, Hindu, Buddhist and Christian minorities
CURRENCY: taka (BDT)
ORGANIZATIONS: Col. Plan, Comm., UN

Bangladesh is one of the poorest and most densely populated countries of the world. Most of its territory, except for bamboo-forested hills in the southeast, comprises the vast river systems of the Ganges and Brahmaputra which drain from the Himalayan mountains into the Bay of Bengal, frequently changing course and flooding the flat delta plain. This land is, however, extremely fertile and attracts a high concentration of the population. The climate is tropical, and agriculture is dependent on monsoon rainfall. When the monsoon fails there is drought. Eighty-two per cent of the population are farmers, the

main crops being rice and jute. Bangladesh is the world's leading supplier of jute, which accounts for 25 per cent of the country's exports. The main industry and number one export is clothing. Natural gas reserves, under the Bay of Bengal, are beginning to be exploited.

BARBADOS

STATUS: Commonwealth State
AREA: 430 sq km (166 sq miles)
POPULATION: 259,000
ANNUAL NATURAL INCREASE: 0.3%
CAPITAL: Bridgetown
LANGUAGE: English
RELIGION: Anglican Christian majority, Methodist and Roman Catholic minorities
CURRENCY: Barbados dollar (BBD)
ORGANIZATIONS: Caricom, Comm., OAS, UN

The former British colony of Barbados in the Caribbean is the most eastern island of the Antilles chain. The gently rolling landscape of the island is lush and fertile, the temperature ranging from 25–28°C (77–82°F) with 1270–1900 mm (50–75 inches) of rainfall per year. Sugar and its by-products, molasses and rum, are traditional cash crops. These are being overtaken in importance by tourism which provides an occupation for one-third of the population. This is a growth sector, although it has suffered recently from world recession. An oilfield supplies one-third of domestic oil requirements.

BELARUS

STATUS: Republic
AREA: 208,000 sq km (80,290 sq miles)
POPULATION: 10,280,000
ANNUAL NATURAL INCREASE: 0.5%
CAPITAL: Minsk
LANGUAGE: Belorussian, Russian
RELIGION: Roman Catholic, Uniate
CURRENCY: rouble
ORGANIZATIONS: CIS, UN

Belarus achieved independence in 1991. The country is mainly flat with forests covering more than one-third of the area. Swamps and marshlands cover large areas but, when drained, the soil is very fertile. The climate is continental with fairly cold winters (-7°C or 20°F). Grain, flax, potatoes and sugar beet are the main crops but livestock production accounts for more than half the value of agricultural output. Large areas of Belarus are thinly populated; most people live in the central area. The republic is comparatively poor in mineral resources and suffered terrible devastation during the Second World War. Postwar industrialization has been based on imported raw materials and semi-manufactured goods, concentrating on the production of trucks, tractors, agricultural machinery and other heavy engineering equipment. However, these industries are heavily reliant on imported Russian energy and output has declined since independence.

BELGIUM

STATUS: Kingdom
AREA: 30,520 sq km (11,780 sq miles)
POPULATION: 10,020,000
ANNUAL NATURAL INCREASE: 0.3%
CAPITAL: Brussels (Bruxelles/Brussel)
LANGUAGE: French, Dutch (Flemish), German
RELIGION: Roman Catholic majority, Protestant and Jewish minorities
CURRENCY: Belgium franc (BEF)
ORGANIZATIONS: Council of Europe, EEA, EU, NATO, OECD, UN, WEU

Over two-thirds of Belgium comprises the Flanders plain, a flat plateau covered by fertile wind-blown loess which extends from the North Sea coast down to the forested mountains of the Ardennes in the south. The climate is mild, maritime temperate with 720–1200 mm (28–47 inches) of rainfall a year. Over half the country is intensively farmed – cereals, root crops, vegetables and flax are the main crops and the country is nearly self-sufficient in meat and dairy products. Belgium's tradition as an industrialized nation dates back to the 19th century and Flanders has historically been famed for its textiles. The main industries now are metal-working (including motor vehicle assembly), chemicals, iron and steel, textiles, food and drink processing and diamonds. In recent years many companies have embarked on high-technology specialization including computer software, micro-electronics and telecommunications. Belgium is a trading nation, exporting more than half its national production. Most trade passes through the port of Antwerp, and an efficient communications network links it with the rest of Europe.

BELIZE

STATUS: Commonwealth Nation

AREA: 22,965 sq km (8,865 sq miles)
POPULATION: 230,000
ANNUAL NATURAL INCREASE: 2.6%
CAPITAL: Belmopan
LANGUAGE: English, Spanish, Maya
RELIGION: 60% Roman Catholic, 40% Protestant
CURRENCY: Belizean dollar (BZD)
ORGANIZATIONS: CARICOM, Comm., OAS, UN

Bordering the Caribbean Sea, in Central America, sub-tropical Belize is dominated by its dense forest cover. Principal exports are sugar cane, citrus concentrates and bananas. Since independence from Britain in 1973 the country has developed agriculture to lessen reliance on imported food products. Other commodities produced include tropical fruits, vegetables, fish and timber.

BENIN

STATUS: Republic
AREA: 112,620 sq km (43,470 sq miles)
POPULATION: 5,010,000
ANNUAL NATURAL INCREASE: 3.2%
CAPITAL: Porto Novo
LANGUAGE: French, Fon, Adja
RELIGION: majority traditional beliefs, 15% Roman Catholic, 13% Muslim
CURRENCY: CFA franc (W Africa) (XOF)
ORGANIZATIONS: ECOWAS, OAU, UN

Benin, formerly Dahomey, is a small strip of country descending from the wooded savannah hills of the north to the forested and cultivated lowlands fringing the Bight of Benin. The economy is agricultural, with palm oil, cotton, cocoa, coffee, groundnuts and copra as main exports. The developing offshore oil industry has proven reserves of over 20 million barrels.

BERMUDA

STATUS: Self-governing UK Crown Colony
AREA: 54 sq km (21 sq miles)
POPULATION: 74,837
CAPITAL: Hamilton

BHUTAN

STATUS: Kingdom
AREA: 46,620 sq km (17,995 sq miles)
POPULATION: 600,000
ANNUAL NATURAL INCREASE: 2.2%
CAPITAL: Thimphu
LANGUAGE: Dzongkha, Nepali, English
RELIGION: Mahayana Buddhist, 30% Hindu
CURRENCY: ngultrum (BTN), Indian rupee (INR)
ORGANIZATIONS: Col. Plan, UN

Bhutan is a small country in the Himalayan foothills between China and India, and to the east of Nepal. Rainfall is high at over 3000 mm (118 inches) a year but temperatures vary between the extreme cold of the northern ranges to a July average of 27°C (81°F) in the southern forests. Long isolated, the economy of Bhutan is dominated by agriculture and small local industries. All manufactured goods are imported.

BOLIVIA

STATUS: Republic
AREA: 1,098,575 sq km (424,050 sq miles)
POPULATION: 7,832,396
ANNUAL NATURAL INCREASE: 2.5%
CAPITAL: La Paz
LANGUAGE: Spanish, Quechua, Aymara
RELIGION: Roman Catholic majority
CURRENCY: Boliviano (BOB)
ORGANIZATIONS: OAS, UN

Bolivia, where the average life expectancy is 51 years, is one of the world's poorest nations. Landlocked and isolated, the country stretches from the eastern Andes across high cool plateaux before dropping to the dense forest of the Amazon basin and the grasslands of the southeast. Bolivia was once rich, its wealth based on minerals (in recent decades tin) but in 1985 world tin prices dropped and the industry collapsed. Oil and gas and agriculture now dominate the economy. Crops include soya, cotton, coca (cocaine shrub), sugar and coffee. Mining is still important, with the emphasis on zinc.

BOSNIA-HERZEGOVINA

STATUS: Republic
AREA: 51,130 sq km (19,736 sq miles)
POPULATION: 2,900,000
ANNUAL NATURAL INCREASE: 0.2%
CAPITAL: Sarajevo
LANGUAGE: Serbo-Croat
RELIGION: Muslim, Christian
CURRENCY: dinar
ORGANIZATIONS: UN

Bosnia-Herzegovina achieved independence in April 1992, but international recognition did not spare the Republic from savage ethnic warfare between Muslims, Serbs and Croats. Partitioning of the country into a new federation acceptable to all warring parties appears to be a necessity for peace. Before the war Bosnia's economy was based predominantly on agriculture – sheep rearing and the cultivation of vines, olives and citrus fruits. The country is mainly mountainous with the Sava valley in the north being the only lowland of consequence. The climate is Mediterranean towards the Adriatic, but continental and cooler inland.

BOTSWANA

STATUS: Republic
AREA: 582,000 sq km (224,652 sq miles)
POPULATION: 1,291,000
ANNUAL NATURAL INCREASE: 3.4%
CAPITAL: Gaborone
LANGUAGE: Setswana, English
RELIGION: traditional beliefs majority,
Christian minority
CURRENCY: pula (BWP)
ORGANIZATIONS: Comm., OAU, UN

The arid high plateau of Botswana, with its poor soils and low rainfall, supports little arable agriculture, but over 2.3 million cattle graze the dry grasslands. Diamonds are the chief export, providing 80 per cent of export earnings. Copper, nickel, potash, soda ash, salt and coal are also important. The growth of light industries around the capital has stimulated trade with neighbouring countries.

BRAZIL

STATUS: Federal Republic
AREA: 8,511,965 sq km (3,285,620 sq miles)
POPULATION: 156,275,000
ANNUAL NATURAL INCREASE: 2.2%
CAPITAL: Brasília
LANGUAGE: Portuguese
RELIGION: 90% Roman Catholic,
Protestant minority
CURRENCY: cruzeiro real (BRC),URV
ORGANIZATIONS: Mercosur, OAS, UN

Brazil is the largest country in South America with the Amazon basin tropical rain forest covers roughly a third of the country. It is one of the world's leading agricultural exporters, with coffee, soya beans, sugar, bananas, cocoa, tobacco, rice and cattle major commodities. Brazil is an industrial power but with development limited to the heavily populated urban areas of the eastern coastal lowlands. Mineral resources, except for iron ore, do not play a significant role in the economy at present, but recent economic policies have concentrated on developing the industrial base – road and rail communications, light and heavy industry and expansion of energy resources, particularly hydro-electric power harnessed from the three great river systems. Unlike other South American countries Brazil still has a serious inflation rate, introducing the 'real', on 1 July 1994 (the fifth new currency in a decade), in an attempt to slow the rate down.

BRITISH ANTARCTIC TERRITORY

STATUS: UK Dependent Territory
AREA: 1,544,000 sq km (599,845 sq miles)
POPULATION: no permanent population

BRITISH INDIAN OCEAN TERRITORY

STATUS: UK Dependency comprising the
Chagos Archipelago
AREA: 5,765 sq km (2,225 sq miles)
POPULATION: 266,000

BRUNEI

STATUS: Sultanate
AREA: 5,765 sq km (2,225 sq miles)
POPULATION: 270,000
ANNUAL NATURAL INCREASE: 3.2%
CAPITAL: Bandar Seri Begawan
LANGUAGE: Malay, English, Chinese
RELIGION: 65% Sunni Muslim, Buddhist and
Christian minorities
CURRENCY: Brunei dollar (BND)
ORGANIZATIONS: ASEAN, Comm, UN

The Sultanate of Brunei is situated on the northwest coast of Borneo. Its tropical climate is hot and humid with annual rainfall ranging from 2500 mm (98 inches) on the narrow coastal strip to 5000 mm (197 inches) in the mountainous interior. Oil and gas reserves, mostly offshore, are the basis of the Brunei economy. Half the oil and nearly all the natural gas (in liquefied form) are exported to Japan.

BULGARIA

STATUS: Republic
AREA: 110,910 sq km (42,810 sq miles)
POPULATION: 8,467,000
ANNUAL NATURAL INCREASE: 0.0%
CAPITAL: Sofia (Sofiya)
LANGUAGE: Bulgarian, Turkish
RELIGION: Eastern Orthodox majority,
Muslim minority
CURRENCY: lev (BGL)
ORGANIZATIONS: Council of Europe, EFTA,
OIEC, UN

Bulgaria exhibits great variety in its landscape. In the north, the land from the plains of the Danube slope upwards into the Balkan mountains (Stara Planina), which run east-west through central Bulgaria. The Rhodope mountains dominate the west, with the lowlands of Thrace and the Maritsa valley in the south. Climate is continental with temperatures ranging from -5°C (23°F) in winter to 28°C (82°F) in summer. The economy is based on agricultural products, with cereals, tobacco, cotton, fruits and vines dominating. Wine is a particularly successful export. Nuclear power is the main domestic power source, however the reactors are becoming elderly and other sources of energy are being sought, in particular oil and gas in the Black Sea. The heavy industry sector, which thrived in close association with the former USSR, is declining.

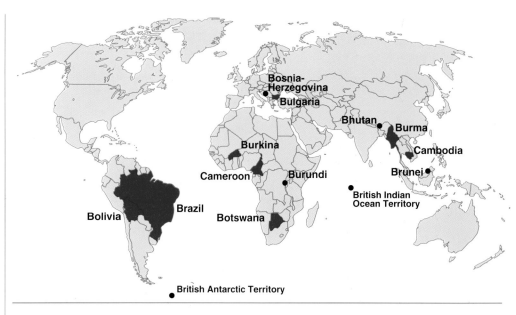

BURKINA
STATUS: Republic
AREA: 274,122 sq km (105,811 sq miles)
POPULATION: 9,490,000
ANNUAL NATURAL INCREASE: 2.8%
CAPITAL: Ouagadougou
LANGUAGE: French, Moré (Mossi), Dyula
RELIGION: 60% animist, 30% Muslim,
10% Roman Catholic
CURRENCY: CFA franc (W Africa) (OXF)
ORGANIZATIONS: ECOWAS, OAU, UN

Situated on the southern edge of the Sahara, Burkina, previously known as Upper Volta, is a poor, landlocked country with thin soils supporting savannah grasslands. Frequent droughts, particularly in the north, seriously affect the economy, which is mainly subsistence agriculture with livestock herding, and the export of groundnuts and cotton. There is virtually no industry. Some minerals are exported and manganese exports began in 1993.

BURMA (MYANMAR)
STATUS: Union of states and divisions
AREA: 678,030 sq km (261,720 sq miles)
POPULATION: 42,330,000
ANNUAL NATURAL INCREASE: 2.2%
CAPITAL: Rangoon (Yangon)
LANGUAGE: Burmese
RELIGION: 85% Buddhist. Animist, Muslim,
Hindu and Christian minorities
CURRENCY: kyat (BUK)
ORGANIZATIONS: Col. Plan, UN

Much of Burma (renamed Myanmar by its military leaders in 1989) is covered by tropical rainforest divided by the central valley of the Irrawaddy, the Sittang and the Salween rivers. The western highlands are an extension of the Himalaya mountains; hills to the east and south

are a continuation of the Yunnan plateau of China. The economy is based on the export of rice and forestry products. The irrigated central basin and the coastal region to the east of the Irrawaddy delta are the main rice-growing areas. Hardwoods, particularly teak, cover the highlands. There is potential for greater exploitation of tin, copper, gold, oil and natural gas deposits.

BURUNDI
STATUS: Republic
AREA: 27,835 sq km (10,745 sq miles)
POPULATION: 5,786,000
ANNUAL NATURAL INCREASE: 2.9%
CAPITAL: Bujumbura
LANGUAGE: French, Kirundi, Swahili
RELIGION: 60% Roman Catholic, animist minority
CURRENCY: Burundi franc (BIF)
ORGANIZATIONS: OAU, UN

This small central African republic is densely populated and one of the world's poorest nations. Although close to the equator, temperatures are modified because of altitude. Coffee is the main export, followed by tea, cotton and manufactured goods. The country has a history of ethnic fighting between the Hutu farming people, who make up 85 per cent of the population, and the Tutsi, originally pastoralists, who have dominated the army and the running of the country. Massacres of thousands of people in 1993-4 resulted from ethnic war, ignited by a Hutu election victory marking an end to 31 years of Tutsi domination.

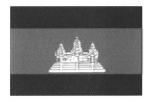

CAMBODIA
STATUS: Kingdom
AREA: 181,000 sq km (69,865 sq miles)
POPULATION: 12,000,000

ANNUAL NATURAL INCREASE: 2.7%
CAPITAL: Phnom Penh
LANGUAGE: Khmer
RELIGION: Buddhist majority, Roman Catholic
and Muslim minorities
CURRENCY: reil (KHR)
ORGANIZATIONS: Col. Plan, UN

Cambodia, in southeast Asia, is mostly a lowland basin. Over 70 per cent of the country is covered by the central plain of the Mekong river. The climate is tropical, with average annual temperatures exceeding 25°C (77°F). Monsoon rainfall occurs from May to October. These provide ideal conditions for the country's rice production and fish harvesting. The economy has been damaged since the 1970s by almost constant civil war. Power shortages hamper industrial development, the roads are badly damaged and land mines buried in the countryside make farming hazardous.

CAMEROON
STATUS: Republic
AREA: 475,500 sq km(183,545 sq miles)
POPULATION: 12,198,000
ANNUAL NATURAL INCREASE: 3.0%
CAPITAL: Yaoundé
LANGUAGE: English, French
RELIGION: 40% Christian, 39% traditional
beliefs, 21% Muslim
CURRENCY: CRA franc (C Africa) (XAF)
ORGANIZATIONS: OAU, UN

Cameroon, in west Africa, is situated between the Gulf of Guinea in the south and the shores of Lake Chad in the north. In the south, coastal lowlands rise to densely forested plateaux, whereas further northwards savannah takes over, and aridity increases towards the Sahara. Oil products, once the main export, have declined in importance and now agricultural products account for most export revenue. Coffee, cocoa, bananas and avocados are the main cash crops. Mineral resources are underdeveloped but Cameroon is one of Africa's main producers of bauxite (aluminium ore) and aluminium is smelted at Edea.

CANADA
STATUS: Commonwealth Nation
AREA: 9,922,385 sq km (3,830,840 sq miles)
POPULATION: 28,866,000
ANNUAL NATURAL INCREASE: 1.4%
CAPITAL: Ottawa
LANGUAGE: English, French
RELIGION: 46% Roman Catholic,
Protestant and Jewish minorities
CURRENCY: Canadian dollar (CAD)
ORGANIZATIONS: Col. Plan, Comm., G7, OAS,
OECD, NATO, NAFTA, UN

Canada is the world's second largest country stretching from the great barren islands of the Arctic north to the vast grasslands of the central south, and from the Rocky Mountains in the west to the farmlands of the Great Lakes in the east. This huge area experiences great climatic differences but basically a continental climate prevails with extremes of heat and cold particularly in the central plains. The Arctic tundra of the far north provides summer grazing for caribou. Further south coniferous forests grow on the thin soils of the ancient shield landscape and on the extensive foothills of the Rocky Mountains. In contrast, the rich soils of the central prairies support grasslands and grain crops. The Great Lakes area provides fish, fruit, maize, root crops and dairy products; the prairies produce over 20 per cent of the worlds wheat; and the grasslands of Alberta support a thriving beef industry. Most minerals are mined and exploited in Canada with oil and natural gas, iron ore, bauxite, nickel, zinc, copper, gold and silver the major exports. Recently, diamonds have been discovered in the Northwest Territories. The country's vast rivers provide huge amounts of hydro-electric power but most industry is confined to the Great Lakes and St Lawrence margins. The principal manufactured goods for export are steel products, motor vehicles and paper for newsprint. The USA is Canada's main trading partner, taking 80 per cent of exports. Following a free trade agreement (NAFTA) in 1993 between the USA, Canada and Mexico, even closer economic ties will be made with the USA.

ALBERTA
STATUS: Province
AREA: 661,190 sq km (255,220 sq miles)
POPULATION: 2,672,000
CAPITAL: Edmonton

BRITISH COLUMBIA
STATUS: Province
AREA: 948,565 sq km (366,160 sq miles)
POPULATION: 3,570,000
CAPITAL: Victoria

MANITOBA
STATUS: Province
AREA: 650,090 sq km (250,935 sq miles)
POPULATION: 1,117,000
CAPITAL: Winnipeg

NEW BRUNSWICK
STATUS: Province
AREA: 73,435 sq km (28,345 sq miles)
POPULATION: 751,000
CAPITAL: Fredericton

NEWFOUNDLAND AND LABRADOR
STATUS: Province
AREA: 404,520 sq km (156,145 sq miles)
POPULATION: 581,000
CAPITAL: St John's

NORTHWEST TERRITORIES
STATUS: Territory
AREA: 3,379,685 sq km (1,304,560 sq miles)
POPULATION: 63,000
CAPITAL: Yellowknife

NOVA SCOTIA
STATUS: Province
AREA: 55,490 sq km (21,420 sq miles)
POPULATION: 925,000
CAPITAL: Halifax

ONTARIO
STATUS: Province
AREA: 1,068,630 sq km (412,490 sq miles)
POPULATION: 10,795,000
CAPITAL: Toronto

PRINCE EDWARD ISLAND
STATUS: Province
AREA: 5,655 sq km (2,185 sq miles)
POPULATION: 132,000
CAPITAL: Charlottetown

QUEBEC
STATUS: Province
AREA: 1,540,680 sq km (594,705 sq miles)
POPULATION: 7,226,000
CAPITAL: Quebec

SASKATCHEWAN
STATUS: Province
AREA: 651,900 sq km (251,635 sq miles)
POPULATION: 1,002,000
CAPITAL: Regina

YUKON TERRITORY
STATUS: Province
AREA: 482,515 sq km (186,250 sq miles)
POPULATION: 33,000
CAPITAL: Whitehorse

CANARY ISLANDS
STATUS: Island Provinces of Spain
AREA: 7,275 sq km (2,810 sq miles)
POPULATION: 1,493,784
CAPITAL: Las Palmas (Gran Canaria) and
Santa Cruz (Tenerife)

CAPE VERDE
STATUS: Republic
AREA: 4,035 sq km (1,560 sq miles)
POPULATION: 350,000
ANNUAL NATURAL INCREASE: 2.7%
CAPITAL: Praia
LANGUAGE: Portuguese, Creole
RELIGION: 98% Roman Catholic
CURRENCY: Cape Verde escudo (CVE)
ORGANIZATIONS: ECOWAS, OAU, UN

Independent since 1975, the ten inhabited volcanic islands of the republic are situated in the Atlantic 500 km (310 miles) west of Senegal. Rainfall is low but irrigation encourages growth of sugar cane, coffee, coconuts, fruit (mainly bananas) and maize. Fishing accounts for about 70 per cent of export revenue and all consumer goods are imported.

CAYMAN ISLANDS
STATUS: UK Dependent Territory
AREA: 259 sq km (100 sq miles)
POPULATION: 29,000
CAPITAL: George Town

CENTRAL AFRICAN REPUBLIC
STATUS: Republic
AREA: 624,975 sq km (241,240 sq miles)
POPULATION: 3,173,000
ANNUAL NATURAL INCREASE: 2.7%
CAPITAL: Bangui
LANGUAGE: French, Sango (national)
RELIGION: Animist majority, Christian minority
CURRENCY: CFA franc (C Africa) (XAF)
ORGANIZATIONS: OAU, UN

The republic is remote from both east and west Africa. It has a tropical climate with little variation in temperature. Savannah covers the rolling plateaux with rainforest in the southeast. To the north lies the Sahara Desert. Most farming is at subsistence level with a small amount of crops grown for export – cotton, coffee, groundnuts and tobacco. Hardwood forests in the southwest provide timber for export. Diamonds are the major export, accounting for over half of foreign earnings.

CHAD
STATUS: Republic
AREA: 1,284,000 sq km (495,625 sq miles)
POPULATION: 6,288,000
ANNUAL NATURAL INCREASE: 2.5%
CAPITAL: Ndjamena
LANGUAGE: French, Arabic, local languages
RELIGION: 50% Muslim, 45% animist
CURRENCY: CRA franc (C Africa) (XAF)
ORGANIZATIONS: OAU, UN

Chad is a vast state of central Africa stretching deep into the Sahara. The economy is based on agriculture but only the south, with 1,000 mm (39 in) of rainfall, can support crops for export – cotton, rice and groundnuts. Severe droughts, increasing desertification and border disputes have severely restricted development. Life expectancy at birth is still only 43 years. Salt is mined around Lake Chad where the majority of the population live.

CHANNEL ISLANDS
STATUS: British Crown Dependency
AREA: 194 sq km (75 sq miles)
POPULATION: 145,796
CAPITAL: St Hélier (Jersey)
St Peter Port (Guernsey)

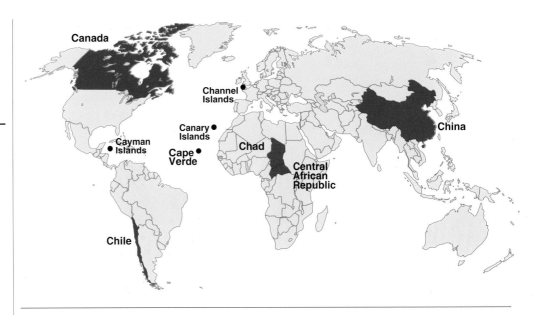

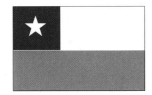

CHILE
STATUS: Republic
AREA: 751,625 sq km (290,125 sq miles)
POPULATION: 13,813,000
ANNUAL NATURAL INCREASE: 1.7%
CAPITAL: Santiago
LANGUAGE: Spanish
RELIGION: 85% Roman Catholic,
Protestant minority
CURRENCY: Chilean peso (CLP)
ORGANIZATIONS: OAS, UN

Chile is a long narrow country on the west coast of South America, stretching through 38° of latitude from the Atacama desert of the north to the sub-polar islands of Tierra del Fuego. Apart from a coastal strip of lowland, the country is dominated by the Andes mountains. Most energy is provided by hydro-electric power. The economy is based upon the abundance of natural resources with copper (the world's largest reserve), iron ore, nitrates, gold, timber, coal, oil and gas. Light and heavy industries are based around Concepción and Santiago. Traditional major exports are copper, fishmeal and cellulose. In the early 1990s farm production increased dramatically and food products now account for 29 per cent of export earnings.

CHINA
STATUS: People's Republic
AREA: 9,597,000 sq km (3,704,440 sq miles)
POPULATION: 1,154,887,381
ANNUAL NATURAL INCREASE: 1.3%
CAPITAL: Beijing (Peking)
LANGUAGE: Mandarin Chinese,
regional languages
RELIGION: Confucianist, Buddhist, Taoist,
Christian and Muslim minorities
CURRENCY: yuan (CNY)
ORGANIZATIONS: UN

The land of China is one of the most diverse on Earth and has vast mineral and agricultural resources. The majority of the people live in the east where the economy is dictated by the great drainage basins of the Yellow River (Huang He) and the Yangtze (Chang Jiang). Here, intensively irrigated agriculture produces one-third of the world's rice as well as wheat, maize, sugar, cotton, soya beans and oil seeds. Pigs are reared and fish caught throughout China. The country is basically self-sufficient in foodstuffs.

Western and northern China are much less densely populated as cultivation is restricted to oases and sheltered valleys. In the southwest, the Tibetan plateau averages 4,900 m (16,000 ft) and supports scattered sheep herding. To the north are Sinkiang and the desert basins of Tarim (Tarim Pendi) and Dzungaria, and bordering Mongolia the vast dry Gobi desert. In the far north only in Manchuria does a more temperate climate allow extensive arable cultivation, of mainly wheat, barley and maize.

The natural mineral resources of China are immense, varied and under-exploited. The Yunnan plateau of the southeast is rich in tin, copper, and zinc; Manchuria possesses coal and iron ore; and oil is extracted from beneath the Yellow Sea. The main industrial centres concentrate on the production of iron, steel, cement, light engineering and textile manufacturing.

With a population of over one billion, China has made tremendous efforts since the late 1970s to erase the negative economic effects of the collectivization policy implemented from 1955, and the cultural revolution of the late 1960s. In 1978 the Chinese leader, Deng Xiaoping, launched an economic revolution (creating special economic zones and encouraging foreign investment). The country is now experiencing phenomenal economic growth, a new consumer revolution and waves of entrepreneurial activities. A growing inequality in living standards between the rural provinces and the richer urban areas has led to a surge of migrants from the countryside to the cities.

ANHUI (ANHWEI)
STATUS: Province
AREA: 139,900 sq km (54,000 sq miles)
POPULATION: 57,600,000
CAPITAL: Hefei

BEIJING (PEKING)
STATUS: Municipality
AREA: 17,800 sq km (6,870 sq miles)
POPULATION: 10,900,000

FUJIAN (FUKIEN)
STATUS: Province
AREA: 123,000 sq km (47,515 sq miles)
POPULATION: 30,800,000
CAPITAL: Fuzhou

GANSU (KANSU)
STATUS: Province
AREA: 530,000 sq km (204,580 sq miles)
POPULATION: 22,900,000
CAPITAL: Lanzhou

GUANGDONG (KWANGTUNG)
STATUS: Province
AREA: 231,400 sq km (89,320 sq miles)
POPULATION: 64,400,000
CAPITAL: Guangzhou (Canton)

GUANGXI (KWANGSI-CHUANG)
STATUS: Autonomous Region
AREA: 220,400 sq km (85,075 sq miles)
POPULATION: 43,200,000
CAPITAL: Nanning

GUIZHOU (KWEICHOW)
STATUS: Province
AREA: 174,000 sq km (67,165 sq miles)
POPULATION: 33,200,000
CAPITAL: Guiyang

HAINAN
STATUS: Province
AREA: 34,965 sq km (13,500 sq miles)
POPULATION: 6,700,000
CAPITAL: Haikou

HEBEI (HOPEI)
STATUS: Province
AREA: 202,700 sq km (78,240 sq miles)
POPULATION: 62,200,000
CAPITAL: Schijiazhuang

HEILONGJIANG (HEILUNGKIANG)
STATUS: Province
AREA: 710,000 sq km (274,060 sq miles)
POPULATION: 35,800,000
CAPITAL: Harbin

HENAN (HONAN)
STATUS: Province
AREA: 167,000 sq km (64,460 sq miles)
POPULATION: 87,600,000
CAPITAL: Zhengzhou

HUBEI (HUPEH)
STATUS: Province
AREA: 187,500 sq km (72,375 sq miles)
POPULATION: 55,100,000
CAPITAL: Wuhan

HUNAN

STATUS: Province
AREA: 210,500 sq km (81,255 sq miles)
POPULATION: 62,100,000
CAPITAL: Changsha

JIANGSU (KIANGSU)

STATUS: Province
AREA: 102,200 sq km (39,450 miles)
POPULATION: 68,400,000
CAPITAL: Nanjing (Nanking)

JIANGXI (KIANGSI)

STATUS: Province
AREA: 164,800 sq km (63,615 sq miles)
POPULATION: 38,700,000
CAPITAL: Nanchang

JILIN (KIRIN)

STATUS: Province
AREA: 290,000 sq km (111,940 sq miles)
POPULATION: 25,100,000
CAPITAL: Changchun

LIAONING

STATUS: Province
AREA: 230,000 sq km (88,780 sq miles)
POPULATION: 39,900,000
CAPITAL: Shenyang

NEI MONGOL (INNER MONGOLIA)

STATUS: Autonomous Region
AREA: 450,000 sq km (173,700 sq miles)
POPULATION: 21,800,000
CAPITAL: Hohhot

NINGXIA HUI (NINGHSIA HUI)

STATUS: Autonomous Region
AREA: 170,000 sq km (65,620 sq miles)
POPULATION: 4,800,000
CAPITAL: Yinchuan

QINGHAI (CHINGHAI)

STATUS: Province
AREA: 721,000 sq km (278,305 sq miles)
POPULATION: 4,500,000
CAPITAL: Xining

SHAANXI (SHENSI)

STATUS: Province
AREA: 195,800 sq km (75,580 sq miles)
POPULATION: 33,600,000
CAPITAL: Xian (Xi'an)

SHANDONG (SHANTUNG)

STATUS: Province
AREA: 153,300 sq km (59,175 sq miles)
POPULATION: 83,430,000
CAPITAL: Jinan

SHANGHAI

STATUS: Municipality
AREA: 5,800 sq km (2,240 sq miles)
POPULATION: 13,400,000

SHANXI (SHANSI)

STATUS: Province
AREA: 157,100 sq km (60,640 sq miles)
POPULATION: 29,400,000
CAPITAL: Taiyuan

SICHUAN (SZECHWAN)

STATUS: Province
AREA: 569,000 sq km (219,635 sq miles)
POPULATION: 109,000,000
CAPITAL: Chengdu

TIANJIN (TIENTSIN)

STATUS: Municipality
AREA: 4,000 sq km (1,545 sq miles)
POPULATION: 9,100,402

XINJIANG UYGUR (SINKIANG-UIGHUR)

STATUS: Autonomous Region
AREA: 1,646,800 sq km (635,665 sq miles)
POPULATION: 15,600,000
CAPITAL: Urumchi (Ürümqi)

XIZANG (TIBET)

STATUS: Autonomous Region
AREA: 1,221,600 sq km (471,540 sq miles)
POPULATION: 2,300,000
CAPITAL: Lhasa

YUNNAN

STATUS: Province
AREA: 436,200 sq km (168,375 sq miles)
POPULATION: 37,800,000
CAPITAL: Kunming

ZHEJIANG (CHEKIANG)

STATUS: Province
AREA: 101,800 sq km (39,295 sq miles)
POPULATION: 42,000,000
CAPITAL: Hangzhou

CHRISTMAS ISLAND

STATUS: External Territory of Australia
AREA: 135 sq km (52 sq miles)
POPULATION: 1,275

COCOS (KEELING) ISLANDS

STATUS: External Territory of Australia
AREA: 14 sq km (5 sq miles)
POPULATION: 647

COLOMBIA

STATUS: Republic
AREA: 1,138,915 (439,620 sq miles)
POPULATION: 13,813,000
ANNUAL NATURAL INCREASE: 1.8%
CAPITAL: Bogotá
LANGUAGE: Spanish, Indian languages
RELIGION: 95% Roman Catholic,
Protestant and Jewish minorities
CURRENCY: Colombian peso (COP)
ORGANIZATIONS: OAS, UN

Colombia is bounded by both the Caribbean Sea and Pacific Ocean. The northernmost peaks of the Andes chain runs from north to south through its western half and the eastern plains, beyond the Andes, contain the headwaters of the Amazon and Orinoco rivers. Almost half of Colombia is covered by the Amazon jungle. Colombia has a tropical climate and temperatures that vary with climate. The fertile river valleys in the uplands produce most of the famous Colombian coffee. Bananas, tobacco, cotton, sugar and rice are grown at lower altitudes. Coffee has always been the major export crop, but manufacturing industry and oil, coal, gold and precious stones are becoming more dominant in the economy. An oil boom is predicted following the discovery of new oil fields at Cusiana and Cupiagua. Immense illegal quantities of cocaine are exported to the US and elsewhere.

COMOROS

STATUS: Federal Islamic Republic
AREA: 1,860 sq km (718 sq miles)
POPULATION: 585,000
ANNUAL NATURAL INCREASE: 3.7%
CAPITAL: Moroni
LANGUAGE: French, Arabic, Comoran
RELIGION: Muslim majority,
Christian minority
CURRENCY: Comoro franc (KMF)
ORGANIZATIONS: OAU, UN

The Comoro Islands, comprising Grand Comore, Anjouan, and Móheli, are situated between Madagascar and the east African coast. The climate is tropical and humid all year round, with a moderate average annual rainfall ranging from 1,000–1140 mm (40–45 inches). Less than half the land is cultivated and the country is dependent on imports for food supplies. The island's economy is based on the export of vanilla, copra, cloves and ylang-ylang essence (exported for the French perfume industry). Mangoes, coconuts and bananas are grown around the coastal lowlands. Timber and timber products are important to local development. There is no manufacturing of any importance.

CONGO

STATUS: Republic
AREA: 342,000 sq km (132,010 sq miles)
POPULATION: 2,690,000
ANNUAL NATURAL INCREASE: 3.3%
CAPITAL: Brazzaville
LANGUAGE: French, Kongo, Teke, Sanga
RELIGION: 50% traditional beliefs,
30% Roman Catholic, Protestant
and Muslim minorities
CURRENCY: CFA franc (C Africa) (XAF)
ORGANIZATIONS: OAU, UN

The Congo, Africa's first communist state still has strong economic ties with the west, especially France, its former colonial ruler. Situated on the coast of west Africa, it contains over

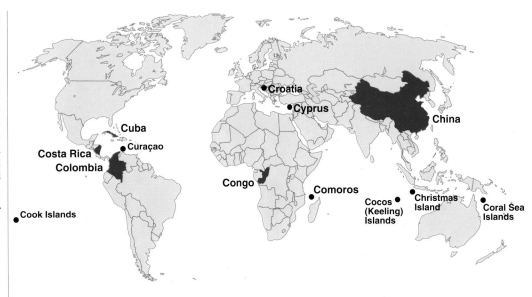

two-thirds swamp and forest, with wooded savannah on the highlands of the Bateké plateau near the Gabon border. Its climate is hot and humid with average rainfall of 1220–1280 mm (48–50 inches). Over 60 per cent of the population is employed in subsistence farming, while sugar, coffee, palm oil and cocoa are all exported. Timber and timber products are major exports but the main source of export revenue is oil from offshore oilfields. Mineral resources are considerable, including industrial diamonds, gold, lead and zinc. Manufacturing industry is concentrated in the major towns and is primarily food processing and textiles.

COOK ISLANDS

STATUS: Self-governing Territory Overseas in Free Association with New Zealand
AREA: 233 sq km (90 sq miles)
POPULATION: 18,617
CAPITAL: Avarua on Rarotonga

CORAL SEA ISLANDS

STATUS: External Territory of Australia
AREA: 22 sq km (8.5 sq miles)
POPULATION: no permanent population

COSTA RICA

STATUS: Republic
AREA: 50,900 sq km (19,650 sq miles)
POPULATION: 3,099,000
ANNUAL NATURAL INCREASE: 2.5%
CAPITAL: San José
LANGUAGE: Spanish
RELIGION: 95% Roman Catholic
CURRENCY: Costa Rican colón (CRC)
ORGANIZATIONS: CACM, OAS, UN

Costa Rica is a narrow country, situated between Nicaragua and Panama, with both a Pacific and a Caribbean coastline. Its coastal regions experience hot, humid, tropical conditions, but in upland areas its climate is more equable. The mountain chains that run the length of the country form the fertile uplands where coffee is grown and cattle are kept. Bananas, grown on the Pacific coast, and coffee are the major cash crops for export. Although gold, silver, iron ore and bauxite are mined, the principal industries are food processing and the manufacture of textiles and chemicals, fertilizers and furniture.

CROATIA

STATUS: Republic
AREA: 56,540 sq km (21,825 sq miles)
POPULATION: 4,764,000
ANNUAL NATURAL INCREASE: 0.4%

CAPITAL: Zagreb
LANGUAGE: Serbo-Croat
RELIGION: Roman Catholic majority
CURRENCY: kuna
ORGANIZATIONS: UN

Croatia is an oddly shaped country which runs in a narrow strip along the Adriatic coast and extends inland in a broad curve. Its climate varies from Mediterranean along the coast to continental further inland. Once part of the Yugoslavian Federation, Croatia achieved recognition as an independent nation in 1992 following the 1991 civil war between Serb and Croat factions. The conflict left the country with a damaged economy, disruption of trade, loss of tourist revenue and a huge reconstruction bill. Traditionally the fertile plains of central and eastern Croatia have been intensively farmed, producing surplus crops, meat and dairy products. The mountainous and barren littoral has been developed for tourism. Croatia used to be the most highly developed part of Yugoslavia, concentrating on electrical engineering, metal working, machine building, chemicals and rubber. Economic recovery is dependent upon political stability and an accommodation with the Serbs over the UN-supervised areas still under ethnic Serb control.

CUBA

STATUS: Republic
AREA: 114,525 sq km (44,205 sq miles)
POPULATION: 10,870,000
ANNUAL NATURAL INCREASE: 1.0%
CAPITAL: Havana (Habana)
LANGUAGE: Spanish
RELIGION: Roman Catholic majority
CURRENCY: Cuban peso (CUP)
ORGANIZATIONS: OIEC, UN

Cuba, the largest of the Greater Antilles islands, dominates the entrance to the Gulf of Mexico. It consists of one large and over 1,500 small islands, and is a mixture of fertile plains, mountain ranges and gentle countryside. Temperatures range from 22–28°C (72–82°F) and an there is an average annual rainfall of 1,200 mm (47 inches).

Sugar, tobacco and nickel are the main exports. Being a communist state, most of Cuba's trade has been with the former USSR and in the three years following the collapse of the Soviet Union the Cuban economy contracted by over 30 per cent (having lost its principal market for sugar, which it had bartered for oil, food and machinery). The economy was already suffering from US sanctions. Severe shortages of food, fuel and basic necessities were tolerated and in 1993 the government was forced to permit limited private enterprise and the use of American dollars.

CURAÇAO

STATUS: Self-governing Island of the Netherlands Antilles
AREA: 444 sq km (171 sq miles)
POPULATION: 707,000

CYPRUS

STATUS: Republic
(Turkish unilateral declaration of independence in northern area)
AREA: 9,250 sq km (3,570 sq miles)
POPULATION: 725,000
ANNUAL NATURAL INCREASE: 1.1%
CAPITAL: Nicosia
LANGUAGE: Greek, Turkish, English
RELIGION: Greek Orthodox majority, Muslim minority
CURRENCY: Cyprus pound (CYP), Turkish lira (TL)
ORGANIZATIONS: Comm., Council of Europe, UN

Cyprus is a prosperous Mediterranean island. The summers are very hot (38°C or 100°F) and dry, and the winters warm and wet. About two-thirds of the island is under cultivation and citrus fruit, potatoes, barley, wheat and olives are produced. Sheep, goats and pigs are the principal livestock. Copper is mined but the mining industry is declining. The main exports are manufactured goods, clothing and footwear, fruit, wine and vegetables. Tourism is an important source of foreign exchange.

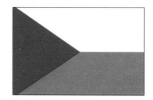

CZECH REPUBLIC

STATUS: Federal Republic
AREA: 127,870 sq km (49,360 sq miles)
POPULATION: 10,330,000
ANNUAL NATURAL INCREASE: 0.3%
CAPITAL: Prague (Praha)
LANGUAGE: Czech
RELIGION: 40% Roman Catholic,
55% no stated religion
CURRENCY: Czech crown or koruna (CSK)
ORGANIZATIONS: Council of Europe,
OIEC, UN

Following the break up of Czechoslovakia, the Czech Republic came into being in January 1993. It is a country that lies at the heart of central Europe and has a diversity of landscapes. In Bohemia, to the west of the country, the upper Elbe drainage basin is surrounded by mountains. Moravia, separated from Bohemia by hills and mountains, is a lowland area centred on the town of Brno. The climate is temperate but with continental characteristics. Rain falls mainly in spring and autumn. This is historically one of the most highly industrialized regions of Europe, whose heavy industry once specialized in producing arms for the Soviet Union. Now the main products include cars, aircraft, tramways and locomotive diesel engines. There are raw materials (coal, minerals and timber) and a nuclear power station is being built to replace some polluting coal-fired stations.

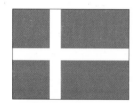

DENMARK

STATUS: Kingdom
AREA: 43,075 sq km (16,625 sq miles)
POPULATION: 5,181,000
ANNUAL NATURAL INCREASE: 0.1%
CAPITAL: Copenhagen (København)
LANGUAGE: Danish
RELIGION: 94% Lutheran, Roman Catholic minority
CURRENCY: Danish krone (DKK)
ORGANIZATIONS: Council of Europe, EU,
NATO, OECD, UN

Denmark is the smallest of the Scandinavian countries. It consists of the Jutland Peninsula and over 400 islands of which only one quarter are inhabited. The country is low-lying with a mixture of fertile and sandy soils, generally of glacial origin. Climate is temperate, with rainfall all the year round. Denmark's economy stems traditionally from agriculture and dairy products; bacon and sugar are still particularly important. An extensive fishing industry is centred on the shallow lagoons along the western coastline. Danish North Sea oil and gas provide self-sufficiency in energy and gas exports began in 1991. Food processing, beer, pharmaceuticals and specialist biotechnological equipment contribute to the industrial sector which provides 75 per cent of Danish exports.

DJIBOUTI

STATUS: Republic
AREA: 23,000 sq km (8,800 sq miles)
POPULATION: 467,000
ANNUAL NATURAL INCREASE: 2.9%
CAPITAL: Djibouti
LANGUAGE: French, Somali, Dankali, Arabic
RELIGION: Muslim majority,
Roman Catholic minority
CURRENCY: Djibouti franc (DJF)
ORGANIZATIONS: Arab League, OAU, UN

Situated at the mouth of the Red Sea, Djibouti consists almost entirely of low-lying desert. There are mountains in the north of which Musa Ālī Terara reaches 2,063 m (6,768 feet). Its climate is very hot all year with annual temperatures between 25–35°C (78–96°F). The annual rainfall is as low as 130 mm (5 inches). The land is barren so Djibouti's economy must rely on activities based on its deep natural port and position along a major shipping route. It therefore acts as a trade outlet for Ethiopia, as well as serving Red Sea shipping. Main exports are cattle and hides.

DOMINICA

STATUS: Commonwealth State
AREA: 751 sq km (290 sq miles)
POPULATION: 72,000
ANNUAL NATURAL INCREASE: -0.3%
CAPITAL: Roseau
LANGUAGE: English, French patois
RELIGION: 80% Roman Catholic
CURRENCY: East Caribbean dollar (XCD)
ORGANIZATIONS: Comm., OAS, UN

Dominica is located in the Windward Islands of the east Caribbean. It is mountainous and forested with a coastline of steep cliffs. Tropical rainforest covers nearly half of the island. The climate is tropical with average temperatures exceeding 25°C (77°F) and has abundant rainfall. Bananas are the major export, followed by citrus fruits, coconuts and timber. Coffee and cocoa production is developing. Tourism is the most rapidly expanding industry.

DOMINICAN REPUBLIC

STATUS: Republic
AREA: 48,440 sq km (18,700 sq miles)
POPULATION: 7,471,000
ANNUAL NATURAL INCREASE: 1.9%
CAPITAL: Santo Domingo
LANGUAGE: Spanish
RELIGION: 90% Roman Catholic,
Protestant and Jewish minorities
CURRENCY: Dominican peso (DOP)
ORGANIZATIONS: OAS, UN

The Dominican Republic is situated on the eastern half of the Caribbean island of Hispaniola. The landscape is dominated by a series of mountain ranges, thickly covered with rainforest, reaching up to 3,000 m (9,843 feet). To the south there is a coastal plain where the capital, Santo Domingo, lies. Minerals, in particular nickel, are important but agricultural products account for 70 per cent of export earnings. The traditional dependence on sugar has diminished, with coffee, tobacco and newer products including cocoa, fruit and vegetables gaining importance.

ECUADOR

STATUS: Republic
AREA: 461,475 sq km (178,130 sq miles)
POPULATION: 10,741,000
ANNUAL NATURAL INCREASE: 2.5%
CAPITAL: Quito
LANGUAGE: Spanish, Quechua,
other Indian languages
RELIGION: 90% Roman Catholic
CURRENCY: sucre (ECS)
ORGANIZATIONS: OAS, UN

Ecuador falls into two distinctive geographical zones, the coastal lowlands which border the Pacific Ocean and inland, the Andean highlands. The highlands stretch about 400 km (250 miles) north-south, and here limited quantities of maize, wheat and barley are cultivated. Ecuador's main agricultural export, bananas, coffee and cocoa, are all grown on the fertile coastal lowlands. The rapidly growing fishing industry, especially shrimps, is becoming more important. Large resources of crude oil have been found in the thickly-forested lowlands on the eastern border and Ecuador has now become South America's second largest oil producer after Venezuela. Mineral reserves include silver, gold, copper and zinc.

EGYPT

STATUS: Republic
AREA: 1,000,250 sq km
(386,095 sq miles)
POPULATION: 55,163,000
ANNUAL NATURAL INCREASE: 2.4%
CAPITAL: Cairo (El Qâhira)
LANGUAGE: Arabic, Berber, Nubian,
English, French
RELIGION: 80% Muslim (mainly Sunni),
Coptic Christian minority
CURRENCY: Egyptian pound (EGP)
ORGANIZATIONS: Arab league, OAU, UN

The focal point of Egypt, situated on the Mediterranean coast of northeast Africa, is the fertile, irrigated Nile river valley, sandwiched between two deserts. Egypt is virtually dependent on the Nile for water as average rainfall varies between only 200 mm (8 inches) in the north and zero in the deserts. Cotton and Egyptian clover are the two most important crops, with increasing cultivation of cereals, fruits, rice, sugar cane and vegetables. Agriculture is concentrated around the Nile flood plain and delta. In spite of this, however, Egypt has to import over half the food it needs. Buffalo, cattle, sheep, goats and camels are the principal livestock. Tourism is an important source of revenue together with the tolls from the Suez Canal. Major industries include the manufacture of cement, cotton goods, iron and steel, and processed foods. The main mineral deposits are phosphates, iron ore, salt, manganese and chromium. Egypt has sufficient oil and natural gas reserves for its own needs and exports crude oil. Gas is now replacing oil in Egyptian power stations in order to release more crude oil for export.

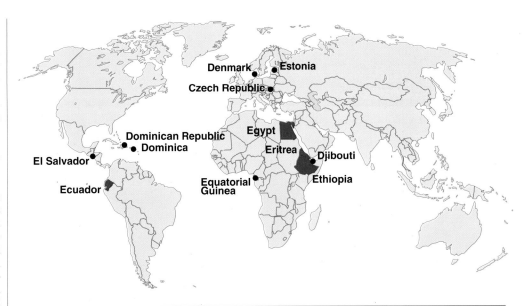

EL SALVADOR

STATUS: Republic
AREA: 21,395 sq km (8,260 sq miles)
POPULATION: 5,048,000
ANNUAL NATURAL INCREASE: 1.8%
CAPITAL: San Salvador
LANGUAGE: Spanish
RELIGION: 80% Roman Catholic
CURRENCY: El Salvador colón (SVC)
ORGANIZATIONS: CACM, OAS, UN

El Salvador is a small, densely populated country on the Pacific coast of Central America. Most of the population live around the lakes in the central plain. Temperatures range from 24–26°C (75–79°F) with an average annual rainfall of 1,780 mm (70 inches). Coffee provides about 50 per cent of export revenue. Other products include sugar, cotton, bananas and balsam. Industry has expanded considerably with the production of textiles, shoes, cosmetics, cement, processed foods, chemicals and furniture. Geothermal and hydro-electric resources are being developed and there are copper deposits as yet unexploited.

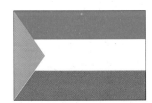

EQUATORIAL GUINEA

STATUS: Republic
AREA: 28,050 sq km (10,825 sq miles)
POPULATION: 369,000
ANNUAL NATURAL INCREASE: 2.3%
CAPITAL: Malabo
LANGUAGE: 85% Fang, Spanish, Bubi,
other tribal languages

RELIGION: 96% Roman Catholic, 4% Animist
CURRENCY: CFA franc (C Africa) (XAF)
ORGANIZATIONS: OAU, UN

Independent from Spain since 1968, Equatorial Guinea consists of two separate regions – a mainland area with a tropical, humid climate and dense rainforest but little economic development, and the volcanic island of Bioko. Agriculture is the principal source of revenue. Cocoa and coffee from the island plantations are the main exports with wood products, fish and processed foods manufactured near the coast on the mainland.

ERITREA

STATUS: Republic
AREA: 91,600 sq km (35,370 sq miles)
POPULATION: 3,500,000
CAPITAL: Asmara (Āsmera)
LANGUAGE: Arabic, native languages, English
RELIGION: 50% Christian, 50% Muslim
CURRENCY: Ethiopian birr
ORGANIZATIONS: OAU, UN

Eritrea gained formal recognition of its independence from Ethiopia in 1993. The landscape consists of an arid coastal plain, which borders the Red Sea, and the highlands of the central area, which rise to over 2000 m (6,562 feet). There are few natural resources, with what industry there is being concentrated around Asmara. The consequences of continuing drought and the protracted civil war will affect the population and economy for some time to come.

ESTONIA

STATUS: Republic
AREA: 45,100 sq km (17,413 sq miles)
POPULATION: 1,516,000

ANNUAL NATURAL INCREASE: 0.2%
CAPITAL: Tallinn
LANGUAGE: Estonian, Russian
RELIGION: Lutheran, Roman Catholic
CURRENCY: kroon (EKR)
ORGANIZATIONS: Council of Europe, UN

With the mainland situated on the southern coast of the Gulf of Finland and encompassing a large number of islands, Estonia is the smallest and most northerly of the Baltic States. The generally flat and undulating landscape is characterised by extensive forests and many lakes. The climate is temperate. Agriculture, mainly livestock production, woodworking and textiles are also important. The economy is currently undergoing a transformation from central planning and state-ownership to a free market system based on private enterprise. Incorporated into the Soviet Union in 1940, Estonia regained its independence in 1991.

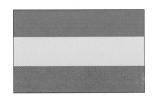

ETHIOPIA

STATUS: Republic
AREA: 1,023,050 sq km (394,895 sq miles)
POPULATION: 51,980,000
ANNUAL NATURAL INCREASE: 3.4%
CAPITAL: Addis Ababa (Ādīs Ābeba)
LANGUAGE: Amharic, English, Arabic
RELIGION: Ethiopian Orthodox,
Muslim and animist
CURRENCY: birr (ETB)
ORGANIZATIONS: OAU, UN

Ethiopia's landscape consists of heavily dissected plateaux and plains of arid desert. Rainfall in these latter areas is minimal and unreliable, and drought and starvation are ever-present problems. Farming, in the high rural areas, accounts for 90 per cent of export revenue with coffee as the principal crop and main export together with fruit and vegetables, oil-seeds, hides and skins. Gold is mined on a small scale. The most important industries are cotton textiles, cement, canned foods, construction materials and leather goods. These are concentrated around the capital. In recent years the economy has been devastated by almost constant civil war.

FAEROES

STATUS: Self-governing Island Region
of Denmark
AREA: 1,399 sq km (540 sq miles)
POPULATION: 47,000
CAPITAL: Tórshavn

FALKLAND ISLANDS

STATUS: UK Crown Colony
AREA: 12,175 sq km (4,700 sq miles)
POPULATION: 2,121
CAPITAL: Stanley

FIJI

STATUS: Republic
AREA: 18,330 sq km (7,075 sq miles)
POPULATION: 758,275
ANNUAL NATURAL INCREASE: 1.8%
CAPITAL: Suva
LANGUAGE: Fijian, English, Hindi
RELIGION: 51% Methodist Christian,
40% Hindu, 8% Muslim
CURRENCY: Fiji dollar (FJD)
ORGANIZATIONS: Col. Plan, UN

A country of some 320 tropical islands, of which over 100 are inhabited, the Republic of Fiji is located in Melanesia, in the south-central Pacific Ocean. The islands range from tiny coral reefs and atolls to the two largest Vanua Levu and Viti Levu, which are mountainous and of volcanic origin. The climate is tropical with temperatures ranging from 16–33°C (60–90°F) and annual rainfall being 236 mm (60 inches). Fiji's economy is geared to production of sugar cane, which provides 45 per cent of export revenue. Coconuts, bananas and rice are grown and livestock raised. Main industries are sugar processing, gold-mining, copra processing and fish canning. Tourism is also an important revenue earner.

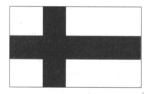

FINLAND

STATUS: Republic
AREA: 337,030 sq km
(130,095 sq miles)
POPULATION: 5,076,000
ANNUAL NATURAL INCREASE: 0.4%
CAPITAL: Helsinki
LANGUAGE: Finnish, Swedish
RELIGION: 87% Evangelical Lutheran,
Eastern Orthodox minority
CURRENCY: markka (Finnmark) (FIM)
ORGANIZATIONS: Council of Europe, EEA,
EFTA, OECD, UN

Finland is a flat land of lakes and forests. Over 70 per cent of the land supports coniferous woodland with a further 10 per cent being water. The Saimaa lake area is Europe's largest inland water system. Its soils are thin and poor on ice-scarred granite plateaux. Most of Finland's population live in towns in the far south because of the harsh northern climate. In the north temperatures can range from -30°C (-22°F) in the winter to 27°C (81°F) in summer. The Baltic Sea can freeze for several miles from the coast during winter months. There is 600 mm (24 inches) of rain per annum throughout the country. Forestry products (timber, pulp and paper) once dominated the economy (80 per cent in 1980) but now account for 40 per cent of the export total and engineering, in particular shipbuilding and forest machinery, is almost equal in importance. Finland is virtually self-sufficient in basic foodstuffs. The country depends heavily on imported energy, producing only 30 per cent of its total consumption (20 per cent by its four nuclear power stations).

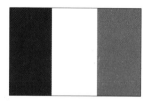

FRANCE

STATUS: Republic
AREA: 543,965 sq km (209,970 sq miles)
POPULATION: 57,800,000
ANNUAL NATURAL INCREASE: 0.6%
CAPITAL: Paris
LANGUAGE: French
RELIGION: 90% Roman Catholic. Protestant,
Muslim, Jewish minorities
CURRENCY: French franc (FRF)
ORGANIZATIONS: Council of Europe, EEA, EU,
G7, NATO, OECD, UN, WEU

France encompasses a great variety of landscapes, ranging from mountain ranges, high plateaux to lowland plains and river basins. The Pyrenees, in the southwest, form the border with Spain and the Jura mountains, in the west, form a border with Switzerland. The highest mountain range is the Alps, south of the Jura. The Massif Central is the highest of the plateaux, which also include the Vosges bordering the plain of Alsace, and Armorica occupying the granite moors of the Brittany peninsula. The French climate is moderated by proximity to the Atlantic, and is generally mild. The south has a Mediterranean climate with hot dry summers, the rest of the country has rain all year round. (Paris has an average annual rainfall of 600 mm or 24 inches). Much of the French countryside is agricultural and it is estimated that one-third of the population derives an income from the land. France is self-sufficient in cereals, dairy products, meat, fruit and vegetables, and is a leading exporter of wheat, barley and sugar beet. Wine is also a major export. Over the past years there has been a steady drift of labour, mainly of younger people from the countryside to the industrialized areas. France is the fourth industrial power in the world after USA, Japan and Germany. It has reserves of coal, oil and natural gas, and is one of the world's leading producers of iron ore. It has large steel-making and chemical refining industries. Its vehicle, aeronautical and armaments industries are among the world's most important. Leading light industries are fashion, perfumes and luxury goods. Most of its heavy industry is concentrated in the major industrial zone of the northeast. In the past, sources of energy have been provided from its reserves of fossil fuels, however in recent years other sources have increased in importance, such as nuclear power using uranium from French mines, tidal power, and hydro-electricity. Tourism is an important source of income, that will be further encouraged by the opening of the Channel Tunnel.

FRENCH GUIANA

STATUS: Overseas Department
of France
AREA: 91,000 sq km (35,125 sq miles)
POPULATION: 114,808
CAPITAL: Cayenne

FRENCH POLYNESIA

STATUS: Overseas Territory
of France
AREA: 3,940 sq km (1,520 sq miles)
POPULATION: 199,031
CAPITAL: Papeete

GABON

STATUS: Republic
AREA: 267,665 sq km (103,320 sq miles)
POPULATION: 1,012,000
ANNUAL NATURAL INCREASE: 2.7%
CAPITAL: Libreville
LANGUAGE: French, Bantu dialects, Fang
RELIGION: 60% Roman Catholic.
CURRENCY: CFA franc (C Africa) (XAF)
ORGANIZATIONS: OAU, OPEC, UN,

Gabon, which lies on the equator, consists of the Ogooué river basin covered with tropical rain forest. It is hot and wet all year with average annual temperatures of 25°C (77°F). It is one of the most prosperous states in Africa with valuable timber (mahogany, ebony and walnut) and mineral (manganese and uranium) resources. State-run plantations growing oil palms, bananas, sugar cane and rubber are also important. Gabon's economy, however, is heavily dependent on its oil industry. It is the third largest producer in sub-Saharan Africa after Nigeria and Angola. France supplies nearly half the country's imports and French influence is evident everywhere.

GAMBIA, THE

STATUS: Republic
AREA: 10,690 sq km (4,125 sq miles)
POPULATION: 1,026,000
ANNUAL NATURAL INCREASE: 3.2%
CAPITAL: Banjul
LANGUAGE: English, Madinka, Fula, Wolof

RELIGION: 90% Muslim,
Christian and animist minorities
CURRENCY: dalasi (GMD)
ORGANIZATIONS: Comm., ECOWAS, OAU, UN

The Gambia is the smallest country in Africa. An enclave within Senegal, it is 470 km (292 miles) long, averages 24 km (15 miles) wide and occupies land bordering the Gambia river. The climate has two distinctive seasons. November to May is dry but July to October sees monsoon rainfall of up to 1,300 mm (51 inches). The temperatures average about 23–27°C (73–81°F) throughout the year. Groundnuts and subsidiary products are the mainstay of the economy but tourism is developing rapidly. The production of cotton, livestock, fish and rice is increasing to change the present economic reliance on groundnuts.

GEORGIA

STATUS: Republic
AREA: 69,700 sq km (26,905 sq miles)
POPULATION: 5,471,000
ANNUAL NATURAL INCREASE: 0.5%
CAPITAL: Tbilisi
LANGUAGE: 70% Georgian, 8% Armenian,
6% Russian, 6% Azeri
RELIGION: Orthodox Christian
CURRENCY: coupon
ORGANIZATIONS: CIS

Georgia, covering part of the southern Caucasus, is a mountainous country with forests covering one-third of its area. The climate ranges from sub-tropical on the shores of the Black Sea, to perpetual ice and snow on the Caucasian crests. Rich deposits of coal are mainly unexploited. Cheap oil and gas imports, hydro-electric power and minerals, in particular rich manganese deposits, have led to industrialization successfully concentrated on metallurgy and machine-building. With the exception of the fertile plain to the east, agricultural land is in short supply and difficult to work. This is partly compensated by the cultivation of labour-intensive and profitable crops such as tea, grapes, tobacco and citrus fruit. The break-up of the Soviet Union brought independence for Georgia in 1991. The question of regional autonomy for the Abkhaz, Adzhar and South Ossetian minorities has repeatedly led to violent ethnic conflict in recent years, causing economic collapse.

GERMANY

STATUS: Federal Republic
AREA: 356,840 sq km (137,740 sq miles)
POPULATION: 81,051,000
ANNUAL NATURAL INCREASE: 0.6%
CAPITAL: Berlin
(seat of government Berlin/Bonn)
LANGUAGE: German

RELIGION: 45% Protestant
40% Roman Catholic
CURRENCY: Deutsch-mark (DM)
ORGANIZATIONS: Council of Europe, EEA, EU,
G7, NATO, OECD, UN, WEU

Germany has three main geographical regions: the Northern plain, stretching from the rivers Oder and Neisse in the east to the Dutch border; the central uplands with elevated plateaux intersected by river valleys and relieved by isolated mountains, gradually rising to peaks of up to nearly 1500 m (5000 feet) in the Black Forest: finally the Bavarian Alps stradling the Austrian border. With exception of the Danube, all German river systems run northwards into the North or the Baltic Seas. The climate is mainly continental with temperatures ranging from -3°–1°C (27–34°F) in January to 16°–19°C (61°–66°F) in July. Only in the north-western corner of the country does the climate become more oceanic in character. Germany on the whole has large stretches of very fertile farmland.

Politically, the division of Germany, a product of the post-1945 Cold War between the victorious Allies against Hitler, was rapidly overcome after the collapse of communism in Eastern Europe, and the unification of the two German states was effected in 1990. Economically, the legacy of 40 years of socialist rule in the East ensures that, in terms of both structure and performance, Germany will encompass two vastly different halves for a long time to come. Having lost its captive markets in what used to be the Soviet Bloc, the eastern economy then all but collapsed under the weight of superior western competition. The task of reconstruction is proving more difficult, more protracted and, most of all, more costly than expected. In the West, the Ruhr basin, historically the industrial heartland of Germany, with its emphasis on coal mining and iron and steel works, has long since been overtaken by more advanced industries elsewhere, notably in the Rhine-Main area and further south in the regions around Stuttgart and Munich. The rapidly expanding services sector apart, the German economy is now dominated by the chemical, pharmaceutical, mechanical engineering, motor and high-tech industries. To lessen the country's dependence on oil imports, an ambitious nuclear energy programme has been adopted. Although poor in minerals and other raw materials with the exception of lignite and potash, Germany has managed to become one of the world's leading manufacturers and exporters of vehicles, machine tools, electrical and electronic products and of consumer goods of various description, in particular textiles. But the massive balance of trade surplus West Germany used to enjoy has now disappeared due to the sucking in of imports by, and the redistribution of output to, the newly acquired territories in the East.

GHANA

STATUS: Republic
AREA: 238,305 sq km (91,985 sq miles)
POPULATION: 15,959,000
ANNUAL NATURAL INCREASE: 3.3%
CAPITAL: Accra
LANGUAGE: English, tribal languages
RELIGION: 42% Christian
CURRENCY: cedi (GHC)
ORGANIZATIONS: Comm., ECOWAS, OAU, UN

Ghana, the west African state once known as the Gold Coast, gained independence from Britain in 1957. The landscape varies from tropical rainforest to dry scrubland, with the terrain becoming hillier to the north, culminating in a plateau averaging some 500 m (1,600 feet). The climate is tropical with the annual rainfall ranging from over 2,000 mm (79 inches) on the coast to less than 1,000 mm (40 inches) inland. The temperature averages 27°C (81°F) all year. Cocoa is the principal crop but although most Ghanaians farm, there is also a thriving industrial base around Tema, where local bauxite is smelted into aluminium. Tema has the largest artificial harbour in Africa. In recent years gold production has surged, Ghana having some of the world's richest gold deposits. Besides gold, Ghana's major exports are cocoa and timber. Principal imports are fuel, food and manufactured goods. Offshore oil has yet to be economically developed.

GIBRALTAR

STATUS: UK Crown Colony
AREA: 6.5 sq km (2.5 sq miles)
POPULATION: 31,000

GREECE

STATUS: Republic
AREA: 131,985 sq km (50,945 sq miles)
POPULATION: 10,269,074
ANNUAL NATURAL INCREASE: 0.4%
CAPITAL: Athens (Athínai)
LANGUAGE: Greek
RELIGION: 97% Greek Orthodox
CURRENCY: drachma (GRD)
ORGANIZATIONS: Council of Europe,
EC, NATO, OECD, UN

Greece is a mountainous country and over one-fifth of its area comprises numerous islands, 154 of which are inhabited. The climate is Mediterranean with temperatures averaging 28°C (82°F) in summer. The mountains experience some heavy snowfall during winter. Poor irrigation and drainage mean that much of the agriculture is localized. The main products of olives, fruit and vegetables, cotton, tobacco and wine are exported. The surrounding seas are important, providing two-thirds of Greece's fish requirements and supporting an active merchant fleet. Athens is the main manufacturing base and at least one quarter of the population lives there. Greece is a very popular tourist destination which helps the craft industries – tourism is a prime source of national income.

GREENLAND

STATUS: Self-governing Island Region
of Denmark
AREA: 2,175,600 sq km (836,780 sq miles)
POPULATION: 55,558
CAPITAL: Godthåb (Nuuk)

GRENADA

STATUS: Commonwealth State
AREA: 345 sq km (133 sq miles)
POPULATION: 95,343
ANNUAL NATURAL INCREASE: -0.2%
CAPITAL: St George's
LANGUAGE: English, French patois
RELIGION: Roman Catholic majority
CURRENCY: E Caribbean dollar (XCD)
ORGANIZATIONS: Caricom, Comm., OAS, UN

The Caribbean island of Grenada, whose territory includes the southern Grenadines, is the most southern of the Windward Islands. It is mountainous and thickly forested, with a settled warm climate and an average temperature of 27°C (81°F). Rainfall varies with altitude, ranging from 760 mm (30 inches) to 3,560 mm (140 inches) on the higher ground. The island is famous for its spices and nutmeg is the main export. Cocoa and bananas are also important, together with some citrus fruits and vegetables. Tourism is important and continues to expand.

GUADELOUPE

STATUS: Overseas Department
of France
AREA: 1,780 sq km (687 sq miles)
POPULATION: 406,000
CAPITAL: Basse-Terre

GUAM

STATUS: External Territory of USA
AREA: 450 sq km (174 sq miles)
POPULATION: 139,000
CAPITAL: Agaña

GUATEMALA

STATUS: Republic
AREA: 108,890 sq km (42,030 sq miles)
POPULATION: 9,745,000
ANNUAL NATURAL INCREASE: 2.9%
CAPITAL: Guatemala City (Guatemala)
LANGUAGE: Spanish, Indian languages
RELIGION: 75% Roman Catholic,
25% Protestant
CURRENCY: quetzal (GTQ)
ORGANIZATIONS: CACM, OAS, UN

The central American country of Guatemala has both a Pacific and a Caribbean coastline. The mountainous interior, with peaks reaching up to 4,000 m (13,120 feet), covers two-thirds of the country while to the north there is the thickly forested area known as the Petén. The northern lowland and the smaller coastal plains have a hot tropical climate, but the central highlands are more temperate. A rainy season lasts from May to October. Annual rainfall reaches up to 5,000 mm (200 inches) in some lowland areas but decreases to an average of 1,150 mm (45 inches) in the mountains. Agricultural products form the bulk of Guatemala's exports, notably coffee, sugar cane, cotton and bananas, but there is also a substantial industrial base. Manufacturing includes textiles, paper and pharmaceuticals. Mineral resources include nickel, antimony, lead, silver and in the north crude oil.

GUINEA

STATUS: Republic
AREA: 245,855 sq km
(94,900 sq miles)
POPULATION: 6,116,000
ANNUAL NATURAL INCREASE: 2.8%
CAPITAL: Conakry
LANGUAGE: French, Susu, Manika
RELIGION: 85% Muslim
10% animist, 5% Roman Catholic
CURRENCY: Guinea franc (GNF)
ORGANIZATIONS: ECOWAS, OAU, UN

Guinea, a former French colony, is situated on the west African coast. Its drowned coastline, lined with mangrove swamps, contrasts strongly with its interior highlands containing the headwaters of the Gambia, Niger and Senegal rivers. Agriculture occupies 80 per cent of the workforce, the main exports being coffee, bananas, pineapple and palm products. Guinea has some of the largest resources of bauxite (aluminium ore) in the world as well as gold and diamonds. Bauxite accounts for 80 per cent of export earnings.

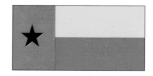

GUINEA-BISSAU

STATUS: Republic
AREA: 36,125 sq km (13,945 sq miles)
POPULATION: 1,006,000
ANNUAL NATURAL INCREASE: 1.9%
CAPITAL: Bissau
LANGUAGE: Portuguese, Creole,
Guinean dialects
RELIGION: Animist and Muslim majority,
Roman Catholic minority
CURRENCY: Guinea-Bissau peso (GWP)
ORGANIZATIONS: ECOWS, OAU, UN

Guinea-Bissau, on the west African coast, was once a centre for the Portuguese slave trade. The coast is swampy and lined with mangroves, and the interior consists of a low-lying plain densely covered with rain forest. The coast is hot and humid with annual rainfall of 2,000–3,000 mm (79–118 inches) a year, although the interior is cooler and drier. Eighty per cent of the country's exports comprise groundnut oil, palm kernels and palm oil. Fish, fish products and coconuts also make an important contribution to trade.

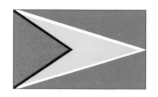

GUYANA

STATUS: Co-operative Republic
AREA: 214,970 sq km (82,980 sq miles)
POPULATION: 808,000
ANNUAL NATURAL INCREASE: 0.3%
CAPITAL: Georgetown
LANGUAGE: English, Hindi, Urdu,
Amerindian dialects
RELIGION: Christian majority, Muslim
and Hindu minorities
CURRENCY: Guyana dollar (GYD)
ORGANIZATIONS: Caricom, Comm., UN

Guyana, formerly the British colony of British Guiana, borders both Venezuela and Brazil. Its Atlantic coast, the most densely-populated area, is flat and marshy, while towards the interior the landscape gradually rises to the Guiana Highlands – a region densely covered in rainforest. The climate is tropical, with hot, wet and humid conditions, which are modified along the coast by sea breezes. Agriculture, dominated by sugar and rice, is the basis of the economy. Bauxite deposits provide a valuable export and in the mid-1990s gold production increased.

Greenland
Iceland
Hungary
Greece
India
Haiti
Guadeloupe
Grenada
Guinea-Bissau
Hong Kong
Guam
Guatemala
Honduras
Guinea
Guyana
Heard and McDonald Islands

HAITI

STATUS: Republic
AREA: 27,750 sq km (10,710 sq miles)
POPULATION: 6,764,000
ANNUAL NATURAL INCREASE: 2.0%
CAPITAL: Port-au-Prince
LANGUAGE: French, Creole
RELIGION: 80% Roman Catholic,
Voodoo folk religion minority
CURRENCY: gourde (HTG)
ORGANIZATIONS: OAS, UN

Haiti occupies the western part of the island of Hispaniola in the Caribbean. It is the poorest country in Central America. The country is mountainous with three main ranges, the highest reaching 2,680 m (8,793 feet). Agriculture is restricted to the plains which divide the ranges. The climate is tropical. Ninety per cent of the workforce are farmers and traditional exports have been coffee, sugar, cotton, and cocoa. In the early to mid-1990s national poverty worsened as a result of UN embargoes imposed against an illegal military regime. Thousands of Haitians fled the country. New sanctions in 1994 threatened to bring an end to all manufacturing and exporting activities.

HEARD AND McDONALD ISLANDS

STATUS: External Territory of Australia
AREA: 412 sq km (159 sq miles)
POPULATION: no permanent population
CAPITAL: Edmonton

HONDURAS

STATUS: Republic
AREA: 112,085 sq km (43,265 sq miles)
POPULATION: 5,462,000
ANNUAL NATURAL INCREASE 3.1%
CAPITAL: Tegucigalpa
LANGUAGE: Spanish, Indian dialects
RELIGION: Roman Catholic majority
CURRENCY: lempira (HNL) or peso
ORGANIZATIONS: CACM, OAS, UN

The central American republic of Honduras is a poor, sparsely populated country which consists substantially of rugged mountains and high plateaux with, on the Caribbean coast, an area of hot and humid plains, densely covered with tropical vegetation. These low-lying plains are subject to high annual rainfall, averaging 2,500 mm (98 inches), and it is in this region that bananas and coffee, accounting for over half the nation's exports, are grown. Other crops include sugar, rice, maize, beans and tobacco. There has been growth in new products such as shrimps, melons and tomatoes. Most industries are concerned with processing local products. Lead and zinc are exported.

HONG KONG

STATUS: UK Dependent Territory
AREA: 1,067 sq km (412 sq miles)
POPULATION: 5,920,000

HUNGARY

STATUS: Republic
AREA: 93,030 sq km (35,910 sq miles)
POPULATION: 10,289,000
ANNUAL NATURAL INCREASE: -0.6%
CAPITAL: Budapest
LANGUAGE: Hungarian (Magyar)
RELIGION: 60% Roman Catholic,
20% Hungarian Reformed Church, Lutheran
and Orthodox minorities
CURRENCY: forint (HUF)
ORGANIZATIONS: Council of Europe, OIEC, UN

Hungary is situated in the heartland of Europe. Its geomorphology consists mainly of undulating fertile plains with the highest terrain in the northeast of the country. The country is bisected north to south by the Danube. It has a humid continental climate, with warm summers that can become very hot on the plains, averaging 20°C (68°F), and cold winters, averaging 0°C (32°F). There is an annual rainfall of 500–750 mm (20–30 inches). Bauxite is Hungary's only substantial mineral resource, and less than 15 per cent of the gross national product is now derived from agriculture. The massive drive for industrialization has fundamentally transformed the structure of the economy since 1945. Both capital and consumer goods industries were developed, and during the 1980s engineering accounted for more than half the total industrial output. After a series of more or less unsuccessful attempts to introduce market elements into what essentially remained a centrally planned and largely state-owned economy, the communist regime finally gave up in 1989/90. However, their democratically elected successors have yet to prove that privatization and free competition will eventually bring general prosperity as well as political stability to what is now a profoundly troubled society.

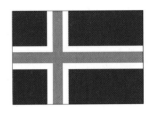

ICELAND

STATUS: Republic
AREA: 102,820 sq km (39,690 sq miles)
POPULATION: 260,000
ANNUAL NATURAL INCREASE: 1.2%
CAPITAL: Reykjavík
LANGUAGE: Icelandic
RELIGION: 93% Evangelical Lutheran
CURRENCY: Icelandic krona (ISK)
ORGANIZATIONS: Council of Europe, EEA,
EFTA, NATO, OECD, UN

One of the most northern islands in Europe, Iceland is 798 km (530 miles) away from Scotland, its nearest neighbour. The landscape is entirely volcanic – compacted volcanic ash has been eroded by the wind and there are substantial ice sheets and lava fields as well as many still active volcanoes, geysers and hot springs. The climate is mild for its latitude, with average summer temperatures of 9–10°C (48–50°F), and vegetation is sparse. Fishing is the traditional mainstay of the economy. An average of some 1,540,000 tonnes of fish are landed each year and 80 per cent of Iceland's exports consist of fish and fish products. Tourism is becoming an increasing source of income.

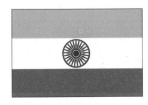

INDIA

STATUS: Federal Republic
AREA: 3,166,830 sq km (1,222,395 sq miles)
POPULATION: 870,000,000
ANNUAL NATURAL INCREASE: 2.1%
CAPITAL: New Delhi
LANGUAGE: Hindi, English, regional languages
RELIGION: 83% Hindu, 11% Muslim
CURRENCY: Indian rupee (INR)
ORGANIZATIONS: Col. Plan, Comm., UN

Occupying most of the Indian subcontinent, India is second only to China in the size of its population. This vast country contains an extraordinary variety of landscapes, climates and resources. The Himalayas, in the north, are the world's highest mountain range with many peaks reaching over 6,000 km (19,685 feet). The Himalayan foothills, are covered with lush vegetation, water is in abundant supply (rainfall in Assam reaches 10,700 mm or 421 inches in a year) and the climate is hot, making this region a centre for tea cultivation. To the south lies the vast expanse of the Indo-Gangetic plain, 2,500 km (1,550 miles) east-west, divided by the Indus, Ganges and Brahmaputra rivers. This is one of the world's most fertile regions, although it is liable to flooding, and failure of monsoon rainfall (June to September) can result in severe drought. In the pre-monsoon season the heat becomes intense – average temperatures in New Delhi reach 38°C (110°F). Rice, wheat, cotton, jute, tobacco and sugar are the main crops. To the south lies the Deccan plateau, bordered on either side by the Eastern and Western Ghats, and in the northwest lies the barren Thar Desert. India's natural resources are immense – timber, coal, iron ore and nickel – and oil has been discovered in the Indian Ocean. There has been a rapid expansion of light industry, notably in the food processing sector, and the manufacturing of consumer goods. Nevertheless, 70 per cent of the population live by subsistence farming. Main exports by value are precious stones and jewelry, engineering goods, clothing, leather goods, chemicals and cotton. Tourism is a valuable source of revenue.

INDONESIA
STATUS: Republic
AREA: 1,919,445 sq km
(740,905 sq miles)
POPULATION: 187,870,000
ANNUAL NATURAL INCREASE: 1.8%
CAPITAL: Jakarta
LANGUAGE: Bahasa Indonesian, Dutch
RELIGION: 88% Muslim, 9% Christian,
Hindu and Buddhist minorities
CURRENCY: rupiah (IDR)
ORGANIZATIONS: ASEAN, Col. Plan,
OPEC, UN

Indonesia consists of thousands of islands in equatorial southeast Asia which include Kalimantan (the central and southern parts of Borneo), Sumatera, Irian Jaya (the western part of New Guinea), Sulawesi (Celebes) and Java. The climate is tropical: hot (temperatures averaging 24°C or 75°F per year), humid and subject to monsoons. Most of its people live along the coast and river valleys of Java, leaving parts of the other islands virtually uninhabited. It is a Muslim nation and has the fourth largest population in the world. Over three-quarters of the people farm and live in small villages. Oil and gas, manufactured goods and coal are the chief exports. Indonesia is also a leading supplier of forest products, palm oil, rubber, spices, tobacco, tea, coffee and tin. With the use of modern techniques, the country has achieved self-sufficiency in rice.

IRAN
STATUS: Republic
AREA: 1,648,000 sq km (636,130 sq miles)
POPULATION: 56,964,000
ANNUAL NATURAL INCREASE: 3.7%
CAPITAL: Tehran
LANGUAGE: Farsi, Kurdish, Arabic,
Baluchi, Turkic
RELIGION: Shi'a Muslim majority, Sunni Muslim
and Armenian Christian minorities
CURRENCY: Iranian rial (IRR)
ORGANIZATIONS: Col. Plan, OPEC, UN

Iran is a large mountainous country north of The Gulf. The climate is one of extremes with temperatures ranging from -20–55°C (-4–131°F) and rainfall varying from 2,000 mm (79 inches) to almost zero. Iran is rich in oil and gas and the revenues have been used to improve communications and social conditions generally. The war with Iraq between 1980 and 1988 seriously restricted economic growth and particularly affected the Iranian oil industry in The Gulf. Oil is the source of 85 per cent of Iran's revenue and thus when world oil prices fall, as in the early–mid 1990s, the economy suffers. Agricultural conditions are poor, except around the Caspian Sea, and wheat is the main crop though fruit (especially dates) and nuts are grown and exported. The main livestock is sheep and goats. Iran has substantial mineral deposits relatively underdeveloped

IRAQ
STATUS: Republic
AREA: 438,317 sq km (169,235 sq miles)
POPULATION: 19,410,000
ANNUAL NATURAL INCREASE: 3.3%
CAPITAL: Baghdad
LANGUAGE: Arabic, Kurdish, Turkoman
RELIGION: 50% Shi'a, 45% Sunni Muslim
CURRENCY: Iraqi dinar (IQD)
ORGANIZATIONS: Arab League, OPEC, UN

Iraq is mostly desert, marsh and mountain, but there are substantial areas of fertile land between the Tigris and the Euphrates. The two great rivers join and become the Shatt al-Arab which flows into The Gulf. The climate is arid with rainfall of less than 500 mm (20 inches) and summers are very hot (averaging 35° or 95°F). Iraq has a short coastline with Basra the only port. Light industry is situated around Baghdad, and there are major petro-chemical complexes around the Basra and Kirkuk oilfields. The war with Iran (1980–8) and the Gulf conflict (1991) wrecked the economy with exports of oil and natural gas, formerly accounting for 95 per cent of export earnings, severely restricted by sanctions. Meanwhile, Arabs living in the Tigris-Euphrates marsh regions are being deprived of their livelihood as the marshes are drained in government reclamation schemes.

IRELAND
(EIRE)
STATUS: Republic
AREA: 68,895 sq km (26,595 sq miles)
POPULATION: 3,548,000
ANNUAL NATURAL INCREASE: -0.1%
CAPITAL: Dublin (Baile Átha Cliath)
LANGUAGE: Irish, English
RELIGION: 95% Roman Catholic, 5% Protestant
CURRENCY: punt or Irish pound (IEP)
ORGANIZATIONS: Council of Europe, EEA, EU,
OECD, UN

The Irish Republic, forming 80 per cent of the island of Ireland, is a lowland country of wide valleys, lakes and marshes, but with some hills of significance, such as the Wicklow Mountains, south of Dublin and Macgillicuddy's Reeks, in the southwest. The Irish climate is maritime and influenced by the Gulf Stream. Temperatures average 5°C (40°F) in winter to 16°C (60°F) in summer, with annual rainfall at about 1,400 mm (55 inches) in the west and half that in the east. There is much rich pastureland and livestock farming predominates. Meat and dairy produce is processed in the small market towns where there are also breweries and mills. Large-scale manufacturing, in which food processing, electronics and textiles have shown recent growth, is centred around Dublin, the capital and main port. The Irish Republic possesses reserves of oil and natural gas, peat and deposits of lead and zinc. A large zinc mine at Galmoy is expected to come into production in 1996.

ISRAEL
STATUS: State
AREA: 20,770 sq km (8,015 sq miles)
POPULATION: 5,287,000
ANNUAL NATURAL INCREASE: 2.7%
CAPITAL: Jerusalem
LANGUAGE: Hebrew, Arabic, Yiddish
RELIGION: 85% Jewish, 13% Muslim
CURRENCY: shekel (ILS)
ORGANIZATIONS: UN

Israel, in the eastern Mediterranean littoral, contains a varied landscape – a coastal plain, interior hills, a deep valley extending from the river Jordan to the Dead Sea, and the Negev semi-desert in the south. Efficient water management is crucial as two-thirds of rainfall, which falls mostly in the mild winters, is lost by evaporation. Fuel needs to be imported (mainly oil from Egypt). Economic development in Israel is the most advanced in the Middle East. Manufacturing, particularly diamond finishing, electronics and science based products are important, although Israel also has flourishing agriculture specializing in exporting fruit, flowers and vegetables to western Europe. The only viable mineral resources are phosphates in the Negev and potash from the Dead Sea.

ITALY

STATUS: Republic
AREA: 301,245 sq km (116,280 sq miles)
POPULATION: 56,767,000
ANNUAL NATURAL INCREASE: 0.2%
CAPITAL: Rome (Roma)
LANGUAGE: Italian, German, French
RELIGION: 90% Roman Catholic
CURRENCY: Italian lira (ITL)
ORGANIZATIONS: Council of Europe, EEA, EU,
G7, NATO, OECD, UN, WEU

Italy, separated from the rest of Europe by the great divide of the Alps, thrusts southeastwards into the Mediterranean Sea, in its famous boot-shaped peninsula. Including the large islands of Sicily and Sardinia, over 75 per cent of the landscape is either hill or mountain. The north is dominated by the plain of the river Po rising to the high Alps. Further along the peninsula the Apennine mountains run from north to south. Climate varies with altitude, but generally there is a Mediterranean regime in the south; in the north the climate becomes more temperate. Agriculture flourishes with cereals, vegetables, olives, and cheese the principal products and Italy is the world's largest wine producer. Tourism is a major source of revenue. In spite of the lack of mineral and power resources, Italy has become a trading nation with a sound industrial base. Manufacturing of textiles, cars, machine tools, textile machinery and engineering, mainly in the north, is expanding rapidly and accounts for nearly 50 per cent of the work force. This is increasing the imbalance between the north and south where the average income is far less per head, and where investment is lacking.

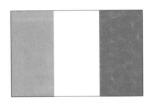

IVORY COAST (CÔTE D'IVOIRE)

STATUS: Republic
AREA: 322,465 sq km (124,470 sq miles)
POPULATION: 12,910,000
ANNUAL NATURAL INCREASE: 4.0%
CAPITAL: Yamoussoukro
LANGUAGE: French, tribal languages
RELIGION: 65% traditional beliefs,
23% Muslim, 12% Roman Catholic
CURRENCY: CFA franc (W Africa) (XOF)
ORGANIZATIONS: ECOWAS, OAU, UN,

Independent from the French since 1960, the Ivory Coast rises from low plains in the south to plateaux in the north. The climate is tropical with rainfall in two wet seasons in the south. Much of the population is engaged in subsistence agriculture. The two chief exports are cocoa and coffee. Other products include cotton, timber, fruit and tobacco. Gold mining began in 1990, diamonds are extracted and by 1995 the Ivory Coast is expected to become self-sufficient in oil and gas from the offshore fields.

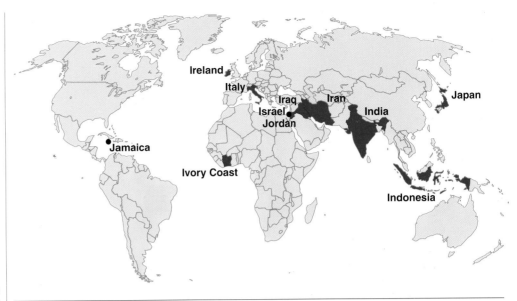

JAMAICA

STATUS: Commonwealth State
AREA: 11,425 sq km (4,410 sq miles)
POPULATION: 2,469,000
ANNUAL NATURAL INCREASE: 0.8%
CAPITAL: Kingston
LANGUAGE: English, local patois
RELIGION: Anglican Christian majority.
Rastafarian minority
CURRENCY: Jamaican dollar (JMD)
ORGANIZATIONS: Caricom, Comm., OAS, UN

Jamaica, part of the Greater Antilles chain of islands in the Caribbean, is formed from the peaks of a submerged mountain range. The climate is tropical with an annual rainfall of over 5,000 mm (197 inches) on the high ground. There is a plentiful supply of tropical fruits such as melons, bananas and guavas. Principal crops include sugar cane, bananas, cocoa and coffee. Jamaica is rich in bauxite which, with the refined product alumina, is the main export. Major industries are food processing, textiles, cement and agricultural machinery. Since 1988 tourism has developed rapidly and is now the biggest single source of foreign earnings.

JAPAN

STATUS: Constitutional monarchy
AREA: 369,700 sq km (142,705 sq miles)
POPULATION: 123,653,000
ANNUAL NATURAL INCREASE: 0.4%
CAPITAL: Tokyo (Tōkyō)
LANGUAGE: Japanese
RELIGION: Shintoist, Buddhist,
Christian minority
CURRENCY: yen (JPY)
ORGANIZATIONS: Col. Plan, G7, OECD, UN

Japan consists of the main islands of Hokkaido, Honshu, Shikoku and Kyushu which stretch over 1,600 km (995 miles). The land is mountainous and heavily forested with small, fertile patches and a climate ranging from harsh to tropical. The highest mountain is Mt Fuji (Fuji-san) at 3,776 m (12,388 feet). The archipelago is also subject to monsoons, earthquakes, typhoons and tidal waves. Very little of the available land is cultivable. Most food has to be imported but the Japanese both catch and eat a lot of fish. The Japanese fishing fleet is the largest in the world. Japan is a leading economic power. Because of the importance of trade, industry has grown up around the major ports especially Yokohama, Osaka and Tokyo, the capital. The principal exports are motor vehicles, chemicals, iron and steel products and electronic, electric and optical equipment. Japan relies heavily on imported fuel and raw materials and is developing the country's nuclear power resources to reduce this dependence. Production of coal, oil and natural gas is also being increased. In the early–mid 1990s, after four decades of phenomenal growth, industrial output declined as Japan experienced its worst recession for half a century.

JORDAN

STATUS: Kingdom
AREA: 90,650 sq km (35,000 sq miles)
POPULATION: 4,291,000
ANNUAL NATURAL INCREASE: 5.8%
CAPITAL: Amman ('Ammān)
LANGUAGE: Arabic
RELIGION: 90% Sunni Muslim,
Christian and Shi'ite Muslim minorities
CURRENCY: Jordanian dinar (JOD)
ORGANIZATIONS: Arab League, UN

Jordan, one of the few kingdoms in the Middle East, is mostly desert, but has fertile pockets. The climate is predominantly arid. Temperatures rise to 49°C (120°F) in the eastern valleys but it is cooler and wetter in the west. Fruit and vegetables account for 20 per cent of Jordan's exports and phosphate, the most valuable mineral, accounts for over 40 per cent of export revenue. Amman is the manufacturing centre, processing bromide and potash from the Dead Sea. Other important industries are food processing and textiles.

KAZAKHSTAN

STATUS: Republic
AREA: 2,717,300 sq km (1,048,880 sq miles)
POPULATION: 17,035,000
ANNUAL NATURAL INCREASE: 1.0%
CAPITAL: Alma-Ata
LANGUAGE: Kazakh, Russian
RELIGION: Muslim majority, Orthodox minority
CURRENCY: tenge
ORGANIZATIONS: CIS, UN

Stretching across central Asia, Kazakhstan is Russia's southern neighbour. Consisting of lowlands, hilly plains and plateaux, with small mountainous areas, the country has a continental climate with hot summers (30°C or 86°F in July) alternating with equally extreme winters. Exceptionally rich in raw materials, extractive industries have played a major role in the country's economy. Vast oil and gas reserves near the Caspian Sea are now being exploited. Rapid industrialization in recent years has focused on iron and steel, cement, chemicals, fertilizers and consumer goods. Although three-quarters of all agricultural land is used for pasture, the nomadic ways of the Kazakh people have all but disappeared. Economic development during the Soviet period brought a massive influx of outside labour which swamped the indigenous population. The proportion of Kazakhs employed in the industrial sector has, until recently, been small, but with the move to towns and better training, the balance is starting to be redressed. Since Kazakhstan's independence in 1991, its economic prospects appear favourable; but the Soviet legacy includes many environmental problems, such as the ruthless exploitation of the Aral Sea for irrigation.

KENYA

STATUS: Republic
AREA: 582,645 sq km (224,900 sq miles)
POPULATION: 25,700,000
ANNUAL NATURAL INCREASE: 3.5%
CAPITAL: Nairobi
LANGUAGE: Kiswahili, English, Kikuyu, Luo
RELIGION: majority traditional beliefs,
25% Christian, 6% Muslim
CURRENCY: Kenya shilling (KES)
ORGANIZATIONS: Comm., OAU, UN

Kenya lies on the equator but as most of the country is on a high plateau the temperatures range from 10–27°C (50–81°F). Rainfall varies from 760–2,500 mm (30–98 inches) depending on altitude. Arable land is scarce but agriculture is the only source of livelihood for over three-quarters of the population. Tea, coffee, flowers and vegetables are the main products for export. Tea, however, has replaced coffee as the chief export and is second only to tourism as a source of foreign revenue. Manufacturing, centred at Nairobi and Mombasa, is dominated by food processing.

KIRGHIZIA (KYRGYZSTAN)

STATUS: Republic
AREA: 198,500 sq km (76,620 sq miles)
POPULATION: 4,502,000
ANNUAL NATURAL INCREASE: 1.7%
CAPITAL: Bishkek
LANGUAGE: Kirghizian, Russian
RELIGION: Muslim
CURRENCY: som
ORGANIZATIONS: CIS, UN

Located in the heart of Asia, to the south of Kazakhstan, Kirghizia is a mountainous country. Traditionally an agrarian-based economy with stock-raising prevalent, the country underwent rapid industrialization during the Soviet period becoming a major producer of machinery and, more recently, producing consumer goods. Valuable mineral deposits include gold, silver, antimony, mercury with the gold deposits believed to be among the world's largest. The cultivation of cotton, sugar beet, tobacco and opium poppies is expanding and provides the basis for a growing processing industry. Independence came unexpectedly in 1991, although Kirghizia had long wanted to control its own affairs.

KIRIBATI

STATUS: Republic
AREA: 717 sq km (277 sq miles)
POPULATION: 72,298
ANNUAL NATURAL INCREASE: 2.1%
CAPITAL: Bairiki (on Tarawa Atoll)
LANGUAGE: I-Kirbati, English
RELIGION: Christian majority
CURRENCY: Australian dollar (AUD)
ORGANIZATIONS: Comm., UN

Kiribati consists of 16 Gilbert Islands, eight Phoenix Islands, three Line Islands and Ocean Island. These four groups are spread over 5 million sq km (1,930,000 miles) in the central and west Pacific. The temperature is a constant 27°–32°C (80–90°F). The islanders grow coconut, breadfruit, bananas and babia (a coarse vegetable). Copra is a major export and fish, particularly tuna, accounts for one-third of total exports. Main imports are machinery and manufactured goods.

KOREA, NORTH

STATUS: Republic
AREA: 122,310 sq km (47,210 sq miles)
POPULATION: 22,618,000
ANNUAL NATURAL INCREASE: 1%
CAPITAL: P'yŏngyang
LANGUAGE: Korean
RELIGION: Chundo Kyo, Buddhism,
Confucianism, Daoism
CURRENCY: North Korean won (KPW)
ORGANIZATIONS: OIEC, UN

High, rugged mountains and deep valleys typify North Korea. Climate is extreme with severe winters and warm, sunny summers. Cultivation is limited to the river valley plains where rice, millet, maize and wheat are the principal crops. North Korea, rich in minerals including iron ore and copper, has developed a heavy industrial base. Industry has, however, since the early 1990s, been severely curtailed, firstly by the loss of Soviet aid following the break-up of the Soviet Union and then by losing imports through its isolationist policies and secretive nuclear industries. Its coal supplies, the main energy source for factories, are running out. Complete economic collapse is only salvaged by remittances from Koreans in Japan.

KOREA, SOUTH

STATUS: Republic
AREA: 98,445 sq km (38,000 sq miles)
POPULATION: 44,190,000
ANNUAL NATURAL INCREASE: 1.9%
CAPITAL: Seoul (Sŏul)
LANGUAGE: Korean
RELIGION: 26% Mahayana Buddhism,
22% Christian, Confucianism,
Daoism, Chundo Kyo
CURRENCY: won (KPW)
ORGANIZATIONS: Col. Plan, UN

The terrain of South Korea, although mountainous, is less rugged than that of North Korea. The flattest parts lie along the west coast and the extreme south of the peninsula. Its climate is continental, with an average temperature range of -5°C (23°F) in winter to 27°C (81°F) in summer. The majority of the population live in the arable river valleys and along the coastal plain. Agriculture is very primitive, with rice the principal crop. Tungsten, coal and iron ore are the main mineral deposits. Despite having to import oil and industrial materials, the country is a major industrial nation producing iron and steel, textiles, aircraft, chemicals, machinery, vehicles and, in recent years, specializing in electronics and computers. South Korea, with Japan, leads the world in ship-building.

KUWAIT

STATUS: State
AREA: 24,280 sq km (9,370 sq miles)
POPULATION: 1,500,000
ANNUAL NATURAL INCREASE: -2.3%
CAPITAL: Kuwait (Al Kuwayt)
LANGUAGE: Arabic, English
RELIGION: 95% Muslim, 5% Christian and Hindu

CURRENCY: Kuwaiti dinar (KWD)
ORGANIZATIONS: Arab League, UN

Kuwait comprises low, undulating desert, with summer temperatures as high as 52°C (126°F). Since the discovery of oil, Kuwait has been transformed into one of the world's wealthiest nations, exporting oil to Japan, France, the Netherlands and the UK since 1946. The natural gas fields have also been developed. Other industries include fishing (particularly shrimp), food processing, chemicals and building materials. In agriculture, the aim is to produce half the requirements of domestic vegetable consumption by expanding the irrigated area. The invasion and attempted annexation of Kuwait by Iraq in 1990–1 had severe effects on the country's economy, but by 1994 the oil industry was restored to its pre-Gulf war efficiency.

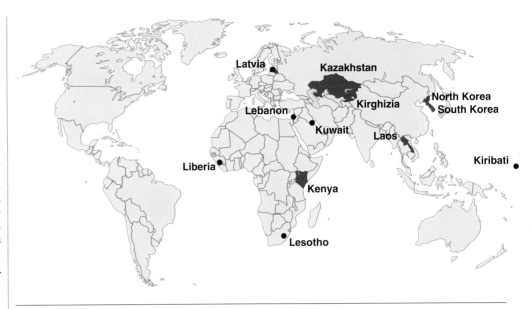

LAOS

STATUS: Republic
AREA: 236,725 sq km (91,375 sq miles)
POPULATION: 4,469,000
ANNUAL NATURAL INCREASE: 2.9%
CAPITAL: Vientiane (Viangchan)
LANGUAGE: Lao, French, tribal languages
RELIGION: Buddhist majority,
Christian and animist minorities
CURRENCY: kip (LAK)
ORGANIZATIONS: Col. Plan, UN

Laos is a landlocked, mostly mountainous and forested country in Indo-China. Temperatures range from 15°C (59°F) in winter, to 32°C (90°F) before the rains, and 26°C (79°F) during the rainy season from May to October. Most of the sparse population are subsistence farmers growing rice, maize, sweet potatoes and tobacco. Mineral resources include tin, iron ore, gold, bauxite and lignite. The major exports are coffee, tin and teak. Almost constant warfare since 1941 has hindered any possible industrial development, and Laos has become one of the world's poorest countries.

LATVIA

STATUS: Republic
AREA: 63,700 sq km (24,590 sq miles)
POPULATION: 2,577,000
ANNUAL NATURAL INCREASE: 0.0%
CAPITAL: Riga
LANGUAGE: Latvian, Lithuanian, Russian
RELIGION: Lutheran, Roman Catholic
and Orthodox minorities
CURRENCY: roublis (Latvian rouble), lats
ORGANIZATIONS: UN

Latvia is situated on the shores of the Baltic Sea and the Gulf of Riga. Forests cover more than a third of the total territory, a second third being made up of meadows and marsh, and there are some 4,000 lakes. Farmland supports dairy and meat production and grain crops. The country

possesses no mineral resources of any value. Industrial development has been sustained by a massive influx of Russian labour since Latvia's incorporation into the Soviet Union in 1940. Under the Soviets, Latvia was assigned the production of consumer durables such as refrigerators and motorcycles as well as ships, rolling stock and power generators. Latvia regained its independence in 1991. The main industries are now radio engineering, electronics, engineering, instruments and industrial robots.

LEBANON

STATUS: Republic
AREA: 10,400 sq km (4,015 sq miles)
POPULATION: 2,838,000
ANNUAL NATURAL INCREASE: 2.3%
CAPITAL: Beirut (Beyrouth)
LANGUAGE: Arabic, French, English
RELIGION: 62% Shi'a and Sunni Muslim,
38% Roman Catholic and Maronite Christian
CURRENCY: Lebanese pound (LBP)
ORGANIZATIONS: Arab League, UN

Physically, Lebanon can be divided into four main regions: a narrow coastal plain; a narrow, fertile interior plateau; the west Lebanon (Jebel Liban) and the Anti-Lebanon (Jebel esh Sharqi) mountains. It has a Mediterranean climate. Trade and tourism have been severely affected by civil war for 17 years from 1975. Agriculture accounts for nearly half of employment and cement, fertilisers, jewelry, sugar and tobacco products are all manufactured on a small scale.

LESOTHO

STATUS: Kingdom
AREA: 30,345 sq km (11,715 sq miles)

POPULATION: 1,836,000
ANNUAL NATURAL INCREASE: 2.7%
CAPITAL: Maseru
LANGUAGE: Sesotho, English
RELIGION: 80% Christian
CURRENCY: loti (LSL), S African rand (ZAR)
ORGANIZATIONS: Comm., OAU, UN

Lesotho, formerly Basutoland, is completely encircled by South Africa. This small country is rugged and mountainous, with southern Africa's highest mountain, Thabana Ntlenyana (3,482 m or 11,424 feet) to be found in the east of the Drakensberg. From these peaks the land slopes westwards in the form of dissected plateaux. The climate is generally sub-tropical although influenced by altitude; rainfall, sometimes variable, falls mainly in the summer months. Because of the terrain, agriculture is limited to the lowlands and foothills. Sorghum, wheat, barley, maize, oats and legumes are the main crops. Cattle, sheep and goats graze on the highlands.

LIBERIA

STATUS: Republic
AREA: 11,370 sq km (42,990 sq miles)
POPULATION: 2,580,000
ANNUAL NATURAL INCREASE: 3.1%
CAPITAL: Monrovia
LANGUAGE: English, tribal languages
RELIGION: traditional beliefs, Christian,
5% Muslim
CURRENCY: Liberian dollar (LRD)
ORGANIZATIONS: ECOWAS, OAU, UN

The west African republic of Liberia is the only nation in Africa never to have been ruled by a foreign power. The hot and humid coastal plain with its savannah vegetation and mangrove swamps rises gently towards the Guinea Highlands, and the interior is densely covered by tropical rainforest. Until the civil war, which ravaged the country, broke out in 1989 the country enjoyed some prosperity from its rubber plantations, rich iron ore deposits, diamonds and gold. Liberia has the world's largest merchant fleet due to its flag of convenience register and this is the only source of revenue relatively unscathed by the war.

LIBYA
STATUS: Republic
AREA: 1,759,540 sq km (679,180 sq miles)
POPULATION: 4,875,000
ANNUAL NATURAL INCREASE: 3.6%
CAPITAL: Tripoli (Ṭarābulus)
LANGUAGE: Arabic, Italian, English
RELIGION: Sunni Muslim
CURRENCY: Libyan dinar (LYD)
ORGANIZATIONS: Arab League, OAU, OPEC, UN

Libya is situated on the lowlands of north Africa which rise southwards from the Mediterranean Sea. Ninety-five per cent of its territory is hot, dry desert or semi-desert with average rainfall of less then 130 mm (5 inches). The coastal plains, however, have a more moist Mediterranean climate with annual rainfall of around 200–610 mm (8–24 inches). In these areas, a wide range of crops are cultivated including grapes, groundnuts, oranges, wheat and barley. Only 30 years ago Libya was classed as one of the world's poorest nations but the exploitation of oil has transformed Libya's economy and now accounts for over 95 per cent of its exports.

LIECHTENSTEIN
STATUS: Principality
AREA: 160 sq km (62 sq miles)
POPULATION: 30,000
ANNUAL NATURAL INCREASE: 1.1%
CAPITAL: Vaduz
LANGUAGE: Alemannish, German
RELIGION: 87% Roman Catholic
CURRENCY: franken (Swiss franc)(CHF)
ORGANIZATIONS Council of Europe, EFTA, UN

Situated in the central Alps between Switzerland and Austria, Liechtenstein is one of the smallest states in Europe. Its territory is divided into two zones – the flood plains of the Rhine to the north and Alpine mountain ranges to the southeast, where cattle are reared. Liechtenstein's other main sources of revenue comprise light industry, chiefly the manufacture of precision instruments, and also textile production, food products, tourism, postage stamps and a fast-growing banking sector.

LITHUANIA
STATUS: Republic
AREA: 65,200 sq km (25,165 sq miles)
POPULATION: 3,742,000
ANNUAL NATURAL INCREASE: 0.7%
CAPITAL: Vilnius

LANGUAGE: Lithuanian, Russian, Polish
RELIGION: 80% Roman Catholic
CURRENCY: litas
ORGANIZATIONS: Council of Europe, UN

Lithuania is one of the three small ex-Soviet states lying on the shores of the Baltic Sea. The country consists of a low-lying plain with many lakes. Its climate is transitional, ranging between the oceanic type of western Europe and continental conditions. Temperatures range between -5–-3°C (24–28°F) in winter to 17–18°C (62–66°F) in summer. There is on average 510 mm–610 mm (20–24 inches) of rainfall per year. Agriculture is dominated by beef and dairy produce; major crops are potatoes and flax. There is a large fishing industry. Industrial products include paper, chemicals, electronics and electrical goods. After almost 50 years' involuntary incorporation into the Soviet Union, Lithuania regained its independence in 1991. The economy is still linked to ex-Soviet countries and the change to a market economy is slow.

LUXEMBOURG
STATUS: Grand Duchy
AREA: 2,585 sq km (998 sq miles)
POPULATION: 395,200
ANNUAL NATURAL INCREASE: 0.8%
CAPITAL: Luxembourg
LANGUAGE: Letzeburgish, French, German
RELIGION: 95% Roman Catholic
CURRENCY: Luxembourg franc (LUF)
Belgian Franc (BEF)
ORGANIZATIONS: Council of Europe, EEA, EU, NATO, OECD, UN, WEU

The Grand Duchy of Luxembourg is situated between France, Belgium and Germany. The climate is mild and temperate with rainfall ranging from 700–1,000 mm (28–40 inches) a year. Just over half the land is arable, mainly cereals, dairy produce and potatoes. Wine is produced in the Moselle valley. Iron ore is found in the south and is the basis of the thriving steel industry. Other industries are textiles, chemicals and pharmaceutical products. Banking and financial services are growing sectors.

MACAU (MACAO)
STATUS: Chinese Territory under Portuguese Administration
AREA: 16 sq km (6 sq miles)
POPULATION: 374,000
CAPITAL: Macau

MACEDONIA
Former Yugoslav Republic of,
STATUS: Republic
AREA: 25,715 sq km (9,925 sq miles)
POPULATION: 2,066,000

ANNUAL NATURAL INCREASE: 1.1%
CAPITAL: Skopje
LANGUAGE: Macedonian, Albanian
RELIGION: Orthodox
CURRENCY: denar
ORGANIZATIONS: UN,
Council of Europe (non-voting member)

The landlocked Balkan state of the Former Yugoslav Republic of Macedonia is a rugged country crossed from north to south by the Vardar valley. The climate is continental with fine hot summers but bitterly cold winters. The economy is basically agricultural. Cereals, tobacco, fruit and vegetables are grown and livestock raised. Heavy industries include chemicals and textiles, which are the county's major employers. Following a Greek economic blockade in 1994, heavy industry – which had already declined through the loss of markets in other former Yugoslav republics – suffered further collapse

MADAGASCAR
STATUS: Republic
AREA: 594,180 sq km (229,345 sq miles)
POPULATION: 12,827
ANNUAL NATURAL INCREASE: 3.1%
CAPITAL: Antananarivo
LANGUAGE: Malagasy, French, English
RELIGION: 47% animist, 48% Christian, 2% Muslim
CURRENCY: Malagasy franc (MGF)
ORGANIZATIONS: OAU, UN

Madagascar, the world's fourth largest island, is situated 400 km (250 miles) east of the Mozambique coast. The terrain consists largely of a high plateau with steppe and savannah vegetation and desert in the south. Much of the hot humid east coast is covered by tropical rainforest – here rainfall reaches 1,500–2,000 mm (59–79 inches) per annum. Although farming is the occupation of about 85 per cent of the population, only 3 per cent of the land is cultivated. Coffee and vanilla are the major exports, and the shellfish trade is growing rapidly. Much of Madagascar's unique plant and animal life are under increasing threat due to widespread deforestation, caused by the rapid development of forestry and soil erosion.

MADEIRA
STATUS: Self-governing Island Region of Portugal
AREA: 796 sq km (307 sq miles)
POPULATION: 253,400
CAPITAL: Funchal

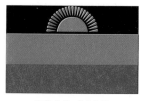

MALAWI
STATUS: Republic
AREA: 94,080 sq km (35,315 sq miles)
POPULATION: 8,823,000
ANNUAL NATURAL INCREASE: 3.4%

CAPITAL: Lilongwe
LANGUAGE: Chichewa, English
RELIGION: traditional beliefs majority,
10% Roman Catholic, 10% Protestant
CURRENCY: kwacha (MWK)
ORGANIZATIONS: Comm., OAU, UN

Malawi is located at the southern end of the east African Rift Valley. The area around Lake Malawi is tropical and humid with swampy vegetation. In the highlands to the west and south-east conditions are cooler. Malawi has an intensely rural economy – 96 per cent of the population work on the land. Maize is the main subsistence crop, and tea, tobacco, sugar and groundnuts are the main exports. Malawi has deposits of both coal and bauxite, but they are under-exploited at present. Manufacturing industry concentrates on consumer goods and building and construction materials. All energy is produced by hydro-electric power.

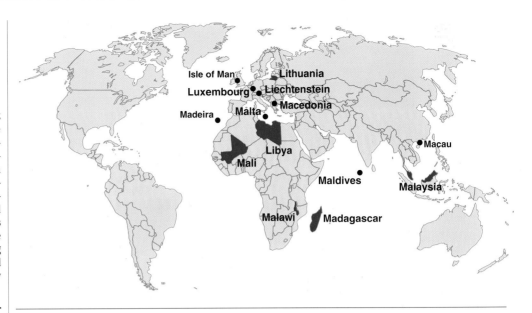

MALAYSIA

STATUS: Federation
AREA: 332,665 sq km
(128,405 sq miles)
POPULATION: 18,606,000
ANNUAL NATURAL INCREASE: 2.5%
CAPITAL: Kuala Lumpur
LANGUAGE: 58% Bahasa Malaysian,
English, Chinese
RELIGION: 53% Muslim, 25% Buddhist, Hindu,
Christian and animist minorities
CURRENCY: Malaysian dollar or ringgit (MYR)
ORGANIZATIONS: ASEAN, Col. Plan,
Comm., UN

The Federation of Malaysia consists of two separate parts; west Malaysia is located on the Malay Peninsula, while east Malaysia consists of Sabah and Sarawak on the island of Borneo 700 km (435 miles) across the South China Sea. Despite this distance, both areas share a similar landscape, which is mountainous and covered with lush tropical rainforest. The climate is tropical, hot and humid all the year round, with annual average rainfall of 2,500 mm (98 inches). At one time the economy was dominated by tin, rubber and timber. Now manufactured goods, in particular electronics, account for over two-thirds of the nation's exports in terms of value. Malaysia is rich in natural resources and other major exports include crude oil, timber, palm oil, pepper, rubber and tin. The fast-growing industrial sector demands increased power supplies which are being met by new power stations and hydro-electric power projects.

PENINSULAR MALAYSIA

STATUS: State
AREA: 131,585 sq km (50,790 sq miles)
POPULATION: 15,286,098
CAPITAL: Kuala Lumpur

SABAH

STATUS: State
AREA: 76,115 sq km (29,380 sq miles)
POPULATION: 1,736,902
CAPITAL: Kota Kinabalu

SARAWAK

STATUS: State
AREA: 124,965 sq km (48,235 sq miles)
POPULATION: 1,583,000
CAPITAL: Kuching

MALDIVES

STATUS: Republic
AREA: 298 sq km (115 sq miles)
POPULATION: 238,363
ANNUAL NATURAL INCREASE: 3.3%
CAPITAL: Male
LANGUAGE: Dhivehi
RELIGION: Sunni Muslim majority
CURRENCY: rufiyaa (MVR)
ORGANIZATIONS: Col. Plan, Comm., UN

The Maldives are one of the world's poorest nations. They consist of a series of coral atolls stretching 885 km (550 miles) across the Indian Ocean. Although there are 2,000 islands, only about 215 are inhabited. The main island, Male, is only 1½ miles long. Fishing is the main activity and fish and coconut fibre are both exported. Most staple foods have to be imported but coconuts, millet, cassava, yams and fruit are grown locally. Tourism is developing and this is now the main source of revenue.

MALI

STATUS: Republic
AREA: 1,240,140 sq km (478,695 sq miles)
POPULATION: 9,818,000
ANNUAL NATURAL INCREASE: 2.8%
CAPITAL: Bamako
LANGUAGE: French, native languages
RELIGION: 65% Muslim,

30% traditional beliefs, 1% Christian
CURRENCY: CFA franc (W Africa) (XOF)
ORGANIZATIONS: ECOWAS, OAU, UN

Mali is one of the world's most underdeveloped countries. Over half the area is barren desert. South of Timbuktu (Tombouctou) the savannah-covered plains support a wide variety of wildlife. Most of the population live in the Niger valley and grow cotton, oil seeds and groundnuts. Fishing is important. Mali has few mineral resources, although a gold mine opened in 1994. Droughts have taken their toll of livestock and agriculture. Main exports are cotton, groundnuts and livestock.

MALTA

STATUS: Republic
AREA: 316 sq km (122 sq miles)
POPULATION: 364,593
ANNUAL NATURAL INCREASE: 0.7%
CAPITAL: Valletta
LANGUAGE: Maltese, English, Italian
RELIGION: Roman Catholic majority
CURRENCY: Maltese lira (MTL)
ORGANIZATIONS: Comm., Council of Europe, UN

Malta lies about 96 km (60 miles) south of Sicily, and consists of three islands; Malta, Gozo and Comino. It has a Mediterranean climate with summer temperatures averaging 25°C (77°F). About 40 per cent of the land is under cultivation with wheat, potatoes, tomatoes and vines the main crops. The large natural harbour at Valletta has made it a major transit port, and shipbuilding and repair are traditional industries. Principal exports are machinery, beverages, tobacco, flowers, wine, leather goods and potatoes. Tourism and light manufacturing are booming sectors of the economy.

MAN, ISLE OF

STATUS: British Crown Dependency
AREA: 588 sq km (227 sq miles)
POPULATION: 71,000
CAPITAL: Douglas

MARSHALL ISLANDS

STATUS: Self-governing state in Compact of
Free Association with USA
AREA: 605 sq km (234 sq miles)
POPULATION: 48,000
CAPITAL: Majuro
LANGUAGE: English, local languages
RELIGION: Roman Catholic majority
CURRENCY: US dollar (USD)
ORGANIZATIONS: UN

The Marshall Islands, formerly UN Trust
Territory under US administration, consist of
over 1,000 atolls and islands which in total
account for only 181 sq km (70 sq miles) but are
spread over a wide area of the Pacific. The climate is hot all year round with a heavy rainfall
averaging 4,050 mm (160 inches). Fishing, subsistence farming and tourism provide occupation for most. The economy is heavily dependent
on grants from the USA for use of the islands as
military bases.

MARTINIQUE

STATUS: Overseas Department
of France
AREA: 1,079 sq km (417 sq miles)
POPULATION: 373,000
CAPITAL: Fort-de-France

MAURITANIA

STATUS: Islamic Republic
AREA: 1,030,700 sq km
(397,850 sq miles)
POPULATION: 2,143,000
ANNUAL NATURAL INCREASE: 2.7%
CAPITAL: Nouakchott
LANGUAGE: Arabic, French
RELIGION: Muslim
CURRENCY: ouguiya (MRO)
ORGANIZATIONS: Arab League, ECOWAS,
OAU, UN

Situated on the west coast of Africa, Mauritania
consists of savannah, steppes and vast areas of
the Sahara desert. It has high temperatures, low
rainfall and frequent droughts. There is very little arable farming except in the Senegal river
valley where millet and dates are grown. Most
Mauritanians raise cattle, sheep, goats or
camels. The country has only one railway which
is used to transport the chief export, iron ore,
from the mines to the coast at Nouadhibou.
Mauritania has substantial copper reserves
which are mined at Akjoujt. A severe drought
during the last decade decimated the livestock
population and forced many nomadic tribesmen
into the towns. Coastal fishing contributes nearly 50 per cent of foreign earnings. Exports are
almost exclusively confined to iron ore, copper
and fish products.

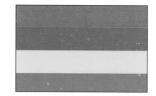

MAURITIUS

STATUS: Republic
AREA: 1,865 sq km (720 sq miles)
POPULATION: 1,098,000
ANNUAL NATURAL INCREASE: 1.1%
CAPITAL: Port Louis
LANGUAGE: English, French Creole, Hindi,
Bhojpuri
RELIGION: 51% Hindu, 31% Christian,
17% Muslim
CURRENCY: Mauritian rupee (MUR)
ORGANIZATIONS: Comm., OAU, UN

Mauritius is a mountainous island in the Indian
Ocean. It has a varied climate with temperatures
ranging from 7–36°C (45–97°F) and annual rainfall of between 1,530–5,080 mm (60–200 inches).
The economy of Mauritius once depended wholly on sugar. Although this is still important, with
tea as a second crop, earnings from the manufacturing of clothing now surpass those from
sugar. Tourism and financial services are also
expanding.

MAYOTTE

STATUS: 'Territorial collectivity' of France
AREA: 376 sq km (145 sq miles)
POPULATION: 85,000
CAPITAL: Dzaoudzi

MEXICO

STATUS: Federal Republic
AREA: 1,972,545 sq km (761,400 sq miles)
POPULATION: 89,538,000
ANNUAL NATURAL INCREASE: 1.8%
CAPITAL: Mexico City
LANGUAGE: Spanish
RELIGION: 96% Roman Catholic
CURRENCY: Mexican peso (MXP)
ORGANIZATIONS: NAFTA, OAS, OECD, UN

Mexico consists mainly of mountain ranges and
dissected plateaux. The only extensive flat lands
are in the Yucatan Peninsula. Temperature and
rainfall are modified by altitude – the north is
arid but the south is humid and tropical. Mexico
has one of the world's fastest growing populations and, with extreme poverty in many rural
areas, migration to the cities continues to be
prevalent. One-third of the land is used for livestock ranching and only 20 per cent farmed.
Communal farms were abolished in 1991 and
peasants are encouraged, with private owner-
ship, to vary crops from the traditional corn and
beans. Mexico has great mineral wealth, e.g. silver, strontium and gold, but much is still unexploited. There are considerable reserves of oil,
natural gas, coal and uranium. Ten years ago
petroleum products accounted for 70 per cent of
exports. Now oil accounts for 30 per cent and
the major exports are manufactured goods from

an industrial base of vehicle production, steel,
textiles, breweries and food processing. Other
exports are coffee, fruit, vegetables and shrimps.
Tourism brings in important foreign revenue.
Trading should be enhanced by Mexico's deci-
sion to join the USA and Canada in the North
American Free Trade Association (NAFTA).

MICRONESIA
Federated States of,

STATUS: Self-governing Federation of States in
Compact of Free Association with USA
AREA: 702 sq km (271 sq miles)
POPULATION: 109,000
ANNUAL NATURAL INCOME: 2.4%
CAPITAL: Palikir
LANGUAGE: English, eight indigenous
languages
RELIGION: Christian majority
CURRENCY: US dollar (USD)
ORGANIZATIONS: UN

Micronesia, a former UN Trust Territory administered by the USA, is a federation of 607 islands
and atolls spread over some 3,200 km (2,000
miles) of the Pacific. Being near the equator, the
climate is hot and humid all year round with a
high annual rainfall of 9,300 mm (194 inches).
Subsistence farming and fishing are the traditional occupations while income is derived from
the export of phosphates and copper, a growing
tourist industry and revenue from foreign fleets
fishing within its territorial waters.

MOLDOVA

STATUS: Republic
AREA: 33,700 sq km (13,010 sq miles)
POPULATION: 4,356,000
ANNUAL NATURAL INCREASE: 0.6%
CAPITAL: Kishinev
LANGUAGE: Moldovan, Russian, Romanian
RELIGION: Orthodox
CURRENCY: rouble
ORGANIZATIONS: CIS, UN

A country of hilly plains, Moldova enjoys a warm
and dry climate with relatively mild winters.
Temperatures range from 5–7°C (23–26°F) during winter , to 20–23°C (68°–72°F) for summer
and rainfall averages 305–457mm (12–18 inches)
per year. It has very fertile soil, so arable farming dominates agricultural output with viticul-
ture, fruit and vegetables especially important.
Sunflower seeds are the main industrial crop;
wheat and maize the chief grain crops.
Traditionally, food processing has been the
major industry but recently light machine building and metal working industries have been
expanding. Moldova, part of the Soviet Union
between 1939 and 1991, has close ethnic, lin-
guistic and historical ties with neighbouring
Romania. Any moves towards re-unification
have been fiercely resisted by the Russian
minority in the eastern region of Trans-Dniester.

MONACO

STATUS: Principality
AREA: 1.6 sq km (0.6 sq miles)
POPULATION: 28,000
ANNUAL NATURAL INCREASE: 1.4%
CAPITAL: Monaco-ville
LANGUAGE: French, Monegasque, Italian, English
RELIGION: 90% Roman Catholic
CURRENCY: French franc (FRF)
ORGANIZATIONS: UN

The tiny principality is the world's smallest independent state after the Vatican City. It occupies a rocky peninsula on the French Mediterranean coast near the Italian border and is backed by the Maritime Alps. The climate is Mediterranean. It comprises the towns of Monaco, la Condamine, Fontvieille and Monte Carlo. Most revenue comes from tourism, casinos, light industry and financial services. Land has been reclaimed from the sea to extend the area available for commercial development.

MONGOLIA

STATUS: People's Republic
AREA: 1,565,000 sq km (604,090 sq miles)
POPULATION: 2,310,000
ANNUAL NATURAL INCREASE: 2.8%
CAPITAL: Ulan Bator (Ulaanbaatar)
LANGUAGE: Khalkha Mongolian
RELIGION: some Buddhist Lamaism
CURRENCY: tugrik (MNT)
ORGANIZATIONS: OIEC, UN

Situated between China and the Russian Federation, Mongolia has one of the lowest population densities in the world. Much of the country consists of a high undulating plateau reaching 1,500 m (4,920 feet) covered with grassland. To the north, mountain ranges reaching 4,231 m (13,881 feet) bridge the border with the Russian Federation, and to the south is the vast Gobi desert. The climate is very extreme with January temperatures falling to -34°C (-29°F). Mongolia is predominantly a farming economy, based on rearing cattle and horses. Its natural resources include some oil, rich coal deposits, iron ore, gold, tin and copper. About half the country's exports originate from the Erdanet copper mine. The break-up of the Soviet Union in 1991 brought an end to a partnership whereby Mongolia supplied raw materials in exchange for aid. A year later communism was abandoned. The country is now forced to reform its economy, but is isolated and in need of investment.

MONTSERRAT

STATUS: UK Crown Colony
AREA: 106 sq km (41 sq miles)
POPULATION: 11,000
CAPITAL: Plymouth

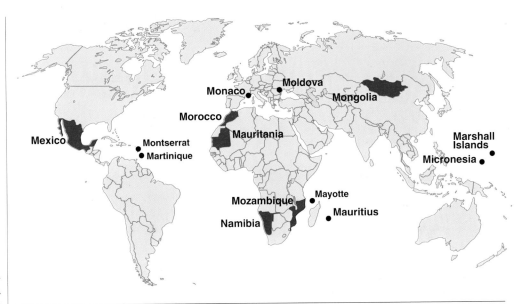

MOROCCO

STATUS: Kingdom
AREA: 710,895 sq km
(274,414 sq miles)
POPULATION: 26,318,000
ANNUAL NATURAL INCREASE: 2.5%
CAPITAL: Rabat
LANGUAGE: Arabic, French, Spanish, Berber
RELIGION: Muslim majority, Christian
and Jewish minorities
CURRENCY: Moroccan dirham (MAD)
ORGANIZATIONS: Arab League, UN

One-third of Morocco consists of the Atlas Mountains, reaching 4,165 m (13,665 feet). Beyond the coastal plains and the mountains lies the Sahara. The north of the country has a Mediterranean climate with some winter rainfall, but elsewhere conditions are mostly desert like and arid. Agriculture has diversified in recent years and as well as tomatoes and citrus fruits exports now include a variety of fruit and vegetables. Morocco has considerable phosphate deposits, which in value account for a quarter of total exports. Manufacturing industries include textiles, leather, food processing and chemicals and a growing mechanical and electronic sector. Income from tourism and remittances from Moroccans abroad are the main sources of foreign revenue.

MOZAMBIQUE

STATUS: Republic
AREA: 784,755 sq km
(302,915 sq miles)
POPULATION: 14,872,000
ANNUAL NATURAL INCREASE: 2.7%
CAPITAL: Maputo
LANGUAGE: Portuguese, tribal languages

RELIGION: majority traditional beliefs,
15% Christian, 15% Muslim
CURRENCY: metical (MZM)
ORGANIZATIONS: OAU, UN

The ex-Portuguese colony of Mozambique consists of a large coastal plain, rising towards plateaux and mountain ranges which border Malawi, Zambia and Zimbabwe. The highlands in the north reach 2,436 m (7,992 feet). The climate is tropical on the coastal plain, although high altitudes make it cooler inland. Over 90 per cent of the population are subsistence farmers cultivating coconuts, cashews, cotton, maize and rice. Cashew nuts and shrimps are the main exports. Mozambique also acts as an entrepôt, handling exports from South Africa, and landlocked Zambia and Malawi. Natural resources include large reserves of coal, also iron ore, copper, bauxite, gold and offshore gas, but most are unexploited.

NAMIBIA

STATUS: Republic
AREA: 825,419 sq km
(318,614 sq miles)
POPULATION: 1,534,000
ANNUAL NATURAL INCREASE: 3.1%
CAPITAL: Windhoek
LANGUAGE: Afrikaans, German, English,
regional languages
RELIGION: 90% Christian
CURRENCY: Namibian dollar, SA rand
ORGANIZATIONS: Comm., OAU, UN

The southwest African country of Namibia is one of the driest in the world. The Namib desert, on the coast, has less than 50 mm (2 inches) average rainfall per year, the Kalahari, to the northeast, has 100–250 mm (4–10 inches). The vegetation is sparse. Maize and sorghum are grown in the northern highlands and sheep are reared in the south. Namibia, however, is rich in mineral resources, with large deposits of lead, tin and zinc, and the world's largest uranium mine. The rich coastal waters are the basis of a successful fishing industry.

NAURU

STATUS: Republic
AREA: 21.2 sq km (8 sq miles)
POPULATION: 9,919
ANNUAL NATURAL INCREASE: -0.3%
CAPITAL: Yaren
LANGUAGE: Nauruan, English
RELIGION: Nauruan Protestant majority
CURRENCY: Australian dollar (AUD)
ORGANIZATIONS: Comm. (special member)

Nauru, a small island only 19 km (12 miles) in circumference, is situated in the Pacific, 2,100 km (1,3000 miles) northeast of Australia. The flat coastal lowlands, encircled by coral reefs, rise gently to a central plateau. The country was once rich in phosphates which were exported to Australia and Japan. However these deposits will soon become exhausted.

NEPAL

STATUS: Kingdom
AREA: 141,415 sq km (54,585 sq miles)
POPULATION: 20,577,000
ANNUAL NATURAL INCREASE: 2.6%
CAPITAL: Katmandu (Kathmandu)
LANGUAGE: Nepali, Maithir, Bhojpuri
RELIGION: 90% Hindu, 5% Buddhist, 3% Muslim
CURRENCY: Nepalese rupee (NPR)
ORGANIZATIONS: Col. Plan, UN

Nepal is a Himalayan kingdom sandwiched between China and India. Some of the highest mountains in the world, including Everest, are to be found along its northern borders. The climate changes sharply with altitude from the mountain peaks southwards to the Tarai plain. Central Kathmandu varies between 2–30°C (35–86°F). Most rain falls between June and October and can reach 2,500 mm (100 inches). Agriculture concentrates on rice, maize, cattle, buffaloes, sheep and goats. The small amount of industry processes local products, with carpets and clothing showing particular economic growth.

NETHERLANDS

STATUS: Kingdom
AREA: 41,160 sq km (15,890 sq miles)
POPULATION: 15,269,000
ANNUAL NATURAL INCREASE: 0.7%
CAPITAL: Amsterdam
(seat of Government: The Hague)
LANGUAGE: Dutch
RELIGION: 40% Roman Catholic,
30% Protestant, Jewish minority
CURRENCY: gulden (guilder or florin) (NLG)
ORGANIZATIONS: Council of Europe, EEA, EU,
NATO, OECD, UN, WEU

The Netherlands is exceptionally low-lying, with about 25 per cent of its territory being reclaimed from the sea. The wide coastal belt consists of flat marshland, mud-flats, sand-dunes and dykes. Further inland, the flat alluvial plain is drained by the Rhine, Maas and Ijssel. A complex network of dykes and canals prevents the area from flooding. To the south and east the land rises. Flat and exposed to strong winds, the Netherlands has a maritime climate with mild winters and cool summers. The Dutch are the leading world producers of dairy goods and also cultivate crops such as cereals, sugar beet and potatoes. Lacking mineral resources, much of the industry of the Netherlands is dependent on natural gas. Most manufacturing industry has developed around Rotterdam, where there are oil refineries, steel-works and chemical and food processing plants.

NETHERLANDS ANTILLES

STATUS: Self-governing Part of Netherlands Realm
AREA: 993 sq km (383 sq miles)
POPULATION: 191,311
CAPITAL: Willemstad

NEW CALEDONIA

STATUS: Overseas Territory of France
AREA: 19,105 sq km (7,375 sq miles)
POPULATION: 164,173
CAPITAL: Nouméa

NEW ZEALAND

STATUS: Commonwealth Nation
AREA: 265,150 sq km (102,350 sq miles)
POPULATION: 3,470,000
ANNUAL NATURAL INCREASE: 0.7%
CAPITAL: Wellington
LANGUAGE: English, Maori
RELIGION: 35% Anglican Christian,
22% Presbyterian, 16% Roman Catholic
CURRENCY: New Zealand dollar (NZD)
ORGANIZATIONS: ANZUS, Col. Plan,
Comm., OECD, UN

New Zealand consists of two main and several smaller islands, lying in the south Pacific Ocean. South Island is mountainous, with the Southern Alps running along its length. It has many glaciers and a coast line that is indented by numerous sounds and fjords. On the more heavily populated North Island, mountain ranges, broad fertile valleys and volcanic plateaux predominate. The overall climate is temperate, with an annual average temperature of 9°C (40°F) on South Island and 15°C (59°F) on the North Island. In terms of value the chief exports are meat, dairy produce and forestry products, followed by wood, fruit and vegetables. In the mineral sector there are deposits of coal, iron ore, oil and natural gas. Hydro-electric and geothermal power are well developed. Manufacturing industries are of increasing importance and in the early 1990s tourism expanded rapidly.

NICARAGUA

STATUS: Republic
AREA: 148,000 sq km (57,130 sq miles)
POPULATION: 4,130,000
ANNUAL NATURAL INCREASE: 2.8%
CAPITAL: Managua
LANGUAGE: Spanish
RELIGION: Roman Catholic
CURRENCY: cordoba (NIO)
ORGANIZATIONS: CACM, OAS, UN

Nicaragua, the largest of the Central America republics, is situated between the Caribbean and the Pacific. Active volcanic mountains run parallel with the western coast. The south is dominated by Lakes Managua and Nicaragua. Climate is tropical, with average daily temperatures in excess of 25°C (77°F) throughout the year. On the west coast wet summer months contrast with a dry period from December to April. Agriculture is the main occupation with cotton, coffee, sugar cane and fruit the main exports. Gold, silver and copper are mined.

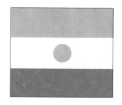

NIGER

STATUS: Republic
AREA: 1,186,410 sq km (457,955 sq miles)
POPULATION: 8,252,000
ANNUAL NATURAL INCREASE: 3.2%
CAPITAL: Niamey
LANGUAGE: French, Hausa and other
native languages
RELIGION: 85% Muslim, 15% traditional beliefs
CURRENCY: CFA franc (W Africa) (XOF)
ORGANIZATIONS: ECOWAS, OAU, UN

Niger is a vast landlocked southern republic. Apart from savannah in the south and in the Niger valley, most of the vast country lies within the Sahara desert. Rainfall is low, and decreases from 560 mm (22 inches) in the south to near zero in the north. Temperatures are above 35°C (95°F) for much of the year. Most of the population are farmers, particularly of cattle, sheep, and goats. Recent droughts have affected both cereals and livestock. The only significant export is uranium. and phosphates, coal, and tungsten are also mined. The economy depends largely on foreign aid.

NIGERIA

STATUS: Federal Republic
AREA: 923,850 sq km (356,605 sq miles)
POPULATION: 88,515,000
ANNUAL NATURAL INCREASE: 2.9%
CAPITAL: Abuja

LANGUAGE: English, Hausa, Yoruba, Ibo
RELIGION: Muslim majority, 35% Christian, animist minority
CURRENCY: naira (NGN)
ORGANIZATIONS: Comm., ECOWAS, OAU, OPEC, UN

The most populous nation in Africa, Nigeria is bounded to the north by the Sahara and to the west, east and southeast by tropical rainforest. The southern half of the country is dominated by the Niger and its tributaries, the north by the interior plateaux. Temperatures average 32°C (90°F) with high humidity. From a basic agricultural economy, Nigeria is only slowly being transformed by the vast oil discoveries in the Niger delta and coastal regions, which account for 95 per cent of exports. Gas reserves are relatively underdeveloped.

NIUE
STATUS: Self-governing Territory Overseas in Free Association with New Zealand
AREA: 259 sq km (100 sq miles)
POPULATION: 2,267
CAPITAL: Aloli

NORFOLK ISLAND
STATUS: External Territory of Australia
AREA: 36 sq km (14 sq miles)
POPULATION: 1,977
CAPITAL: Kingston

NORTHERN MARIANA ISLANDS
STATUS: Self-governing Commonwealth of USA
AREA: 471 sq km (182 sq miles)
POPULATION: 45,200
CAPITAL: Saipan

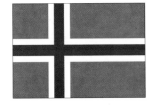

NORWAY
STATUS: Kingdom
AREA: 323,895 sq km (125,025 sq miles)
POPULATION: 4,305,000
ANNUAL NATURAL INCREASE: 0.4%
CAPITAL: Oslo
LANGUAGE: Norwegian, Lappish
RELIGION: 92% Evangelical Lutheran Christian
CURRENCY: Norwegian krone (NOK)
ORGANIZATIONS: Council of Europe, EEA, EFTA, NATO, OECD, UN

Norway is a mountainous country stretching from 58° to 72°N. The climate along its indented western coast is modified by the Gulf Stream, with high rainfall and relatively mild winters. Temperatures average -3.9°C (25°F) in January and 17°C (63°F) in July. Rainfall may be as high as 1,960 mm (79 inches). Most settlements are scattered along the fjords, the coast and around Oslo in the south. Norway is rich in natural resources. Oil and natural gas predominate in exports, but are supplemented by metal products, timber, pulp and paper, fish and machinery. The advanced production of hydro-electric power has helped develop industry, particularly chemicals, metal products and paper.

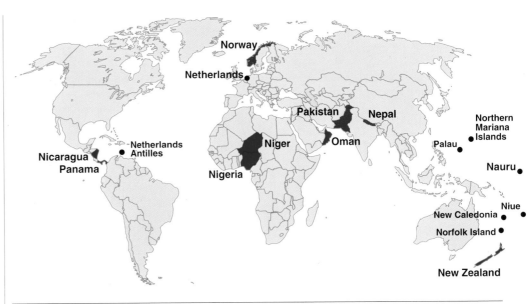

OMAN
STATUS: Sultanate
AREA: 271,950 sq km (104,970 sq miles)
POPULATION: 1,637,000
ANNUAL NATURAL INCREASE: 3.8%
CAPITAL: Muscat (Masqaṭ)
LANGUAGE: Arabic, English
RELIGION: 75% Ibadi Muslim, 25% Sunni Muslim
CURRENCY: rial Omani (OMR)
ORGANIZATIONS: Arab League, UN

The Sultanate of Oman occupies the northeast coast of the Arabian peninsula, with an enclave overlooking the Strait of Hormuz. Its desert landscape consists of a coastal plain and low hills rising to plateau in the interior, and has two fertile areas; Batinah in the north and Dhofar in the south. Copper ores are being mined and exported and oil provides over 95 per cent of export revenue. New discoveries of gas suggest that this will eventually supplant oil in importance.

PAKISTAN
STATUS: Republic
AREA: 803,940 sq km (310,320 sq miles)
POPULATION: 119,107,000
ANNUAL NATURAL INCREASE: 3.1%
CAPITAL: Islamabad
LANGUAGE: Urdu, Punjabi, Sindhi, Pushtu, English
RELIGION: 90% Muslim
CURRENCY: Pakistan rupee (PKR)
ORGANIZATIONS Col. Plan, Comm., UN

The landscape of Pakistan is dominated by the river Indus which flows south through the country flanked by the plateau of Balochistan and the Sulaiman mountains to the west and the Thar desert to the east. The climate is arid with temperatures averaging 27°C (80°F). Rainfall can be

less than 127 mm (5 inches) in the southwest and only in the northern mountains does it reach appreciable amounts; 900 mm (36 inches). Over 50 per cent of the population are engaged in agriculture which is confined to the irrigated areas near rivers. Main crops are wheat, cotton, maize, rice and sugar cane. There are many types of low-grade mineral deposits, such as coal and copper, which are little developed. Main industries are textiles, food processing and oil refining but these only contribute about 20 per cent to the economy.

PALAU
STATUS: Self-governing state in Compact of Free Association with USA
AREA: 497 sq km (192 sq miles)
POPULATION: 15,450
CAPITAL: Babelthuap

PANAMA
STATUS: Republic
AREA: 78,515 sq km (30,305 sq miles)
POPULATION: 2,535,000
ANNUAL NATURAL INCREASE: 2.1%
CAPITAL: Panama City (Panamá)
LANGUAGE: Spanish, English
RELIGION: Roman Catholic majority
CURRENCY: balboa (PAB), US dollar (USD)
ORGANIZATIONS: OAS, UN

Panama is situated at the narrowest part of central American isthmus. Mountain ranges, reaching heights exceeding 3,000 m (9,800 feet), run the country's length. Much of its tropical forest has now been cleared, but some remains towards the border with Colombia. Its climate is tropical with little variation throughout the year. The average temperature is around 27°C (80°F). There is a rainy season from April to December. Most of its foreign income is earned from revenues derived from the Panama Canal and from a large merchant fleet that is registered in its name. Petroleum products, bananas and shrimps are the main exports.

PAPUA NEW GUINEA

STATUS: Commonwealth Nation
AREA: 462,840 sq km (178,655 sq miles)
POPULATION: 4,056,000
ANNUAL NATURAL INCREASE: 2.3%
CAPITAL: Port Moresby
LANGUAGE: English, Pidgin English,
RELIGION: Pantheist, Christian minority
CURRENCY: kina (PGK)
ORGANIZATIONS: Col. Plan, Comm., UN

Papua New Guinea (the eastern half of New Guinea and neighbouring islands) is a mountainous country. It has an equatorial climate with temperatures of 21–32°C (70–90°F) and annual rainfall of over 2,000 mm (79 inches). The country is rich in minerals, in particular copper, gold and silver, but development is restricted by rainforest and lack of roads. Exports include coconuts, cocoa, coffee, rubber, tea and sugar. Logging was once dominant but exports are now being reduced in order to preserve forest resources.

PARAGUAY

STATUS: Republic
AREA: 406,750 sq km (157,055 sq miles)
POPULATION: 4,500,000
ANNUAL NATURAL INCREASE: 2.9%
CAPITAL: Asunción
LANGUAGE: Spanish, Guarani
RELIGION: 90% Roman Catholic
CURRENCY: guarani (PYG)
ORGANIZATIONS: OAS, UN

Paraguay is a landlocked country in South America with hot rainy summers, when temperatures reach over 27°C (80°F), and mild winters with an average temperature of 18°C (64°F). Lush, fertile plains and heavily forested plateau east of the River Paraguay contrast with the scrubland of the Chaco to the west. Cassava, cotton, soya beans and maize are the main crops but the rearing of livestock – cattle, horses, pigs and sheep – and food processing, dominate the export trade. The largest hydro-electric power dam in the world is at Itaipú, constructed as a joint project with Brazil, and another massive hydro-electric development is being constructed at Yacyreta in conjunction with Argentina.

PERU

STATUS: Republic
AREA: 1,285,215 sq km (496,095 sq miles)
POPULATION: 22,454,000
ANNUAL NATURAL INCREASE: 2.1%
CAPITAL: Lima
LANGUAGE: Spanish, Quechua, Aymara
RELIGION: Roman Catholic majority
CURRENCY: new sol (PES)
ORGANIZATIONS: OAS, UN

Peru exhibits three geographical regions. The Pacific coastal region is very dry but with fertile oases producing cotton, sugar, fruit and fodder crops. This is the most prosperous and heavily populated area and includes the industrial centres around Lima. In the ranges and plateaux of the Andes and in the Amazon lowlands to the northeast, the soils are thin with the inhabitants depending on cultivation and grazing. Poor communications have hindered the development of Peru and there are great differences between the rich and poor. Peru has rich mineral deposits of copper, gold, lead, zinc and silver and there are oil and gas reserves in the interior.

PHILIPPINES

STATUS: Republic
AREA: 300,000 sq km (115,800 sq miles)
POPULATION: 65,650,000
ANNUAL NATURAL INCREASE: 2.3%
CAPITAL: Manila
LANGUAGE: Filipino (Tagalog), English,
Spanish, Cebuano
RELIGION: 90% Christian, 7% Muslim
CURRENCY: Philippine peso (PHP)
ORGANIZATIONS: ASEAN, Col. Plan, UN

The Philippine archipelago consists of some 7,000 islands and is subject to earthquakes and typhoons. It has a monsoonal climate, with up to 6,350 mm (250 inches) of rainfall per annum in some areas. This once supported tropical rain forest but, apart from Palawan island, this has now been destroyed. Fishing is important but small farms dominate the economy, producing rice and copra for domestic consumption and other coconut and sugar products for export. Main exports are textiles, fruit and electronic products. Remittances from Filipinos working overseas are important to the economy. There is high unemployment and the extent of poverty is widespread.

PITCAIRN ISLAND

STATUS: UK Dependent Territory
AREA: 45 sq km (17.25 sq miles)
POPULATION: 71
CAPITAL: Adamstown

POLAND

STATUS: Republic
AREA: 312,685 sq km (120,695 sq miles)
POPULATION: 38,310,000
ANNUAL NATURAL INCREASE: 0.4%
CAPITAL: Warsaw (Warszawa)
LANGUAGE: Polish
RELIGION: 90% Roman Catholic
CURRENCY: zloty (PLZ)
ORGANIZATIONS: Council of Europe,
OIEC, UN,

Much of Poland lies in the north European plain south of the Baltic Sea. It is a land of woods and lakes, gently rising southwards from the coast towards the Tartry mountains in the south and Sudety mountains in Silesia. The climate is continental with short, warm summers and long severe winters, when average temperatures can drop below freezing point (32°F). Rainfall occurs mainly in the summer months and averages between 520 and 730 mm (21–29 inches). Both agriculture and natural resources play an important part in the economy and Poland is nearly self-sufficient in cereals, sugar beet and potatoes. There are large reserves of coal, copper, sulphur and natural gas. Its major industries are ship-building in the north and the production of machinery, transport equipment, metals and chemicals in the major mining centres of the south. Manufacturing industries in both the private and public sectors are expanding rapidly and the government is committed to a programme of economic reforms and privatization.

PORTUGAL

STATUS: Republic
AREA: 91,630 sq km (35,370 sq miles)
POPULATION: 9,846,000
ANNUAL NATURAL INCREASE: -0.7%
CAPITAL: Lisbon (Lisboa)
LANGUAGE: Portuguese
RELIGION: Roman Catholic majority
CURRENCY: escudo (PTE)
ORGANIZATIONS: Council of Europe, EEA, EU,
NATO, OECD, UN, WEU

Portugal occupies the western Atlantic coast of the Iberian Peninsula. The river Tagus, on whose estuary is Lisbon, divides the country physically. In the north the land lies mainly above 4,000 m (1,220 feet) with plateaux cut by westward flowing rivers. Here, the climate is modified by westerly winds and the Gulf Stream. This is reflected in the lush mixed deciduous/coniferous forests. Land to the south is generally less than 300 m (1,000 feet) and the climate becomes progressively more arid further south, with Mediterranean scrub predominating in the far south. A quarter of the population are farmers growing vines, olives, wheat and maize. Wines, cork and fruit are important exports. In industry the chief exports are textiles, clothing, footwear and wood products. Mineral deposits include coal, copper, kaolinite and uranium. Tourism is an important source of revenue, with many visitors coming to the Algarve region in the far south of the country.

PUERTO RICO

STATUS: Self-governing Commonwealth of USA
AREA: 8,960 sq km (3,460 sq miles)
POPULATION: 3,580,000
CAPITAL: San Juan

QATAR

STATUS: State
AREA: 11,435 sq km (4,415 sq miles)
POPULATION: 453,000
ANNUAL NATURAL INCREASE: 6%
CAPITAL: Doha (Ad Dawḥah)
LANGUAGE: Arabic, English
RELIGION: Muslim
CURRENCY: Qatari riyal (QAR)
ORGANIZATIONS: Arab League, OPEC, UN

The country occupies all of the Qatar peninsula in the Gulf and is a land of flat, arid desert. July temperatures average 37°C (98°F) and annual rainfall averages 62mm (2.5 inches). The main source of revenue is from the exploitation of oil and gas reserves. The North Field gas reserves are the world's largest single field and the development of these has a high priority.

RÉUNION

STATUS: Overseas Department of France
AREA: 2,510 sq km (969 sq miles)
POPULATION: 624,000
CAPITAL: Saint-Denis

ROMANIA

STATUS: Republic
AREA: 237,500 sq km (91,699 sq miles)
POPULATION: 22,767,000
ANNUAL NATURAL INCREASE: 0.1%
CAPITAL: Bucharest (Bucureşti)
LANGUAGE: Romanian, Magyar
RELIGION: 85% Romanian Orthodox,
CURRENCY: leu (ROL)
ORGANIZATIONS: Council of Europe, OIEC, UN

Romania is dominated by the great curve of the Carpathians, flanked by rich agricultural lowlands and has a continental climate. Forced industrialization has taken the economy from one based on agriculture to one dependent on heavy industry, notably chemicals, metal processing and machine-building. Since the fall of the communist dictatorship in 1989, most land has been privatized and there has been a re-emergence of Romania's traditional agriculture, with exports of cereals, fruit and wine. There are natural resources including oil, gas and minerals but industrial reform is slow and the economy is sluggish. Living standards are among the lowest in Europe.

RUSSIAN FEDERATION

STATUS: Federation
AREA: 17,078,005 sq km (6,592,110 sq miles)

POPULATION: 148,673,000
ANNUAL NATURAL INCREASE: 0.5%
CAPITAL: Moscow (Moskva)
LANGUAGE: Russian
RELIGION: Russian Orthodox,
Jewish and Muslim minorities
CURRENCY: rouble
ORGANIZATIONS: CIS, UN

Covering much of east and northeast Europe and all of north Asia, the Russian Federation (Russia) displays an enormous variety of landforms and climates. The Arctic deserts of the north give way to tundra wastes and taiga which cover two-thirds of the country. In the far south, beyond the steppes, some areas assume subtropical and semi-desert landscapes. The majority of the population live west of the north-south spine of the Urals but in recent decades there has been a substantial migration eastwards to the Siberian basin in order to exploit its vast natural resources. Massive oil fields off the east coast of Sakhalin north of Japan and also in the Russian Arctic (Timan Pechora basin) are now to be developed. Russia's extraordinary wealth of natural resources was a key factor in the country's speedy industrialization during the Soviet period. Heavy industry still plays a decisive role in the economy, while light and consumer industries have remained relatively under-developed. Agricultural land covers one-sixth of Russia's territory but there remains great potential for increase through drainage and clearance. By the mid-1980s the Soviet system was finally acknowledged to have reached an impasse, and the failure of the *perestroika* programme for reform precipitated the disintegration of the Soviet Union, which finally broke up in 1991. A transition from a state-run Communist economy to a market economy is taking place. Between 1992 and 1994 70 per cent of state-owned enterprises were privatized and farms are also starting to be re-organized.

RWANDA

STATUS: Republic
AREA: 26,330 sq km (10,165 sq miles)

POPULATION: 7,526,000
ANNUAL NATURAL INCREASE: 3%
CAPITAL: Kigali
LANGUAGE: French, Kinyarwanda (Bantu),
tribal languages
RELIGION: 50% animist, 50% Christian
(mostly Roman Catholic)
CURRENCY: Rwanda franc (RWF)
ORGANIZATIONS: OAU, UN

Small and isolated, Rwanda supports a high density of population on the mountains and plateaux east of the Rift Valley. It has a tropical climate with a dry season between June and August. Agriculture is basically subsistence with coffee the major export. Tin is mined and there are major natural gas reserves. Since 1990 a civil war has raged between the Tutsi and Hutu tribes, creating many thousands of casualties and well over one million refugees. The country has become reliant on foreign aid, and will require a massive international relief effort to avert disease and famine.

ST HELENA

STATUS: UK Dependent Territory
AREA: 122 sq km (47 sq miles)
POPULATION: 5,564
CAPITAL: Jamestown

ST KITTS-NEVIS

STATUS: Commonwealth State
AREA: 262 sq km (101 sq miles)
POPULATION: 40,618
ANNUAL NATURAL INCREASE: -0.4%
CAPITAL: Basseterre
LANGUAGE: English
RELIGION: Christian (mostly Protestant)
CURRENCY: E Caribbean dollar (XCD)
ORGANIZATIONS: CARICOM, Comm., OAS, UN

St Kitts-Nevis, in the Leeward Islands, comprises two volcanic islands: St Kitts and Nevis. The climate is tropical with temperatures of 16–33°C (61–91°F) and an average annual rainfall of 1,400 mm (55 inches). Main exports are sugar, molasses and cotton. Tourism is an important industry.

ST LUCIA

STATUS: Commonwealth State
AREA: 616 sq km (238 sq miles)
POPULATION: 136,000
ANNUAL NATURAL INCREASE: 1.9%
CAPITAL: Castries
LANGUAGE: English, French patois
RELIGION: 82% Roman Catholic
CURRENCY: E. Caribbean dollar (XCD)
ORGANIZATIONS: Caricom, Comm., OAS, UN

Independent since 1979 this small tropical Caribbean island in the Lesser Antilles grows coconuts, cocoa and fruit. Bananas account for over 40 per cent of export earnings. Main industries are food and drink processing and all consumer goods are imported. Tourism is a major growth sector.

ST PIERRE AND MIQUELON

STATUS: Territorial Collectivity of France
AREA: 241 sq km (93 sq miles)
POPULATION: 6,392
CAPITAL: St Pierre

ST VINCENT AND THE GRENADINES

STATUS: Commonwealth State
AREA: 389 sq km (150 sq miles)
POPULATION: 107,598
ANNUAL NATURAL INCREASE: 0.9%
CAPITAL: Kingstown
LANGUAGE: English
RELIGION: Christian
CURRENCY: E. Caribbean dollar (XCD)
ORGANIZATIONS: Caricom, Comm., OAS, UN

St Vincent in the Lesser Antilles comprises a forested main island and the northern part of the Grenadines. It has a tropical climate. Most exports are foodstuffs: arrowroot, sweet potatoes, coconut products and yams, but the principal crop is bananas. Some sugar cane is grown for the production of rum and other drinks. Tourism is well-established.

SAN MARINO

STATUS: Republic
AREA: 61 sq km (24 sq miles)
POPULATION: 24,003
ANNUAL NATURAL INCREASE: 1.2%
CAPITAL: San Marino
LANGUAGE: Italian

RELIGION: Roman Catholic
CURRENCY: Italian lira (ITL),
San Marino coinage
ORGANIZATIONS: Council of Europe, UN

An independent state within Italy, San Marino straddles a limestone peak in the Apennines south of Rimini. The economy is centred around tourism and the sale of postage stamps. Most of the population are farmers growing cereals, olives and vines and tending herds of sheep and goats.

SÃO TOMÉ AND PRÍNCIPE

STATUS: Republic
AREA: 964 sq km (372 sq miles)
POPULATION: 124,000
ANNUAL NATURAL INCREASE: 2.3%
CAPITAL: São Tomé
LANGUAGE: Portuguese, Fang
RELIGION: Roman Catholic majority
CURRENCY: dobra (STD)
ORGANIZATIONS: OAU, UN

This tiny state, independent from Portugal since 1975, comprises two large and several small islands near the equator, 200 km (125 miles) off west Africa. The climate is tropical with temperatures averaging 25°C (77°F) and rainfall of between 1,000–5,000 mm (40–197 inches). Cocoa (which provides 90 per cent of revenue), coconuts and palm oil are the main crops grown on the rich volcanic soil. Other foods and consumer goods are imported.

SAUDI ARABIA

STATUS: Kingdom
AREA: 2,400,900 sq km (926,745 sq miles)
POPULATION: 16,900,000
ANNUAL NATURAL INCREASE: 3.5%
CAPITAL: Riyadh (Ar Riyāḍ)
LANGUAGE: Arabic
RELIGION: 90% Sunni Muslim,
5% Roman Catholic
CURRENCY: Saudi riyal (SAR)
ORGANIZATIONS: Arab League, OPEC, UN

Saudi Arabia occupies the heart of the vast arid Arabian Peninsula. The country is mostly desert and there are no rivers which flow all year round. To the west, the Hejaz and Asir mountains fringe the Red Sea but even here rainfall rarely exceeds 380 mm (15 inches). Temperatures rise beyond 44°C (111°F) in the summer. The interior plateau slopes gently eastwards down to the Gulf and supports little vegetation. The southeast of the country is well named as the 'Empty Quarter'; it is almost devoid of population. Only in the coastal strips and oases are cereals and date palms grown. Oil is the most important resource – Saudi Arabia has a quarter of the world's known oil reserves – and export commodity and economic development is dependent on its revenue.

SENEGAL

STATUS: Republic
AREA: 196,720 sq km (75,935 sq miles)
POPULATION: 7,970,000
ANNUAL NATURAL INCREASE: 3.0%
CAPITAL: Dakar
LANGUAGE: French, native languages
RELIGION: 94% Sunni Muslim,
animist minority
CURRENCY: CFA franc (W Africa) (XOF)
ORGANIZATIONS: ECOWAS, OAU, UN

Senegal is a flat, dry country cut through by the Gambia, Casamance and Senegal rivers. Rainfall rarely exceeds 580 mm (23 inches) on the wetter coast. The interior savannah supports varied wildlife but little agriculture. Cultivation is mainly confined to the south where groundnuts account for nearly half of the agricultural output. Cotton and millet are also grown, but frequent droughts have reduced their value as cash crops. Phosphate mining, ship-repairing, textiles, petroleum products and food processing are the major industries. Both tourism and fishing are becoming increasingly important.

SEYCHELLES

STATUS: Republic
AREA: 404 sq km (156 sq miles)
POPULATION: 72,000
ANNUAL NATURAL INCREASE: 0.8%
CAPITAL: Victoria
LANGUAGE: English, French, Creole
RELIGION: 92% Roman Catholic
CURRENCY: Seychelles rupee (SCR)
ORGANIZATIONS: Comm., OAU, UN

This archipelago in the Indian Ocean comprises over 100 granite or coral islands. Main exports are copra, coconuts and cinnamon and in recent years tea and tuna. All domestic requirements, including most foodstuffs, have to be imported. Tourism has developed rapidly in the 1990s and is now the dominant sector in the economy.

SIERRA LEONE

STATUS: Republic
AREA: 72,325 sq km
(27,920 sq miles)
POPULATION: 4,376,000
ANNUAL NATURAL INCREASE: 2.4%
CAPITAL: Freetown
LANGUAGE: English, Krio Temne, Mende
RELIGION: 52% animist, 39% Muslim and
8% Christian

CURRENCY: leone (SLL)
ORGANIZATIONS: Comm., ECOWAS, OAS, UN

Sierra Leone, a former British colony, has a coast dominated by swamps but is essentially a flat plain some 70 miles wide which extends to interior plateaux and mountains. Three-quarters of the population are employed in subsistence farming. Cash crops include cocoa and coffee but the main source of revenue is from minerals. Diamonds, gold, bauxite and iron ore are mined but the most important export is now rutile (titanium ore). Manufacturing in the form of processing local products has developed around Freetown.

SINGAPORE

STATUS: Republic
AREA: 616 sq km (238 sq miles)
POPULATION: 2,874,000
ANNUAL NATURAL INCREASE: 1.2%
CAPITAL: Singapore
LANGUAGE: Malay, Chinese (Mandarin),
Tamil, English
RELIGION: Daoist, Buddist, Muslim, Christian
and Hindu
CURRENCY: Singapore dollar (SGD)
ORGANIZATIONS: ASEAN, Col. Plan,
Comm., UN

The republic of Singapore, independent from Britain since 1959, has been transformed from an island of mangrove swamps into one of the world's major entrepreneurial centres. The island, connected to Peninsular Malaysia by a man-made causeway, has a tropical, humid climate with 2,240 mm (96 inches) of rain per year. With few natural resources, Singapore depends on manufacturing precision goods, electronic products, financial services and activities associated with its port, which is one of the world's largest.

SLOVAKIA

STATUS: Republic
AREA: 49,035 sq km (18,932 sq miles)
POPULATION: 5,320,000
ANNUAL NATURAL INCREASE: 0.4%
CAPITAL: Bratislava
LANGUAGE: Slovak, Hungarian
RELIGION: Roman Catholic
CURRENCY: Slovak crown or koruna
ORGANIZATIONS: Council of Europe, UN

On 1 January 1993 Czechoslovakia ceased to exist and Slovakia and the Czech Republic came into being. Slovakia's geomorphology is dominated by the Tatry mountains in the north. Bratislava, the capital, lies in the extreme southwest, on the north bank of the Danube. Natural resources include iron ore, copper, antimony, mercury, magnesite and oil. Under Communism large manufacturing complexes developed,

many of which specialized in arms and tanks. The end of the Cold War in 1989 brought a collapse in demand for these products. This, and a decline in trade with the Czech Republic, has forced Slovakia to restructure existing industry and look to new developments such as aluminium smelting and car assembly.

SLOVENIA

STATUS: Republic
AREA: 20,250 sq km
(7,815 sq miles)
POPULATION: 1,990,000
ANNUAL NATURAL INCREASE: 0.7%
CAPITAL: Ljubljana
LANGUAGE: Slovene
RELIGION: Roman Catholic
CURRENCY: Slovenian tolar (SLT)
ORGANIZATIONS: Council of Europe, UN

The northernmost republic of the former Yugoslav federation, Slovenia, has always been one of the key gateways from the Balkans to central and western Europe. Much of the country is mountainous, its heartland and main centre of population being the Ljubljana basin. The climate generally shows continental tendencies, with warm summers and cold winters, when snow is plentiful on the ground. The small coastal region has a Mediterranean regime. Extensive mountain pastures provide profitable dairy-farming, but the amount of cultivable land is restricted. There are large mercury mines in the northwest and, in recent decades, this area has also developed a broad range of light industries. Combined with tourism, this has given the country a well-balanced economy. After a brief military conflict Slovenia won its independence in 1991.

SOLOMON ISLANDS

STATUS: Commonwealth Nation
AREA: 29,790 sq km (11,500 sq miles)

POPULATION: 349,500
ANNUAL NATURAL INCREASE: 2.9%
CAPITAL: Honiara
LANGUAGE: English, Pidgin English,
native languages
RELIGION: 95% Christian
CURRENCY: Solomon Islands dollar (SBD)
ORGANIZATIONS: Comm., UN

Situated in the South Pacific Ocean the Solomon Islands consist of a 1400 km (870 miles) archipelago of six main and many smaller islands. The mountainous large islands are covered by tropical rain forest reflecting the high temperatures, on average 22–34°C (72–95°F) and heavy rainfall, about 3,050 mm (120 inches). The main crops are coconuts, cocoa and rice, with copra, timber and palm oil being the main exports. Mineral deposits include reserves of bauxite, gold and phosphate, mined on the small island of Bellona south of Guadalcanal. Once a British protectorate, the Solomons became independent in 1978.

SOMALIA

STATUS: Republic
AREA: 6300,000sq km (243,180 sq miles)
POPULATION: 7,497,000
ANNUAL NATURAL INCREASE: 3.0%
CAPITAL: Mogadishu (Muqdisho)
LANGUAGE: Somali, Arabic, English, Italian
RELIGION: Muslim, Roman Catholic minority
CURRENCY: Somali shilling (S0S)
ORGANIZATIONS: UN, Arab League, OAU

Independent since 1960, Somalia is a hot and arid country in northeast Africa. The semi-desert of the northern mountains contrasts with the plains of the south where the bush country is particularly rich in wildlife. Most of the population are nomadic, following herds of camels, sheep, goats and cattle. Little land is cultivated but cotton, maize, millet and sugar cane are grown. Bananas are a major export. Iron ore, gypsum and uranium deposits are as yet unexploited. Five years of inter-clan warfare and a lack of coherent government have led to the collapse of the economy.

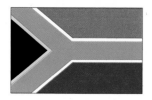

SOUTH AFRICA
STATUS: Republic
AREA: 1,220,845 sq km (471,369 sq miles)
POPULATION: 37,600,000
ANNUAL NATURAL INCREASE: 2.4%
CAPITAL: Pretoria (administrative)
Cape Town (legislative)
LANGUAGE: Afrikaans, English,
various African languages
RELIGION: mainly Christian, Hindu,
Jewish and Muslim minorities
CURRENCY: rand (ZAR)
ORGANIZATIONS: Comm., OAU, UN

The interior of South Africa consists of a plateau of over 900 m (2,955 feet) drained by the Orange and Limpopo rivers. Surrounding the plateau is a pronounced escarpment below which the land descends by steps to the sea. Rainfall in most areas is less than 500 mm (20 inches) and the land is increasingly drier towards the west. Agriculture is limited by poor soils but sheep and cattle are extensively grazed. Main crops are maize, wheat, sugar cane, vegetables, cotton and vines. Wine is an important export commodity. South Africa abounds in minerals. Diamonds, gold, platinum, silver, uranium, copper, manganese and asbestos are mined and nearly 80 per cent of the continent's coal reserves are in South Africa. Manufacturing and engineering is concentrated in the southern Transvaal area and around the ports. In 1994 the first ever multi-racial elections were held resulting in Nelson Mandela coming to power. In a post-apartheid era, economic sanctions have been lifted, boosting exports, but the country faces adaptation, beginning with a rush of complicated land-ownership claims.

EASTERN CAPE
STATUS: Province
AREA: 174,405 sq km (67,338 sq miles)
POPULATION: 5,900,000
CAPITAL: East London

EASTERN TRANSVAAL
STATUS: Province
AREA: 73,377 sq km (28,311 sq miles)
POPULATION: 2,600,000
CAPITAL Nelspruit

KWAZULU-NATAL
STATUS: Province
AREA: 90,925 sq km (35,106 sq miles)
POPULATION: 8,000,000
CAPITAL: Durban

NORTHERN CAPE
STATUS: Province
AREA: 369,552 sq km (142,684 sq miles)
POPULATION: 700,000
CAPITAL: Kimberley

NORTHERN TRANSVAAL
STATUS: Province
AREA: 121,766 sq km (47,014 sq miles)
POPULATION: 4,700,000
CAPITAL: Pietersburg

NORTH WEST
STATUS: Province
AREA: 120,170 sq km (46,398 sq miles)
POPULATION: 3,300,000
CAPITAL: Klerksdorp

ORANGE FREE STATE
STATUS: Province
AREA: 123,893 sq km (47,835 sq miles)
POPULATION: 2,500,000
CAPITAL: Bloemfontein

PRETORIA-WITWATERSRAND-VEREENIGING (PWV)
STATUS: Province
AREA: 18,078 sq km (6,980 sq miles)
POPULATION: 6,500,000
CAPITAL: Johannesburg

WESTERN CAPE
STATUS: Province
AREA: 128,679 sq km
(49,683 sq miles)
POPULATION: 3,400,000
CAPITAL: Cape Town

SOUTHERN AND ANTARCTIC TERRITORIES
STATUS: Overseas Territory of France
AREA: 439,580 sq km (169,680 sq miles)
POPULATION: 180

SOUTH GEORGIA AND THE SOUTH SANDWICH ISLANDS
STATUS: UK Dependent Territory
AREA: 3,755 sq km (1,450 sq miles)
POPULATION: no permanent population

SPAIN
STATUS: Kingdom
AREA: 504,880 sq km (194,885 sq miles)
POPULATION: 39,166,000
ANNUAL NATURAL INCREASE: 0.5%
CAPITAL: Madrid
LANGUAGE: Spanish (Castilian), Catalan,
Basque, Galician
RELIGION: Roman Catholic
CURRENCY: Spanish peseta (ESP)
ORGANIZATIONS: Council of Europe, EEA, EU,
NATO, OECD, UN, WEU

Spain occupies most of the Iberian Peninsula, from the Bay of Biscay and the Pyrenees mountains in the north, to the Strait of Gibraltar in the south. It includes in its territory the Balearic Islands in the Mediterranean Sea, and the Canary Islands in the Atlantic. The mainland of Spain is mostly plateaux, often forested in the north, but becoming more arid and open further south. Climate is affected regionally by latitude and proximity to the Atlantic Ocean and Mediterranean Sea. Although the climate and terrain are not always favourable, agriculture is important to the Spanish economy. Wheat and other cereals such as maize, barley and rice are cultivated while grapes, citrus fruits and olives are important cash crops. Textile manufacturing in the northeast and steel, chemicals, consumer goods and vehicle manufacturing in the towns and cities have proved a magnet for great numbers of the rural population. The main minerals found are coal, iron ore, uranium and zinc. Tourism is of vital importance to the economy.

SRI LANKA
STATUS: Republic
AREA: 65,610 sq km (25,325 sq miles)
POPULATION: 17,405,000
ANNUAL NATURAL INCREASE: 1.5%
CAPITAL: Colombo
LANGUAGE: Sinhala, Tamil, English
RELIGION: 70% Buddhist, 15% Hindu, Roman
Catholic and Muslim minorities
CURRENCY: Sri Lanka rupee (LKR)
ORGANIZATIONS: Col. Plan, Comm., UN

The island of Sri Lanka is situated only 19 km (12 miles) from mainland India. The climate is tropical along the coastal plain and temperate in the central highlands. Annual rainfall averages only 1,000 mm (39 inches) in the north and east while the south and west receive over 2,000 mm (79 inches). The traditional economy of Sri Lanka is based on agriculture in which rubber, coffee, coconuts and particularly tea are dominant. The nation is also self-sufficient in rice. In recent years, however, manufacturing, especially of clothing and textiles, has become the main export earner. Gemstones and tourism are also important, but the tourist industry has suffered because of the activities of Tamil separatists.

SUDAN
STATUS: Republic
AREA: 2,505,815 sq km (967,245 sq miles)
POPULATION: 24,941,000
ANNUAL NATURAL INCREASE: 3.0%
CAPITAL: Khartoum
LANGUAGE: Arabic, tribal languages
RELIGION: 60% Sunni Muslim,
animist and Christian
CURRENCY: Sudanese pound (SDP)
ORGANIZATIONS: Arab League, OAU, UN

Sudan, in the upper Nile basin, is Africa's largest country. The land is mostly flat and infertile with a hot, arid climate. The White and Blue Niles are invaluable, serving not only to irrigate cultivated land but also as a potential source of hydro-electric power. Subsistence farming accounts for 80 per cent of Sudan's total production. Major exports include cotton, groundnuts, sugar cane and sesame seed. The principal activity is nomadic herding with over 40 million cattle and sheep and 14 million goats. However, economic activity has been damaged by the effects of drought and civil war.

SURINAM

STATUS: Republic
AREA: 163,820 sq km (63,235 sq miles)
POPULATION: 438,000
ANNUAL NATURAL INCREASE: 2.5%
CAPITAL: Paramaribo
LANGUAGE: Dutch, English, Spanish,
Surinamese (Sranang Tongo), Hindi
RELIGION: 45% Christian, 28% Hindu,
20% Muslim
CURRENCY: Surinam guilder (SRG)
ORGANIZATIONS: OAS, UN

Independent from the Dutch since 1976, Surinam is a small state lying on the northeast coast in the tropics of South America. Physically, there are three main regions: a low-lying, marshy coastal strip; undulating savannah; densely forested highlands. Rice growing takes up 75 per cent of all cultivated land; sugar and pineapples are also grown, while cattle rearing for both meat and dairy products has been introduced. Bauxite accounts for 90 per cent of Surinam's foreign earnings. Timber resources offer great potential but as yet are largely untapped.

SWAZILAND

STATUS: Kingdom
AREA: 17,365 sq km (6,705 sq miles)
POPULATION: 823,000
ANNUAL NATURAL INCREASE: 3.4%
CAPITAL: Mbabane
LANGUAGE: English, Siswati
RELIGION: 60% Christian, 40% traditional beliefs
CURRENCY: lilangeni (SZL),
South African rand (ZAR)
ORGANIZATIONS: Comm., OAU, UN

Landlocked Swaziland in southern Africa, is a sub-tropical, savannah country. It is divided into four main regions: the High, Middle and Low Velds and the Lebombo Mountains. Rainfall is abundant, promoting good pastureland for the many cattle and sheep. Major exports include sugar, meat, citrus fruits, textiles, wood products and asbestos.

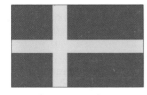

SWEDEN

STATUS: Kingdom
AREA: 449,790 sq km (173,620 sq miles)
POPULATION: 8,721,000
ANNUAL NATURAL INCREASE: 0.2%

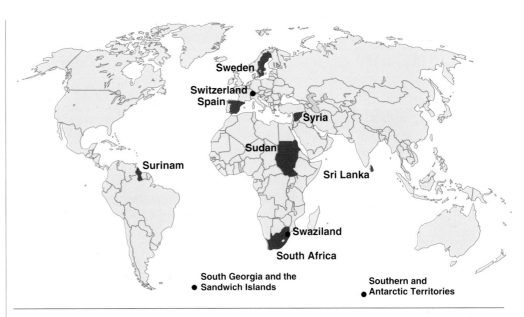

CAPITAL: Stockholm
LANGUAGE: Swedish, Finnish, Lappish
RELIGION: 95% Evangelical Lutheran
CURRENCY: Swedish krona (SED)
ORGANIZATIONS: Council of Europe, EEA, EFTA,
OECD, UN

Glacial debris, glacier-eroded valleys and thick glacial clay are all dominant features of Sweden. Physically, Sweden comprises four main regions: Norrland, the northern forested mountains; the Lake District of the centre south; the southern uplands of Jönköping; the extremely fertile Scania plain of the far south. Summers are short and hot with long, cold winters. Temperatures vary with latitude; in the south from -3–18°C (27–64°F) and in the north from -14–14°C (7–57°F). Annual rainfall varies between 2,000 mm (79 inches) in the southwest, to 500 mm (20 inches) in the east. Over half the land area is forested resulting in a thriving timber industry, but manufacturing industry, particularly cars and trucks, metal products and machine tools, is well established. Mineral resources are also rich and plentiful – iron ore production alone exceeds 17 million tons a year. There are also deposits of copper, lead and zinc.

SWITZERLAND

STATUS: Federation
AREA: 41,285 sq km (15,935 sq miles)
POPULATION: 6,908,000
ANNUAL NATURAL INCREASE: 0.3%
CAPITAL: Bern (Berne)
LANGUAGE: German, French, Italian, Romansch
RELIGION: 48% Roman Catholic,
44% Protestant, Jewish minority
CURRENCY: Swiss franc (CHF)
ORGANIZATIONS: Council of Europe, EFTA,
OECD

Switzerland is a landlocked, mountainous country of great scenic beauty, situated in western Europe. The Alps traverse the southern half of the country, in which are to be found some of Europe's highest peaks. In the north the Jura mountains form a natural border with France.

Winters are cold with heavy snowfall in the highest regions. Summers are mild with an average July temperature of 18–19°C (64–66°F). Most rain falls in the summer months. Agriculture is based mainly on dairy farming. Major crops include hay, wheat, barley and potatoes. Industry plays a major role in Switzerland's economy, centred on metal engineering, watchmaking, food processing, textiles and chemicals. The high standard of living enjoyed by the Swiss owes much to the tourist industry. The financial services sector, especially banking, is also of great importance. Switzerland's history of neutrality has made it an attractive location for the headquarters of several international organizations.

SYRIA

STATUS: Republic
AREA: 185,680 sq km (71,675 sq miles)
POPULATION: 13,400,000
ANNUAL NATURAL INCREASE: 3.6%
CAPITAL: Damascus, (Dimashq, Esh Sham)
LANGUAGE: Arabic
RELIGION: 65% Sunni Muslim, Shi'a Muslim
and Christian minorities
CURRENCY: Syrian pound (SYP)
ORGANIZATIONS: Arab League, UN

Syria is situated in the heart of the Middle East. Its most fertile areas lie along the coastal strip on the Mediterranean Sea which supports the bulk of its population, and in the depressions and plateaux of the northeast which are cut through by the rivers Orontes and Euphrates. In the south the Anti-Lebanon mountains (Jebel esh Sharqi) is bordered to the east by the Syrian desert. While the coast has a Mediterranean climate with dry hot summers and mild winters, the interior becomes increasingly hot and arid – average summer temperatures in the desert reach 43°C (109°F). Rainfall varies between 220–400 mm (9–16 inches). Cotton is Syria's main export crop, and wheat and barley are also grown. Cattle, sheep and goats are the main livestock. Although traditionally an agriculturally-based economy, the country is rapidly becoming industrialized as oil, natural gas, salt, gypsum and phosphate are being exploited.

TAHITI

STATUS: Main Island of French Polynesia
AREA: 1,042 sq km (402 sq miles)
POPULATION: 199,031

TAIWAN

STATUS: Island 'Republic of China'
AREA: 35,990 sq km
(13,890 sq miles)
POPULATION: 20,600,000
ANNUAL NATURAL INCREASE: 1.5%
CAPITAL: Taipei (T'ai-pei)
LANGUAGE: Mandarin Chinese, Taiwanese
RELIGION: Buddhist majority, Muslim,
Daoist and Christian minorities
CURRENCY: New Taiwan dollar (TWD), yuan (CNY)
ORGANIZATIONS: none listed

Taiwan is separated from mainland China by the Taiwan Strait (the former Formosa Channel) in which lie the Pescadores. Two-thirds of Taiwan is mountainous, the highest point is 3,950 m (12,959 feet). The flat to rolling coastal plain in the western part of the island accommodates the bulk of the population and the national commerce, industry and agriculture. The climate is tropical marine, with persistent cloudy conditions. The monsoon rains fall in June to August, with an annual average of 2,600 mm (102 inches). Main crops are rice, tea, fruit, sugar cane and sweet potatoes. Industry has been founded on textiles but in recent years electronic products have gained in importance. The Taiwanese economy is inevitably influenced by its large neighbour and is likely to benefit from improving Chinese performance.

TAJIKISTAN

STATUS: Republic
AREA: 143,100 sq km (55,235 sq miles)
POPULATION: 5,465,000
ANNUAL NATURAL INCREASE: 3.0%
CAPITAL: Dushanbe
LANGUAGE: Tajik, Uzbek, Russian
RELIGION: Sunni Muslim
CURRENCY: Russian rouble
ORGANIZATIONS: CIS, UN

Situated in the mountainous heart of Asia, more than half the territory of Tajikistan lies above 3,000 m (10,000 feet). The major settlement areas lie within the Fergana valley in the west. The climate varies from continental to subtropical according to elevation and shelter. Extensive irrigation, without which agriculture would be severely limited, has made it possible for cotton growing to develop into the leading branch of agriculture, and on that basis textiles have become the largest industry in the country. Tajikistan is rich in mineral and fuel deposits, the exploitation of which became a feature of

economic development during the Soviet era. Preceding full independence in 1991 there was an upsurge of sometimes violent Tajik nationalism as a result of which many Russians and Uzbeks have left the country.

TANZANIA

STATUS: Republic
AREA: 939,760 sq km (362,750 sq miles)
POPULATION: 27,829,000
ANNUAL NATURAL INCREASE: 3.5%
CAPITAL: Dodoma
LANGUAGE: Swahili, English
RELIGION: 40% Christian, 35% Muslim
CURRENCY: Tanzanian shilling
ORGANIZATIONS: Comm., OAU, UN

Much of this east African country consists of high interior plateaux covered by scrub and grassland, bordered to the north by the volcanic Kilimanjaro region and Lake Victoria, to the west by Lake Tanganyika, by highlands to the south and by the Indian Ocean in the east. Despite its proximity to the equator, the altitude of much of Tanzania means that temperatures are reduced, and only on the narrow coastal plain is the climate truly tropical. Average temperatures vary between 19–28°C (67–82°F), and annual rainfall is around 570–1,060 mm (23–43 inches). The economy is heavily based on agriculture and subsistence farming is the main way of life for most of the population, although coffee, cotton, sisal, cashew nuts and tea are exported. Industry is limited, but gradually growing in importance, and involves textiles, food processing and tobacco. Tourism could be a future growth area.

THAILAND

STATUS: Kingdom
AREA: 514,000 sq km (198,405 sq miles)
POPULATION: 57,800,000
ANNUAL NATURAL INCREASE: 1.9%
CAPITAL: Bangkok (Krung Thep)
LANGUAGE: Thai
RELIGION: Buddhist, 4% Muslim
CURRENCY: baht (THB)
ORGANIZATIONS: ASEAN, Col. Plan, UN

Thailand is a land of flat undulating plains and mountains, consisting of the plains of the Chao Phraya and Mae Nam Mun river systems, fringed by mountains, a plateau in the northeast drained by the tributaries of the Mekong river, and the northern half of the Malay peninsula. From May to October, monsoon rains are heavy with an annual average rainfall of 1,500 mm (59 inches). The climate is tropical with temperatures reaching 36°C (97°F) and much of the country is forested. The central plain is well-served with irrigation canals which supply the paddy fields

for rice cultivation; Thailand is the world's leading exporter of this crop. Maize, cassava, sugar and rubber also contribute to the economy. Tin production has declined in importance in recent years and has, in part, been replaced by a small scale petro-chemical industry. Other industries of importance include textiles and clothing. Tourism, which grew at a record rate during the 1980s, has since levelled out after the military coup of 1991.

TOGO

STATUS: Kingdom
AREA: 699 sq km (270 sq miles)
POPULATION: 130,000
ANNUAL NATURAL INCREASE: 3.5%
CAPITAL: Lomé
LANGUAGE: French, Kabre, Ewe
RELIGION: Christian
CURRENCY: pa'anga (TOP)
ORGANIZATIONS: Comm.

Togo, formerly a German protectorate and French colony, is situated between Ghana and Benin in west Africa. A long narrow country, it has only 65 km (40 miles) of coast. The interior consists of mountains and high infertile tableland. The climate is tropical with an average temperature of 27°C (81°F). Most of Togo's farmers grow maize, cassava, yams, groundnuts and plantains, and the country is virtually self-sufficient in food stuffs. Phosphates account for half of export revenue. Cotton, cocoa and coffee are also exported.

TOKELAU ISLANDS

STATUS: Overseas Territory of New Zealand
AREA: 10 sq km (4 sq miles)
POPULATION: 1,577
CAPITAL: none, each island has its own
administration centre

TONGA

STATUS: Kingdom
AREA: 699 sq km (270 sq miles)
POPULATION: 103,000
ANNUAL NATURAL INCREASE: 0.4%
CAPITAL: Nuku'alofa
LANGUAGE: Tongan, English
RELIGION: Christian
CURRENCY: pa'anga (TOP)
ORGANIZATIONS: Comm.

Tonga consists of an archipelago of 169 islands in the Pacific 180 km (112 miles) north of New Zealand. There are seven groups of islands, but the most important are Tongatapu, Ha'apai and Vava'u. All the islands are covered with dense tropical vegetation, and temperatures range from 11–29°C (52–84°F). Main exports are coconut products and bananas.

TRINIDAD & TOBAGO

STATUS: Republic
AREA: 5,130 sq km (1,980 sq miles)
POPULATION: 1,265,000
ANNUAL NATURAL INCREASE: 1.7%
CAPITAL: Port of Spain
LANGUAGE: English, Hindi, French, Spanish
RELIGION: 60% Christian, 25% Hindu,
6% Muslim
CURRENCY: Trinidad and Tobago dollar (TTD)
ORGANIZATIONS: Caricom, Comm., OAS, UN

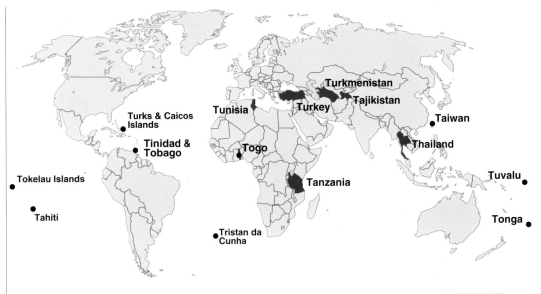

Trinidad and Tobago, the southernmost Caribbean islands of the Lesser Antilles lie only 11 and 30 km (7 and 19 miles) respectively from the Venezuelan coast. Both islands are mountainous, the Northern Range of Trinidad reaching 940 m (3,084 feet) with its highest parts retaining tropical forest cover. The country has a humid, tropical climate with temperatures averaging 25°C (76°F) per annum. Rain falls mostly between June and December and varies between 1,300–3,000 mm (51–118 inches) annually. Sugar was once the mainstay of the economy but oil is now the leading source of revenue accounting for over 70 per cent of export revenue. There is also a petro-chemical industry based on significant gas reserves.

TRISTAN DA CUNHA

STATUS: Dependency of St Helena
AREA: 98 sq km (38 sq miles)
POPULATION: 295

TUNISIA

STATUS: Republic
AREA: 164,150 sq km (63,360 sq miles)
POPULATION: 8,401,000
ANNUAL NATURAL INCREASE: 2.0%
CAPITAL: Tunis
LANGUAGE: Arabic, French
RELIGION: Muslim
CURRENCY: Tunisian dinar (TND)
ORGANIZATIONS: Arab League, OAU, UN

Tunisia, on the southern shores of the Mediterranean is largely an arid, desert country of northern Africa. The eastern limits of the Atlas mountain range extend into northern parts of the country, which are separated from the Sahara desert to the south by a lowland belt of salt pans, called the Chott El Jerid. Average annual temperatures are in the range 10–27°C (50–81°F) and rainfall averages 380–500 mm (15–20 inches) in the north, but drops to virtually nothing in the south. The majority of the population live along the northeast coast. Wheat, barley, olives and citrus fruit are the main crops and oil, natural gas and sugar refining are the main industries. The tourist industry is expanding and is becoming increasingly important to the economy.

TURKEY

STATUS: Republic
AREA: 779,450 sq km (300,870 sq miles)
POPULATION: 59,869,000
ANNUAL NATURAL INCREASE: 2.2%
CAPITAL: Ankara
LANGUAGE: Turkish, Kurdish
RELIGION: 98% Sunni Muslim, Christian minority
CURRENCY: Turkish lira (TRL)
ORGANIZATIONS: Council of Europe, NATO, OECD, UN

Turkey has always occupied a strategically important position linking Europe and Asia. It is a rugged, mountainous country particularly in the east. The central Anatolian plateau is bordered in the north by the Pontine mountains (Anadolu Dağlari) and in the south by the Taurus mountains (Toros Dağlari) which converge in the east, crowned by Mt Ararat (Büyük Ağri). Thrace, in European Turkey is flatter with rolling hills. Coastal regions exhibit Mediterranean conditions with short mild winters with some rainfall and long hot, dry summers. The interior is relatively arid with average rainfall in some places less than 250 mm (10 inches). The main crops are wheat and barley, but tobacco, olives, sugar beet, tea and fruit are also grown, and sheep, goats and cattle are raised. Turkey is becoming increasingly industrialized; textiles account for a third of exports and the car industry is developing. The nation now leads the Middle East in the production of iron, steel, chrome, coal and lignite. Tourism is a rapidly growing industry.

TURKMENISTAN

STATUS: Republic
AREA: 488,100 sq km (188,405 sq miles)
POPULATION: 3,714,000
ANNUAL NATURAL INCREASE: 2.5%
CAPITAL: Ashkhabad
LANGUAGE: Turkmen, Russian, Uzbek
RELIGION: Muslim
CURRENCY: manat
ORGANIZATIONS: CIS, UN

Situated in the far south of the former Soviet Union, Turkmenistan is a desert land except for the lowlands in the west along the Caspian shore, the mountains along its southern borders and the valley of Amudar'ya river in the north. The continental climate is responsible for great fluctuations in temperature, both during the day and throughout the year. Traditionally nomads, the Turkmen tribes under the Soviet regime, turned from pastoral farming to cotton-growing, made possible by extensive irrigation. Turkmenistan enjoys substantial natural resources, principally oil and gas but also potassium, sulphur and salt.

TURKS & CAICOS ISLANDS

STATUS: UK Dependent Territory
AREA: 430 sq km (166 sq miles)
POPULATION: 11,696
CAPITAL: Cockburn Town

TUVALU

STATUS: Special membership of the Commonwealth
AREA: 24.6 sq km (9.5 sq miles)
POPULATION: 10,090
ANNUAL NATURAL INCREASE: 1.5%
CAPITAL: Funafuti
LANGUAGE: Tuvaluan, English
RELIGION: 98% Protestant
CURRENCY: Australian dollar (AUD), Tuvaluan coinage
ORGANIZATIONS: Comm., (special member)

Tuvalu consists of nine dispersed coral atolls, north of Fiji, in the Pacific Ocean. The climate is tropical; hot, with heavy annual rainfall exceeding 3,000 mm (118 inches). Fish is the staple food but coconuts and bread-fruit are cultivated. The sale of postage stamps abroad is, however, the largest source of revenue.

UGANDA

STATUS: Republic
AREA: 236,580 sq km
(91,320 sq miles)
POPULATION: 18,674,000
ANNUAL NATURAL INCREASE: 3.1%
CAPITAL: Kampala
LANGUAGE: English, tribal languages
RELIGION: 62% Christian, 6% Muslim
CURRENCY: Uganda shilling (UGS)
ORGANIZATIONS: Comm., OAU, UN

Uganda is bordered in the west by the great Rift Valley and the Ruwenzori mountain range which reaches 5,220 m (16,765 feet). In the east it is bordered by Kenya and Lake Victoria, from which the Nile flows northwards. Most of the country is high plateau with savannah vegetation although the lands around Lake Victoria have been cleared for cultivation and have become the most populated and developed areas. The climate is warm (21–24°C or 70–75°F), and rainfall ranges from 750–1,500 mm (30–59 inches) per annum. The Ugandan economy is firmly based on agriculture with a heavy dependence on coffee, the dominant export crop, and cotton. Fishing, from the waters of Lake Victoria is also important for local consumption.

UKRAINE

STATUS: Republic
AREA: 603,700 sq km (233,030 sq miles)
POPULATION: 52,194,000
ANNUAL NATURAL INCREASE: 0.3%
CAPITAL: Kiev (Kiyev)
LANGUAGE: Ukrainian, Russian
RELIGION: Russian Orthodox,
Roman Catholic (Uniate)
CURRENCY: karbovanets (coupon)
ORGANIZATIONS: CIS, UN

Ukraine consists mainly of level plains and mountainous border areas. The landscape is, however, diverse, with marshes, forests, wooded and treeless steppe. Deposits of 'black earth', among the most fertile soils, cover about 65 per cent of Ukraine. Grain, potatoes, vegetables and fruits, industrial crops (notably sugar beets and sunflower seeds) and fodder crops are grown. Food processing is important to the economy, and southern regions are renowned for wines. Ukraine is rich in mineral resources, such as iron ore, coal and lignite, and has large reserves of petroleum and gas. Extensive mining, metal production, machine-building, engineering and chemicals dominate Ukrainian industry, most of it located in the Donetsk basin and the Dneiper lowland. These two regions account for four-fifths of the urban population. Despite its natural wealth and industrial development, Ukraine has failed to respond to the economic needs of its independent status and has experienced sharp declines in agricultural and industrial output.

UNITED ARAB EMIRATES (UAE)

STATUS: Federation of seven Emirates
AREA: 75,150 sq km (29,010 sq miles)
POPULATION: 2,083,000
ANNUAL NATURAL INCREASE: 3.1%
CAPITAL: Abu Dhabi (Abū Ẓabī)
LANGUAGE: Arabic, English
RELIGION: Sunni Muslim
CURRENCY: UAE dirham (AED)
ORGANIZATIONS: Arab League, OPEC, UN

The United Arab Emirates (UAE), comprising seven separate emirates, are stretched along the southeastern coast of the Gulf. It is a country covered mostly by flat deserts with the highest land in the Hajar mountains of the Musandam Peninsula. Summer temperatures reach 40°C (104°F); meagre rains of 130 mm (5 inches) fall mainly in the winter. Only the desert oases are fertile, producing fruit and vegetables. The economic wealth of the UAE is founded on its huge reserves of hydrocarbons, mainly within the largest Emirate, Abu Dhabi, with smaller supplies in three others – Dubai, Sharjah and Ras al Khaimah. Natural gas and oil are the major exports for which Japan and the Far East are the major markets. Revenue gained from these has allowed the economy to grow rapidly, with there being huge investment in the service industries. It has a population that is overwhelmingly made up of foreign immigrants.

ABU DHABI

STATUS: Emirate
AREA: 64,750 sq km (24,995 sq miles)
POPULATION: 670,175

AJMAN

STATUS: Emirate
AREA: 260 sq km (100 sq miles)
POPULATION: 64,318

DUBAI

STATUS: Emirate
AREA: 3,900 sq km (1,505 sq miles)
POPULATION: 419,104

FUJAIRAH

STATUS: Emirate
AREA: 1,170 sq km (452 sq miles)
POPULATION: 54,425

RAS AL KHAIMAH

STATUS: Emirate
AREA: 1,690 sq km (625 sq miles)
POPULATION: 116,470

SHARJAH

STATUS: Emirate
AREA: 2,600 sq km (1,005 sq miles)
POPULATION: 268,722

UMM AL QAIWAIN

STATUS: Emirate
AREA: 780 sq km (300 sq miles)
POPULATION: 29,229

UNITED KINGDOM OF GREAT BRITAIN & NORTHERN IRELAND (UK)

STATUS: Kingdom
AREA: 244,755 sq km
(94,475 sq miles)
POPULATION: 57,998,400
ANNUAL NATURAL INCREASE: 0.3%
CAPITAL: London
LANGUAGE: English, Welsh, Gaelic
RELIGION: Protestant majority, Roman Catholic,
Jewish, Muslim, Hindu minorities
CURRENCY: pound sterling (GBP)
ORGANIZATIONS: Col. Plan, Comm.,
Council of Europe, EEA, EU, G7, NATO,
OECD, UN, WEU

The United Kingdom, part of the British Isles, is situated off the northwest European coast, separated from France by the English Channel. It includes the countries of England and Scotland, the principality of Wales, and the region of Northern Ireland in the north of the island of Ireland.

In broad terms Britain can be divided into the upland regions of Wales, Northern England and Scotland, characterized by ancient dissected and glaciated mountain regions, and the lowland areas of southern and eastern England where low ranges of chalk, limestone and sandstone hills are interspersed with wide clay vales. The highest point in the United Kingdom is Ben Nevis in the Grampians of Scotland at 1,344 m (4,409 feet).

The climate of the British Isles is mild, wet and variable. Summer temperatures average 13–17°C (55–63°F) and winter temperatures 5–7°C (41–45°F). Annual rainfall varies between 640–5,000 mm (26–200 inches) with the highest rainfall in the Lake District and the lowest in East Anglia.

Although only a tiny percentage of the nation's workforce is employed in agriculture, farm produce is important to both home and export markets. Seventy-six per cent of the total UK land area is farmland. The main cereal crops are wheat, barley and oats. Potatoes, sugar beet and green vegetable crops are widespread.

About 20 per cent of the land is permanent pasture for raising dairy and beef stock and 28 per cent, mainly hill and mountain areas, is used for rough grazing of sheep. The best fruit-growing areas are the southeast, especially Kent, East Anglia and the central Vale of Evesham. Fishing supplies two-thirds of the nation's requirements but overfishing and encroachment into territorial waters by other countries have created problems.

The major mineral resources of the UK are coal, oil and natural gas. Over two-thirds of deep-mined coal came from the Yorkshire and East Midlands fields and substantial reserves remain. However, the coal industry, which had already been in slow decline for some 30 years, collapsed rapidly in 1993–4 when many of the remaining pits were closed. The number of employees fell from 208,000 in 1983 to 18,000 in early 1994 and by mid-1994 only 16 deep coal mines remained in operation, compared with 50 pits two years earlier.

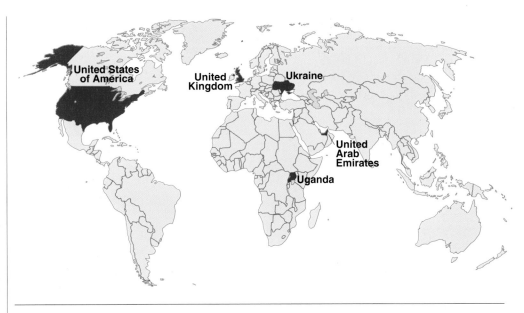

Before the 1970s Britain relied on imports from the Middle East for its oil supplies, but in 1975 supplies of oil and gas from the vast North Sea oil fields began to provide both self-sufficiency and enough to export. Some of the older fields are now nearly worked out and operating costs for these are rising. The major Scott Field came on-stream in 1993 and in 1994 approval was granted for the development of the Fife and Birch oil fields and the Armada gas fields.

Wind farms as a source of energy, often the subject of controversy with environmentalists, contribute less than 1 per cent of Britain's electricity.

Although the UK is an industrialized nation, the traditional mainstays of heavy industry such as coal, iron and steel and shipbuilding no longer figure prominently in the economy. Concurrent with the decline of heavy industry, there has been a substantial growth of light industries. High technology and electronic products predominate, as well as pharmaceuticals, motor parts and food processing. Tourism is an essential part of the economy, especially in London, and in five years up to 1993 the number of visitors to the UK rose by 22 per cent. Financial services is another expanding sector, the 'City' of London having the greatest concentration of banks in the world.

The UK is a trading nation. The balance of trade has changed during the last 30 years because of increasingly closer economic ties with Europe and the move towards a Single European Market. Consequently, trading with Commonwealth nations, particularly Australia, has assumed lower priority. In terms of value, the most important exports from the UK are machinery, chemicals and transport equipment, followed by food, beverages and tobacco, petroleum products, iron and steel.

The transport network in the UK is highly developed. Out of 362,357 km (225,164 miles) of public roads, 9 per cent are motorways and 13 per cent are other major roads. The railway network covers over 16,730 km (10,395 miles) and carries over 150 million tonnes of freight annually. The opening of the Channel Tunnel in 1994 has connected the motorway and rail networks of Britain with those of northern France and southern Belgium. The inland waterway system totals only 563 navigable kilometres (350 miles) but has potential to carry more than its present 4 million tonnes of goods annually.

ENGLAND

STATUS: Constituent Country
AREA: 130,360 sq km (50,320 sq miles)
POPULATION: 48,208,100
CAPITAL: London

NORTHERN IRELAND

STATUS: Constituent Region
AREA: 14,150 sq km (5,460 sq miles)
POPULATION: 1,573,282
CAPITAL: Belfast

SCOTLAND

STATUS: Constituent Country
AREA: 78,750 sq km (30,400 sq miles)
POPULATION: 4,998,567
CAPITAL: Edinburgh

WALES

STATUS: Principality
AREA: 20,760 sq km (8,015 sq miles)
POPULATION: 2,891,500
CAPITAL: Cardiff

UNITED STATES OF AMERICA (USA)

STATUS: Federal Republic
AREA: 9,363,130 sq km (3,614,170 sq miles)
POPULATION: 255,020,000
ANNUAL NATURAL INCREASE: 0.9%
CAPITAL: Washington D.C.
LANGUAGE: English, Spanish
RELIGION: Christian majority, Jewish minority
CURRENCY: US dollar (USD)
ORGANIZATIONS: ANZUS, Col. Plan, G7, NAFTA, NATO, OAS, OECD, UN

The United States of America is the world's fourth largest country after Canada, China and Russia with the world's fourth largest population. The 19th and 20th centuries have brought 42 million immigrants to its shores, and the population of the USA now has the highest living standard of any country in the world. The large land area covers a huge spectrum of different landscapes, environments and climates. The eastern coast of New England, where the European settlers first landed, is rocky, mountainous and richly wooded. South of New England is the Atlantic coastal plain, rising to the west towards the Appalachian mountain system. Beyond the Appalachians lie the central lowlands, a large undulating plain cut through by the Mississippi and Ohio rivers. Further west lie the Great Plains crossed by the Missouri, Red and Arkansas rivers and rising gently towards the mighty Rocky Mountains, a spine of mountains running south from Alaska. Beyond these lie the Great Valley of California, the coastal ranges and the Pacific coast.

Climatic variety within the United States is enormous, ranging from the Arctic conditions of Alaska to the desert of the southwest – winter temperatures in Alaska plummet to -28°C (-19°F); in Florida they maintain a steady 19°C (66°F). The centre of the continent is dry, but both the northwest Pacific and the New England Atlantic coast are humid with heavy rainfall. Many areas of the USA fall prey to exceptional, often disastrous, weather conditions: the northeastern seaboard is susceptible to heavy blizzards, the southern lowlands are vulnerable to spring thaw flooding and the Mississippi valley is prone to tornadoes.

The natural vegetation of the USA reflects its climatic diversity. The northwest coast is rich in coniferous forest, while the Appalachian mountain region is well endowed with hardwoods. In the arid southwest, vegetation is limited to desert scrub whereas the Gulf and South Atlantic coast are fringed with swampy wetlands. The central lowlands are endowed with rich black-earth soils (the agricultural heartland), gradually supplanted, towards the Rockies, by tall-grass prairie. The northeastern states of Illinois, Iowa, Indiana and Nebraska form the 'corn belt', which produces 45 per cent of the world's corn. Further west wheat supplements corn as the main crop. The northeastern states are predominantly dairy country, and the south is famous for cotton and tobacco. Rice is grown in Texas, California and Louisiana, and fruit and vegetables in Florida.

The USA consumes 25 per cent of all the world's energy resources but is well endowed with energy reserves. There are substantial coal resources, particularly in the Appalachians. The great rivers have been harnessed extensively for hydro-electric power. Oil and natural gas fields are found in Texas, Alaska, Louisiana and California and new deep-sea exploratory drilling is underway in the Gulf of Mexico. Oil production, however, has declined steadily since 1983.

The industrial base is diverse, the main industries being steel, motor vehicles, aerospace, chemicals, computers, electronics, telecommunications and consumer goods. The service industries (encompassing tourism and finance) are by far the biggest source of employment in the United States.

ALABAMA

STATUS: State
AREA: 131,485 sq km (50,755 sq miles)
POPULATION: 4,136,000
CAPITAL: Montgomery

ALASKA

STATUS: State
AREA: 1,478,450 sq km (570,680 sq miles)
POPULATION: 587,000
CAPITAL: Juneau

ARIZONA

STATUS: State
AREA: 293,985 sq km (113,480 sq miles)
POPULATION: 3,832,000
CAPITAL: Phoenix

ARKANSAS
STATUS: State
AREA: 134,880 sq km (52,065 sq miles)
POPULATION: 2,399,000
CAPITAL: Little Rock

CALIFORNIA
STATUS: State
AREA: 404,815 sq km (156,260 sq miles)
POPULATION: 30,867,000
CAPITAL: Sacramento

COLORADO
STATUS: State
AREA: 268,310 sq km (103,570 sq miles)
POPULATION: 3,470,000
CAPITAL: Denver

CONNECTICUT
STATUS: State
AREA: 12,620 sq km (4,870 sq miles)
POPULATION: 3,281,000
CAPITAL: Hartford

DELAWARE
STATUS: State
AREA: 5,005 sq km (1,930 sq miles)
POPULATION: 689,000
CAPITAL: Dover

DISTRICT OF COLUMBIA
STATUS: Federal District
AREA: 163 sq km (63 sq miles)
POPULATION: 589,000
CAPITAL: Washington D.C.

FLORIDA
STATUS: State
AREA: 140,255 sq km (54,1405 sq miles)
POPULATION: 13,488,000
CAPITAL: Tallahassee

GEORGIA
STATUS: State
AREA: 150,365 sq km (58,040 sq miles)
POPULATION: 6,751,000
CAPITAL: Atlanta

HAWAII
STATUS: State
AREA: 16,640 sq km (6,425 sq miles)
POPULATION: 1,160,000
CAPITAL: Honolulu

IDAHO
STATUS: State
AREA: 213,445 sq km (82,390 sq miles)
POPULATION: 1,067,000
CAPITAL: Boise

ILLINOIS
STATUS: State
AREA: 144,120 sq km (55,630 sq miles)
POPULATION: 11,631,000
CAPITAL: Springfield

INDIANA
STATUS: State
AREA: 93,065 sq km (35,925 sq miles)
POPULATION: 5,662,000
CAPITAL: Indianapolis

IOWA
STATUS: State
AREA: 144,950 sq km (55,950 sq miles)
POPULATION: 2,812,000
CAPITAL: Des Moines

KANSAS
STATUS: State
AREA: 211,805 sq km (81,755 sq miles)
POPULATION: 2,523,000
CAPITAL: Topeka

KENTUCKY
STATUS: State
AREA: 102,740 sq km (39,660 sq miles)
POPULATION: 3,755,000
CAPITAL: Frankfort

LOUISIANA
STATUS: State
AREA: 115,310 sq km (44,510 sq miles)
POPULATION: 4,287,000
CAPITAL: Baton Rouge

MAINE
STATUS: State
AREA: 80,275 sq km (30,985 sq miles)
POPULATION: 1,235,000
CAPITAL: Augusta

MARYLAND
STATUS: State
AREA: 25,480 sq km (9,835 sq miles)
POPULATION: 4,908,000
CAPITAL: Annapolis

MASSACHUSETTS
STATUS: State
AREA: 20,265 sq km (7,820 sq miles)
POPULATION: 5,998,000
CAPITAL: Boston

MICHIGAN
STATUS: State
AREA: 147,510 sq km (56,940 sq miles)
POPULATION: 9,437,000
CAPITAL: Lansing

MINNESOTA
STATUS: State
AREA: 206,030 sq km (79,530 sq miles)
POPULATION: 4,480,000
CAPITAL: St Paul

MISSISSIPPI
STATUS: State
AREA: 122,335 sq km (47,220 sq miles)
POPULATION: 2,614,000
CAPITAL: Jackson

MISSOURI
STATUS: State
AREA: 178,565 sq km (68,925 sq miles)
POPULATION: 5,193,000
CAPITAL: Jefferson City

MONTANA
STATUS: State
AREA: 376,555 sq km (145,350 sq miles)
POPULATION: 824,000
CAPITAL: Helena

NEBRASKA
STATUS: State
AREA: 198,505 sq km (76,625 sq miles)
POPULATION: 1,606,000
CAPITAL: Lincoln

NEVADA
STATUS: State
AREA: 284,625 sq km (109,865 sq miles)
POPULATION: 1,327,000
CAPITAL: Carson City

NEW HAMPSHIRE
STATUS: State
AREA: 23,290 sq km (8,990 sq miles)
POPULATION: 1,111,000
CAPITAL: Concord

NEW JERSEY
STATUS: State
AREA: 19,340 sq km (7,465 sq miles)
POPULATION: 7,789,000
CAPITAL: Trenton

NEW MEXICO
STATUS: State
AREA: 314,255 sq km (121,300 sq miles)
POPULATION: 1,581,000
CAPITAL: Sante Fe

NEW YORK
STATUS: State
AREA: 122,705 sq km (47,365 sq miles)
POPULATION: 18,119,000
CAPITAL: Albany

NORTH CAROLINA
STATUS: State
AREA: 126,505 sq km (48,830 sq miles)
POPULATION: 6,843,000
CAPITAL: Raleigh

NORTH DAKOTA
STATUS: State
AREA: 179,485 sq km (69,280 sq miles)
POPULATION: 636,000
CAPITAL: Bismarck

OHIO
STATUS: State
AREA: 106,200 sq km (40,995 sq miles)
POPULATION: 11,016,000
CAPITAL: Columbus

OKLAHOMA
STATUS: State
AREA: 177,815 sq km (68,635 sq miles)
POPULATION: 3,212,00
CAPITAL: Oklahoma City

OREGON
STATUS: State
AREA: 249,115 sq km (96,160 sq miles)
POPULATION: 2,977,000
CAPITAL: Salem

PENNSYLVANIA
STATUS: State
AREA: 116,260 sq km (44,875 sq miles)
POPULATION: 12,009,000
CAPITAL: Harrisburg

RHODE ISLAND
STATUS: State
AREA: 2,730 sq km (1,055 sq miles)
POPULATION: 1,005,000
CAPITAL: Providence

SOUTH CAROLINA
STATUS: State
AREA: 78,225 sq km (30,195 sq miles)
POPULATION: 3,603,000
CAPITAL: Columbia

SOUTH DAKOTA
STATUS: State
AREA: 196,715 sq km (75,930 sq miles)
POPULATION: 711,000
CAPITAL: Pierre

TENNESSEE
STATUS: State
AREA: 106,590 sq km (41,145 sq miles)
POPULATION: 5,024,000
CAPITAL: Nashville

TEXAS
STATUS: State
AREA: 678,620 sq km (261,950 sq miles)
POPULATION: 17,656,000
CAPITAL: Austin

UTAH
STATUS: State
AREA: 212,570 sq km (82,050 sq miles)
POPULATION: 1,813,000
CAPITAL: Salt Lake City

VERMONT
STATUS: State
AREA: 24,015 sq km (9,270 sq miles)
POPULATION: 570,000
CAPITAL: Montpelier

VIRGINIA
STATUS: State
AREA: 102,835 sq km (39,695 sq miles)
POPULATION: 6,377,000
CAPITAL: Richmond

WASHINGTON
STATUS: State
AREA: 172,265 sq km (66,495 sq miles)
POPULATION: 5,136,000
CAPITAL: Olympia

WEST VIRGINIA
STATUS: State
AREA: 62,470 sq km (24,115 sq miles)
POPULATION: 1,812,000
CAPITAL: Charleston

WISCONSIN
STATUS: State
AREA: 140,965 sq km (54,415 sq miles)
POPULATION: 5,007,000
CAPITAL: Madison

WYOMING
STATUS: State
AREA: 251,200 sq km (96,965 sq miles)
POPULATION: 466,000
CAPITAL: Cheyenne

URUGUAY
STATUS: Republic
AREA: 186,925 sq km (72,155 sq miles)
POPULATION: 3,131,000
ANNUAL NATURAL INCREASE: 0.6%
CAPITAL: Montevideo
LANGUAGE: Spanish
RELIGION: Roman Catholic
CURRENCY: Uruguayan peso (UYP)
ORGANIZATIONS: Mercosur, OAS, UN

Uruguay is a small country on the southeast coast of south America. Geographically it consists firstly of a narrow plain, fringed with lagoons and dunes, skirting along the coast and the estuary of the river Plate. Further inland, rolling grassland hills are broken by minor ridges of the Brazilian highlands, which reach heights of no more than 500 m (1,600 feet). The climate is temperate and rainfall is spread evenly throughout the year at about 100 mm (4 inches) per month. Monthly temperatures average in the range of 10–22°C (50–72°F). The land has good agricultural potential, however most is given over to the grazing of sheep and cattle. The economy relies heavily on the production of meat and wool with 87 per cent of the area devoted to farming. Uruguay has no oil or gas reserves, and most of its energy requirements are obtained from hydro-electricity.

UZBEKISTAN
STATUS: Republic
AREA: 447,400 sq km (172,695 sq miles)
POPULATION: 20,708,000
ANNUAL NATURAL INCREASE: 2.4%
CAPITAL: Tashkent
LANGUAGE: Uzbek, Russian, Turkish
RELIGION: Muslim
CURRENCY: som
ORGANIZATIONS: CIS, UN

Established in 1924 as a constituent republic of the Soviet Union, Uzbekistan became an independent state in 1991. The majority of the country consists of flat, sun-baked lowlands with mountains in the south and east. The climate is markedly continental and very dry with an abundance of sunshine and mild, short winters. The southern mountains are of great economic importance, providing ample supplies of water for hydro-electric plants and irrigation schemes. The mountain regions also contain substantial reserves of natural gas, oil, coal, iron and other metals. With its fertile soils (when irrigated) and good pastures, Uzbekistan is well situated for cattle raising and the production of cotton. It is also the largest producer of machines and heavy equipment in central Asia, and has been specializing mainly in machinery for cotton cultivation and harvesting, for irrigation projects, for road-building and textile processing. During the Soviet period the urban employment market became increasingly dominated by Russians and other outsiders. The gradual emergence of better educated and better trained Uzbeks has generated fiercely nationalist sentiments.

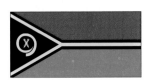

VANUATU
STATUS: Republic
AREA: 14,765 sq km (5,700 sq miles)
POPULATION: 154,000
ANNUAL NATURAL INCREASE: 2.4%
CAPITAL: Port-Vila
LANGUAGE: Bislama (national), English, French,
Melanesian languages
RELIGION: Christian
CURRENCY: vatu (VUV)
ORGANIZATIONS: Comm., UN

Vanuatu is a chain of some 80 densely forested, mountainous, volcanic islands, situated in the Melanesian south Pacific. Its climate is tropical, with a high rainfall and a continuous threat of cyclones. Copra, cocoa and coffee are grown mainly for export, with fish, pigs and sheep as well as yams, taro, manioc and bananas important only for home consumption. Manganese is the only mineral with deposits of economic value. Tourism is becoming important, particularly with Australian and Japanese visitors.

VATICAN CITY

STATUS: Ecclesiastical State
AREA: 0.44 sq km (0.17 sq miles)
POPULATION: 1,000
LANGUAGE: Italian, Latin
RELIGION: Roman Catholic
CURRENCY: Italian lira (ITL), Papal coinage
ORGANIZATIONS: none

The Vatican City, the headquarters of the Roman Catholic Church, is the world's smallest independent state. It is entirely surrounded by the city of Rome, occupying a hill to the west of the river Tiber. It has been the papal residence since the 5th century and a destination for pilgrims and tourists from all over the world. Most income is derived from voluntary contributions (Peter's Pence), tourism and interest on investments. The only industries are those connected with the Church.

VENEZUELA

STATUS: Republic
AREA: 912,045 sq km
(352,050 sq miles)
POPULATION: 20,410,000
ANNUAL NATURAL INCREASE: 2.5%
CAPITAL: Caracas
LANGUAGE: Spanish
RELIGION: Roman Catholic
CURRENCY: bolivar (VEB)
ORGANIZATIONS: OAS, OPEC, UN

Venezuela, one of the richest countries of Latin America, is divided into four topographical regions: the continuation of the Andes in the west; the humid lowlands around Lake Maracaibo in the north; the savannah-covered central plains (Llanos), and the extension of the Guiana Highlands covering almost half the country. The climate varies between tropical in the south to warm temperate along the northern coasts. The majority of the population live along the north coast. Venezuela's economy is built around oil production in the Maracaibo region; over three-quarters of export revenue comes from oil. Bauxite and iron ore are also important. The majority of employment is provided by industrial and manufacturing sectors of the economy.

VIETNAM

STATUS: Republic
AREA: 329,566 sq km (127,246 sq miles)
POPULATION: 69,306,000
ANNUAL NATURAL INCREASE: 2.3%
CAPITAL: Hanoi
LANGUAGE: Vietnamese, French, Chinese
RELIGION: Buddhist
CURRENCY: dong (VND)
ORGANIZATIONS: OIEC, UN

Situated on the eastern coast of the Indo-Chinese peninsula of southeastern Asia, Vietnam is predominantly a rugged, mountainous country. The north-south oriented mountainous spine separates two major river deltas: the Red River (Hong river) in the north and the Mekong in the south. Monsoons bring 1,500 mm (59 inches) of rain every year and temperatures average 15°C (59°F) annually. Rainforest still covers some of the central mountainous areas, but most has been cleared for agriculture and habitation. Rice is grown extensively throughout the north (Vietnam is the world's third largest exporter after the USA and Thailand) along with coffee and rubber in other parts of the country. Vietnam possesses a wide range of minerals including coal, lignite, anthracite, iron ore and tin. Industry is expanding rapidly, but decades of warfare and internal strife have impeded development. The US government has lifted its 20-year-old trade embargo, which will further help strengthen Vietnam's trade position.

VIRGIN ISLANDS (UK)

STATUS: UK Dependent Territory
AREA: 153 sq km (59 sq miles)
POPULATION: 16,749
CAPITAL: Road Town

VIRGIN ISLANDS (USA)

STATUS: External Territory of USA
AREA: 345 sq km (133 sq miles)
POPULATION: 101,809
CAPITAL: Charlotte Amalie

WALLIS & FUTUNA ISLANDS

STATUS: Self-governing Overseas
Territory of France
AREA: 274 sq km (106 sq miles)
POPULATION: 14,100
CAPITAL: Mata-Uta

WESTERN SAHARA

STATUS: Territory in dispute,
administered by Morocco
AREA: 266,000 sq km (102,675 sq miles)
POPULATION: 250,000
CAPITAL: Laayoune

WESTERN SAMOA

STATUS: Commonwealth State
AREA: 2,840 sq km (1,095 sq miles)
POPULATION: 170,000
ANNUAL NATURAL INCREASE: 0.5%
CAPITAL: Apia
LANGUAGE: English, Samoan
RELIGION: Christian
CURRENCY: tala (dollar) (WST)
ORGANIZATIONS: Comm., UN

Western Samoa constitutes a 160 km (100 mile) chain of nine south Pacific islands. The two largest islands, Savaii and Upolu, are mountainous and volcanic. Annual rainfall averages 2,500 mm (100 inches) per year and temperatures average 26°C (79°F) for most months. Only four of the islands are populated – Savaii, Upolu, Manono and Apolima. Main exports are copra, timber, coffee, cocoa and fruit. Western Samoa has some light industries, such as food processing, textiles and cigarette manufacture and a tourist trade is developing. Remittances from citizens abroad are, however, also very important to the economy.

YEMEN

STATUS: Republic
AREA: 527,970 sq km (328,065 sq miles)
POPULATION: 11,092,084
ANNUAL NATURAL INCREASE: 4.4%
CAPITAL: San'a (Şan'ā')
LANGUAGE: Arabic
RELIGION: Sunni and Shi'a Muslim
CURRENCY: Yemeni dinar and rial
ORGANIZATIONS: Arab League, UN

The Yemen Arab Republic and the People's Democratic Republic of Yemen were unified in 1990 to form a single state with its capital at San'a. Situated in the southern part of the Arabian Peninsula the country comprises several contrasting physical landscapes. The north is mainly mountainous and relatively wet with rainfall reaching 890 mm (35 inches) in inland areas which helps to irrigate the cereals, cotton, fruits and vegetables grown on the windward mountain sides and along the coast. The south coast stretches for 1,100 km (685 miles) from the mouth of the Red Sea to Oman. These southern regions are generally arid except along the coastal plain where irrigation schemes support some agriculture and away from the coast in the Hadhramaut valley where sufficient rainfall occurs for cereal cultivation. To the north of the Hadhramaut lies the uninhabited Arabian Desert. The population, most of whom are subsistence farmers or nomadic herders of sheep and goats, are concentrated in western regions. Until recently the only mineral exploited commercially was salt but since the discovery of oil in 1984 and 1991, that commodity is making an important contribution to the economy. Otherwise, industrial activity is limited to small scale manufacturing.

YUGOSLAVIA
Federal Republic of,

STATUS: Federation of former Yugoslav
Republics of Serbia and Montenegro

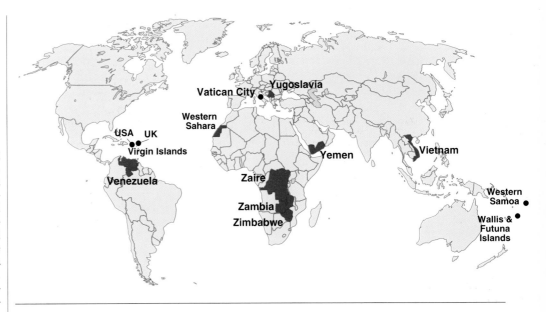

AREA: 102,170 sq km (39,435 sq miles)
POPULATION: 10,479,000
ANNUAL NATURAL INCREASE: 0.8%
CAPITAL: Belgrade (Beograd)
LANGUAGE: Serbo-Croat, Albanian
and Hungarian
RELIGION: Orthodox Christian, 10% Muslim
CURRENCY: new Yugoslav dinar (YUD)
ORGANIZATIONS: UN (suspended)

Serbia and Montenegro are the last remaining elements of the Federal Republic of Yugoslavia. Until 1918, they were separate kingdoms. Union of the two, including Vojvodina, followed by unification with lands freed from the Turkish and Austro-Hungarian Empires, resulted in the creation of the Kingdom of Serbs, Croats and Slovenes, a name which was changed to the Kingdom of Yugoslavia in 1929. Yugoslavia became a Socialist Federal Republic in 1945. Economic difficulties from 1980 onwards, combined with regional and ethnic factors, culminated in the secession of Slovenia and Croatia in 1992. International recognition of their sovereignty did not deter Serbia, with the Serb-dominated army at its disposal, from armed incursion to secure areas inhabited by Serbians. Macedonia's claim for recognition was not so well received internationally because of Greek objection to the name Macedonia. Yet, it has ceased to be a part of Yugoslavia. No such impediment stood in the way of recognizing the independence of Bosnia-Herzegovina. Armed conflict intensified in this ethnically complex republic as rival factions fought to support their kinsfolk.

The climate is essentially continental with hot summers and cold winters. Agriculture, which is largely in private hands, features cotton and cereal cultivation on the fertile plains of Vojvodina in the north, livestock production in central Serbia and fruit and tobacco growing in Kosovo in the south. Industry, however, which had accounted for 80 per cent of economic wealth, has suffered severely from the effects of civil war and United Nations sanctions. Inflation is rife and only the black market flourishes.

MONTENEGRO
STATUS: Constituent Republic
AREA: 13,810 sq km (5,330 sq miles)
POPULATION: 664,000
CAPITAL: Podgorica

SERBIA
STATUS: Constituent Republic
AREA: 88,360 sq km (34,105 sq miles)
POPULATION: 9,815,000
CAPITAL: Belgrade (Beograd)

ZAIRE
STATUS: Republic
AREA: 2,345,410 sq km (905,330 sq miles)
POPULATION: 39,882,000
ANNUAL NATURAL INCREASE: 3.3%
CAPITAL: Kinshasa
LANGUAGE: French, Lingala, Kiswahili,
Tshiluba, Kikongo

RELIGION: 46% Roman Catholic,
28% Protestant, traditional beliefs
CURRENCY: zaire (ZRZ)
ORGANIZATIONS: OAU, UN

Zaire, formerly the Belgian Congo, lies astride the Equator and is Africa's third largest country after Sudan and Algeria. It is dominated by the drainage basin of the Zaire, Kasai, and Oubangui rivers, which join to flow into the Atlantic. The land gradually rises from these basins to the south and east, culminating in the Chaine des Mitumba or Mitumbar mountains. On its eastern border the great Rift Valley forms a natural boundary with Uganda and Tanzania. Tropical rainforest covers most of the basin. Zaire's climate is equatorial with both high temperatures, averaging 27°C (80°F) throughout the year, and high rainfall of about 1,500–2,000 (59–79 inches). The majority of the population is engaged in shifting agriculture. Cassava, cocoa, coffee, cotton, millet, rubber and sugar cane are grown. Although the nation possesses mineral wealth, particularly copper which alone has provided 40 per cent of foreign earnings, political turmoil has reduced the country to bankruptcy. The copper mines are closed and diamonds are the only source of income. Zaire faces expulsion from the IMF because of debt arrears.

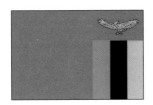

ZAMBIA
STATUS: Republic
AREA: 752,615 sq km (290,510 sq miles)
POPULATION: 8,638,000
ANNUAL NATURAL INCREASE: 3.5%
CAPITAL: Lusaka
LANGUAGE: English, African languages
RELIGION: 75% Christian, animist minority
CURRENCY: kwacha (ZMK)
ORGANIZATIONS: Comm., OAU, UN

Mineral-rich Zambia, is situated in the interior of southern central Africa. Its geography consists mainly of high rolling plateaux, with mountains to the north and northeast. In the south is the Zambezi river basin and the man-made reservoir of Lake Kariba, which forms Zambia's border with Zimbabwe. Altitude moderates the

potentially tropical climate so that the summer temperature averages only 13–27°C (55–81°F). The north receives over 1,250 mm (49 inches) of rain per annum, the south less. Most of the country is grassland with some forest in the north. Farming is now mainly at subsistence level, as droughts have had an adverse effect on many crops, but some cattle rearing still takes on importance in the east. Copper remains the mainstay of the country's economy although reserves are fast running out. Lead, zinc, cobalt, cotton, groundnuts and tobacco are also exported. Wildlife is diverse and abundant and contributes to expanding tourism.

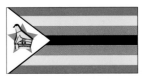

ZIMBABWE
STATUS: Republic
AREA: 390,310 sq km (150,660 sq miles)
POPULATION: 10,402,000
ANNUAL NATURAL INCREASE: 3.0%
CAPITAL: Harare
LANGUAGE: English, native languages
RELIGION: 58% Christian, traditional beliefs
CURRENCY: Zimbabwe dollar (ZWD)
ORGANIZATIONS: Comm., OAU, UN

Landlocked Zimbabwe (formerly southern Rhodesia) in south central Africa consists predominantly of rolling plateaux and valleys. A broad ridge of upland plateaux (the high veld) crosses east-west over the greater part of the country reaching heights of 1,200–1,500 m (3,940–4,920 feet). There are lowland areas (the low veld) formed by the valleys of the Zambezi and Limpopo rivers, in the north and south respectively. The climate varies with altitude and distance from the ocean. Rainfall across the country averages between 600-1,000 mm (24-39 inches). The exploitation of mineral deposits have traditionally supported the economy although recent years have seen a shift in the decline of chrome and coal and a rise in the importance of platinum, nickel and asbestos. Maize is the most important crop as it is the staple food of a large proportion of the population. Tobacco, tea, sugar cane and fruit are also grown. Manufacturing industry is slowly developing and now provides a wide range of consumer products.

North and Central America
25 349 000
9 785 000

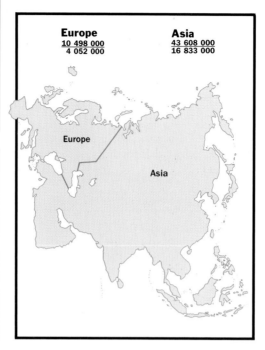

CONTINENTS

land area ▢ = **1 000 000** sq kms
386 000 sq miles

Europe
10 498 000
4 052 000

Asia
43 608 000
16 833 000

Europe

Asia

Africa
30 335 000
11 709 000

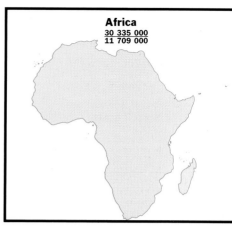

South America
17 611 000
6 798 000

Antarctica
13 340 000
5 149 240

Australasia
8 923 000
3 444 278

METROPOLITAN AREAS

Population	City	Country
2,500,000	Adibjan	Ivory Coast
1,891,000	Addis Ababa	Ethiopia
3,297,655	Ahmadabad	India
3,380,000	Alexandria	Egypt
3,033,000	Algiers	Algeria
1,151,300	Alma-Ata	Kazakhstan
1,091,338	Amsterdam	Netherlands
3,022,236	Ankara	Turkey
1,390,000	Anshan	China
3,096,775	Athens	Greece
3,051,000	Atlanta	USA
896,700	Auckland	New Zealand
4,044,000	Baghdad	Iraq
1,779,500	Baku	Azerbaijan
2,414,000	Baltimore	USA
4,086,548	Bangalore	India
5,876,000	Bangkok	Thailand
1,625,542	Barcelona	Spain
10,900,000	Beijing (Peking)	China
1,500,000	Beirut	Lebanon
1,168,454	Belgrade	Yugoslavia
3,461,905	Belo Horizonte	Brazil
3,446,000	Berlin	Germany
2,310,900	Birmingham	UK
5,025,989	Bogotá	Colombia
12,571,720	Bombay	India
4,497,000	Boston	USA
1,803,478	Brasília	Brazil
950,339	Brussels	Belgium
2,350,984	Bucharest	Romania
2,992,000	Budapest	Hungary
12,200,000	Buenos Aires	Argentina
13,300,000	Cairo	Egypt
10,916,000	Calcutta	India
320,000	Canberra	Australia
2,350,157	Cape Town	South Africa
4,092,000	Caracas	Venezuela
3,210,000	Casablanca	Morocco
2,214,000	Changchun	China
1,362,000	Changsha	China
1,148,000	Chelyabinsk	Russian Federation
3,004,000	Chengdu	China
7,498,000	Chicago	USA
3,010,000	Chongqing	China
1,342,679	Copenhagen	Denmark
2,543,000	Dalian	China
4,135,000	Dallas – Fort Worth	USA
2,913,000	Damascus	Syria
1,657,000	Dar-es-Salaam	Tanzania
8,375,000	Delhi	India
4,285,000	Detroit	USA
6,105,160	Dhaka	Bangladesh
915,516	Dublin	Republic of Ireland
2,720,400	Essen – Dortmund	Germany
1,420,000	Fushun	China
383,900	Geneva	Switzerland
2,846,720	Guadalajara	Mexico
3,620,000	Guangzhou (Canton)	China
1,669,000	Hamburg	Germany

Population	City	Country
1,412,000	Hangzhou	China
3,056,146	Hanoi	Vietnam
2,840,000	Harbin	China
2,099,000	Havana	Cuba
3,924,435	Ho Chi Minh (Saigon)	Vietnam
5,812,000	Hong Kong	UK colony
3,437,000	Houston	USA
4,280,000	Hyderabad	India
6,407,215	Istanbul	Turkey
9,000,000	Jakarta	Indonesia
608,000	Jerusalem	Israel
1,327,000	Jilin	China
2,415,000	Jinan	China
1,916,063	Johannesburg	South Africa
1,300,000	Kābul	Afghanistan
7,702,000	Karachi	Pakistan
1,947,000	Khartoum	Sudan
2,616,000	Kiev	Ukraine
3,505,000	Kinshasa	Zaire
1,711,000	Kuala Lumpur	Malaysia
5,689,000	Lagos	Nigeria
4,092,000	Lahore	Pakistan
1,566,000	Lanzhou	China
6,483,901	Lima	Peru
1,742,000	Lisbon	Portugal
9,277,687	London	UK
11,420,000	Los Angeles	USA
5,361,468	Madras	India
2,909,792	Madrid	Spain
2,578,900	Manchester	UK
8,475,000	Manila – Quezon City	Philippines
1,594,967	Medellín	Colombia
3,178,000	Melbourne	Australia
20,200,000	Mexico City	Mexico
1,814,000	Miami	USA
2,583,000	Minneapolis – St Paul	USA
1,633,000	Minsk	Belarus
2,521,697	Monterrey	Mexico
1,383,660	Montevideo	Uruguay
3,127,100	Montréal	Canada
8,957,000	Moscow	Russian Federation
1,236,000	Munich	Germany
2,095,000	Nagoya	Japan
1,503,000	Nairobi	Kenya
1,415,000	Nanchang	China
2,265,000	Nanjing	China
16,972,000	New York	USA
1,442,000	Novosibirsk	Russian Federation
1,106,000	Odessa	Ukraine
8,520,000	Osaka-Kobe	Japan
473,344	Oslo	Norway
921,000	Ottawa	Canada

Population	City	Country
9,318,000	Paris	France
4,941,000	Philadelphia	USA
2,287,000	Phoenix	USA
2,404,000	Pittsburgh	USA
3,015,960	Pôrto Alegre	Brazil
1,214,174	Prague	Czech Republic
3,797,566	Pusan	South Korea
2,230,000	Pyôngyang	North Korea
645,000	Quebec	Canada
2,060,000	Qingdao	China
1,281,849	Quito	Ecuador
3,295,000	Rangoon	Burma
2,859,469	Recife	Brazil
910,200	Riga	Latvia
9,871,165	Rio de Janeiro	Brazil
1,500,000	Riyadh	Saudi Arabia
2,723,327	Rome	Italy
1,388,000	Sacramento	USA
2,472,131	Salvador	Brazil
2,549,000	San Deigo	USA
5,240,000	San Francisco	USA
1,390,000	San Juan	Puerto Rico
4,628,000	Santiago	Chile
2,055,000	Santo Domingo	Dominican Repul
15,199,423	São Paulo	Brazil
10,627,000	Seoul	South Korea
13,341,896	Shanghai	China
4,763,000	Shenyang	China
2,874,000	Singapore	Singapore
1,221,000	Sofia	Bulgaria
2,507,000	St Louis	USA
5,004,000	St Petersburg	Russian Federati
1,669,840	Stockholm	Sweden
2,473,272	Surabaya	Indonesia
3,700,000	Sydney	Australia
2,228,000	Taegu	South Korea
2,720,000	Taipei	Taiwan
2,199,000	Taiyuan	China
452,000	Tallinn	Estonia
2,094,000	Tashkent	Uzbekistan
1,400,000	Tbilisi	Georgia
6,773,000	Tehran	Iran
1,135,800	Tel Aviv	Israel
9,100,000	Tianjin	China
11,609,735	Tokyo	Japan
3,893,400	Toronto	Canada
2,062,000	Tripoli	Libya
1,603,600	Vancouver	Canada
1,565,000	Vienna	Austria
593,000	Vilnius	Lithuania
1,655,700	Warsaw	Poland
4,293,000	Washington DC	USA
325,700	Wellington	New Zealand
652,000	Winnipeg	Canada
3,921,000	Wuhan	China
2,859,000	Xian	China
1,202,000	Yerevan	Armenia
726,770	Zagreb	Croatia
2,460,000	Zibo	China

MOUNTAIN HEIGHTS

metres	feet		
8,848	29,028	**Everest (Qomolangma Feng)**	*China–Nepal*
8,611	28,250	**K2 (Qogir Feng) (Godwin Austen)**	*India – China*
8,598	28,170	**Kangchenjunga**	*India–Nepal*
8,481	27,824	**Makalu**	*China–Nepal*
8,217	26,958	**Cho Oyu**	*China–Nepal*
8,167	26,795	**Dhaulagiri**	*Nepal*
8,156	26,758	**Manaslu**	*Nepal*
8,126	26,660	**Nanga Parbat**	*India*
8,078	26,502	**Annapurna**	*Nepal*
8,088	26,470	**Gasherbrum**	*India–China*
8,027	26,335	**Xixabangma Feng (Gosainthan)**	*China*
7,885	25,869	**Distaghil Sar**	*Kashmir, India*
7,820	25,656	**Masherbrum**	*India*
7,817	25,646	**Nanda Devi**	*India*
7,788	25,550	**Rakaposhi**	*India*
7,756	25,446	**Kamet**	*China–India*
7,756	25,447	**Namjagbarwa Feng**	*China*
7,728	25,355	**Gurla Mandhata**	*China*
7,723	25,338	**Muztag**	*China*
7,719	25,325	**Kongur Shan (Kungur)**	*China*
7,690	25,230	**Tirich Mir**	*Pakistan*
7,556	24,790	**Gongga Shan**	*China*
7,546	24,757	**Muztagata**	*China*
7,495	24,590	**Pik Kommunizma**	*Tajikistan*
7,439	24,406	**Pik Pobedy (Tomur Feng)**	*Kirghizia–China*
7,313	23,993	**Chomo Lhari**	*Bhutan–Tibet*
7,134	23,406	**Pik Lenina**	*Kirghizia*
6,960	22,834	**Aconcagua**	*Argentina*
6,908	22,664	**Ojos del Salado**	*Argentina–Chile*
6,872	22,546	**Bonete**	*Argentina*
6,800	22,310	**Tupungato**	*Argentina–Chile*
6,770	22,221	**Mercedario**	*Argentina*

metres	feet		
6,768	22,205	**Huascarán**	*Peru*
6,723	22,057	**Llullaillaco**	*Argentina–Chile*
6,714	22,027	**Kangrinboqê Feng (Kailas)**	*Tibet, China*
6,634	21,765	**Yerupaja**	*Peru*
6,542	21,463	**Sajama**	*Bolivia*
6,485	21,276	**Illampu**	*Bolivia*
6,425	21,079	**Coropuna**	*Peru*
6,402	21,004	**Illimani**	*Bolivia*
6,310	20,702	**Chimborazo**	*Ecuador*
6,194	20,320	**McKinley**	*USA*
5,959	19,551	**Logan**	*Canada*
5,896	19,344	**Cotopaxi**	*Ecuador*
5,895	19,340	**Kilimanjaro**	*Tanzania*
5,800	19,023	**Sa. Nevada de Sta. Marta (Cristobal Colon)**	*Columbia*
5,775	18,947	**Bolivar**	*Venezuela*
5,699	18,697	**Citlaltépetl (Orizaba)**	*Mexico*
5,642	18,510	**El'brus**	*Russian Federation*
5,601	18,376	**Damāvand**	*Iran*
5,489	18,008	**Mt St. Elias**	*Canada*
5,227	17,149	**Mt Lucania**	*Canada*
5,199	17,057	**Kenya (Kirinyaga)**	*Kenya*
5,165	16,945	**Ararat (Büyük Ağri Daği)**	*Turkey*
5,140	16,860	**Vinson Massif**	*Antarctica*
5,110	16,763	**Stanley (Margherita)**	*Uganda–Zaire*
5,029	16,499	**Jaya (Carstensz)**	*Indonesia*
5,005	16,421	**Mt Bona**	*USA*
4,949	16,237	**Sandford**	*USA*

metres	feet		
4,936	16,194	**Mt Blackburn**	*Canada*
4,808	15,774	**Mont Blanc**	*France–Italy*
4,750	15,584	**Klyuchevskaya Sopka**	*Russian Federation*
4,634	15,203	**Monte Rosa (Dufour)**	*Italy–Switzerland*
4,565	14,979	**Meru**	*Tanzania*
4,545	14,910	**Dom (Mischabel group)**	*Switzerland*
4,533	14,872	**Ras Dashen**	*Ethiopia*
4,528	14,855	**Kirkpatrick**	*Antarctica*
4,508	14,790	**Wilhelm**	*Papua, New Guinea*
4,507	14,786	**Karisimbi**	*Rwanda–Zaire*
4,477	14,688	**Matterhorn**	*Italy–Switzerland*
4,418	14,495	**Whitney**	*USA*
4,398	14,431	**Elbert**	*USA*
4,392	14,410	**Rainier**	*USA*
4,351	14,275	**Markham**	*Antarctica*
4,321	14,178	**Elgon**	*Kenya–Uganda*
4,307	14,131	**Batu**	*Ethiopia*
4,169	13,677	**Mauna Loa**	*USA, Hawaii*
4,165	13,644	**Toubkal**	*Morocco*
4,095	13,435	**Cameroon (Caméroun)**	*Cameroon*
4,094	13,431	**Kinabalu**	*Malaysia*
3,794	12,447	**Erebus**	*Antarctica*
3,776	12,388	**Fuji**	*Japan*
3,754	12,316	**Cook**	*New Zealand*
3,718	12,198	**Teide**	*Canary Is*
3,482	11,424	**Thabana Ntlenyana**	*Lesotho*
3,482	11,424	**Mulhacén**	*Spain*
3,415	11,204	**Emi Koussi**	*Chad*
3,323	10,902	**Etna**	*Italy, Sicily*
2,743	9,000	**Mt Balbi**	*Bougainville, Papua New Guinea*
2,655	8,708	**Gerlachovsky stit (Tatra)**	*Czech Republic*
2,230	7,316	**Kosciusko**	*Australia*

ISLANDS

land area ▢ = 10 000 sq kms / 3 860 sq miles

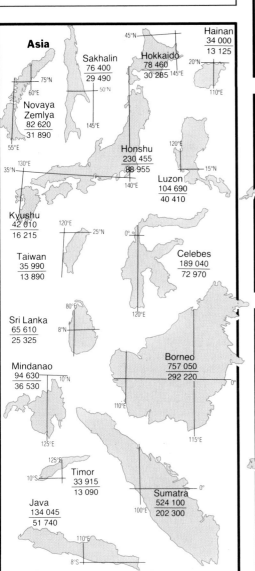

Asia

Sakhalin 76 400 / 29 490
Hokkaido 78 460 / 30 285
Hainan 34 000 / 13 125
Novaya Zemlya 82 620 / 31 890
Honshu 230 455 / 88 955
Luzon 104 690 / 40 410
Kyushu 42 010 / 16 215
Taiwan 35 990 / 13 890
Celebes 189 040 / 72 970
Sri Lanka 65 610 / 25 325
Borneo 757 050 / 292 220
Mindanao 94 630 / 36 530
Timor 33 915 / 13 090
Sumatra 524 100 / 202 300
Java 134 045 / 51 740

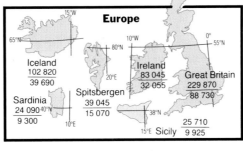

Europe

Iceland 102 820 / 39 690
Ireland 83 045 / 32 055
Great Britain 229 870 / 88 730
Sardinia 24 090 / 9 300
Spitsbergen 39 045 / 15 070
Sicily 25 710 / 9 925

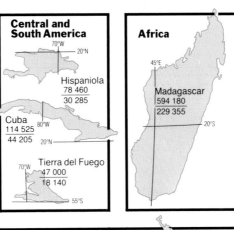

Central and South America

Hispaniola 78 460 / 30 285
Cuba 114 525 / 44 205
Tierra del Fuego 47 000 / 18 140

Africa

Madagascar 594 180 / 229 355

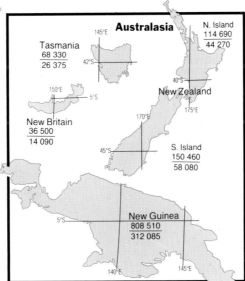

Australasia

Tasmania 68 330 / 26 375
N. Island 114 690 / 44 270
New Zealand
New Britain 36 500 / 14 090
S. Island 150 460 / 58 080
New Guinea 808 510 / 312 085

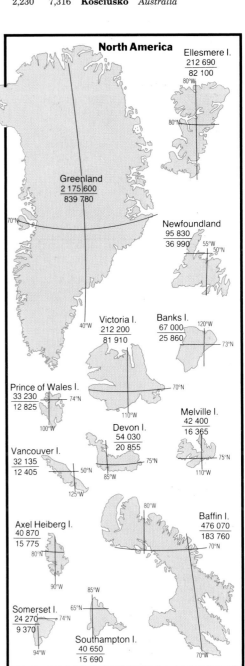

North America

Ellesmere I. 212 690 / 82 100
Greenland 2 175 600 / 839 780
Newfoundland 95 830 / 36 990
Victoria I. 212 200 / 81 910
Banks I. 67 000 / 25 860
Prince of Wales I. 33 230 / 12 825
Devon I. 54 030 / 20 855
Melville I. 42 400 / 16 365
Vancouver I. 32 135 / 12 405
Axel Heiberg I. 40 870 / 15 775
Baffin I. 476 070 / 183 760
Somerset I. 24 270 / 9 370
Southampton I. 40 650 / 15 690

OCEANS AND SEAS

water area ▣ = $\dfrac{1\,000\,000\quad \text{sq km}}{386\,000\quad \text{sq miles}}$

OCEAN FACTS AND FIGURES

The area of the Earth covered by sea is estimated to be 361,740,000 sq km (139,670,000 sq miles), or 70.92% of the total surface. The mean depth is estimated to be 3554 m (11,660 ft), and the volume of the oceans to be 1,285,600,000 cu. km (308,400,000 cu. miles).

INDIAN OCEAN

Mainly confined to the southern hemisphere, and at its greatest breadth (Tasmania to Cape Agulhas) 9600 km. Average depth is 4000 m; greatest depth is the Amirante Trench (9000 m).

ATLANTIC OCEAN

Commonly divided into North Atlantic (36,000,000 sq km) and South Atlantic (26,000,000 sq km). The greatest breadth in the North is 7200 km (Morocco to Florida) and in the South 9600 km (Guinea to Brazil). Average depth is 3600 m; the greatest depths are the Puerto Rico Trench 9220 m, S. Sandwich Trench 8264 m, and Romansh Trench 7728 m.

PACIFIC OCEAN

Covers nearly 40% of the world's total sea area, and is the largest of the oceans. The greatest breadth (E/W) is 16,000 km and the greatest length (N/S) 11,000 km. Average depth is 4200 m; also the deepest ocean. Generally the west is deeper than the east and the north deeper than the south. Greatest depths occur near island groups and include Mindanao Trench 11,524 m, Mariana Trench 11,022 m, Tonga Trench 10,882 m, Kuril-Kamchatka Trench 10,542 m, Philippine Trench 10,497 m, and Kermadec Trench 10,047 m.

Comparisons (where applicable)	greatest distance N/S (km)	greatest distance E/W (km)	maximum depth (m)
Indian Ocean	—	9600	9000
Atlantic Ocean	—	9600	9220
Pacific Ocean	11,000	16,000	11,524
Arctic Ocean	—	—	5450
Mediterranean Sea	960	3700	4846
S. China Sea	2100	1750	5514
Bering Sea	1800	2100	5121
Caribbean Sea	1600	2000	7100
Gulf of Mexico	1200	1700	4377
Sea of Okhotsk	2200	1400	3475
E. China Sea	1100	750	2999
Yellow Sea	800	1000	91
Hudson Bay	1250	1050	259
Sea of Japan	1500	1100	3743
North Sea	1200	550	661
Red Sea	1932	360	2246
Black Sea	600	1100	2245
Baltic Sea	1500	650	460

EARTH'S SURFACE WATERS

Total volume	c.1400 million cu. km
Oceans and seas	1370 million cu. km
Ice	24 million cu. km
Interstitial water (in rocks and sediments)	4 million cu. km
Lakes and rivers	230 thousand cu. km
Atmosphere (vapour)	c.140 thousand cu. km

to convert metric to imperial measurements:
1 m = 3.281 feet
1 km = 0.621 miles
1 sq km = 0.386 sq miles

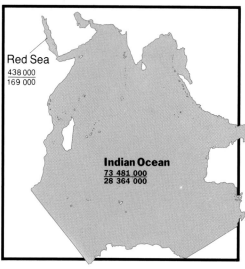

Red Sea
438 000
169 000

Indian Ocean
73 481 000
28 364 000

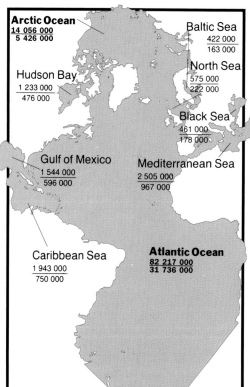

Arctic Ocean
14 056 000
5 426 000

Baltic Sea
422 000
163 000

Hudson Bay
1 233 000
476 000

North Sea
575 000
222 000

Black Sea
461 000
178 000

Gulf of Mexico
1 544 000
596 000

Mediterranean Sea
2 505 000
967 000

Caribbean Sea
1 943 000
750 000

Atlantic Ocean
82 217 000
31 736 000

FEATURES OF THE OCEAN BASIN

The majority of land drainage occurs in the Atlantic, yet this is the most saline ocean due to interchange of waters with its marginal seas. The continental margins (21% of ocean floors) are the most important economic areas.

	PACIFIC	ATLANTIC	INDIAN	WORLD
AVERAGE OCEAN DEPTH (metres)				
OCEAN AREA (million sq km)	180	107	74	361
LAND AREA DRAINED (million sq km)	19	69	13	101
AREA AS PERCENTAGE OF TOTAL				
Continental margin	15.8	27.9	14.8	20.6
Ridges, rises and fracture zones	38.4	33.3	35.6	35.8
Deep ocean floor	42.9	38.1	49.3	41.9
Island arcs and trenches	2.9	0.7	0.3	1.7

AVERAGE OCEAN DEPTH (metres)
3000
3500
4000

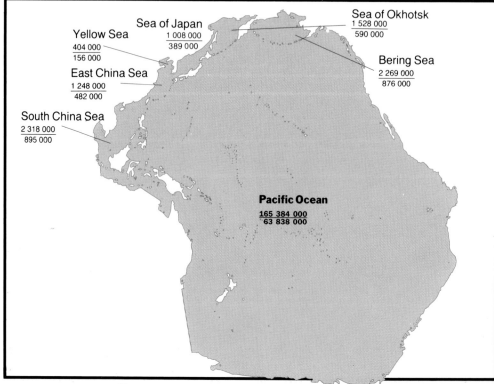

Sea of Japan
1 008 000
389 000

Sea of Okhotsk
1 528 000
590 000

Yellow Sea
404 000
156 000

Bering Sea
2 269 000
876 000

East China Sea
1 248 000
482 000

South China Sea
2 318 000
895 000

Pacific Ocean
165 384 000
63 838 000

RIVER LENGTHS

km	miles		
6,695	4,160	**Nile**	*Africa*
6,515	4,050	**Amazon**	*South America*
6,380	3,965	**Yangtze (Chang Jiang)**	*Asia*
6,019	3,740	**Mississippi-Missouri**	*North America*
5,570	3,460	**Ob'-Irtysh**	*Asia*
5,550	3,450	**Yenisei-Angara**	*Asia*
5,464	3,395	**Yellow River (Huang He)**	*Asia*
4,667	2,900	**Congo (Zaire)**	*Africa*
4,500	2,800	**Paraná**	*South America*
4,440	2,775	**Irtysh**	*Asia*
4,425	2,750	**Mekong**	*Asia*
4,416	2,744	**Amur**	*Asia*
4,400	2,730	**Lena**	*Asia*
4,250	2,640	**Mackenzie**	*North America*
4,090	2,556	**Yenisei**	*Asia*
4,030	2,505	**Niger**	*Africa*
3,969	2,466	**Missouri**	*North America*
3,779	2,348	**Mississippi**	*North America*
3,750	2,330	**Murray-Darling**	*Australasia*
3,688	2,290	**Volga**	*Europe*
3,218	2,011	**Purus**	*South America*
3,200	1,990	**Madeira**	*South America*
3,185	1,980	**Yukon**	*North America*
3,180	1,975	**Indus**	*Asia*
3,078	1,913	**Syrdar'ya**	*Asia*
3,060	1,901	**Salween**	*Asia*
3,058	1,900	**St Lawrence**	*North America*
2,900	1,800	**São Francisco**	*South America*
2,870	1,785	**Rio Grande**	*North America*
2,850	1,770	**Danube**	*Europe*
2,840	1,765	**Brahmaputra**	*Asia*
2,815	1,750	**Euphrates**	*Asia*
2,750	1,710	**Pará-Tocantins**	*South America*
2,750	1,718	**Tarim**	*Asia*
2,650	1,650	**Zambezi**	*Africa*
2,620	1,630	**Amudar'ya**	*Asia*
2,620	1,630	**Araguaia**	*South America*
2,600	1,615	**Paraguay**	*South America*
2,570	1,600	**Nelson-Saskatchewan**	*North America*

RIVER LENGTHS & DRAINAGE BASINS

km	miles		
2,534	1,575	**Ural**	*Asia*
2,513	1,562	**Kolyma**	*Asia*
2,510	1,560	**Ganges (Ganga)**	*Asia*
2,500	1,555	**Orinoco**	*South America*
2,490	1,550	**Shabeelle**	*Africa*
2,490	1,550	**Pilcomayo**	*South America*
2,348	1,459	**Arkansas**	*North America*
2,333	1,450	**Colorado**	*North America*
2,285	1,420	**Dneper**	*Europe*
2,250	1,400	**Columbia**	*North America*
2,150	1,335	**Irrawaddy**	*Asia*
2,129	1,323	**Pearl River (Xi Jiang)**	*Asia*
2,032	1,270	**Kama**	*Europe*
2,000	1,240	**Negro**	*South America*
1,923	1,195	**Peace**	*North America*
1,899	1,186	**Tigris**	*Asia*
1,870	1,162	**Don**	*Europe*
1,860	1,155	**Orange**	*Africa*
1,809	1,124	**Pechora**	*Europe*
1,800	1,125	**Okavango**	*Africa*
1,609	1,000	**Marañón**	*South America*
1,609	1,095	**Uruguay**	*South America*
1,600	1,000	**Volta**	*Africa*
1,600	1,000	**Limpopo**	*Africa*
1,550	963	**Magdalena**	*South America*
1,515	946	**Kura**	*Asia*
1,480	925	**Oka**	*Europe*
1,480	925	**Belaya**	*Europe*
1,445	903	**Godavari**	*Asia*
1,430	893	**Senegal**	*Africa*
1,410	876	**Dnester**	*Europe*
1,400	875	**Chari**	*Africa*
1,368	850	**Fraser**	*North America*
1,320	820	**Rhine**	*Europe*
1,314	821	**Vyatka**	*Europe*
1,183	735	**Donets**	*Europe*
1,159	720	**Elbe**	*Europe*
1,151	719	**Kizilirmak**	*Asia*

km	miles		
1,130	706	**Desna**	*Europe*
1,094	680	**Gambia**	*Africa*
1,080	675	**Yellowstone**	*North America*
1,049	652	**Tennessee**	*North America*
1,024	640	**Zelenga**	*Asia*
1,020	637	**Duena**	*Europe*
1,014	630	**Vistula (Wisła)**	*Europe*
1,012	629	**Loire**	*Europe*
1,006	625	**Tagus (Tejo)**	*Europe*
977	607	**Tisza**	*Europe*
925	575	**Meuse (Maas)**	*Europe*
909	565	**Oder**	*Europe*
761	473	**Seine**	*Europe*
354	220	**Severn**	*Europe*
346	215	**Thames**	*Europe*
300	186	**Trent**	*Europe*

DRAINAGE BASINS

sq km	sq miles		
7,050,000	2,721,000	**Amazon**	*South America*
3,700,000	1,428,000	**Congo**	*Africa*
3,250,000	1,255,000	**Mississippi-Missouri**	*North America*
3,100,000	1,197,000	**Paraná**	*South America*
2,700,000	1,042,000	**Yenisei**	*Asia*
2,430,000	938,000	**Ob'**	*Asia*
2,420,000	934,000	**Lena**	*Asia*
1,900,000	733,400	**Nile**	*Africa*
1,840,000	710,000	**Amur**	*Asia*
1,765,000	681,000	**Mackenzie**	*North America*
1,730,000	668,000	**Ganges-Brahmaputra**	*Asia*
1,380,000	533,000	**Volga**	*Europe*
1,330,000	513,000	**Zambezi**	*Africa*
1,200,000	463,000	**Niger**	*Africa*
1,175,000	454,000	**Yangtze**	*Asia*
1,020,000	394,000	**Orange**	*Africa*
980,000	378,000	**Yellow River**	*Asia*
960,000	371,000	**Indus**	*Asia*
945,000	365,000	**Orinoco**	*South America*
910,000	351,000	**Murray-Darling**	*Australasia*
855,000	330,000	**Yukon**	*North America*
815,000	315,000	**Danube**	*Europe*
810,000	313,000	**Mekong**	*Asia*
225,000	86,900	**Rhine**	*Europe*

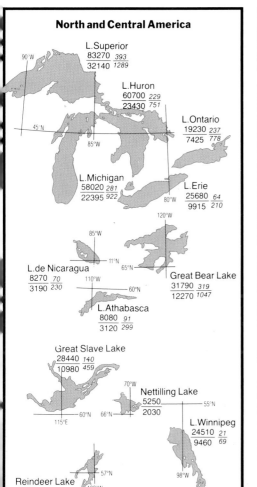

North and Central America

L.Superior 83270 *393* / 32140 *1289*

L.Huron 60700 *229* / 23430 *751*

L.Ontario 19230 *237* / 7425 *778*

L.Michigan 58020 *281* / 22395 *922*

L.Erie 25680 *64* / 9915 *210*

L.de Nicaragua 8270 *70* / 3190 *230*

Great Bear Lake 31790 *319* / 12270 *1047*

L.Athabasca 8080 *91* / 3120 *299*

Great Slave Lake 28440 *140* / 10980 *459*

Nettilling Lake 5250 / 2030

L.Winnipeg 24510 *21* / 9460 *69*

Reindeer Lake 6390 / 2470

INLAND WATERS

water surface area ☐ = 1 000 sq km / 386 sq miles

deepest point 229 metres / 751 feet

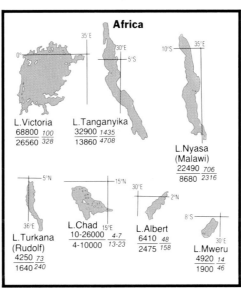

Africa

L.Victoria 68800 *100* / 26560 *328*

L.Tanganyika 32900 *1435* / 13860 *4708*

L.Nyasa (Malawi) 22490 *706* / 8680 *2316*

L.Turkana (Rudolf) 4250 *73* / 1640 *240*

L.Chad 10-26000 *4-7* / 4-10000 *13-23*

L.Albert 6410 *48* / 2475 *158*

L.Mweru 4920 *14* / 1900 *46*

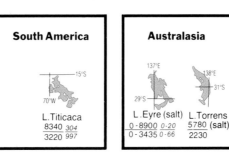

South America

L.Titicaca 8340 *304* / 3220 *997*

Australasia

L.Eyre (salt) 0 - 8900 *0-20* / 0 - 3435 *0-66*

L.Torrens 5780 (salt) / 2230

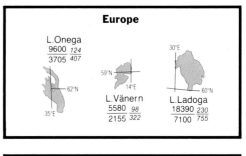

Europe

L.Onega 9600 *124* / 3705 *407*

L.Vänern 5580 *98* / 2155 *322*

L.Ladoga 18390 *230* / 7100 *755*

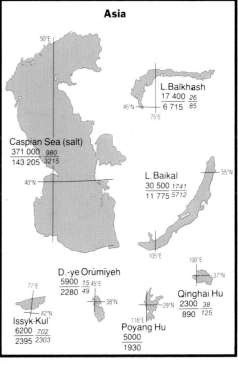

Asia

Caspian Sea (salt) 371 000 *980* / 143 205 *3215*

L.Balkhash 17 400 *26* / 6 715 *85*

L.Baikal 30 500 *1741* / 11 775 *5712*

D.-ye Orūmiyeh 5900 *15* / 2280 *49*

Issyk-Kul 6200 *702* / 2395 *2303*

Poyang Hu 5000 / 1930

Qinghai Hu 2300 *38* / 890 *125*

SIBERIA

Kolyu

Lena

Honshu

Sakhalin

Laptev
Sea

New Siberian
Islands

ARCTIC

Hokkaido

Kurii Islands

Sea of Okhotsk

Kolyma

East
Siberian
Sea

OCEAN

Kamchatka

Anadyr

Wrangel
Island

Chukchi
Sea

Bering

Sea

Chukotskiy
Peninsula

Bering Strait

Point Barrow

Brooks Range

Beaufort
Sea

Mely
Islan

Aleutian Islands

Yukon

Banks
Island

Victo

Alaska Range
Mount
McKinley

Mackenzie Mountains

Mackenzie

Great
Bear
Lake

Aleutian Range

Kodiak Island

Gulf
of
Alaska

Coast Mountains

ROCKY

Great
Slave Lake

NORTH

Midway Islands

Lake
Athabas

Queen
Charlotte
Islands

Peace

Athabasca

PACIFIC

Hawaiian Islands

Vancouver
Island

Fraser

Mountains

Saskatchew

Mount Rainier
Mount St Helens

Cascade Ranges

Columbia

OCEAN

Coast Ranges

Sierra Nevada

Snake

Great Salt
Lake

Mount
Whitney

Colorado

Gulf of California

Sierra Madre Occidental

Lower California

48

A

Ob'

Urals

Black Sea

Kara
Sea

Novaya
Zemlya

Barents
Sea

SCANDINAVIA

Baltic Sea

vernaya
Zemlya

North Cape

Franz
Josef
Land

Bear
Island

Norwegian
Sea

North
Sea

Mediterranean Sea

Svalbard

Jan Mayen

BRITISH
ISLES

NORTH AFRICA

Limit of permanent pack ice

NORTH POLE

Wandell
Sea

Greenland Sea

Bay
of
Biscay

Lincoln
Sea

Denmark Strait

Iceland

Ellesmere
Island

Greenland

Madeira

Axel
Heiburg
Island

NORTH

Canary
Islands

Queen
Elizabeth
Islands

rry Islands

Devon
Island

Baffin Bay

Davis Strait

Azores

Prince of
Wales Island

Somerset
Island

nd

Baffin Island

Nettiling
Lake

Labrador
Sea

Foxe

Basin

Southampton
Island

Hudson Strait

Cape Chidley

Cape Farewell

Hudson
Bay

Labrador

Reindeer
Lake

Churchill

Churchill

Southern
Indian
Lake

Nelson

La Grande Rivière

Laurentian
Highlands

Newfoundland

Cape Race

ATLANTIC

James
Bay

Rupert

Lake
Winnipeg

Nova
Scotia

Lake
Manitoba

Lake
of the
Woods

Lake Superior

St. Lawrence

Lake
Huron

Lake Ontario

Cape Cod

Missouri

Mississippi

Lake Michigan

Lake Erie

Mountains

Great

Ohio

Appalachian

Bermuda

OCEAN

Plains

Cape Hatteras

platte

Ozark
Plateaus

Tennessee

Arkansas

Mississippi

Savannah

Red River

Florida

The
Bahamas

Rio Grande

Gulf of Mexico

West Indies

Sierra

Madre
Oriental

Yucatan

Caribbean Sea

Orinoco

Florida

GULF
OF
MEXICO

W
C

G R E

Gulf of Campeche

Y
u
c
a
t
a
n

Gulf
of
Honduras

Sierra Madre Occidental

Sierra Madre Oriental

Gulf of California

Lower California

Rio Grande

Mississippi

Popocatépetl

Sierra Madre del Sur

Islas Revillagigedo

Lake
Nicaragua

Isthmus

G
o
Pana

Clipperton
Island

P A C I F I C

Isla del Coco

Isla de Malpelo

Cotop

Chimborazo

Galapagos Islands

O C E A N

Bermuda

NORTH

BAHAMAS

ATLANTIC

Sargasso
Sea

W E S T   I N D I E S

OCEAN

Hispaniola

Puerto
Rico

Gulf
of
Darien

CARIBBEAN

SEA

LESSER   ANTILLES

Trinidad

Lake
Maracaibo

Cordillera Occidental

Cauca

Magdalena

Cordillera Oriental

L L A N O S

Orinoco

Guiana   Highlands

Roraima▲

Branco

Mouths
of the
Amazon

Negro

Japurá

Amazon

Putumayo

Amazon

Marañón

Juruá

Purus

Madeira

Tapajós

Xingu

Tocantins

Ucayali

Madre de Dios

MATO

GROSSO

Araguaia

Tocantins

Parnaíba

São Francisco

A N D E S

Lake
Titicaca

Ancohuma▲

Lake
Poopó

Brazilian   Highlands

Salar
de
Uyuni

GRAN   CHACO

Paraguay

Paraná

Atacama Desert

Pilcomayo

Galapagos Islands

Gran Chaco

Bermejo

Uruguay

San Félix   San Ambrosio

Aconcagua

Salado

Paraná

Plate

N

Colorado

Negro

Juan Fernández

S O U T H

D

Chubut

E

Chico

S

Patagonia

Deseado

Falkland
Islands

Sala y Gomez

Tierra del
Fuego

Easter Island

Cape Horn

Drake   Passage

P A C I F I C

Elephant Island

South
Shetland
Islands

King
George I.

Ducie Island

Graham Land

Henderson Island

Palmer Land

ANTARCTIC PENINSULA

Pitcairn Island

Peter I Island

Bellingshausen

Sea

O C E A N

Ro

Rapa

Ellsworth
Land

A N T

Amundsen
Sea

Lesser
Antarctica

Marie   Byrd
Land

Rockefeller
Plateau

Ross
Ice
Shelf

R o s s

Mount Erebus

S e a

Scott Island

Oates
Land

Chatham
Islands

Balleny Islands

Bounty
Islands   Antipodes

New
Zealand   Campbell Island

INDIA

St Helena

S O U T H

Tristan da Cunha

Gough Island

Cunene

Kalahari
Desert

Orange River

South Georgia

A T L A N T I C

Cape
of
Good Hope

South
Sandwich
Islands

South Orkney
Islands

Bouvet Island

Limpopo

Madagascar

Weddell

Sea

Lazarev
Sea

Prince Edward
Islands

Limit of permanent pack ice

O C E A N

Shelf

Queen Maud Land

R C T I C A

Îles Crozet

SOUTH POLE

Antarctica

Greater

Enderby Land

Îles Kerguelen

Macdonald Islands
Heard Island

St Paul
Amsterdam Island

orge V
and

Wilkes Land

OCEAN

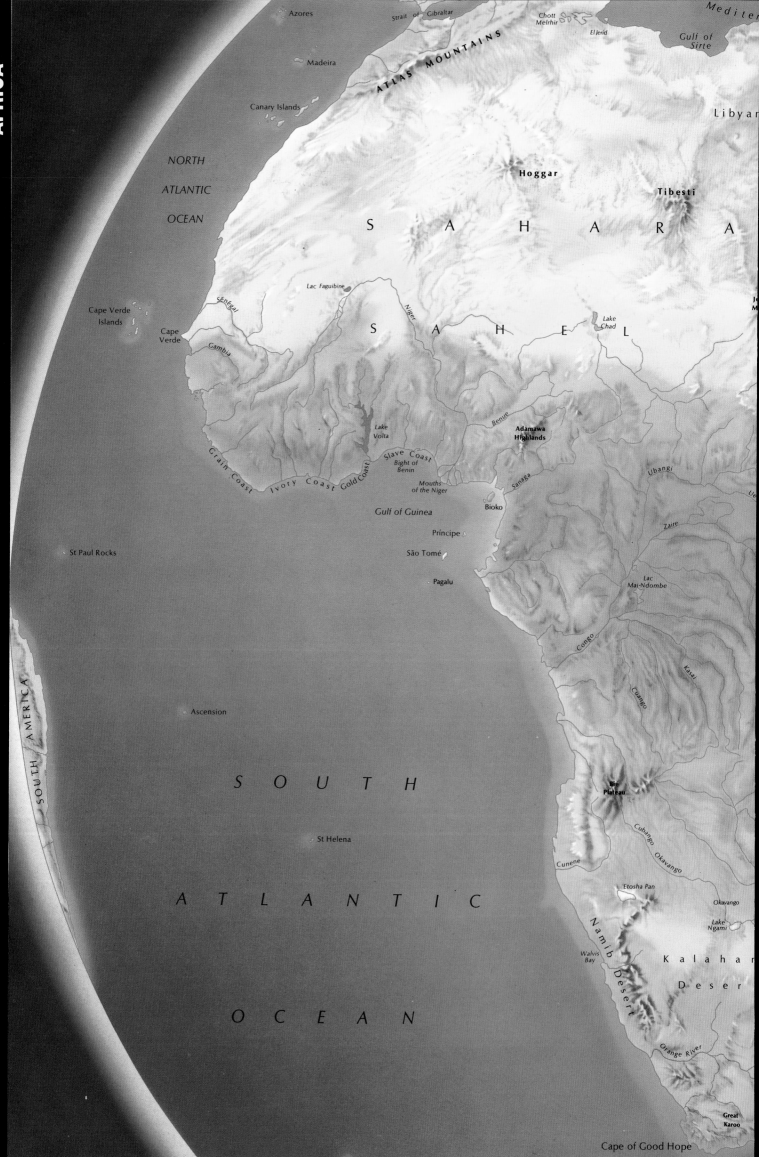

Azores

Strait of Gibraltar

Chott
Melrhir

El Jerid

Gulf of
Sirte

Mediter

Madeira

ATLAS MOUNTAINS

Libyar

Canary Islands

Hoggar

Tibesti

NORTH

ATLANTIC

OCEAN

S   A   H   A   R   A

J-
M

Lac Faguibine

Sénégal

Niger

S   A   H   E   L

Lake
Chad

Cape Verde
Islands

Cape
Verde

Gambia

Lake
Volta

Benue

**Adamawa
Highlands**

Ubangi

Uc

Grain Coast

Slave Coast

Bight of
Benin

Sanaga

Ivory Coast Gold Coast

Mouths
of the Niger

Zaire

Gulf of Guinea

Bioko

St Paul Rocks

Príncipe

São Tomé

Lac
Mai-Ndombe

Pagalu

Congo

Kasai

Ascension

Cuango

SOUTH AMERICA

S   O   U   T   H

Bie
Plateau

St Helena

Cubango Okavango

Cunene

A   T   L   A   N   T   I   C

Etosha Pan

Okavango

Lake
Ngami

Namib Desert

Walvis
Bay

K a l a h a r

O   C   E   A   N

D e s e r

Orange River

Great
Karoo

Cape of Good Hope

Cyprus

Daryācheh-ye-Namak

Hindu Kush

Karakoram

an Sea

Euphrates
Tigris

Zagros Mountains

Plateau
of
Iran

HIMALAYAS

Plateau
of
Tibet

Nile
Delta

Dead
Sea

Helmand

Qattāra
Depression

Sinai

Gulf of
Suez

Gulf of
Aqaba

Persian Gulf

Makran

Indus

Thar
Desert

Brahmaputra

ARABIAN

R
E
D

S
E
A

Al Liwá'

Gulf of Oman

Ganges
(Ganga)

The
Great
Oasis
Lake
Nasser

Nile

Desert

Umm
as Samim

Maṣirah

Narmada

Nubian Desert

PENINSULA

ARABIAN

Deccan

Godavari

AR RUB AL KHĀLÍ

SEA

Krishna

Hadhramaut

Bāb el Mandeb

Lake
Tana

Danakil
Desert

Gulf of Aden

Socotra

Socotra

Laccadive
Islands

Ethiopian
Plateau

White Nile

Blue Nile

Ogaden

Ceylon

Deccan

White Nile

Shabeelle

Maldive Islands

Lake
Turkana

Juba

Lake
Albert

Lake
Kyoga

INDIAN

Mt Stanley

Mount Kenya
Tana

Lake
Edward

Lake
Victoria

Lake
Kivu

Seychelles

Lake
Eyasi

Lake
Natron

Kilimanjaro

Amirante Islands

Chagos
Archipelago

Pemba Island

Lake
Tanganyika

Zanzibar

Coëtivy Island

Mafia Island

Lake
Rukwa

emba

Lake
Mweru

Aldabra
Islands

Providence Islands

Agalega Islands

Lake
Bangweulu

Lake
Nyasa

Comoro Islands

O C E A N

Lake
Chilwa

Zambezi

Rift Valley

Mozambique Channel

Madagascar

Tromelin

Lake
Kariba

Rodrigues

adikgadi
Pan

Réunion

Mauritius

Limpopo

Vaal

Drakensberg

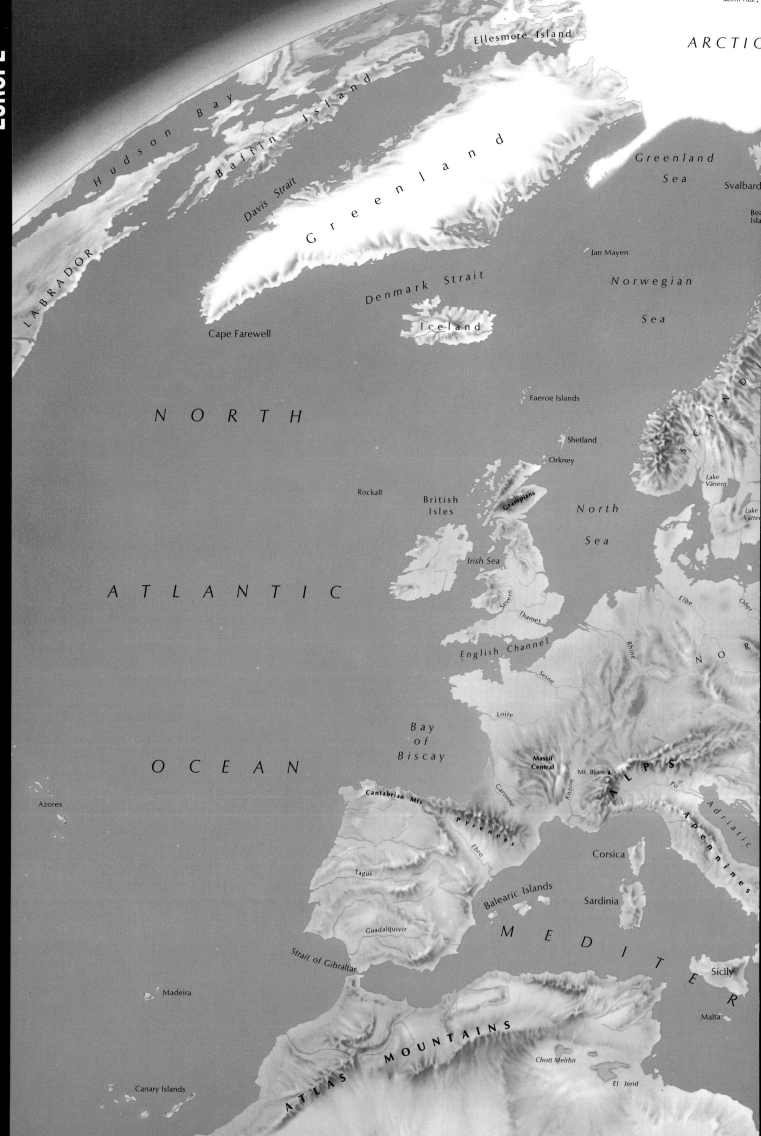

NORTH POLE

ARCTIC

Ellesmere Island

Hudson Bay

Baffin Island

Davis Strait

Greenland

Greenland
Sea

Svalbard

LABRADOR

Jan Mayen

Denmark Strait

Norwegian

Cape Farewell

Iceland

Sea

Bear
Isla

Faeroe Islands

NORTH

Shetland

Orkney

Rockall

British
Isles

Grampians

North

Sea

SCANDI

Lake
Vänern

Lake
Vätter

ATLANTIC

Irish Sea

Severn

Thames

Rhine

Elbe

Oder

English Channel

Seine

N O R

Loire

OCEAN

Bay
of
Biscay

Massif
Central

Mt. Blanc

ALPS

Po

Adriatic

Azores

Cantabrian Mts

Garonne

Rhône

Apennines

Pyrenees

Ebro

Corsica

Tagus

Balearic Islands

Sardinia

Guadalquivir

M E D I T E R

Strait of Gibraltar

Sicily

Madeira

Malta

ATLAS MOUNTAINS

Chott Melrhir

Canary Islands

El Jerid

CEAN

Severnaya
Zemlya

Limit of permanent pack ice

Franz
Josef
Land

Kara
Sea

bergen

Novaya
Zemlya

Barents
Sea

n Cape

White
Sea

Pechora

URAL MOUNTAINS

WEST SIBERIAN PLAIN

Lena

CENTRAL SIBERIAN PLATEAU

Nizhnyaya Tunguska

Lena

Yenisey

Ob'

Ob'

Angara

Lake
Baikal

Irtysh

Bothnia

Lake
Onega

Severnaya Dvina

Lake
Ladoga

Gulf of Finland

Volga

KIRGHIZ STEPPE

Lake
Balkhash

Sea

Dvina

E U R O P E A N P L A I N

Central

Russian

Uplands

Ural

Kyzylkum

Aral
Sea

Syrdar'ya

Dnieper

Volga

CARPATHIANS

Dniester

Don

Amudar'ya

garian Plain

Tisza

Sea of Azov

Caspian Sea

Karakumy

Caucasus

Balkan Mountains

Danube

Black   Sea

Rhodope

Thtace

Bosporus

Araxes

Pindus

Sea of
Marmara

Dardanelles

Aegean

Sea

ASIA MINOR

Kizil Irmak

Tuz
Gölü

Taurus

Lake
Van

Lake
Urmia

Elbruz Mts

Daryācheh-ye-Namak

Zagros Mountains

Plateau
of
Iran

Cyprus

Crete

Mesopotamia

Tigris

Euphrates

A N S E A

Jordan

Syrian Desert

Dead Sea

Persian Gulf

Gulf
of
Oman

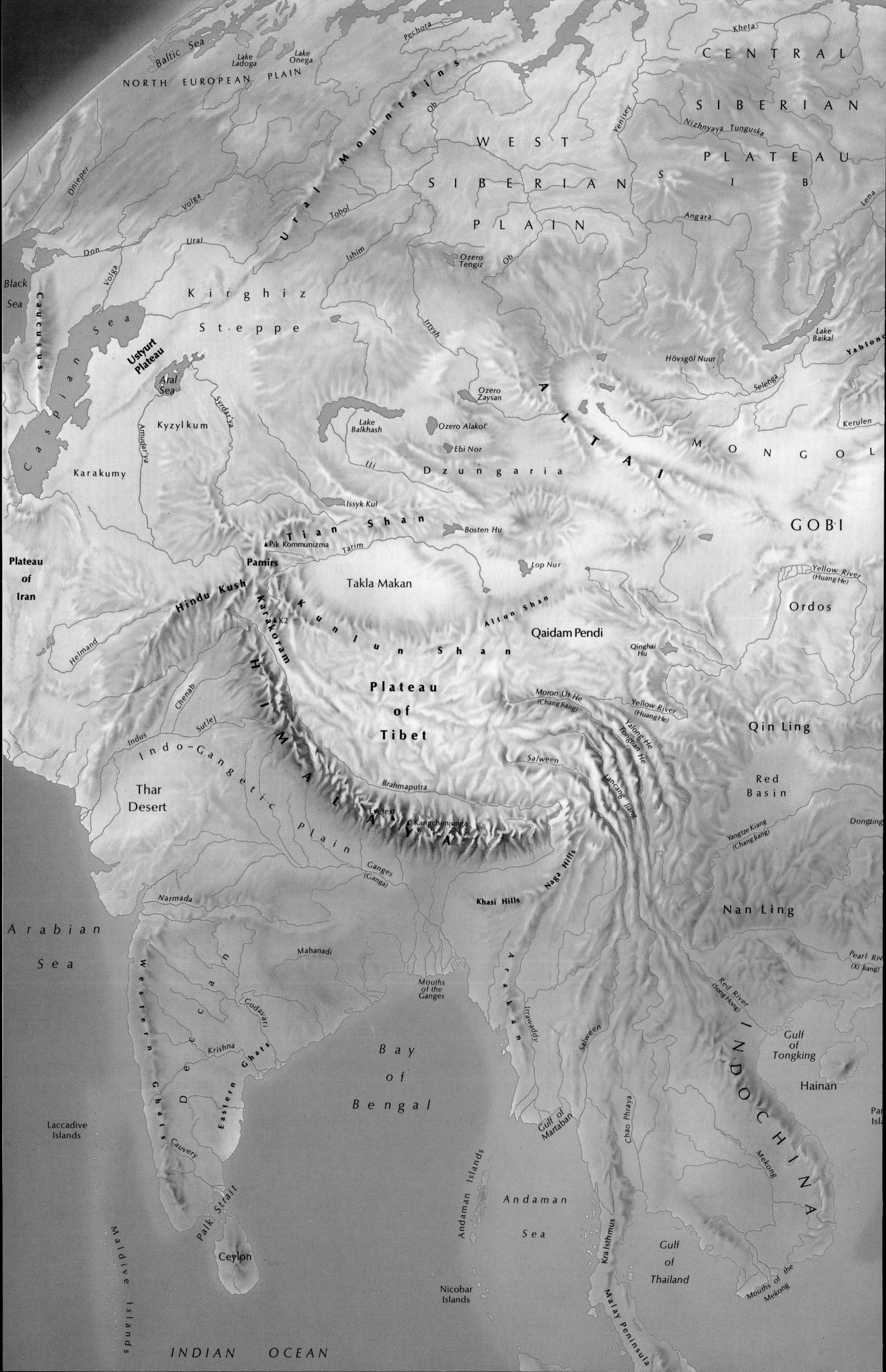

Baltic Sea

NORTH EUROPEAN PLAIN

Lake Ladoga

Lake Onega

Pechora

Kheta

CENTRAL

SIBERIAN

PLATEAU

S I B

Ob

WEST

SIBERIAN

PLAIN

Nizhnyaya Tunguska

Dnieper

Volga

Ural Mountains

Tobol

Ishim

Ob

Ozero Tengiz

Angara

Lena

Don

Volga

Ural

Irtysh

Lake Baikal

Yablon

Black Sea

Caucus

Caspian Sea

KIRGHIZ

St·eppe

Ustyurt Plateau

Aral Sea

Kyzylkum

Lake Balkhash

Ozero Zaysan

Ozero Alakol'

Ebi Nor

ALTAI

Hövsgöl Nuur

MONGOL

Selenga

Kerulen

Karakumy

Amudar'ya

Syrdar'ya

Ili

Dzungaria

GOB·I

Issyk Kul

Tian Shan

Bosten Hu

Tarim

Lop Nur

Yellow River (Huang He)

Pik Kommunizma

Plateau of Iran

Pamirs

Takla Makan

Ordos

Hindu Kush

K2

Karakoram

Kunlun Shan

Altun Shan

Qaidam Pendi

Qinghai Hu

Qin Ling

Helmand

Chenab

Sutlej

Moron Us He (Chang Jiang)

Yellow River (Huang He)

Yalong Jiang

Tongtian He

Red Basin

Indus

Plateau of Tibet

Lancang Jiang

Indo-Gangetic

Salween

Dongting

Thar Desert

Brahmaputra

Yangtze Kiang (Chang Jiang)

Plain

Everest

Kangchenjunga

HIMALAYA

Nan Ling

Narmada

Ganges (Ganga)

Naga Hills

Khasi Hills

Arabian Sea

Mahanadi

Mouths of the Ganges

Pearl Riv (Xi Jiang)

Godavari

Eastern Ghats

Western Ghats

Krishna

Deccan

Arakan

Irrawaddy

Red River (Sang Hong)

Gulf of Tongking

Laccadive Islands

Cauvery

Bay

of

Bengal

Salween

Hainan

INDOCHINA

Palk Strait

Maldive Islands

Ceylon

Andaman Islands

Andaman Sea

Gulf of Martaban

Chao Phraya

Mekong

Par Isla

Nicobar Islands

Kra Isthmus

Gulf of Thailand

Mouths of the Mekong

Malay Peninsula

INDIAN OCEAN

Yana

Indigirka

Kolyma

Anadyr

Nunivak
Island

Verkhoyanskiy Khrebet

Lena

A

R

Aldan

Kamchatka

B e r i n g

S e a

Aleutian Islands

Komandorskiye
Ostrova

Kht.Dzhugdzhur

S e a
of
O k h o t s k

Sakhalin

Tatarskiy Proliv

Kuril Islands

Greater Khingan Range

Hulun
Nur

Manchuria

Amur

Songhua

Ussuri

Oz
Khanka

Sikhote Alin

Hokkaido

N O R T H

Midway
Islands

Changbai Shan

Bo Hai

Korea

S e a
of
J a p a n

Honshu

P A C I F I C

Yellow River
(Huang He)

Yellow
Sea

Korea Strait

Shikoku

Kyushu

O C E A N

Great Plain of China

Yangtze Kiang
(Chang Jiang)

Poyang Hu

E a s t

C h i n a

S e a

Ryukyu Islands

Bonin Islands

Volcano
Islands

Taiwan Strait

Taiwan

M
a
r
i
a
n
a
s

Marshall Islands

S o u t h

C h i n a

S e a

P
H
I
L
I
P
P
I
N
E
S

Luzon

Guam

Kiribati

Mindoro

Samar

Caroline Islands

Panay

Palawan

Negros

S u l u

S e a

Mindanao

New Ireland

Nicobar
Islands

South
China
Sea

Celebes
Sea

NOR

Halmahera

Malay Peninsula

Strait of Malacca

Borneo

Makassar Strait

Celebes

Moluccas

Seram

Sumatra

Java
Sea

Banda
Sea

E
A
S
T

Java

Bali

Sumbawa

Flores

Arafura
Sea

Christmas Island

Sumba

Timor

S

I
N
D
I
E
S

Timor
Sea

Cocos–Keeling Island

Arnhem Land

Victoria

Barkly Tabl

I N D I A N

Kimberley
Plateau

Fitzroy

Tanami
Desert

Great
Sandy
Desert

Lake
Mackay

Ashburton

Macdonnell Ranges

Simps
Des

Gibson
Desert

Lake
Amadeus

Finke

Gascoyne

Murchison

Great Victoria Desert

Lak
Eyr

Lake
Barlee

La
Torr

Lake
Moore

Nullarbor Plain

Lake
Gairdner

O C E A N

Great Australian Bight

Sp

Amsterdam Island

St Paul

Kerguelen

Heard Island
Macdonald Islands

A N T A R C T I C A

PACIFIC OCEAN

MICRONESIA

Marshall Islands

MELANESIA

SOUTH

POLYNESIA

Admiralty Islands

Nauru

Banaba

Kiribati

New Ireland

Bismarck Sea

New Britain

Bougainville

Solomon Islands

Guinea

Tokelau Islands

Tuvalu

Torres Strait

Santa Cruz Islands

PACIFIC

Great Barrier Reef

Cape York Peninsula

Coral

Sea

Vanuatu

Samoan Islands

Fiji

Tahiti

'f of

ntaria

Flinders

New Caledonia

Tonga

Great Dividing Range

OCEAN

Diamantina

Cooper Creek

Fraser Island

Warrego

Culgoa

Barwon

Lake Frome

Darling

Murray

Lachlan

Murrumbidgee

Murray

Norfolk Island

Lord Howe Island

Kermadec Islands

Murray

Murray

Australian Alps

Mount Kosciusko

Tasman

Sea

New Zealand

King Island

Bass Strait

Flinders Island

Tasmania

Cook Strait

Chatham Islands

Foveaux Strait

Stewart Island

Bounty Islands

Antipodes Islands

Auckland Islands

Campbell Island

Macquarie Island

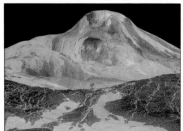

Far left The Caloris basin of Mercury is the largest impact feature on the planet.

Left Radar mapping of Venus has provided this computer-generated image of the volcano, Maat Mons.

Top right Io (left) and Europa are clearly visible as they cross the face of Jupiter.

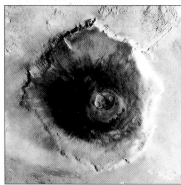

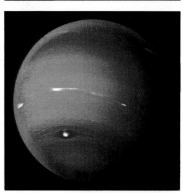

Far left Olympus Mons on Mars is the largest known volcano in the solar system. It is 550 km across at the base and more than 26 km high.

Right The rings of Saturn lie in the equatorial plane and consist of countless ice-covered particles, perhaps up to several metres across.

Left Voyager 2 produced this false-colour image of Neptune in August 1989. A planet-wide haze (red) and white clouds are visible.

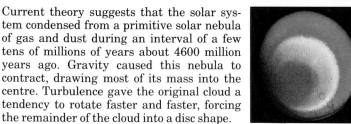

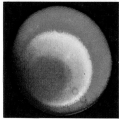

Left This image of Uranus in false-colour was taken from 9.1 million km by Voyager 2. The atmosphere is deep, cold and remarkably clear, but the false colours enhance the polar region. Here, the suggestion is that a brownish haze of smog is concentrated over the pole.

Current theory suggests that the solar system condensed from a primitive solar nebula of gas and dust during an interval of a few tens of millions of years about 4600 million years ago. Gravity caused this nebula to contract, drawing most of its mass into the centre. Turbulence gave the original cloud a tendency to rotate faster and faster, forcing the remainder of the cloud into a disc shape.

The centre of the cloud heated up as it compressed, and so eventually became hot enough for the Sun to begin to shine, through nuclear energy released at its core. Meanwhile the surrounding disc of cloud cooled, allowing material to condense into solid form. Particles stuck together as they collided and progressively larger bodies were built up. These swept up most of the debris to form the planets, which now orbit the Sun.

EARTHLIKE PLANETS

Mercury is the nearest planet to the Sun, spinning three times for every two orbits around the Sun. It has an exceptionally large metallic core which may be responsible for Mercury's weak magnetic field. Mercury is an airless world subject to vast extremes of temperature, from −180°C (−292°F) at night to 430°C (806°F) near the middle of its long day. The Mariner 10 space probe, during the mid-1970s, revealed the surface to be dominated by heavily cratered areas.

Venus has a dense atmosphere with a surface pressure 90 times that of the Earth. Made up of 96% carbon dioxide, the lower layers are rich in sulphur dioxide while sulphuric acid droplets populate the higher clouds. The clouds maintain a mean surface temperature of about 480°C (896°F). The hidden surface has been mapped by radar from orbiting probes and shows a rugged surface with some volcanoes, possibly still active.

Mars has a thin atmosphere of about 96% carbon dioxide mixed with other minor gasses. The polar caps consist of semi-permanent water-ice and solid carbon dioxide. Day and night surface temperatures vary between about −120°C (−184°F) and −20°C (−4°F). Mars has two small satellites, Phobos and Deimos, each less than about 25km (15.5 miles) across, probably captured asteroids.

Mars also shows evidence of erosional processes. The effect of winds is seen in the form of the deposition of sand dunes. Dust storms frequently obscure the surface. The large channels, such as the 5000km (3107 miles) long Valles Marineris, may have been cut by flowing water. Water is abundant in the polar caps and may be widespread, held in as permafrost.

GAS GIANTS

Jupiter has at least 16 satellites and a debris ring system about 50,000km (31,070 miles) above the cloud tops. The outer atmosphere is all that can be directly observed of the planet itself. It is mostly hydrogen with less amounts of helium, ammonia, methane and water vapour. Jupiter's rapid rotation causes it to be flattened towards the poles. This rotation and heat flow from the interior causes complex weather patterns. Where cloud systems interact vast storms can occur in the form of vortices. Some last only a few days but the most persistent of these, the Great Red Spot, has been present since it was first detected in the 17th century.

Saturn is the least dense of the planets. It has a stormy atmosphere situated above 30,000km (18,640 miles) layer of liquid hydrogen and helium distorted by rotation.

The rings of Saturn are thought to be mostly made of icy debris, from 10m (33 ft) down to a few microns in size, derived from the break-up of a satellite. The rings are less than 1km thick.

Uranus, consisting mainly of hydrogen, was little known until Voyager 2 flew by it in 1986. The probe discovered ten new satellites and provided images of the planet's eleven ice rings of debris.

Neptune was visited by Voyager 2 in 1989. Six new satellites were discovered, one larger than Nereid, the smaller of the two known satellites. Triton, the largest satellite, was found to be smaller than previous estimates. The turbulent atmosphere is a mixture of hydrogen, helium and methane.

Pluto is now 4500 million km from the Sun, closer than Neptune until 1999, but its eccentric orbit will take it to 7500 million km by 2113. A tenuous atmosphere has been found above a surface of frozen methane. Charon, the satellite, is half Pluto's diameter.

	SUN	MERCURY	VENUS	EARTH	(MOON)	MARS	JUPITER	SATURN	URANUS	NEPTUNE	PLUTO
Mass (Earth = 1)	333 400	0.055	0.815	1 (5.97 10²⁴kg)	0.012	0.107	317.8	95.2	14.5	17.2	0.003
Volume (Earth = 1)	1 306 000	0.06	0.88	1	0.020	0.150	1 323	752	64	54	0.007
Density (water = 1)	1.41	5.43	5.24	5.52	3.34	3.94	1.33	0.70	1.30	1.64	2.0
Equatorial diameter (km)	1 392 000	4878	12 104	12 756	3476	6794	142 800	120 000	52 000	48 400	2 302
Polar flattening	0	0	0	0.003	0	0.005	0.065	0.108	0.060	0.021	0
'Surface' gravity (Earth = 1)	27.9	0.37	0.88	1	0.16	0.38	2.69	1.19	0.93	1.22	0.05
Number of satellites greater than 100 km diameter	—	0	0	1	—	0	7	13	7	6	1
Total number of satellites	—	0	0	1	—	2	16	17	15	8	1
Period of rotation (in Earth days)	25.38	58.65	−243 (retrograde)	23hr 56m 4 secs	27.32	1.03	0.414	0.426	−0.74 (retrograde)	0.67	−6.39 (retrograde)
Length of year (in Earth days and years)	—	88 days	224.7 days	365.26 days	—	687 days	11.86 years	29.46 years	84.01 years	164.8 years	247.7 years
Distance from Sun (mean) Mkm	—	57.9	108.9	149.6	—	227.9	778.3	1 427	2 870	4 497	5 900

EARTH STRUCTURE

Internally, the Earth may be divided broadly into crust, mantle and core (*see right*).

The crust is a thin shell constituting only 2% of the mass of the Earth. The continental crust varies in thickness from 20 to 90km (12 to 56 miles) and is less dense than ocean crust. Two-thirds of the continents are overlain by sedimentary rocks of average thickness less than 2km (1.2 miles). Ocean crust is on average 7km (4.4 miles) thick. It is composed of igneous rocks, basalts and gabbros.

Crust and mantle are separated by the Mohorovičić Discontinuity (Moho). The mantle differs from the crust. It is largely igneous. The upper mantle extends to 350km (218 miles). The lower mantle has a more uniform composition. A sharp discontinuity defines the meeting of mantle and core. The inability of the outer core to transmit seismic waves suggests it is liquid. It is probably of metallic iron with other elements – sulphur, silicon, oxygen, potassium and hydrogen have all been suggested. The inner core is solid and probably of nickel-iron. Temperature at the core-mantle boundary is about 3700°C (6430°F) and 4000°–4500°C (7230°–8130°F) in the inner core.

THE ATMOSPHERE

The ancient atmosphere lacked free oxygen. Plant life added oxygen to the atmosphere and transferred carbon dioxide to the crustal rocks and the hydrosphere. The composition of air today at 79% nitrogen and 20% oxygen remains stable by the same mechanism.

Solar energy is distributed around the Earth by the atmosphere. Most of the weather and climate processes occur in the troposphere at the lowest level. The atmosphere also shields the Earth. Ozone exists to the extent of 2 parts per million and is at its maximum at 30km (19 miles). It is the only gas which absorbs ultra-violet radiation. Water-vapour and CO_2 keep out infra-red radiation.

Above 80km (50 miles) nitrogen and oxygen tend to separate into atoms which become ionized (an ion is an atom lacking one or more of its electrons). The ionosphere is a zone of ionized belts which reflect radio waves back to Earth. These electrification belts change their position dependent on light and darkness and external factors.

Beyond the ionosphere, the magnetosphere extends to outer space. Ionized particles form a plasma (a fourth state of matter, ie. other than solid, liquid, gas) held in by the Earth's magnetic field.

ORIGIN AND DEVELOPMENT OF LIFE

Primitive life-forms (blue-green algae) are found in rocks as old as 3500Ma (million years) and, although it cannot yet be proved, the origin of life on Earth probably dates back to about 4000Ma. It seems likely that the oxygen levels in the atmosphere increased only slowly at first, probably to about 5 of the present amount by 2000Ma. As the atmospheric oxygen built up so the protective ozone layer developed to allow organisms to live in shallower waters. More highly developed photosynthesising organisms led to the development of oxygen breathing animals. The first traces of multicellular life occur about 1000Ma; by 700Ma complex animals, such as jellyfish, worms and primitive molluscs, had developed.

Organisms developed hard parts that allowed their preservation as abundant fossils at about 570Ma. This coincided with a

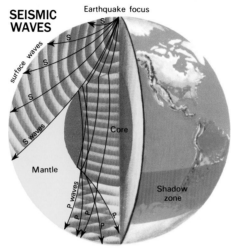

THE EARTH'S SHELLS

oceanic crust — Lithosphere — continental crust
depth (km) 350 — transition zone — Moho — upper mantle
900 — seismic discontinuities
lower mantle
2900 — core-mantle discontinuity
outer core
4700
5150 — transition zone
inner core
6370

SEISMIC WAVES

Earthquake focus
surface waves
S waves
Mantle
Core
P waves
Shadow zone

Above In an earthquake the shock generates vibrations, or seismic waves, which radiate in all directions from the focus. The slowest waves are Surface waves which transmit the bulk of the energy in shallow earthquakes.

Other waves known as body waves pass through the body of the Earth. Primary (P) waves are compressional. They are able to travel through solids and fluids and cause the particles of the Earth to vibrate in the direction of travel. Secondary (S) waves are transverse, or shear, waves. They can only pass through solids and do not penetrate the Earth's outer core.

period of explosive evolution of marine life. Fishes appeared about 475Ma and by 400Ma land plants had developed. Between 340 and 305Ma dense vegetation covered the land, amphibians emerged from the sea, and by about 250Ma had given rise to reptiles and the first mammals. These expanded hugely about 65Ma.

EARTHQUAKES

Earthquakes are the manifestation of a slippage at a geological fault. The majority occur at tectonic plate boundaries. The interior of a plate tends to be stable and less subject to earthquakes. When plates slide past each other strain energy is suddenly released. Even though the amount of movement is very small the energy released is colossal. It

is transferred in shock waves.

Some earthquakes originate at depths as shallow as 5km (3 miles) below the surface. Others, however, may be as deep as 700km (435 miles). The precise cause of these very deep earthquakes is not known. The point from which the earthquake is generated is the focus and the point on the surface immediately above the focus is the epicentre.

The Richter Scale is used to define the magnitude of earthquakes. Each unit represents an increase in the amount of energy released by a factor of around 30 over the preceding point on the Scale. There is no upper limit, but the greatest magnitude yet recorded is 8.9.

VOLCANOES

Almost all the world's active volcanoes, numbering 500–600 are located at convergent plate boundaries. Those are the volcanoes which give spectacular demonstrations of volcanic activity. Yet far greater volcanic activity continues unnoticed and without cessation at mid-ocean ridges where magma from the upper mantle is quietly being extruded on to the ocean floor to create new crustal material.

Chemical composition of magmas and the amount of gas they contain determine the nature of a volcanic eruption. Gas-charged basalts produce cinder cones. Violent eruptions usually occur when large clouds of lava come into contact with water to produce fine-grained ash. When andesites are charged with gas they erupt with explosive violence.

Nuées ardentes (burning clouds) are extremely destructive. They are produced by magmas which erupt explosively sending molten lava fragments and gas at great speeds down the mountain sides.

In spite of the destructiveness of many volcanoes people still live in their vicinity because of the fertile volcanic soils. Geothermal energy in regions of volcanic activity is another source of attraction.

GRAVITY AND MAGNETISM

The Earth is spheroidal in form because it is a rotating body. Were it not so it would take the form of a sphere. The shape is determined by the mass of the Earth and its rate of rotation. Centrifugal force acting outwards reduces the pull of gravity acting inwards so that gravity at the equator is less than at the poles. Uneven distribution of matter within the Earth distorts the shape taken up by the mean sea-level surface (the geoid). Today the belief is that electric currents generated in the semi-molten outer core are responsible for the magnetic field. The Earth's magnetic poles have experienced a number of reversals, the north pole becoming the south and vice-versa.

ROCK AND HYDROLOGICAL CYCLES

Right In the most familiar cycle rain falls onto the land, drains to the sea, evaporates, condenses into cloud and is precipitated onto the land again. Water is also released and recirculated. In the rock cycle rocks are weathered and eroded, forming sediments which are compacted into rocks that are eventually exposed and then weathered again.

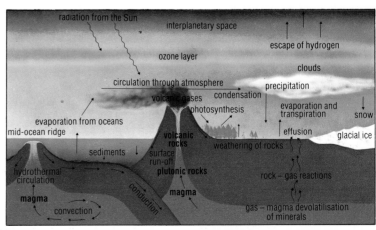

radiation from the Sun — interplanetary space
escape of hydrogen
ozone layer
clouds
circulation through atmosphere — precipitation
volcanic gases — condensation
evaporation and transpiration
evaporation from oceans — photosynthesis — snow
mid-ocean ridge
effusion — glacial ice
volcanic rocks
sediments — surface run-off — weathering of rocks
hydrothermal circulation — plutonic rocks — conduction
rock – gas reactions
magma — magma
convection — gas – magma devolatilisation of minerals

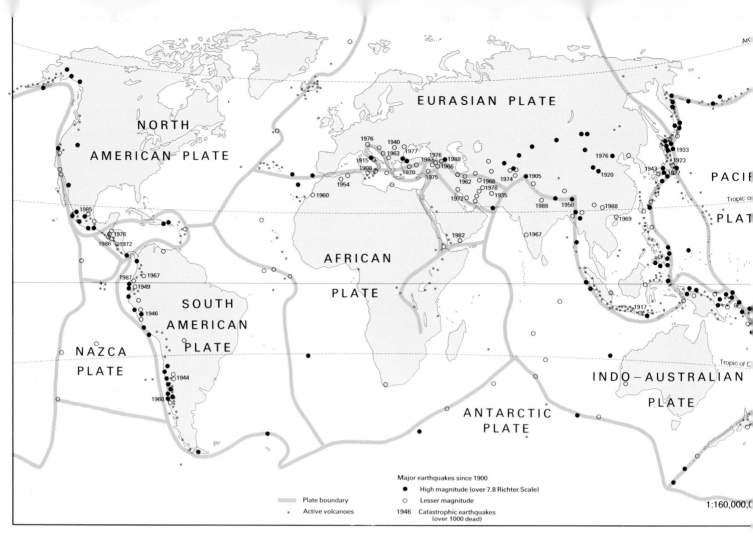

NORTH
AMERICAN PLATE

EURASIAN PLATE

1976 1940
1963 1977
1915 1983 1976 1988
1908 1966
1970
1954 1975 1962 1968 1974 1905
1960 1978
1972 1935
1982 1988 1950 1988
1967 1969

PACIFIC

PLATE

PLATE

AFRICAN

PLATE

NAZCA
PLATE

SOUTH
AMERICAN
PLATE

INDO–AUSTRALIAN

PLATE

1987 1967
1949
1946
1944
1960

1917

ANTARCTIC
PLATE

Tropic of

Tropic of C

Arc

Major earthquakes since 1900
● High magnitude (over 7.8 Richter Scale)
○ Lesser magnitude
1946 Catastrophic earthquakes
(over 1000 dead)

Plate boundary
Active volcanoes

1:160,000,0

ECONOMIC MINERALS

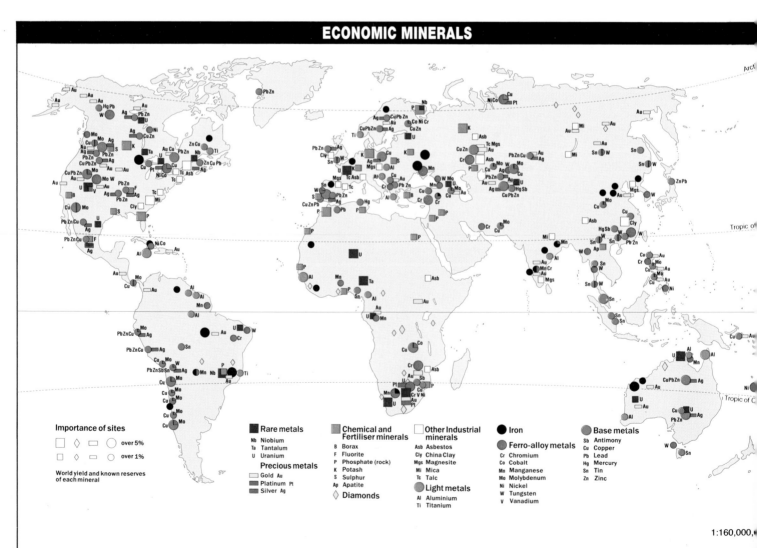

Importance of sites

☐ ◇ ▭ ◯ over 5%
▭ ◇ ▭ ◯ over 1%

World yield and known reserves
of each mineral

Rare metals
Nb Niobium
Ta Tantalum
U Uranium

Precious metals
Gold Au
Platinum Pt
Silver Ag

◇ Diamonds

**Chemical and
Fertiliser minerals**
B Borax
F Fluorite
P Phosphate (rock)
K Potash
S Sulphur
Ap Apatite

**Other Industrial
minerals**
Asb Asbestos
Cly China Clay
Mgs Magnesite
Mi Mica
Tc Talc

Light metals
Al Aluminium
Ti Titanium

● Iron

● **Ferro-alloy metals**
Cr Chromium
Co Cobalt
Mn Manganese
Mo Molybdenum
Ni Nickel
W Tungsten
V Vanadium

● **Base metals**
Sb Antimony
Cu Copper
Pb Lead
Hg Mercury
Sn Tin
Zn Zinc

1:160,000,

TEMPERATURE: JANUARY

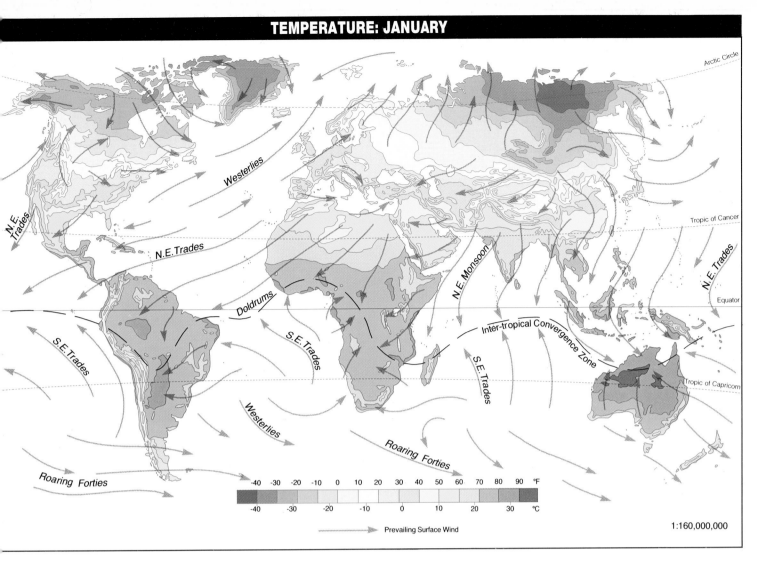

Arctic Circle

N.E. Trades

Westerlies

N.E. Trades

Tropic of Cancer

N.E. Trades

N.E. Monsoon

Doldrums

Equator

S.E. Trades

Inter-tropical Convergence Zone

S.E. Trades

S.E. Trades

Tropic of Capricorn

Westerlies

Roaring Forties

Roaring Forties

| -40 | -30 | -20 | -10 | 0 | 10 | 20 | 30 | 40 | 50 | 60 | 70 | 80 | 90 | °F |

| -40 | -30 | -20 | -10 | 0 | 10 | 20 | 30 | °C |

Prevailing Surface Wind

1:160,000,000

TEMPERATURE: JULY

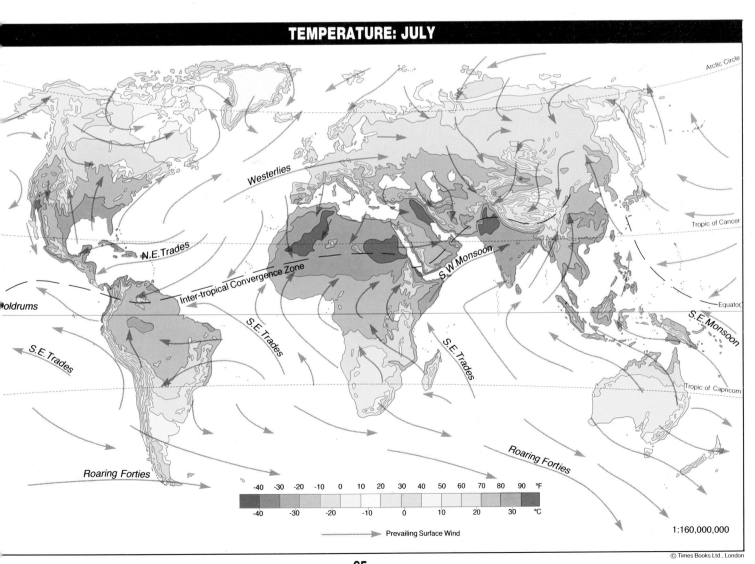

Arctic Circle

Westerlies

N.E. Trades

Tropic of Cancer

Inter-tropical Convergence Zone

S.W. Monsoon

Doldrums

S.E. Trades

Equator

S.E. Monsoon

S.E. Trades

S.E. Trades

Tropic of Capricorn

Roaring Forties

Roaring Forties

| -40 | -30 | -20 | -10 | 0 | 10 | 20 | 30 | 40 | 50 | 60 | 70 | 80 | 90 | °F |

| -40 | -30 | -20 | -10 | 0 | 10 | 20 | 30 | °C |

Prevailing Surface Wind

1:160,000,000

© Times Books Ltd., London

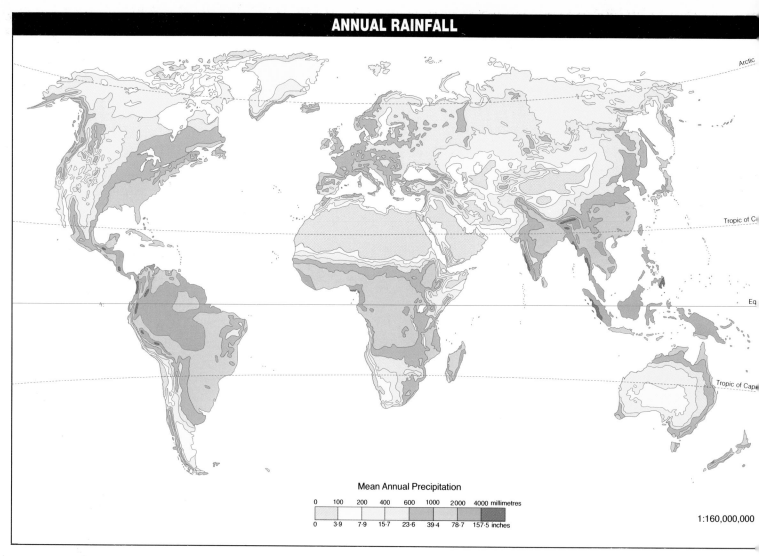

Mean Annual Precipitation

0	100	200	400	600	1000	2000	4000 millimetres
0	3·9	7·9	15·7	23·6	39·4	78·7	157·5 inches

1:160,000,000

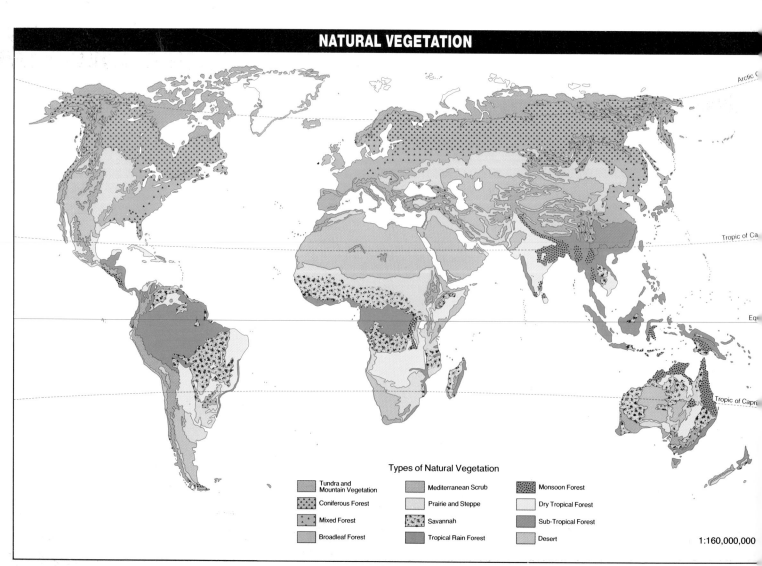

Types of Natural Vegetation

Tundra and Mountain Vegetation	Mediterranean Scrub	Monsoon Forest
Coniferous Forest	Prairie and Steppe	Dry Tropical Forest
Mixed Forest	Savannah	Sub-Tropical Forest
Broadleaf Forest	Tropical Rain Forest	Desert

1:160,000,000

POPULATION DENSITY

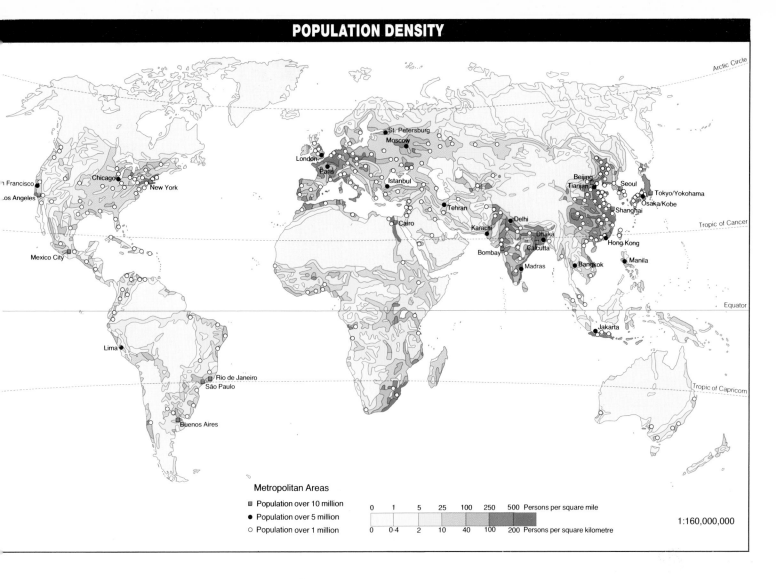

Metropolitan Areas

■ Population over 10 million
● Population over 5 million
○ Population over 1 million

| 0 | 1 | 5 | 25 | 100 | 250 | 500 | Persons per square mile |
| 0 | 0·4 | 2 | 10 | 40 | 100 | 200 | Persons per square kilometre |

1:160,000,000

POPULATION CHANGE

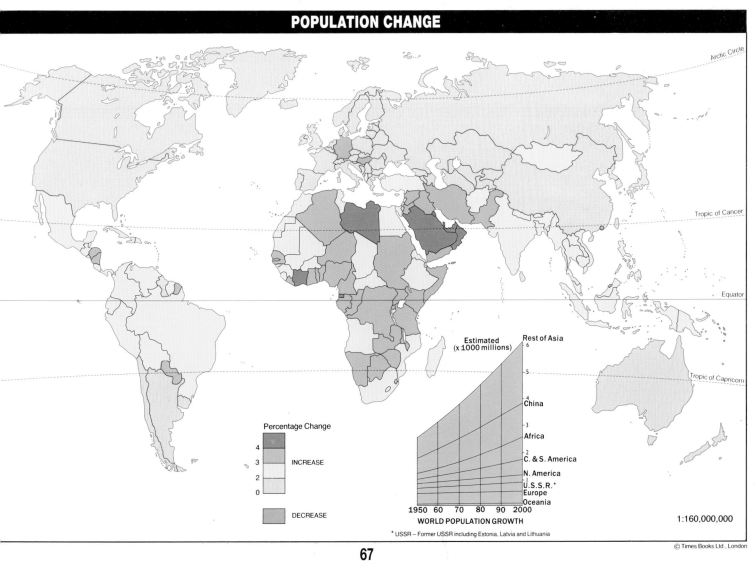

Percentage Change

4
3   INCREASE
2
0

DECREASE

Estimated (x 1000 millions)

Rest of Asia
China
Africa
C. & S. America
N. America
U.S.S.R.*
Europe
Oceania

1950 60 70 80 90 2000
WORLD POPULATION GROWTH

1:160,000,000

* USSR – Former USSR including Estonia, Latvia and Lithuania

© Times Books Ltd., London

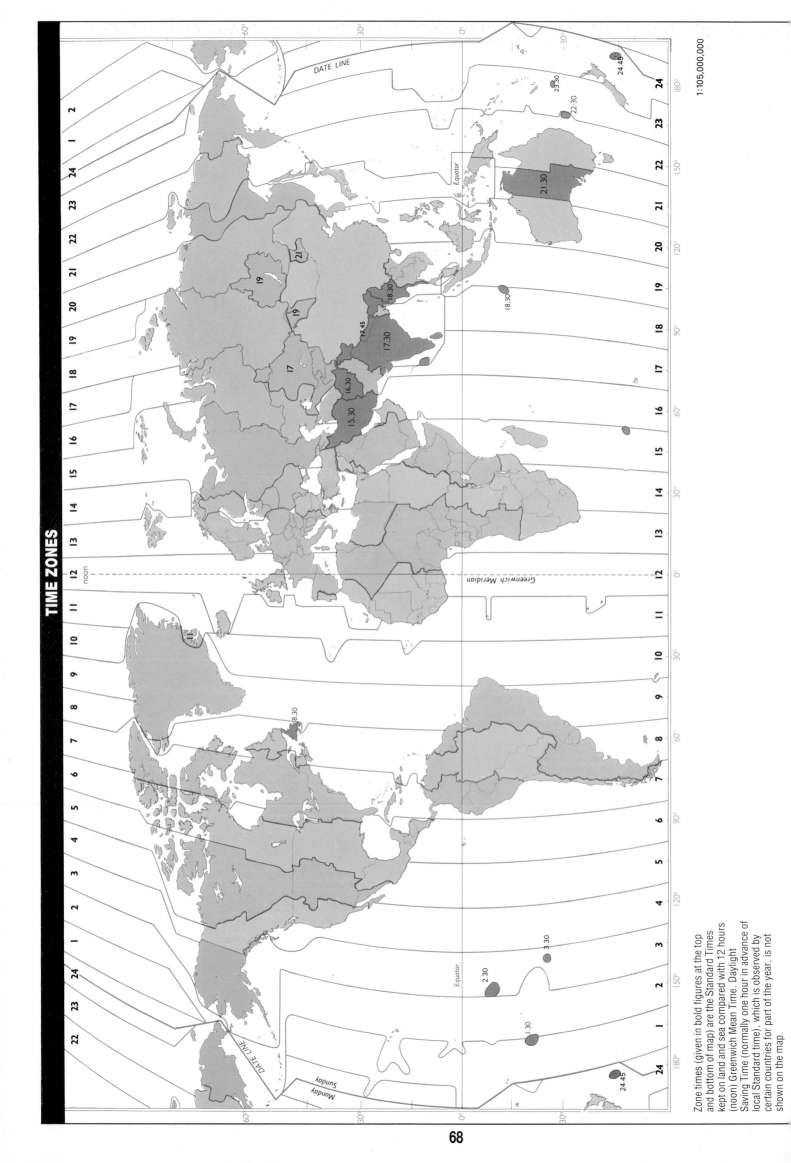

TIME ZONES

DATE LINE

24.45

23.30

22.30

21.30

18.30

noon

Greenwich Meridian

Equator

DATE LINE

Monday
Sunday

2.30

3.30

1.30

24.45

8.30

Zone times (given in bold figures at the top
and bottom of map) are the Standard Times
kept on land and sea compared with 12 hours
(noon) Greenwich Mean Time. Daylight
Saving Time (normally one hour in advance of
local Standard time), which is observed by
certain countries for part of the year, is not
shown on the map.

1:105,000,000

This page explains the main symbols, lettering style and height/depth colours used on the reference maps on pages 2 to 76. The scale of each map is indicated at the foot of each page. Abbreviations used on the maps appear at the beginning of the index.

BOUNDARIES

———————	International
— — — —	International under Dispute
· · · · · · ·	Cease Fire Line
———————	Autonomous or State
———————	Administrative
— · — · — ·	Maritime (National)
— — — —	International Date Line

COMMUNICATIONS

———————	Motorway/Express Highway
= = = = =	Under Construction
———————	Major Highway
———————	Other Roads
— — — —	Under Construction
· · · · · · ·	Track
→=====←	Road Tunnel
— — — —	Car Ferry
———·—	Main Railway
———————	Other Railway
— — — —	Under Construction
→— — —←	Rail Tunnel
— — — —	Rail Ferry
—ı—ı—ı—	Canal
⊕	International Airport
✈	Other Airport

LAKE FEATURES

	Freshwater
	Saltwater
	Seasonal
	Salt Pan

LANDSCAPE FEATURES

	Glacier, Ice Cap
	Marsh, Swamp
	Sand Desert, Dunes

OTHER FEATURES

	River
	Seasonal River
≍	Pass, Gorge
	Dam, Barrage
	Waterfall, Rapid
	Aqueduct
	Reef
▲4231	Summit, Peak
·217	Spot Height, Depth
⌣	Well
△	Oil Field
▲	Gas Field
Gas/Oil	Oil/Natural Gas Pipeline
Gemsbok Nat. Pk	National Park
∴UR	Historic Site

LETTERING STYLES

CANADA	Independent Nation
FLORIDA	State, Province or Autonomous Region
Gibraltar (U.K.)	Sovereignty of Dependent Territory
Lothian	Administrative Area
LANGUEDOC	Historic Region
Loire **Vosges**	Physical Feature or Physical Region

TOWNS AND CITIES

Square symbols denote capital cities. Each settlement is given a symbol according to its relative importance, with type size to match.

■	●	**New York**	Major City
■	●	**Montréal**	City
□	○	Ottawa	Small City
■	●	Québec	Large Town
□	○	St John's	Town
□	○	Yorkton	Small Town
□	○	Jasper	Village
			Built-up-area

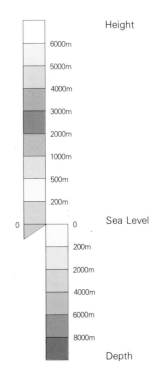

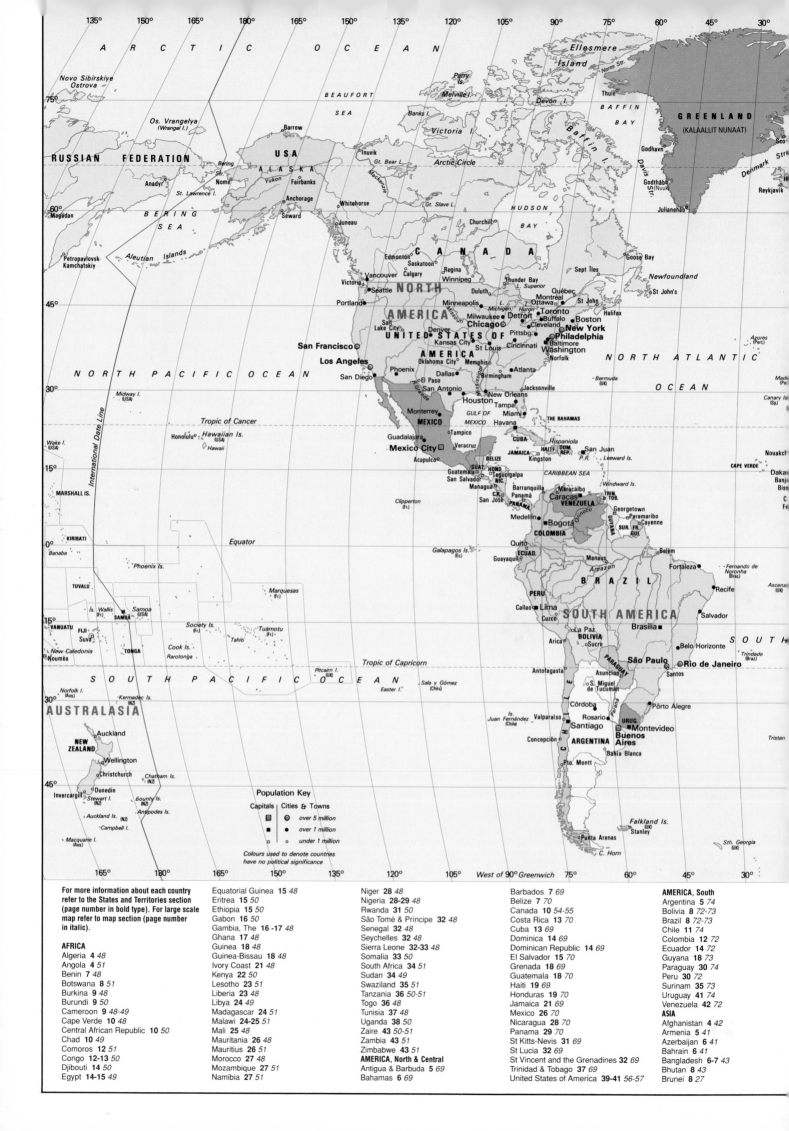

Population Key
Capitals / Cities & Towns
over 5 million
over 1 million
under 1 million
Colours used to denote countries have no political significance

1:70 000 000
(45° N & S)

A · 40 · B · ② · 30 · C · 20 · 70 · D · 10 · E · ⑦ · F · 10 · G

Greenland
(Dan)
Cape Farewell

Jan Mayen
(Nor.)

ARCTI
ARCTI

③

ICELAND

Reykjavík

NORWEGIAN

SEA

Vesterålen
Lofoten

Nar

ATLANTIC

Faeroes

Rockall

Shetland

Orkney

UNITED KINGDOM
OF GREAT BRITAIN AND
NORTHERN IRELAND

Dundee
Glasgow   Aberdeen
Edinburgh

Trondheim

Bergen

Stavanger

NORWAY

Oslo

SWEDEN

Uppsala

Västerås
Örebro

Norrk

Stock

OCEAN

④

50

NORTH

SEA

Belfast

IRELAND

Dublin

Cork

Newcastle
Middlesborough

Blackpool   Leeds   Hull
Liverpool   Manchester
Sheffield
Wolverhampton   Derby
Birmingham   Leicester
Northampton   Norwich
Oxford
Swansea   Reading   Luton
Cardiff   Ipswich
Bristol   London
Southampton   Brighton
Plymouth

Göteborg   Borås   Linköping   Jönköping   Alborg   Ólar
Århus   Helsingborg
DENMARK
Copenhagen   Malmö
(København)   Odense   Bornholm   Balti
Kiel   Rostock   Schwerin   Szczecin
Bremerhaven   Lübeck
Wilhelmshaven   Hamburg
Bremen   Wolfsburg   Berlin
Gronigen   Hannover   Hildesheim   Gorzów Wlkp.   Poznań
Amsterdam   Enschede   Magdeburg   PO
NETHERLANDS   Paderborn   Essen   Leipzig   Cottbus   Zielona Góra
The Hague   Dortmund   Göttingen   Jena   Dresden   Wrocław
s-Gravenhage   GERMANY
Rotterdam   Düsseldorf   Kassel   Zwickau   Chemnitz
Antwerp   Cologne   Bonn   Erfurt
BELGIUM   (Köln)   Koblenz   Frankfurt   Plzeň   Prague
Brussels   Namur   Mainz   Darmstadt   CZECH REP   (Praha)   Brno
(Bruxelles)   LUXEMBOURG   Heidelberg   Erlangen
Lille   Luxembourg   Nürnberg   Regensburg

ENGLISH CHANNEL

Isles of Scilly

Channel Islands

Le Havre
Amiens   Valenciennes
Boulogne
Brest   Rouen   Reims   Metz   Nancy   Karlsruhe
Caen   Seine   Heilbronn   Ulm
Rennes   Paris   Troyes   Strasbourg   Stuttgart   Augsburg   Munich
Orléans   Freiburg   (München)
Angers   Le Mans   Dijon   Mulhouse   AUSTRIA   Vienna   (Wien)
St. Nazaire   Loire   Besançon   Berne   Basle   Salzburg   Bratis
Nantes   Tours   (Bern)   Zurich   Innsbruck   SI
FRANCE   SWITZERLAND   LIECHTENSTEIN   Graz   HU
Limoges   Clermont-   Geneva   Lausanne   Bolzano
Ferrand   (Genève)   SLOVENIA   Pécs
Bordeaux   St-Étienne   Lyon   Bergamo   Udine   Ljubljana
Villeurbanne   Novara   Brescia   Trieste   Zagreb
Bayonne   Toulouse   Valence   Milan   Verona   CROATIA
San Sebastián   Pau   Montpellier   (Milano)   Padova
Santander   Nîmes   Turin   Piacenza   Venice   BOS
La Coruña   Baracaldo   (Torino)   Alessandria   Parma   (Venezia)   HERZEG
Gijón   Bilbao   Marseilles   Genoa   Ferrara
Vigo   Oviedo   Vitoria   (Marseille)   Nice   (Genova)   Reggio   Bologna   Rimini   Split   Sara
León   Burgos   Logroño   Toulon   La Spezia   ITALY   Ancona   Adriatic
Oporto   ANDORRA   MONACO   Livorno   SAN
(Porto)   Valladolid   Sabadell   Pisa   MARINO
Salamanca   Zaragoza   Tarrasa   Corsica   Florence   Perugia   Pescara
PORTUGAL   Madrid   (Corse)   (Firenze)   Terni
Lisbon   SPAIN   Alcalá de H.   Badalona   Bastia   Rome
(Lisboa)   Tajo   Barcelona   (Roma)
Badajoz   Toledo   Tarragona   Ajaccio   Sassari   Olbia   Naples
Córdoba   Castellón   Olbia   (Napoli)   Foggia
Faro   de la P.   Sardinia   Salerno   Bari
⑤   Albacete   Valencia   (Sardegna)   TYRRHENIAN
Sevilla   Balearic   Islands   Cagliari   SEA   Cosenza
Huelva   Granada   Murcia   Minorca
Jerez de la F.   Alicante   Elche   (Menorca)   Palermo   Messina
Cádiz   Majorca   Reggio di Calabria
Málaga   Cartagena   Ibiza   (Mallorca)   Sicily
Tangiers   Gibraltar (U.K.)   Almería   (Sicilia)   Syracuse
(Tanger)   Ceuta (Sp.)
Casablanca   Tetouan   MEDITERRANEAN   Algiers
Rabat   Melilla   (Alger)   MALTA
(Sp.)   Oran   SE
MOROCCO   ALGERIA   TUNISIA
Marrakech   Tunis

Madeira
(Port.)

Canary Is.

D · 10 · E · 0 · F · 10 · G

1:15M   200   400   600 km
100   200   300 mls

O C E A N

Barents Sea

H 30 J 40 K 50 L 60 M 70 ② N 80

O.Kolguyev

Vorkuta M

③

Ob'

Murmansk

White Sea

Apatity

O.Kolguyev

Pechora

Ukhta

Pechora

Ob'

Tavda

Irtysh

Irtysh

Omsk

Luleå

Oulu

Severodvinsk

Arkhangel'sk

Sev Dvina

Syktyvkar

Kamskoye Vdkhr.

Perm'

Yekaterinburg

Vaasa

Kuopio

Jyväskylä

FINLAND

Petrozavodsk

Lake Onega

Kotlas

Kirov

Ufa

Chelyabinsk

Magnitogorsk

Tampere

Vyborg

Lake Ladoga

Kazan'

50

Pori

Turku

Helsinki

Gulf of Finland

St Petersburg (Leningrad)

Cherepovets

Vologda

Rybinskoye Vdkhr.

Yaroslavl'

Volga

Kuybyshevskoye Vdkhr.

Tol'yatti

Samara

R U S S I A N   F E D E R A T I O N

Tallinn

ESTONIA

Pskov

Tver

Sergiyev Posad

KAZAKHSTAN

Riga LATVIA

Daugava

Nizhniy Novgorod

Ural

Daugavpils

Moscow

Tula

Aral Sea (Aral'skoye More)

④

LITHUANIA

Nemunas

RUS. FED.

Kaunas

Kaliningrad

Vilnius

Orsha

Minsk

Voronezh

Saratov

Volgogradskoye Vdkhr.

Gur'yev

UZBEKISTAN

saw awa)

BELARUS (BELORUSSIA)

Kursk

Brest

Grodno

Volgograd

Tsimlyanskoye Vdkhr.

Volga

Astrakhan'

Shevchenko

Khar'kov

acow

L'vov

Kiev

UKRAINE

Kremenchugskoye Vdkhr.

Dnepar' (Dnepr)

Dnepropetrovsk

Rog

Zaporozh'ye

Mariupol'

Donetsk

Don

Rostov

Makhachkala

C A S P I A N   S E A

40

KIA

MOLDOVA

Kishinev (Chisinau)

Odessa

Kakhovskoye Vdkhr.

Kerch'

Krasnodar

Vladikavkaz

Baku

TURKMENISTAN

est

Oradea

Cluj

Tîrgu Mureş

ROMANIA

Arad

Timişoara

Galaţi

Sevastopol

B L A C K   S E A

Batumi

GEORGIA

Tbilisi

AZERBAIJAN

 y

Belgrade (Beograd)

Bucharest Bucureşti

Danube (Dunav)

Constanţa

ARMENIA

Yerevan

AZER.

AVIA

Niš

Pleven

Varna

Samsun

Trabzon

Erzurum

Tabriz

I R A N

Sofiya

Burgas

Tehrān

⑤

A

Skopje

Plovdiv

BULGARIA

Edirne

Istanbul

Üsküdar

Ankara

T U R K E Y

Urumyeh

Mosul

MACEDONIA

Thessaloniki

Bursa

Firat

GREECE

Lárisa

Eskişehir

Esfahan

Pátrai

Athens (Athina)

Izmir

Denzil

Adana

Halab

Baghdād

Kalamai

Cyclades

Antalya

Adana

Hims

S Y R I A

Tigris

I R A Q

Khaniá

Crete

Dodecanese

CYPRUS

Nicosia

LEBANON

Beirūt

Damascus

Euphrates

Basra

Abadan

The Gulf

H 30 J 40 K 50

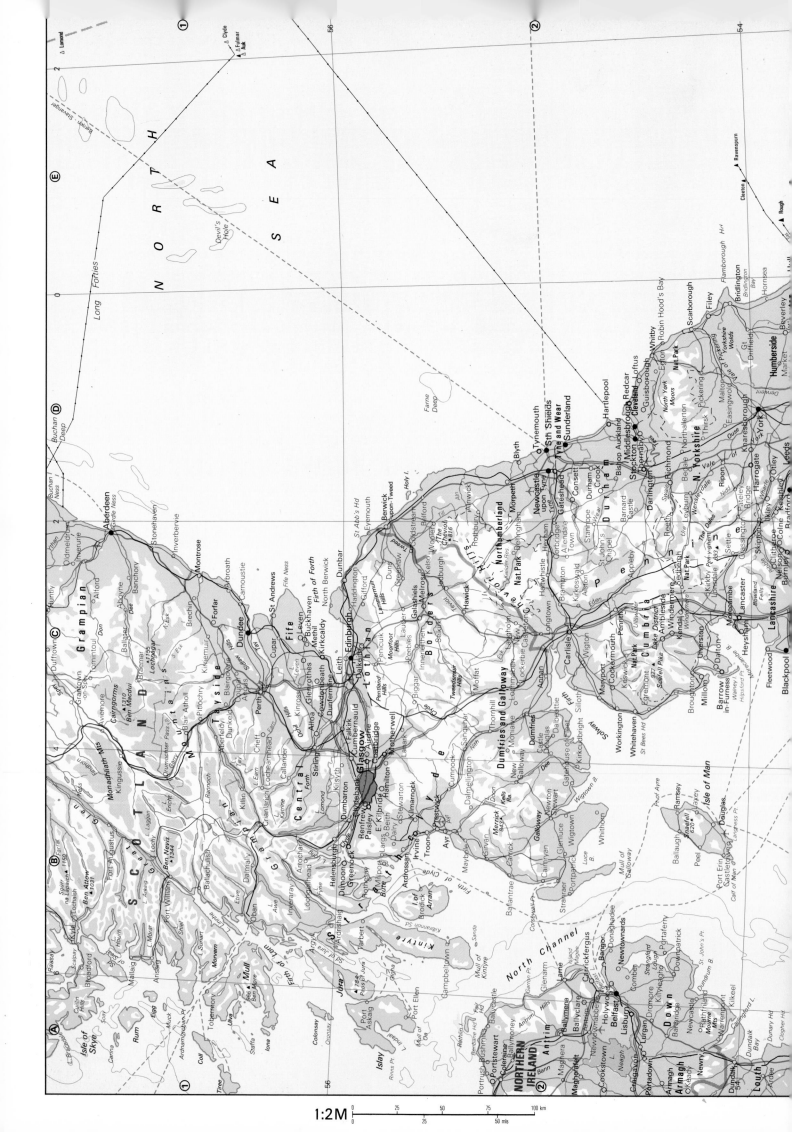

1:2M

0   25   50   75   100 km

0   25   50 mls

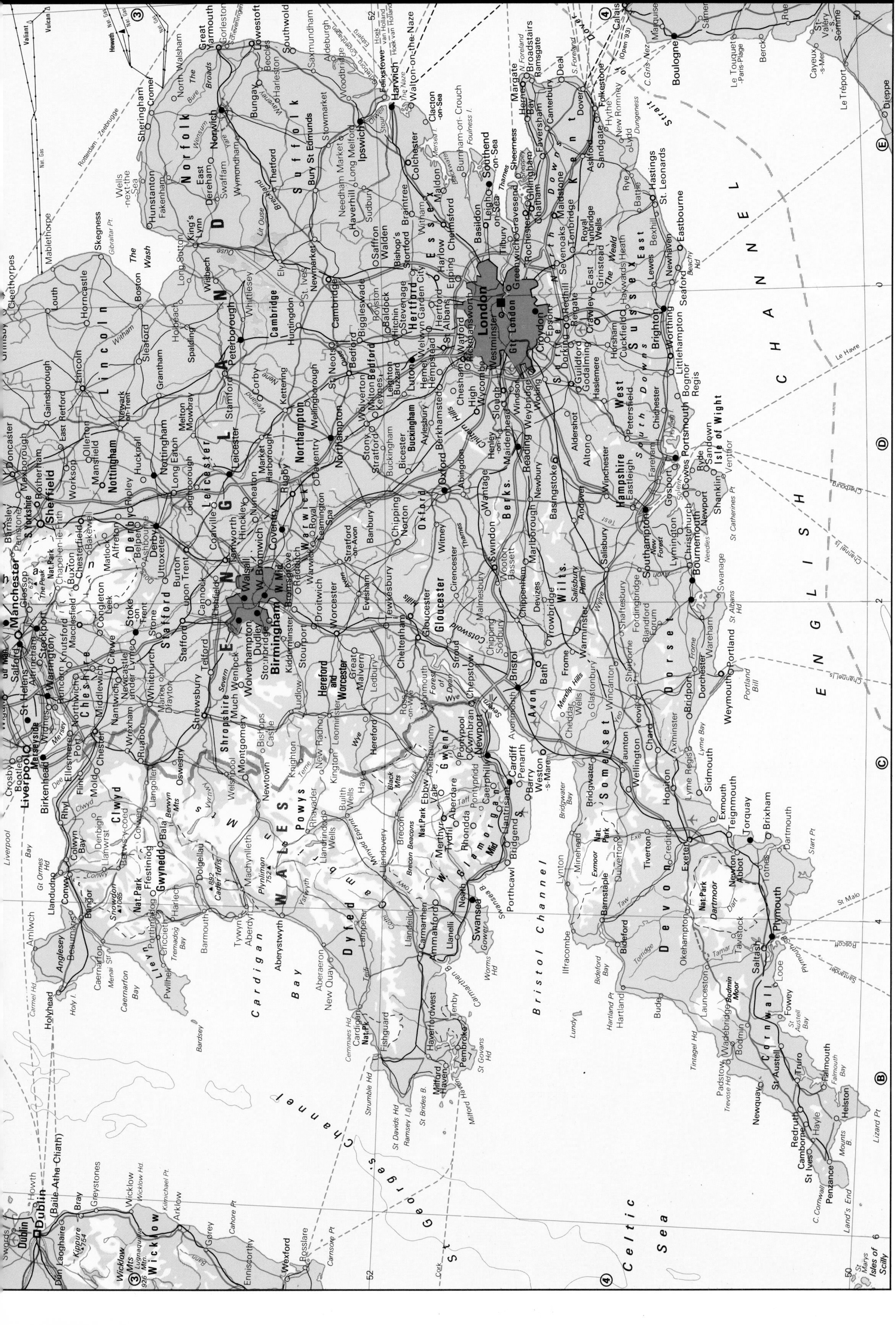

Liverpool
Manchester
Sheffield
Birmingham
Nottingham
Leicester
Derby
Stoke-on-Trent
Coventry
Northampton
Peterborough
Cambridge
Norwich
Ipswich
Colchester
Oxford
Reading
London
Gt London
Croydon
Southend-on-Sea
Brighton
Portsmouth
Southampton
Bournemouth
Bristol
Cardiff
Newport
Swansea
Exeter
Plymouth
Torquay
Dublin
Calais
Boulogne
Dieppe
Norfolk
Suffolk
Essex
Kent
Lincoln
Leicester
Hampshire
Dorset
Devon
Cornwall
Somerset
Wilts.
Berks.
Gloucester
Powys
Clwyd
Gwynedd
Dyfed
Gwent
Isle of Wight
Wicklow
The Wash
Bristol Channel
Cardigan Bay
St George's Channel
Celtic Sea
English Channel
Strait of Dover

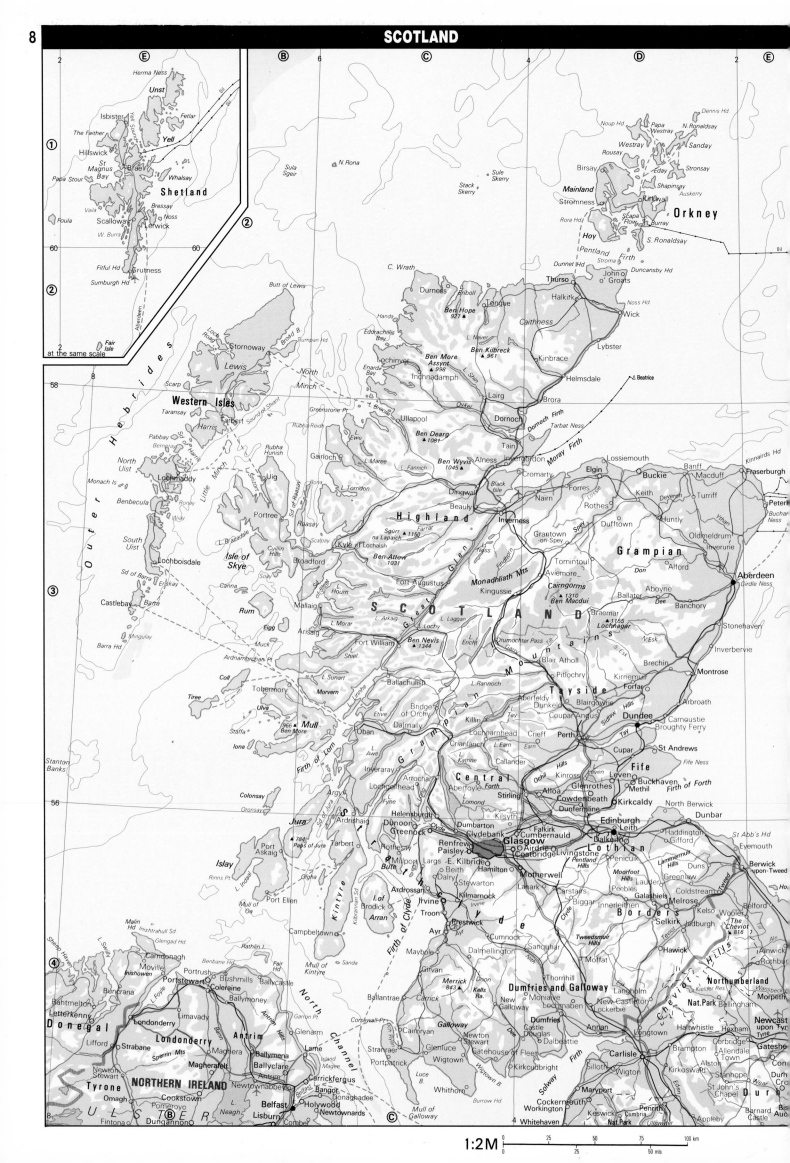

Inset map (top left): Shetland

Herma Ness
Unst
Isbister
The Faither
Fetlar
Yell
Yell Sound
Oil
Oil
Hillswick
St Magnus Bay
Brae
Whalsay
Papa Stour
Vaila
Shetland
Bressay
Foula
Noss
Scalloway
Lerwick
W. Burra
60
Fitful Hd
Grutness
Sumburgh Hd
Fair Isle
Aberdeen
at the same scale

Main map

Outer Hebrides

Butt of Lewis
Loch Road
Stornoway
Broad B.
Lewis
North Minch
Scarp
Western Isles
Taransay
Tarbert
Sound of Shiant
Greenstone Pt
Harris
Rubha Reidh
Pabbay
Sd of Harris
Berneray
Rubha Hunish
North Uist
Monach Is
Lochmaddy
Benbecula
Ronay
Uig
Wiay
Rona
L. Snizort
Sd of Raasay
South Uist
Raasay
Portree
Scalpay
Lochboisdale
L. Bracadale
Cuillin Hills
Broadford
Isle of Skye
Soay
Eriskay
Canna
Sd of Barra
Castlebay
Barra
Rum
Mingulay
Eigg
Barra Hd
Muck
Ardnamurchan Pt
Coll
Tiree
Tobermory
Morvern
Ulva
Staffa
Mull
966 Ben More
Iona

C. Wrath
Durness
Eriboll
Ben Hope 927
Tongue
Handa
Eddrachillis Bay
Lochinver
Ben More Assynt 998
Inchnadamph
Ben Kilbreck 961
L. Maver
Halkirk
Thurso
Caithness
Wick
Noss Hd
John o' Groats
Duncansby Hd
Kinbrace
Lybster
Helmsdale
Brora
Lairg
Enard Bay
L. Shin
Trumpan Hd
L. Broom
Ullapool
Oykel
Dornoch
Dornoch Firth
Tarbat Ness
Beatrice
Ben Dearg 1081
Ben Wyvis 1045
Alness
Invergordon
Tain
Moray Firth
Cromarty
L. Ewe
Gairloch
L. Maree
L. Fannich
Dingwall
Black Isle
Beauly
Nairn
Lossiemouth
Elgin
Buckie
Banff
Macduff
Fraserburgh
L. Torridon
Forres
Rothes
Keith
Deveron
Turriff
Peter
Ben Attow 1031
Highland
Inverness
Ness
Findhorn
Grantown-on-Spey
Spey
Dufftown
Huntly
Oldmeldrum
Inverurie
Buchan Ness
Sgurr na Lapaich 1150
Farrar
Fort Augustus
Great Glen
Monadhliath Mts
Aviemore
Tomintoul
Don
Alford
Grampian
Aberdeen
Girdle Ness
Kingussie
Cairngorms
Ben Macdui 1310
Ballater
Aboyne
Banchory
SCOTLAND
Mallaig
L. Arkaig
L. Lochy
L. Laggan
Dee
Braemar 1155
Lochnagar
Stonehaven
L. Hourn
Fort William
Ben Nevis 1344
Ericht
Drumochter Pass
Tilt
Garry
S. Esk
Inverbervie
Arisaig
L. Morar
L. Shiel
Blair Atholl
Pitlochry
Brechin
Montrose
Ardnarmurchan Pt
L. Sunart
Ballachulish
L. Linnhe
L. Rannoch
Tayside
Kirriemuir
Forfar
Arbroath
Bridge of Orchy
Aberfeldy
Blairgowrie
L. Etive
Dunkeld
Coupar Angus
Sidlaw Hills
Dundee
Carnoustie
Broughty Ferry
Dalmally
Killin
L. Tay
Perth
Tay
Oban
Ben More 966
Crianlarich
Lochearnhead
L. Earn
Crieff
Cupar
St Andrews
Iona
L. Awe
Inveraray
L. Katrine
Callander
Hills
Kinross
Leven
Fife
Fife Ness
Colonsay
Oronsay
Arrochar
Central
L. Lomond
Aberfoyle
Forth
Ochil Hills
Glenrothes
Buckhaven
Firth of Forth
Lochgilphead
Stirling
Alloa
Methil
Jura
Sd of Jura
Ardrishaig
Helensburgh
Dunoon
Clyde
Dumbarton
Clydebank
Falkirk
Cumbernauld
Dunfermline
Cowdenbeath
Kirkcaldy
North Berwick
Dunbar
784 Paps of Jura
Tarbert
Rothesay
Greenock
Renfrew
Paisley
Glasgow
Airdrie
Coatbridge
Edinburgh
Leith
Haddington
Gifford
St Abb's Hd
Eyemouth
Islay
Gigha
Bute
Milport
Largs
E. Kilbride
Hamilton
Cumbernauld
Livingstone
Penicuik
Pentland Hills
Lothian
Lammermuir Hills
Duns
Berwick-upon-Tweed
Ho
L. Indaal
Port Askaig
Beith
Dalry
Stewarton
Motherwell
Lamark
Carstairs
Moorfoot Hills
Lauder
Greenlaw
Kintyre
Kilbrannan Sd
I. of Brodick
Arran
Ardrossan
Kilmarnock
Irvine
Biggar
Peebles
Innerleithen
Galashiels
Coldstream
Tweed
Kelso
Melrose
Borders
Belford
Rinns Pt
Port Ellen
Troon
Prestwick
Irvine
Stewarton
Clyde
Tweedsmuir Hills
Selkirk
Jedburgh
The Cheviot 816
Wooler
Mull of Oa
Ayr
Ayr
Cumnock
Sanquhar
Hawick
Teviot
Cheviot Hills
Alnwick
Rothbury
Campbeltown
Maybole
Dalmellington
Moffat
Northumberland
Mull of Kintyre
Sanda
Girvan
Doon
Merrick 843
Kells Ra.
Thornhill
New Galloway
Dumfries and Galloway
Langholm
Kielder Res.
Wansbeck
Nat. Park
Bellingham
Morpeth
Carrick
Ballantrae
Galloway
Loch Maben
New Castleton
Newcast upon Tyne
Corsewall Pt
Cairnryan
Newton Stewart
Dee
Dumfries
Gatehouse of Fleet
Castle Douglas
Dalbeattie
Annan
Longtown
Brampton
Corbridge
Gateshe
Stranraer
Portpatrick
Wigtown
Luce B.
Wigtown B.
Kirkcudbright
Solway
Firth
Carlisle
Hexham
Allendale Town
Alston
Con
Durh
Bis
Whithorn
Burrow Hd
Silloth
Cockermouth
Maryport
Workington
Wigton
Penrith
Keswick
Cumbria
Nat. Park
Ullswater
Appleby
Barnard Castle
St John's Chapel
Wear
Stanhope
Weardale
Whitehaven
Mull of Galloway

Northern Ireland / Ireland

Malin Hd
Inishtrahull Sd
Sheep Haven
Inishowen
L. Swilly
Camdonagh
Moville
Fair Hd
Benbane Hd
Rathlin I.
Portstewart
Portrush
Coleraine
Bushmills
Ballycastle
Rahtmelton
Buncrana
Londonderry
Ballymoney
Antrim Hills
Glenarm
Letterkenny
Lifford
Strabane
Limavady
Bann
Donegal
Londonderry
L. Foyle
Magilligan
Magherafelt
Ballymena
Antrim
Island Magee
Larne
North Channel
Tyrone
Sperrin Mts
Cookstown
Pomeroy
Maghera
Ballyclare
Carrickfergus
Omagh
Newtownabbey
Bangor
Donaghadee
Newtownards
Dungannon
Fintona
NORTHERN IRELAND
Belfast
Holywood
Combe
ULSTER
Dunganvon
Lisburn
L. Neagh
Lisburn

Scale

1:2M
0 25 50 75 100 km
0 25 50 mls

Islands (top right)

Noup Hd
Papa Westray
N. Ronaldsay
Dennis Hd
Westray
Rousay
Eday
Sanday
Shapinsay
Auskerry
Stronsay
Birsay
Mainland
Stromness
Kirkwall
Orkney
Rora Hd
Scapa Flow
Burray
Hoy
Pentland Firth
Dunnet Hd
Stroma
S. Ronaldsay
Oil
Kinnairds Hd
N. Rona
Sula Sgeir
Sule Skerry
Stack Skerry

58
56
60

Stanton Banks

① 56

Colonsay
Oronsay
Jura
Firth of Lorn
Inveraray
Lochgoilhead
Arrochar
Argyll
L. Awe
L. Fyne
Tarbert
Ardrishaig
Helensburgh
Dunoon
Greenock
Clyde
Rothesay
Bute
Largs
Millport
Ardrossan
Irvine
Troon
Prestwick
Ayr
Maybole
Girvan
Ballantrae
Carrick
Cairnryan
Stranraer
Portpatrick
Glenluce
Luce B.

Islay
Port Askaig
Rinns Pt.
L. Indaal
Gigha
Port Ellen
Mull of Oa
Sanda
Campbeltown
Mull of Kintyre
Kintyre
Sd. of Jura
Paps of Jura
Kilbrannan Sd.
Brodick
Arran
I. of Arran
Firth of Clyde

Malin Hd.
Inishtrahull Sd.
Glengad Hd.
Tory I.
Tory Sound
Sheep Haven
L. Swilly
Carndonagh
Inishowen
Moville
L. Foyle
Portrush
Portstewart
Bushmills
Coleraine
Ballycastle
Benbane Hd.
Rathlin I.
Fair Hd.
Garron Pt.
Corsewall Pt.

Bloody Foreland
Gola
Errigal ▲752
Donegal Mts
Rathmelton
Buncrana
Letterkenny
Ballymoney
Limavady
Londonderry
Antrim
Antrim Hills
Glenarm

Aran I.
Gweebarra B.
Glenties
Donegal Mts
Blue Stack ▲676
Lifford
Strabane
Newton Stewart
LONDONDERRY
Sperrin Mts
Maghera
Ballymena
Ballyclare
Larne
Island Magee
Glenarm
Glenluce

Rossan Pt.
Killybegs
Donegal
TYRONE
Omagh
Pomeroy
Cookstown
Magherafelt
NORTHERN IRELAND
Newtownabbey
Carrickfergus
Belfast
Bangor
Donaghadee

Muckros Hd.
Donegal Bay
Bundoran
Ballyshannon
ULSTER
Fintona
Dungannon
Portadown
Lurgan
Craigavon
Lisburn
Holywood
Newtownards
Comber
Strangford Lough
Isle of Man
Peel

Erris Hd.
The Mullet
Belmullet
Ballycastle
Benwee Hd.
Broad Haven
Inishkea
Blacksod B.
Achill Hd.
Achill

Sligo Bay
Killala B.
Ballina
Ox Mts
Sligo
Leitrim
L. Melvin
Enniskillen
Upper L. Erne
L. Erne
FERMANAGH
Monaghan
Clones
MONAGHAN
Castleblayney
Cootehill
ARMAGH
Keady
Newry
Mourne Mts
Warrenpoint
Rathfriland
Newcastle
Dundrum B.
St. John's Pt.
Downpatrick
Killyleagh
Portaferry
Ballynahinch
Bambridge
DOWN

Inishmurray
Carrowmore L.
Leitrim
L. Allen
L. Gara
Boyle
Carrick on Shannon
Cavan
L. Oughter
Cavan
L. Sheelin
Carrickmacross
LOUTH
Dundalk
Dundalk Bay
Carlingford L.
Kilkeel
Mull of Galloway
Port Erin
Calf of Man

Mts of Mayo
Nephin ▲807
L. Conn
SLIGO
Swinford
Ballaghaderreen
L. Boderg
CAVAN
Kells
 LOUTH
Ardee
Dunany Pt.
Clogher Hd.

Clare
Inishturk
Clew Bay
Westport
Castlebar
MAYO
Claremorris
Ballyhaunis
Castlerea
ROSCOMMON
Longford
L. Ramor
An Uaimh
MEATH
Drogheda

Inishbofin
Inishshark
Corraun Pen
Party Mts
L. Mask
Ballinrobe
Tuam
ROSCOMMON
Roscommon
LONGFORD
L. Ree
Trim
Balbriggan
Skerries
Slyne Hd.
IRISH SEA

Mts of Connemara
Clifden
CONNAUGHT
L. Corrib
GALWAY
Athenry
Ballinasloe
Suck
Athlone
WESTMEATH
Moate
Clara
Mullingar
Royal Canal
Swords
Howth
Dublin

Bertraghboy B.
Kilkieran B.
Inishmore
Aran Is
Inishmaan
Black Hd.
Galway B.
Galway
Loughrea
Portumna
OFFALY
Banagher
Birr
Tullamore
Edenderry
KILDARE
Liffey
Dublin (Baile Atha Cliath)
Dún Laoghaire
Holyhead
Holy I.

Hags Hd.
Ennistimon
Gort
Slieve Aughty Mts
Lough Derg
Roscrea
Mountmellick
Port Laoise
Naas
Droichead Nua
Portarlington
Kippure ▲754
Bray
Greystones
Caernarfon Bay

Liscannor B.
Muttons I.
CLARE
Scarriff
Ennis
Killaloe
Nenagh
Slieve Bloom Mts
LAOIS
Athy
LEINSTER
Wicklow Mts ▲926
Lugnaquillia Mtn
Wicklow
Wicklow Hd.
③

Donegal Pt.
Milltown Malbay
Shannon
Foynes
LIMERICK
Templemore
Thurles
Roscrea
Carlow
CARLOW
Tullow
Arklow
Kilmichael Pt.
Bardsey

Loop Hd.
Mouth of the Shannon
Kilrush
Kilkee
Limerick
Rathkeale
TIPPERARY
Cashel
Tipperary
Fethard
Kilkenny
KILKENNY
Thomastown
Muine Bheag
Gorey
Cahore Pt.

Kerry Hd.
Tralee Bay
Listowel
Newcastle
Abbeyfeale
Rath Luirc
MUNSTER
Tipperary
Galty Mts
Cahir
Carrick-on-Suir
Clonmel
New Ross
WEXFORD
Enniscorthy

Dingle
Tralee
Castleisland
Kilmallock
Mitchelstown
Fethard
Comeragh Mts
Clonmel
Wexford
Rosslare

KERRY
Killorglin
Killarney
Newmarket
Kanturk
Fermoy
Knockmealdown Mts
Lismore
WATERFORD
Cappoquin
Dungarvan
Tramore
Ballyteige Bay
Saltee
Carnsore Pt.

▲1041
MacGillycuddy's Reeks
Cahersiveen
Sneem
Millstreet
Boggeragh Mts
Mallow
Blackwater
CORK
Lee
Macroom
Cork
Youghal
Youghal Harb.
Helvick Hd.
Mine Hd.
Waterford Harb.
Hook Hd.
Cardigan
Nat. Pk
Strumble Hd.
Fishguard
52

Kenmare
Ceha Mts
Bantry
Dunmanway
Bandon
Midleton
Cobh
Passage West
Ballycotton Bay
St Davids Hd
Ramsey I.
St Davids
Milford Haven
Haverfordwest

Castletown Bere
Dursey
Bantry Bay
Dunmanus Bay
Schull
Skibbereen
Clonakilty
Kinsale
Old Head of Kinsale
Milford Haven
Pembroke
Tenby
Caldy
St Govans Hd

Mizen Hd.
Roaringwater B.
Baltimore
C. Clear
Fastnet Rock
Clonakilty Bay
St George's Channel

Kinsale

Lundy

1:2M   0 25 50 75 100 km
       0 25   50 mls

Map of the British Isles and part of northwestern Europe.

A B ① C D ②

Shetland
St Magnus B. Fetlar
Yell
Whalsay
Lerwick
Foula
Sumburgh Hd
Viking Bank

Westray
Sanday Fair Isle
Rousay Stronsay
Sule Skerry Stromness Kirkwall
Stack Skerry Hoy Scapa Flow Orkney

Flannan Is
Sula Sgeir N. Rona
St Kilda
Butt of Lewis
C. Wrath Thurso Duncansby Hd Wick
Helmsdale
Ben Hope 927
Lewis Stornoway
Outer Hebrides
Harris
N. Uist
S. Uist
Barra
Ben More Assynt 998
Ullapool
The Minch
Portree Skye
Kyle of Lochalsh
L. Ness Dingwall Inverness Elgin Banff Fraserburgh
Peterhead
Buchan Ness
Moray Firth
Dornoch Dornoch Firth
Spey
Rum
Mallaig Fort Augustus
Ben Macdui 1309
Coll
Fort William Ben Nevis 1344
Tiree
SCOTLAND
Braemar Aberdeen
Dee Stonehaven
Don
Grampian Mts
Ben Lawers 1214 Pitlochry
Mull Oban
F. of Lorn
L. Awe Perth Dundee Arbroath
F. of Tay St Andrews
Montrose
Colonsay Jura
L. Lomond Stirling Kirkcaldy
Islay
Greenock Paisley Glasgow Edinburgh
F. of Forth
Motherwell St Abbs Hd
Berwick-upon-Tweed
Holy I.

NORTH

SEA

Long Forties

Great Fisher Bank

Malin Hd
Tory I.
Aran I.
Rossan Pt
Donegal
Errigal 752 Londonderry Coleraine
L. Foyle
Errris Hd
Donegal B.
Ballina
Achill Head
Sligo B.
L. Conn
Clew B.
Castlebar
L. Mask
Slyne Hd
L. Corrib
Galway
Aran Is
Galway B.
Slieve
Campbeltown
Arran
Irvine
Ayr
Kilmarnock
White Coomb 822
Girvan Moffat Hawick
Merrick 843 Nith
Dumfries
Cheviots
Moffat
N. IRELAND
Ballymena Belfast Bangor
Omagh
Enniskillen Monaghan Armagh Portadown
L. Neagh
Sligo Newry
L. Erne
Boyle Cavan
Roscommon Longford
L. Ree
Athlone
Monasterevin Mullingar
Shannon
REP. OF IRELAND
Stranraer Larne
Kirkcudbright Carlisle
Solway Firth
Luce B.
Douglas Isle of Man
Penrith
Scafell Pike 977
Kendal
Barrow-in-Furness
Morecambe
Blackpool Lancaster
Preston
Penrith Alnwick
Morpeth Blyth
Newcastle upon Tyne
Gateshead S. Shields
Durham Sunderland
Darlington Hartlepool
Middlesbrough
Yorkshire Moors Scarborough
Flamborough Hd
Harrogate York
Leeds Hull
Bradford Humber
Huddersfield Grimsby
Spurn Hd

Dogger Bank

Dublin (Baile Átha Cliath)
Dún Laoghaire
Bray
Wicklow Mts
IRISH SEA
Drogheda Dundalk
Ennis
Nenagh Port Laoise
Limerick Carlow
Tipperary Kilkenny
Clonmel
Waterford
Barrow
Killarney Blackwater
Dungarvan
Youghal
Cork
Bantry B.
Bantry
C. Clear
Old Hd of Kinsale
Cartauntoohill 1041
Dingle
Dingle B.
Tralee
Kilrush
Mouth of the Shannon

Holyhead
Anglesey
Bangor
Pwllheli
Snowdon 1085
Aberystwyth
Cardigan Bay
St George's Channel
Fishguard
St David's Hd
Carmarthen
Pembroke
Swansea
WALES
Builth Wells
Brecon
Newport
Cardiff
Bristol Chan.
Lundy I.
Barnstaple
Bude
Newquay
Truro
Penzance
Isles of Scilly
Land's End
Lizard Pt
Prawle Pt

Liverpool Birkenhead
Bolton Manchester
Warrington Doncaster
Chester
Crewe Stoke-on-Trent Sheffield
Lincoln
Derby
Shrewsbury Nottingham
Wolverhampton Leicester
Birmingham
ENGLAND
Coventry
Worcester Northampton
Gloucester Bedford
Milton Keynes
Oxford Luton
Swindon
Bristol
Bath Reading
Weston-super-Mare
Taunton
Salisbury
Exeter
Bournemouth
Plymouth Torquay
Weymouth
Isle of Wight
Southampton Portsmouth
Winchester
Guildford
London
Windsor
Maidstone
Crawley
Brighton Hastings
Eastbourne

Dee
Trent
Ouse
Trent
Severn
Wye
Avon
Nene Ouse
The Wash
King's Lynn
Norwich Great Yarmouth
Peterborough Lowestoft
Newmarket
Cambridge Ipswich
Colchester Felixstowe
Harwich
Chelmsford
Southend-on-Sea
Canterbury
Folkestone Dover
Thames

Den Helder
Vlieland
Texel
Terse
Hoorn
Alkmaar Zaanstad
Haarlem Amst
Hilvers
Leiden Amer
The Hague ('s-Gravenhage) Utrecht
Rotterdam
Dordrecht
's-Hertoger
Breda
N
B
E
Antwerp (Antwe
Mech
Leuve
Brussels (Bruxelles)
Vlissingen
Zeebrugge
Oostende Bruges Gent
Calais Dunkirk
St-Omer Tourcoing Roubaix
Béthune Lille Tournai Mons
Lens Douai Denain Maubeuge
St-Quentin
Valenciennes
Charleville-Mézières
Boulogne

ENGLISH CHANNEL

C. de la Hague
Alderney
Guernsey Sark
Channel Is (To U.K.)
Jersey St Helier
Golfe de St-Malo
Roscoff
Morlaix
Brest
I. d'Ouessant
Carhaix-Plouguer
Châteaulin
Quimper
Concarneau
Quimperlé
Lorient

Pte de Barfleur
Cherbourg
Valognes
St-Lô
Bayeux
Caen Lisieux
Coutances
Granville
St-Malo
Dinan
Mont-St-Michel
Domfront
Fougères
Mayenne
Vitré
Laval
Rennes
Ploërmel
Pontivy
Loudéac
St-Brieuc
BRITTANY
MAINE
Le Mans
Châteaudun

Montreuil
Le Tréport
Dieppe
Abbeville
Cambrai
Fourmies
Amiens
Neufchâtel Montdidier
Beauvais
Le Havre Fécamp
Bolbec Rouen
Deauville
Elbeuf Louviers
Seine
Soissons
Senlis Laon
Compiègne
Aisne
Reims
NORMANDY
Argentan
Évreux
Dreux Mantes
Versailles
Alençon
Chartres Étampes
Rambouillet
Fontainebleau
Cergy Pontoise
Paris
Meaux
Château-Thierry
Epernay
Provins
Melun
Sézanne
Romilly-s.-S.
FRANCE
Troyes
Sens
Chaumo
Vitry

PICARDIE
ARTOIS

③ ④

B ① C ② F R A N C D

1:5M
0 50 100 150 200 km
0 50 100 mls

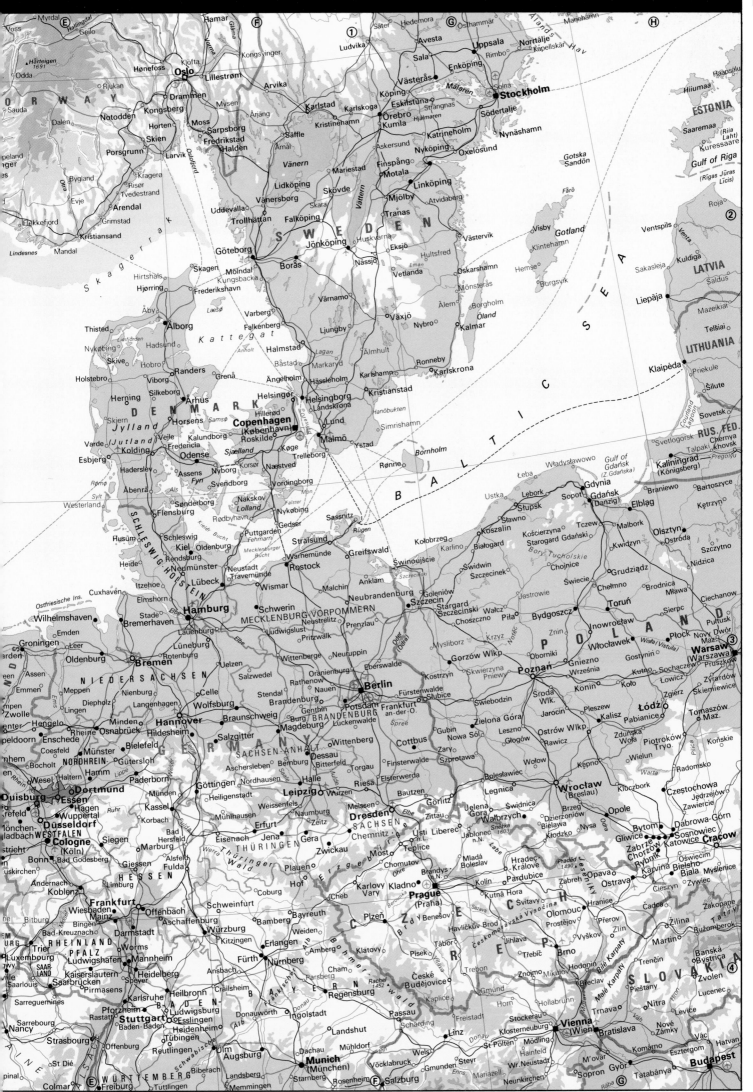

Inset maps

Iceland (at the same scale)

25W · Arctic Circle · 20 · 15

Bolungarvik · Ísafjörður · Dranga jökull · Grímsey · Bakkaflói
Siglufjörður · Olafsfjörður · Húsavík · Njarðvík
Húna flói · Sauðárkrókur · Akureyri · Seyðisfjörður
Biargtangar · *Gláma 945 · Blönduós · Neskaupstaður · Eskifjörður
Breiðafjörður · Stykkishólmur
Faxaflói · Akranes · Langjökull · Hofs jökull · Tungnafells jökull · Snæfell 1833
Reykjavík · Kópavogur · Þjórsá · Vatnajökull
Keflavík · Hafnarfjörður · Öræfajökull 2119
Grindavík · Selfoss · Mýrdalsjökull · Ingólfshöfði
Vestmannaeyjar · Surtsey

ICELAND

Faeroes (Færøerne)(Den.) (at the same scale)

Streymoy · Vágar · Tórshavn · Sandoy · Suðuroy
62 · 7W · 5

Main map

NORWEGIAN SEA

ARCTIC OCEAN

BARENTS SEA

Nordkapp · Honningsvåg · Vardø · Pov Rybachiy
Søroya · Hammerfest · Vadsø
Tromsø · Alta · Lakselv · Kirkenes · Pechenga · Nikel · Polyarnyy · Murmansk
Andenes · Kautokeino · Inari · Kola · Kol'skiy Poluostrov
Harstad · Karasjok · Monchegorsk · Apatity
Narvik · Karesuando · Kiruna · Nivskiy · Kandalaksha
Bodø · Gällivare · Rovaniemi · Kemijärvi · Kandalakshskaya Guba

FINLAND

Trondheim · Östersund · Umeå · Vaasa · Kuopio · Joensuu
Tampere · Pori · Turku · Helsinki · St Petersburg (Leningrad)

Bergen · Oslo · Stockholm · Tallinn · Narva

ESTONIA

Göteborg · Jönköping · Visby · Gotland · Riga · LATVIA

Copenhagen · Malmö · Karlskrona · Klaipeda · LITHUANIA · Minsk · BELARUS

DENMARK · Kaliningrad · Kaunas · Vilnius

Hamburg · Rostock · Gdańsk (Danzig) · Warsaw

GERMANY · Berlin · POLAND

BALTIC SEA

1:7.5M

0 · 50 · 100 · 200 · 300 km
0 · 50 · 100 · 150 mls

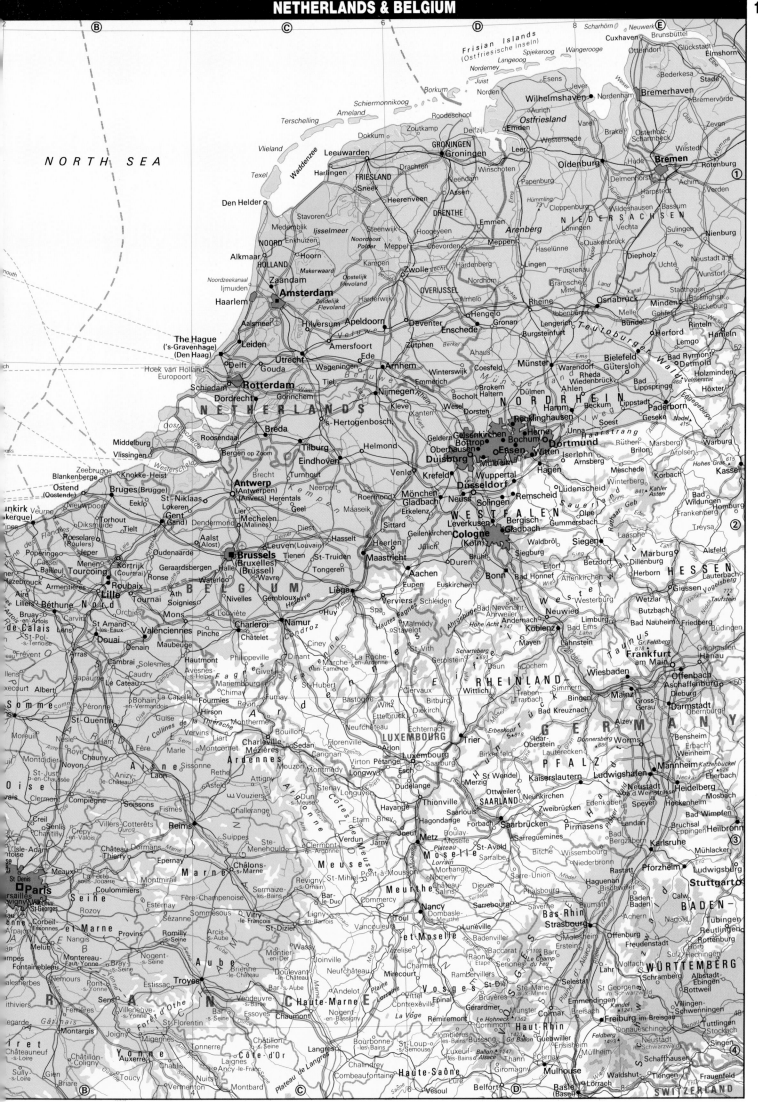

1:2.5M

1:5M

| | 50 | 100 | 150 | 200 km |

100 mls

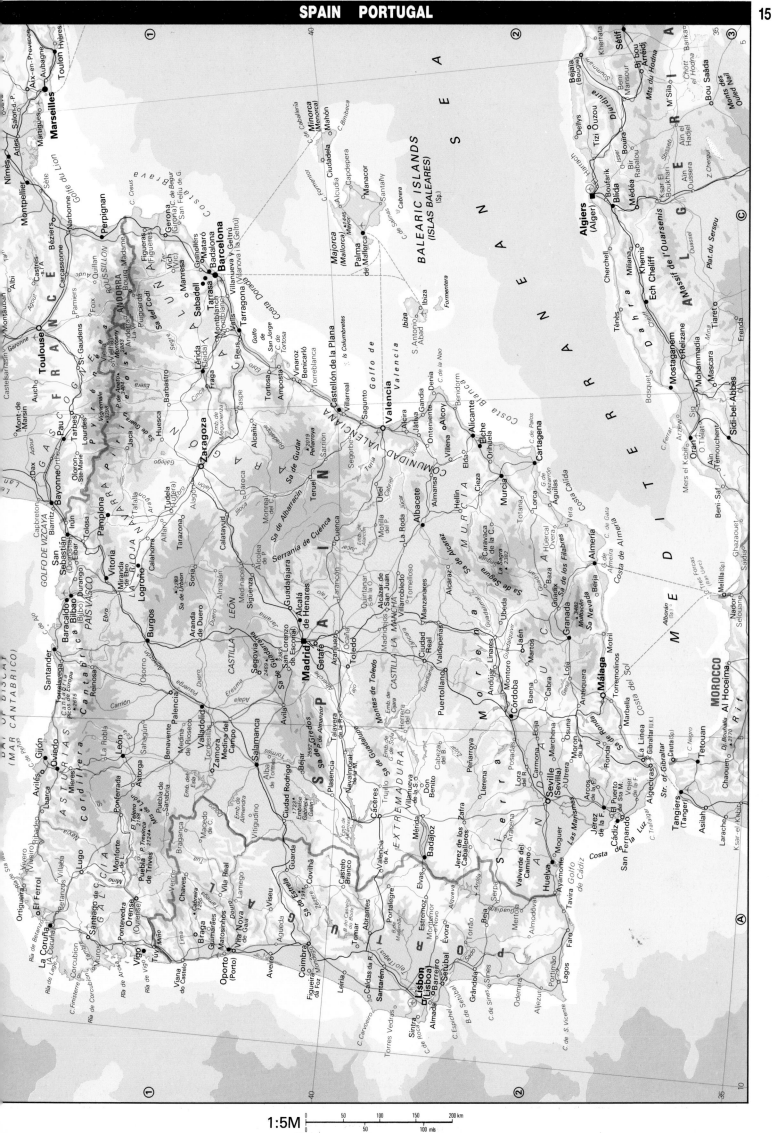

1:5M

| 0 | 50 | 100 | 150 | 200 km |
| 0 | 50 | 100 mls | | |

1:5M

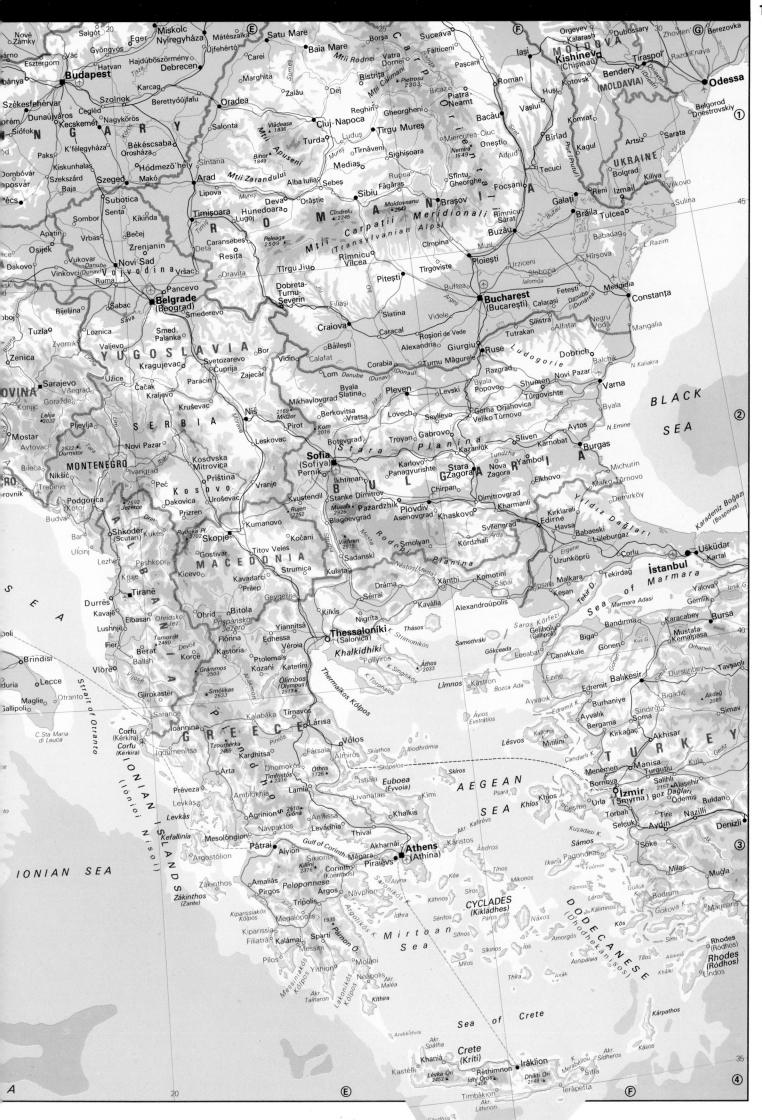

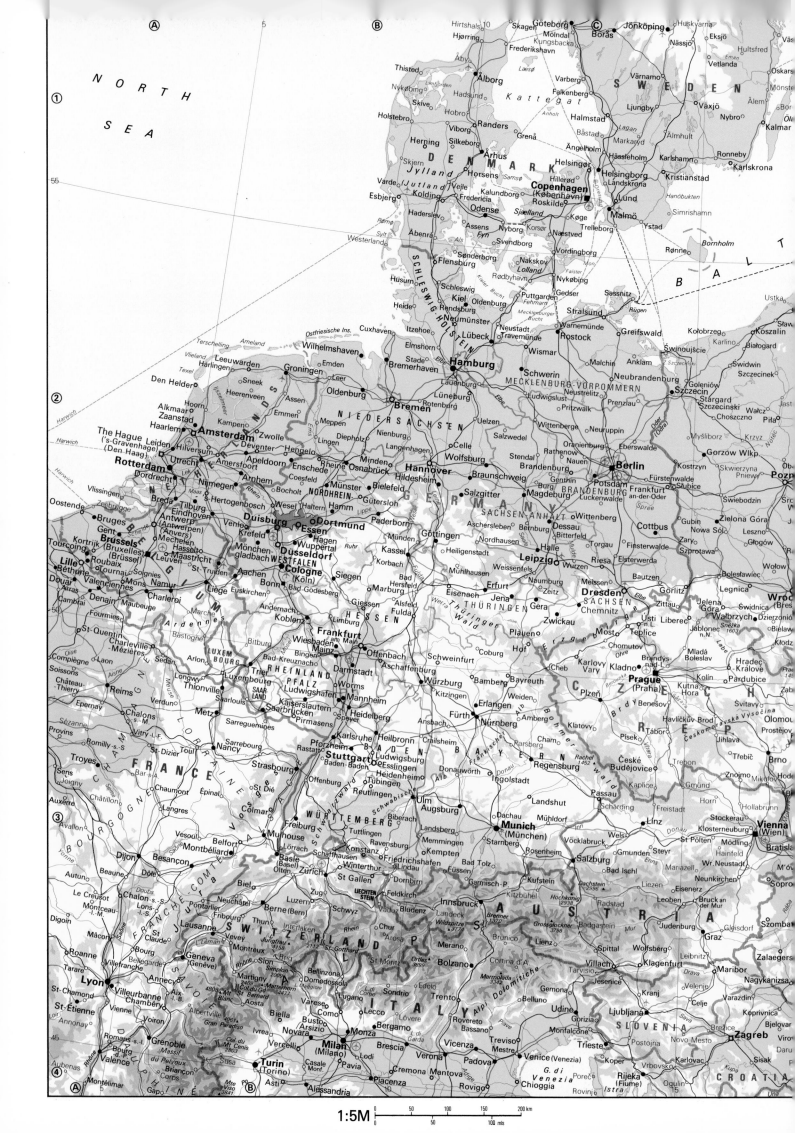

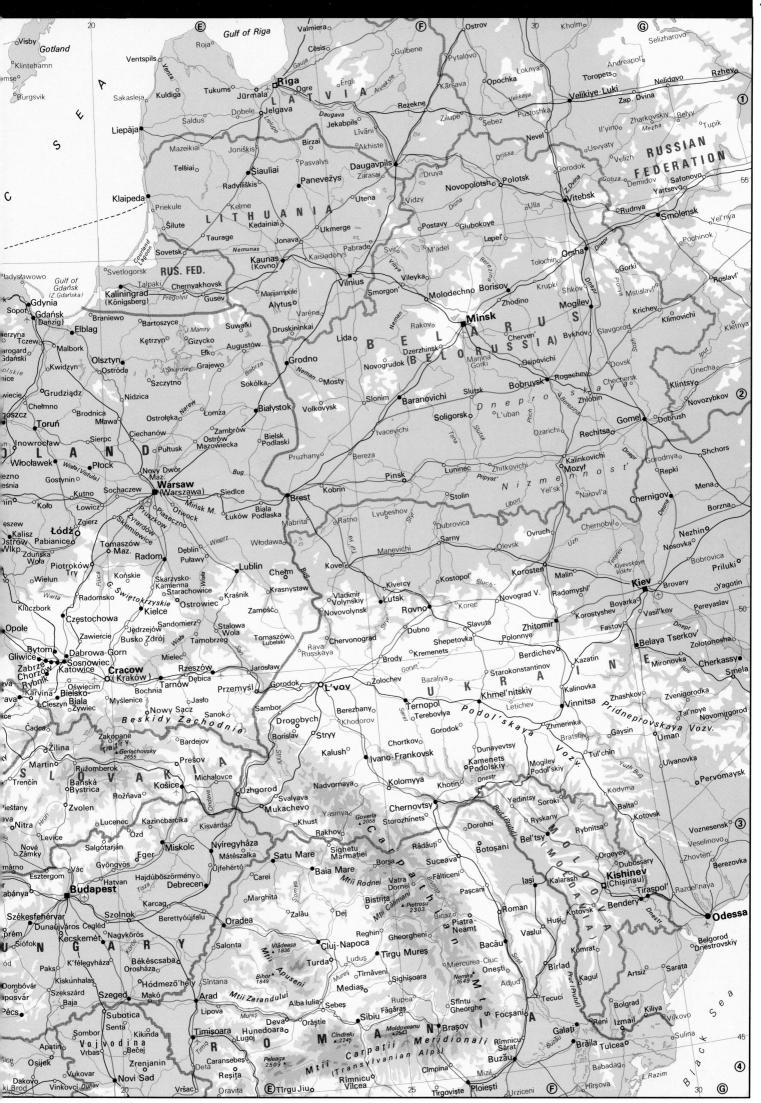

1:10M

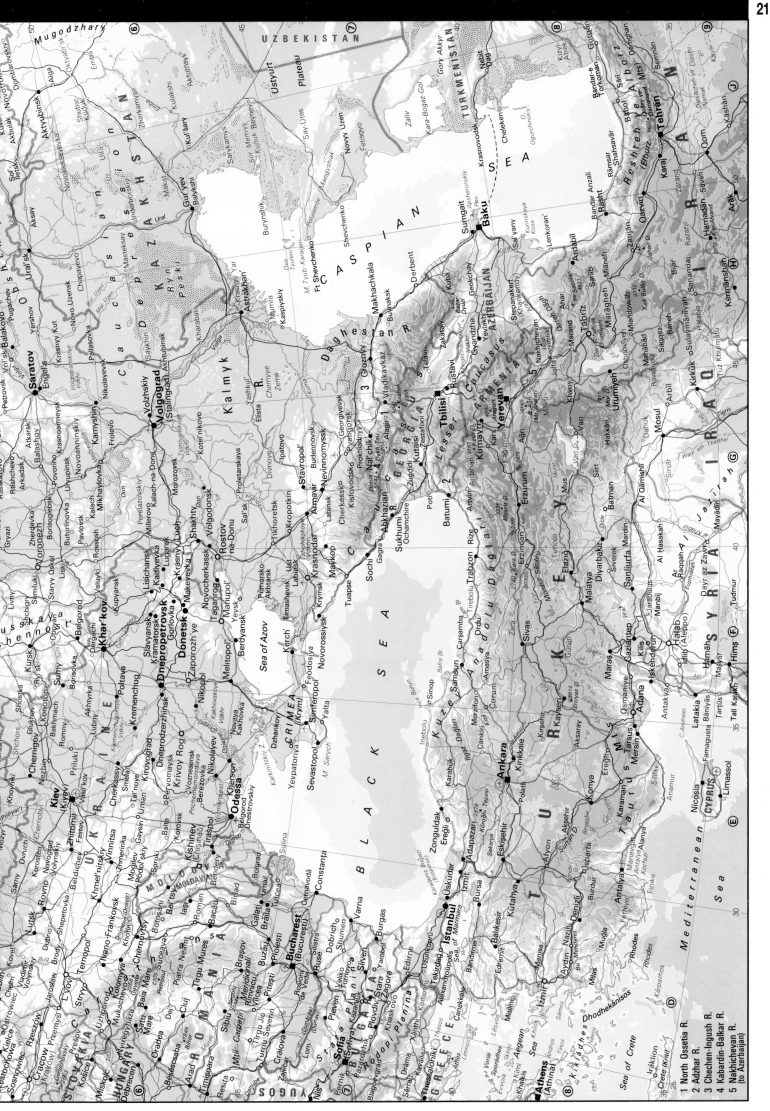

Mugodzhary ⑥

UZBEKISTAN ⑦

⑧

⑨

KAZAKHSTAN

Ustyurt Plateau

C A S P I A N

TURKMENISTAN

S E A

A N

I R A N

Reshteh-ye Alborz Mts

Tehrān

Saratov

Volgograd (Stalingrad)

Astrakhan'

Kalmyk

Daghestan

Makhachkala

Derbent

Sumgait

Baku

AZERBAIJAN

Tabrīz

 Orūmiyeh

Qom

Kāshān

U K R A I N E

Khar'kov

Dnepropetrovsk

Donetsk

Rostov na-Donu

Stavropol'

3 Grozny

Vladikavkaz

C a u c a s u s

Caucasus

GEORGIA

Tbilisi

ARMENIA

Yerevan

Mosul

I R A Q

Kirkūk

Arbīl

Kiev (Kiyev)

Odessa

CRIMEA

Sea of Azov

Novorossiysk

Sochi

Sukhumi

Abkhazian

Batumi

Lesser Caucasus

Erzurum

Van

Tigris

Euphrates

S Y R I A

Ḥalab (Aleppo)

MOLDAVIA

B L A C K   S E A

Zonguldak

T U R K E Y

Sivas

Malatya

Diyarbakir

Gaziantep

Adana

Ḥimṣ

ROMANIA

Bucharest (Bucureşti)

Istanbul

Ankara

Konya

Latakia

CYPRUS

Nicosia

Bucharest

BULGARIA

Sofia

Edirne

İzmir

Antalya

Mediterranean Sea

YUGOS.

GREECE

Athens (Athinai)

Aegean Sea

Crete (Kriti)

Sea of Crete

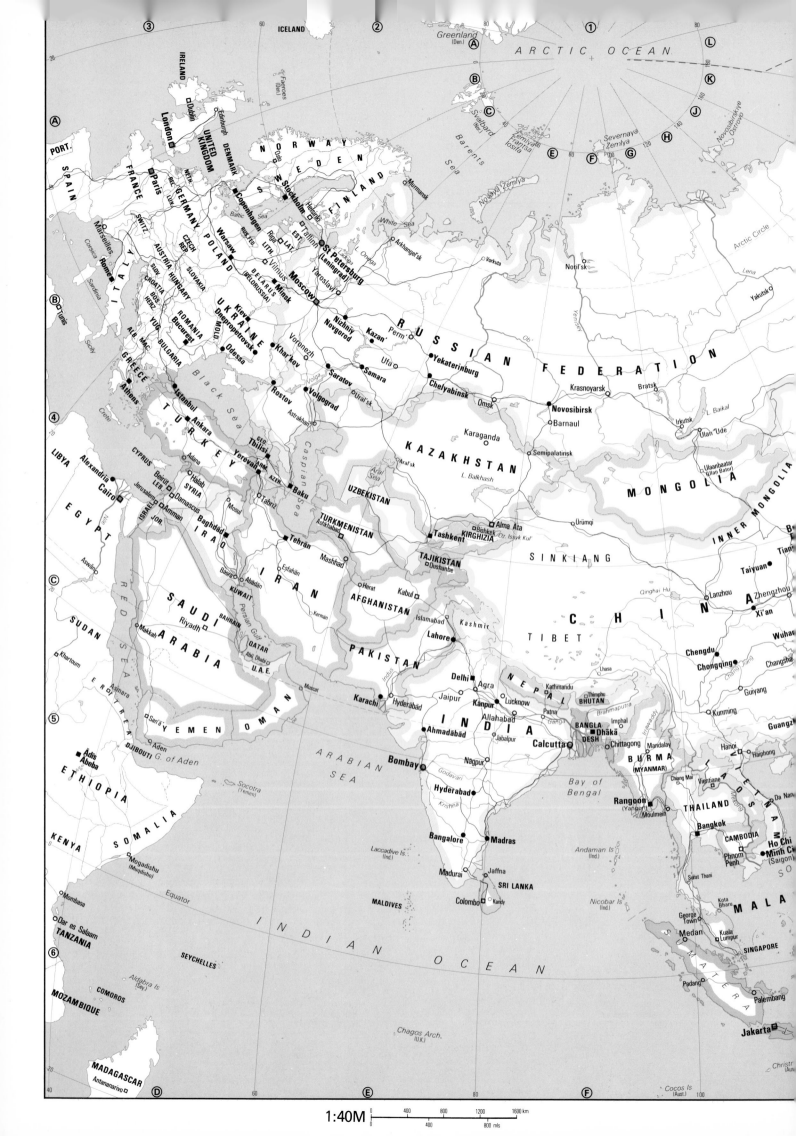

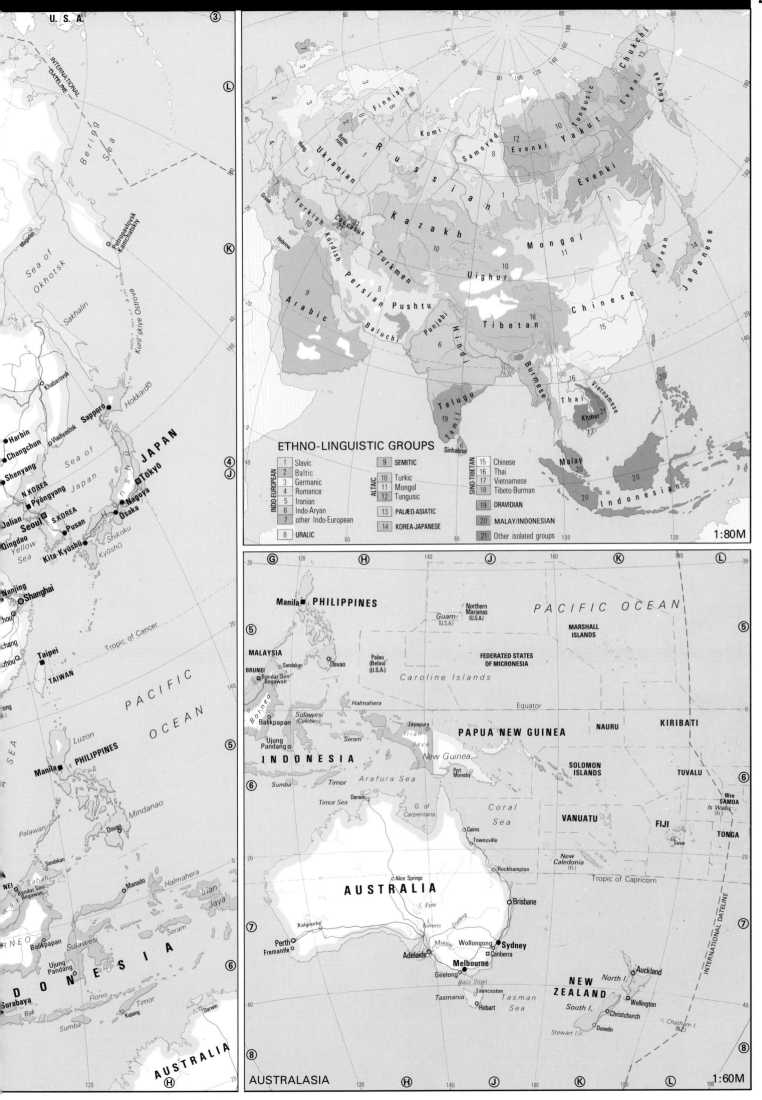

U.S.A.

INTERNATIONAL DATELINE

Bering Sea

Sea of Okhotsk

Magadan

Petropavlovsk-Kamchatskiy

Sakhalin

Kuril'skiye Ostrova

Khabarovsk

Harbin
Changchun
Shenyang
Vladivostok
Sapporo
Hokkaidō

N.KOREA
Pyongyang
Dalian
Seoul
S.KOREA
Pusan
Qingdao
Kita-Kyūshū
Yellow Sea
Kyūshū

Sea of Japan

Honshu

JAPAN
Tokyo
Nagoya
Osaka
Shikoku

Nanjing
Shanghai
zhou

Taipei
TAIWAN

Tropic of Cancer

PACIFIC OCEAN

Luzon

PHILIPPINES
Manila

SEA

Sabah
Bandar Seri Begawan
BORNEO
Balikpapan
Ujung Pandang
Sulawesi

Mindanao

Palawan

Sandakan

Manado
Halmahera

Irian Jaya

DONESIA

NEI

Surabaya
Bali
Flores
Timor
Kupang
Sumba
Darwin

AUSTRALIA

ETHNO-LINGUISTIC GROUPS

Finnish
Komi
Samoyed
Evenki
Yakut
Tungusic
Chukchi
Koryak
Eveni

Byelo Russ.
Ukranian
Russian
Evenki
Evenki
Korean
Japanese
Mongol
Greek
Turkish
Caucasus
Kazakh
Hebrew
Kurdish
Turkmen
Uighur
Persian
Pushtu
Tibetan
Chinese
Arabic
Baluchi
Punjabi
Hindi
Burmese
Telugu
Tamil
Vietnamese
Thai
Khmer
Sinhalese
Malay
Indonesian

INDO-EUROPEAN		ALTAIC		SINO-TIBETAN	
1	Slavic	9	SEMITIC	15	Chinese
2	Baltic	10	Turkic	16	Thai
3	Germanic	11	Mongol	17	Vietnamese
4	Romance	12	Tungusic	18	Tibeto-Burman
5	Iranian	13	PALÆO-ASIATIC	19	DRAVIDIAN
6	Indo-Aryan	14	KOREA-JAPANESE	20	MALAY/INDONESIAN
7	other Indo-European			21	Other isolated groups
8	URALIC				

1:80M

PHILIPPINES
Manila

Northern Marianas (U.S.A.)
Guam (U.S.A.)

PACIFIC OCEAN

MARSHALL ISLANDS

MALAYSIA
BRUNEI
Bandar Seri Begawan
Sandakan
Davao
Palau (Belau) (U.S.A.)

FEDERATED STATES OF MICRONESIA

Caroline Islands

Borneo
Balikpapan
Sulawesi (Celebes)
Halmahera
Seram

Equator

Jayapura
Irian Jaya

PAPUA NEW GUINEA

New Guinea
Port Moresby

NAURU

KIRIBATI

INDONESIA

Sumba
Timor
Arafura Sea
Darwin

SOLOMON ISLANDS

TUVALU

Timor Sea

G. of Carpentaria

Coral Sea

VANUATU

New Caledonia (Fr.)

FIJI
Suva

Wm SAMOA
Is Wallis (Fr.)

TONGA

Cairns
Townsville

Tropic of Capricorn

Alice Springs

Rockhampton

AUSTRALIA

L. Eyre

Brisbane

Kalgoorlie

L. Torrens
Darling

Perth
Fremantle

Murray
Wollongong
Sydney
Adelaide
Canberra
Melbourne
Geelong

Bass Strait

North I.

Auckland

NEW ZEALAND

Launceston
Tasmania
Hobart

Tasman Sea

South I.
Wellington
Christchurch
Dunedin

Chatham I. (N.Z.)

Stewart I.

INTERNATIONAL DATELINE

AUSTRALASIA

1:60M

Bering Str.

ARCTIC OCEAN

Ostrov Komsomolets

SEVERNAYA ZEMLYA (NORTH LAND)

Ostrov Bol'shevik

O. Malyy Taymyr

Mys Chelyushin

Zaliv Faddeya

O. Petra

NOVOSIBIRSKYE OSTROVA (NEW SIBERIAN ISLANDS)

Ostrova De Longa

O. Bennetta

Ostrov Faddeyevskiy

O. Kotel'nyy

O. Novaya Sibir

O. Bol'shoy Lyakhovskiy

O. Malyy Lyakhovskiy

O. Bel'kovskiy

Proliv Dmitrya Lapteva

LAPTEV SEA

EAST SIBERIAN SEA

Wrangel I.

Proliv Longa

CHUKCHI SEA

Mys Shmidta

Mys Shalaurova

Pevek

Mys Shelagskiy

Iul'tin

Uelen

Providencia

M. Chaplino

St Lawrence I. (USA)

St Matthew I. (USA)

BERING SEA

Chukotskiy

Poluostrov

Anadyrskiy Zaliv

Anadyr'

Beringovskiy

Khatyrka

Koryakskoye Nagor'ye

Kolymskoye Nagor'ye

Bilibino

Cherskiy

Ambarchik

Anyuysk

Markovo

Il'pyrskiy

Ossora

O. Karaginskiy

Mys Ozernoy

KAMCHATKA

Sredinnyy Khrebet

Klyuchi

Ust'-Kamchatsk

Petropavlovsk-Kamchatskiy

Kronotskiy

Mys Lopatka

Paramushir

Kuril Islands (Kuril'skiye Ostrova)

SEA OF OKHOTSK

Magadan

Ust'-Nera

Oymyakon

Khrebet Cherskogo

Verkhoyanskiy Khrebet

Khrebet Orulgan

YAKUT R.

Zyryanka

Srednekolymsk

Omolon

Kolyma

Indigirka

Zhigansk

Tiksi

Kyusyur

Yana

Olenek

Saskylakh

Udzha

Khatanga

Novorybnoye

Nordvik

Gory Byrranga

Ozero Taymyr

Poluostrov Taymyr

Dudypta

Volochanka

Gory Putorana

Norilsk

Yessey

Tura

Podkamennaya Tunguska

Baykit

Vanavara

Yartsevo

Yeniseyskiy Kryazh

Lesosibirsk

Pit Gorodok

Kezhma

Sredne Sibirskoye Ploskogor'ye

FEDERATION

SIBERIAN

Yakutsk

Vilyuysk

Verkhnevilyuysk

Nyurba

Mirnyy

Suntar

Lensk

Olekminsk

Peleduy

Nepa

Mama

Bodaybo

Aldan

Tommot

Chulman

Stanovoy Khrebet

Aldanskoye Nagor'ye

Patomskoye Nagor'ye

Kirensk

Ust'-Kut

Ilimsk

Neftelensk

Severo Baykal'skoye Nagor'ye

Nizhneangarsk

Ust' Nyukzha

Chara

Tynda

Tukuringra

Khrebet

Zeya

Skovorodino

Yerofey Pavlovich

Mogocha

Chernyshevsk

Shilka

Sretensk

Nerchinsk

Chita

Borzya

Zabaykal'sk

Yablonovyy Khrebet

Petrovsk-Zabaykal'skiy

Ulan Ude

Angarsk

Irkutsk

Slyudyanka

Lake Baikal

Baykalsk

Bratsk

Tayshet

Zima

Tulun

Cheremkhovo

Usolye Sibirskoye

Kansk

Achinsk

Krasnoyarsk

Uyar

Minusinsk

Abakan

Sayanogorsk

Sayan

Gora Munku Sardyk 3491

Kyzyl

Tuva

Tannu Ola

Turan

Chaa-Khol

Uvs Nuur

Ulaangom

Tsagan Tologoy

Hyargas Nuur

Baylik Shan

Altun Shan

Qilian Shan

Karlik Shan 4925

Hami

Yumen

Jiayuguan

Zhangye

Anxi

Dunhuang

Lop Nur

Xingxingxia

Qijiaotang

Wuwei

Yinchuan

Ordos

Lanzhou

Baotou

Hohhot

Datong

Zhangjiakou

BEIJING (Peking)

TIANJIN (Tientsin)

Baoding

Shijiazhuang

Tangshan

Qinhuangdao

Chengde

Xuanhua

Jining

Bo Hai

Yantai

Qingdao

Weifang

Jinan

Zibo

Dezhou

Handan

Anyang

Xinxiang

Jining

Xuzhou

Lianyungang

Qingjiang

Linyi

Yanzhou

Taiyuan

Yangquan

Xingtai

Fenyang

Linfen

Changzhi

Yan'an

YELLOW SEA

Dalian

Lüshun

Liaodong Bandao

Jinzhou

Yingkou

Jinxi

Anshan

Benxi

Shenyang

Fushun

Liaoyang

Liaoyuan

Tieling

Fuxin

Chifeng

Duolun

Erenhot

Saihan Tal

Dzamin Uüd

S.ainshand

Mandalgovi

Dalandzadgad

Bayan Obo

Linxi

Ulanhot

Baicheng

Da'an

Changchun

Jilin

Siping

Tongliao

Harbin

Qiqihar

Daqing

Nenjiang

Hailar

Manzhouli

Choybalsan

Öndörhaan

Baruun-Urt

Tamsagbulag

Buyr Nuur

Hulun Nuur

De Hinggan Ling (Greater Khingan Range)

Da Hinggan Ling

Nen Jiang

Bei'an

Suihua

Hegang

Jiamusi

Shuangyashan

Jixi

Mudanjiang

Mishan

Suifenhe

Boli

MANCHURIA

Tonghua

Dandong

Kuandian

Tumen

Yanji

Hunchun

Vladivostok

Ussuriysk

Nakhodka

Partizansk

Spassk-Dal'niy

Dal'nerechensk

Bikin

Sikhote Alin

Khor

Khabarovsk

Birobidzhan

Obluchye

Blagoveshchensk

Svobodnyy

Belogorsk

Shimanovsk

Zavitinsk

Raychikhinsk

Komsomol'sk na Amure

Amur

Nikolayevsk

Bogorodskoye

De Kastri

Tatarskiy Proliv

SAKHALIN

Aleksandrovsk-Sakhalinskiy

Uglegorsk

Poronaysk

Yuzhno-Sakhalinsk

Korsakov

Zaliv Terpeniya

Zaliv Aniva

La Pérouse Strait

Sovetskaya Gavan

Vanino

Okha

Moskal'vo

Nogliki

Nikolayevsk-na-Amure

Ayan

Nel'kan

Chumikan

Udskaya Guba

Okhotsk

Magadan

Ust' Omchug

Atka

SEA OF OKHOTSK

Wakkanai

Asahikawa

HOKKAIDO

Sapporo

Otaru

Muroran

Hakodate

Aomori

Hirosaki

Noshiro

Akita

Morioka

Ishinomaki

Sendai

Yamagata

Sakata

Niigata

Nagaoka

Fukushima

Mito

TOKYO

Yokohama

Chiba

Nagano

Takaoka

Kanazawa

Fukui

Toyama

Gifu

Nagoya

Shizuoka

Kyoto

Osaka

Kobe

Nara

Wakayama

Okayama

Hiroshima

Matsue

Tottori

Matsuyama

Kochi

Takamatsu

SHIKOKU

Kitakyushu

Fukuoka

Saga

Sasebo

Nagasaki

Kumamoto

Miyazaki

Kagoshima

KYUSHU

Osumi-shoto

Tanega

Yaku

Osumi-Kaikyo

JAPAN

SEA OF JAPAN

NORTH KOREA

P'yongyang

Nampo

Sinuiju

Kanggye

Hamhung

Hungnam

Wonsan

Ch'ongjin

Najin

Hoeryong

Kimch'aek

SOUTH KOREA

SEOUL (Soul)

Inch'on

Suwon

Ch'unch'on

Kangnung

Taejon

Chonju

Kwangju

Mokp'o

Kunsan

Taegu

Pusan

Masan

Chinju

Ulsan

P'ohang

Cheju

Cheju Do

Korea Strait

Tsushima

Dalian

Kaesong

Haeju

Osan

Kimch'aek

Chech'on

Andong

Ch'ongju

Wonju

Uijongbu

Pohang

Yosu

Goto-Retto

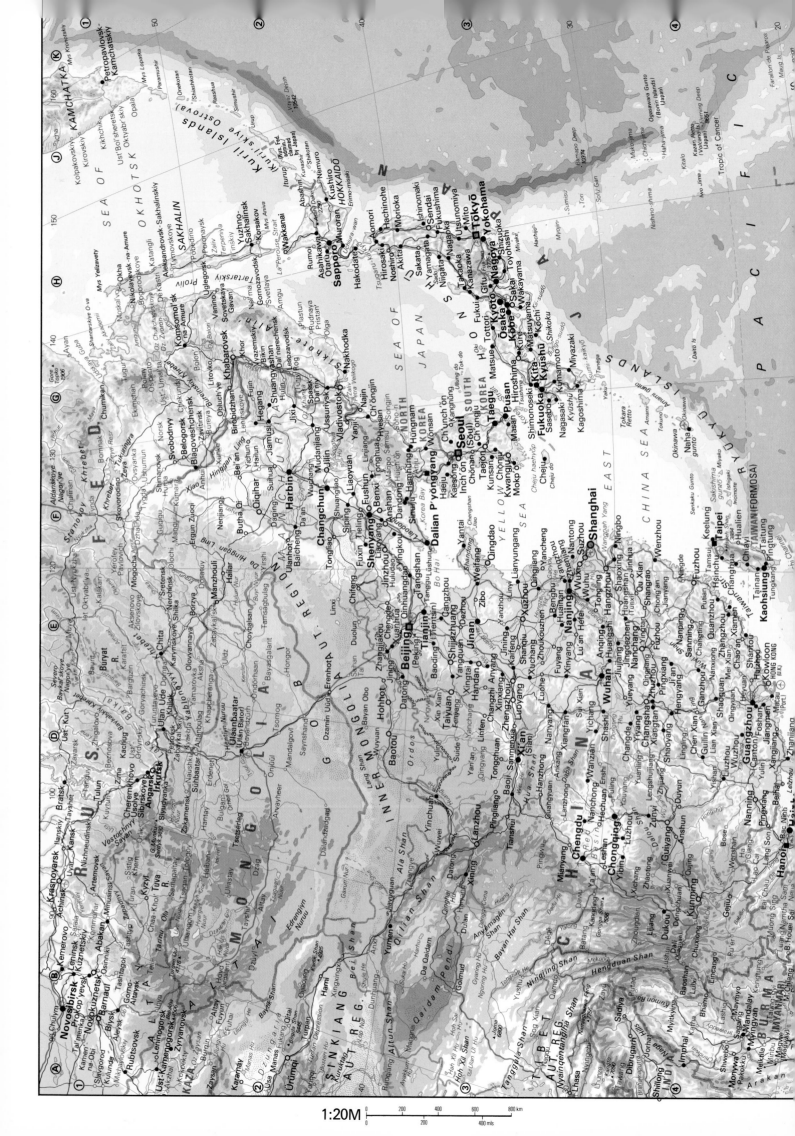

1:20M

200   400   600   800 km
200   400 mls

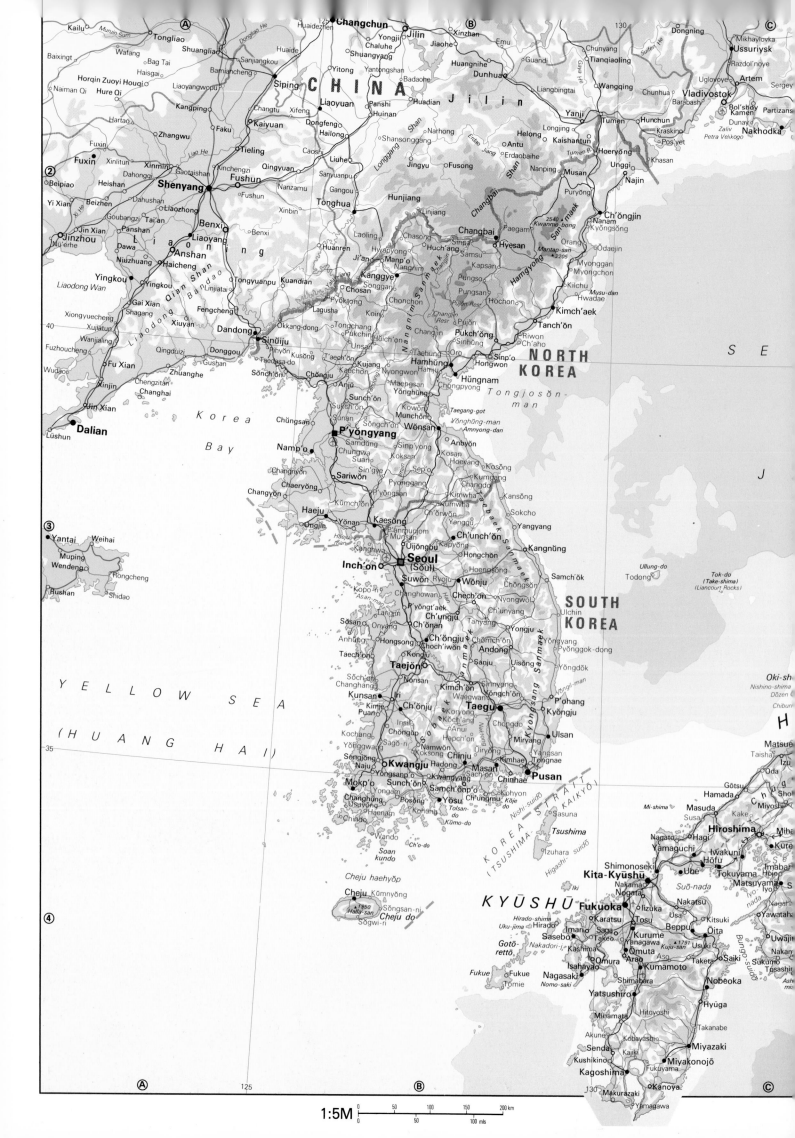

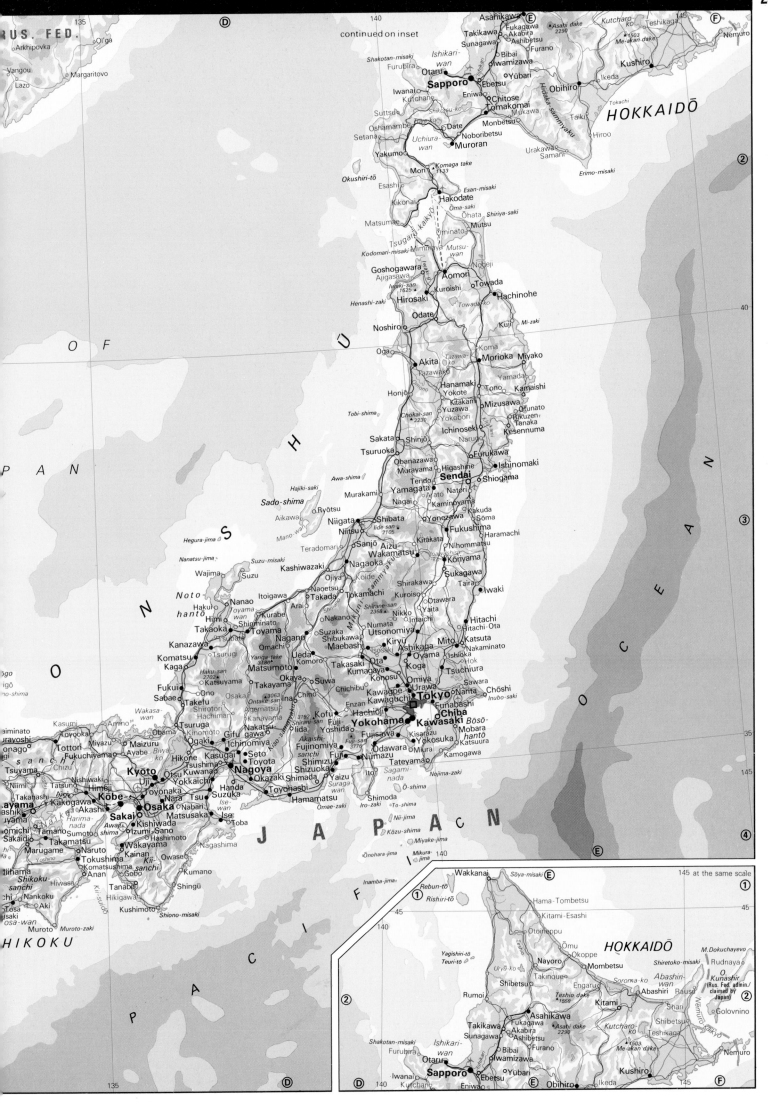

RUS. FED.
Arkhipovka
Vangou
Lazo
Ol'ga
Margaritovo

continued on inset

Asahikawa
Takikawa
Sunagawa
Fukagawa
Akabira
Ashibetsu
Furano
Asahi dake 2290
Kutcharo-ko
Teshikaga
Nemuro

Shakotan-misaki
Furubira
Ishikari-wan
Iwamizawa
Bibai
Yubari
Iwanai
Kutchan
Otaru
Sapporo
Ebetsu
Eniwa
Chitose
Tomakomai
Mukawa
Ikeda
Obihiro
Kushiro

Suttsu
Shikotsu-ko
Date
Noboribetsu
Monbetsu
Toya-ko
Muroran
Uchiura-wan
Taiki
Hiroo

HOKKAIDŌ
Hidaka-sammyaku
Tokachi
Urakawa
Samani
Erimo-misaki

Oshamambe
Setana
Yakumo
Mori
Komaga take 1133

Okushiri-tō
Esashi
Esan-misaki
Ōma-saki
Shiriya-saki

Kikonai
Hakodate
Ōhata
Mutsu

Matsumae
Tsugaru-kaikyō
Minmaya
Ōminato

Kodomari-misaki
Mutsu-wan
Noheji

Goshogawara
Ajigasawa
Aomori
Towada
Hachinohe

Iwaki-san 1625
Hirosaki
Kuroishi
Towada-ko

Henashi-zaki
Odate
Kuji
Mi-zaki

Noshiro
Koma

Oga
Akita
Tazawa-ko
Morioka
Miyako

Honjō
Tazawako
Omono
Hanamaki
Tono
Kamaishi

Tobi-shima
Chokai-san 2230
Yokote
Kitakami
Mizusawa
Ōfunato

Sakata
Yuzawa
Yokobori
Ichinoseki
Rikuzen-Tanaka
Kesennuma

Shinjō
Narugo

Tsuruoka
Obanazawa
Furukawa

Murayama
Higashine
Ishinomaki

Tendo
Sendai
Shiogama

Awa-shima
Yamagata
Natori

Hajiki-saki
Nagai
Kaminoyama
Kakuda
Sōma

Sado-shima
Aikawa
Ryōtsu
Murakami
Yonezawa
Fukushima
Haramachi

Mano-wan
Niigata
Shibata
Iide san 2105
Kitakata
Nihommachi

Hegura-jima
Niitsu
Aizu-Wakamatsu
Kōriyama

Nanatsu-jima
Teradomari
Sanjō
Ojiya
Shirakawa
Sukagawa

Suzu-misaki
Wajima
Kashiwazaki
Nagaoka
Taira
Iwaki

Suzu
Koide
Otawara

Noto hantō
Nanao
Itoigawa
Takada
Tokamachi
Kuroiso
Hitachi

Haku-san
Himi
Toyama-wan
Arai
Nakano
Shirane-san 2368
Nikko
Imaichi
Hitachi-Ota

Takaoka
Shinminato
Toyama
Suzaka
Numata
Utsunomiya
Mito
Katsuta

Kanazawa
Tsubata
Nagano
Shibukawa
Kiryū
Ashikaga
Nakaminato

Komatsu
Tsurugi
Omachi
Maebashi
Ōta
Oyama
Ishioka

Kaga
Yariga-take 3180
Matsumoto
Komoro
Ueda
Takasaki
Koga
Tsuchiura

Fukui
Haku-san 2702
Katsuyama
Okaya
Suwa
Kumagaya
Konosu
Omiya

Sabae
Osaka
Ontake-san 3063
Inа
Chichibu
Enzan
Kawagoe
Urawa
Narita
Chōshi

Takefu
Shirotori
Nakatsu-gawa
Iida
Kōfu
Kawaguchi
Tokyo
Inubo-saki

Tsuruga
Obama
Kinomoto
Agematsu
Shirani-san 3192
Fuji Yoshida
Hachioji
Funabashi
Chiba

Kasumi
Ogaki
Ichinomiya
Kiso-sammyaku
Akaishi sanchi
Fuji-san 3776
Yokohama
Kawasaki
Bōsō-hantō

Toyooka
Miyazu
Maizuru
Ayabe
Biwa-ko
Hikone
Kasugai
Seto
Toyota
Odawara
Kisarazu
Mobara
Katsuura

Tottori
Fukuchiyama
Kuwana
Nagoya
Shimizu
Numazu
Yokosuka
Kamogawa

Tsuyama
Kyōto
Ōtsu
Yokkaichi
Handa
Suzuka
Okazaki
Shimada
Fuji
Miura
Nojima-zaki

Niimi
Nishiwaki
Uji
Nara
Tsu
Shizuoka
Yaizu
Itō
Sagami-nada

Takahashi
Himeji
Kōbe
Akashi
Nabari
Matsusaka
Ise
Toyohashi
Hamamatsu
Shimoda
Ō-shima

Aioi
Sakai
Kishiwada
Ise-wan
Toba
Ōmae-zaki
Iro-zaki
To-shima

Kakogawa
Osaka
Izumi-Sano
Nagashima
Nii-jima

Tamano
Sumoto
Wakayama
Kumano
Kōzu-shima
Miyake-jima

Marugame
Takamatsu
Naruto
Kainan
Owase

Tokushima
Komatsushima
Hashimoto
Gobo
Shingū
Ōnohara-jima
Mikura-jima

Anan
Tanabe
Hikigawa
Kushimoto
Shiono-misaki

Muroto
Muroto-zaki

SHIKOKU

JAPAN

PACIFIC OCEAN

SEA OF JAPAN

C H Ū G O K U

H O N S H Ū

Inset:

145 at the same scale

Wakkanai
Sōya-misaki
Inamba-jima
Rebun-tō
Rishiri-tō
Hama-Tombetsu
Kitami-Esashi

Yagishiri-tō
Teuri-tō
Otoineppu
Ōmu
Koppe

Uryū-ko
Nayoro
Mombetsu

Rumoi
Shibetsu
Takinoue
Engaru
Teshio dake 1558
Sorома-ko
Abashiri-wan
Shiretoko-misaki
Rudnaya

HOKKAIDŌ
M. Dokuchayevo
O. Kunashir
(Rus. Fed. admin./ claimed by Japan)

Takikawa
Fukagawa
Asahikawa
Akabira
Ashibetsu
Asahi dake 2290
Kitami
Abashiri
Shari
Shibetsu
Teshikaga

Shakotan-misaki
Furubira
Ishikari-wan
Sunagawa
Bibai
Iwamizawa
Furano
Kutcharo-ko
Me-akan dake 1503
Golovnino

Otaru
Sapporo
Ebetsu
Yūbari
Kushiro

Iwanai
Kutchan
Eniwa
Obihiro
Ikeda
Nemuro

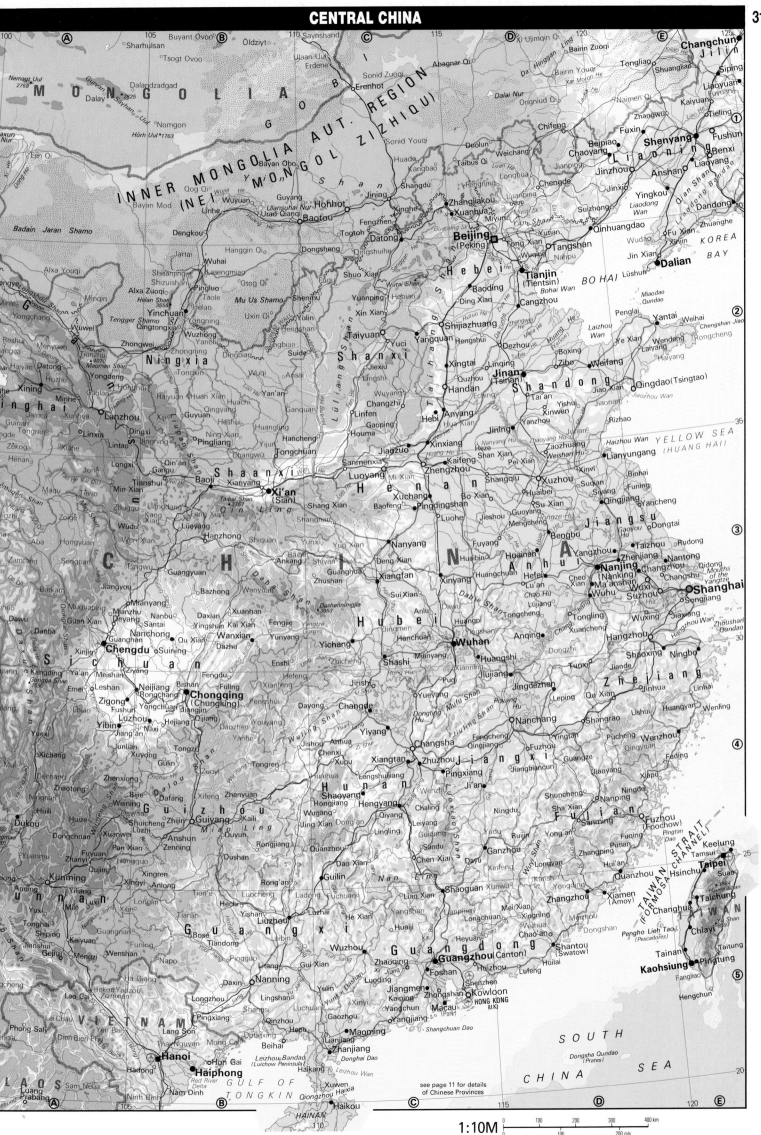

1:10M

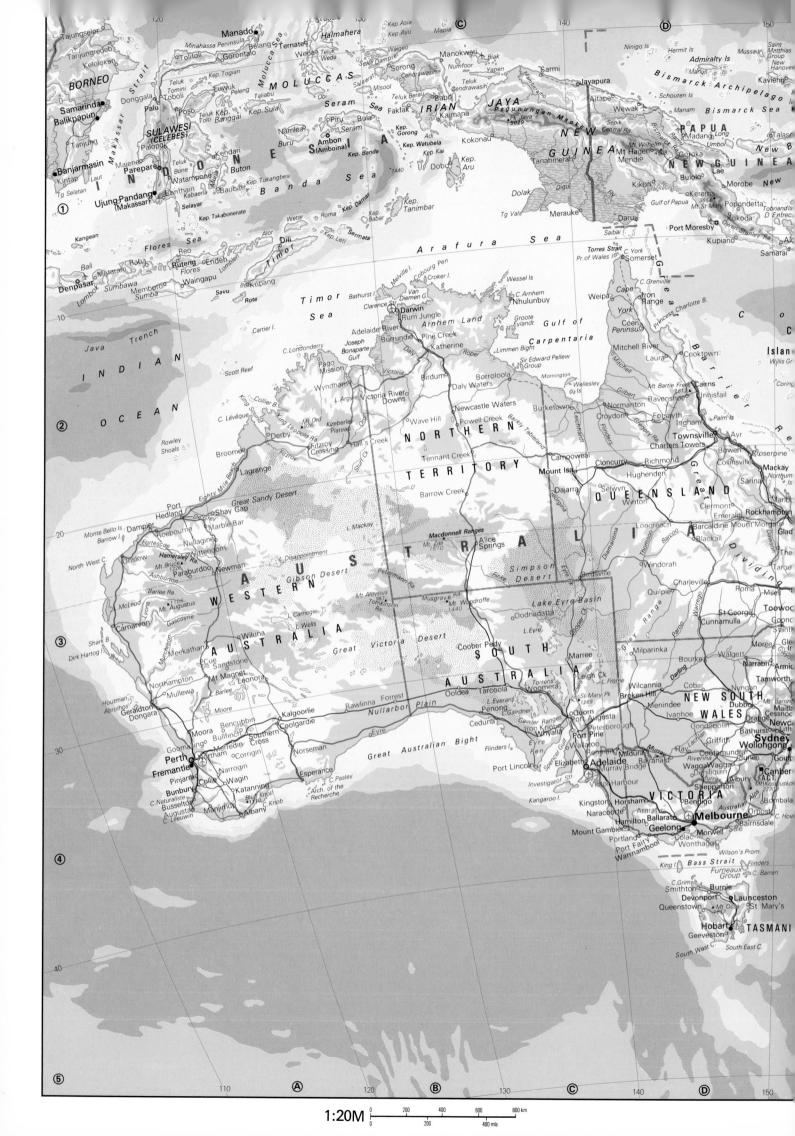

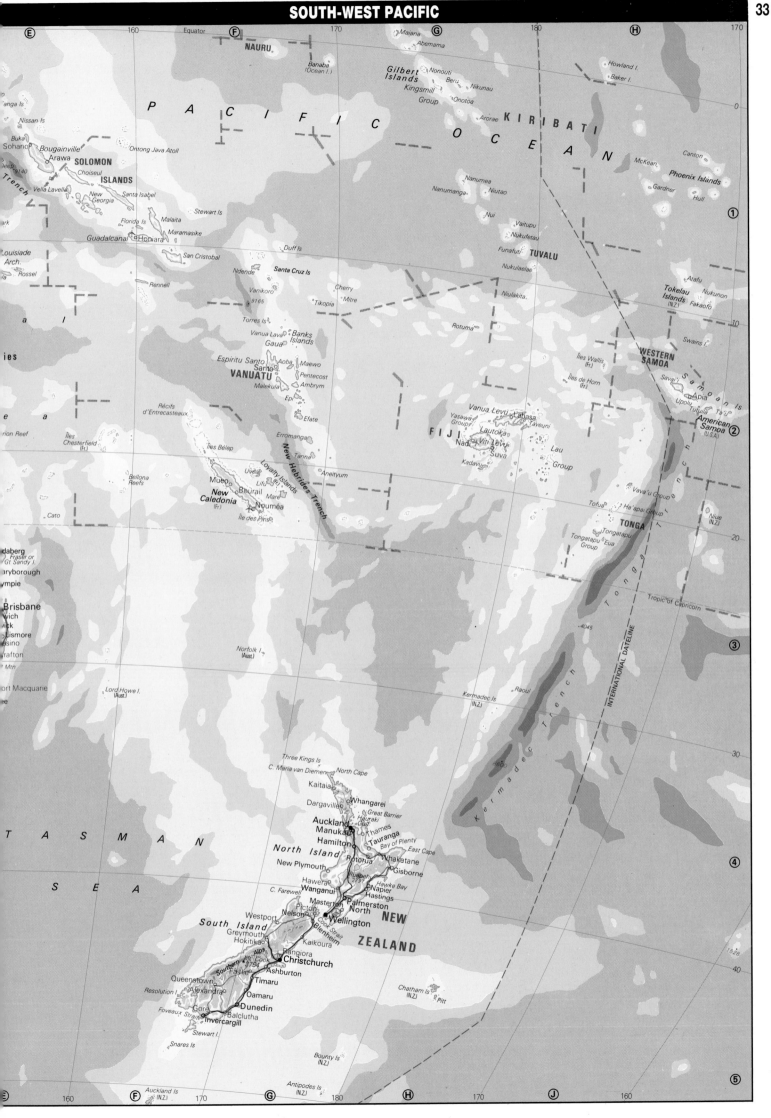

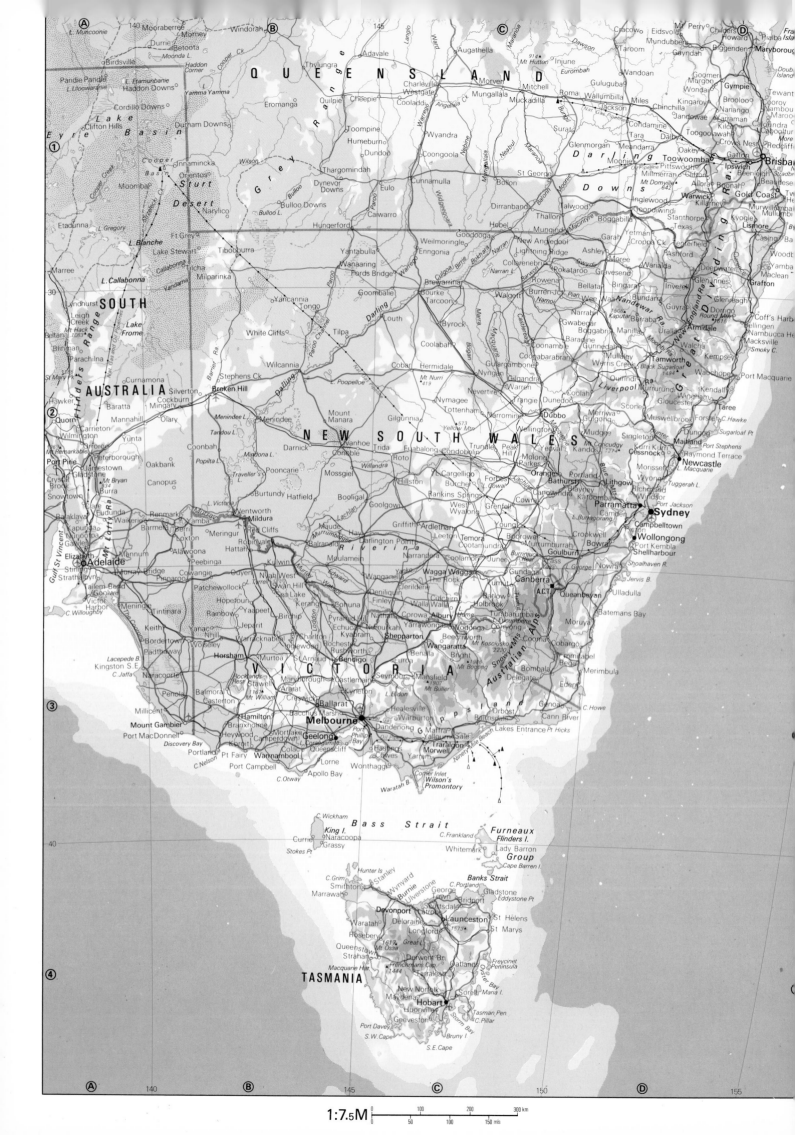

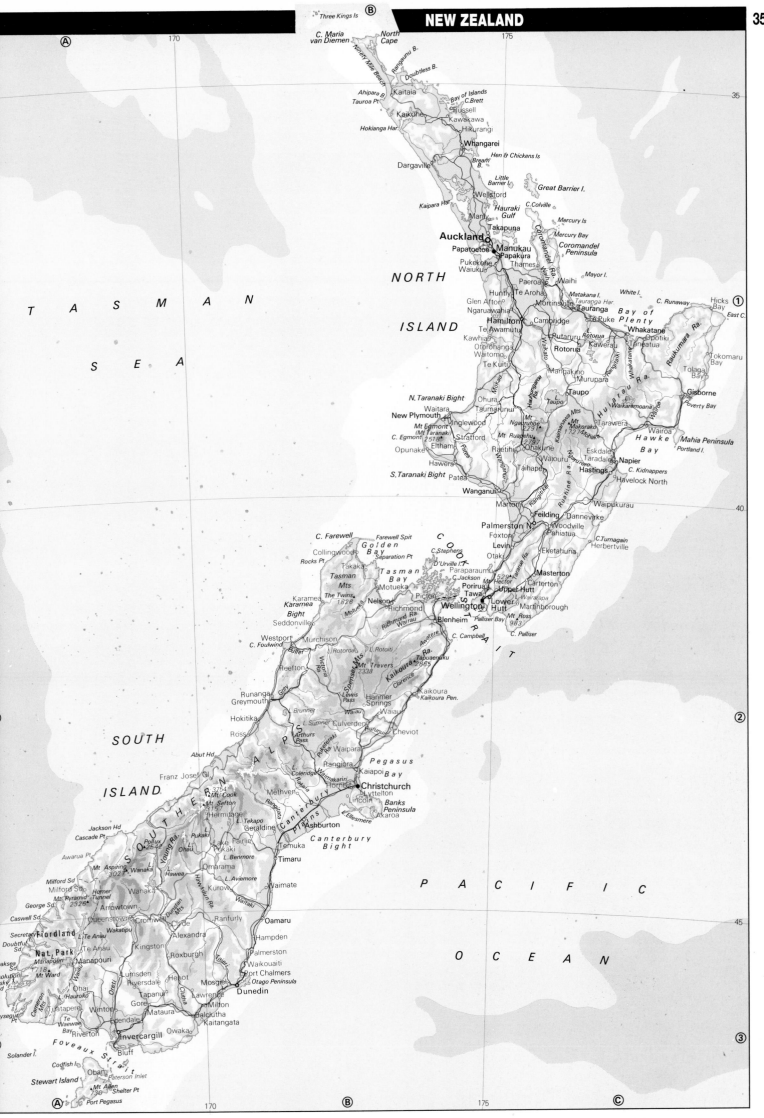

1:5M

0   50   100   150   200 km

0   50   100 mils

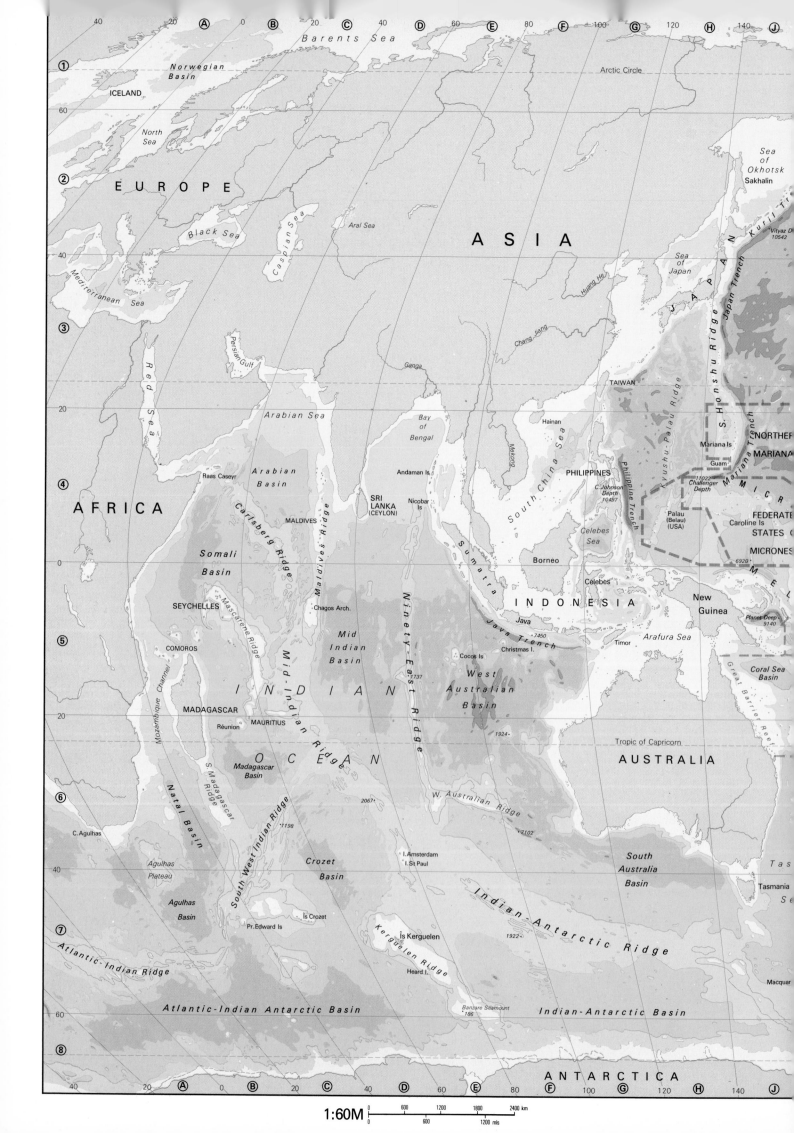

Barents Sea

40 20 Ⓐ 0 Ⓑ 20 Ⓒ 40 Ⓓ 60 Ⓔ 80 Ⓕ 100 Ⓖ 120 Ⓗ 140 Ⓙ

① Norwegian Basin
Arctic Circle

ICELAND
60

North Sea
② EUROPE

Black Sea
Caspian Sea
Aral Sea
ASIA

40
Mediterranean Sea
Sea of Japan

③ Red Sea
Persian Gulf
Chang Jiang
Huang He
JAPAN
Kuril Tr
S. Honshu Ridge
Japan Trench
•Vityaz D 10542

Ganga
TAIWAN
Kyushu-Palau Ridge
Mariana Trench

20
Arabian Sea
Bay of Bengal
Hainan
NORTHER
Mariana Is
MARIANA
Guam

Arabian Basin
Andaman Is
South China Sea
PHILIPPINES
Philippine Trench
11022 Challenger Depth
C. Johnson Depth 10497
MICR

④ AFRICA
Raas Caseyr
Carlsberg Ridge
Maldives Ridge
SRI LANKA (CEYLON)
Nicobar Is
Mekong
Palau (Belau) (USA)
Caroline Is
FEDERATE
STATES C

MALDIVES
Somali Basin
Celebes Sea
MICRONES

Chagos Arch.
Borneo
6920
M

SEYCHELLES
Mascarene Ridge
Celebes
ME
New Guinea
L

COMOROS
Mid Indian Basin
Ninety-East Ridge
INDONESIA
Planet Deep 9140

⑤
West Australian Basin
Java
•7450
Arafura Sea
Coral Sea Basin

Mozambique Channel
Cocos Is
Christmas I.
Timor

MADAGASCAR
•7737
Great Barrier Reef

20
Réunion
MAURITIUS
I N D I A N
O C E A N
Mid-Indian Ridge
•1924
Tropic of Capricorn

S. Madagascar Ridge
Madagascar Basin
AUSTRALIA

⑥
2067•
W. Australian Ridge
•7102

C.Agulhas
Natal Basin
South West Indian Ridge
•1198
I. Amsterdam
I. St Paul
South Australia Basin
Tas

Agulhas Plateau
Crozet Basin
40
Indian-Antarctic Ridge
Tasmania
Se

Agulhas Basin
Ìs Crozet
Kerguelen Ridge
Ìs Kerguelen
1922•

⑦
Atlantic-Indian Ridge
Pr.Edward Is
Heard I.
Macquar

Banzare Seamount 186
60
Atlantic-Indian Antarctic Basin
Indian-Antarctic Basin

⑧
ANTARCTICA

40 20 Ⓐ 0 Ⓑ 20 Ⓒ 40 Ⓓ 60 Ⓔ 80 Ⓕ 100 Ⓖ 120 Ⓗ 140 Ⓙ

Sea of Okhotsk
Sakhalin

1:60M   0   600   1200   1800   2400 km
0   600   1200 mls

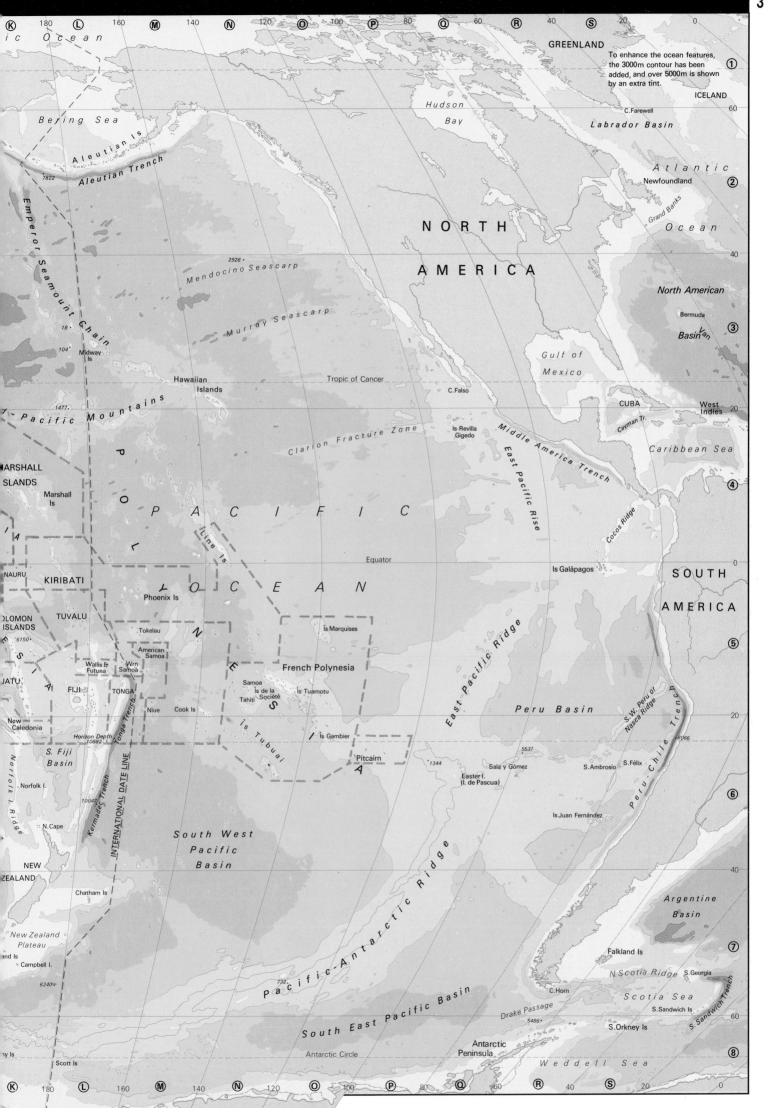

K 180 L 160 M 140 N 120 O 100 P 80 Q 60 R 40 S 20 0

ic Ocean

GREENLAND

To enhance the ocean features,
the 3000m contour has been
added, and over 5000m is shown
by an extra tint.

①

Hudson

Bay

C.Farewell

ICELAND

60

Bering Sea

Labrador Basin

Aleutian Is

Atlantic

Aleutian Trench

Newfoundland

②

7822

Grand Banks

Ocean

NORTH

Emperor Seamount Chain

2926·

Mendocino Seascarp

40

AMERICA

North American

Bermuda

③

18·

Murray Seascarp

Basin   Van

104·

Midway
Is

Gulf of

Hawaiian

Tropic of Cancer

Mexico

Islands

C.Falso

CUBA

West

20

1477·

─ Pacific   Mountains

Clarion Fracture Zone

Is Revilla
Gigedo

Cayman Tr.

Indies

P

Middle America Trench

Caribbean Sea

④

MARSHALL
ISLANDS

P

A   C   I   F   I   C

East Pacific Rise

Marshall
Is

Cocos Ridge

IA

O

Line Is

Equator

Is Galápagos

0

NAURU

L

KIRIBATI

SOUTH

Phoenix Is

Y

O   C   E   A   N

AMERICA

SOLOMON
ISLANDS

TUVALU

N

Îs Marquises

East Pacific Ridge

⑤

6150·

Tokelau

E

French Polynesia

Peru Basin

S.W. Peru or
Nasca Ridge

American
Samoa

JATU

Wallis &
Futuna

W'rn
Samoa

S

Samoa
Îs de la
Société

Îs Tuamotu

FIJI

Tahiti

Peru-Chile Trench

TONGA

8066

New
Caledonia

Niue

Cook Is

Îs Gambier

20

Horizon Depth
10882

Îs Tubuai

A

5537

S.Ambrosio S.Félix

Norfolk I. Ridge

10042

Pitcairn

·1344

Sala y Gómez

Norfolk I.

Easter I.
(I. de Pascua)

Is Juan Fernández

⑥

N.Cape

South West

NEW

Pacific

ZEALAND

Basin

40

Chatham Is

Argentine

Basin

New Zealand
Plateau

Pacific-Antarctic Ridge

Falkland Is

⑦

and Is

Campbell I.

N Scotia Ridge S.Georgia

6240▽

C.Horn

Scotia Sea

732·

S.Sandwich Is

South East Pacific Basin

Drake Passage

S.Orkney Is

S.Sandwich Trench

60

5486·

ny Is

Scott Is

Antarctic Circle

Antarctic
Peninsula

Weddell Sea

⑧

K 180 L 160 M 140 N 120 O 100 P 80 Q 60 R 40 S 20 0

S. Fiji
Basin

Kermadec Trench

Tonga Trench

INTERNATIONAL DATE LINE

YUGOS.
B.H.
Belgrade
Sarajevo
Split
Dubrovnik
Nikšić
Shkodër
Tiranë
ALB.
MAC.
Skopje
Niš
Sofia
BULGARIA
Plovdiv
Burgas
Edirne
Rodopi Pl.
Thessaloniki
GREECE
Trikkala
Ólimpos
Patrai
Peloponnisos
Kalamai
Athens (Athina)
Crete (Kriti)
Rhodes (Ródhos)
Rhodes
Izmir
Denizli
Aydin
Antalya
Ak Dağ
Toros Dağlari
Konya
Adana
Ankara
Afyon
Kayseri
Eskişehir
Bursa
Üsküdar
Istanbul
Zonguldak
Ereğli
Sinop
Samsun
Trabzon
Kuzey Anadolu Dağlari
Kizil Irmak
Sivas
Malatya
Diyarbakir
Gaziantep
Erzurum
Murat
Van Gölü
Van
Büyük Ağri
TURKEY

ROMANIA
Sibiu
Meridionali
Carpații
Galați
Ploiești
Bucharest
Ruse
Constanța
Varna
Dunărea
Sulina

Nikolayev
Odessa
Krym
Sevastopol
Simferopol
Melitopol'
Berdyansk
Zaporozh'ye
Mariupol'
Taganrog
Kerch
Sea of Azov
Novorossiysk
Krasnodar
Sochi
Sukhumi
Batumi
Kutaisi
GEORGIA
Kumayri
Tbilisi
Vladikavkaz
ARMENIA
Yerevan
Gyandzha
AZERBAIJAN
Nakhichevan
Tabriz
Ardabil

Donetsk
Shakhty
Rostov-na-Donu
RUS. FED.
Don
Volgograd
Kalmyk R.
Stavropol'
Maykop
Kislovodsk
Groznyy
Makhachkala
Daghestan R.
Elbrus 5642
Astrakhan'
Ism', ynskoye
Divnoye
Gur'yev
Kul'sary
CASPIAN SEA
Ft Shevchenko
Shevchenko
Plato Ustyurt

KAZAK
Chelkar
Dzhezkazgan
Aral'sk
Novokazalinsk
Aral Sea
Chimbay
Nukus
Tashauz
Urgench
Turtkul'
UZBEKISTAN
K'yzyl-kum
Bukhara
Karshi
Chardzhou
TURKMENISTAN
Nebit-Dag
Kizyl-Arvat
Ashkhabad
Mary
Kerki
Tedzhen
Kushka
AFGHANISTAN
Herat
Shindand
Daulat Yar

MEDITERRANEAN SEA
Nicosia
CYPRUS
Famagusta
Latakia
Hamah
Hims
Beirut
LEBANON
Damascus
Haifa
Tel Aviv
ISRAEL
Jerusalem
Amman
JORDAN
Dar'a
Ma'an
'Aqaba
Tabuk
Al Wajh

Halab
SYRIA
Al Hasakah
Dayr az Zawr
Tudmur
Ar Ramadi
Ar Rutbah
Badanah
IRAQ
Mosul
Arbil
Kirkuk
Samarra
Baghdad
Karbala'
An Najaf
Al Amarah
Basra
Kuwait
KUWAIT
Ad Diwaniyah

Mosul
Zanjan
Qazvin
Tehran
Hamadan
Qom
D. Namak
Kermanshah
Khorramabad
Arak
Kashan
Esfahan
Dezful
Ahvaz
Abadan
Bandar Khomeyni
IRAN
Yazd
Shiraz
Kerman
Zahedan
Bam
Kuh-e-Taftan 4042
Baluchistan
Rasht
Babol
Bojnurd
Shahrud
Sabzevar
Mashhad
Meymaneh
AFGHAN
Farah
Dilaram
Zaranj
Helmand
Kandahar
Girishk

LIBYA
Darnah
Tubruq
Matruh
Alexandria
Siwa
Qattara Depression
Cairo
Tanta
Ismailiya
Suez
El Faiyum
Beni Suef
Sinai
EGYPT
Asyut
El Minya
Farafra Oasis
El Kharga
El Kharga Oasis
Libyan Desert
Luxor
Aswan
L. Nasser
Wadi Halfa
Nubian Desert
Dongola
Merowe
Berber
Atbara
Ed Damer
Omdurman
Khartoum
Kassala
Wad Medani
Sennar
Singa
SUDAN
En Nahud
El Obeid
Ed Dueim
Kosti
Rumbek
Malakal
Sudd
Juba
Nimule
ZAIRE
Watsa
Pakwach

An Nafud
Al Jawf
Tayma
Ha'il
'Unayzah
Buraydah
Shaqra
SAUDI ARABIA
Ar Riyad
As Salamiyah
As Salamiyah
Layla'
Ar Rub' al Khali
Medina
Yanbu al Bahr
Rabigh
Jiddah
Makkah
At Ta'if
Al Lith
Al Qunfidhah
Abha
Jizan
Sa'dah
San'a'
YEMEN
Al Hudaydah
Ta'izz
Al Mukha
Aden ('Adan)
Hadramawt
Al Mukalla
Ash Shihr
Sayhut
Al Ghaydah

Kharg I.
Bushehr
Safaniyah
Dhahran
Dammam
BAHRAIN
Manamah
QATAR
Doha
Abu Dhabi
UNITED ARAB EMIRATES
Dubai
Al Khaburah
Suhar
Muscat
GULF OF OMAN
Al Liwa
Nazwa
OMAN
Bandar 'Abbas
Jask
Makran
Chah Bahar
Gwadar
Turbat
Ras al Hadd
Masirah
Gulf of Masirah
Salalah
Ra's Fartak
Kuria Muria Is.

Persian Gulf
Str. of Hormuz

Hurghada
Bur Safaga
Port Sudan
Suakin
Massawa (Mits'iwa)
Keren
Asmara
ERITREA
Adigrat
Mekele
Gonder
L. Tana
Ras Dashan 4533
Debre Mark'os
ETHIOPIA
Adis Abeba
Dembi Dolo
Gore
Jima
Nazret
Harer
Dese
Dire Dawa
Djibouti
DJIBOUTI
Gulf of Aden
Berbera
Hargeysa
Ceerigaabo
Raas Xaafuun
Raas Caseyr
Socotra (Suqutra) (Yemen)
Hadiboh

SOMALIA
Hobyo
Muqdisho (Mogadishu)
Marka
Baraawe
Kismaayo

UGANDA
Kampala
Entebbe
Jinja
Tororo
Mbale
Soroti
Lira
Gulu
Arua
Bunia
Eldoret
Kisumu
KENYA
Nakuru
Nanyuki
Nairobi
Kirinyaga (Mt Kenya) 5200
Meru
Garissa
Wajir
Moyale
Negele
Dolo
Ginir
Batu 4307
L. Abaya
Gidde
L. Rudolf
TANZANIA
Arusha
Moshi
Kilimanjaro 5895
Mt Elgon 4321
Bukoba
Lake Victoria
Mwanza
L. Eyasi
L. Natron
Musoma

RWANDA
Kigali
Butare
BURUNDI
Bujumbura
Gitega
Kigoma
Mbarara
Kasese
Kabale
L. Kivu
L. Kyoga
L. Albert
Ituri
Fort Portal

BLACK SEA
Aegean Sea
Sea of Marmara

ARAB SEA
Carlsberg
Somali Basin
INDIAN
Equator
Tropic of Cancer

Red Sea
Nile
Blue Nile
White Nile
Atbara
Shebele
Juba (Guba)

1:20M
200 400 600 800 km
200 400 mls

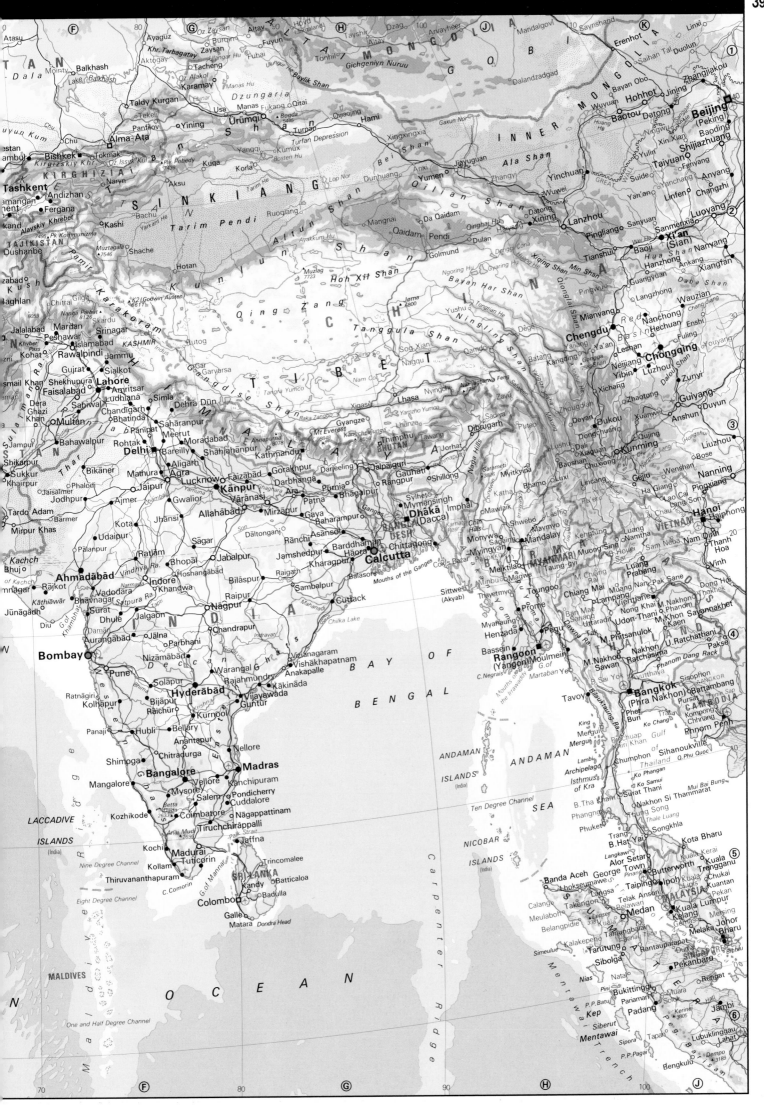

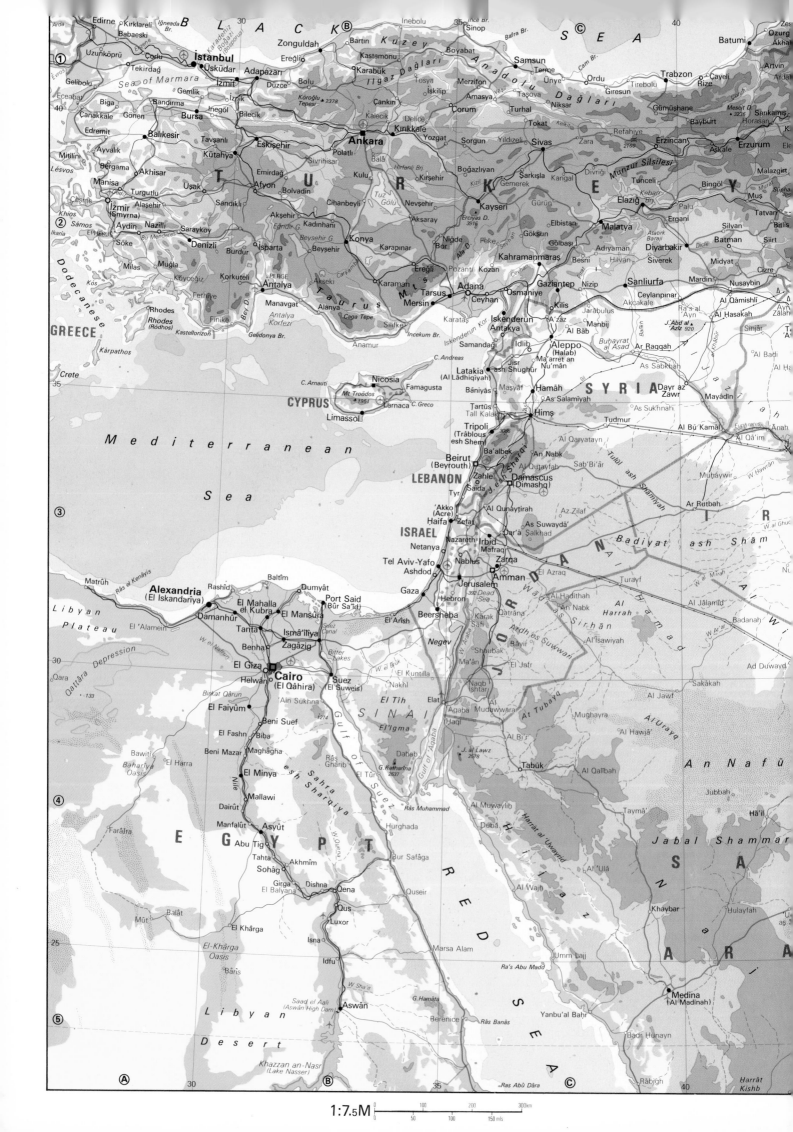

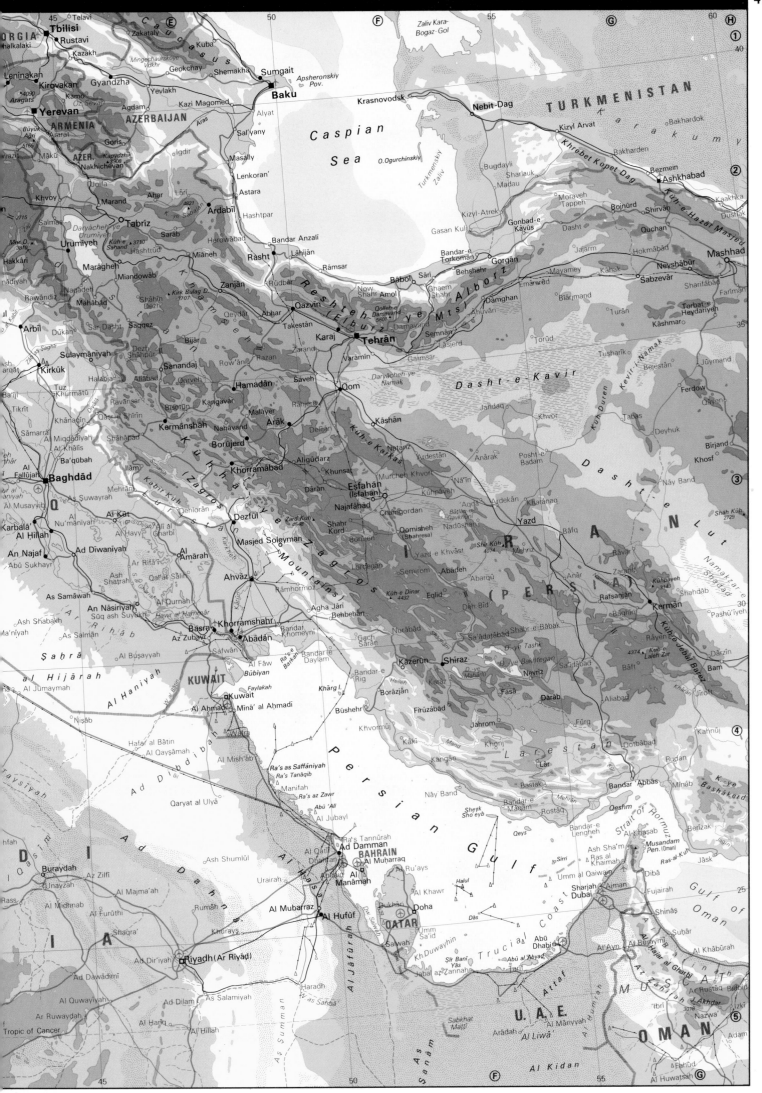

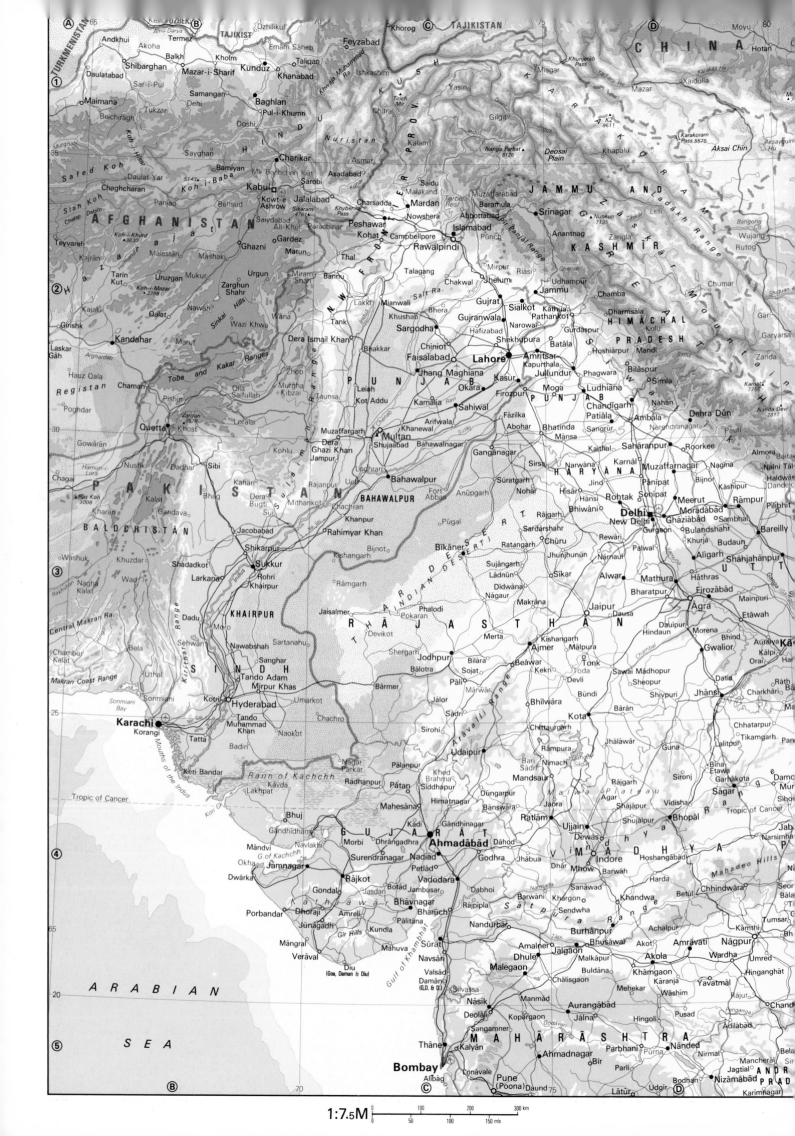

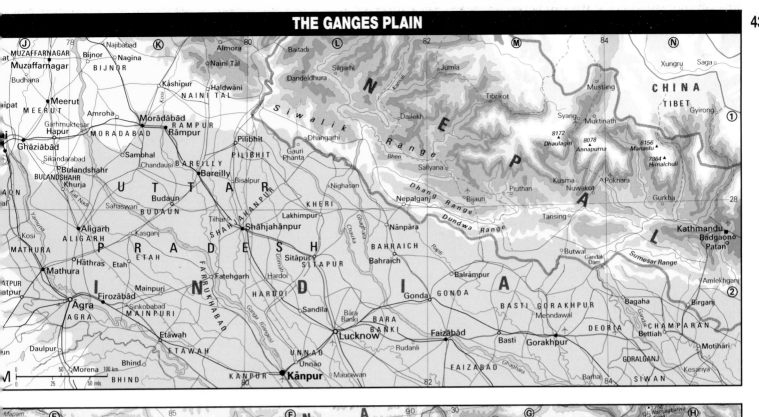

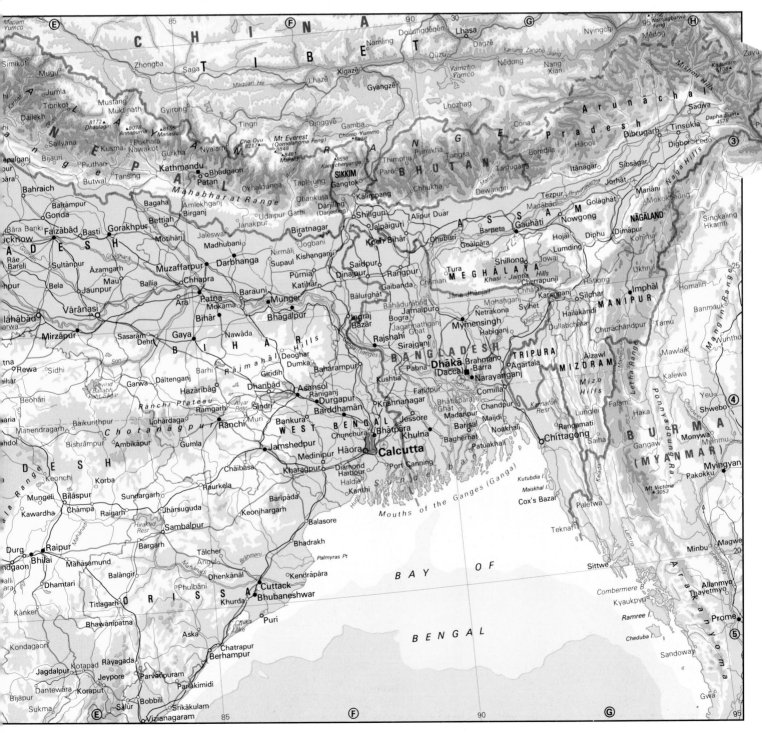

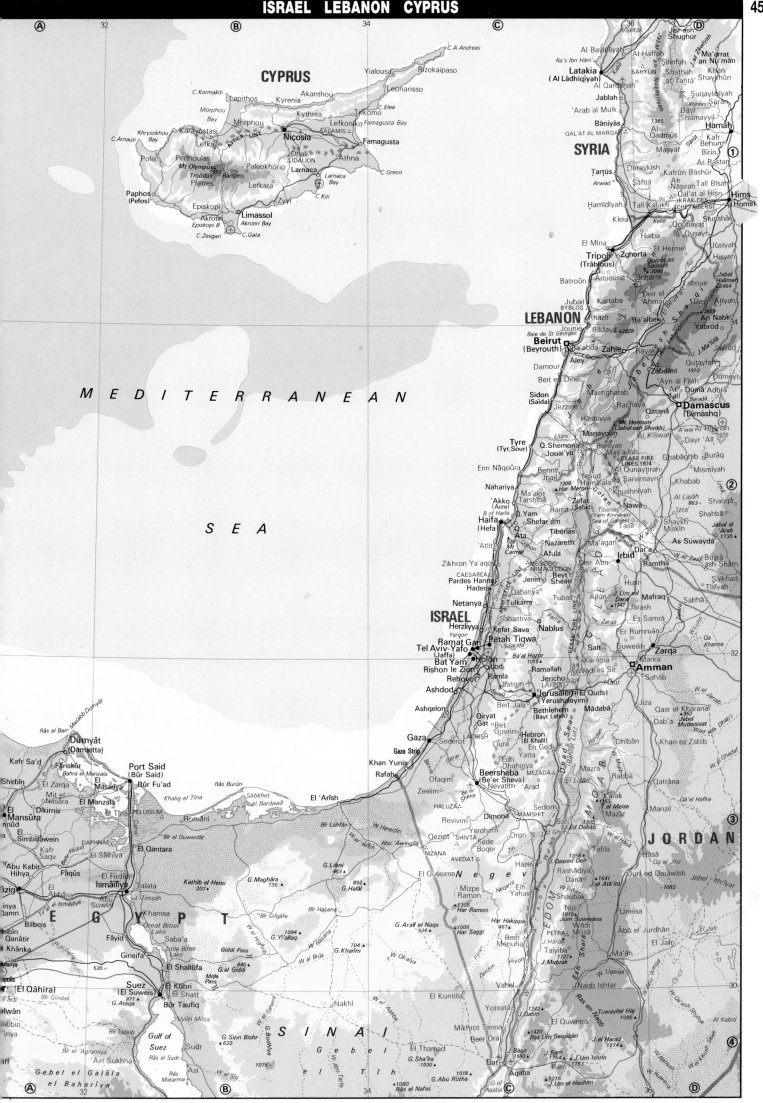

CYPRUS

C.A.Andreas
Yialousa
Rizokaipaso
C.Kormakiti
Lapithos Kyrenia Acanthou
Morphou Kythrea Trikomo C.Elea
Bay Morphou Lefkoniko Famagusta Bay
Khrysokhou Karavostasi SALAMIS
Bay Lefka Nicosia Famagusta
C.Arnauti Polis Pedhoulas Dhali Athna
Mt Olympus 1951 IDALION C.Greco
Troödos Paleokhório
Platres Larnaca
Lefkara
Episkopi Zyyi C.Kiti
Paphos Larnaca
(Pefos) Bay
Limassol
Akrotiri Akrotiri Bay
Episkopi B C.Gata
C.Zevgari

SYRIA

Jisr ash Shughūr
Seraï Al Baylūliyah Al Haffah
Ma'arrat an Nu'mān
Al Qardāhah Shilinfah Shathah Khān
Latakia SAHYŪN at Tahtā Shaykhūn
(Al Lādhiqiyah) Suqaylibiyah
Jablah Dayr Sūrān
'Arab al Mulk Orontes
Bāniyās 1385 Hamāh
QAL'AT AL MARQAB Al Qadmūs Hamāh
Ţarţūs Maşyāf Birin
Arwad Dur:ykish Kafrūn Bashūr Ar Rastan
Şāfītā An Nasirah Tall Bīsah
Tall Kalakh Qal'at al Hisn Hims
Ḥamīdīyah KRAK-DES (Homs)
CHEVALIERST Shinshār

MEDITERRANEAN

El Mīna Kleia Kebir Qoubayat
Tripoli Halba El Hermel
(Trâblous) Zghorta Yūsīyah
Batroûn Amioune Qournet es Hisyah
Saouda 3096 Jabal
Jubail Kartaba Ba'albek Halîman
BYBLOS Ghazīr Deir el 2464
Ahmar An Nabk
Jounié 2559 Yabrūd
LEBANON Bikfaya 2628
Baie de St Georges Ba'abda Rayak Al J.Ma'lūla
Beirut Zahle Az Zabdāni Jayrūd
(Beyrouth) Aley Dūmayr
Machgharab Qutayfah 1910
Damour At Fijah
Beit ed Dîne Duma 'Adhrā
Sidon Barada
(Saida) Rachaya **Damascus**
Jezzîne Qatana (Dimashq)
Haspaiya Mt Hermon A'waj Al Hijanah
SEA (Jebel esh Sheikh) Dayr 'Alī
Tyre Q.Shemona Baniyas Ghabāghib Burāq
(Tyr,Sour) Jouai'ya Mas'adah
Litani CEASE FIRE Al Qunaytirah Mismiyah
Enn Nâqoûra Bennt LINES 1974 Khabab
Jbail 1208 Al Sanamayn
Nahariya Ma'alot Hama Kala Nawa Al Lajāh 863 Shaqqā
Tarshīha Har Meron Khushniyah
'Akko Zefat Izra' Shahbā
(Acre) Q. Yam (Safad) Tiberias Tasil Jabal al
Haifa Rama (Yam Kinneret) Shaykh 'Arab
(Hefa) Shefar'am (Sea of Galilee) Fīq Miskīn 1735
'Atlit Q. Ata Tiberias Dar'a As Suwaydā
526 Oron Ma'agan W. az Zaydi Buşrā
Zikhron Ya'aqov Mt Afula Yarmūk ash Shām
Carmel Nazareth Dar'a
MEGIDDO Deir Abu Irbid Salkhad
CAESAREA ARMAGEDDON Sa'id Tişfah
Pardes Hanna Beyt Husn
Hadera Jenin Shean Ajlūn W.Luhf
Qabatiya J.Um ed Es Samrā
Netanya Tubas Jarash Dara Mafraq
Tulkarm Zarqa Er Rummān Sabhā
Sabastiya Farā'a Salt Qa
ISRAEL Nablus Suweilih Khanna
Herzliyya Kefar Sava Karama Marka Zarqa
Ramat Gan Petah Tiqwa Ba'al Hazor Amman
Tel Aviv-Yafo Holon 1016 Wadi es Sir Sahāb
(Jaffa) Lud Ramallah Na'ūr
Bat Yam Ramla Jericho Jiza
Rishon le Zion Latrun ('Arīha) Mādabā Qasr el Kharāna
Rehovot 963 Dab'a Jebel
Ashdod Beit Jala **Jerusalem**(El Quds) Mudeisisat Dhab'i
(Yerushalayim)
Ashqelon Bethlehem
Qiryat (Bayt Lahm)
Gat Bet
LACHISH Guvrin Hebron
Gaza Sederot (El Khalil) Dhībān Khan ez Zabib
Gaza Strip Gat Dura Yatta
Khan Yunis Edh En Gedi
Rafah Dhahiriya MEZADA
Beersheba Sedom Karak Manzil
Otaqim (Be'er Sheva) T.el Meise
Be er Arad Safi Rabba
Zeelim Sheva Ed Dabāb Qatrāna
Nevatim W.el Ghadaf
HALUZA Dimona MAMSHIT Mazra
Revivim Sedom
DAPHNAE Qeziot Yeroham El Ghor **JORDAN**
SHIVTA Sede Zin 1305 J.Qasred Deir Hāsā
Boqer Rashādīya Qa'el Jinz
NIZANA Oron Hazeva Dana 1356 Jurf ed Darāwīsh
AVEDAT Negev Tafila J.el Atā'ita
El Quseima 1641 Jebel Ithrīyat
G.Libni Mizpe Ein 1082
463 Ramon Yahav
892 Negarot Shaubak
G.Maghâra G.Halâl 1305 Abū el Jurdhān
735 Har Ramon PETRA
207 G.Karîm Har Hakippa Niijl J.el Jafr
G.Yi'allaq 467 Jum Suwwāna El Jafr
1094 G.Arnif el Naqa Beer Wādī Mūsa
Kathīb el Henu Bîr Hasana 934 Menuha
El Arish 1006 Taiyiba Ma'ān
G.Saggi 1727
Bîr Gifgâfa Hiyon J.Mubrak
Beer Ora Uneisa
G.el Giddi 1242
840 G.Khârim J.Qatim
Mikhrot Timna 1615 J.Um Ishrin Al Kabid
G.Sinn Bishr 1420 Ras Um Seisabān
622 Gebel Beer Ora J.el Harad
el Tîh 1274

EGYPT

Dumyât
(Damietta)
Kafr Sa'd Masabb Dumyât
Fâriskûr
Bahra el Manzala Port Said
El Zarqa (Bûr Saïd)
Mit el El Matariya Bûr Fu'ad
Nasâra Ras Burûn
El Manzala Khalig el Tîna
El Mansûra Dikirnis El Tîna Khalig el Tīna El 'Arîsh
El Simbillawein PELUSIUM Români
Kafr El Salhîya Bîr el Duweidâr
Saqr El Qantara
Abu Kebir Faqûs
Hihya El Firdân Bîr Lahfân W.Haredin
Ismâilîya Talata W.Arish
El Ismâilîya L.Timsah
Bilbeis Khamsa Bîr Hasana
Saba'a G.Gifgâfa
Qanâtir El Abbâsa Great Bitter Zenith
Khânka Fâyid Lake Abu Aweigila
Gineifa Little Bitter NIZANA
Lake G.Arraf el Naqa
Suez Saba'a Mitla Pass
El Kûbri G.el Giddi
(El Suweis) El Shallûfa Giddi Pass
Bîr Gindali El Shatt Bîr Udeib
Bûr Taufiq Nakhl W.el Brūk
Uyûn Mûsa
Gulf of El Thamad
Suez Bîr el 'Agramîya **SINAI**
Sudr G.Sinn Bishr El Kuntilla
'Ain Sukhna Ras el Sudr 622 Yotvatā
Asl W.el Sig El Quweitra
1076 Mikhrot Timna
Gebel el Galâla 1080 G.Sha'ira Beer Ora Aqaba
el Baharîya 871 1030 J.Baqir 1592 J.Um Ishrin Al Kabid
G.Abu Rûtha 1754 J.el Harad
Ras en Nafas Elat 1216 Naqb Ishtar
G.of 1754 J.Um el Hashim
Aqaba Aqaba

SEA

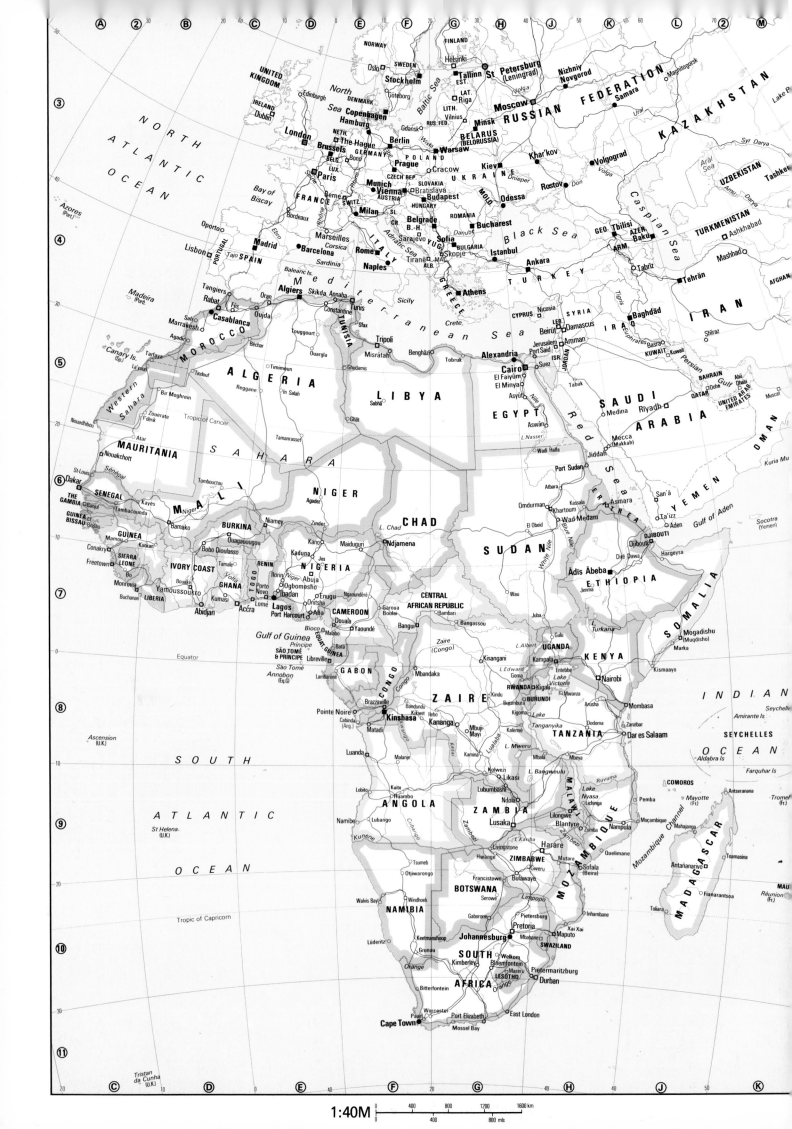

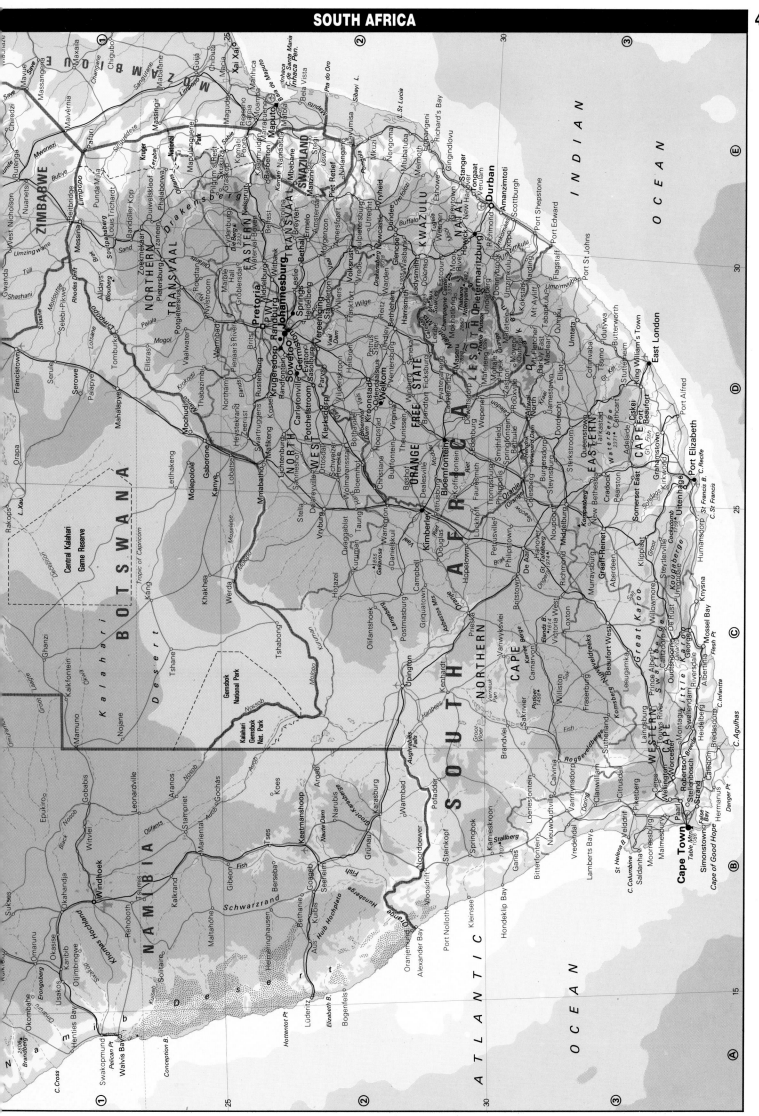

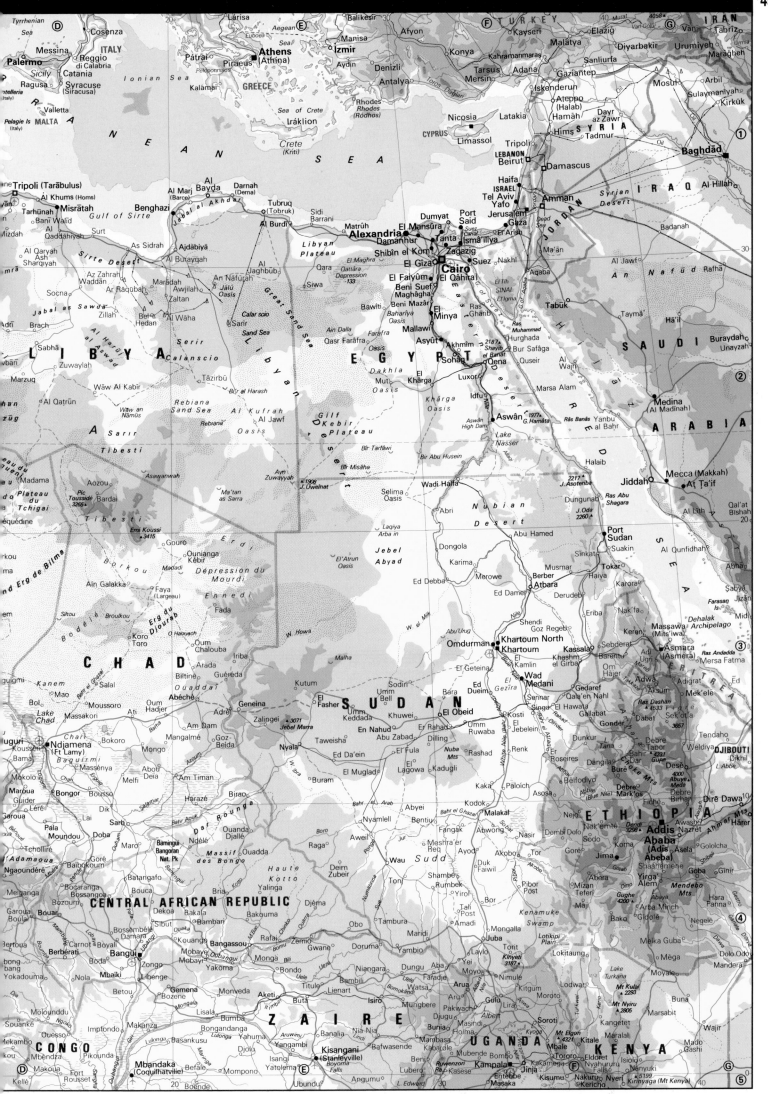

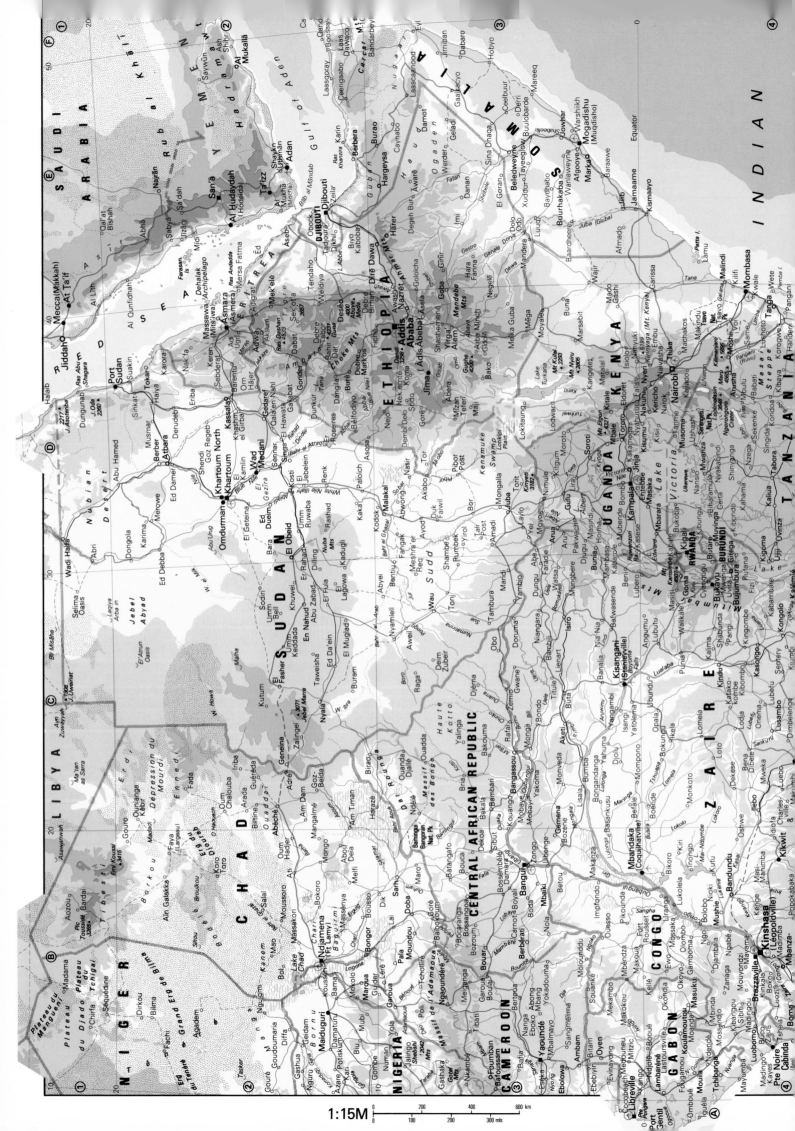

1:15M

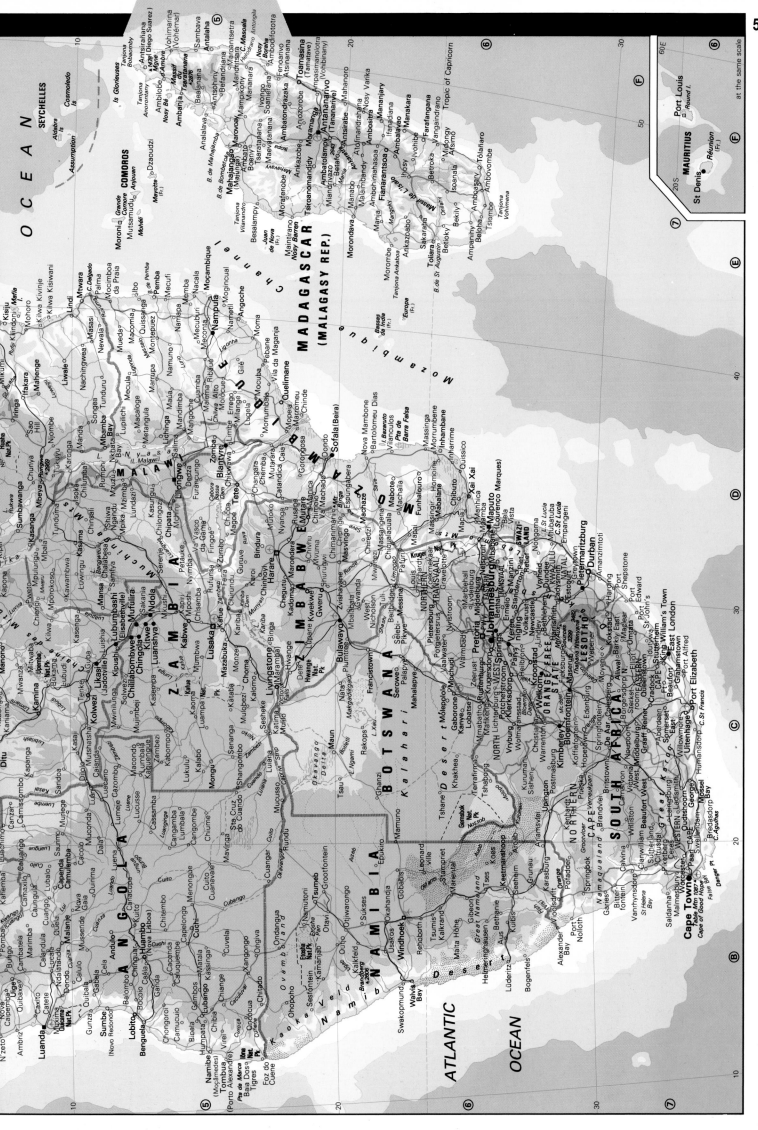

51

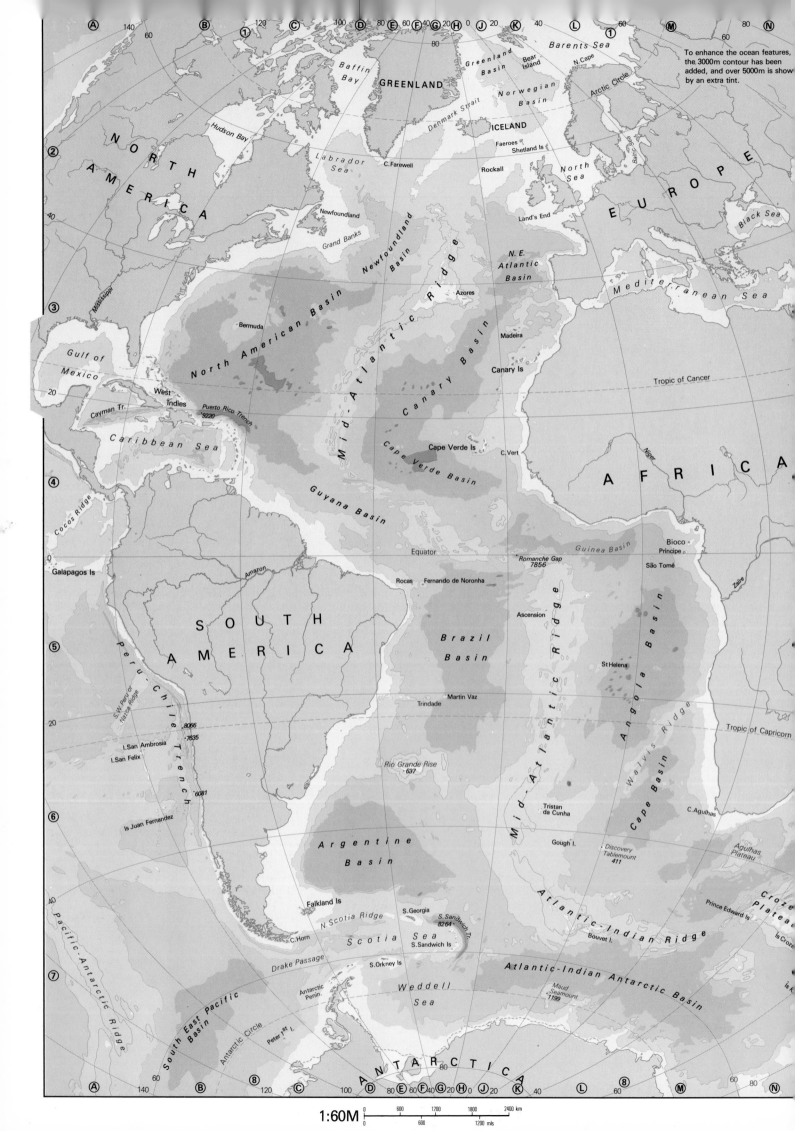

Ⓐ 140 60 Ⓑ 120 Ⓒ 100 Ⓓ 80 Ⓔ 60 Ⓕ 40 Ⓖ Ⓗ 0 Ⓙ 20 Ⓚ 40 Ⓛ 60 Ⓜ 80 Ⓝ
① ① 80 ①

To enhance the ocean features,
the 3000m contour has been
added, and over 5000m is show
by an extra tint.

Baffin
Bay

GREENLAND

Greenland
Basin

Bear
Island

Barents Sea

N.Cape

Arctic Circle

Denmark Strait

Norwegian
Basin

Hudson Bay

ICELAND

Faeroes
Shetland Is

Rockall

North
Sea

Black Sea

②

N O R T H

Labrador
Sea

C.Farewell

Land's End

E U R O P E

A M E R I C A

Newfoundland

Newfoundland
Basin

N. E.
Atlantic
Basin

Mediterranean Sea

40

Grand Banks

Mid-Atlantic Ridge

Azores

③

Mississippi

North American Basin

Bermuda

Madeira

Canary
Basin

Tropic of Cancer

Gulf of
Mexico

West
Indies

Canary Is

20

Cayman Tr.

Puerto Rico Trench
·9220

Cape Verde Is

C.Vert

A F R I C A

Caribbean Sea

Cape Verde Basin

④

Cocos Ridge

Guyana Basin

Guinea Basin

Bioco
Principe

Niger

0

Galapagos Is

Amazon

Equator

Romanche Gap
7856

São Tomé

Zaire

Rocas Fernando de Noronha

⑤

S O U T H

Ascension

Brazil
Basin

Mid-Atlantic Ridge

St Helena

Angola Basin

A M E R I C A

Peru-Chile Trench

S.W.Peru or
Nazca Ridge

Martin Vaz

Trindade

20

·8066

·7635

I.San Ambrosia

Rio Grande Rise
·637

Walvis Ridge

Cape Basin

Tropic of Capricorn

I.San Felix

·6081

Tristan
da Cunha

C.Agulhas

⑥

Is Juan Fernandez

Gough I.

Discovery
Tablemount
411

Agulhas
Plateau

Argentine
Basin

Mid-Atlantic Ridge

Croze
Plateau

40

Pacific-Antarctic Ridge

Falkland Is

N.Scotia Ridge

S.Georgia

S.Sandwich Tr.
8264

Atlantic-Indian Ridge

Prince Edward Is

Is Croze

Bouvet I.

C.Horn

Scotia Sea

S.Sandwich Is

Is K

Drake Passage

S.Orkney Is

⑦

South East Pacific Basin

Antarctic
Penin.

Weddell
Sea

Atlantic-Indian Antarctic Basin

Maud
Seamount
1199

Antarctic Circle

Peter 1st I.

80

A N T A R C T I C A

Ⓐ 140 Ⓑ 120 Ⓒ 100 Ⓓ 80 Ⓔ 60 Ⓕ Ⓖ 20 Ⓗ Ⓙ 20 Ⓚ 40 Ⓛ 60 Ⓜ 80 Ⓝ
⑧ 60 ⑧ 60

1:60M   600   1200   1800   2400 km
         600   1200 mls

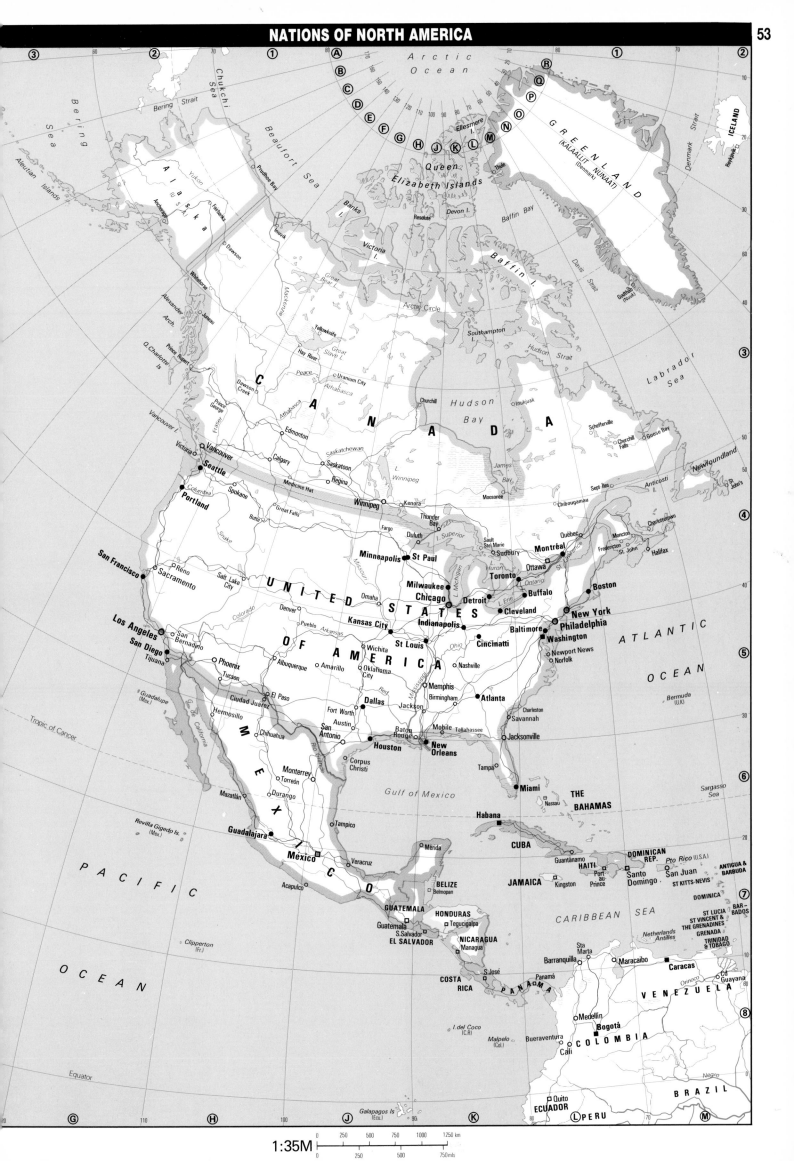

1:35M

GREENLAND (KALAALLIT NUNAAT) (Denmark)

ICELAND

BAFFIN BAY

DAVIS STRAIT

DENMARK STRAIT

Arctic Circle

Lancaster Sound

Devon Island

Baffin Island

Baffin Basin

Foxe Peninsula

Foxe Basin

Foxe Channel

Southampton Island

Coral Harbour

HUDSON STRAIT

Ungava Bay

Labrador Sea

NEWFOUNDLAND

HUDSON BAY

James Bay

QUEBEC

ONTARIO

Labrador

Newfoundland

LAKE SUPERIOR

NOVA SCOTIA

NEW BRUNSWICK

PRINCE EDWARD I.

MAINE

NEW HAMPSHIRE

VERMONT

NEW YORK

MASS.

CONN.

ATLANTIC OCEAN

Gulf of Saint Lawrence

Cape Breton I.

St John's

Montréal

Ottawa

Hull

Toronto

Hamilton

Buffalo

Detroit

Milwaukee

St Paul

Thunder Bay

Sudbury

Quebec

Halifax

Boston

Providence

Hartford

Cumberland Sound

Frobisher Bay

Resolution I.

Cape Farewell (Kap Farvel)

Reykjavik

Churchill

Reykjavik

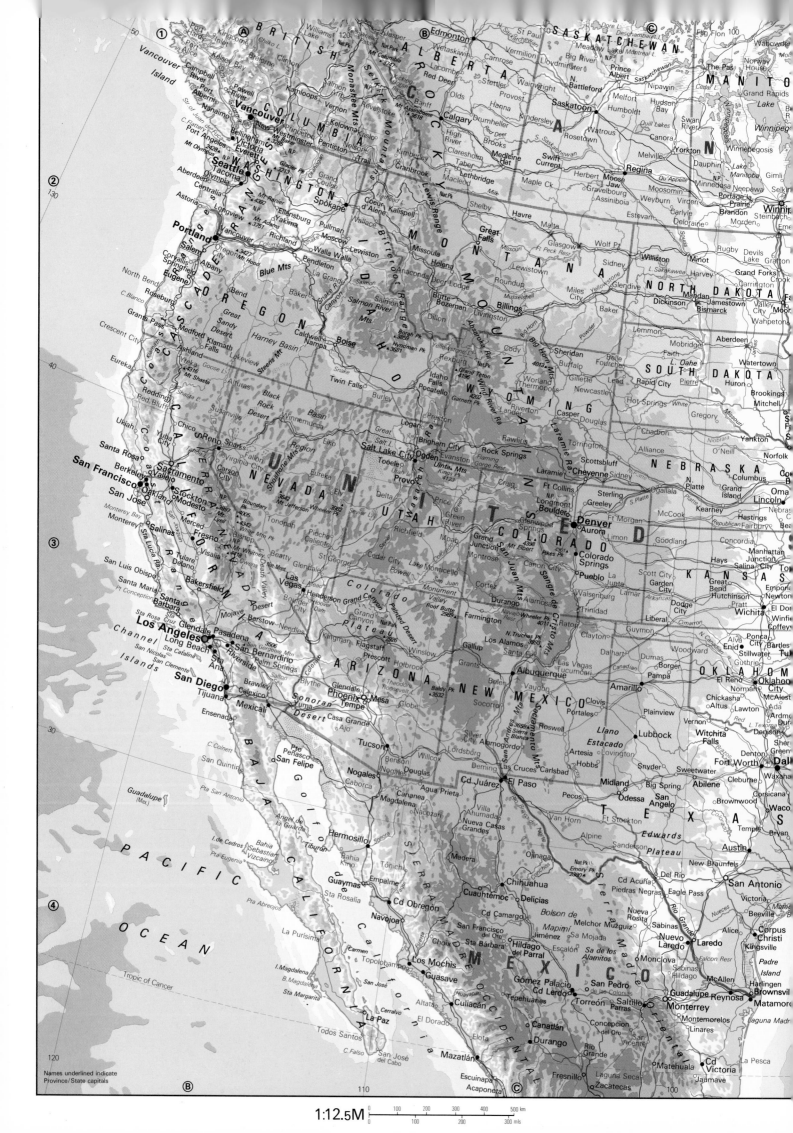

1:12.5M

Names underlined indicate
Province/State capitals

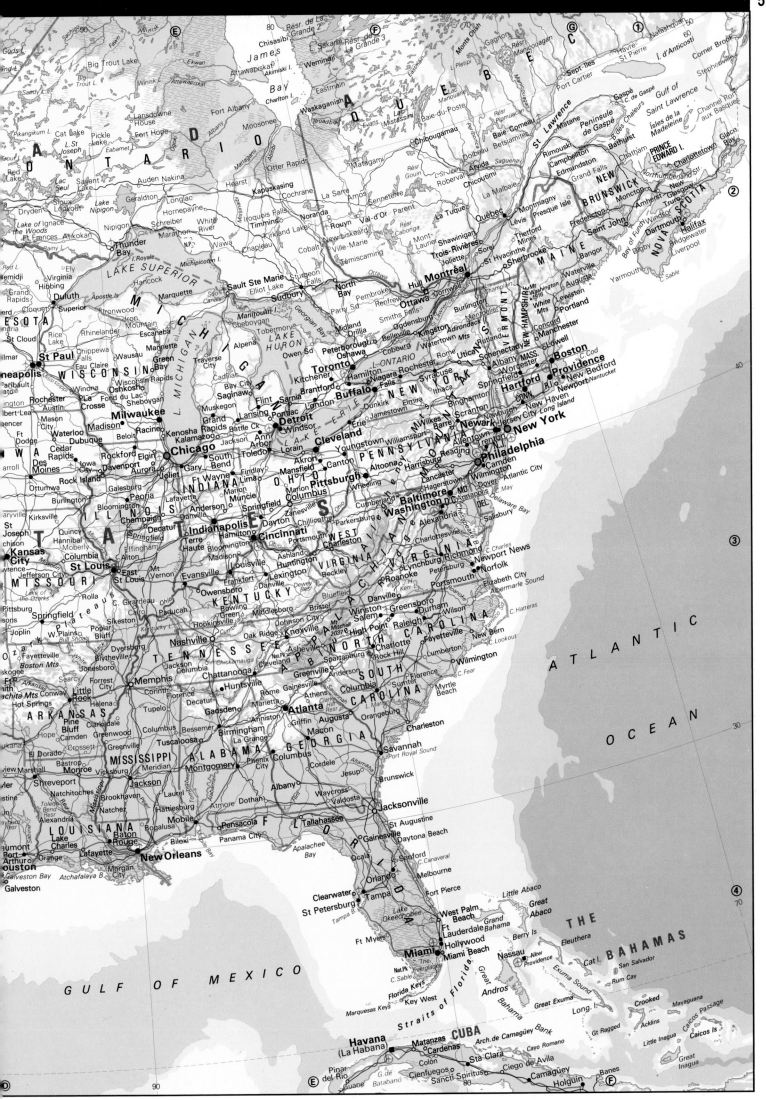

1:5M

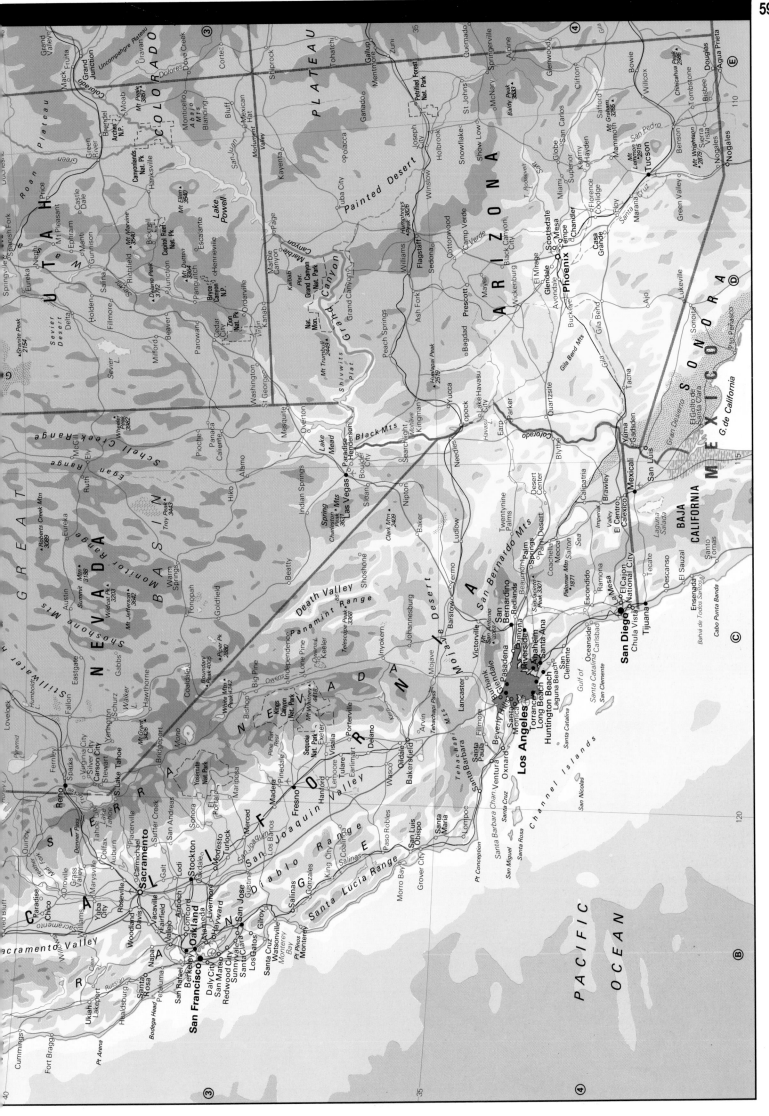

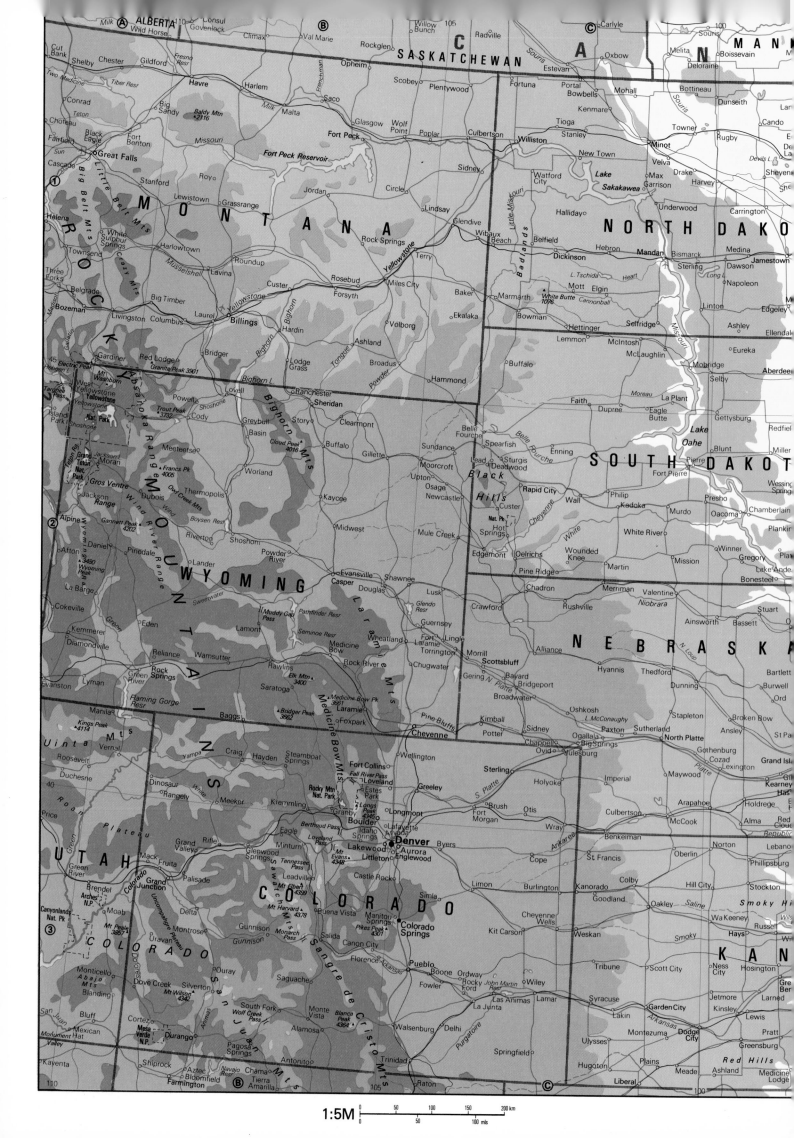

1:5M

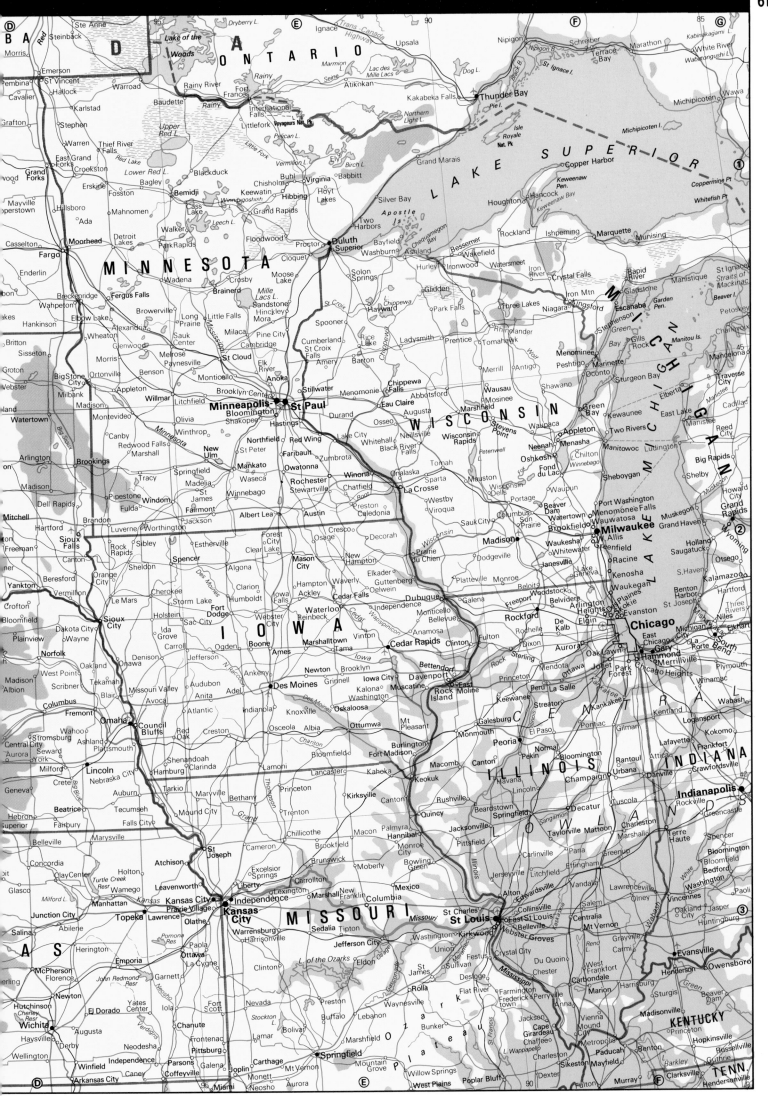

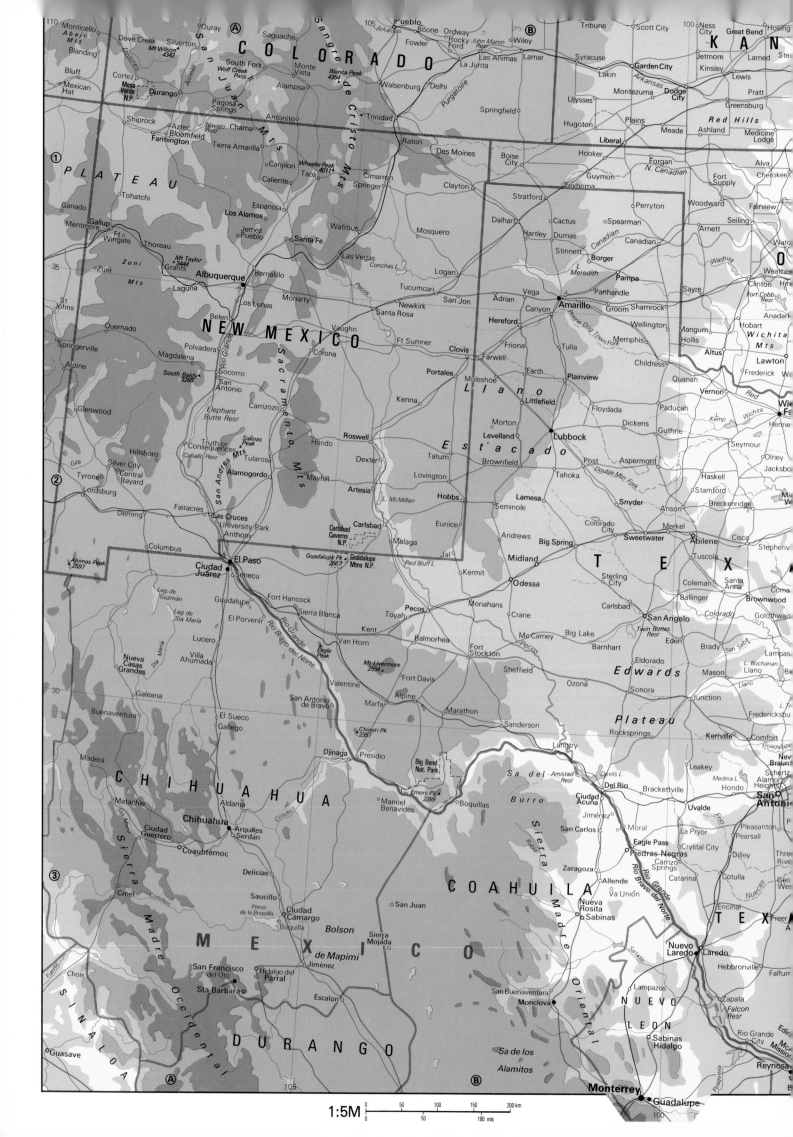

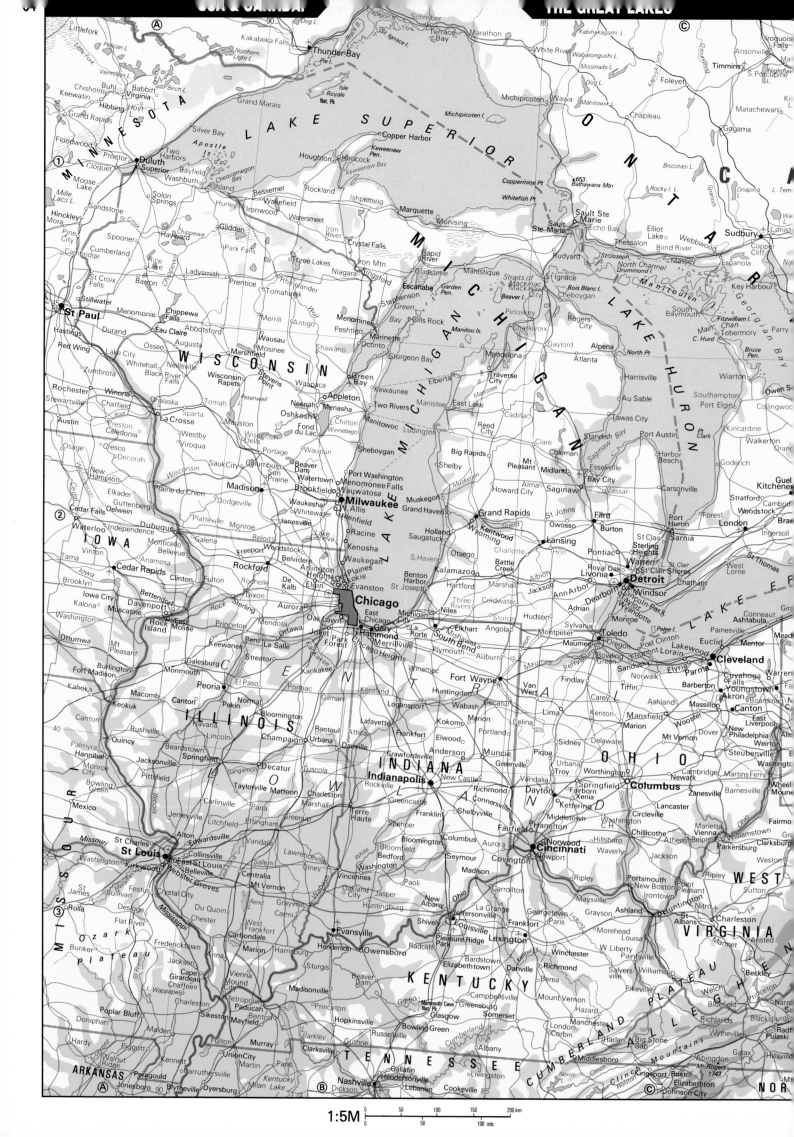

1:5M

0   50   100   150   200 km

0   50   100 mls

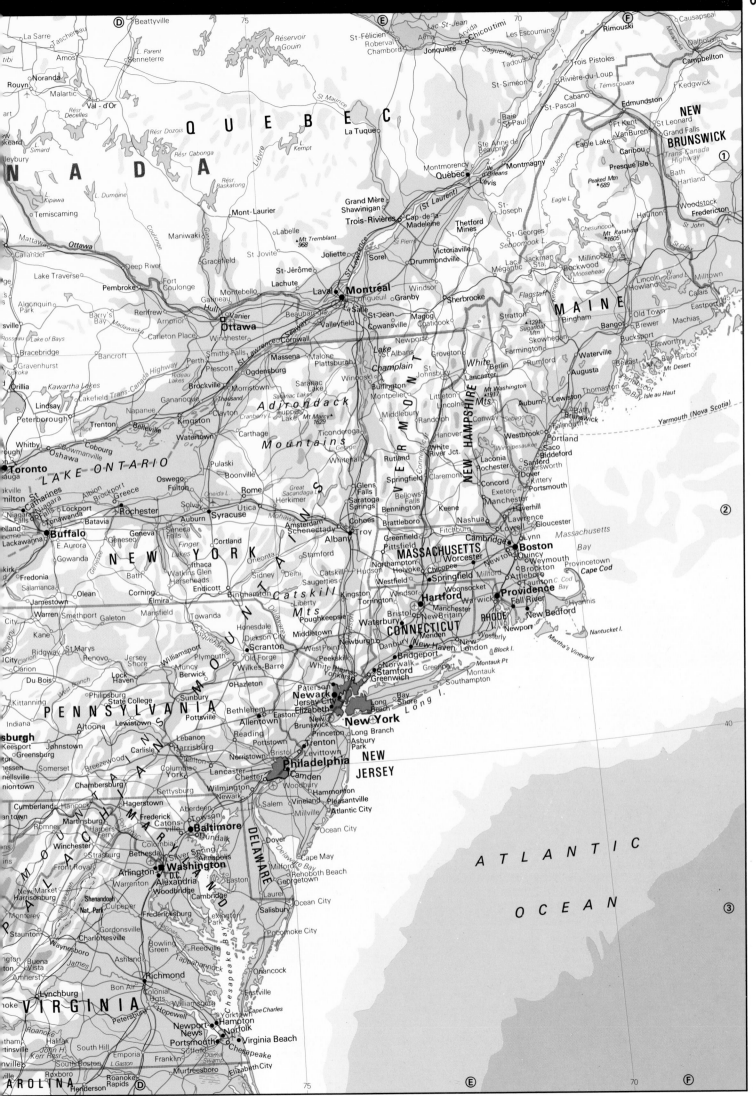

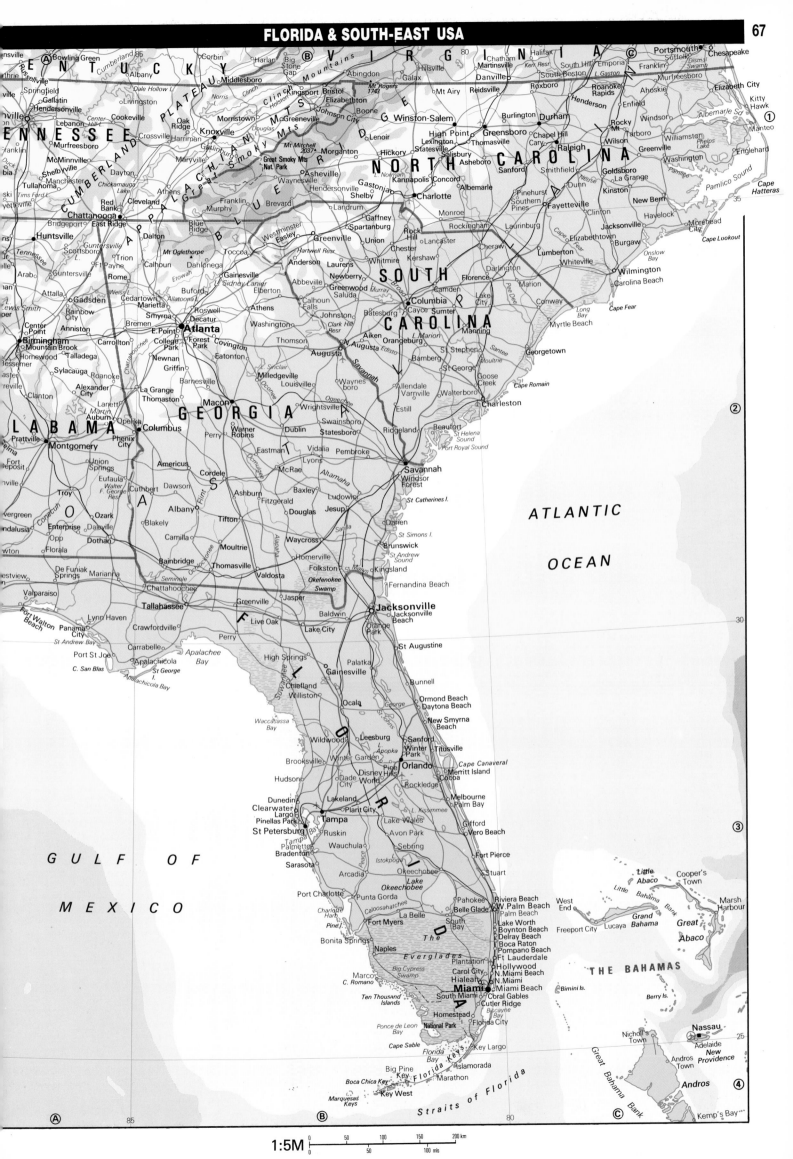

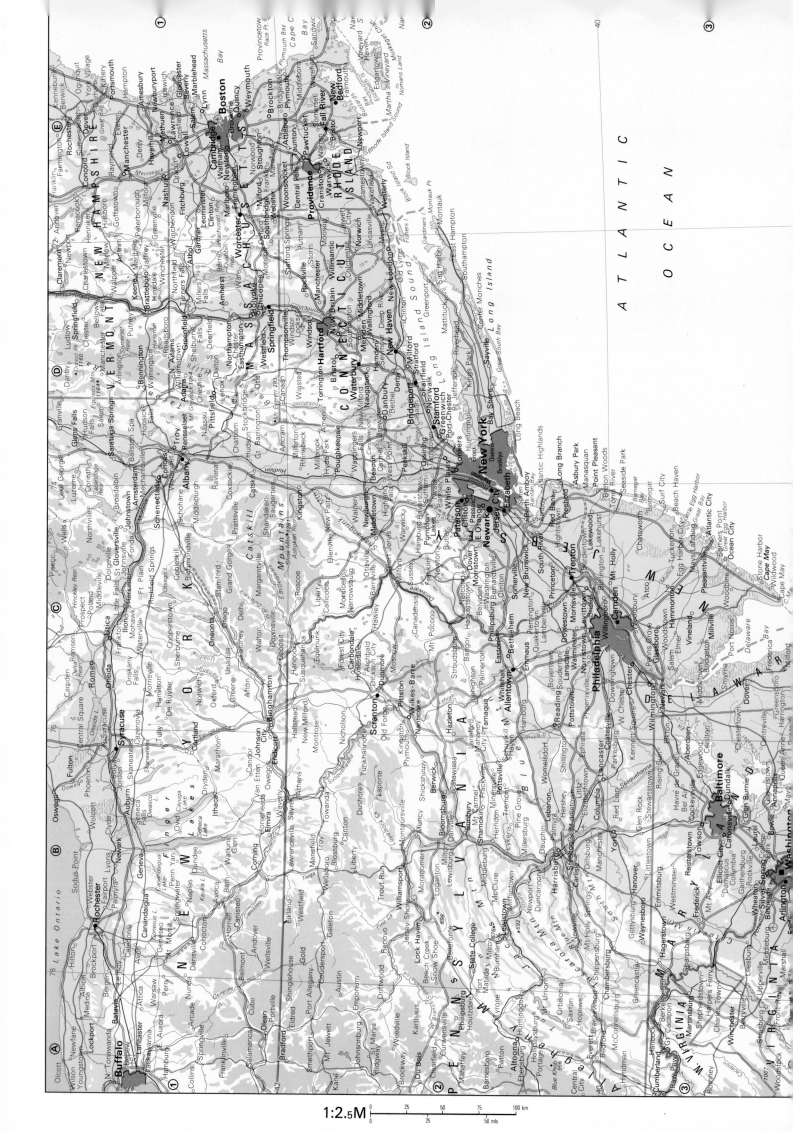

1:2.5M

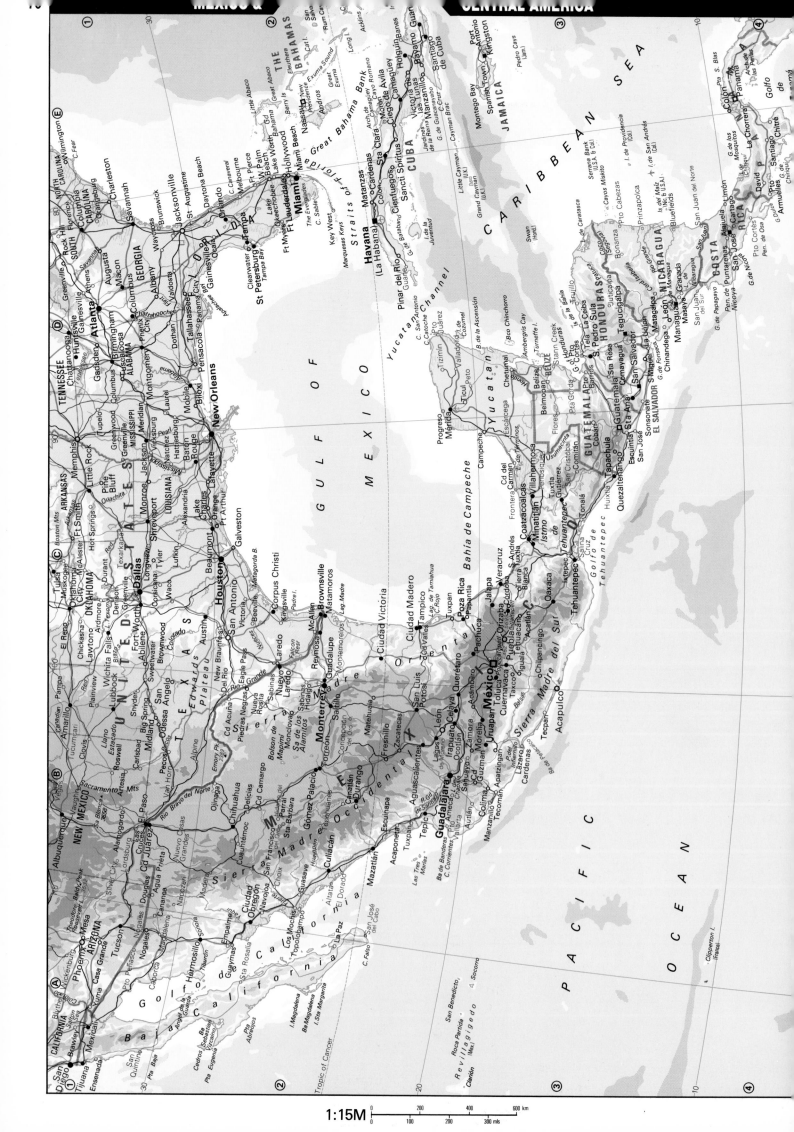

1:15M

200 400 600 km
100 200 300 mls

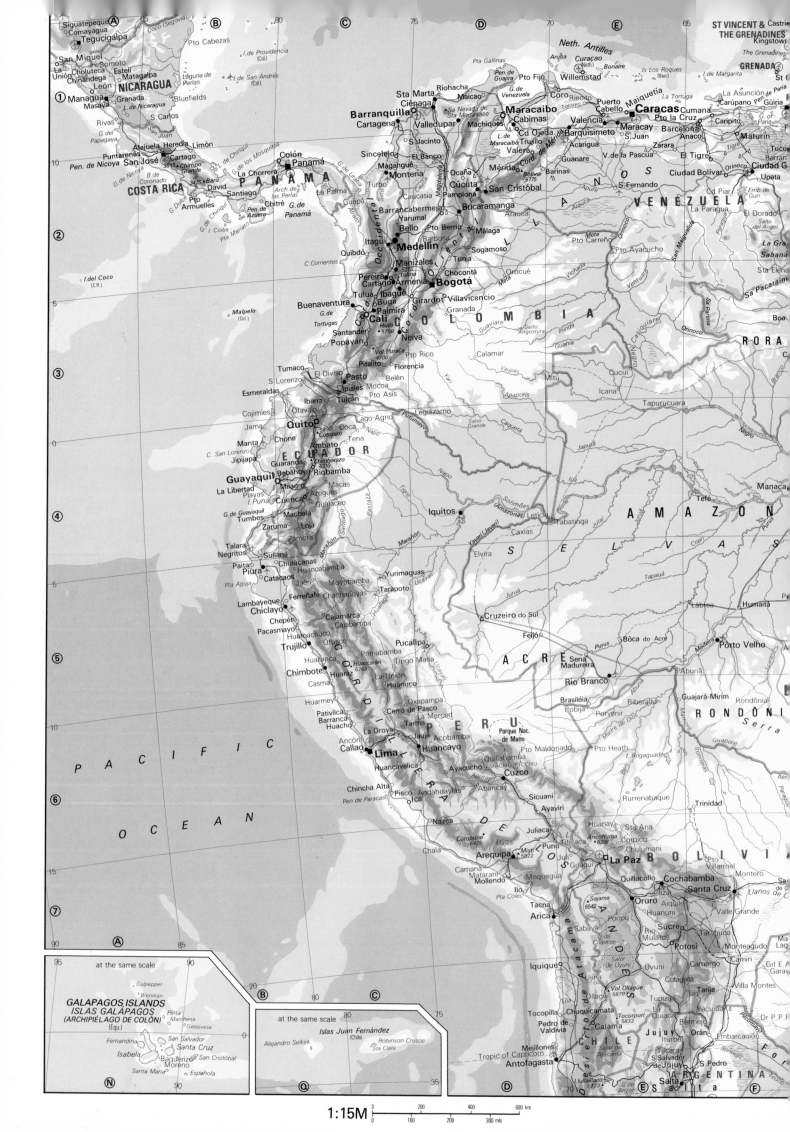

ST VINCENT & Castri
THE GRENADINES
The Grenadines
Kingstown
GRENADA
St G
I. de Margarita

NICARAGUA
Siguatepeque
Comayagua
Tegucigalpa
Coco (Segovia)
Pto Cabezas
I. de Providencia (Col.)
San Miguel
La Unión
Choluteca
Somoto
Estelí
Matagalpa
Chinandega
León
Managua
Granada
Masaya
Rivas
S. Carlos
L. de Nicaragua
Bluefields
Laguna de Perlas
I. de San Andrés (Col.)

Pta Gallinas
Pen. de Guajira
Aruba
Neth. Antilles
Curaçao (Neth.)
Bonaire
Willemstad
Is Los Roques (Ven)
La Tortuga

Pto Fijo
G. de Venezuela
Coro
Riecito
Puerto Cabello
Maiquetía
Caracas
Cumaná
Carúpano
Güiria
Gof. of Pa

Sta Marta
Ciénaga
Ríohacha
Maicao
Sa Nevada de Sta Marta 5800
Maracaibo
Cabimas
Cd Ojeda
L. de Maracaibo
Valencia
Maracay
S. Juan
Barcelona
Anaco
Maturín
Tigre

Puntarenas
Alajuela Heredia Limón
San José Cartago
3815 Chirripó Grande
Pen. de Nicoya
B. de Coronado
2475 Barú
David
Santiago
Pto Armuelles
Chitré
Pen. de Azuero
G. de Chiriquí
I. Coiba
Pta Mariato

COSTA RICA
PANAMÁ
Colón
Panamá
G. de Panamá
Arch. de las Perlas
La Palma
Turbo
G. de Urabá

Barranquilla
Cartagena
Valledupar
Machiques
S. Jacinto
El Banco
Sincelejo
Magangué
Montería
Caucasia
Ocaña
Cúcuta
Pamplona
San Cristóbal
Mérida
Cord. de Mérida
Barinas
Valera
Trujillo
Barquisimeto
Acarigua
Guanare
V. de la Pascua
El Tigre
Zárara

VENEZUELA
Apure
S. Fernando
Ciudad Bolívar
Upata
Cd Piar
Emb. de Gurí

Quibdó
C. Corrientes
Itagüí
Medellín
Yarumal
Pto Berrío
Barbosa
Bello
Málaga
Sogamoso
Tunja
Arauca
Pto Carreño
Pto Ayacucho
La Paragua
El Dorado
Salto del Angel

Barrancabermeja
Manizales
5215 Tolima
Pereira
Cartago
Armenia
Ibagué
Bogotá
Chocontá
Orocué
Meta

COLOMBIA
Buenaventura
G. de Tortugas
Tuluá
Buga
Palmira
Cali
Girardot
Villavicencio
Granada
Guaviare
Inírida
Vichada
Sta Elena
Sa Pacaraim
RORA

Santander
Huila 5750
Popayán
Neiva
Pto Rico
Calamar
Guania
Orinoco

Tumaco
S. Lorenzo
El Diviso
Pasto
Pitalito
Florencia
Belén
Yarí
Guaviare
Mitú
Icana
Tapurucuara
Negro
Boa

Esmeraldas
Ibarra
Ipiales
Mocoa
Tulcán
Pto Asis
Leguízamo
Putumayo
Caquetá
Salto Grande
Vaupés
Apaporis
Içá
Solimões
(Amazonas)

Cojimíes
Otavalo
Quito
5896 Cotopaxi
Coca
Napo
Leticia
Tabatinga
Jutaí
Tefé
AMAZON
Manaca

Jama
Chone
Tena
Ambato
ECUADOR
Chimborazo 6310
Riobamba
Napo
Manta
C. San Lorenzo
Jipijapa

Guayaquil
Babahoyo
Milagro
Macas
Iquitos
Caxias
Elvita
SELVAS
Coarí
Tapauá
Juruá

La Libertad
Playas
I. Puná
Cuenca
Azogues
Gualaceo
Yavari (Javari)
Marañón

G. de Guayaquil
Machala
Tumbes
Zaruma
Loja
Zamora
Santiago
Pastaza
Tigre
Yurimaguas
Ucayali
Juruá
Lábrea
Humaitá

Talara
Negritos
Paita
Sullana
Chulucanas
Huancabamba
Tarapoto
Moyobamba
Cruzeiro do Sul
Feijó
Purus
Bôca do Acre
Madeira
Pôrto Velho

Piura
Catacaos
Jaén
Chachapoyas
Pta Aguja
Lambayeque
Ferreñafe
Cajamarca
Huallaga
Pucallpa
Abunã
ACRE
Sena Madureira
Rio Branco
Guajará-Mirim
RONDÔNIA
Serra

Chiclayo
Chepén
Pacasmayo
Cajabamba
Huamachuco
Otuzco
Pomabamba
Tingo María
Brasiléia
Cobija
Riberalta
Porvenir
Abunã

Trujillo
Huallanca
Huascarán 6768
Huaraz
La Unión
Huánuco
CORDILLERA
Ucayali
Madre de Dios
Pto Maldonado
Pto Heath
L. Rogaguado
Iténez

Chimbote
Casma
Huarmey
Oxapampa
Cerro de Pasco
La Merced
Tarma
Jauja
Acobamba
Parque Nac. de Manu
Rurrenabaque
Trinidad
Guaporé

Pativilca
Barranca
Huacho
Ancón
Callao
Lima
La Oroya
PERU
Huancayo
Quillabamba
MACHU PICCHU
**Chincha Alta
Pisco
Ica
Huancavelica
Andahuaylas
Ayacucho
Abancay
Apurímac
Cuzco
Sicuani
Ayaviri
Huanay
Sta Ana
Ancohuma 6358
Corpico
Chulumani

PACIFIC
Pen. de Paracas
Nazca
Juliaca
L. Titicaca
Puno
La Paz
BOLIVIA
Cochabamba

OCEAN
Chala
Coropuna 6425
Majes
Arequipa
Misti 5822
Juli
Guaqui
Quillacollo
Oruro
Santa Cruz
Montero
Llanos de

Camaná
Matarani
Mollendo
Moquegua
Ilo
Desaguadero
Sajama 6542
Aiquile
Sucre
Valle Grande
Sa

Tacna
Arica
Tocopilla
Poopó
Huanuni
Río Mulatos
Potosí
Tarabuco
Monteagudo
Camiri
Lag

Galapagos Islands
at the same scale
**GALAPAGOS ISLANDS
ISLAS GALAPAGOS
(ARCHIPIÉLAGO DE COLÓN)**
(Equ.)
Culpepper
Wenman
Pinta
Marchena
Genovesa
San Salvador
Santa Cruz
Fernandina
Baquerizo Moreno
San Cristóbal
Isabela
Santa María
Española

at the same scale
Islas Juan Fernández
(Chile)
Alejandro Selkirk
Robinson Crusoe
Sta Clara

Iquique
Pedro de Valdivia
Chuquicamata
Tocorpuri 5833
Vol. Ollagüe 5870
Ujina
Uyuni
Calama
Chiza
CHILE
S Pedro
Tupiza
Tarija
Bermejo
Yacuiba
Villa Montes

Mejillones
Tropic of Capricorn
Pedro de Valdivia
Salar de Atacama
Vol. Licancábur
S Salvador de Jujuy
Tilcara
S. Pedro
JUJUY
Orán
Embarcación
Antofagasta
Llullaillaco 6723
ARGENTINA
Salta

1:15M
0 200 400 600 km
0 100 200 300 mls

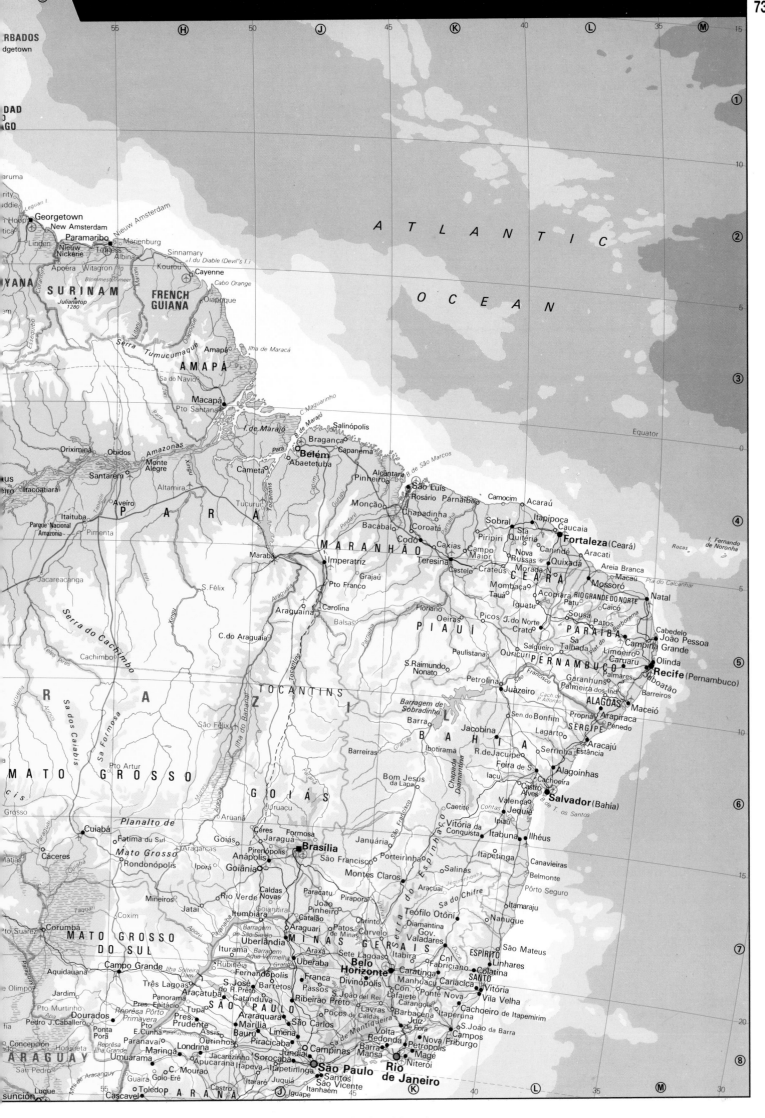

G · 55 · H · 50 · J · 45 · K · 40 · L · 35 · M · 15

① ⑩ ② ③ ④ ⑤ ⑥ ⑦ ⑧

ATLANTIC

OCEAN

RBADOS
dgetown

DAD
O
GO

ruma

rity
ddie
ddie

Hoop

Georgetown
New Amsterdam

Paramaribo
Nieuw
Nickerie
Totness
Albina

GUYANA

SURINAM

Julianatop
1280

FRENCH
GUIANA

Cayenne

I. du Diable (Devil's I.)

Cabo Orange

Olapoque

Leguan I.

Linden

Nieuw Amsterdam

Marienburg

Sinnamary

Kourou

Blommestein meer

Apoera
Witagron

Serra
Tumucumaque

Amapá

Ilha de Maracá

AMAPÁ

Sa. do Navio

Macapá

Pto Santana

Amapá

Oriximiná
Óbidos

Santarém

Monte
Alegre

Amazonas

I. de Marajó

B. de Marajó

C. Maguarinho

Salinópolis

Bragança

Belém

Abaetetuba

Capanema

Pará

Alcântara

B. de São Marcos

Camocim

Acaraú

Equator

Pinheiro

São Luís

Rosário

Parnaíba

Itacoatiara

Itaituba

Parque Nacional
Amazonia

Pimenta

PARÁ

Altamira

Tucurui

Tocantins

Maraba

Imperatriz

S. Félix

Xingu

Aveiro

Tapajós

Teles Pires

Serra do Cachimbo

Cachimbo

Jacareacanga

Iriri

Cametá

Monção

Chapadinha

Coroatá

Bacabal

MARANHÃO

Codó

Caxias

Grajaú

Pto Franco

Carolina

Balsas

C. do Araguaia

Araguaína

Araguaia

São Félix

Ilha do Bananal

TOCANTINS

Teresina

Castelo

Floriano

Oeiras

Piripiri

Sta
Quitéria

Sobral

Itapipoca
Caucaia

Fortaleza (Ceará)

Aracati

Canindé

Nova
Russas

Morada N.

Quixadá

Mombaça

CEARÁ

Tauá

Iguatu

Acopiara

Crateús

Campo
Maior

Picos
J. do Norte

Patu

RIO GRANDE DO NORTE

Caicó

Macau

Mossoró

Areia Branca

Pta do Calcanhar

Natal

I. Fernando
de Noronha

Rocas

S.Raimundo
Nonato

PIAUÍ

Crato

Sousa

Patos

Sorobema

Cabedelo

João Pessoa

Salgueiro

PARAÍBA

Talhada

Campina Grande

Paulistana

Ouricuri

PERNAMBUCO

Limoeiro

Caruaru

Olinda

Recife (Pernambuco)

Petrolina

Juàzeiro

São Francisco

Garanhuns

Palmeira dos Ind.

Palmares

ALAGOAS

Barreiros

Abôatão

Barragem de
Sobradinho

Cach. de
P. Afonso

Propriá

Arapiraca

Maceió

Barra

Sen. do Bonfim

BAHIA

Jacobina

R. de Jacuipe

Lagarto

SERGIPE

Penedo

Aracajú

Estância

Barreiras

Ibotirama

Grande

Feira de S.

Chapada Diamantina

Iaçu

Serrinha

Alagoinhas

Cachoeira

Bom Jesus
da Lapa

MATO GROSSO

Sa dos Caiabis

Sa Formosa

Pto Artur

Cuiabá

Fátima du Sul

Mato Grosso

Cáceres

Rondonópolis

Planalto de

GOIÁS

Iporá

Goiânia

Aruanã

Goiás

Céres
Jaraguá

Pirenópolis

Anápolis

Formosa

Brasília

São Francisco

Januária

Porteirinha

Contas

Caetité

Vitória da
Conquista

Valença

Jequié

Ipiaú

Itabuna

Ilhéus

Canavieiras

Belmonte

Montes Claros

Araçuaí

Sa do Chifre

Itapetinga

Itamaraju

Pôrto Seguro

Nanuque

São Mateus

Cuiabá

Corumbá

MATO GROSSO
DO SUL

Aquidauana

Campo Grande

Três Lagoas

Ilha Solteira
Dam

Matias

Grosso

Olimpo

Pto Murtinho

Jardim

Dourados

Pedro J. Caballero

Concepción

Horqueta

PARAGUAY

San Pedro

sunción

Luque

fia

Mineiros

Jataí

Coxim

Rio Verde

Caldas
Novas

Itumbiara

Goiandira

Catalão

Paracatu

João
Pinheiro

Pirapora

Corinto

Araguari

Uberlândia

Barragem de
São Simão

Iturama

Uberaba

Ituiutaba

Barragem
Água Vermelha

Araxá

Patos
de Minas

Curvelo

MINAS GERAIS

Sete Lagoas

Itabira

Belo
Horizonte

Divinópolis

Caratinga

Teófilo Otôni

Diamantina
Gov.
Valadares

Serra do Espinhaço

Salinas

Araçuaí

Jequitinhonha

ESPÍRITO

Linhares

São Mateus

Cnl
Fabriciano
Colatina

Vila Velha

Vitória

SANTO

Cachoeiro de Itapemirim

Rubinéia

Fernandópolis

Franca

Passos

S.João del Rei

Carangola

Ponte Nova

Manhuaçu

Lafaiete

Três Lagoas

S.José
do R. Prêto

Barretos

Catanduva

Araçatuba

Tupã

SÃO PAULO

Ribeirão Prêto

Poços
de Caldas

Lavras

Barbacena

Juiz
de Fora

S.João da Barra

Campos

Panorama

Pres.
Epitácio

Pres.
Prudente

Marília

Bauru

São Carlos

Araraquara

Limeira

Piracicaba

Pôço de Caldas

Serra de Mantiqueira

Volta
Redonda

Nova
Friburgo

Petrópolis

Ourinhos

Assis

Maringá

Londrina

Jacarezinho

Apucarana

Sorocaba

Campinas

Jundiaí

Itapeva

Itapetininga

Barra
Mansa

Magé

Niterói

Rio
de Janeiro

São Paulo

Santos

São Vicente

Umuarama

C. Mourão

Goio-Erê

Guaíra

Paranavaí

Toledo

PARANÁ

Cascavel

Castro

Itararé

Juquiá

Itanhaém

Iguape

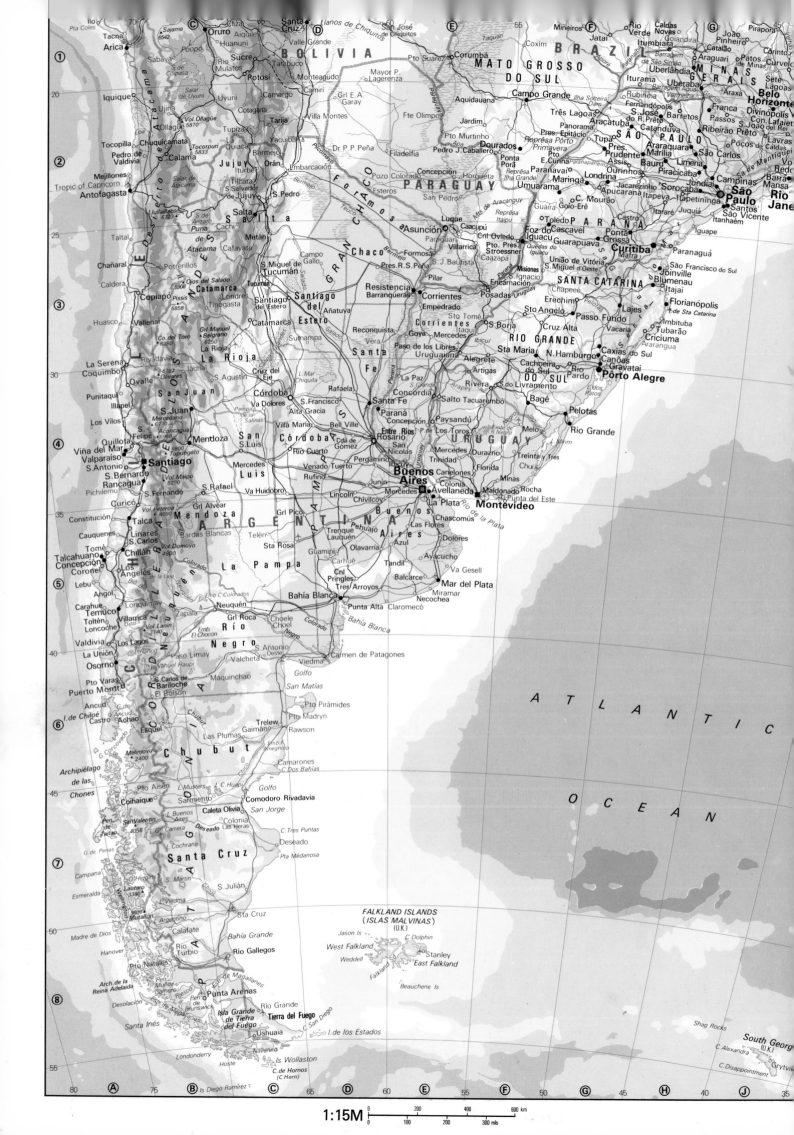

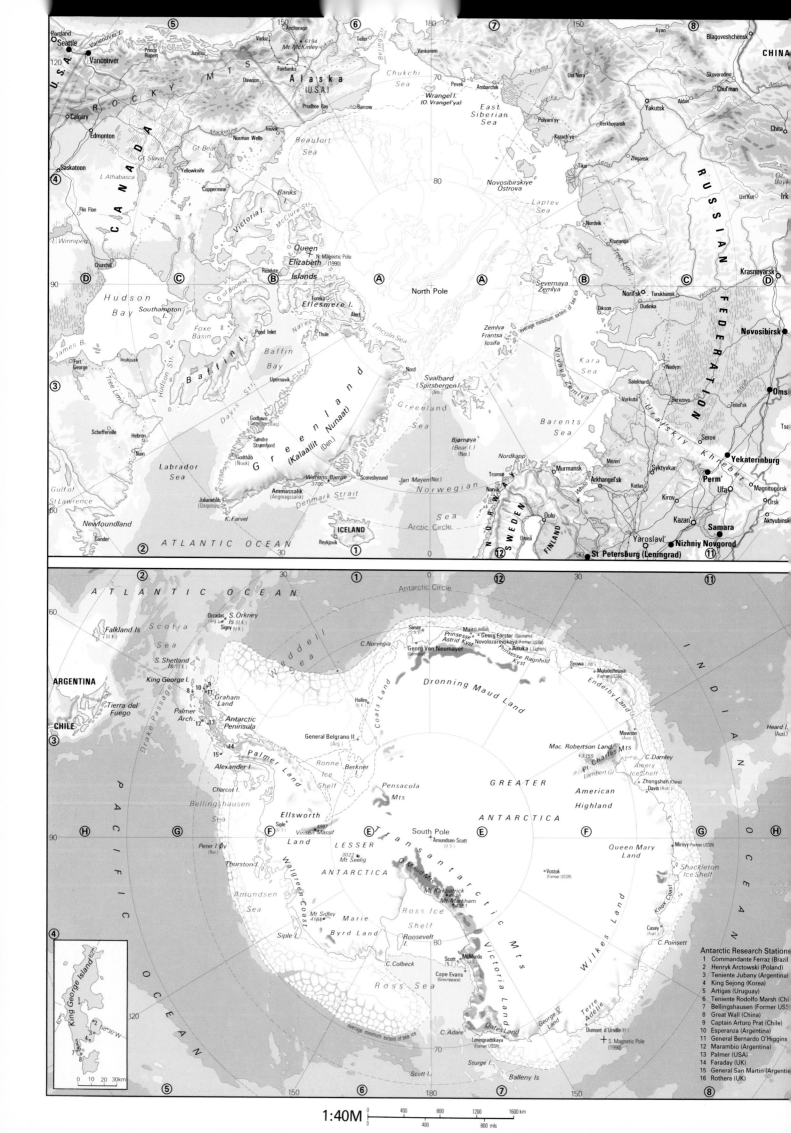

International Boundary
State Boundary
Department Boundary
City Limits
Borough, District Boundary
Military Zones
Armistice, Ceasefire Line
Demilitarised Zone
Station Main Railways
Other Railways
Bridge Projected Railways
Underground Railway
Station Aerial Cableway, Funicular
Metro Stations
M
Projected Special Highway
Main Road
Secondary Road
Other Road, Street
Track
Road Tunnel
Bridge, Flyover

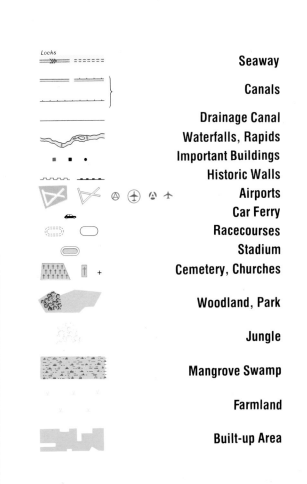

Locks Seaway
Canals
Drainage Canal
Waterfalls, Rapids
Important Buildings
Historic Walls
Airports
Car Ferry
Racecourses
Stadium
Cemetery, Churches
Woodland, Park
Jungle
Mangrove Swamp
Farmland
Built-up Area

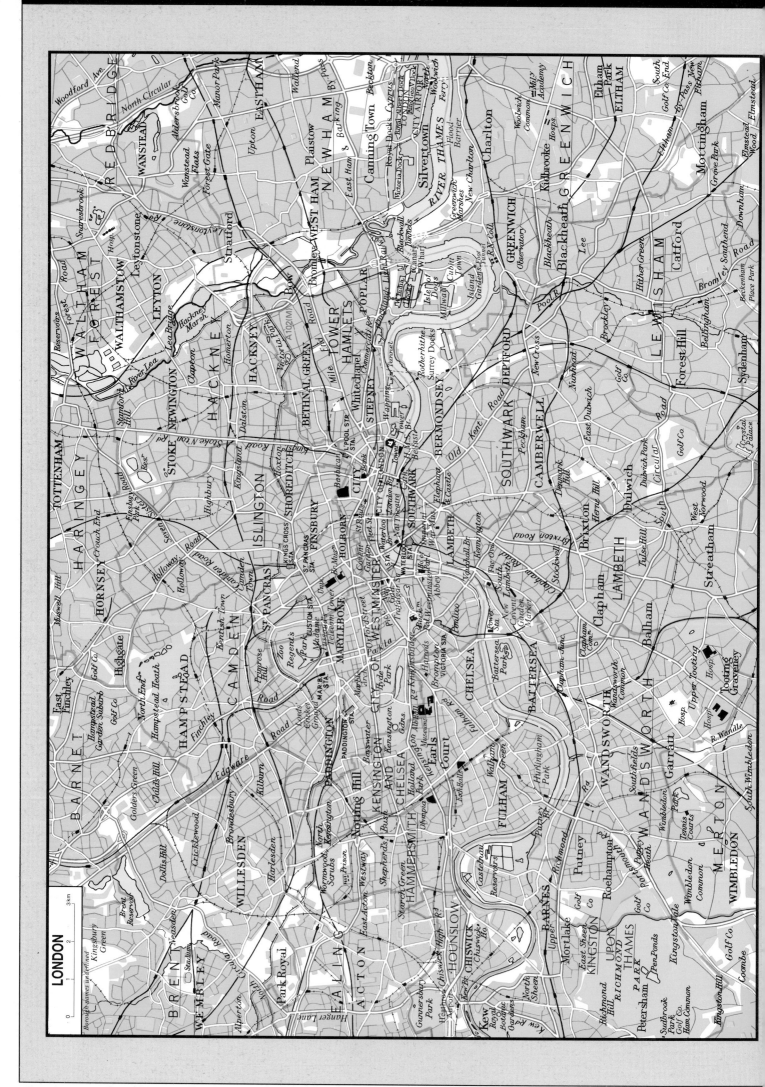

London

3 km

Borough names underlined

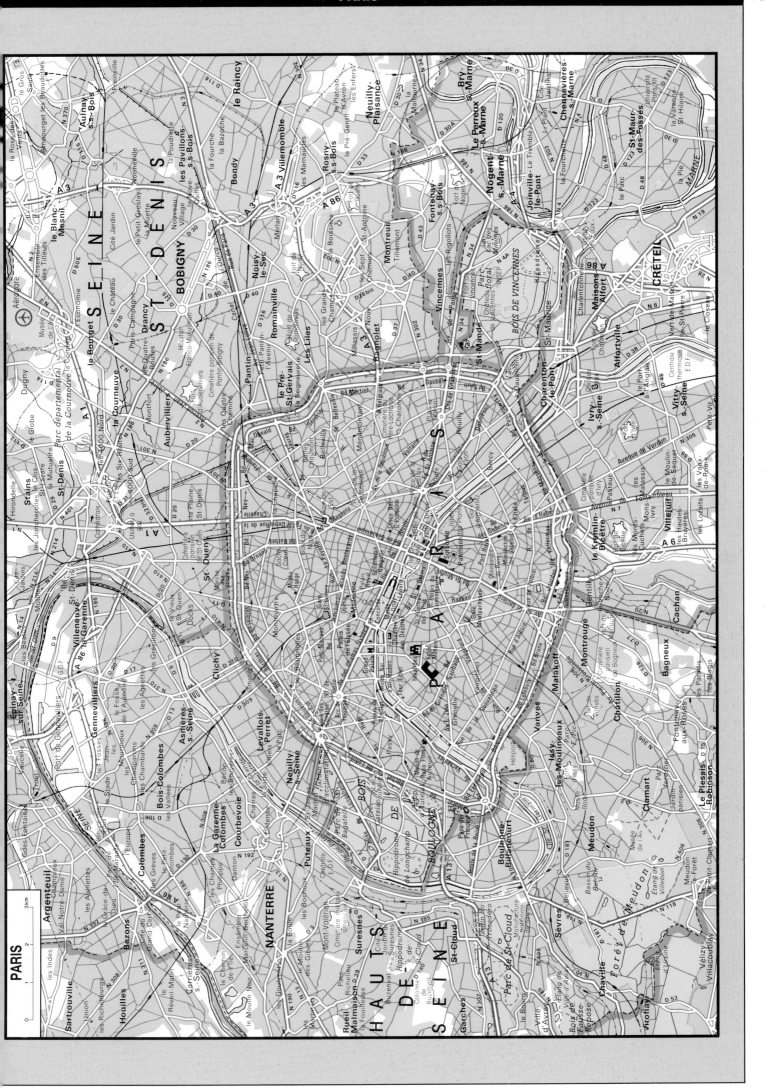

PARIS
3km
2
1
0

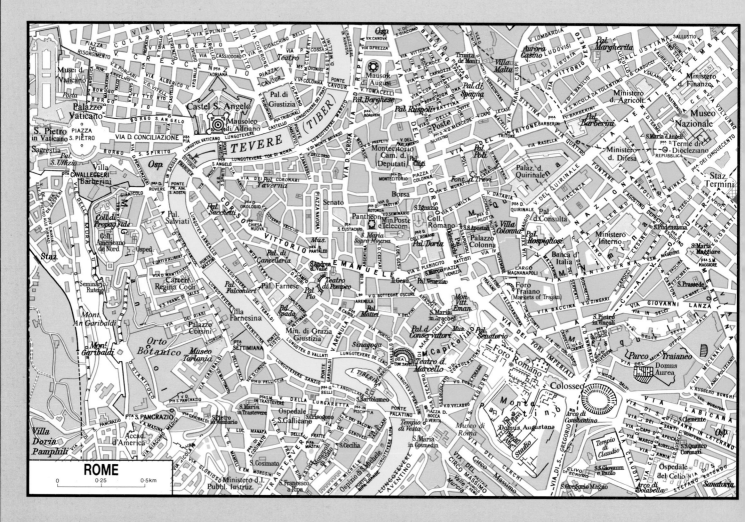

ROME

0   0·25   0·5km

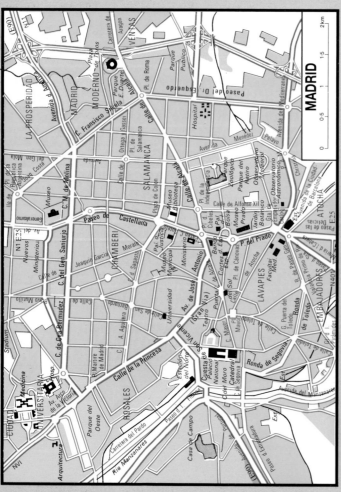

MADRID

2km
1·5
1
0·5
0

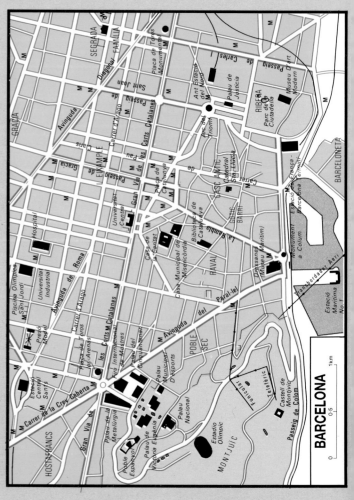

BARCELONA

1km
0·5
0

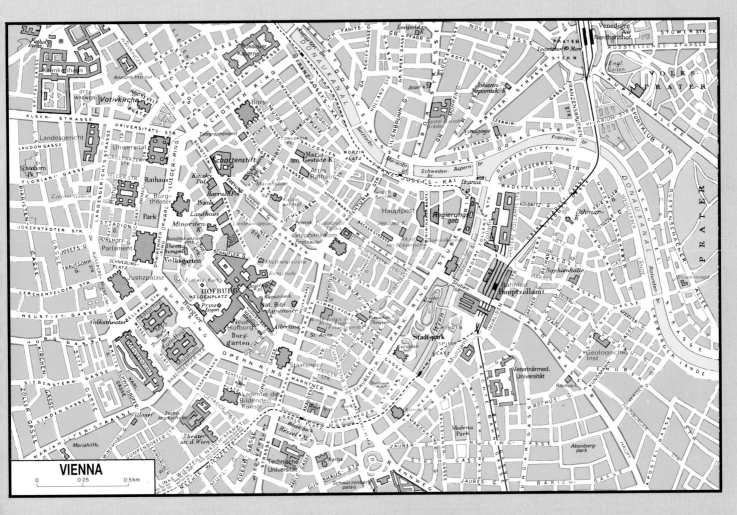

VIENNA

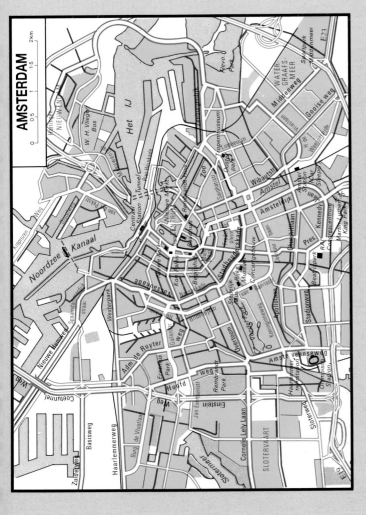

AMSTERDAM

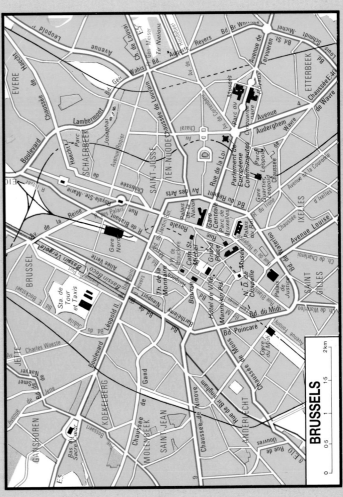

BRUSSELS

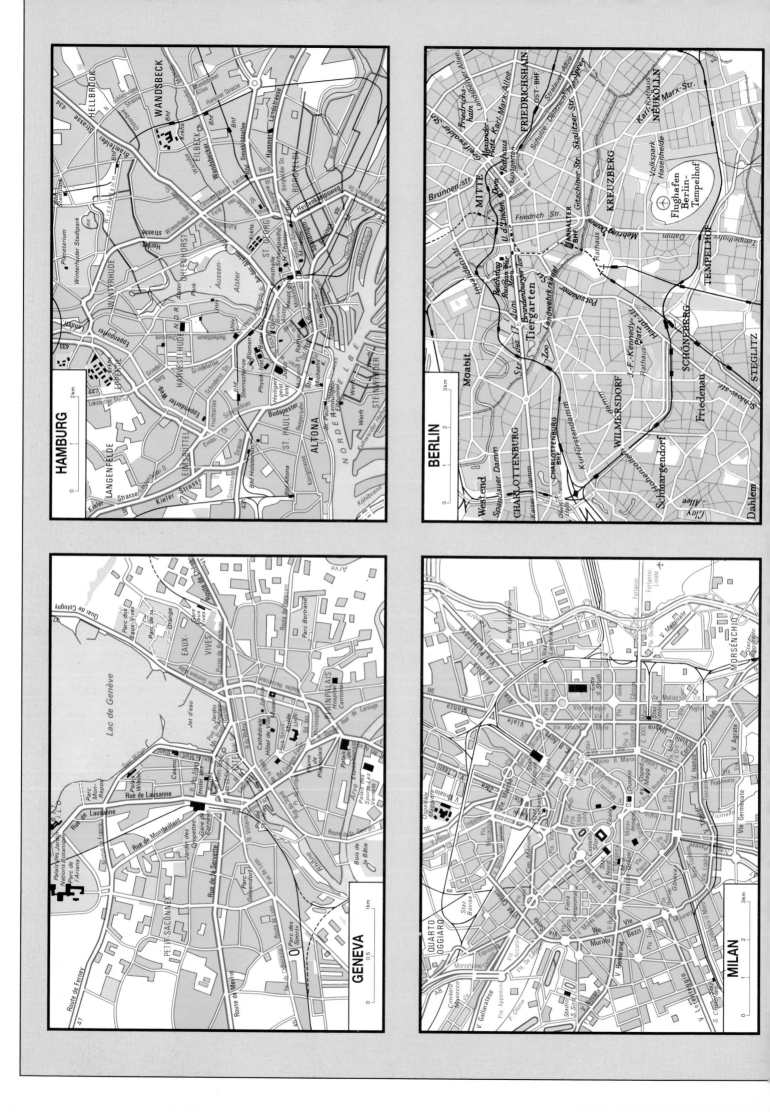

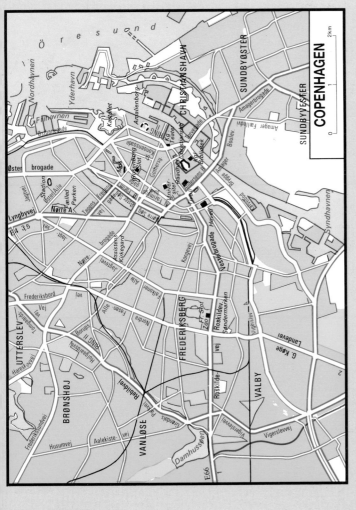

COPENHAGEN

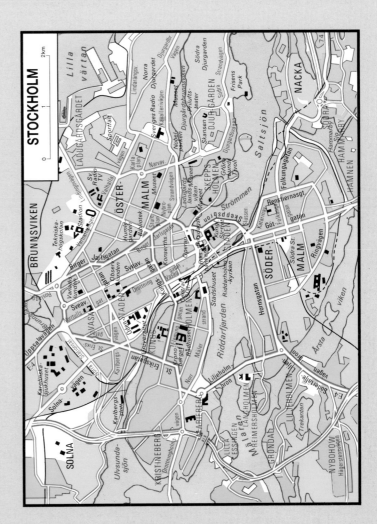

STOCKHOLM

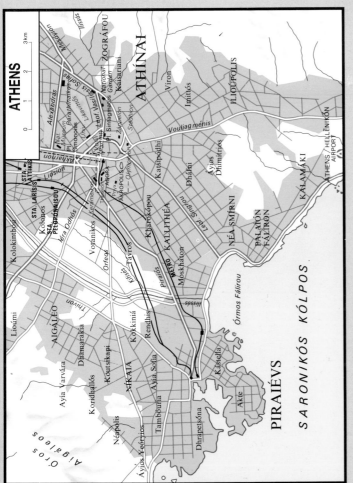

ATHENS

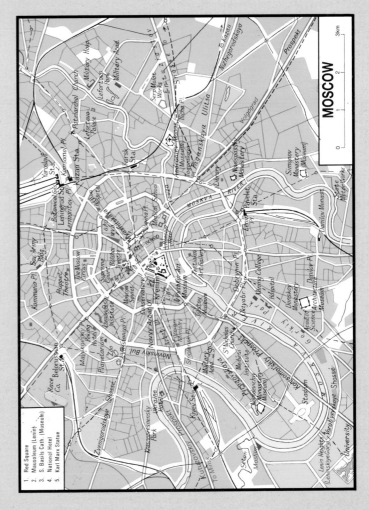

MOSCOW

1. Red Square
2. Mausoleum (Lenin)
3. S. Basil's Cath. (Museum)
4. National Hotel
5. Karl Marx Statue

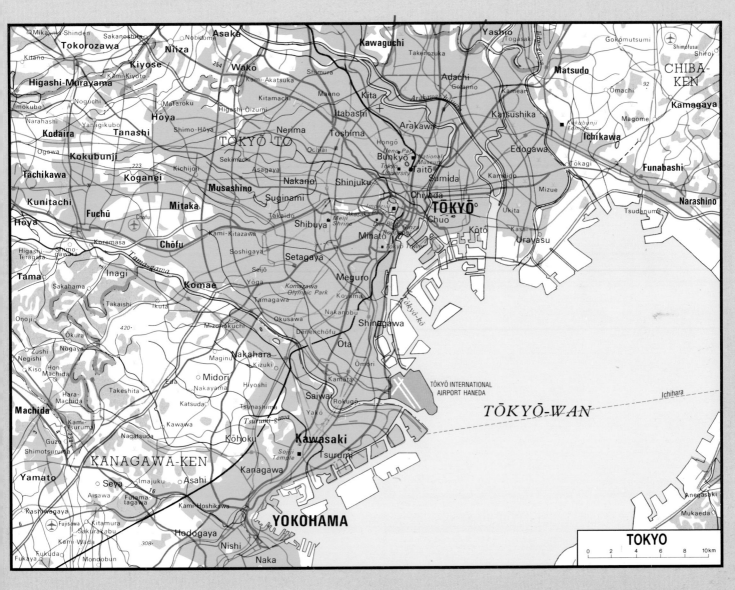

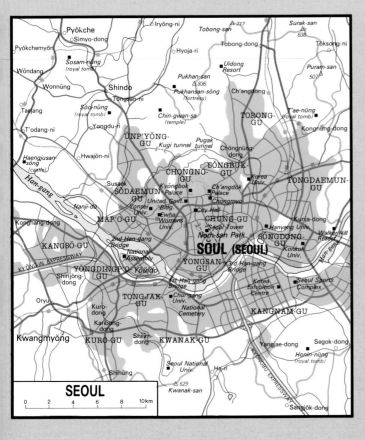

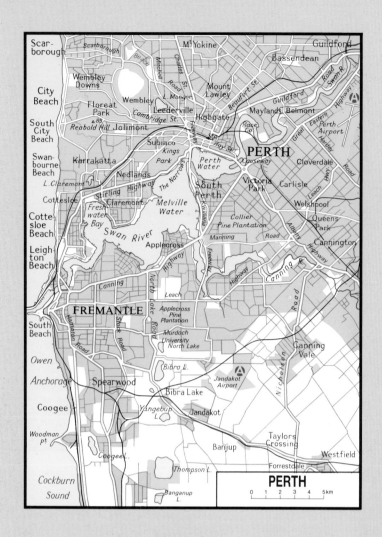

PERTH

Scarborough, Mt Yokine, Guildford, Bassendean, Mt Lawley, Beaufort St, Great Eastern Highway, Perth Airport, City Beach, Wembley Downs, Mitchell Rd, L. Monger, Charles St, Maylands, Belmont, Guildford Rd, Swan R, Floreat Park, Wembley, Cambridge St, Leederville, Highgate, Reabold Hill, Jolimont, Stirling Highway, Subiaco, Kings Park, PERTH, Causeway, Cloverdale, Karrakatta, Nedlands, Claremont, The Narrows, Perth Water, South Perth, Victoria Park, Carlisle, L. Claremont, Cottesloe, Melville Water, Applecross, Welshpool, Fresh water Bay, Swan River, Manning, Canning R, Queens Park, Cannington, Cottesloe Beach, Leighton Beach, Canning, Leach, Albany Highway, Owen Anchorage, Applecross Pine Plantation, Murdoch University North Lake, Canning Vale, Spearwood, Bibra L, Jandakot Airport, Coogee, Yangebup L, Bibra Lake, Jandakot, Taylors Crossing, Woodman Pt, Banjup, Westfield, Coogee L, Thompson L, Forrestdale, Cockburn Sound, Banganup L

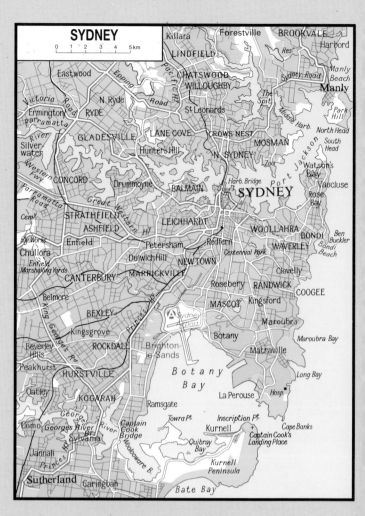

SYDNEY

0 1 2 3 4 5km

Killara, Forestville, BROOKVALE, Harbord, LINDFIELD, Res, Manly Beach, Eastwood, CHATSWOOD, WILLOUGHBY, Sydney Road, Manly, Ermington, N. Ryde, RYDE, Epping Road, St Leonards, CROWS NEST, The Spit, Park Hill, Parramatta, Silverwater, GLADESVILLE, LANE COVE, MOSMAN, Middle Harb, North Head, Hunters Hill, N. SYDNEY, Zoo, South Head, CONCORD, Harb. Bridge, Watson's Bay, Drummoyne, BALMAIN, SYDNEY, Vaucluse, Parramatta Road, Rose Bay, Great Western Hy, STRATHFIELD, LEICHHARDT, WOOLLAHRA, BONDI, Cem, ASHFIELD, Ben Buckler, Enfield, Petersham, Redfern, Centennial Park, WAVERLEY, Bondi Beach, Chullora, Dulwich Hill, NEWTOWN, Clovelly, Enfield Marshalling Yards, CANTERBURY, MARRICKVILLE, Roseberry, RANDWICK, COOGEE, Belmore, King George's Rd, MASCOT, Kingsford, BEXLEY, Maroubra, Kingsgrove, Sydney Airport, Botany, Beverley Hills, Princes Hy, Maroubra Bay, Brighton-le-Sands, ROCKDALE, Matraville, Peakhurst, HURSTVILLE, Botany Bay, Long Bay, Oatley, KOGARAH, La Perouse, Hosp, Como, Georges River, Ramsgate, George's R, Towra Pt, Inscription Pt, Cape Banks, Jannali, Princes Hy, Captain Cook Bridge, River, Woolooware B, Kurnell, Quibray Bay, Captain Cook's Landing Place, Sutherland, Caringbah, Sylvania, Kurnell Peninsula, Bate Bay

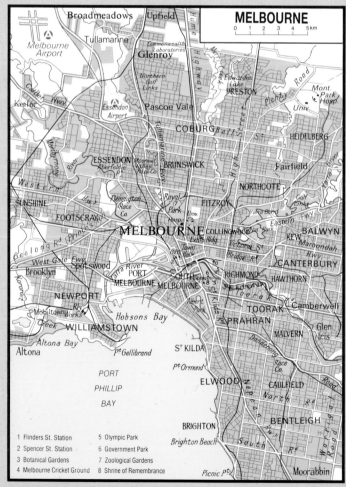

MELBOURNE

0 1 2 3 4 5km

Broadmeadows, Upfield, Melbourne Airport, Tullamarine, Commonwealth Laboratories, Glenroy, Keilor, Essendon Airport, Northern Golf Links, Edwardes Lake Park, PRESTON, Mont. Park Hosp, Univ, Pascoe Vale, Hume Highway, Plenty Road, Merri Creek, COBURG, HEIDELBERG, Maribyrnong, ESSENDON, Aberfeldie, Moonee Valley Race Co, BRUNSWICK, Yarra, Fairfield, NORTHCOTE, High Street, Golf Links, SUNSHINE, Flemington Race Co, Royal Park, FITZROY, BALWYN, FOOTSCRAY, Univ, COLLINGWOOD, Yarra Bend Park, KEW, Maroondah Hwy, Geelong Rd, Princes Hwy, Town Hall, Exhib. Bldg, Eastern Fwy, CANTERBURY, MELBOURNE, West Gate Fwy, Spotswood, Yarra River, PORT MELBOURNE, SOUTH MELBOURNE, RICHMOND, HAWTHORN, Brooklyn, Mobiltown Works, Rly, Hobsons Bay, Albert Park, St Kilda Rd, TOORAK, Camberwell, NEWPORT, Glen Iris, Creek, WILLIAMSTOWN, Dandenong Rd, PRAHRAN, MALVERN, Altona Bay, Pt Gellibrand, ST KILDA, Altona, PORT PHILLIP BAY, Pt Ormond, ELWOOD, Nepean Highway, CAULFIELD, North Rd, BRIGHTON, BENTLEIGH, Brighton Beach, South Rd, Picnic Pt, Moorabbin

1 Flinders St. Station
2 Spencer St. Station
3 Botanical Gardens
4 Melbourne Cricket Ground
5 Olympic Park
6 Government Park
7 Zoological Gardens
8 Shrine of Remembrance

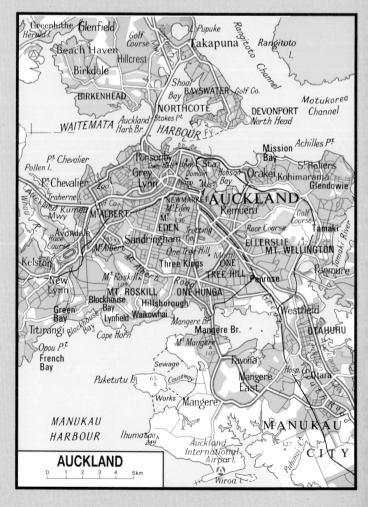

AUCKLAND

0 1 2 3 4 5km

Greenhithe, Glenfield, L. Pupuke, Rangitoto Channel, Rangitoto I, Herald I, Beach Haven, Golf Course, Takapuna, Hillcrest, Birkdale, Shoal Bay, BAYSWATER, Golf Co, Motukorea, BIRKENHEAD, NORTHCOTE, DEVONPORT, Devonport Channel, WAITEMATA, Auckland Harb. Br, Stokes Pt, North Head, HARBOUR, Achilles Pt, Pt Chevalier, Ponsonby, Mission Bay, Pollen I, Town Hall, Univ, Sta, Domain, Hobson Bay, S. Heliers, Pt Chevalier, Zoo, Grey Lynn, Mus, Orakei, Kohimarama, Traherne I, Golf Co, Auckland, Kumeu, AUCKLAND, Glendowie, Whau R, NEWMARKET, Mt Eden, Remuera, Avondale Race Course, Mt ALBERT, EDEN, Trotting Co, Race Course, Tamaki, Kelston, Sandringham, One Tree Hill, ELLERSLIE, MT WELLINGTON, Mt Roskill, Three Kings, ONE TREE HILL, New Lynn, MT ROSKILL, ONE HUNGA, Penrose, Panmure, Green Bay, Blockhouse Bay, Hillsborough, Westfield, Titirangi, Lynfield, Waikowhai, Mangere Br, OTAHUHU, Blockhouse Bay, Cape Horn, Mt Mangere, Opou Pt, French Bay, Puketutu I, Sewage, Tavona, Mangere East, Hosp, Otara, MANUKAU HARBOUR, Ihumatao, Causeway, Mangere, MANUKAU CITY, Works, Auckland International Airport, Wiroa I, Puhinui C

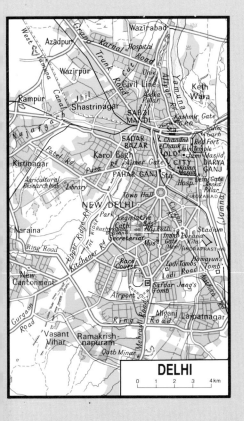

DELHI

0 1 2 3 4km

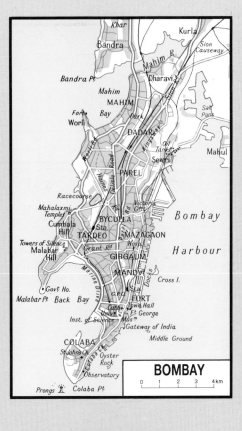

BOMBAY

0 1 2 3 4km

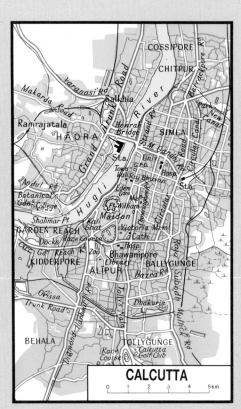

CALCUTTA

0 1 2 3 4 5km

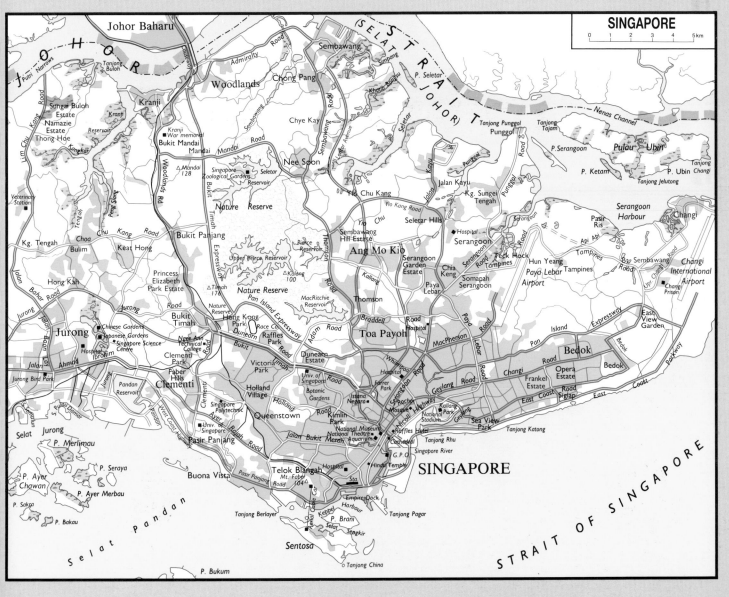

SINGAPORE

0 1 2 3 4 5km

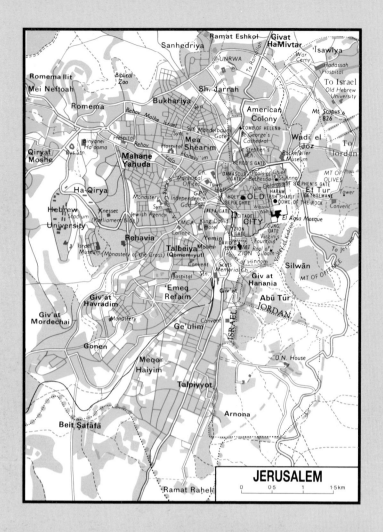

JERUSALEM

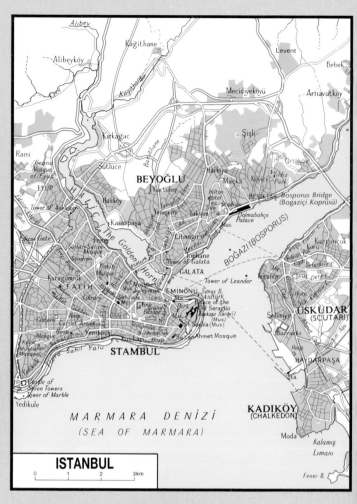

ISTANBUL

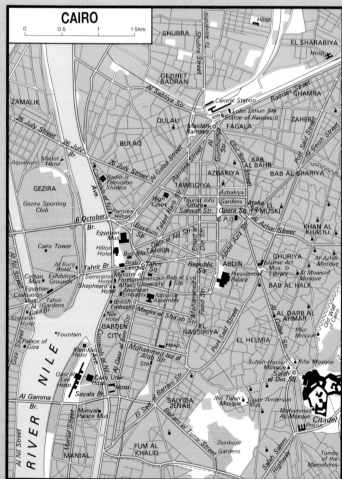

CAIRO

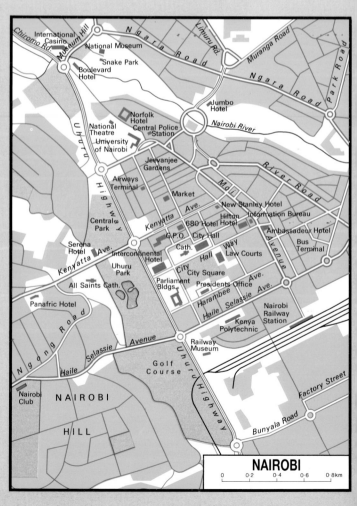

NAIROBI

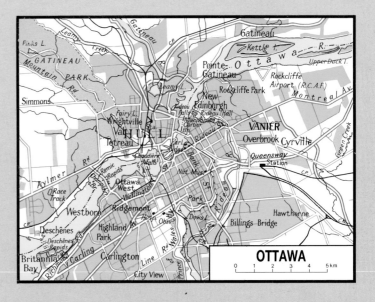

OTTAWA

0 1 2 3 4 5km

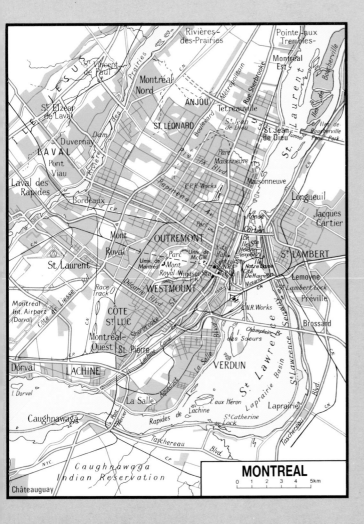

MONTREAL

0 1 2 3 4 5km

TORONTO

0 1 2 3 4 5km

CHICAGO

0 1 2 3 4 5km

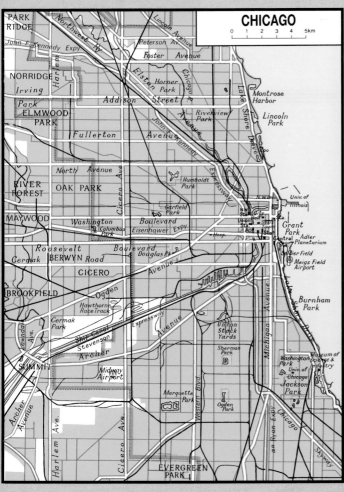

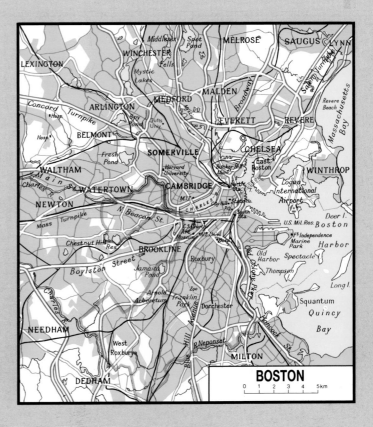

BOSTON

0 1 2 3 4 5km

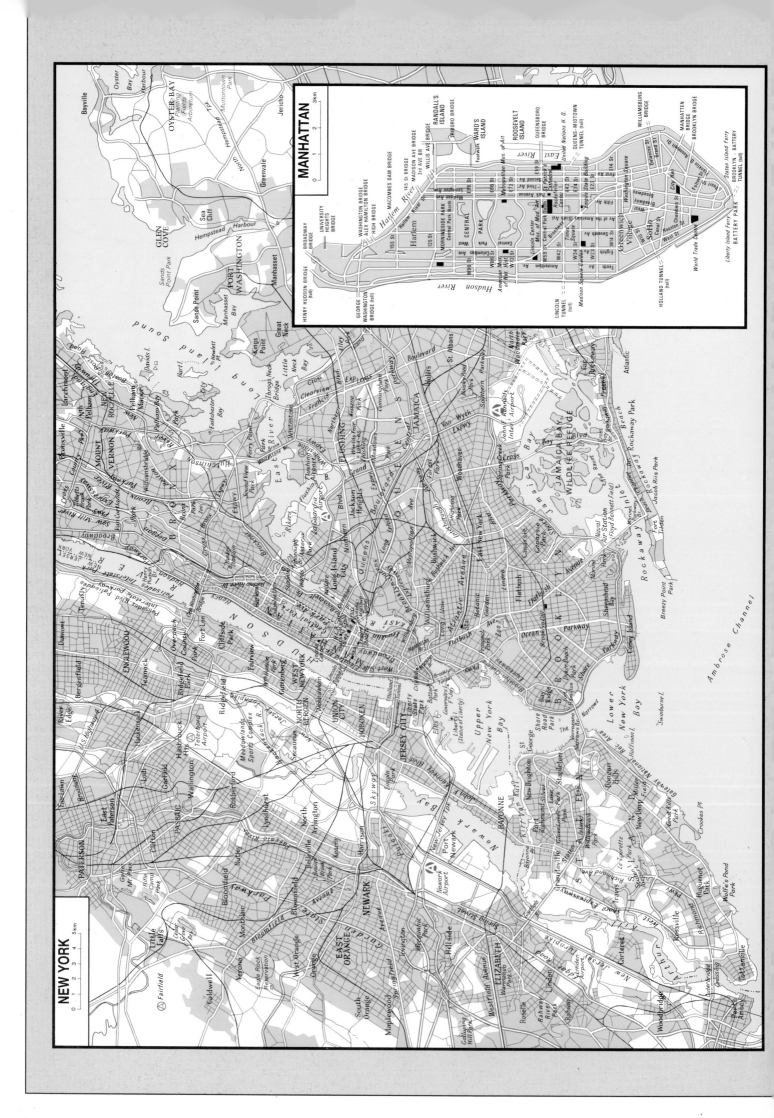

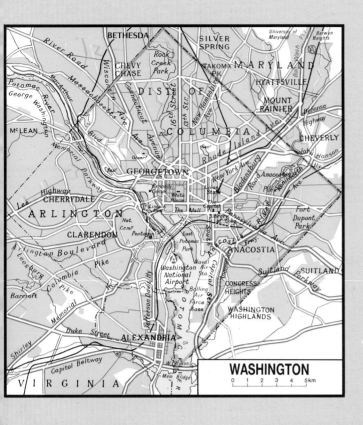

WASHINGTON

0 1 2 3 4 5km

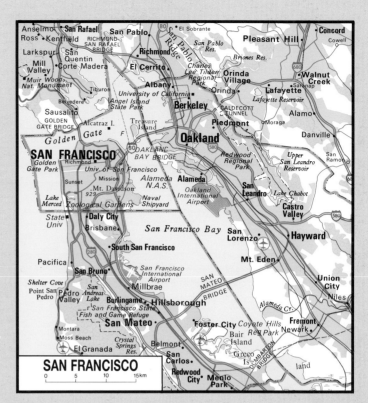

SAN FRANCISCO

0 5 10 15km

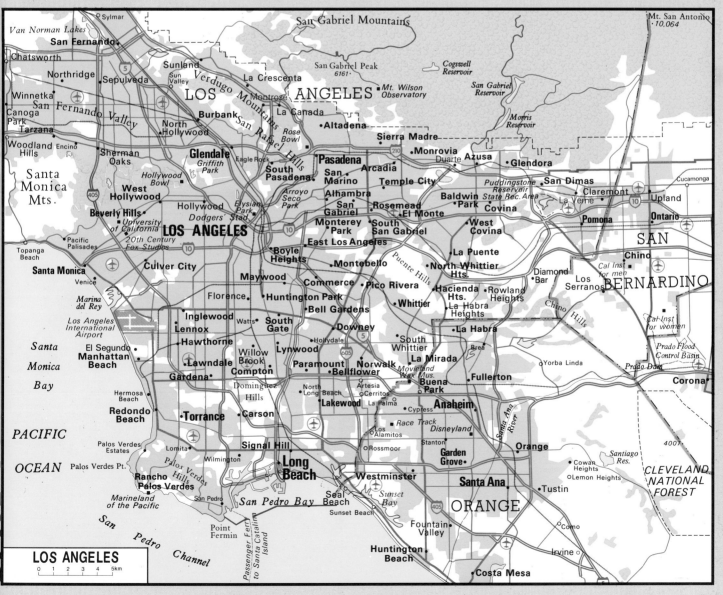

LOS ANGELES

0 1 2 3 4 5km

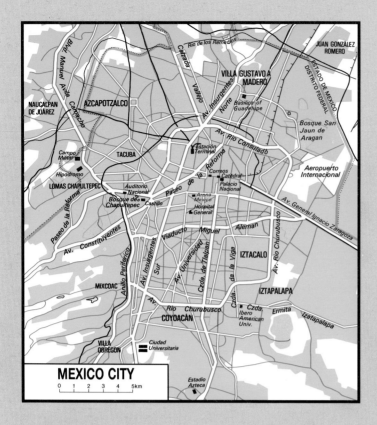

MEXICO CITY

SAO PAULO

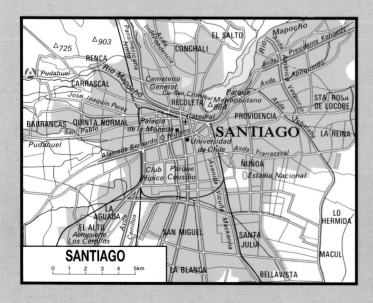

SANTIAGO

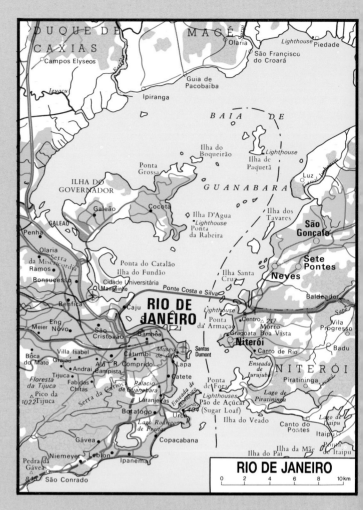

RIO DE JANEIRO

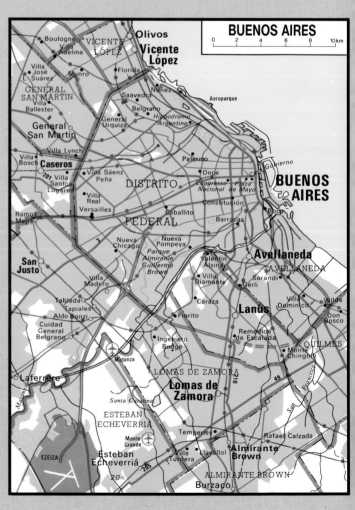

BUENOS AIRES

The roman alphabet is used world-wide. Yet the sounds of Latin from which it was inherited were far too few to allow the alphabet to be applied unaltered to the languages of the world. As a result numerous modifications have been made by adding supplementary letters, by changing the original letters or by adding accents or other diacritical signs.

This brief guide is intended to give no more than an indication of the English language equivalents of the more important letters or combinations of letters in the various alphabets used in the Atlas. An English word is added in brackets to illustrate the sound intended.

zh = s in measure;
kh = ch in Scottish loch
   = German ch in achtung

S-C = Serbo-Croat
Pol = Polish
Cz = Czech

FRENCH
There are four nasal vowels:
am an aen em en aon   ã
aim ain en en eim ein im in ẽ
om on   õ
um un   eũ
ã ẽ õ eũ are like a in hart; e in met; o in corn; oo in book pronounced nasally.
au, eau = o (no); é = ay (lay); è, ê, = e (met);
oi oî = wa (wand)
c + a = k; c + e or i = ç = s (sit)
ch = sh (fresh); g + a, o or u = g (got)
g + e or i = j = zh*; gn = ni (onion)
gu = g (got); gü = gw (iguana)
ll = l or y; qu = k; th = t
u = between e in few and oo in too

SPANISH
c + a, o or u = k; c + e or i = th (thin) or s (sit)
ch = ch (cheese); g + a, o or u = g (got)
g + e or i = kh*; gu + a, o or u = gw (iguana)
gu + e or i = g (got); j = kh*; ñ = ny (canyon);
ll = y (yes)
qu + a, o or u = kw (quick); qu + e or i = k (kite)
y = y (yes); z = th (thin) or z depending on dialect

ITALIAN
c + a, o or u = k; c + e or i = ch (cheese)
ch = k
g + a, o or u = g (got); g + e or i = j (jet)
gh = g (got); gli = lli (million)
qu = kw (quick); z = ts or dz

ROMANIAN
ă = a in relative
â = i in ravine
c + a, o or u = k
c + e or i = ch (cheese); ch = k
g + a, o or u = g (got); g + e or i = j (jet)
ş = sh (fresh); ţ = ts (sits)

PORTUGUESE
ã, ãe = French ẽ
õa, õe = French õ
c + a, o or u = k; c + e or i = s
ç = s; ch = sh (fresh)
ih = lli (million)
x = sh (fresh); z = z but = zh when final

GERMAN
ä = e (met); au = ow (down)
äu = oy (boy); c = ts (sits)
ch = kh*; ei, ey = eye (= y in why)
eu = oy (boy); g = g (got)
ie = ie (retrieve); j = y (yes)
ö = oo (book); s = z but s when final
sch = sh (fresh); sp, st = shp, sht
ü = French u; v = f; w = v; z = ts (sits)

DUTCH
aa ee are long vowels
c + e or i or z = s, otherwise k
ij = eye (= y in why)

SCANDINAVIAN
å = aw (law); ä = e (met)
ø = oo (book); øj = oy (boy)
j = y (yes)

ICELANDIC
ð = dh = th (then)
hv = kw; ll = tl; p = th

FINNISH
ay = eye (= y in why)
j = y; y = French u; w = v

HUNGARIAN
a = aw (law); cs = ch (cheese); ccs = chch;
gy = d + y (dew)
j = y; ny = ny (canyon)
s = sh (fresh); ss = shsh
sz = s (sit); ty = t + y (yes)
zs = zh*
ai = e (met); av = au or av
dh = th (then); th = th (thin)
kh = kh*; oi = i (ravine)
ou = oo (too)

TURKISH
c = j (jet); ç = ch (cheese)
ö = oo (book); ş = sh
ü = French u
ı and i = i (ravine)

RUSSIAN
ay = a + y (yes)
e = e or ye
ë = yaw; ëy = yoy
ch = ch (cheese); sh = sh (fresh)
sh ch = sh ch (fresh cheese)
ts = ts (sits)
ya = ya (yam); z = z (zoo)
zh = zh (measure)
' = sound of y (yes)
'' = silent

OTHER SLAVONIC

S-C	Pol	Cz	
c	c	c	= ts (sits)
	ć		= ts + y (yes)
č	cz	č	= ch (cheese)
ć			= t + y (yes)
đ		ď	= d + y (yes)
		ě	= e (mother)
h	ch	ch	= kh*
j	j	j	= y (yes)
	l		= w (wood)
nj	ń	ň	= ny (canyon)
		ř	= rzh*
š	sz	š	= sh (fresh)
		ť	= t + y (yes)
ž	ž, rz, ź	ž	= zh*

ARABIC
long vowels have a macron (bar), ā
dh = th (then)
h = h (hat); j = (jet)
gh = French r, pronounce as g (got)
kh = kh* q = g (got)
' and ' are best treated as glottal stops
ḍ ḥ ṣ ẓ = d, h, s, t, z
Note: 1. in Egypt and Sudan g = g (got)
         2. in NW Africa Dj = j (jet)
                         ou = w (wadi)

FARSI (IRAN)
Can be read as Arabic above. Stress is on the last syllable.

SOMALI
long vowels are aa, ee, ii, oo, uu
c is silent = glottal stop
dh = th (then)
g = g (got); q = k (kite)
sh = sh (fresh); w = w (wadi)
x = kh*

MALAY – INDONESIAN
As English except
c = ch (cheese)

CHINESE (PINYIN)
q = ch (church); c = ts (sits)
x = hs = h + s

A

ABLATION The loss of water from ice and snow surfaces, by melting and run-off, calving of icebergs, evaporation and snow-blowing.

ABRASION The wearing down or away of rocks by friction.

ABSOLUTE HUMIDITY The amount of water vapour in a specified amount of air, frequently expressed as grams of water vapour per kilogram of dry air containing the vapour.

ABYSSAL Usually applied to the very deep parts of the oceans, over 3km below the surface.

ACCRETION The growth of objects by collection of additional material, usually of smaller size. Ice particles in the atmosphere can grow by this process.

ACID PRECIPITATION Rain and snow with a pH of less than 5.6.

ADVECTION Movement of a property in air and water by their motion. Usually applied to horizontal rather than vertical motion.

AEOLIAN Related to winds. Thus aeolian geomorphology is concerned with the processes whereby wind removes, distributes and deposits materials of the earth's surface.

AGGLOMERATE A rock made of small pieces of lava that have been fused by heat.

AGGRADATION The building up of a land surface by deposition of material by wind, water or ice.

AGGREGATE A loose collection of rock fragments.

ALLUVIAL PLAIN A plain, usually at low altitude, made of alluvium.

ANTICYCLONE An extensive region of relatively high atmospheric pressure, usually a few thousand kilometres across, in which the low level winds spiral outwards, clockwise in the northern hemisphere and anticlockwise in the southern hemisphere.

ARCHIPELAGO A sea or lake containing numerous islands, such as the area between Sumatra and the Philippines.

ARTESIAN WELL A well which taps water held under pressure in rocks below the surface. The pressure results in a well water level higher than the highest part of the water-bearing rocks.

ATOLL A coral reef surrounding a lagoon found in the tropical oceans.

AURORA BOREALIS (Northern Lights) Flashing lights in the atmosphere some 400km above polar regions caused by solar particles being trapped in the earth's magnetic field.

AVALANCHE The sudden and rapid movement of ice, snow, earth and rock down a slope.

AZIMUTH Horizontal angle between two directions.

B

BADLANDS Highly dissected landscapes, usually associated with poorly consolidated materials and sparse vegetation cover.

BAR A usually sandy feature, lying parallel to the coast and frequently underwater.

BARCHAN A crescentic sand dune whose horns point in the direction of dune movement.

BAROGRAPH An instrument for recording atmospheric pressure. The output is a graph of pressure changes through time.

BAROMETER An instrument for measuring atmospheric pressure. The reading is either by measuring the height of a column of mercury or by the compression or expansion of a series of vacuum chambers.

BARRIER REEF A coral reef characterized by the presence of a lagoon or body of water between it and the associated coastline.

BASALT A fine-grained and dark coloured igneous rock.

BASE LEVEL The lower limit to the operation of erosional processes generating on land – usually defined with reference to the role of running water. Sea level is the most general form of base level.

BASIN An area of land encompassing the water flow into any specific river channel – hence usually known as a drainage basin.

BATHOLITH A large mass of intrusive igneous rock.

BATHYMETRY Measurement of water depth.

BAUXITE The main ore of aluminium.

BEACH A coastal accumulation of various types of sediment, usually sands and pebbles.

BEAUFORT SCALE A scale of wind speed devised by Admiral Sir Francis Beaufort based on effects of winds on ships. Later modified to include land-based phenomena.

BENCH MARK A reference point used in the measurement of land height in topographic surveying.

BENTHIC Relating to plants, animals and other organisms that inhabit the floors of lakes, seas and oceans.

BERGSCHRUND The crevasse existing at the head of a glacier because of the movement of glacier ice away from the rock wall.

BIGHT A bend in a coast forming an open bay, or the bay itself.

BIOMASS The mass of biological material present per plant or animal, per community or per unit area.

BIOME A mixed community of plants and animals occupying a large area of continental size.

BIOSPHERE The zone at the interface of the earth's surface, ocean and atmosphere where life is found.

BIOTA The entire collection of species or organisms, plants and animals found in a given region.

BISE A cold, dry northerly to north-easterly wind occurring in the mountains of Central Europe in winter.

BLACK EARTH A black soil rich in humus, found extensively in temperate grasslands such as the Russian Steppes.

BLOW HOLE Vertical shaft leading from a sea cave to the surface. Air and water are frequently forced through it by advancing seas.

BORE A large solitary wave which moves up funnel-shaped rivers and estuaries.

BOREAL A descriptive term, usually of climate and forest, to characterize conditions in middle to high latitudes.

BOURNE A river channel on chalk terrain that flows after heavy rain.

BUTTE A small, flat-topped and often steep-sided hill standing isolated on a flat plain. *(see picture below)*

C

CALDERA A depression, usually several kilometres across.

CALVING The breaking away of a mass of ice from a floating glacier or ice shelf to form an iceberg.

CANYON A steep sided valley, usually found in semi-arid and arid areas.

CAPE An area of land jutting out into water, frequently as a peninsula or promontory.

CARDINAL POINTS The four principal compass points, north, east, south and west.

CATARACT A large waterfall over a precipice.

CHINOOK A warm, dry wind that blows down the eastern slopes of the Rocky Mountains of North America.

Above Butte, Monument Valley, Arizona USA. This type of flat-topped, steep sided hill is characteristic of the arid plateau region of the western United States.

CIRQUE OR CORRIE A hollow, open downstream but bounded upstream by a curved, steep headwall, with a gently sloping floor. Found in areas that have been glaciated.

CLIMATE The long-term atmospheric characteristics of a specified area.

CLOUD A collection of a vast number of small water droplets or ice crystals or both in the atmosphere.

COL A pass or saddle between two mountain peaks.

COLD FRONT A zone of strong horizontal temperature gradient in the atmosphere moving such that, for the surface observer, cold air replaces warm.

CONDENSATION The process of formation of liquid water from water vapour.

CONFLUENCE The 'coming together' of material

flows, most usually used in fluids such as the atmosphere and oceans.

CONGLOMERATE A rock which comprises or contains rounded pebbles more than about 2mm in diameter.

CONTINENTAL DRIFT The movement of continents relative to each other. (See *Plate Tectonics*)

CONTINENTAL SHELF A portion of the continental crust below sea level that slopes gently seaward forming an extension of the adjacent coastal plain separated from the deep ocean by the steeply sloping continental slope.

CONTINENTAL SLOPE Lies on the seaward edge of the continental shelf and slopes steeply to the ocean floor.

CONTOUR A line on a map that joins points of equal height or equal depth.

CONVECTION CURRENT A current resulting from convection which is a mode of mass transport within a fluid (especially heat) resulting in movement and mixing of properties of that fluid.

CONVERGENCE The opposite of divergence which is the outflowing mass of fluid. Hence convergence is the inflowing of such mass.

CORAL REEF Large structures fringing islands and coastlines consisting mostly of corals and algae.

CORDILLERA A system of mountain ranges consisting of a number of more or less parallel chains of mountain peaks – such as in the Rocky Mountains.

CRATER A depression at the top of a volcano where a vent carrying lava and gasses reaches the surface.

CRATON A continental area that has experienced little internal deformation in the last 600 million years.

CREVASSE A deep fissure in the surface of a body of ice.

CYCLONE A region of relatively low atmospheric pressure about 2000 km across around which air rotates anticlockwise in the northern hemisphere and clockwise in the southern.

D

DATUM LEVEL Something (such as a fixed point or assumed value) used as a basis for calculating or measuring. Frequently a height of ground relative to which other heights are assessed.

DECLINATION Angular distance north or south from the equator measured along a line of longitude.

DECIDUOUS FOREST Forest in which the trees shed their leaves at a particular time, season or growth stage. The most common manifestation is the shedding in winter.

DEFLATION The process whereby the wind removes fine materials from the surface of a beach or desert.

DEGRADATION The lowering and often flattening of a land surface by erosion.

DELTA Accumulations of sediment deposited at the mouths of rivers. The Nile and Mississippi deltas are two famous examples.

DENUDATION The laying bare of underlying rocks or strata by the removal of overlying material.

DEPOSITION The laying down of material, which, in geomorphological terms, was previously carried by wind, liquid water or ice.

DEPRESSION See *cyclone*

DESALINIZATION To take out the salt content of a material. Usually applied to the extraction of salt from sea water to give fresh water.

DESERT An area in which vegetation cover is sparse or absent and precipitation is low in amount. Deserts can be hot or cold.

DISCHARGE The volume of flow of fluid in a given time period.

DISSECTED PLATEAU A relatively flat, high level area of land which has been cut by streams.

DIURNAL Occurring everyday or having a daily cycle.

DIVERGENCE A spreading of material. Frequently found in high pressure areas (anticyclones) in the atmosphere where air spirals outwards from the centre.

DOLDRUMS A zone of light, variable winds and low atmospheric pressure near or slightly north of the equator.

DRAINAGE The flow of material (usually a fluid) over the earth's surface due to the force of gravity. Most familiarly seen as rivers.

DRIFT ICE Ice bodies drifting in ocean currents.

DROUGHT Dryness caused by lack of precipitation, most easily seen in the hot, dry desert areas of the world.

DROWNED VALLEY A valley which has been filled with water due to a rise of sea level relative to the level with which the river mouth was previously in accord.

DRUMLIN A depositional landform, usually made of glacially-derived material, which has been streamlined by the passage of overlying ice.

DRY VALLEY A valley which is seldom, if ever, occupied by a stream channel.

DUNE An accumulation of sand deposited and shaped by wind.

DUST Solid particles carried in suspension by the atmosphere.

DYKE A sheet-like intrusion of igneous rock, usually oriented vertically, which cuts across the structural planes of the host rocks.

E

EARTH PILLAR A pinnacle of soil or other unconsolidated material that is protected from erosion by the presence of a stone at the top.

EARTHQUAKE A series of shocks and tremors resulting from the sudden release of pressure along active faults and in areas of volcanic activity.

EBB TIDE Tide receding to or at its lowest point.

ECLIPSE, LUNAR The total or partial obscuring of the Moon by the Earth lying on a line between the Moon and the Sun.

ECLIPSE, SOLAR The total or partial obscuring of the Sun by the Moon lying on a line between the Sun and the Earth.

ECOLOGY A branch of science that studies the relations of plants and animals with each other and with their non-living environment.

ECOSYSTEM An entity within which ecological relations operate.

EPICENTRE The point on the earth's surface which lies directly above the focus of an earthquake.

EQUINOX The time of year when the sun is directly overhead at noon at the equator.

ERG A sand desert.

EROSION The group of processes whereby debris is loosened or dissolved and removed from any part of the earth's surface.

ERRATIC A rock that has been carried to its present location by a glacier.

ESCARPMENT A linear land form with one steep side (scarp slope) and one less steep side (dip slope).

ESKER A sinuous ridge of coarse gravel which has been deposited by a meltwater stream normally flowing underneath a glacier.

ESTUARY The sections of a river which flow into the sea and are influenced by tidal currents.

EVAPORATION The diffusion of water vapour into the atmosphere from freely exposed water surfaces.

EXFOLIATION The weathering of a rock by the peeling off of surface layers.

F

FATHOM A unit of length equal to six feet, most usually used in measuring depth of water.

FAULT A crack or fissure in rock, resulting from tectonic movement.

FAUNA Animals or animal life of an area.

FEN A low lying area partially covered by water which is characterized by accumulations of peat.

FJORD A glacially eroded valley whose floor is occupied by the sea.

FIRTH A sea inlet, particularly in Scotland.

FLORA Plants or plant life in an area.

FLUVIOGLACIAL The activity of rivers which are fed by water melted from glaciers.

FOG An accumulation of water droplets or ice crystals in the atmosphere such that visibility is reduced to 1km or less.

FÖHN WIND A strong, gusty, warm, down-slope wind which occurs on the lee side of a mountain range.

FOLD A bend in rock strata resulting from movement of the crustal rocks.

FOOD CHAIN The transfer of food from one type of organism to another in a sequence.

FORD A shallow part of a river that allows easy crossing.

FRACTURE The splitting of material into parts: usually concerned with geological materials.

FRAZIL ICE Fine spikes of ice in suspension in water, usually associated with the freezing of sea water.

FRONT A transition zone between air of different density, temperature and humidity.

FROST A situation resulting from air temperatures falling to 0°C – either in the air (air frost) or at the ground (ground frost).

FUMAROLE A small, volcanic vent through which hot gasses are emitted.

G

GABBRO A basic igneous rock, usually coarse grained and dark grey to black in colour.

GEEST Ancient alluvial sediments which still cover the land surfaces on which they were originally deposited.

GEODESY The determination of the size and shape of the earth by survey and calculation.

GEOID The shape of the earth at mean sea level.

GEOLOGY Science that deals with the nature and origin of the earth's rocks and sediments.

GEOMORPHOLOGY Science that deals with the nature and origin of landforms of the earth's surface.

GEOSYNCLINE A very large depression, tens or hundreds of kilometres across and up to ten kilometres deep, the floor of which is built up by sedimentation.

GEYSER A spring of geothermally heated water that erupts intermittently due to pressures beneath the surface. Old Faithful in Yellowstone National Park, USA, is the most famous example.

GLACIATION The incursion of ice into (or over) a landscape resulting in a whole suite of glacial processes operating thereupon.

GLACIER A large body of ice, in a valley or covering a much larger area. The largest are found in polar regions.

GLEN Valley. Term especially used in Scotland.

GNEISS A coarse-grained igneous rock that has been metamorphosed.

GONDWANALAND A large continent which it is thought was split very early in geological time to form parts of Africa, Australia, Antarctica, South America and India.

GORGE A deep and narrow section of a river valley, usually with very steep sides.

GRAVEL Loose, rounded fragments of rock.

GREAT CIRCLE A circle formed on the surface of the earth by the intersection of a plane through the centre of the earth with the surface. Lines of longitude and the Equator are great circles.

GROUND FROST See *frost*

GROUND WATER All water (gaseous, liquid or solid) lying below the earth's surface and not chemically combined with the minerals present.

GROYNE A man-made barrier running across a beach and into the sea; constructed to reduce erosion of the beach by longshore currents.

GULF A part of the sea that is partly or almost completely enclosed by land.

GULLY A linear depression worn in the earth by running water after rains.

GUYOT A flat-topped mountain on the sea floor which does not reach the sea surface.

GYRE Large circulations of water in the world's oceans, involving the major currents.

H

HAFF A coastal lagoon separated from the open seas by a sand spit.

HAIL Solid precipitation which falls as ice particles from cumulonimbus clouds. Contrasts markedly with snow.

HEMISPHERE Half of the earth, usually thought of in terms of its surface. The most familiar are the northern and southern hemispheres, bounded by the Equator.

HORIZON Apparent junction of earth and sky.

HORSE LATITUDE The latitude belts over the oceans at latitudes of 30–35° where winds are predominantly calm or light and weather is often hot and dry.

HOT SPOT A small area of the earth's crust where an unusually high heat flow is associated with volcanic activity.

HOT SPRING An emission of hot water at the land surface.

HURRICANE A severe cyclone occurring in the tropics, characterized by high wind speeds and heavy precipitation.

HYDROLOGICAL CYCLE The continuous movement of all forms of water (vapour, liquid and solid) on, in and above the earth.

HYDROSPHERE The earth's water – saline, fresh, gaseous, liquid and solid.

HYGROMETER A device for measuring the relative humidity of the atmosphere.

HYPSOGRAPHIC CURVE A generalized profile of the earth and ocean floors which represents the proportions of the area of the surface at various altitudes above or below a datum.

I

ICEBERG A large floating mass of ice detached from a glacier, usually tens of metres deep and can be several kilometres across.

ICE-CAP A dome-shaped glacier with a generally outward flow of ice.

ICE FLOE A piece of floating ice which is not attached to the land and is usually 2–3 metres thick.

ICE SHELF A floating sheet of ice attached to an embayment in the coast.

IGNEOUS ROCK Rock formed when molten material solidifies, either within the earth's crust or at the surface.

INSELBERG A large, residual hill which overlooks a surrounding eroded plain.

INSOLATION The amount of solar radiation received over a specified area and a specified time.

INTERNATIONAL DATE LINE An arbitary line, roughly along the 180° longitude line, east and west of which the date differs by one day.

INVERSION (temperature) An increase of temperature with height.

IRRIGATION The supply of water to land by artificial means. Usually to improve agricultural productivity.

ISLAND ARC A chain of islands with an arcuate plan form. The islands are usually volcanic in origin.

ISOBAR A line drawn on diagrams joining equal values of atmospheric pressure. A particular kind of isopleth.

ISOPLETH A line drawn on diagrams joining equal values of the plotted element.

ISOSTASY The condition of balance between the rigid crustal elements of the earth's surface and the underlying, denser and more mobile material.

Above Limestone towers in the world's most spectacular karst region – Li River near Guilin, Guangxi Province, China. The towers are the result of erosional processes.

ISTHMUS A narrow strip of land which connects two islands or two large land masses.

J

JOINT A fracture or crack in a rock.

JUNGLE An area of land overgrown with dense vegetation, usually in the tropics.

K

KAME An irregular mound of stratified sediment deposited by, in association with stagnant ice.

KARST Limestone areas which have distinctive landforms such as caves, sinks and frequently a lack of surface water. *(see picture above)*

KELP A mass of large brown seaweeds.

KETTLE HOLE An enclosed depression resulting from the melting of buried ice.

KNOT A measure of speed – one nautical mile per hour (1.15 mi hr^{-1}; 0.85 km hr^{-1}).

KOPJE A small hill or rock outcrop; term used particularly in South Africa.

KRILL Small marine animals, resembling shrimps.

L

LACCOLITH A mass of intrusive rock, usually with a horizontal base and causing the doming of overlying strata.

LAGOON A shallow pool separated from a larger body of water by a bar or reef.

LANDSAT An unmanned satellite that carries sensors to record the resources of the earth.

LANDSLIDE The movement downward under the influence of gravity of a mass of rock debris.

LATERITE A red clay formed by the weathering of rock that consists especially of compounds of iron and aluminium.

LAURASIA The northern part of Pangaea, a super-continent thought to have been broken up by continental drift.

LAVA Molten rock material that emerges from volcanoes and volcanic fissures.

LEACHING The downward movement of water through soil resulting in the removal of water-soluble materials from upper layers and their accumulation in lower layers.

LEEWARD To the lee (downwind, downstream) of an obstacle lying in a flow.

LEVEE A broad, long ridge running parallel and adjacent to a river on its flood-plain.

LIGNITE A brownish black coal in which the texture of the original wood is distinct.

LITHOSPHERE The earth's crust and a portion of the upper mantle that together comprise a layer of strength relative to the more easily deformable layer below.

LITTORAL A coastal region.

LLANOS An open grassy plain in S. America.

LOAM A crumbly soil consisting of a mixture of clay, silt and sand.

LOCH A lake or narrow sea inlet in Scotland.

LOESS Unconsolidated and frequently unstratified material deposited after transport by wind.

LONGSHORE CURRENT A current that runs along a coast. It may result in longshore drift, the transport of beach material along the coast.

LOW See *cyclone*

LUNAR MONTH The period of time between two successive new moons, being about 29½ days.

M

MAGMA Fused, molten rock material beneath the earth's crust from which igneous rocks are formed.

MAGNETIC ANOMALIES Areas with local surface variations in the earth's magnetic field relative to large-scale values.

MAGNETIC FIELD The field of force exerted by the earth by virtue of its being like a giant magnet. Its most familiar manifestation is in the behaviour of a compass.

MAGNETIC REVERSAL The reversal of the earth's magnetic field, such that a north-seeking compass points toward the South Pole. Such reversals have occurred in geological time.

MANTLE The zone within the earth's interior extending from 25 to 70km below the surface to a depth of 2900km.

MAP PROJECTION A mathematical device for representing a portion of all of the earth's curved surface on a flat surface.

MAP SCALE A measure of the ratio of distances represented on a map to their true value.

MAQUIS Scrub vegetation of evergreen shrubs characteristic of the western Mediterranean.

MARL A fine grained mixture of clay and silt with a high proportion of calcium carbonate.

MASSIF A large mountainous area, often quite distinct, containing several individual substantial mountains.

MEANDER A sinuously winding portion of a river channel; also applied to similar forms within larger flows, such as the atmosphere and oceans.

MEAN SEA LEVEL The level of the sea determined from a mean of the tidal ranges over periods of several months to several years.

METAMORPHIC ROCKS Rocks in which their composition, structure and texture have been significantly altered by the action of heat and pressure greater than that produced normally by burial.

METEOROLOGY The study of the workings of the atmosphere.

MILLIBAR A unit of pressure, most widely used in meteorology. The average pressure exerted by the atmosphere on the surface of the earth is just over 1013 millibars.

MISTRAL A cold, dry, north or northwest wind affecting the Rhone Valley.

MONSOON A wind regime with marked seasonal reversal in direction, most famously found in the Indian sub-continent.

MORAINE A landform resulting from the deposition of till by glaciers, taking on several distinctive forms depending upon the location and mode of deposition.

N

NADIR A point that is vertically below the observer.

NASA National Aeronautics and Space Administration (USA).

NEAP TIDE A tide of minimum height occurring at the first and third quarter of the moon.

NÉVÉ Snow that is being compacted into ice, as found in the birth place of glaciers.

NUNATAK A mountain completely surrounded by an ice cap or ice sheet.

O

OASIS An area within a desert region where there is sufficient water to sustain animal and plant life throughout the year.

OCEAN BASIN A large depression in the ocean floor analogous to basins on land.

OCEANIC CRUST The portion of the earth's surface crust comprising largely sima (silica-magnesia rich rocks) about 5km thick. Underlies most of the world's oceans.

OCEAN RIDGE A ridge in the ocean floor, sometimes 150 to 1500 km wide and hundreds of metres high.

OCCLUSION The coming together of warm and cold fronts in cyclones in the latest stages of its evolution.

OROGENESIS The formation of mountains, such as the Andes and Rocky Mountains. The mechanism is still uncertain but is probably related to plate tectonics.

OUTWASH PLAIN Stratified material deposited by glacio-fluvial waters beyond the ice margin.

OXBOW LAKE A lake, usually curved in plan, occupying an abandoned section of meandering river.

P

PACK ICE Ice formed on sea surface when water temperatures fall to about −2°C and floating free under the influence of currents and wind.

PAMPAS An extensive, generally grass-covered plain of temperate South America east of the Andes.

PANGAEA The name given to a postulated continental landmass which split up to produce most of the present northern hemisphere continents.

PASS A narrow passage over relatively low ground in a mountain range.

PEDIMENT A smooth, erosional land surface typically sloping from the foot of a high-land area to a local base level.

PELAGIC The part of an aquatic system that excludes its margins and substrate; it is essentially the main part of the water body.

PENEPLAIN The supposed end land form resulting from erosional processes wearing down an initially uplifted block.

PENUMBRA A region of partial darkness in a shadow surrounding the region of total darkness (umbra), such as seen in an eclipse.

PERIHELION   The point in its orbit about the sun that a planet is closest to the sun.

PIEDMONT GLACIER   A glacier which spreads out into a lobe as it flows onto a lowland.

PILLOW LAVA   Lava that has solidified, probably under water, in rounded masses.

PLACER DEPOSIT   A sediment, such as in the bed of a stream, which contains particles of valuable minerals.

PLAIN   Extensive area of level or rolling treeless country.

PLANKTON   Small freshwater and marine organisms that tend to move with water currents and comprise the food of larger and higher order organisms.

PLATE TECTONICS   A theory which holds that the earth's surface is divided into several major rigid plates which are in motion with respect to each other and the underlying mantle. Continental drift results from plate motion and earthquakes, volcanoes and mountain-building tend to occur at the plate boundaries.

PLUTONIC ROCK   Rock material that has formed at depth where cooling and crystallization have occurred slowly.

POLAR WANDERING   The movements of the North and South Poles throughout geological time relative to the positions of the continents.

POLDER   A low lying area of land that has been reclaimed from the sea or a lake by artificial means and is kept free of water by pumping.

PRECIPITATION   The deposition of water from the atmosphere in liquid and solid form. Rain, snow, hail and dew are the most familiar forms.

PRAIRIE   An extensive area of level or rolling, almost treeless grassland in North America.

PRESSURE GRADIENT   The change per unit distance of pressure, perhaps most frequently met in atmospheric studies. The cause of winds.

Q

QUARTZ   A crystalline mineral consisting of silicon dioxide that is a major constituent of many rocks.

QUICKSAND   Water-saturated sand that is semi-liquid and cannot bear the weight of heavy objects.

R

RADAR   A device that transmits radio waves and locates objects in the vicinity by analysis of the waves reflected back from them (radio detection and ranging).

RADIATION   The transmission of energy in the form of electromagnetic waves and requiring no intervening medium.

RAIN SHADOW   An area experiencing relatively low rainfall because of its position on the leeward side of a hill.

RAISED BEACH   An emerged shoreline represented by stranded marine deposits and wave cut platforms, usually backed by former cliffs.

RANGE   An open region over which livestock may roam and feed, particularly in North America.

RAVINE   A narrow, steep sided valley usually formed by running water.

REEF   A rocky construction found at or near sea-level; coral reefs are perhaps the most familiar type.

RELATIVE HUMIDITY   The amount of water vapour in an air sample relative to the amount the sample could hold if it were saturated at the same temperature; expressed as a percentage.

REMOTE SENSING   The observation and measurement of an object without touching it.

RHUMB LINE   An imaginary line on the surface of the earth which makes equal oblique angles with all lines of longitude so that it forms a spiral coiling round the poles but never reaching them. This would be the course sailed by a ship following a single compass direction.

RIA   An inlet of the sea formed by the flooding of river valleys by rising sea or sinking land. Contrast to fjords which are drowned glacial valleys.

RIFT VALLEY   A valley formed when the area between two parallel faults sinks.

RIVER TERRACE   A step like land form in the flood plain of rivers due to the river incising further into the plain and leaving remnants of its former flood plain at levels higher than the present level of the river channel.

ROARING FORTIES   The area between 40° and 50°S, so called because of the high speeds of the winds occurring there. Sometimes applied to the winds themselves.

RUN-OFF   The section of the hydrological cycle connecting precipitation to channel flow.

S

SALINITY   The presence of salts in the waters and soils of arid, semi-arid and coastal areas.

SALT-MARSH   Vegetated mud-flats found commonly on many low-lying coasts in a wide range of temperate environments.

SANDBANK   A large deposit of sand, usually in a river or coastal waters.

SANDSTORM   A wind storm driving clouds of sand, most usually in hot, dry deserts.

SAVANNAH   A grassland region of the tropics and sub-tropics.

SCHIST   Medium to coarse-grained crystalline metamorphic rock.

SEA-FLOOR SPREADING   The phenomenon when tectonic plates move apart.

SEAMOUNT   A mountain or other area of high relief on the sea-floor which does not reach the surface.

SEASAT   A satellite especially designed to sense remotely wind and sea conditions on the oceans.

SEDIMENTARY ROCK   Rock composed of the fragments of older rocks which have been eroded and the debris deposited by wind and water, often as distinct strata.

SEISMIC WAVE   Wave resulting from the movements of materials in earthquakes.

SEISMOLOGY   Science that deals with earthquakes and other vibrations of the earth.

SHALE   A compacted sedimentary rock, usually with fine-grained particles.

SHALLOW-FOCUS EARTHQUAKE   An earthquake with a focus (or centre) at a shallow level relative to the earth's surface.

SIAL   The part of the earth's crust with a composition dominated by minerals rich in silicon and aluminium.

SIDEREAL DAY   A period of complete rotation of the earth on its axis, about 23 hours 56 minutes.

SILL   A tabular sheet of igneous rock injected along the bedding planes of sedimentary and volcanic formations.

SILT   An unconsolidated material of small particles ranging in size from about 2 to 60 micrometres.

SIMA   The part of the earth's crust with a composition dominated by minerals rich in silicon and magnesium.

SOIL CREEP   The slow movement downslope of soil, usually resulting in thinning of soils on the upper reaches and accumulations on the lower.

SOLIFLUCTION   The slow movement downslope of water saturated, seasonally thawed materials.

SOLSTICE   The days of maximum declination of the sun measured relative to the equator. When

Above On May 18 1980, Mt St Helens demonstrated a plinian eruption (a kind first described by Pliny the Elder). The apparent smoke cloud is pulverised ash.

the midday sun is overhead at 23½°N it gives the longest day in the northern hemisphere and the shortest day in the southern. The reverse applies when the sun is overhead at 23½°S.

SPIT   Usually linear deposits of beach material attached at one end to land and free at the other.

SPRING TIDE   A tide of greater than average range occurring at or around the times of the new and full moon.

SQUALL   A sudden, violent wind, often associated with rain or hail; frequently occurs under cumulonimbus clouds.

STALACTITE   A deposit of calcium carbonate, rather like an icicle, hanging from the roof of a cave.

STALAGMITE   A deposit of calcium carbonate growing up from the floor of a cave due to the constant drip of water from the roof.

STANDARD TIME The officially established time, with reference to Greenwich Mean Time, of a region or country.

STEPPE Mid-latitude grasslands with few trees, most typically found in USSR.

STORM SURGE Changes in sea level caused by extreme weather events, notably the winds in storms.

STRAIT A narrow passage joining two large bodies of water.

STRIAE Scratches of a rock surface due to the passage over it of another rock of equal or greater hardness.

SUBDUCTION ZONE An area where the rocks comprising the sea floor are forced beneath continental rocks at a plate margin to be reincorporated in the magma beneath the earth's crust.

SUBSEQUENT RIVER A stream which follows a course determined by the structure of the local bedrock.

SUBSIDENCE Usually applied to the sinking of air in the atmosphere or the downward movement of the earth's surface.

SUBSOIL The layer of weathered material that underlies the surface soil.

SUDD Floating vegetable matter that forms obstructive masses in the upper White Nile.

SUNSPOT Relatively dark regions on the disk of the sun with surface temperature of about 4500K compared to the more normal 6000K of the rest of the surface.

SURGE A sudden excess over the normal value, usually of a flow of material (soil, ice, water).

SWELL A long, perturbation (usually wavelike) of a water surface that continues beyond its cause (eg a strong wind).

T

TAIGA The most northerly coniferous forest of cold temperature regions found in Canada, Alaska and Eurasia.

TECTONIC Concerned with the broad structures of the earth's rocks and the processes of faulting, folding and warping that form them.

TETHYS OCEAN An ocean formed in the Palaeozoic Era which extended from what is now the Mediterranean Sea eastwards as far as South-east Asia.

THERMOCLINE A layer of water or a lake or sea that separates an upper, warmer, oxygen-rich zone from a lower, colder, oxygen-poor zone and in which temperature decreases by 1°C for every metre of increased depth.

THRUST FAULT A low-angle reverse fault.

THUNDERSTORM A cloud in which thunder and lightning occur, usually associated with heavy precipitation and strong winds.

TIDAL BORE A large solitary wave that moves up funnel-shaped rivers and estuaries with the rising tide, especially spring tides.

TIDAL CURRENT The periodic horizontal motions of the sea, generated by the gravitational attraction of the moon and sun, typically of $1ms^{-1}$ on continental shelves.

TIDE The regular movements of the seas due to the gravitational attraction of the moon and sun, most easily observed as changes in coastal sea levels.

TOPOGRAPHY The configuration of a land surface, including its relief and the position of its natural and man-made features.

TOR An exposure of bedrock usually as blocks and boulders, forming an abrupt, steep sided culmination of a more gentle rise to the summits of hills. Famous tors exist on Dartmoor.

TORNADO A violent, localized rotating storm with winds of $100ms^{-1}$ circulating round a funnel cloud some 100m in diameter. Frequent in mid-western USA.

TRADE WIND Winds with an easterly component which blow from the subtropic high pressure areas around 30° toward the equator.

TROPICAL CYCLONE *See hurricane*

TROPOSPHERE The portion of the earth's atmosphere between the earth's surface and a height about 15–20km. This layer contains virtually all the world's weather. Mean temperatures decrease and mean wind speeds increase with height in the troposphere.

TSUNAMI Sea-surface waves caused by submarine earthquakes and volcanic activity. Popularly called tidal waves.

TURBULENCE Chaotic and apparently random fluctuations in fluid flow, familiarly seen in the behaviour of smoke, either from a cigarette, a chimney or a volcano.

TUNDRA Extensive, level, treeless and marshy regions lying polewards of the taiga.

TYPHOON A term used in the Far East to describe tropical cyclones or hurricanes.

U

UMBRA A region of total shadow, especially in an eclipse.

UPWELLING The upward movement of deeper water towards the sea surface.

V

VARVE A sediment bed deposited in a body of water within the course of one year.

VOE An inlet or narrow bay of the Orkney or Shetland Islands.

VOLCANIC ASH Ash emitted from a volcano.

VOLCANO An opening through which magma, molten rock ash or volatiles erupts onto the earth's surface. Also used to describe the landform produced by the erupted material. *(see picture below left)*

W

WADI An ephemeral river channel in deserts.

WARM FRONT An atmospheric front whereby, as it passes over an individual on the ground, warm air replaces cold.

WATERFALL A vertical or very steep descent of water in a stream.

WATERSHED A boundary dividing and separating the areas drained by different rivers.

WATERSPOUT A funnel-shaped, rotating cloud that forms occasionally over water when the atmosphere is very unstable. Akin to tornadoes which occur over land.

WATER TABLE The level below which the ground is wholly and permanently saturated with water.

WAVE HEIGHT The vertical extent of a wave.

WAVE LENGTH The horizontal extent of a wave, most easily seen as the distance along the direction of wave movement between crests or troughs.

WAVE PERIOD The time taken for a complete cycle of the oscillation occurring within a wave.

WAVE VELOCITY The velocity of a wave form, best seen by concentrating on one part of the wave such as its crest or trough.

WEATHERING The alteration by physical, chemical and biological processes of rocks and sediments in the top metres of the earth's crust. So called because this material is exposed to the effects of atmospheric and atmospherically related conditions.

WEATHER ROUTEING Choosing a route for a ship or aeroplane to minimise the deleterious effects of weather.

WESTERLIES Winds with a westerly component occurring between latitudes of about 35° and 60°. The whole regime forms a 'vortex' around each of the poles and forms a major element in world climate.

WHIRLWIND A general term to describe rotating winds of scales up to that of a tornado, usually a result of intense convection over small areas.

WILLY-WILLY Australasian term for a tropical cyclone or hurricane.

WINDSHEAR The variation of speed or direction or both of wind over a distance.

Y

YARDANG A desert landform, usually but not always, of unconsolidated material, shaped by and lying roughly along the direction of the wind.

Z

ZENITH A point that is vertically above the observer: the opposite of nadir.

ZOOPLANKTON One of the three kinds of plankton, including mature representatives of many animal groups such as Protozoa and Crustacea.

ABBREVIATIONS	FULL FORM	ENGLISH FORM
A		
a.d.	an der	on the
Akr.	Ákra, Akrotírion	cape
Appno	Appennino	mountain range
Arch.	Archipelago	
	Archipiélago	archipelago
B		
B.	1. Bahía, Baía, Baie, Bay, Bucht, Bukhta, Bugt	bay
	2. Ban	village
	3. Barrage,	dam
	4. Bir, Bîr, Bi'r	well
Bol.	Bol'sh, -oy	big
Br.	1. Branch	branch
	2. Bridge, Brücke	bridge
	3. Burun	cape
Brj	Baraj, -i	dam
C		
C.	Cabo, Cap, Cape	cape
Can.	Canal	canal
Cd	Ciudad	town
Chan.	Channel	channel
Ck	Creek	creek
Co., Cord.	Cordillera	mountain chain
D		
D.	1. Dağ, Dagh, Dağı, Dağları	mountain, range
	2. Daryācheh	lake
Dj.	Djebel	mountain
Dr.	doctor	doctor
E		
E.	East	east
Emb.	Embalse	reservoir
Escarp.	Escarpment	escarpment
Estr.	Estrecho	strait
F		
F.	Firth	estuary
Fj.	Fjord, Fjörður	fjord
Ft	Fort	fort
G		
G.	1. Gebel	mountain
	2. Göl, Gölü	lake
	3. Golfe, Golfo, Gulf	Gulf
	4. Gora, -gory	mountain, range
	5. Gunung	mountain
Gd, Gde	Grand, Grande	grand
Geb.	Gebirge	mountain range
Gl.	Glacier	glacier
Grl	General	general
Gt, Gtr	Great, Groot, -e, Greater	greater
H		
Har.	Harbour, Harbor	harbour
Hd	Head	head
I		
I.	Ile, Ilha, Insel, Isla, Island, Isle Isola,	island
	Isole	islands
In.	1. Inner	inner
	2. Inlet	inlet
Is	Iles, Ilhas, Islands, Isles, Islas	islands
Isth.	Isthmus	isthmus
J		
J.	Jabal, Jebel,	mountain
K		
K.	1. Kaap, Kap, Kapp	cape
	2. Kūh(hā)	mountain(s)
	3. Kólpos	gulf
Kep.	Kepulauan	islands
Khr.	Khrebet	mountain range
Kör.	Körfez, -i	gulf, bay
L		
L.	Lac, Lago, Lagoa, Lake, Liman, Limni, Loch, Lough	lake
Lag.	Lagoon, Laguna, Lagune, Lagoa	lagoon
Ld.	Land	land
Lit.	Little	little

ABBREVIATIONS	FULL FORM	ENGLISH FORM
M		
M.	1. Muang	town
	2. Mys	cape
m	metre, -s	metre(s)
Mal.	Malyy	small
Mf	Massif	mountain group
Mgne	Montagne(s)	mountain(s)
Mt	Mont, Mount	mountain
Mte	Monte	mountain
Mti	Monti	mountains, range
Mtn	Mountain	mountain
Mts	Monts, Mountains, Montañas, Montes	mountains
N		
N.	1. Neu-, Ny-	new
	2. Noord, Nord, Norte, North, Norra, Nørre	north
	3. Nos	cape
Nat.	National	national
Nat. Pk	National Park	national park
Ndr	Nieder	lower
N.E.	North East	north east
N.M.	National Monument	national monument
N.P.	National Park	national park
N.W.	North West	north west
O		
O.	1. Oost, Ost	east
	2. Ostrov	island
Ø	-øy	island
Oz.	Ozero, Ozera	lake(s)
P		
P.	1. Pass, Passo	pass
	2. Pic, Pico, Pizzo	peak
	3. Pulau	island
Pass.	Passage	passage
Peg.	Pegunungan	mountains
Pen.	Peninsula, Penisola	peninsula
Pk	1. Park	park
	2. Peak, Pik	peak
Plat.	Plateau, Planalto	plateau
Pov	Poluostrov	peninsula
Pr.	Prince	prince
P.P.	Pulau-pulau	islands
Pres.	Presidente	president
Promy	Promontory	promontory
Pt	Point	point
Pta	1. Ponta, Punta	point
	2. Puerta	pass
Pte	Pointe	point
Pto	Porto, Puerto	port
R		
R.	Rio, Río, River, Rivière	river
Ra.	Range	range
Rap.	Rapids	rapids
Res.	Reserve, Reservation	reserve, reservation
Resp.	Respublika	Republic
Resr	Reservoir	reservoir
S		
S.	1. Salar, Salina	salt marsh
	2. San, São	saint
	3. See	sea, lake
	4. South, Sud	south
s.	sur	on
Sa	Serra, Sierra	mountain range
Sd	Sound, Sund	sound
S.E.	South East	south east
Sev.	Severo-, Severnaya, -nyy	north
		peak
Sp.	Spitze	saint
St	Saint	saint
Sta	Santa	saint
Ste	Sainte	saint
Sto	Santo	strait
Str.	Strait	south west
S.W.	South West	
T		
T.	Tall, Tell	hill, mountain
Tg	Tanjung	cape
Tk	Teluk	bay
Tr.	Trench, Trough	trench, trough
U		
U.	Uad	wadi
Ug	Ujung	cape
Upr	Upper	upper

ABBREVIATIONS	FULL FORM	ENGLISH FORM
V		
V.	1. Val, Valle	valley
	2. Ville	town
Va	Villa	town
Vdkhr.	Vodokhranilishche	reservoir
Vol.	Volcán, Volcano, Vulkan	volcano
Vozv.	Vozvyshennost'	upland
W		
W.	1. Wadi	wadi
	2. Water	water
	3. Well	well
	4. West	west
Y		
Yuzh.	Yuzhno-, Yuzhnyy	south
Z		
Z	1. Zaliv	gulf, bay
	2. Zatoka	
Zap.	Zapad-naya, Zapadno-, Zapadnyy	western
Zem.	Zemlya	country, land

Introduction to the index

In the index, the first number refers to the page, and the following letter and number to the section of the map in which the index entry can be found.
For example, 14C2 **Paris** means that Paris can be found on page 14 where column C and row 2 meet.

Abbreviations used in the index

Arch	Archipelago
B	Bay
C	Cape
Chan	Channel
Gl	Glacier
I(s)	Island(s)
Lg	Lagoon
L	Lake
Mt(s)	Mountain(s)
P	Pass
Pass	Passage
Pen	Peninsula
Plat	Plateau
Pt	Point
Res	Reservoir
R	River
S	Sea
Sd	Sound
Str	Strait
UAE	United Arab Emirates
UK	United Kingdom
USA	United States of America
V	Valley

A

18B2 **Aachen** Germany
13C1 **Aalsmeer** Netherlands
13C2 **Aalst** Belgium
12K6 **Äänekoski** Finland
31A3 **Aba** China
48C4 **Aba** Nigeria
50D3 **Aba** Zaïre
41E3 **Abādān** Iran
41F3 **Abādeh** Iran
48B1 **Abadla** Algeria
75C2 **Abaeté** Brazil
75C2 **Abaeté** *R* Brazil
73J4 **Abaetetuba** Brazil
31D1 **Abagnar Qi** China
59E3 **Abajo Mts** USA
48C4 **Abakaliki** Nigeria
25L4 **Abakan** Russian Federation
48C3 **Abala** Niger
48C2 **Abalessa** Algeria
72D6 **Abancay** Peru
41F3 **Abarqū** Iran
29E2 **Abashiri** Japan
29E2 **Abashiri-wan** *B* Japan
27H7 **Abau** Papua New Guinea
50D3 **Abaya, L** Ethiopia
50D2 **Abbai** *R* Ethiopia/Sudan
50E2 **Abbe, L** Djibouti/Ethiopia
14C1 **Abbeville** France
63D3 **Abbeville** Louisiana, USA
67B2 **Abbeville** S Carolina, USA
58B1 **Abbotsford** Canada
64A2 **Abbotsford** USA
42C2 **Abbottabad** Pakistan
40D2 **'Abd al 'Azīz, Jebel** *Mt* Syria
20J5 **Abdulino** Russian Federation
50C2 **Abéché** Chad
48B4 **Abengourou** Ivory Coast
18B1 **Åbenrå** Denmark
48C4 **Abeokuta** Nigeria
50D3 **Abera** Ethiopia
7B3 **Aberaeron** Wales
7C4 **Aberdare** Wales
66C2 **Aberdeen** California, USA
65D3 **Aberdeen** Maryland, USA
63E2 **Aberdeen** Mississippi, USA
47C3 **Aberdeen** South Africa
8D3 **Aberdeen** Scotland
56D2 **Aberdeen** S Dakota, USA
56A2 **Aberdeen** Washington, USA
54J3 **Aberdeen L** Canada
7B3 **Aberdyfi** Wales
8D3 **Aberfeldy** Scotland
8C3 **Aberfoyle** Scotland
7C4 **Abergavenny** Wales
7B3 **Aberystwyth** Wales
20L2 **Abez'** Russian Federation
50E2 **Abhā** Saudi Arabia
41E2 **Abhar** Iran
48B4 **Abidjan** Ivory Coast
61D3 **Abilene** Kansas, USA
62C2 **Abilene** Texas, USA
7D4 **Abingdon** England
64C3 **Abingdon** USA
55K4 **Abitibi** *R* Canada
55L5 **Abitibi,L** Canada
21G7 **Abkhazian Republic** Georgia
42C2 **Abohar** India
48C4 **Abomey** Benin
50B3 **Abong Mbang** Cameroon
50B2 **Abou Deïa** Chad
8D3 **Aboyne** Scotland
41E4 **Abqaiq** Saudi Arabia
15A2 **Abrantes** Portugal
70A2 **Abreojos, Punta** *Pt* Mexico
50D1 **'Abri** Sudan
32A3 **Abrolhos** *I* Australia
75E2 **Abrolhos, Arquipélago dos** *Is* Brazil
56B2 **Absaroka Range** *Mts* USA
41F5 **Abū al Abyaḍ** *I* UAE
41E4 **Abū 'Alī** *I* Saudi Arabia
45D3 **Abu 'Amūd, Wadi** Jordan
45C3 **Abu 'Aweigîla** *Well* Egypt
41F5 **Abū Dhabi** UAE
45C3 **Ābū el Jurdhān** Jordan
50D2 **Abu Hamed** Sudan
48C4 **Abuja** Nigeria
45A3 **Abu Kebir Hihya** Egypt
72E5 **Abunã** Brazil
72E6 **Abunã** *R* Bolivia/Brazil
45C4 **Abu Rûtha, Gebel** *Mt* Egypt
41D3 **Abū Sukhayr** Iraq
45B3 **Abu Suweir** Egypt
45B4 **Abu Tarfa, Wadi** Egypt
35B2 **Abut Head** *C* New Zealand
40B4 **Abu Tig** Egypt
50D2 **Abu'Urug** *Well* Sudan
50D2 **Abuye Meda** *Mt* Ethiopia
50C2 **Abu Zabad** Sudan
50D3 **Abwong** Sudan
18B1 **Åby** Denmark
50C3 **Abyei** Sudan
65F2 **Acadia Nat Pk** USA
70B2 **Acámbaro** Mexico
69B5 **Acandí** Colombia
70B2 **Acaponeta** Mexico
70B3 **Acapulco** Mexico
73L4 **Acaraú** Brazil
72E2 **Acarigua** Venezuela
70C3 **Acatlán** Mexico
48B4 **Accra** Ghana
6C3 **Accrington** England
42D4 **Achalpur** India
74B6 **Achao** Chile
13E3 **Achern** Germany
9A3 **Achill Hd** *Pt* Irish Republic
10A3 **Achill I** Irish Republic
13E1 **Achim** Germany
25L4 **Achinsk** Russian Federation
16D3 **Acireale** Sicily, Italy
61E2 **Ackley** USA
69C2 **Acklins** *I* The Bahamas
72D6 **Acobamba** Peru
74B4 **Aconcagua** *Mt* Chile
73L5 **Acopiara** Brazil
Açores *Is* = **Azores**
A Coruña = La Coruña
Acre = 'Akko
72D5 **Acre** *State* Brazil
66C3 **Acton** USA
63C2 **Ada** USA
15B1 **Adaja** *R* Spain
41G5 **Adam** Oman
50D3 **Adama** Ethiopia
75B3 **Adamantina** Brazil
50B3 **Adamaoua** *Region* Cameroon/Nigeria
50B3 **Adamaoua, Massif de l'** *Mts* Cameroon
68D1 **Adams** USA
44B4 **Adam's Bridge** India/Sri Lanka
56A2 **Adams,Mt** USA
44C4 **Adam's Peak** *Mt* Sri Lanka
'Adan = Aden
21F8 **Adana** Turkey
21E7 **Adapazarı** Turkey
76F7 **Adare,C** Antarctica
34B1 **Adavale** Australia
41E4 **Ad Dahnā'** *Region* Saudi Arabia
41F4 **Ad Damman** Saudi Arabia
41D5 **Ad Dawādimī** Saudi Arabia
41E4 **Ad Dibdibah** *Region* Saudi Arabia
41E5 **Ad Dilam** Saudi Arabia
41E5 **Ad Dir'iyah** Saudi Arabia
50D3 **Addis Ababa** Ethiopia
41D3 **Ad Dīwanīyah** Iraq
40D3 **Ad Duwayd** Saudi Arabia
61E2 **Adel** USA
32C4 **Adelaide** Australia
67C4 **Adelaide** Bahamas
76G3 **Adelaide** *Base* Antarctica
54J3 **Adelaide Pen** Canada
27G8 **Adelaide River** Australia
66D3 **Adelanto** USA
38C4 **Aden** Yemen
38C4 **Aden,G of** Somalia/Yemen
48C3 **Aderbissinat** Niger
45D2 **Adhrā'** Syria
27G7 **Adi** *I* Indonesia
16C1 **Adige** *R* Italy
50D2 **Adigrat** Ethiopia
42D5 **Adilābād** India
58B2 **Adin** USA
65E2 **Adirondack Mts** USA
50D2 **Adi Ugrī** Eritrea
40C2 **Adıyaman** Turkey
17F1 **Adjud** Romania
54E4 **Admiralty I** USA
55K2 **Admiralty Inlet** *B* Canada
32D1 **Admiralty Is** Papua New Guinea
44B2 **Ādoni** India
14B3 **Adour** *R* France
48B2 **Adrar** Algeria
48C2 **Adrar** *Mts* Algeria
48A2 **Adrar** *Region* Mauritius
48A2 **Adrar Soutouf** *Region* Morocco
50C2 **Adré** Chad
49D2 **Adri** Libya
64C2 **Adrian** Michigan, USA
62B1 **Adrian** Texas, USA
16C2 **Adriatic S** Italy/Yugoslavia
50D2 **Adwa** Ethiopia
25P3 **Adycha** *R* Russian Federation
48B4 **Adzopé** Ivory Coast
20K2 **Adz'va** *R* Russian Federation
20K2 **Adz'vavom** Russian Federation
17E3 **Aegean Sea** Greece
38E2 **Afghanistan** *Republic* Asia
50E3 **Afgooye** Somalia
41D5 **'Afif** Saudi Arabia
48C4 **Afikpo** Nigeria
12G6 **Åfjord** Norway
48C1 **Aflou** Algeria
50E3 **Afmado** Somalia
48A3 **Afollé** *Region* Mauritius
68C1 **Afton** New York, USA
58D2 **Afton** Wyoming, USA
45C2 **Afula** Israel
21E8 **Afyon** Turkey
45A3 **Aga** Egypt
50B2 **Agadem** Niger
48C3 **Agadez** Niger
48B1 **Agadir** Morocco
42D4 **Agar** India
43G4 **Agartala** India
58B1 **Agassiz** Canada
48B4 **Agboville** Ivory Coast
40E1 **Agdam** Azerbaijan
29C3 **Agematsu** Japan
14C3 **Agen** France
41E3 **Agha Jārī** Iran
48B4 **Agnibilékrou** Ivory Coast
14C3 **Agout** *R* France
42D3 **Āgra** India
41D2 **Ağrı** Turkey
16D2 **Agri** *R* Italy
16C3 **Agrigento** Sicily, Italy
26H5 **Agrihan** *I* Marianas
17E3 **Agrínion** Greece
16C2 **Agropoli** Italy
20J4 **Agryz** Russian Federation
55N3 **Agto** Greenland
75B3 **Agua Clara** Brazil
69D3 **Aguadilla** Puerto Rico
70B1 **Agua Prieta** Mexico
75A3 **Aguaray Guazú** Paraguay
70B2 **Aguascalientes** Mexico
75D2 **Aguas Formosas** Brazil
75C2 **Agua Vermelha, Barragem** Brazil
15A1 **Agueda** Portugal
48C3 **Aguelhok** Mali
48A2 **Agüenit** *Well* Morocco
15B2 **Águilas** Spain
72B5 **Aguja, Puerta** Peru
36C7 **Agulhas Basin** Indian Ocean
51C7 **Agulhas,C** South Africa
36C6 **Agulhas Plat** Indian Ocean
Ahaggar = Hoggar
21H8 **Ahar** Iran
13D1 **Ahaus** Germany
35B1 **Ahipara B** New Zealand
13D2 **Ahlen** Germany
42C4 **Ahmadābād** India
44A2 **Ahmadnagar** India
50E3 **Ahmar Mts** Ethiopia
67C1 **Ahoskie** USA
13D2 **Ahr** *R* Germany
13D2 **Ahrgebirge** *Mts* Germany
12G7 **Åhus** Sweden
41F2 **Āhuvān** Iran
41E3 **Ahvāz** Iran
69A4 **Aiajuela** Costa Rica
14C3 **Aigoual, Mount** France
29C3 **Aikawa** Japan
67B2 **Aiken** USA
31A5 **Ailao Shan** *Upland* China
75D2 **Aimorés** Brazil
16B3 **Aïn Beïda** Algeria
48B1 **Aïn Beni Mathar** Morocco
49E2 **Aïn Dalla** *Well* Egypt
15C2 **Aïn el Hadjel** Algeria
50B2 **Aïn Galakka** Chad
15C2 **Aïn Oussera** Algeria
48B1 **Aïn Sefra** Algeria
40B4 **'Ain Sukhna** Egypt
60D2 **Ainsworth** USA
15B2 **Aïn Témouchent** Algeria
29B4 **Aioi** Japan
48B2 **Aïoun Abd el Malek** *Well* Mauritius
48B3 **Aïoun El Atrouss** Mauritius
72E7 **Aiquile** Bolivia
48C3 **Aïr** *Desert Region* Niger
8D4 **Airdrie** Scotland
13B2 **Aire** France
6D3 **Aire** *R* England
13C3 **Aire** *R* France
55L3 **Airforce I** Canada
54E3 **Aishihik** Canada
13B3 **Aisne** *Department* France
14C2 **Aisne** *R* France
27H7 **Aitape** Papua New Guinea
19F1 **Aiviekste** *R* Latvia
14D3 **Aix-en-Provence** France
14D2 **Aix-les-Bains** France
43F4 **Aiyar Res** India
17E3 **Aíyion** Greece
17E3 **Aíyna** *I* Greece
43G4 **Āīzawl** India
51B6 **Aizeb** *R* Namibia
29D3 **Aizu-Wakamatsu** Japan
16B2 **Ajaccio** Corsica, Italy
16B2 **Ajaccio, G d'** Corsica, Italy
49E1 **Ajdābiyā** Libya
29E2 **Ajigasawa** Japan
45C2 **Ajlūn** Jordan
41G4 **Ajman** UAE
42C3 **Ajmer** India
59D4 **Ajo** USA
15B1 **Ajo, Cabo de** *C* Spain
17F3 **Ak** *R* Turkey
29D2 **Akabira** Japan
29C3 **Akaishi-sanchi** *Mts* Japan
44B2 **Akalkot** India
45B1 **Akanthou** Cyprus
35B2 **Akaroa** New Zealand
29B4 **Akashi** Japan
21K5 **Akbulak** Russian Federation
40C2 **Akçakale** Turkey
48A2 **Akchar** *Watercourse* Mauritius
50C3 **Aketi** Zaïre
41D1 **Akhalkalaki** Georgia
40D1 **Akhalsikhe** Georgia
17E3 **Akharnái** Greece
49E1 **Akhdar, Jabal al** *Mts* Libya
41G5 **Akhdar, Jebel** *Mt* Oman
40A2 **Akhisar** Turkey
19F1 **Akhiste** Latvia
49F2 **Akhmîm** Egypt
21H6 **Akhtubinsk** Russian Federation
21E5 **Akhtyrka** Ukraine
29B4 **Aki** Japan
55K4 **Akimiski I** Canada
29E3 **Akita** Japan
48A3 **Akjoujt** Mauritius
45C2 **'Akko** Israel
54E3 **Aklavik** Canada
48B3 **Aklé Aouana** *Desert Region* Mauritius
50D3 **Akobo** Ethiopia
50D3 **Akobo** *R* Ethiopia/Sudan
42B1 **Akoha** Afghanistan
42D4 **Akola** India
42D4 **Akot** India
55M3 **Akpatok I** Canada
17E3 **Ákra Kafirévs** *C* Greece
17E4 **Ákra Líthinon** *C* Greece
17E3 **Ákra Maléa** *C* Greece
12A2 **Akranes** Iceland
17F3 **Ákra Sídheros** *C* Greece
17E3 **Ákra Spátha** *C* Greece
17E3 **Ákra Taínaron** *C* Greece
57E2 **Akron** USA
45B1 **Akrotiri** Cyprus
45B1 **Akrotiri B** Cyprus
42D1 **Aksai Chin** *Mts* China
21E8 **Aksaray** Turkey
21J5 **Aksay** Kazakhstan
42D1 **Aksayquin Hu** *L* China
40B2 **Akşehir** Turkey
40B2 **Akseki** Turkey
25N4 **Aksenovo Zilovskoye** Russian Federation
26E1 **Aksha** Russian Federation
39G1 **Aksu** China
50D2 **Aksum** Ethiopia
24J5 **Aktogay** Kazakhstan
21K6 **Aktumsyk** Kazakhstan
21K5 **Aktyubinsk** Kazakhstan
12B1 **Akureyri** Iceland
Akyab = Sittwe
24K5 **Akzhal** Kazakhstan
63E2 **Alabama** *R* USA
57E3 **Alabama** *State* USA
67A2 **Alabaster** USA
40C2 **Ala Dağları** *Mts* Turkey
21G7 **Alagir** Russian Federation
73L5 **Alagoas** *State* Brazil
73L6 **Alagoinhas** Brazil
15B1 **Alagón** Spain
41E4 **Al Ahmadi** Kuwait
70D3 **Alajuela** Costa Rica
54B3 **Alakanuk** USA
24K5 **Alakol, Ozero** *L* Kazakhstan/Russian Federation
12L5 **Alakurtti** Russian Federation
27H5 **Alamagan** *I* Pacific Ocean
41E3 **Al Amārah** Iraq
59B3 **Alameda** USA
59C3 **Alamo** USA
62A2 **Alamogordo** USA
62C3 **Alamo Heights** USA
62A1 **Alamosa** USA
12H6 **Åland** *I* Finland
21E8 **Alanya** Turkey
67B2 **Alapaha** *R* USA
42L4 **Alapayevsk** Russian Federation
15B2 **Alarcón, Embalse de** *Res* Spain
40A2 **Alaşehir** Turkey
26D3 **Ala Shan** *Mts* China
54C3 **Alaska** *State* USA
54D4 **Alaska,G of** USA
54C3 **Alaska Range** *Mts* USA
16B2 **Alassio** Italy
20H5 **Alatyr'** Russian Federation
34B2 **Alawoona** Australia
41G5 **Al'Ayn** UAE
39F2 **Alayskiy Khrebet** *Mts* Tajikistan
25R3 **Alazeya** *R* Russian Federation
14D3 **Alba** Italy
15B2 **Albacete** Spain
15A1 **Alba de Tormes** Spain
40D2 **Al Badi** Iraq
17E1 **Alba Iulia** Romania
17D2 **Albania** *Republic* Europe
32A4 **Albany** Australia
67B2 **Albany** Georgia, USA
64B3 **Albany** Kentucky, USA
65E2 **Albany** New York, USA
56A2 **Albany** Oregon, USA
55K4 **Albany** *R* Canada
15B1 **Albarracin, Sierra de** *Mts* Spain
41G5 **Al Bātinah** *Region* Oman
27H8 **Albatross B** Australia
49E1 **Al Baydā** Libya
45C1 **Al Baylūlīyah** Syria
67B1 **Albemarle** USA
67C1 **Albemarle Sd** USA
15B1 **Alberche** *R* Spain
13B2 **Albert** France
54G4 **Alberta** *Province* Canada
27H7 **Albert Edward** *Mt* Papua New Guinea
47C3 **Albertinia** South Africa
50D3 **Albert,L** Uganda/Zaïre
57D2 **Albert Lea** USA
50D3 **Albert Nile** *R* Uganda
58D1 **Alberton** USA
14D2 **Albertville** France
14C3 **Albi** France
61E2 **Albia** USA
73H2 **Albina** Surinam
64C2 **Albion** Michigan, USA
61D2 **Albion** Nebraska, USA
65D2 **Albion** New York, USA
40C4 **Al Bi'r** Saudi Arabia
15B2 **Alborán** *I* Spain
12G7 **Ålborg** Denmark
13E3 **Albstadt-Ebingen** Germany
40D3 **Al Bū Kamāl** Syria
56C3 **Albuquerque** USA
41G5 **Al Buraymī** Oman
49D1 **Al Burayqah** Libya
49E1 **Al Burdī** Libya
32D4 **Albury** Australia
41E3 **Al Buşayyah** Iraq
15B1 **Alcalá de Henares** Spain
16C3 **Alcamo** Sicily, Italy
15B1 **Alcañiz** Spain
73K4 **Alcântara** Brazil
15A2 **Alcántara, Embalse de** *Res* Spain
15B2 **Alcaraz** Spain

Alcaraz, Sierra de Animas Peak

15B2 Alcaraz, Sierra de *Mts* Spain
15B2 Alcázar de San Juan Spain
15B2 Alcira Spain
75E2 Alcobaça Brazil
15B1 Alcolea de Pinar Spain
15B2 Alcoy Spain
15C2 Alcudia Spain
46J8 Aldabra Is Indian Ocean
62A3 Aldama Mexico
25O4 Aldan Russian Federation
25P4 Aldan *R* Russian Federation
25O4 Aldanskoye Nagor'ye *Upland* Russian Federation
7E3 Aldeburgh England
14B2 Alderney *I* Channel Islands
7D4 Aldershot England
48A3 Aleg Mauritius
75A2 Alegre *R* Brazil
74E3 Alegrete Brazil
25Q4 Aleksandrovsk Sakhalinskiy Russian Federation
24J4 Alekseyevka Kazakhstan
20F5 Aleksin Russian Federation
18D1 Älem Sweden
75D3 Além Paraíba Brazil
14C2 Alençon France
66E5 Alenuihaha Chan Hawaiian Islands
21F8 Aleppo Syria
55M1 Alert Canada
14C3 Alès France
16B2 Alessandria Italy
24B3 Ålesund Norway
54C4 Aleutian Ra *Mts* USA
37L2 Aleutian Trench Pacific Ocean
54E4 Alexander Arch USA
47B2 Alexander Bay South Africa
67A2 Alexander City USA
76G3 Alexander I Antarctica
35A3 Alexandra New Zealand
74J8 Alexandra,C South Georgia
55L2 Alexandra Fjord Canada
49E1 Alexandria Egypt
57D3 Alexandria Louisiana, USA
57D2 Alexandria Minnesota, USA
57F3 Alexandria Virginia, USA
17F2 Alexandroúpolis Greece
45C2 Aley Lebanon
24K4 Aleysk Russian Federation
41D3 Al Fallūjah Iraq
15B1 Alfaro Spain
17F2 Alfatar Bulgaria
41E4 Al Fāw Iraq
75C3 Alfensas Brazil
17E3 Alfiós *R* Greece
75D3 Alfonso Cláudio Brazil
8D3 Alford Scotland
75D3 Alfredo Chaves Brazil
7D3 Alfreton England
41E4 Al Furūthi Saudi Arabia
21K6 Alga Kazakhstan
15A2 Algeciras Spain
Alger = Algiers
48B2 Algeria *Republic* Africa
16B2 Alghero Sardinia, Italy
15C2 Algiers Algeria
62B2 Algona USA
65D1 Algonquin Park Canada
38D3 Al Ḩadd Oman
40D3 Al Hadīthah Iraq
40C3 Al Hadīthah Saudi Arabia
40D2 Al Ḩaḑr Iraq
45D1 Al Haffah Syria
41G5 Al Ḩajar al Gharbī *Mts* Oman
40C3 Al Hamad *Desert Region* Jordan/Saudi Arabia
41E4 Al Haniyah *Desert Region* Iraq
41E5 Al Ḩarīq Saudi Arabia
40C3 Al Harrah *Desert Region* Saudi Arabia
49D2 Al Harūj al Aswad *Upland* Libya
41E4 Al Hasa *Region* Saudi Arabia
40D2 Al Ḩasakah Syria
40C4 Al Hawjā' Saudi Arabia
41E3 Al Hayy Iraq
45D2 Al Hījānah Syria
41D3 Al Ḩillah Iraq
41E5 Al Ḩillah Saudi Arabia
15B2 Al Hoceima Morocco
50E2 Al Ḩudaydah Yemen
41E4 Al Hufūf Saudi Arabia
41F5 Al Humrah *Region* UAE
41G5 Al Huwatsah Oman
41E2 Alīābad Iran
41G4 Aliabad Iran
17E2 Aliákmon *R* Greece
41E3 Alī al Gharbī Iraq
44A2 Alībāg India
15B2 Alicante Spain
56D4 Alice USA
16D3 Alice, Punta *Pt* Italy
32C3 Alice Springs Australia
16C3 Alicudi *I* Italy
42D3 Aligarh India
41E3 Aligūdarz Iran
42B2 Ali-Khel Afghanistan
17F3 Alimniá *I* Greece
43F3 Alīpur Duār India
64C2 Aliquippa USA
40C3 Al' Īsawiyah Saudi Arabia
47D3 Aliwal North South Africa
49E2 Al Jaghbūb Libya
40D3 Al Jālamīd Saudi Arabia
49E2 Al Jawf Libya
40C4 Al Jawf Saudi Arabia
40D2 Al Jazīrah *Desert Region* Iraq/Syria
15A2 Aljezur Portugal
41E4 Al Jubayl Saudi Arabia
41D4 Al Jumaymah Saudi Arabia
45D4 Al Kabid *Desert* Jordan
41D4 Al Kahfah Saudi Arabia
41E4 Al Kāmil Oman
40D2 Al Khābūr *R* Syria
41G5 Al Khābūrah Oman
41D3 Al Khālis Iraq
41G4 Al Khaşab Oman
41F4 Al Khawr Qatar
49D1 Al Khums Libya
41F5 Al Kidan *Region* Saudi Arabia
45D2 Al Kiswah Syria
18A2 Alkmaar Netherlands
49E2 Al Kufrah Oasis Libya
41E3 Al Kūt Iraq
Al Lādhiqīyah = Latakia
43E3 Allahābād India
45D2 Al Lajāh *Mt* Syria
54C3 Allakaket USA
30B2 Allanmyo Burma
67B2 Allatoona L USA
47D1 Alldays South Africa
65D2 Allegheny *R* USA
57F3 Allegheny Mts USA
67B2 Allendale USA
6C2 Allendale Town England
9B2 Allen, Lough *L* Irish Republic
35A3 Allen,Mt New Zealand
65D2 Allentown USA
44B4 Alleppey India
14C2 Aller *R* France
60C2 Alliance USA
50E1 Al Līth Saudi Arabia
41F5 Al Liwā' *Region* UAE
8D3 Alloa Scotland
34D1 Allora Australia
65E1 Alma Canada
64C2 Alma Michigan, USA
60D2 Alma Nebraska, USA
39F1 Alma Ata Kazakhstan
15A2 Almada Portugal
41E4 Al Majma'ah Saudi Arabia
41F4 Al Manāmah Bahrain
41D3 Al Ma'nīyah Iraq
59B2 Almanor,L USA
15B2 Almansa Spain
41F5 Al Māriyyah UAE
49E1 Al Marj Libya
75C2 Almas *R* Brazil
15B1 Almazán Spain
13E2 Alme *R* Germany
13D1 Almelo Netherlands
75D2 Almenara Brazil
15A1 Almendra, Embalse de *Res* Spain
15B2 Almería Spain
15B2 Almería, Golfo de Spain
20J5 Al'met'yevsk Russian Federation
18C1 Älmhult Sweden
41D4 Al Midhnab Saudi Arabia
41E3 Al Miqdādīyah Iraq
17E3 Almirós Greece
41E4 Al Mish'āb Saudi Arabia
15A2 Almodôvar Portugal
42D3 Almora India
41E4 Al Mubarraz Saudi Arabia
40C4 Al Mudawwara Jordan
41F4 Al Muḩarraq Bahrain
38C4 Al Mukallā Yemen
50E2 Al Mukhā Yemen
41D3 Al Musayyib Iraq
40C4 Al Muwayliḩ Saudi Arabia
8C3 Alness Scotland
6D2 Aln, R England
41E3 Al Nu'mānīyah Iraq
6D2 Alnwick England
27F7 Alor *I* Indonesia
30C4 Alor Setar Malaysia
Alost = Aalst
32E2 Alotau Papua New Guinea
32B3 Aloysius,Mt Australia
64C1 Alpena USA
16C1 Alpi Dolomitiche *Mts* Italy
59E4 Alpine Arizona, USA
62B2 Alpine Texas, USA
58D2 Alpine Wyoming, USA
16B1 Alps *Mts* Europe
49D1 Al Qaddāhiyah Libya
45D1 Al Qadmūs Syria
40D3 Al Qā'im Iraq
40C4 Al Qalībah Saudi Arabia
40D2 Al Qāmishlī Syria
45D1 Al Qardāḩah Syria
49D1 Al Qaryah Ash Sharqīyah Libya
40C3 Al Qaryatayn Syria
41D4 Al Qasīm *Region* Saudi Arabia
41E4 Al Qatīf Saudi Arabia
49D2 Al Qatrūn Libya
41E4 Al Qayşāmah Saudi Arabia
15A2 Alquera *Res* Portugal/Spain
40C3 Al Qunayţirah Syria
50E2 Al Qunfidhah Saudi Arabia
41E3 Al Qurnah Iraq
45D1 Al Quşayr Syria
45D2 Al Quţayfah Syria
41E5 Al Quwayīyah Saudi Arabia
18B1 Als *I* Denmark
14D2 Alsace *Region* France
13D3 Alsace, Plaine d' France
18B2 Alsfeld Germany
6C2 Alston England
12J5 Alta Norway
74D4 Alta Gracia Argentina
69D5 Altagracia de Orituco Venezuela
26B2 Altai *Mts* Mongolia
67B2 Altamaha *R* USA
73H4 Altamira Brazil
16D2 Altamura Italy
26D1 Altanbulag Mongolia
70B2 Altata Mexico
24K5 Altay China
25L5 Altay Mongolia
24K4 Altay *Mts* Russian Federation
13D2 Altenkirchen Germany
75B2 Alto Araguaia Brazil
51D5 Alto Molócue Mozambique
7D4 Alton England
64A3 Alton USA
65D2 Altoona USA
75B2 Alto Sucuriú Brazil
7C3 Altrincham England
39G2 Altun Shan *Mts* China
58B2 Alturas USA
62C2 Altus USA
40C4 Al'Ulā Saudi Arabia
40C4 Al Urayq *Desert Region* Saudi Arabia
62C1 Alva USA
63C2 Alvarado USA
12G6 Älvdalen Sweden
63C3 Alvin USA
12J5 Älvsbyn Sweden
49D2 Al Wāha Libya
40C4 Al Wajh Saudi Arabia
42D3 Alwar India
40D3 Al Widyān *Desert Region* Iraq/Saudi Arabia
31A2 Alxa Youqi China
31B2 Alxa Zuoqi China
41E2 Alyat Azerbaijan
12J8 Alytus Lithuania
13E3 Alzey Germany
50D3 Amadi Sudan
41D2 Amādīyah Iraq
55L3 Amadjuak L Canada
12G7 Åmål Sweden
25N4 Amalat *R* Russian Federation
17E3 Amaliás Greece
42C4 Amalner India
75A3 Amambaí Brazil
75B3 Amambaí *R* Brazil
75A3 Amamba, Serra *Mts* Brazil/Paraguay
26F4 Amami *I* Japan
26F4 Amami gunto *Arch* Japan
73H3 Amapá Brazil
73H3 Amapá *State* Brazil
62B1 Amarillo USA
21F7 Amasya Turkey
73H4 Amazonas *R* Brazil
72E4 Amazonas *State* Brazil
42D2 Ambāla India
44C4 Ambalangoda Sri Lanka
51E6 Ambalavao Madagascar
50B3 Ambam Cameroon
51E5 Ambanja Madagascar
25S3 Ambarchik Russian Federation
72C4 Ambato Ecuador
51E5 Ambato-Boeny Madagascar
51E5 Ambatolampy Madagascar
51E5 Ambatondrazaka Madagascar
18C3 Amberg Germany
70D3 Ambergris Cay *I* Belize
43E4 Ambikāpur India
51E5 Ambilobe Madagascar
6C2 Ambleside England
51E6 Amboasary Madagascar
51E5 Ambodifototra Madagascar
51E6 Ambohimahasoa Madagascar
Amboina = Ambon
27F7 Ambon Indonesia
51E6 Ambositra Madagascar
51E6 Ambovombe Madagascar
27E6 Amboyna Cay *I* S China Sea
51E5 Ambre, Montagne d' *Mt* Madagascar
51B4 Ambriz Angola
33F2 Ambrym *I* Vanuatu
50C2 Am Dam Chad
20L2 Amderma Russian Federation
70B2 Ameca Mexico
18B2 Ameland *I* Netherlands
68D2 Amenia USA
58D2 American Falls USA
58D2 American Falls Res USA
59D2 American Fork USA
76F10 American Highland *Upland* Antarctica
37L5 American Samoa *Is* Pacific Ocean
67B2 Americus USA
18B2 Amersfoort Netherlands
47D2 Amersfoort South Africa
61E1 Amery USA
76G10 Amery Ice Shelf Antarctica
61E2 Ames USA
68E1 Amesbury USA
17E3 Amfilokhía Greece
17E3 Amfissa Greece
25P3 Amga Russian Federation
25P3 Amgal *R* Russian Federation
26G2 Amgu Russian Federation
26G1 Amgun' *R* Russian Federation
50D2 Amhara *Region* Ethiopia
55M5 Amherst Canada
68D1 Amherst Massachusetts, USA
65D3 Amherst Virginia, USA
44B3 Amhūr India
16C2 Amiata, Monte *Mt* Italy
14C2 Amiens France
29C3 Amino Japan
45C1 Amioune Lebanon
46K8 Amirante Is Indian Ocean
62B3 Amistad Res Mexico
43F3 Amlekhganj Nepal
7B3 Amlwch Wales
40C3 Amman Jordan
7C4 Ammanford Wales
12K6 Ämmänsaari Finland
55P3 Ammassalik Greenland
28A3 Amnyong-dan *C* N Korea
41F2 Amol Iran
17F3 Amorgós *I* Greece
55L5 Amos Canada
Amoy = Xiamen
51E6 Ampanihy Madagascar
75C3 Amparo Brazil
51E5 Ampasimanolotra Madagascar
15C1 Amposta Spain
42D4 Amrāvati India
42C4 Amreli India
42C2 Amritsar India
43K1 Amroha India
36E6 Amsterdam *I* Indian Ocean
18A2 Amsterdam Netherlands
47E2 Amsterdam South Africa
65E2 Amsterdam USA
50C2 Am Timan Chad
24H5 Amu Darya *R* Uzbekistan
55J2 Amund Ringnes I Canada
54F2 Amundsen G Canada
76E Amundsen-Scott *Base* Antarctica
76F4 Amundsen Sea Antarctica
27E7 Amuntai Indonesia
26F1 Amur *R* Russian Federation
25N2 Anabar *R* Russian Federation
66C4 Anacapa Is USA
72F2 Anaco Venezuela
56B2 Anaconda USA
58B1 Anacortes USA
62C1 Anadarko USA
25T3 Anadyr' Russian Federation
25T3 Anadyr' *R* Russian Federation
25U3 Anadyrskiy Zaliv *S* Russian Federation
25T3 Anadyrskoye Ploskogor'ye *Plat* Russian Federation
17F3 Anáfi *I* Greece
75D1 Anagé Brazil
40D3 'Ānah Iraq
59C4 Anaheim USA
44B3 Anaimalai Hills India
44C2 Anakāpalle India
51E5 Analalava Madagascar
27D6 Anambas, Kepulauan *Is* Indonesia
64A2 Anamosa USA
21E8 Anamur Turkey
29B4 Anan Japan
44B3 Anantapur India
42D2 Anantnag India
73J7 Anápolis Brazil
41G3 Anār Iran
41F3 Anārak Iran
27H5 Anatahan *I* Pacific Ocean
74D3 Añatuya Argentina
28B3 Anbyŏn N Korea
54D3 Anchorage USA
72E7 Ancohuma *Mt* Bolivia
72C6 Ancón Peru
16C2 Ancona Italy
68D1 Ancram USA
74B6 Ancud Chile
74B6 Ancud, Golfo de *G* Chile
13C4 Ancy-le-Franc France
72D6 Andahuaylas Peru
12F6 Åndalsnes Norway
15A2 Andalucia *Region* Spain
67A2 Andalusia USA
39H4 Andaman Is India
75D1 Andaraí Brazil
13C3 Andelot France
12H5 Andenes Norway
18B2 Andernach Germany
64B2 Anderson Indiana, USA
63D1 Anderson Missouri, USA
67B2 Anderson S Carolina, USA
54F3 Anderson *R* Canada
72C5 Andes, Cordillera de los *Mts* Peru
44B2 Andhra Pradesh *State* India
17E3 Andikíthira *I* Greece
24J5 Andizhan Uzbekistan
24H6 Andkhui Afghanistan
28B3 Andong S Korea
15C1 Andorra *Principality* SW Europe
15C1 Andorra-La-Vella Andorra
7D4 Andover England
68E1 Andover New Hampshire, USA
68B1 Andover New York, USA
75B3 Andradina Brazil
19G1 Andreapol' Russian Federation
40B2 Andreas,C Cyprus
62B2 Andrews USA
16D2 Andria Italy
17E3 Ándros *I* Greece
57F4 Andros *I* The Bahamas
67C4 Andros Town Bahamas
44A3 Androth *I* India
15B2 Andújar Spain
51B5 Andulo Angola
48C3 Anéfis Mali
48C4 Anécho Togo
33F3 Aneityum *I* Vanuatu
25M4 Angarsk Russian Federation
20A3 Ånge Sweden
70A2 Angel de la Guarda *I* Mexico
12G7 Ängelholm Sweden
34C1 Angellala Creek *R* Australia
66B1 Angels Camp USA
27G7 Angemuk *Mt* Indonesia
14B2 Angers France
13B3 Angerville France
30C3 Angkor *Hist Site* Cambodia
10C3 Anglesey *I* Wales
63C3 Angleton USA
Angmagssalik = Ammassalik
51E5 Angoche Mozambique
74B5 Angol Chile
64C2 Angola Indiana, USA
51B5 Angola *Republic* Africa
52J5 Angola Basin Atlantic Ocean
14C2 Angoulême France
48A1 Angra do Heroismo Azores
75D3 Angra dos Reis Brazil
69E3 Anguilla *I* Caribbean Sea
69B2 Anguilla Cays *Is* Caribbean Sea
43F4 Angul India
50C4 Angumu Zaïre
18C1 Anholt *I* Denmark
31C4 Anhua China
26F2 Anhui China
31D3 Anhui *Province* China
75B2 Anhumas Brazil
28A3 Anhŭng S Korea
54C3 Aniak USA
75C2 Anicuns Brazil
62A1 Animas *R* USA
62A2 Animas Peak *Mt* USA

Anita Atafu

61E2 **Anita** USA
26H2 **Aniva, Mys** *C* Russian Federation
13B3 **Anizy-le-Château** France
14B2 **Anjou** *Region* France
51E5 **Anjouan** *I* Comoros
51E5 **Anjozorobe** Madagascar
28B3 **Anju** N Korea
31B3 **Ankang** China
21E8 **Ankara** Turkey
51E5 **Ankaratra** *Mt* Madagascar
51E6 **Ankazoabo** Madagascar
51E5 **Ankazobe** Madagascar
61E2 **Ankeny** USA
18C2 **Anklam** Germany
30D3 **An Loc** Vietnam
31B4 **Anlong** China
31C3 **Anlu** China
64B3 **Anna** USA
16B3 **'Annaba** Algeria
40C3 **An Nabk** Saudi Arabia
40C3 **An Nabk** Syria
40D4 **An Nafūd** *Desert* Saudi Arabia
49E2 **An Nāfūrah** Libya
41D3 **An Najaf** Iraq
8D4 **Annan** Scotland
65D3 **Annapolis** USA
43E3 **Annapurna** *Mt* Nepal
64C2 **Ann Arbor** USA
45D1 **An Nāsirah** Syria
41E3 **An Nāsirīyah** Iraq
14D2 **Annecy** France
30D3 **An Nhon** Vietnam
31A5 **Anning** China
67A2 **Anniston** USA
48C4 **Annobon** *I* Equatorial Guinea
14C2 **Annonay** France
69J1 **Annotto Bay** Jamaica
31D3 **Anqing** China
31B2 **Ansai** China
18C3 **Ansbach** Germany
69C3 **Anse d'Hainault** Haiti
31E1 **Anshan** China
31B4 **Anshun** China
60D2 **Ansley** USA
62C2 **Anson** USA
27F8 **Anson B** Australia
48C3 **Ansongo** Mali
64C1 **Ansonville** Canada
64C3 **Ansted** USA
21F8 **Antakya** Turkey
51F5 **Antalaha** Madagascar
21E8 **Antalya** Turkey
21E8 **Antalya Körfezi** *B* Turkey
51E5 **Antananarivo** Madagascar
76G1 **Antarctic Circle** Antarctica
76G3 **Antarctic Pen** Antarctica
15B2 **Antequera** Spain
62A2 **Anthony** USA
48B1 **Anti-Atlas** *Mts* Morocco
55M5 **Anticosti, Ī. de** Canada
64B1 **Antigo** USA
69E3 **Antigua** *I* Caribbean Sea
Anti Lebanon = Sharqi, Jebel esh
59B3 **Antioch** USA
33G5 **Antipodes Is** New Zealand
63C2 **Antlers** USA
74B2 **Antofagasta** Chile
75C4 **Antonina** Brazil
62A1 **Antonito** USA
9C2 **Antrim** Northern Ireland
68E1 **Antrim** USA
9C2 **Antrim** *County* Northern Ireland
9C2 **Antrim Hills** Northern Ireland
51E5 **Antsirabe** Madagascar
51E5 **Antsirañana** Madagascar
51E5 **Antsohiny** Madagascar
28B2 **Antu** China
30D3 **An Tuc** Vietnam
13C2 **Antwerp** Belgium
Antwerpen = Antwerp
9C3 **An Uaimh** Irish Republic
28A3 **Anui** S Korea
42C3 **Anūpgarh** India
44C4 **Anuradhapura** Sri Lanka
Anvers = Antwerp
54B3 **Anvik** USA
25L5 **Anxi** China
31C2 **Anyang** China
31A3 **A'nyêmaqên Shan** *Mts* China
25S3 **Anyuysk** Russian Federation
24K4 **Anzhero-Sudzhensk** Russian Federation
16C2 **Anzio** Italy
33F2 **Aoba** *I* Vanuatu
29E2 **Aomori** Japan
16B1 **Aosta** Italy
48B3 **Aouker** *Desert Region* Mauritius
48C2 **Aoulef** Algeria
50B1 **Aozou** Chad
74E2 **Apa** *R* Brazil/Paraguay
57E4 **Apalachee B** USA
67B3 **Apalachicola** USA
67A3 **Apalachicola B** USA
72D3 **Apaporis** *R* Brazil/Colombia
75B3 **Aparecida do Taboado** Brazil
27F5 **Aparri** Philippines
17D1 **Apatin** Croatia
20E2 **Apatity** Russian Federation
70B3 **Apatzingan** Mexico
18B2 **Apeldoorn** Netherlands
33H2 **Apia** Western Samoa
75C3 **Apiaí** Brazil
73G2 **Apoera** Surinam
34B3 **Apollo Bay** Australia
67B3 **Apopka,L** USA
73H7 **Aporé** *R* Brazil
64A1 **Apostle Is** USA
57E3 **Appalachian Mts** USA
16C2 **Appennino Abruzzese** *Mts* Italy
16B2 **Appennino Ligure** *Mts* Italy
16D2 **Appennino Lucano** *Mts* Italy
16D2 **Appennino Napoletano** *Mts* Italy
16C2 **Appennino Tosco-Emilliano** *Mts* Italy
16C2 **Appennino Umbro-Marchigiano** *Mts* Italy
6C2 **Appleby** England
61D1 **Appleton** Minnesota, USA
64B2 **Appleton** Wisconsin, USA
21J7 **Apsheronskiy Poluostrov** *Pen* Azerbaijan
74F2 **Apucarana** Brazil
72E2 **Apure** *R* Venezuela
72D6 **Apurimac** *R* Peru
40C4 **'Aqaba** Jordan
40B4 **'Aqaba,G of** Egypt/Saudi Arabia
45C4 **'Aqaba, Wadi el** Egypt
41F3 **'Aqdā** Iran
73G8 **Aqidauana** Brazil
75A3 **Aquidabán** *R* Paraguay
74E2 **Aquidauana** Brazil
75A2 **Aquidauana** *R* Brazil
43E3 **Ara** India
67A2 **Arab** USA
45C1 **'Arab al Mulk** Syria
45C3 **'Araba, Wadi** Israel
36E4 **Arabian Basin** Indian Ocean
38E4 **Arabian Sea** SW Asia
45D2 **'Arab, Jabal al** *Mt* Syria
73L6 **Aracajú** Brazil
75A3 **Aracanguy,Mts de** Paraguay
73L4 **Aracati** Brazil
75D1 **Aracatu** Brazil
73H8 **Araçatuba** Brazil
15A2 **Aracena** Spain
73K7 **Araçuaí** Brazil
45C3 **'Arad** Israel
21C6 **Arad** Romania
50C2 **Arada** Chad
41F5 **'Arādah** UAE
32C1 **Arafura S** Indonesia/Australia
73H7 **Aragarças** Brazil
21G7 **Aragats** *Mt* Armenia
15B1 **Aragon** *R* Spain
15B1 **Aragón** *Region* Spain
75C1 **Araguaçu** Brazil
73H6 **Araguaia** *R* Brazil
73J5 **Araguaina** Brazil
73J7 **Araguari** Brazil
75C2 **Araguari** *R* Brazil
29C3 **Arai** Japan
45C3 **Araif el Naqa, Gebel** *Mt* Egypt
48C2 **Arak** Algeria
41E3 **Arāk** Iran
30A2 **Arakan Yoma** *Mts* Burma
44B3 **Arakkonam** India
24G5 **Aral S** Kazakhstan
24H5 **Aral'sk** Kazakhstan
15B1 **Aranda de Duero** Spain
10B2 **Aran I** Irish Republic
10B3 **Aran Is** Irish Republic
15B1 **Aranjuez** Spain
47B1 **Aranos** Namibia
63C3 **Aransas Pass** USA
28B4 **Arao** Japan
48B3 **Araouane** Mali
60D2 **Arapahoe** USA
74E4 **Arapey** *R* Uruguay
73L5 **Arapiraca** Brazil
75B3 **Araporgas** Brazil
74G3 **Ararangua** Brazil
73J8 **Araraquara** Brazil
75C3 **Araras** Brazil
32D4 **Ararat** Australia
41D2 **Ararat** Armenia
Ararat, Mt = Büyük Ağri Daği
75D3 **Araruama, Lagoa de** Brazil
40D3 **Ar'ar, Wadi** *Watercourse* Saudi Arabia
41D1 **Aras** *R* Turkey
41E2 **Aras** *R* Azerbaijan/Iran
29D3 **Arato** Japan
72E2 **Arauca** *R* Venezuela
72D2 **Arauea** Colombia
42C3 **Arāvalli Range** *Mts* India
33E1 **Arawa** Papua New Guinea
73J7 **Araxá** Brazil
21G8 **Araxes** *R* Iran
50D3 **Arba Minch** Ethiopia
16B3 **Arbatax** Sardinia, Italy
21G8 **Arbīl** Iraq
12H6 **Arbrå** Sweden
8D3 **Arbroath** Scotland
14B3 **Arcachon** France
68A1 **Arcade** USA
67B3 **Arcadia** USA
58B2 **Arcata** USA
66D1 **Arc Dome** *Mt* USA
20G3 **Archangel** Russian Federation
68C2 **Archbald** USA
59E3 **Arches Nat Pk** USA
13C3 **Arcis-sur-Aube** France
58D2 **Arco** USA
75C3 **Arcos** Brazil
15A2 **Arcos de la Frontera** Spain
55K2 **Arctic Bay** Canada
76C1 **Arctic Circle**
54E3 **Arctic Red** *R* Canada
54E3 **Arctic Red River** Canada
54D3 **Arctic Village** USA
76G2 **Arctowski** *Base* Antarctica
17F2 **Arda** *R* Bulgaria
21H8 **Ardabīl** Iran
21G7 **Ardahan** Turkey
12F6 **Årdal** Norway
48C2 **Ardar des Iforas** *Upland* Algeria/Mali
9C3 **Ardee** Irish Republic
41F3 **Ardekān** Iran
13C3 **Ardennes** *Department* France
18B2 **Ardennes** *Region* Belgium
41F3 **Ardestāh** Iran
40C3 **Ardh es Suwwan** *Desert Region* Jordan
15A2 **Ardila** *R* Portugal
34C2 **Ardlethan** Australia
56D3 **Ardmore** USA
8B3 **Ardnamurchan Pt** Scotland
13A2 **Ardres** France
8C3 **Ardrishaig** Scotland
8C4 **Ardrossan** Scotland
69D3 **Arecibo** Puerto Rico
73L4 **Areia Branca** Brazil
59B3 **Arena,Pt** USA
13D1 **Arenberg** *Region* Germany
12F7 **Arendal** Norway
72D7 **Arequipa** Peru
16C2 **Arezzo** Italy
16C2 **Argenta** Italy
14C2 **Argentan** France
13B3 **Argenteuil** France
71D7 **Argentina** *Republic* S America
52F7 **Argentine Basin** Atlantic Ocean
74B8 **Argentino, Lago** Argentina
14C2 **Argenton-sur-Creuse** France
17F2 **Argeş** *R* Romania
42B2 **Arghardab** *R* Afghanistan
17E3 **Argolikós Kólpos** *G* Greece
13C3 **Argonne** *Region* France
17E3 **Árgos** Greece
17E3 **Argostólion** Greece
66B3 **Arguello,Pt** USA
66D3 **Argus Range** *Mts* USA
32B2 **Argyle,L** Australia
8C3 **Argyll** Scotland
18C1 **Århus** Denmark
51C6 **Ariamsvlei** Namibia
48B3 **Aribinda** Burkina
74B1 **Arica** Chile
42C2 **Arifwala** Pakistan
Arihā = Jericho
60C3 **Arikaree** *R* USA
69L1 **Arima** Trinidad
75C2 **Arinos** Brazil
73G6 **Arinos** *R* Brazil
69L1 **Aripo,Mt** Trinidad
72F5 **Aripuanã** Brazil
72F5 **Aripuanã** *R* Brazil
8C3 **Arisaig** Scotland
45B3 **'Arîsh, Wadi el** *Watercourse* Egypt
56B3 **Arizona** *State* USA
12G7 **Årjäng** Sweden
25Q4 **Arka** Russian Federation
21G5 **Arkadak** Russian Federation
63D2 **Arkadelphia** USA
8C3 **Arkaig, L** Scotland
24H4 **Arkalyk** Kazakhstan
57D3 **Arkansas** *R* USA
57D3 **Arkansas** *State* USA
63C1 **Arkansas City** USA
29C2 **Arkhipovka** Russian Federation
25K2 **Arkipelag Nordenshelda** *Arch* Russian Federation
10B3 **Arklow** Irish Republic
15B1 **Arlanzón** *R* Spain
14C3 **Arles** France
61D2 **Arlington** S Dakota, USA
63C2 **Arlington** Texas, USA
65D3 **Arlington** Virginia, USA
58B1 **Arlington** Washington, USA
64B2 **Arlington Heights** USA
18B3 **Arlon** Belgium
Armageddon = Megiddo
9C2 **Armagh** Northern Ireland
9C2 **Armagh** *County* Northern Ireland
13B4 **Armançon** *R* France
21G7 **Armavir** Russian Federation
72C3 **Armenia** Colombia
21G7 **Armenia** *Republic* Europe
13B2 **Armentières** Belgium
32E4 **Armidale** Australia
55L3 **Arnaud** *R* Canada
40B2 **Arnauti** *C* Cyprus
62C1 **Arnett** USA
18B2 **Arnhem** Netherlands
32C2 **Arnhem,C** Australia
32C2 **Arnhem Land** Australia
66B1 **Arnold** USA
65D1 **Arnprior** Canada
13E2 **Arnsberg** Germany
47B2 **Aroab** Namibia
13E2 **Arolsen** Germany
33G1 **Arorae** *I* Kiribati
16B1 **Arosa** Switzerland
13B3 **Arpajon** France
75C1 **Arraias** Brazil
75C1 **Arraias, Serra de** *Mts* Brazil
41D3 **Ar Ramādī** Iraq
8C4 **Arran, I of** Scotland
40C2 **Ar Raqqah** Syria
49D2 **Ar Rāqūbah** Libya
14C1 **Arras** France
41D4 **Ar Rass** Saudi Arabia
45D1 **Ar Rastan** Syria
48A2 **Arrecife** Canary Islands
41E3 **Ar Rifā'ī** Iraq
41E3 **Ar Rihāb** *Desert Region* Iraq
Ar Riyād = Riyadh
8C3 **Arrochar** Scotland
75C1 **Arrojado** *R* Brazil
58C2 **Arrowrock Res** USA
35A2 **Arrowtown** New Zealand
66B3 **Arroyo Grande** USA
41F4 **Ar Ru'ays** Qatar
41G5 **Ar Rustāq** Oman
40D3 **Ar Rutbah** Iraq
41D5 **Ar Ruwayḍah** Saudi Arabia
44B3 **Arsikere** India
20H4 **Arsk** Russian Federation
17E3 **Árta** Greece
28C2 **Artem** Russian Federation
25L4 **Artemovsk** Russian Federation
25N4 **Artemovskiy** Russian Federation
56C3 **Artesia** USA
35B2 **Arthurs P** New Zealand
74E4 **Artigas** Uruguay
54H3 **Artillery L** Canada
14C1 **Artois** *Region* France
19F3 **Artsiz** Ukraine
76G2 **Arturo Prat** *Base* Antarctica
21G7 **Artvin** Turkey
50D3 **Aru** Zaïre
73H6 **Aruanã** Brazil
69C4 **Aruba** *I* Caribbean Sea
27G7 **Aru, Kepulauan** *Arch* Indonesia
43F3 **Arun** *R* Nepal
43G3 **Arunāchal Pradesh** *Union Territory* India
44B4 **Aruppukkottai** India
50D4 **Arusha** Tanzania
50C3 **Aruwimi** *R* Zaïre
60B3 **Arvada** USA
26D2 **Arvayheer** Mongolia
55L5 **Arvida** Canada
12H5 **Arvidsjaur** Sweden
12G7 **Arvika** Sweden
59C3 **Arvin** USA
45C1 **Arwad** *I* Syria
20G4 **Arzamas** Russian Federation
15B2 **Arzew** Algeria
42C2 **Asadabad** Afghanistan
29B4 **Asahi** *R* Japan
29E2 **Asahi dake** *Mt* Japan
29E2 **Asahikawa** Japan
28A3 **Asan-man** *B* S Korea
43F4 **Asansol** India
49D2 **Asawanwah** *Well* Libya
20L4 **Asbest** Russian Federation
47C2 **Asbestos Mts** South Africa
65E2 **Asbury Park** USA
52H5 **Ascension** *I* Atlantic Ocean
70D3 **Ascensión, B de la** Mexico
18B3 **Aschaffenburg** Germany
18C2 **Aschersleben** Germany
16C2 **Ascoli Piceno** Italy
50E2 **Āseb** Eritrea
48C2 **Asedjrad** *Upland* Algeria
50D3 **Asela** Ethiopia
12H6 **Åsele** Sweden
17E2 **Asenovgrad** Bulgaria
13C3 **Asfeld** France
20K4 **Asha** Russian Federation
7D3 **Ashbourne** England
67B2 **Ashburn** USA
33G5 **Ashburton** New Zealand
32A3 **Ashburton** *R* Australia
40B3 **Ashdod** Israel
63D2 **Ashdown** USA
67A1 **Asheboro** USA
57E3 **Asheville** USA
34D1 **Ashford** Australia
7E4 **Ashford** England
59D3 **Ash Fork** USA
29D2 **Ashibetsu** Japan
29D3 **Ashikaga** Japan
28B4 **Ashizuri-misaki** *Pt* Japan
24G6 **Ashkhabad** Turkmenistan
62C1 **Ashland** Kansas, USA
57E3 **Ashland** Kentucky, USA
60B1 **Ashland** Montana, USA
61D2 **Ashland** Nebraska, USA
64C2 **Ashland** Ohio, USA
56A2 **Ashland** Oregon, USA
65D3 **Ashland** Virginia, USA
61E1 **Ashland** Wisconsin, USA
34C1 **Ashley** Australia
60D1 **Ashley** USA
68C2 **Ashokan Res** USA
45C3 **Ashqelon** Israel
41D3 **Ash Shabakh** Iraq
41G4 **Ash Sha'm** UAE
41D2 **Ash Sharqāṭ** Iraq
41E3 **Ash Shaṭrah** Iraq
38C4 **Ash Shiḥr** Yemen
41E4 **Ash Shumlūl** Saudi Arabia
64C2 **Ashtabula** USA
55M4 **Ashuanipi L** Canada
21F8 **Asi** *R* Syria
15A2 **Asilah** Morocco
16B2 **Asinara** *I* Sardinia, Italy
24K4 **Asino** Russian Federation
50E1 **Asīr** *Region* Saudi Arabia
43E5 **Aska** India
40D2 **Aşkale** Turkey
12G7 **Askersund** Sweden
45B4 **Asl** Egypt
42C1 **Asmar** Afghanistan
50D2 **Asmara** Eritrea
Āsmera = Asmara
28B4 **Aso** Japan
50D2 **Asosa** Ethiopia
50D1 **Asoteriba, Jebel** *Mt* Sudan
62B2 **Aspermont** USA
35A2 **Aspiring,Mt** New Zealand
40C2 **As Sabkhah** Syria
41E5 **As Salamiyah** Saudi Arabia
40C2 **As Salamīyah** Syria
41D3 **As Salmān** Iraq
43G3 **Assam** *State* India
41E3 **As Samāwah** Iraq
41F5 **Aş Şanām** *Region* Saudi Arabia
45D2 **Aş Şanamayn** Syria
18B2 **Assen** Netherlands
18C1 **Assens** Denmark
49D1 **As Sidrah** Libya
54H5 **Assiniboia** Canada
54G4 **Assiniboine,Mt** Canada
73H8 **Assis** Brazil
40C3 **As Sukhnah** Syria
41E5 **Aş Şumman** *Region* Saudi Arabia
51E4 **Assumption** *I* Seychelles
40C3 **As Suwaydā'** Syria
41D3 **Aş Şuwayrah** Iraq
41E2 **Astara** Azerbaijan
16B2 **Asti** Italy
17F3 **Astipálaia** *I* Greece
15A1 **Astorga** Spain
56A2 **Astoria** USA
21H6 **Astrakhan'** Russian Federation
15A1 **Asturias** *Region* Spain
76F12 **Asuka** *Base* Antarctica
74E3 **Asunción** Paraguay
26H5 **Asuncion** *I* Marianas
50D3 **Aswa** *R* Uganda
40B5 **Aswân** Egypt
49F2 **Aswân High Dam** Egypt
49F2 **Asyût** Egypt
74C2 **Atacama, Desierto de** *Desert* Chile
33H1 **Atafu** *I* Tokelau Islands

45C3 Atā'ita, Jebel el *Mt* Jordan
48C4 Atakpamé Togo
27F7 Atambua Indonesia
55N3 Atangmik Greenland
45B4 Ataqa, Gebel *Mt* Egypt
48A2 Atar Mauritius
40C2 Atatürk Baraji *Res* Turkey
66B3 Atascadero USA
24J5 Atasu Kazakhstan
50D2 Atbara Sudan
24H4 Atbasar Kazakhstan
57D4 Atchafalaya B USA
57D3 Atchison USA
68C3 Atco USA
16C2 Atessa Italy
13B2 Ath Belgium
54G4 Athabasca Canada
54G4 Athabasca *R* Canada
54H4 Athabasca,L Canada
67A2 Athens Alabama, USA
57E3 Athens Georgia, USA
17E3 Athens Greece
64C3 Athens Ohio, USA
68B2 Athens Pennsylvania, USA
67B1 Athens Tennessee, USA
63C2 Athens Texas, USA
Athína = Athens
10B3 Athlone Irish Republic
45B1 Athna Cyprus
68D1 Athol USA
17E3 Áthos *Mt* Greece
9C3 Athy Irish Republic
50B2 Ati Chad
55J5 Atikokan Canada
25R3 Atka Russian Federation
21G5 Atkarsk Russian Federation
63D1 Atkins USA
57E3 Atlanta Georgia, USA
64C2 Atlanta Michigan, USA
61D2 Atlantic USA
57F3 Atlantic City USA
68C2 Atlantic Highlands USA
52H8 Atlantic-Indian Antarctic Basin Atlantic Ocean
52H7 Atlantic Indian Ridge Atlantic Ocean
Atlas Mts = Haut Atlas, Moyen Atlas
48C1 Atlas Saharien *Mts* Algeria
54E4 Atlin Canada
54E4 Atlin L Canada
45C2 'Atlit Israel
57E3 Atmore USA
51E6 Atofinandrahana Madagascar
63C2 Atoka USA
72C2 Atrato *R* Colombia
41F5 Attaf *Region* UAE
50E1 Aţ Ţā'if Saudi Arabia
45D2 At Tall Syria
67A2 Attalla USA
55K4 Attawapiskat Canada
55K4 Attawapiskat *R* Canada
41D3 At Taysīyah *Desert Region* Saudi Arabia
64B2 Attica Indiana, USA
68A1 Attica New York, USA
13C3 Attigny France
45B1 Attila Line Cyprus
65E2 Attleboro Massachusetts, USA
30D3 Attopeu Laos
40C4 At Tubayq *Upland* Saudi Arabia
12H7 Atvidaberg Sweden
66B2 Atwater USA
14D3 Aubagne France
13C3 Aube *Department* France
13C3 Aube *R* France
14C3 Aubenas France
67A2 Auburn Alabama, USA
59B3 Auburn California, USA
64B2 Auburn Indiana, USA
65E2 Auburn Maine, USA
61D2 Auburn Nebraska, USA
65D2 Auburn New York, USA
58B1 Auburn Washington, USA
14C3 Auch France
33G4 Auckland New Zealand
37K7 Auckland Is New Zealand
14C3 Aude *R* France
55K4 Auden Canada
61E2 Audubon USA
34C1 Augathella Australia
9C2 Aughnacloy Northern Ireland
47B2 Aughrabies Falls South Africa
18C3 Augsburg Germany
32A4 Augusta Australia
57E3 Augusta Georgia, USA
63C1 Augusta Kansas, USA
57G2 Augusta Maine, USA
58B1 Augusta Montana, USA
64A2 Augusta Wisconsin, USA
19E2 Augustów Poland
32A3 Augustus,Mt Australia
47B1 Auob *R* Namibia
42D3 Auraiya India

42D5 Aurangābād India
48C1 Aurès *Mts* Algeria
16B3 Aurès, Mt de l' Algeria
13D1 Aurich Germany
14C3 Aurillac France
56C3 Aurora Colorado, USA
64B2 Aurora Illinois, USA
64C3 Aurora Indiana, USA
63D1 Aurora Mississippi, USA
61D2 Aurora Nebraska, USA
47B2 Aus Namibia
64C2 Au Sable USA
48A2 Ausert *Well* Morocco
8D2 Auskerry, I Scotland
57D2 Austin Minnesota, USA
59C3 Austin Nevada, USA
68A2 Austin Pennsylvania, USA
56D3 Austin Texas, USA
32D4 Australian Alps *Mts* Australia
18C3 Austria *Federal Republic* Europe
70B3 Autlán Mexico
14C2 Autun France
14C2 Auvergne *Region* France
14C2 Auxerre France
13A2 Auxi-le-Château France
14C2 Avallon France
66C4 Avalon USA
55N5 Avalon Pen Canada
75C3 Avaré Brazil
13E1 Ave *R* Germany
45C3 Avedat *Hist Site* Israel
73G4 Aveiro Brazil
15A1 Aveiro Portugal
74E4 Avellaneda Argentina
16C2 Avellino Italy
66B3 Avenal USA
13B2 Avesnes-sur-Helpe France
12H6 Avesta Sweden
16C2 Avezzano Italy
8D3 Aviemore Scotland
35B2 Aviemore,L New Zealand
14C3 Avignon France
15B1 Avila Spain
15A1 Avilés Spain
61D2 Avoca Iowa, USA
68B1 Avoca New York, USA
34B3 Avoca *R* Australia
68B1 Avon USA
7C4 Avon *County* England
7D4 Avon *R* Dorset, England
7D3 Avon *R* Warwick, England
59D4 Avondale USA
7C4 Avonmouth Wales
67B3 Avon Park USA
13B3 Avre *R* France
17D2 Avtovac Bosnia-Herzegovina
45D2 A'waj *R* Syria
29D4 Awaji-shima *I* Japan
50E3 Awarē Ethiopia
35A2 Awarua Pt New Zealand
50E3 Awash Ethiopia
50E3 Awash *R* Ethiopia
29C3 Awa-shima *I* Japan
35B2 Awatere *R* New Zealand
49D2 Awbārī Libya
50C3 Aweil Sudan
8C3 Awe, Loch *L* Scotland
49E2 Awjilah Libya
55J1 Axel Heiberg I Canada
7C4 Axminster England
29C3 Ayabe Japan
74E5 Ayacucho Argentina
69C5 Ayacucho Colombia
72D6 Ayacucho Peru
24K5 Ayaguz Kazakhstan
39G2 Ayakkum Hu *L* China
15A2 Ayamonte Spain
25P4 Ayan Russian Federation
72D6 Ayaviri Peru
21D8 Aydin Turkey
17F3 Áyios Evstrátios *I* Greece
25N3 Aykhal Russian Federation
7D4 Aylesbury England
45D2 'Ayn al Fijah Syria
40D2 Ayn Zālah Iraq
49E2 Ayn Zuwayyah *Well* Libya
50D3 Ayod Sudan
32D2 Ayr Australia
8C4 Ayr Scotland
8C4 Ayr *R* Scotland
6B2 Ayre,Pt of Isle of Man, British Islands
17F2 Aytos Bulgaria
30C3 Ayutthaya Thailand
17F3 Ayvacık Turkey
17F3 Ayvalık Turkey
43E3 Azamgarh India
48B3 Azaouad *Desert Region* Mali
48C3 Azaouak, Vallée de l' Niger
48D3 Azare Nigeria
40C2 A'zāz Syria
Azbine = Aïr
48A2 Azeffal *Watercourse* Mauritius

21H7 Azerbaijan *Republic* Europe
72C4 Azogues Ecuador
20H2 Azopol'ye Russian Federation
46B4 Azores *Is* Atlantic Ocean
50C2 Azoum *R* Chad
21F6 Azov, S of Russian Federation/Ukraine
48B1 Azrou Morocco
62A1 Aztec USA
72B2 Azuero,Pen de Panama
74E5 Azul Argentina
75B1 Azul, Serra *Mts* Brazil
16B3 Azzaba Algeria
45D2 Az-Zabdānī Syria
41G5 Aẓ Ẓāhirah *Mts* Oman
49D2 Az Zahrah Libya
40C3 Az Zilaf Syria
41D4 Az Zilfi Saudi Arabia
41E3 Az Zubayr Iraq

B

45C2 Ba'abda Lebanon
40C3 Ba'albek Lebanon
45C3 Ba'al Hazor *Mt* Israel
50E3 Baardheere Somalia
17F2 Babadag Romania
40A1 Babaeski Turkey
72C4 Babahoyo Ecuador
50E2 Bāb al Mandab *Str* Djibouti/Yemen
32B1 Babar, Kepulauan *I* Indonesia
50D4 Babati Tanzania
20F4 Babayevo Russian Federation
61E1 Babbitt USA
64C2 Baberton USA
54F4 Babine L Canada
32C1 Babo Indonesia
41F2 Bābol Iran
27F5 Babuyan Is Philippines
73J4 Bacabal Brazil
27F7 Bacan *I* Indonesia
21D6 Bacău Romania
30D1 Bac Can Vietnam
13D3 Baccarat France
34B3 Baccchus Marsh Australia
39F2 Bachu China
54J3 Back *R* Canada
30D1 Bac Ninh Vietnam
27F5 Bacolod Philippines
6C3 Bacup England
44B3 Badagara India
31A1 Badain Jaran Shamo *Desert* China
15A2 Badajoz Spain
15C1 Badalona Spain
40D3 Badanah Saudi Arabia
28B2 Badaohe China
13E3 Bad Bergzabern Germany
13D2 Bad Ems Germany
18B3 Baden-Baden Germany
13D3 Badenviller France
18B3 Baden-Württemberg *State* Germany
18C3 Badgastein Austria
66C2 Badger USA
18B2 Bad-Godesberg Germany
18B2 Bad Hersfeld Germany
13D2 Bad Honnef Germany
42B4 Badin Pakistan
16C1 Bad Ischl Austria
40C3 Badiyat ash Sham *Desert Region* Iraq/Jordan
18B3 Bad-Kreuznach Germany
60C1 Badlands *Region* USA
13E2 Bad Lippspringe Germany
13E2 Bad Nauheim Germany
13D2 Bad Nevenahr-Ahrweiler Germany
40C5 Badr Ḥunayn Saudi Arabia
13E2 Bad Ryrmont Germany
18C3 Bad Tolz Germany
44C4 Badulla Sri Lanka
13E2 Bad Wildungen Germany
13E3 Bad Wimpfen Germany
15B2 Baena Spain
48A3 Bafatá Guinea-Bissau
55L2 Baffin B Canada/Greenland
63C3 Baffin B USA
55L2 Baffin I Canada
50B3 Bafia Cameroon
48A3 Bafing *R* Mali
48A3 Bafoulabé Mali
50B3 Bafoussam Cameroon
41G3 Bāfq Iran
21F7 Bafra Burun *Pt* Turkey
41G4 Bāft Iran
50C3 Bafwasende Zaïre
43E3 Bagaha India
44B2 Bāgalkot India
51D4 Bagamoyo Tanzania
59D4 Bagdad USA
74F4 Bagé Brazil
60B2 Baggs USA
41D3 Baghdād Iraq
43F4 Bagherhat Bangladesh
41G3 Bāghīn Iran
42B1 Baghlan Afghanistan

61D1 Bagley USA
48B4 Bagnoa Ivory Coast
14C3 Bagnols-sur-Cèze France
Bago = Pegu
48B3 Bagoé *R* Mali
28A2 Bag Tai China
27F5 Baguio Philippines
43F3 Bāhādurābād Bangladesh
57F4 Bahamas,The *Is* Caribbean Sea
43F4 Baharampur India
40A4 Baharīya Oasis Egypt
42C3 Bahawalnagar Pakistan
42C3 Bahawalpur Pakistan
42C3 Bahawalpur *Division* Pakistan
Bahia = Salvador
73K6 Bahia *State* Brazil
74D5 Bahia Blanca Argentina
70D3 Bahía, Islas de la Honduras
56B4 Bahia Kino Mexico
74C6 Bahias, Cabo dos Argentina
50D2 Bahir Dar Ethiopia
45A3 Bahra el Manzala *L* Egypt
43E3 Bahraich India
38D3 Bahrain *Sheikhdom* Arabian Pen
41D3 Bahr al Milh *L* Iraq
50C3 Bahr Aouk *R* Chad/Central African Republic
Bahrat Lut = Dead Sea
Bahr el Abiad = White Nile
50C3 Bahr el Arab *Watercourse* Sudan
Bahr el Azraq = Blue Nile
50D3 Bahr el Ghazal *R* Sudan
50B2 Bahr el Ghazal *Watercourse* Chad
45A3 Bahr Fāqūs *R* Egypt
15A2 Baia de Setúbal *B* Portugal
51B5 Baia dos Tigres Angola
21C6 Baia Mare Romania
50B3 Baïbokoum Chad
26F2 Baicheng China
55M5 Baie-Comeau Canada
45C2 Baie de St Georges *B* Lebanon
55L4 Baie-du-Poste Canada
65E1 Baie St Paul Canada
55N5 Baie-Verte Canada
31B3 Baihe China
31C3 Bai He *R* China
41D3 Ba'ijī Iraq
25M4 Baikal, L Russian Federation
43E4 Baikunthpur India
Baile Atha Cliath = Dublin
17E2 Băileşti Romania
13B2 Bailleul France
31A3 Baima China
67B2 Bainbridge USA
54B3 Baird Mts USA
31D1 Bairin Youqi China
31D1 Bairin Zuoqi China
32D4 Bairnsdale Australia
43E3 Baitadi Nepal
28A2 Baixingt China
17D1 Baja Hungary
70A1 Baja California *Pen* Mexico
59C4 Baja California *State* Mexico
70A2 Baja, Punta *Pt* Mexico
20K5 Bakal Russian Federation
50C3 Bakala Central African Republic
48A3 Bakel Senegal
59C3 Baker California, USA
56C2 Baker Montana, USA
56B2 Baker Oregon, USA
55J3 Baker Foreland *Pt* Canada
54J3 Baker L Canada
54J3 Baker Lake Canada
56A2 Baker,Mt USA
56B3 Bakersfield USA
7D3 Bakewell England
41G2 Bakharden Turkmenistan
41G2 Bakhardok Turkmenistan
21E5 Bakhmach Ukraine
12C1 Bakkaflói *B* Iceland
50D3 Bako Ethiopia
50C3 Bakouma Central African Republic
21H7 Baku Azerbaijan
40B2 Balā Turkey
7C3 Bala Wales
27E6 Balabac *I* Philippines
27E6 Balabac Str Malaysia/Philippines
43E4 Bālaghāt India
34A2 Balaklava Australia
21H5 Balakovo Russian Federation
43E4 Balāngīr India
21G5 Balashov Russian Federation
43F4 Balasore India

17D1 Balaton *L* Hungary
9C3 Balbriggan Irish Republic
74E5 Balcarce Argentina
17F2 Balchik Bulgaria
33F5 Balclutha New Zealand
63D1 Bald Knob USA
7D4 Baldock England
67B2 Baldwin USA
58E1 Baldy Mt USA
56C3 Baldy Peak *Mt* USA
15C2 Balearic Is Spain
75E2 Baleia, Ponta da *Pt* Brazil
55M4 Baleine, Rivière de la *R* Canada
27F5 Baler Philippines
20J4 Balezino Russian Federation
32A1 Bali *I* Indonesia
40A2 Balıkesir Turkey
40C2 Balīkh *R* Syria/Turkey
27E7 Balikpapan Indonesia
75B2 Baliza Brazil
42B1 Balkh Afghanistan
24J5 Balkhash Kazakhstan
24J5 Balkhash, L Kazakhstan
8C3 Ballachulish Scotland
8C4 Ballantrae Scotland
54G2 Ballantyne Str Canada
44B3 Ballāpur India
32D4 Ballarat Australia
8D3 Ballater Scotland
6B2 Ballaugh England
76G7 Balleny Is Antarctica
43E3 Ballia India
34D1 Ballina Australia
10B3 Ballina Irish Republic
62C2 Ballinger USA
9A4 Ballinskelligs B Irish Republic
13D4 Ballon d'Alsace *Mt* France
17D2 Ballsh Albania
68D1 Ballston Spa USA
9C2 Ballycastle Northern Ireland
9D2 Ballyclare Northern Ireland
9C4 Ballycotton B Irish Republic
9B3 Ballyhaunis Northern Ireland
9C2 Ballymena Northern Ireland
9C2 Ballymoney Northern Ireland
9C2 Ballynahinch Northern Ireland
9B2 Ballyshannon Irish Republic
9C3 Ballyteige B Irish Republic
34B3 Balmoral Australia
62B2 Balmorhea USA
42B3 Balochistān *Region* Pakistan
51B5 Balombo Angola
34C1 Balonn *R* Australia
42C3 Bālotra India
43E3 Balrāmpur India
32D4 Balranald Australia
73J5 Balsas Brazil
70B3 Balsas *R* Mexico
21D6 Balta Ukraine
12H7 Baltic S N Europe
40B3 Baltim Egypt
57F3 Baltimore USA
43F3 Bālurghāt India
21J6 Balykshi Kazakhstan
41G4 Bam Iran
50B2 Bama Nigeria
48B3 Bamako Mali
50C3 Bambari Central African Republic
67B2 Bamberg USA
18C3 Bamberg Germany
50C3 Bambili Zaïre
75C3 Bambuí Brazil
50B3 Bamenda Cameroon
28A2 Bamiancheng China
50B3 Bamingui *R* Central African Republic
50B3 Bamingui Bangoran National Park Central African Republic
42B2 Bamiyan Afghanistan
33F1 Banaba *I* Kiribati
50C3 Banalia Zaïre
48B3 Bamba Mali
44E4 Bananga Nicobar Is, Indian Ocean
30C3 Ban Aranyaprathet Thailand
30C2 Ban Ban Laos
30C4 Ban Betong Thailand
9C2 Banbridge Northern Ireland
7D3 Banbury England
8D3 Banchory Scotland
70D3 Banco Chinchorro *Is* Mexico
65D1 Bancroft Canada
43E3 Bānda India
27C6 Banda Aceh Indonesia

Banda, Kepulauan **Belfast**

27G7 **Banda, Kepulauan** *Arch* Indonesia
48B4 **Bandama** *R* Ivory Coast
41G4 **Bandar 'Abbās** Iran
21H8 **Bandar Anzalī** Iran
41F4 **Bandar-e Daylam** Iran
41F4 **Bandar-e Lengheh** Iran
41F4 **Bandar-e Māqām** Iran
41F4 **Bandar-e Rig** Iran
21J8 **Bandar-e Torkoman** Iran
41E3 **Bandar Khomeynī** Iran
27E6 **Bandar Seri Begawan** Brunei
27F7 **Banda S** Indonesia
75D3 **Bandeira** *Mt* Brazil
75B1 **Bandeirantes** Brazil
70B2 **Banderas, B de** Mexico
48B3 **Bandiagara** Mali
21D7 **Bandırma** Turkey
47D1 **Bandolier Kop** South Africa
50B4 **Bandundu** Zaïre
27D7 **Bandung** Indonesia
21H8 **Baneh** Iran
70E2 **Banes** Cuba
8D3 **Banff** Scotland
54G4 **Banff** *R* Canada
44B3 **Bangalore** India
50C3 **Bangassou** Central African Republic
32B1 **Banggai, Kepulauan** *I* Indonesia
27E6 **Banggi** *I* Malaysia
30D2 **Bang Hieng** *R* Laos
27D7 **Bangka** *I* Indonesia
30C3 **Bangkok** Thailand
30C3 **Bangkok, Bight of** *B* Thailand
39G3 **Bangladesh** *Republic* Asia
42D2 **Bangong Co** *L* China
57G2 **Bangor** Maine, USA
9D2 **Bangor** Northern Ireland
68C2 **Bangor** Pennsylvania, USA
7B3 **Bangor** Wales
30B3 **Bang Saphan Yai** Thailand
50B3 **Bangui** Central African Republic
51D5 **Bangweulu, L** Zambia
30C4 **Ban Hat Yai** Thailand
30C2 **Ban Hin Heup** Laos
30C1 **Ban Houei Sai** Laos
30B3 **Ban Hua Hin** Thailand
48B3 **Bani** *R* Mali
48C3 **Bani Bangou** Niger
49D1 **Banī Walīd** Libya
40C2 **Bāniyās** Syria
16D2 **Banja Luka** Bosnia-Herzegovina
27E7 **Banjarmasin** Indonesia
48A3 **Banjul** The Gambia
30B4 **Ban Kantang** Thailand
30D2 **Ban Khemmarat** Laos
30B4 **Ban Khok Kloi** Thailand
27H8 **Banks I** Australia
54E4 **Banks I** British Columbia, Canada
54F2 **Banks I** Northwest Territories, Canada
33F2 **Banks Is** Vanuatu
58C1 **Banks L** USA
35B2 **Banks Pen** New Zealand
34C4 **Banks Str** Australia
43F4 **Bankura** India
30B2 **Ban Mae Sariang** Thailand
30B2 **Ban Mae Sot** Thailand
43H4 **Banmauk** Burma
30D3 **Ban Me Thuot** Vietnam
9C3 **Bann** *R* Irish Republic
9C2 **Bann** *R* Northern Ireland
30B4 **Ban Na San** Thailand
42C2 **Bannu** Pakistan
30C2 **Ban Pak Neun** Laos
30C4 **Ban Pak Phanang** Thailand
30D3 **Ban Pu Kroy** Cambodia
30B3 **Ban Sai Yok** Thailand
30C3 **Ban Sattahip** Thailand
19D3 **Banská Bystrica** Slovakia
42C4 **Bānswāra** India
30B4 **Ban Tha Kham** Thailand
30D2 **Ban Thateng** Laos
30C2 **Ban Tha Tum** Thailand
10B3 **Bantry** Irish Republic
10A3 **Bantry** *B* Irish Republic
27C6 **Banyak, Kepulauan** *Is* Indonesia
30D3 **Ban Ya Soup** Vietnam
27E7 **Banyuwangi** Indonesia
36E7 **Banzare Seamount** Indian Ocean
31D2 **Baoding** China
31C3 **Baofeng** China
30C1 **Bao Ha** Vietnam
31B3 **Baoji** China
30D3 **Bao Loc** Vietnam
26C4 **Baoshan** China
31C1 **Baotou** China
44C2 **Bāpatla** India
13B2 **Bapaume** France
45C4 **Bāqir, Jebel** *Mt* Jordan
41D3 **Ba'qūbah** Iraq
17D2 **Bar** Montenegro, Yugoslavia
50D2 **Bara** Sudan
50E3 **Baraawe** Somalia
43E3 **Bāra Banki** India
28C2 **Barabash** Russian Federation
24J4 **Barabinsk** Kazakhstan/Russian Federation
24J4 **Barabinskaya Step** *Steppe* Kazakhstan/Russian Federation
15B1 **Baracaldo** Spain
69C2 **Baracoa** Cuba
45D2 **Baradá** *R* Syria
34C2 **Baradine** Australia
44A2 **Bārāmati** India
42C2 **Baramula** Pakistan
42D3 **Bārān** India
54E4 **Baranof I** USA
20D5 **Baranovichi** Belarus
34A2 **Baratta** Australia
43F3 **Barauni** India
73K8 **Barbacena** Brazil
69F4 **Barbados** *I* Caribbean Sea
15C1 **Barbastro** Spain
47E2 **Barberton** South Africa
14B2 **Barbezieux** France
72D2 **Barbosa** Colombia
69E3 **Barbuda** *I* Caribbean Sea
32D3 **Barcaldine** Australia
Barce = Al Marj
16D3 **Barcellona** Sicily, Italy
15C1 **Barcelona** Spain
72F1 **Barcelona** Venezuela
32D3 **Barcoo** *R* Australia
50B1 **Bardai** Chad
74C5 **Bardas Blancas** Argentina
43F4 **Barddhamān** India
19E3 **Bardejov** Slovakia
7B3 **Bardsey** *I* Wales
64B3 **Bardstown** USA
42D3 **Bareilly** India
Barentsovo More *S* = **Barents Sea**
24D2 **Barentsøya** *I* Svalbard
20F1 **Barents S** Russian Federation
50D2 **Barentu** Eritrea
14B2 **Barfleur, Pointe de** France
43E4 **Bargarh** India
25M4 **Barguzin** Russian Federation
25N4 **Barguzin** *R* Russian Federation
65F2 **Bar Harbor** USA
43F4 **Barhi** India
16D2 **Bari** Italy
15D2 **Barika** Algeria
72D2 **Barinas** Venezuela
43F4 **Baripāda** India
40B5 **Bârîs** Egypt
42C4 **Bari Sādri** India
43G4 **Barisal** Bangladesh
27D7 **Barisan, Pegunungan** *Mts* Indonesia
27E7 **Barito** *R* Indonesia
49D2 **Barjuj** *Watercourse* Libya
31A3 **Barkam** China
64B3 **Barkley,L** USA
47D3 **Barkly East** South Africa
32C2 **Barkly Tableland** *Mts* Australia
13C3 **Bar-le-Duc** France
32A3 **Barlee,L** Australia
32A3 **Barlee Range** *Mts* Australia
16D2 **Barletta** Italy
42C3 **Bārmer** India
34B2 **Barmera** Australia
7B3 **Barmouth** Wales
6D2 **Barnard Castle** England
24K4 **Barnaul** Russian Federation
68C3 **Barnegat** USA
68C3 **Barnegat B** USA
68A2 **Barnesboro** USA
55L2 **Barnes Icecap** Canada
67B2 **Barnesville** Georgia, USA
64C3 **Barnesville** Ohio, USA
62B2 **Barnhart** USA
7D3 **Barnsley** England
7B4 **Barnstaple** England
48C4 **Baro** Nigeria
43G3 **Barpeta** India
72E1 **Barquisimeto** Venezuela
13D3 **Barr** France
73K6 **Barra** Brazil
8B3 **Barra** *I* Scotland
34D2 **Barraba** Australia
75D1 **Barra da Estiva** Brazil
75A2 **Barra do Bugres** Brazil
75B2 **Barra do Garças** Brazil
75D3 **Barra do Piraí** Brazil
51D6 **Barra Falsa, Punta de** *Pt* Mozambique
73K6 **Barragem de Sobradinho** *Res* Brazil
15A2 **Barragem do Castelo do Bode** *Res* Portugal
15A2 **Barragem do Maranhão** *Res* Portugal
8B3 **Barra Head** *Pt* Scotland
73K8 **Barra Mansa** Brazil
72C6 **Barranca** Peru
72D2 **Barrancabermeja** Colombia
72F2 **Barrancas** Venezuela
74E3 **Barranqueras** Argentina
72D1 **Barranquilla** Colombia
8B3 **Barra,Sound of** *Chan* Scotland
68D1 **Barre** USA
73J6 **Barreiras** Brazil
15A2 **Barreiro** Portugal
73L5 **Barreiros** Brazil
32D5 **Barren,C** Australia
73J8 **Barretos** Brazil
65D2 **Barrie** Canada
34B2 **Barrier Range** *Mts* Australia
32E4 **Barrington,Mt** Australia
75C2 **Barro Alto** Brazil
27G8 **Barroloola** Australia
64A1 **Barron** USA
69N2 **Barrouallie** St Vincent
54C2 **Barrow** USA
9C3 **Barrow** *R* Irish Republic
32C3 **Barrow Creek** Australia
32A3 **Barrow I** Australia
6C2 **Barrow-in-Furness** England
54C2 **Barrow,Pt** USA
55J2 **Barrow Str** Canada
7C4 **Barry** Wales
65D1 **Barry's Bay** Canada
68C2 **Barryville** USA
44B2 **Barsi** India
13E1 **Barsinghausen** Germany
56B3 **Barstow** USA
14C2 **Bar-sur-Aube** France
13C3 **Bar-sur-Seine** France
73G2 **Bartica** Guyana
40B1 **Bartın** Turkey
32D2 **Bartle Frere,Mt** Australia
56D3 **Bartlesville** USA
60D2 **Bartlett** USA
51D6 **Bartolomeu Dias** Mozambique
6D3 **Barton-upon-Humber** England
19E2 **Bartoszyce** Poland
72B2 **Barú** *Mt* Panama
42D4 **Barwāh** India
42C4 **Barwāni** India
34C1 **Barwon** *R* Australia
20H5 **Barysh** Russian Federation
66C1 **Basalt** USA
50B3 **Basankusu** Zaïre
Basel = Basle
16D2 **Basento** *R* Italy
26F4 **Bashi Chan** Philippines/Taiwan
20J5 **Bashkortostan** *Republic* Russian Federation
27F6 **Basilan** Philippines
27F6 **Basilan** *I* Philippines
7E4 **Basildon** England
58E2 **Basin** USA
7D4 **Basingstoke** England
56B2 **Basin Region** USA
65D1 **Baskatong, Réservoir** Canada
16B1 **Basle** Switzerland
41E3 **Basra** Iraq
13D3 **Bas-Rhin** *Department* France
30D3 **Bassac** *R* Cambodia
16C1 **Bassano** Italy
48C4 **Bassar** Togo
51D6 **Bassas da India** *I* Mozambique Channel
30A2 **Bassein** Burma
69E3 **Basse Terre** Guadeloupe
60D2 **Bassett** USA
48C4 **Bassila** Benin
66C2 **Bass Lake** USA
32D5 **Bass Str** Australia
13E1 **Bassum** Germany
12G7 **Båstad** Sweden
41F4 **Bastak** Iran
43E3 **Basti** India
16B2 **Bastia** Corsica, Italy
18B3 **Bastogne** Belgium
63D2 **Bastrop** Louisiana, USA
63C2 **Bastrop** Texas, USA
48C4 **Bata** Equatorial Guinea
27F5 **Bataan Pen** Philippines
69A2 **Batabanó, G de** Cuba
27E7 **Batakan** Indonesia
42D2 **Batāla** India
26C3 **Batang** China
50B3 **Batangafo** Central African Republic
27F5 **Batangas** Philippines
26F4 **Batan Is** Philippines
75C3 **Batatais** Brazil
65D2 **Batavia** USA
34D3 **Batemans Bay** Australia
67B2 **Batesburg** USA
63D1 **Batesville** Arkansas, USA
63E2 **Batesville** Mississippi, USA
65F1 **Bath** Canada
7C4 **Bath** England
65F2 **Bath** Maine, USA
65D2 **Bath** New York, USA
50B2 **Batha** *R* Chad
64C1 **Bathawana Mt** Canada
32D4 **Bathurst** Australia
55M5 **Bathurst** Canada
54F2 **Bathurst,C** Canada
32C2 **Bathurst I** Australia
54H2 **Bathurst I** Canada
54H3 **Bathurst Inlet** *B* Canada
48B4 **Batié** Burkina
41E4 **Bāţin, Wadi al** *Watercourse* Iraq
41F3 **Bāţlāq-e-Gavkhūnī** *Salt Flat* Iran
34C3 **Batlow** Australia
40D2 **Batman** Turkey
16B3 **Batna** Algeria
57D3 **Baton Rouge** USA
45C1 **Batroûn** Lebanon
30C3 **Battambang** Cambodia
44C4 **Batticaloa** Sri Lanka
44E4 **Batti Malv** *I* Nicobar Is, Indian Ocean
7E4 **Battle** England
57E2 **Battle Creek** USA
55N4 **Battle Harbour** Canada
58C2 **Battle Mountain** USA
21G7 **Batumi** Georgia
30C5 **Batu Pahat** Malaysia
45C2 **Bat Yam** Israel
32B1 **Baubau** Indonesia
48C3 **Bauchi** Nigeria
61E1 **Baudette** USA
55N4 **Bauld,C** Canada
25N4 **Baunt** Russian Federation
73J8 **Bauru** Brazil
75B2 **Baús** Brazil
18C2 **Bautzen** Germany
27E7 **Bawean** *I* Indonesia
49E2 **Bawîti** Egypt
48B3 **Bawku** Ghana
30B2 **Bawlake** Burma
34A2 **Bawlen** Australia
67B2 **Baxley** USA
70E2 **Bayamo** Cuba
43J2 **Bayana** India
26D2 **Bayandzürh** Mongolia
26C3 **Bayan Har Shan** *Mts* China
31A1 **Bayan Mod** China
31B1 **Bayan Obo** China
60C2 **Bayard** Nebraska, USA
62A2 **Bayard** New Mexico, USA
25N2 **Bayasgalant** Mongolia
40D1 **Bayburt** Turkey
57E2 **Bay City** Michigan, USA
63C3 **Bay City** Texas, USA
20M2 **Baydaratskaya Guba** *B* Russian Federation
50E3 **Baydhabo** Somalia
18C3 **Bayern** *State* Germany
14B2 **Bayeux** France
64A1 **Bayfield** USA
40C3 **Bāyir** Jordan
Baykal, Ozero *L* = **Baikal, L**
26D1 **Baykalskiy Khrebet** *Mts* Russian Federation
25L3 **Baykit** Russian Federation
25L5 **Baylik Shan** *Mts* China/Mongolia
20K5 **Baymak** Russian Federation
63E2 **Bay Minette** USA
14B3 **Bayonne** France
18C3 **Bayreuth** Germany
63E2 **Bay St Louis** USA
65E2 **Bay Shore** USA
65D1 **Bays,L of** Canada
26B2 **Baytik Shan** *Mts* China
Bayt Lahm = Bethlehem
63D3 **Baytown** USA
15B2 **Baza** Spain
19F3 **Bazaliya** Ukraine
21H7 **Bazar-Dyuzi** *Mt* Azerbaijan
51D6 **Bazaruto, Ilha** Mozambique
14B3 **Bazas** France
31B3 **Bazhong** China
45D1 **Bcharre** Lebanon
60C1 **Beach** USA
68C3 **Beach Haven** USA
7E4 **Beachy Head** England
68D2 **Beacon** USA
51E5 **Bealanana** Madagascar
58D2 **Bear** *R* USA
64A2 **Beardstown** USA
24C2 **Bear I** Barents Sea
58D2 **Bear L** USA
66B1 **Bear Valley** USA
69C3 **Beata, Cabo** *C* Dominican Republic
69C3 **Beata, Isla** Dominican Republic
56D2 **Beatrice** USA
8D2 **Beatrice** *Oilfield* N Sea
54F4 **Beatton River** Canada
56B3 **Beatty** USA
65D1 **Beattyville** Canada
74E8 **Beauchene Is** Falkland Islands
34D1 **Beaudesert** Australia
67B2 **Beaufort** USA
54D2 **Beaufort S** Canada/USA
47C3 **Beaufort West** South Africa
65E1 **Beauharnois** Canada
8C3 **Beauly** Scotland
7B3 **Beaumaris** Wales
59C4 **Beaumont** California, USA
57D3 **Beaumont** Texas, USA
14C2 **Beaune** France
14C2 **Beauvais** France
54D3 **Beaver** USA
59D3 **Beaver** Utah, USA
54G4 **Beaver** *R* Canada
54D3 **Beaver Creek** Canada
64B3 **Beaver Dam** Kentucky, USA
64B2 **Beaver Dam** Wisconsin, USA
58D1 **Beaverhead Mts** USA
64B1 **Beaver I** USA
63D1 **Beaver L** USA
42C3 **Beāwar** India
75C3 **Bebedouro** Brazil
7E3 **Beccles** England
17E1 **Bečej** Serbia, Yugoslavia
48B1 **Béchar** Algeria
57E3 **Beckley** USA
13E2 **Beckum** Germany
6D2 **Bedale** England
13E1 **Bederkesa** Germany
7D3 **Bedford** England
64B3 **Bedford** Indiana, USA
68A3 **Bedford** Pennsylvania, USA
7D3 **Bedford** *County* England
69M2 **Bedford Pt** Grenada
68B2 **Beech Creek** USA
54D2 **Beechey Pt** USA
34C3 **Beechworth** Australia
34D1 **Beenleigh** Australia
45C3 **Beer Menuha** Israel
45C4 **Beer Ora** Israel
40B3 **Beersheba** Israel
Be'er Sheva = Beersheba
45C3 **Be'er Sheva** *R* Israel
56D4 **Beeville** USA
50C3 **Befale** Zaïre
51E5 **Befandriana** Madagascar
34C3 **Bega** Australia
Begicheva, Ostrov *I* = **Bol'shoy Begichev, Ostrov**
15C1 **Begur, C de** Spain
41F3 **Behbehān** Iran
41F2 **Behshahr** Iran
42B2 **Behsud** Afghanistan
26F2 **Bei'an** China
31B5 **Beihai** China
31D2 **Beijing** China
30E1 **Beiliu** China
31B4 **Beipan Jiang** *R* China
31E1 **Beipiao** China
Beira = Sofala
40C3 **Beirut** Lebanon
26C2 **Bei Shan** *Mts* China
47E1 **Beitbridge** Zimbabwe
45C2 **Beit ed Dīne** Lebanon
8C4 **Beith** Scotland
45C3 **Beit Jala** Israel
28A2 **Beizhen** China
15A2 **Beja** Portugal
16B3 **Béja** Tunisia
15C2 **Bejaïa** Algeria
15A1 **Béjar** Spain
41G3 **Bejestān** Iran
19E3 **Békéscsaba** Hungary
51E6 **Bekily** Madagascar
43E3 **Bela** India
42B3 **Bela** Pakistan
68B3 **Bel Air** USA
44B2 **Belampalli** India
27F6 **Belang** Indonesia
27C6 **Belangpidie** Indonesia
20D5 **Belarus** *Republic* Europe
Belau = Palau
75A3 **Béla Vista** Brazil/Paraguay
47E2 **Bela Vista** Mozambique
27C6 **Belawan** Indonesia
20K4 **Belaya** *R* Russian Federation
19G3 **Belaya Tserkov'** Ukraine
55J2 **Belcher Chan** Canada
55L4 **Belcher Is** Canada
42B1 **Belchiragh** Afghanistan
20J5 **Belebey** Russian Federation
50E3 **Beledweyne** Somalia
73J4 **Belém** Brazil
72C3 **Belén** Colombia
75A3 **Belén** Paraguay
56C3 **Belen** USA
33F2 **Bélep, Îles** Nouvelle Calédonie
16B3 **Belezma, Mts de** Algeria
9C2 **Belfast** Northern Ireland

Belfast

Black

47E2 **Belfast** South Africa
9C2 **Belfast Lough** *Estuary* Northern Ireland
60C1 **Belfield** USA
50D2 **Bēlfodiyo** Ethiopia
6D2 **Belford** England
14D2 **Belfort** France
44A2 **Belgaum** India
18A2 **Belgium** *Kingdom* NW Europe
21F5 **Belgorod** Russian Federation
21E6 **Belgorod Dnestrovskiy** Ukraine
58D1 **Belgrade** USA
17E2 **Belgrade** Serbia, Yugoslavia
49D2 **Bel Hedan** Libya
27D7 **Belitung** *I* Indonesia
70D3 **Belize** Belize
70D3 **Belize** *Republic* Central America
25P2 **Bel'kovskiy, Ostrov** *I* Russian Federation
14C2 **Bellac** France
54F4 **Bella Coola** Canada
63C3 **Bellaire** USA
44B2 **Bellary** India
34C1 **Bellata** Australia
68B2 **Bellefonte** USA
56C2 **Belle Fourche** USA
60C2 **Belle Fourche** *R* USA
14D2 **Bellegarde** France
13B4 **Bellegarde** France
67B3 **Belle Glade** USA
55N4 **Belle I** Canada
14B2 **Belle-Ile** *I* France
55N4 **Belle Isle,Str of** Canada
55L5 **Belleville** Canada
64B3 **Belleville** Illinois, USA
61D3 **Belleville** Kansas, USA
58D2 **Bellevue** Idaho, USA
64A2 **Bellevue** Iowa, USA
58B1 **Bellevue** Washington, USA
34D2 **Bellingen** Australia
6C2 **Bellingham** England
56A2 **Bellingham** USA
76G2 **Bellingshausen** *Base* Antarctica
76G3 **Bellingshausen S** Antarctica
16B1 **Bellinzona** Switzerland
72C2 **Bello** Colombia
33E3 **Bellona Reefs** Nouvelle Calédonie
66B1 **Bellota** USA
65E2 **Bellows Falls** USA
55K3 **Bell Pen** Canada
16C1 **Belluno** Italy
74D4 **Bell Ville** Argentina
68B1 **Belmont** USA
73L7 **Belmonte** Brazil
70D3 **Belmopan** Belize
26F1 **Belogorsk** Russian Federation
51E6 **Beloha** Madagascar
73K7 **Belo Horizonte** Brazil
61D3 **Beloit** Kansas, USA
57E2 **Beloit** Wisconsin, USA
20E3 **Belomorsk** Russian Federation
20K5 **Beloretsk** Russian Federation
Belorussia = Belarus
51E5 **Belo-Tsiribihina** Madagascar
Beloye More *S* **= White Sea**
20F3 **Beloye Ozero** *L* Russian Federation
20F3 **Belozersk** Russian Federation
7D3 **Belper** England
64C3 **Belpre** USA
34A2 **Beltana** Australia
63C2 **Belton** USA
19F3 **Bel'tsy** Moldavia
24K5 **Belukha** *Mt* Russian Federation
20H2 **Belush'ye** Russian Federation
64B2 **Belvidere** Illinois, USA
68C2 **Belvidere** New Jersey, USA
24J2 **Belyy, Ostrov** *I* Russian Federation
51B4 **Bembe** Angola
48C3 **Bembéréké** Benin
57D2 **Bemidji** USA
63E1 **Bemis** USA
50C4 **Bena Dibele** Zaïre
34C3 **Benalla** Australia
8C3 **Ben Attow** *Mt* Scotland
15A1 **Benavente** Spain
8B3 **Benbecula** *I* Scotland
32A4 **Bencubbin** Australia
56A2 **Bend** USA
8C3 **Ben Dearg** *Mt* Scotland
50E3 **Bendarbeyla** Somalia
19F3 **Bendery** Moldavia
32D4 **Bendigo** Australia
18C3 **Benešov** Czech Republic
16C2 **Benevento** Italy
39G4 **Bengal,B of** Asia
49D1 **Ben Gardane** Tunisia
31D3 **Bengbu** China
49E1 **Benghazi** Libya
27D7 **Bengkulu** Indonesia
51B5 **Benguela** Angola
40B3 **Benha** Egypt
8C2 **Ben Hope** *Mt* Scotland
50C3 **Beni** Zaïre
72E6 **Béni** *R* Bolivia
48B1 **Beni Abbès** Algeria
15C1 **Benicarló** Spain
15B2 **Benidorm** Spain
15C2 **Beni Mansour** Algeria
49F2 **Beni Mazâr** Egypt
48B1 **Beni Mellal** Morocco
48C4 **Benin** *Republic* Africa
48C4 **Benin City** Nigeria
15B2 **Beni-Saf** Algeria
49F2 **Beni Suef** Egypt
60C3 **Benkelman** USA
8C2 **Ben Kilbreck** *Mt* Scotland
10C2 **Ben Lawers** *Mt* Scotland
8D3 **Ben Macdui** *Mt* Scotland
8B3 **Ben More** Scotland
8C2 **Ben More Assynt** *Mt* Scotland
35B2 **Benmore,L** New Zealand
25R2 **Bennetta, Ostrov** *I* Russian Federation
8C3 **Ben Nevis** *Mt* Scotland
65E2 **Bennington** USA
45C2 **Bennt Jbail** Lebanon
50B3 **Bénoué** *R* Cameroon
13E3 **Bensheim** Germany
56B3 **Benson** Arizona, USA
61D1 **Benson** Minnesota, USA
27F7 **Benteng** Indonesia
50C3 **Bentiu** Sudan
75A2 **Bento Gomes** *R* Brazil
63D2 **Benton** Arkansas, USA
66C2 **Benton** California, USA
64B3 **Benton** Kentucky, USA
64B2 **Benton Harbor** USA
48C4 **Benue** *R* Nigeria
8C3 **Ben Wyvis** *Mt* Scotland
31E1 **Benxi** China
Beograd = Belgrade
43E4 **Beohāri** India
28C4 **Beppu** Japan
17D2 **Berat** Albania
27G7 **Berau, Teluk** *B* Indonesia
50D2 **Berber** Sudan
50E2 **Berbera** Somalia
50B3 **Berbérati** Central African Republic
19F3 **Berdichev** Ukraine
21F6 **Berdyansk** Ukraine
64C3 **Berea** USA
48B4 **Berekum** Ghana
66B2 **Berenda** USA
40C5 **Berenice** Egypt
54J4 **Berens** *R* Canada
54J4 **Berens River** Canada
61D2 **Beresford** USA
19E3 **Berettyóújfalu** Hungary
19E2 **Bereza** Belarus
19E3 **Berezhany** Ukraine
19F2 **Berezina** *R* Belarus
20G3 **Bereznik** Russian Federation
20K4 **Berezniki** Russian Federation
21E6 **Berezovka** Ukraine
20L3 **Berezovo** Russian Federation
40A2 **Bergama** Turkey
16B1 **Bergamo** Italy
12F6 **Bergen** Norway
68B1 **Bergen** USA
13C2 **Bergen op Zoom** Netherlands
14C3 **Bergerac** France
13D2 **Bergisch-Gladbach** Germany
44C2 **Berhampur** India
25S4 **Beringa, Ostrov** *I* Russian Federation
25T3 **Beringovskiy** Russian Federation
37K2 **Bering S** Russian Federation/USA
76C6 **Bering Str** Russian Federation/USA
41G4 **Berīzak** Iran
15B2 **Berja** Spain
13D1 **Berkel** *R* Germany/ Netherlands
56A3 **Berkeley** USA
68A3 **Berkeley Spring** USA
7D4 **Berkhamsted** England
76F2 **Berkner I** Antarctica
17E2 **Berkovitsa** Bulgaria
7D4 **Berkshire** *County* England
68D1 **Berkshire Hills** USA
18C2 **Berlin** Germany
18C2 **Berlin** *State* Germany
65E2 **Berlin** New Hampshire, USA
72F8 **Bermejo** Bolivia
74E3 **Bermejo** *R* Argentina
53M5 **Bermuda** *I* Atlantic Ocean
Bern = Berne
62A1 **Bernalillo** USA
75B4 **Bernardo de Irigoyen** Argentina
68C2 **Bernardsville** USA
18C2 **Bernburg** Germany
16B1 **Berne** Switzerland
8B3 **Berneray, I** Scotland
55K2 **Bernier B** Canada
18C3 **Berounka** *R* Czech Republic
34B2 **Berri** Australia
48C1 **Berriane** Algeria
14C2 **Berry** *Region* France
66A1 **Berryessa,L** USA
57F4 **Berry Is** The Bahamas
68B3 **Berryville** USA
47B2 **Berseba** Namibia
60B3 **Berthoud P** USA
50B3 **Bertoua** Cameroon
33G1 **Beru** *I* Kiribati
65D2 **Berwick** USA
6C2 **Berwick-upon-Tweed** England
7C3 **Berwyn Mts** Wales
51E5 **Besalampy** Madagascar
14D2 **Besançon** France
19E3 **Beskidy Zachodnie** *Mts* Poland
40C2 **Besni** Turkey
45C3 **Besor** *R* Israel
67A2 **Bessemer** Alabama, USA
64B1 **Bessemer** Michigan, USA
51E5 **Betafo** Madagascar
15A1 **Betanzos** Spain
45C3 **Bet Guvrin** Israel
47D2 **Bethal** South Africa
47B2 **Bethanie** Namibia
61E2 **Bethany** Missouri, USA
63C1 **Bethany** Oklahoma, USA
54B3 **Bethel** Alaska, USA
68D2 **Bethel** Connecticut, USA
64C2 **Bethel Park** USA
65D3 **Bethesda** USA
45C3 **Bethlehem** Israel
47D2 **Bethlehem** South Africa
65D2 **Bethlehem** USA
47D3 **Bethulie** South Africa
14C1 **Béthune** France
51E6 **Betioky** Madagascar
34B1 **Betoota** Australia
50B3 **Betou** Congo
39E1 **Betpak Dala** *Steppe* Kazakhstan
51E6 **Betroka** Madagascar
55M5 **Betsiamites** Canada
64A2 **Bettendorf** USA
43E3 **Bettiah** India
42D4 **Betūl** India
13C2 **Betuwe** *Region* Netherlands
42D3 **Betwa** *R* India
7C3 **Betws-y-coed** Wales
13D2 **Betzdorf** Germany
7D3 **Beverley** England
68E1 **Beverly** USA
66C3 **Beverly Hills** USA
7E4 **Bexhill** England
40B2 **Bey Dağları** Turkey
48B4 **Beyla** Guinea
44B3 **Beypore** India
Beyrouth = Beirut
40B2 **Beyşehir** Turkey
21E8 **Beyşehir Gölü** *L* Turkey
45C2 **Beyt Shean** Israel
20F4 **Bezhetsk** Russian Federation
14C3 **Béziers** France
41G2 **Bezmein** Turkmenistan
26D1 **Beznosova** Russian Federation
43F3 **Bhadgaon** Nepal
44C2 **Bhadrāchalam** India
43F4 **Bhadrakh** India
44B3 **Bhadra Res** India
44B3 **Bhadrāvati** India
42B3 **Bhag** Pakistan
43F3 **Bhāgalpur** India
42C2 **Bhakkar** Pakistan
42D4 **Bhandāra** India
42D3 **Bharatpur** India
42C4 **Bharūch** India
43F4 **Bhātiāpāra Ghat** Bangladesh
42C2 **Bhatinda** India
44A3 **Bhatkal** India
43F4 **Bhātpāra** India
42C4 **Bhāvnagar** India
43E5 **Bhawānipatna** India
42C2 **Bhera** Pakistan
43E3 **Bheri** *R* Nepal
43E4 **Bhilai** India
42C3 **Bhīlwāra** India
44C2 **Bhīmavaram** India
42D3 **Bhind** India
42D3 **Bhiwāni** India
44B2 **Bhongir** India
42D4 **Bhopāl** India
43F4 **Bhubaneshwar** India
42B4 **Bhuj** India
42D4 **Bhusāwal** India
39H3 **Bhutan** *Kingdom* Asia
27G7 **Biak** *I* Indonesia
19E2 **Biala Podlaska** Poland
18D2 **Białogard** Poland
19E2 **Bialystok** Poland
12A1 **Biargtangar** *C* Iceland
41G2 **Bīārjmand** Iran
14B3 **Biarritz** France
40B4 **Biba** Egypt
29E2 **Bibai** Japan
51B5 **Bibala** Angola
18B3 **Biberach** Germany
48B4 **Bibiani** Ghana
17F1 **Bicaz** Romania
7D4 **Bicester** England
59D3 **Bicknell** USA
48C4 **Bida** Nigeria
44B2 **Bīdar** India
41G5 **Bidbid** Oman
65E2 **Biddeford** USA
7C6 **Bideford** England
7B4 **Bideford B** England
48C2 **Bidon 5** Algeria
19E2 **Biebrza** *R* Poland
16B1 **Biel** Switzerland
18D2 **Bielawa** Poland
18B2 **Bielefeld** Germany
16B1 **Biella** Italy
19E2 **Bielsk Podlaski** Poland
30D3 **Bien Hoa** Vietnam
55L4 **Bienville, Lac** Canada
16C2 **Biferno** *R* Italy
40A1 **Biga** Turkey
17F3 **Bigadiç** Turkey
58D1 **Big Belt Mts** USA
62B3 **Big Bend Nat Pk** USA
63E2 **Big Black** *R* USA
61D2 **Big Blue** *R* USA
67B3 **Big Cypress Swamp** USA
54D3 **Big Delta** USA
8D4 **Biggar** Scotland
54H4 **Biggar Kindersley** Canada
34D1 **Biggenden** Australia
7D3 **Biggleswade** England
58D1 **Big Hole** *R* USA
60B1 **Bighorn** *R* USA
60B1 **Bighorn L** USA
60B2 **Bighorn Mts** USA
48C4 **Bight of Benin** *B* W Africa
48C4 **Bight of Biafra** *B* Cameroon
55L3 **Big I** Canada
62B2 **Big Lake** USA
48A3 **Bignona** Senegal
59C3 **Big Pine** USA
67B4 **Big Pine Key** USA
66C3 **Big Pine Mt** USA
64B2 **Big Rapids** USA
54H4 **Big River** Canada
58D1 **Big Sandy** USA
61D2 **Big Sioux** *R* USA
66D1 **Big Smokey V** USA
56C3 **Big Spring** USA
60C2 **Big Springs** USA
61D1 **Big Stone City** USA
64C3 **Big Stone Gap** USA
66B2 **Big Sur** USA
58E1 **Big Timber** USA
55J4 **Big Trout L** Canada
55K4 **Big Trout Lake** Canada
16D2 **Bihać** Bosnia-Herzegovina
43F3 **Bihār** India
43F4 **Bihār** *State* India
50D4 **Biharamulo** Tanzania
21C6 **Bihor** *Mt* Romania
48A3 **Bijagós, Arquipélago dos** *Is* Guinea-Bissau
44B2 **Bijāpur** India
44C2 **Bījāpur** India
41E2 **Bījār** Iran
43E3 **Bijauri** Nepal
17D2 **Bijeljina** Bosnia-Herzegovina
31B4 **Bijie** China
42D3 **Bijnor** India
42C3 **Bijnot** Pakistan
42C3 **Bīkāner** India
45C2 **Bikfaya** Lebanon
26G2 **Bikin** Russian Federation
50B4 **Bikoro** Zaïre
Bilbo = Bilbao
42C3 **Bilāra** India
42D2 **Bilāspur** India
43E4 **Bilāspur** India
30B3 **Bilauktaung Range** *Mts* Burma/Thailand
15B1 **Bilbao** Spain
45A3 **Bilbeis** Egypt
18D3 **Bílé** *R* Czech Republic/ Slovakia
17D2 **Bileća** Bosnia-Herzegovina
40B1 **Bilecik** Turkey
50C3 **Bili** *R* Zaïre
25S3 **Bilibino** Russian Federation
56C2 **Billings** USA
50B2 **Bilma** Niger
57E3 **Biloxi** USA
50C2 **Biltine** Chad
67C3 **Bimini Is** Bahamas
42D4 **Bīna-Etawa** India
51D5 **Bindura** Zimbabwe
51C5 **Binga** Zimbabwe
51D5 **Binga, Mt** Mozambique/ Zimbabwe
34D1 **Bingara** Australia
18B3 **Bingen** Germany
65F1 **Bingham** USA
57F2 **Binghamton** USA
40D2 **Bingöl** Turkey
31D3 **Binhai** China
15C2 **Binibeca, Cabo** *C* Spain
27D6 **Bintan** *I* Indonesia
27E6 **Bintulu** Malaysia
74B5 **Bió Bió** *R* Chile
48C4 **Bioco** *I* Equatorial Guinea
44B2 **Bīr** India
49E2 **Bîr Abu Husein** *Well* Egypt
49E2 **Bi'r al Harash** *Well* Libya
50C2 **Birao** Central African Republic
43F3 **Biratnagar** Nepal
34B3 **Birchip** Australia
61E1 **Birch L** USA
54G4 **Birch Mts** Canada
55J4 **Bird** Canada
32C3 **Birdsville** Australia
32C2 **Birdum** Australia
45A4 **Bîr el 'Agramîya** *Well* Egypt
45B3 **Bîr el Duweidâr** *Well* Egypt
43E3 **Birganj** Nepal
45B3 **Bîr Gifgâfa** *Well* Egypt
45A4 **Bîr Gindali** *Well* Egypt
45B3 **Bîr Hasana** *Well* Egypt
75B3 **Birigui** Brazil
45D1 **Bīrīn** Syria
41G3 **Bīrjand** Iran
40B4 **Birkat Qârûn** *L* Egypt
13D3 **Birkenfeld** Germany
7C3 **Birkenhead** England
21D6 **Bîrlad** Romania
45B3 **Bîr Lahfân** *Well* Egypt
7C3 **Birmingham** England
57E3 **Birmingham** USA
49E2 **Bîr Misâha** *Well* Egypt
48A2 **Bir Moghrein** Mauritius
48C3 **Birnin-Kebbi** Nigeria
26G2 **Birobidzhan** Russian Federation
9C3 **Birr** Irish Republic
15C2 **Bir Rabalou** Algeria
34C1 **Birrie** *R* Australia
8D2 **Birsay** Scotland
20K4 **Birsk** Russian Federation
49E2 **Bîr Tarfâwi** *Well* Egypt
45B4 **Bîr Udelb** *Well* Egypt
25L4 **Biryusa** *R* Russian Federation
12J7 **Biržai** Lithuania
48B2 **Bir Zreigat** *Well* Mauritius
43K1 **Bisalpur** India
59E4 **Bisbee** USA
14A2 **Biscay,B of** France/Spain
67B3 **Biscayne B** USA
13D3 **Bischwiller** France
64C1 **Biscotasi L** Canada
31B4 **Bishan** China
39F1 **Bishkek** Kirgizia
56B3 **Bishop** USA
6D2 **Bishop Auckland** England
7C3 **Bishops Castle** England
7E4 **Bishop's Stortford** England
43E4 **Bishrāmpur** India
48C1 **Biskra** Algeria
56C2 **Bismarck** USA
32D1 **Bismarck Arch** Papua New Guinea
32D1 **Bismarck Range** *Mts* Papua New Guinea
32D1 **Bismarck S** Papua New Guinea
41E3 **Bīsotūn** Iran
48A3 **Bissau** Guinea-Bissau
57D1 **Bissett** Canada
54G4 **Bistcho L** Canada
17F1 **Bistrita** *R* Romania
50B3 **Bitam** Gabon
18B3 **Bitburg** Germany
13D3 **Bitche** France
40D2 **Bitlis** Turkey
17E2 **Bitola** Macedonia, Yugoslavia
18C2 **Bitterfeld** Germany
47B3 **Bitterfontein** South Africa
40B3 **Bitter Lakes** Egypt
56B2 **Bitteroot Range** *Mts* USA
48D3 **Biu** Nigeria
29D3 **Biwa-ko** *L* Japan
50E2 **Biyo Kaboba** Ethiopia
24K4 **Biysk** Russian Federation
16B3 **Bizerte** Tunisia
16D1 **Bjelovar** Croatia
48B2 **Bj Flye Ste Marie** Algeria
Bjørnøya *I* **= Bear I**
63D1 **Black** *R* USA

Blackall Breda

32D3 **Blackall** Australia
64B1 **Black B** Canada
6C3 **Blackburn** England
54D3 **Blackburn, Mt** USA
59D4 **Black Canyon City** USA
61E1 **Blackduck** USA
58D1 **Black Eagle** USA
58D2 **Blackfoot** USA
58D1 **Blackfoot** *R* USA
9B3 **Black Hd** *Pt* Irish Republic
54H5 **Black Hills** USA
8C3 **Black Isle** *Pen* Scotland
69Q2 **Blackman's** Barbados
59D3 **Black Mts** USA
7C4 **Black Mts** Wales
47B1 **Black Nosob** *R* Namibia
6C3 **Blackpool** England
69H1 **Black River** Jamaica
64A2 **Black River Falls** USA
56B2 **Black Rock Desert** USA
21D7 **Black S** Asia/Europe
64C3 **Blacksburg** USA
34D2 **Black Sugarloaf** *Mt* Australia
48B4 **Black Volta** *R* W Africa
63E2 **Black Warrior** *R* USA
7E4 **Blackwater** *R* England
10B3 **Blackwater** *R* Irish Republic
63C1 **Blackwell** USA
17E2 **Blagoevgrad** Bulgaria
25O4 **Blagoveshchensk** Russian Federation
58D1 **Blaikiston,Mt** Canada
58B1 **Blaine** USA
61D2 **Blair** USA
8D3 **Blair Atholl** Scotland
8D3 **Blairgowrie** Scotland
67C2 **Blakely** USA
74D5 **Blanca, Bahía** *B* Argentina
62A1 **Blanca Peak** *Mt* USA
16B3 **Blanc, C** Tunisia
34A1 **Blanche** *L* Australia
16B1 **Blanc, Mont** *Mt* France/Italy
56A2 **Blanco,C** USA
55N4 **Blanc Sablon** Canada
7C4 **Blandford Forum** England
59E3 **Blanding** USA
13B2 **Blankenberge** Belgium
69E4 **Blanquilla, Isla** Venezuela
51D5 **Blantyre** Malawi
9A3 **Blasket Sd** Irish Republic
14B2 **Blaye** France
34C2 **Blayney** Australia
33G5 **Blenheim** New Zealand
15C2 **Blida** Algeria
64C1 **Blind River** Canada
34A2 **Blinman** Australia
65E2 **Block I** USA
68E2 **Block Island Sd** USA
47D2 **Bloemfontein** South Africa
47D2 **Bloemhof** South Africa
47D2 **Bloemhof Dam** *Res* South Africa
73G3 **Blommesteinmeer** *L* Surinam
12A1 **Blönduós** Iceland
64B3 **Bloomfield** Indiana, USA
61E2 **Bloomfield** Iowa, USA
61D2 **Bloomfield** Nebraska,USA
62A1 **Bloomfield** New Mexico, USA
64B2 **Bloomington** Illinois, USA
64B3 **Bloomington** Indiana, USA
61E2 **Bloomington** Minnesota, USA
68B2 **Bloomsburg** USA
68B2 **Blossburg** USA
55Q3 **Blosseville Kyst** *Mts* Greenland
47D1 **Blouberg** *Mt* South Africa
18B3 **Bludenz** Austria
57E3 **Bluefield** USA
72B1 **Bluefields** Nicaragua
60D2 **Blue Hill** USA
68A2 **Blue Knob** *Mt* USA
69J1 **Blue Mountain Peak** *Mt* Jamaica
68B2 **Blue Mt** USA
34D2 **Blue Mts** Australia
56A2 **Blue Mts** USA
69J1 **Blue Mts, The** Jamaica
50D2 **Blue Nile** *R* Sudan
54G3 **Bluenose L** Canada
67C2 **Blue Ridge** USA
57E3 **Blue Ridge Mts** USA
9C2 **Blue Stack** *Mt* Irish Republic
35A3 **Bluff** New Zealand
59E3 **Bluff** USA
32A4 **Bluff Knoll** *Mt* Australia
74G3 **Blumenau** Brazil
60D2 **Blunt** USA
58B2 **Bly** USA
6D2 **Blyth** England
56B3 **Blythe** USA
57E3 **Blytheville** USA
48A4 **Bo** Sierra Leone
27F5 **Boac** Philippines
75D1 **Boa Nova** Brazil
64C2 **Boardman** USA
72F3 **Boa Vista** Brazil
48A4 **Boa Vista** *I* Cape Verde
30E1 **Bobai** China
44C2 **Bobbili** India
48B3 **Bobo Dioulasso** Burkina
19G2 **Bobrovica** Ukraine
20D5 **Bobruysk** Belarus
67B4 **Boca Chica Key** *I* USA
72E5 **Bôca do Acre** Brazil
75D2 **Bocaiúva** Brazil
50B3 **Bocaranga** Central African Republic
67B3 **Boca Raton** USA
19E3 **Bochnia** Poland
18B2 **Bocholt** Germany
13D2 **Bochum** Germany
51B5 **Bocoio** Angola
50B3 **Boda** Central African Republic
25N4 **Bodaybo** Russian Federation
59B3 **Bodega Head** *Pt* USA
50B2 **Bodélé** *Desert Region* Chad
12J5 **Boden** Sweden
9C3 **Boderg, L** Irish Republic
44B2 **Bodhan** India
44B3 **Bodināyakkanūr** India
7B4 **Bodmin** England
7B4 **Bodmin Moor** *Upland* England
12G5 **Bodø** Norway
17F3 **Bodrum** Turkey
50C4 **Boende** Zaïre
48A3 **Boffa** Guinea
30B2 **Bogale** Burma
63E2 **Bogalusa** USA
34C2 **Bogan** *R* Australia
48B3 **Bogande** Burkina
40C2 **Boğazlıyan** Turkey
20L4 **Bogdanovich** Russian Federation
26B2 **Bogda Shan** *Mt* China
47B2 **Bogenfels** Namibia
34D1 **Boggabilla** Australia
34C2 **Boggabri** Australia
7D4 **Bognor Regis** England
34C3 **Bogong** *Mt* Australia
27D7 **Bogor** Indonesia
25Q4 **Bogorodskoye** Russian Federation
20J4 **Bogorodskoye** Russian Federation
72D3 **Bogotá** Colombia
25K4 **Bogotol** Russian Federation
43F4 **Bogra** Bangladesh
31D2 **Bo Hai** *B* China
13B3 **Bohain-en-Vermandois** France
31D2 **Bohai Wan** *B* China
18C3 **Bohmer-wald** *Upland* Germany
27F6 **Bohol** *I* Philippines
27F6 **Bohol S** Philippines
75E1 **Boipeba, Ilha de** Brazil
75B2 **Bois** *R* Brazil
64C1 **Bois Blanc I** USA
56B2 **Boise** USA
62B1 **Boise City** USA
54F3 **Bois, Lac des** Canada
60C1 **Boissevain** Canada
48A2 **Bojador,C** Morocco
27F5 **Bojeador, C** Philippines
41G2 **Bojnürd** Iran
48A3 **Boké** Guinea
34C1 **Bokhara** *R* Australia
12F7 **Boknafjord** *Inlet* Norway
50B4 **Boko** Congo
30C3 **Bokor** Cambodia
50B2 **Bokoro** Chad
50C4 **Bokungu** Zaïre
50B2 **Bol** Chad
48A3 **Bolama** Guinea-Bissau
14C2 **Bolbec** France
48B4 **Bole** Ghana
18D2 **Bolesławiec** Poland
48B3 **Bolgatanga** Ghana
21D6 **Bolgrad** Ukraine
63D1 **Bolivar** Missouri, USA
63E1 **Bolivar** Tennessee, USA
72D2 **Bolívar** *Mt* Venezuela
72E7 **Bolivia** *Republic* S America
12H6 **Bollnäs** Sweden
34C1 **Bollon** Australia
50B4 **Bolobo** Zaïre
16C2 **Bologna** Italy
20E4 **Bologoye** Russian Federation
26G1 **Bolon'** Russian Federation
26G2 **Bolon', Oz** *L* Russian Federation
16C2 **Bolsena, L di** Italy
25M2 **Bol'shevik, Ostrov** *I* Russian Federation
20J2 **Bol'shezemel'skaya Tundra** *Plain* Russian Federation
25S3 **Bol'shoy Anyuy** *R* Russian Federation
25N2 **Bol'shoy Begichev, Ostrov** *I* Russian Federation
21H5 **Bol'shoy Irgiz** *R* Russian Federation
28C2 **Bol'shoy Kamen** Russian Federation
25Q2 **Bol'shoy Lyakhovskiy, Ostrov** *I* Russian Federation
21H6 **Bol'shoy Uzen** *R* Kazakhstan
56C4 **Bolson de Mapimí** *Desert* Mexico
7C3 **Bolton** England
40B1 **Bolu** Turkey
12A1 **Bolungarvik** Iceland
9A4 **Bolus Hd** *Pt* Irish Republic
40B2 **Bolvadin** Turkey
16C1 **Bolzano** Italy
50B4 **Boma** Zaïre
32D4 **Bombala** Australia
44A2 **Bombay** India
51E5 **Bombetoka, Baie de** *B* Madagascar
50D3 **Bombo** Uganda
75C2 **Bom Despacho** Brazil
43G3 **Bomdila** India
48A4 **Bomi Hills** Liberia
73K6 **Bom Jesus da Lapa** Brazil
25O4 **Bomnak** Russian Federation
50C3 **Bomokāndi** *R* Zaïre
50C3 **Bomu** *R* Central African Republic/Zaïre
65D3 **Bon Air** USA
69D4 **Bonaire** *I* Caribbean Sea
70D3 **Bonanza** Nicaragua
55N5 **Bonavista** Canada
16C3 **Bon, C** Tunisia
50C3 **Bondo** Zaïre
48B4 **Bondoukou** Ivory Coast
Bône = 'Annaba
60D2 **Bonesteel** USA
73G3 **Bonfim** Guyana
50C3 **Bongandanga** Zaïre
50C3 **Bongo, Massif des** *Upland* Central African Republic
50B2 **Bongor** Chad
63C2 **Bonham** USA
16B2 **Bonifacio** Corsica, France
16B2 **Bonifacio,Str of** *Chan* Corsica, France/Sardinia, Italy
Bonin Is = Ogasawara Gunto
67B3 **Bonita Springs** USA
75A3 **Bonito** Brazil
18B2 **Bonn** Germany
58C1 **Bonners Ferry** USA
48C4 **Bonny** Nigeria
32A1 **Bonthain** Indonesia
48A4 **Bonthe** Sierra Leone
50E2 **Booaaso** Somalia
34B2 **Booligal** Australia
34D1 **Boonah** Australia
62B1 **Boone** Colorado, USA
61E2 **Boone** Iowa, USA
67B1 **Boone** North Carolina, USA
65D2 **Boonville** USA
34C2 **Boorowa** Australia
55J2 **Boothia,G of** Canada
55J2 **Boothia Pen** Canada
7C3 **Bootle** England
50B4 **Booué** Gabon
47C2 **Bophuthatswana** *Self governing homeland* South Africa
62B3 **Boquillas** Mexico
50D3 **Bor** Sudan
40B2 **Bor** Turkey
17E2 **Bor** Serbia, Yugoslavia
56B2 **Borah Peak** *Mt* USA
12G7 **Borås** Sweden
41F4 **Borāzjān** Iran
14B3 **Bordeaux** France
54G2 **Borden I** Canada
55K2 **Borden Pen** Canada
68C2 **Bordentown** USA
8D4 **Borders** *Region* Scotland
34B3 **Bordertown** Australia
15C2 **Bordj bou Arréidj** Algeria
48C2 **Bordj Omar Driss** Algeria
Borgå = Porvoo
55Q3 **Borgarnes** Iceland
56C3 **Borger** USA
12H7 **Borgholm** Sweden
19E3 **Borislav** Ukraine
21G5 **Borisoglebsk** Russian Federation
20D5 **Borisov** Belarus
21F5 **Borisovka** Russian Federation
75A4 **Borja** Paraguay
50B2 **Borkou** *Desert Region* Chad
13D1 **Borkum** *I* Germany
12H6 **Borlänge** Sweden
27E6 **Borneo** *I* Indonesia/Malaysia
12H7 **Bornholm** *I* Denmark
17F3 **Bornova** Turkey
48D3 **Bornu** *Region* Nigeria
50C3 **Boro** *R* Sudan
25P3 **Borogontsy** Russian Federation
48B3 **Boromo** Burkina
66D3 **Boron** USA
20E4 **Borovichi** Russian Federation
32C2 **Borroloola** Australia
17E1 **Borsa** Romania
41F3 **Borūjen** Iran
41E3 **Borūjerd** Iran
18D2 **Bory Tucholskie** *Region* Poland
19G2 **Borzna** Ukraine
25N4 **Borzya** Russian Federation
31B5 **Bose** China
47D2 **Boshof** South Africa
17D2 **Bosna** *R* Bosnia-Herzegovina
17D2 **Bosnia-Herzegovina** *Republic* Europe
29D3 **Bōsō-hantō** *B* Japan
Bosporus = Karadeniz Boğazi
15C2 **Bosquet** Algeria
50B3 **Bossangoa** Central African Republic
50B3 **Bossèmbélé** Central African Republic
63D2 **Bossier City** USA
24K5 **Bosten Hu** *L* China
7D3 **Boston** England
57F2 **Boston** USA
57D3 **Boston Mts** USA
42C4 **Botād** India
17E2 **Botevgrad** Bulgaria
47D2 **Bothaville** South Africa
20B3 **Bothnia,G of** Finland/Sweden
51C6 **Botletli** *R* Botswana
21D6 **Botoşani** Romania
51C6 **Botswana** *Republic* Africa
16D3 **Botte Donato** *Mt* Italy
60C1 **Bottineau** USA
13D2 **Bottrop** Germany
75C3 **Botucatu** Brazil
75D1 **Botuporã** Brazil
55N5 **Botwood** Canada
48B4 **Bouaké** Ivory Coast
50B3 **Bouar** Central African Republic
48B1 **Bouârfa** Morocco
50B3 **Bouca** Central African Republic
15C2 **Boufarik** Algeria
33E1 **Bougainville** *I* Papua New Guinea
16B3 **Bougaroun, C** Algeria
Bougie = Bejaïa
48B3 **Bougouni** Mali
15A2 **Bouhalla, Djebel** *Mt* Morocco
13C3 **Bouillon** France
15C2 **Bouïra** Algeria
48B2 **Bou Izakarn** Morocco
13D3 **Boulay-Moselle** France
56C2 **Boulder** Colorado, USA
58D1 **Boulder** Montana, USA
56B3 **Boulder City** USA
66A2 **Boulder Creek** USA
14C1 **Boulogne** France
50B3 **Boumba** *R* Cameroon/Central African Republic
48B4 **Bouna** Ivory Coast
56B3 **Boundary Peak** *Mt* USA
48B4 **Boundiali** Ivory Coast
58D2 **Bountiful** USA
33G5 **Bounty Is** New Zealand
33F3 **Bourail** New Caledonia
13C4 **Bourbonne-les-Bains** France
48B3 **Bourem** Mali
14D2 **Bourg** France
14D2 **Bourg de Péage** France
14C2 **Bourges** France
14C3 **Bourg-Madame** France
14C2 **Bourgogne** *Region* France
34C2 **Bourke** Australia
7D4 **Bournemouth** England
15C2 **Bou Saâda** Algeria
50B2 **Bousso** Chad
48A3 **Boutilimit** Mauritius
52J7 **Bouvet I** Atlantic Ocean
60C1 **Bowbells** USA
32D2 **Bowen** Australia
59E4 **Bowie** Arizona, USA
63C2 **Bowie** Texas, USA
6C3 **Bowland Fells** England
57E3 **Bowling Green** Kentucky, USA
63D1 **Bowling Green** Missouri, USA
64C2 **Bowling Green** Ohio, USA
65D3 **Bowling Green** Virginia, USA
60C1 **Bowman** USA
65D2 **Bowmanville** Canada
9C3 **Bowna, L** Irish Republic
34D2 **Bowral** Australia
31D3 **Bo Xian** China
31D2 **Boxing** China
40B1 **Boyabat** Turkey
50B3 **Boyali** Central African Republic
19G2 **Boyarka** Ukraine
54J4 **Boyd** Canada
68C2 **Boyertown** USA
10B3 **Boyle** Irish Republic
9C3 **Boyne** *R* Irish Republic
67B3 **Boynton Beach** USA
50C3 **Boyoma Falls** Zaïre
58E2 **Boysen Res** USA
17D1 **Bozanski Brod** Bosnia-Herzegovina/Croatia
17F3 **Bozca Ada** *I* Turkey
17F3 **Boz Dağları** *Mts* Turkey
56B2 **Bozeman** USA
Bozen = Bolzano
50B3 **Bozene** Zaïre
50B3 **Bozoum** Central African Republic
16D2 **Brač** *I* Croatia
8B3 **Bracadale, Loch** *Inlet* Scotland
16C2 **Bracciano, L di** Italy
65D1 **Bracebridge** Canada
49D2 **Brach** Libya
12H6 **Bräcke** Sweden
62B3 **Brackettville** USA
67B3 **Bradenton** USA
6D3 **Bradford** England
68A2 **Bradford** USA
66B3 **Bradley** USA
62C2 **Brady** USA
8E1 **Brae** Scotland
8D3 **Braemar** Scotland
15A1 **Braga** Portugal
73J4 **Bragança** Brazil
15A1 **Bragança** Portugal
75C3 **Bragança Paulista** Brazil
43G4 **Brahman-Baria** Bangladesh
43F4 **Brāhmani** *R* India
43G3 **Brahmaputra** *R* Bangladesh/India
21D6 **Brăila** Romania
57D2 **Brainerd** USA
7E4 **Braintree** England
47C3 **Brak** *R* South Africa
47D1 **Brak** *R* South Africa
13E1 **Brake** Germany
48A3 **Brakna** *Region* Mauritius
54F4 **Bralorne** Canada
65D2 **Brampton** Canada
6C2 **Brampton** England
13D1 **Bramsche** Germany
72F3 **Branco** *R* Brazil
51B6 **Brandberg** *Mt* Namibia
18C2 **Brandenburg** Germany
18C2 **Brandenburg** *State* Germany
47D2 **Brandfort** South Africa
56D2 **Brandon** Canada
61D2 **Brandon** USA
47C3 **Brandvlei** South Africa
18C2 **Brandýs-nad-Laben** Czech Republic
19D2 **Braniewo** Poland
57E2 **Brantford** Canada
34B3 **Branxholme** Australia
55M5 **Bras d'Or Lakes** Canada
72E6 **Brasiléia** Brazil
73J7 **Brasília** Brazil
75D2 **Brasília de Minas** Brazil
17F1 **Braşov** Romania
18D3 **Bratislava** Slovakia
25M4 **Bratsk** Russian Federation
19F3 **Bratslav** Ukraine
65E2 **Brattleboro** USA
18C2 **Braunschweig** Germany
48A4 **Brava** *I* Cape Verde
56B3 **Brawley** USA
9C3 **Bray** Irish Republic
55L3 **Bray I** Canada
13B3 **Bray-sur-Seine** France
71E5 **Brazil** *Republic* S America
52G5 **Brazil Basin** Atlantic Ocean
56D3 **Brazos** *R* USA
50B4 **Brazzaville** Congo
18C3 **Brdy** *Upland* Czech Republic
35A3 **Breaksea Sd** New Zealand
35B1 **Bream B** New Zealand
8D3 **Brechin** Scotland
13C2 **Brecht** Belgium
61D1 **Breckenridge** Minnesota, USA
62C2 **Breckenridge** Texas, USA
7E3 **Breckland** England
18D3 **Břeclav** Czech Republic
7C4 **Brecon** Wales
7C4 **Brecon Beacons** *Mts* Wales
7B3 **Brecon Beacons Nat Pk** Wales
18A2 **Breda** Netherlands

Bredasdorp
Calabozo

47C3 **Bredasdorp** South Africa
12H6 **Bredbyn** Sweden
20K5 **Bredy** Russian Federation
47B3 **Breede** *R* South Africa
65D2 **Breezewood** USA
12A1 **Breiethafjörethur** *B* Iceland
13D3 **Breisach** Germany
67A2 **Bremen** USA
18B2 **Bremen** Germany
18B2 **Bremerhaven** Germany
58B1 **Bremerton** USA
13E1 **Bremervörde** Germany
59E3 **Brendel** USA
63C2 **Brenham** USA
18C3 **Brenner** *P* Austria/Italy
66B2 **Brentwood** USA
16C1 **Brescia** Italy
Breslau = Wrocław
8E1 **Bressay** *I* Scotland
14B2 **Bressuire** France
14B2 **Brest** France
19E2 **Brest** Belarus
14B2 **Bretagne** *Region* France
13B3 **Breteuil** France
63E3 **Breton Sd** USA
68C2 **Breton Woods** USA
35B1 **Brett,C** New Zealand
67B1 **Brevard** USA
34C1 **Brewarrina** Australia
65F2 **Brewer** USA
68D2 **Brewster** New York, USA
58C1 **Brewster** Washington, USA
67A2 **Brewton** USA
47D2 **Breyten** South Africa
16D1 **Brežice** Slovenia
50C3 **Bria** Central African Republic
14D3 **Briançon** France
14C2 **Briare** France
7C4 **Bridgend** Wales
8C3 **Bridge of Orchy** Scotland
67A2 **Bridgeport** Alabama, USA
59C3 **Bridgeport** California, USA
65E2 **Bridgeport** Connecticut, USA
60C2 **Bridgeport** Nebraska, USA
63C2 **Bridgeport** Texas, USA
66C1 **Bridgeport Res** USA
58E1 **Bridger** USA
60B2 **Bridger Peak** USA
68C3 **Bridgeton** USA
69R3 **Bridgetown** Barbados
55M5 **Bridgewater** Canada
68E2 **Bridgewater** USA
7C4 **Bridgwater** England
7C4 **Bridgwater B** England
6D2 **Bridlington** England
6E3 **Bridlington Bay** England
34C4 **Bridport** Australia
7C4 **Bridport** England
13C3 **Brienne-le-Château** France
13C3 **Briey** France
16B1 **Brig** Switzerland
56B2 **Brigham City** USA
34C3 **Bright** Australia
7D4 **Brighton** England
75A3 **Brilhante** *R* Brazil
13E2 **Brilon** Germany
17D2 **Brindisi** Italy
63D2 **Brinkley** USA
33E3 **Brisbane** Australia
65E2 **Bristol** Connecticut, USA
7C4 **Bristol** England
65E2 **Bristol** Pennsylvania, USA
68E2 **Bristol** Rhode Island, USA
57E3 **Bristol** Tennessee, USA
64C3 **Bristol** USA
7B4 **Bristol Chan** England/Wales
54F4 **British Columbia** *Province* Canada
55K1 **British Empire Range** *Mts* Canada
54E3 **British Mts** Canada
47D2 **Brits** South Africa
47C3 **Britstown** South Africa
61D1 **Britton** USA
14C2 **Brive** France
7C4 **Brixham** England
18D3 **Brno** Czech Republic
67B2 **Broad** *R* USA
68C1 **Broadalbin** USA
55L4 **Broadback** *R* Canada
8B2 **Broad Bay** *Inlet* Scotland
8C3 **Broadford** Scotland
9B2 **Broad Haven, B** Irish Republic
7E4 **Broadstairs** England
60B1 **Broadus** USA
60C2 **Broadwater** USA
54H4 **Brochet** Canada
54G2 **Brock I** Canada
65D2 **Brockport** USA
68E1 **Brockton** USA
65D2 **Brockville** Canada
68A2 **Brockway** USA
55K2 **Brodeur Pen** Canada
8C4 **Brodick** Scotland
19D2 **Brodnica** Poland
21D5 **Brody** Ukraine
13D2 **Brokem Haltern** Germany
60D2 **Broken Bow** Nebraska, USA
63D2 **Broken Bow** Oklahoma, USA
63D2 **Broken Bow L** USA
32D4 **Broken Hill** Australia
7C3 **Bromsgrove** England
12G5 **Brønnøysund** Norway
68D2 **Bronx** *Borough* New York, USA
27E6 **Brooke's Pt** Philippines
61E3 **Brookfield** Missouri, USA
64B2 **Brookfield** Wisconsin, USA
57D3 **Brookhaven** USA
58B2 **Brookings** Oregon, USA
56D2 **Brookings** South Dakota, USA
68E1 **Brookline** USA
61E2 **Brooklyn** USA
68D2 **Brooklyn** *Borough* New York, USA
61E1 **Brooklyn Center** USA
54G4 **Brooks** Canada
54C3 **Brooks Range** *Mts* USA
67B3 **Brooksville** USA
34D1 **Brooloo** Australia
32B2 **Broome** Australia
8C3 **Broom, Loch** *Estuary* Scotland
8D2 **Brora** Scotland
58B2 **Brothers** USA
6C2 **Broughton** England
8D3 **Broughty Ferry** Scotland
50B2 **Broulkou** *Well* Chad
19G2 **Brovary** Ukraine
61E1 **Browerville** USA
62B2 **Brownfield** USA
56D4 **Brownsville** USA
56D3 **Brownwood** USA
27F8 **Browse I** Australia
13B2 **Bruay-en-Artois** France
32A3 **Bruce,Mt** Australia
64C1 **Bruce Pen** Canada
13E3 **Bruchsal** Germany
18D3 **Bruck an der Mur** Austria
Bruges = Brugge
13B2 **Brugge** Belgium
13D2 **Brühl** Germany
45B3 **Brûk, Wadi el** Egypt
75D1 **Brumado** Brazil
13D3 **Brumath** France
58C2 **Bruneau** USA
58C2 **Bruneau** *R* USA
27E6 **Brunei** *State* Borneo
16C1 **Brunico** Italy
35B2 **Brunner,L** New Zealand
13E1 **Brunsbüttel** Germany
57E3 **Brunswick** Georgia, USA
65F2 **Brunswick** Maine, USA
61E3 **Brunswick** Mississippi, USA
74B8 **Brunswick,Pen de** Chile
34C4 **Bruny I** Australia
20G3 **Brusenets** Russian Federation
60C2 **Brush** USA
69A3 **Brus Laguna** Honduras
Brüssel = Brussels
18A2 **Brussels** Belgium
Bruxelles = Brussels
13D3 **Bruyères** France
56D3 **Bryan** USA
34A2 **Bryan,Mt** Australia
20E5 **Bryansk** Russian Federation
63D2 **Bryant** USA
59D3 **Bryce Canyon Nat Pk** USA
18D2 **Brzeg** Poland
41E4 **Būbīyan** *I* Kuwait
50D4 **Bubu** *R* Tanzania
47E1 **Bubye** *R* Zimbabwe
72D2 **Bucaramanga** Colombia
8E3 **Buchan** *Oilfield* N Sea
48A4 **Buchanan** Liberia
62C2 **Buchanan,L** USA
8E3 **Buchan Deep** N Sea
55L2 **Buchan G** Canada
10C2 **Buchan Ness** *Pen* Scotland
55N5 **Buchans** Canada
17F2 **Bucharest** Romania
66B3 **Buchon,Pt** USA
13E1 **Bückeburg** Germany
59D4 **Buckeye** USA
8D3 **Buckhaven** Scotland
8D3 **Buckie** Scotland
7D3 **Buckingham** England
65F2 **Bucksport** USA
50B4 **Buco Zau** Congo
București = Bucharest
19D3 **Budapest** Hungary
42D3 **Budaun** India
7B4 **Bude** England
63D2 **Bude** USA
21G7 **Budennovsk** Russian Federation
43J1 **Budhana** India
45B4 **Budhîya, Gebel** Egypt
13E2 **Büdingen** Germany
17D2 **Budva** Montenegro, Yugoslavia
48C4 **Buéa** Cameroon
66B3 **Buellton** USA
72C3 **Buenaventura** Colombia
62A3 **Buenaventura** Mexico
60B3 **Buena Vista** Colorado, USA
65D3 **Buena Vista** Virginia, USA
66C3 **Buena Vista L** USA
74E4 **Buenos Aires** Argentina
74E5 **Buenos Aires** *State* Argentina
74B7 **Buenos Aires, Lago** Argentina
63D1 **Buffalo** Mississipi, USA
57F2 **Buffalo** New York, USA
60C1 **Buffalo** S Dakota, USA
63C2 **Buffalo** Texas, USA
56C2 **Buffalo** Wyoming, USA
47E2 **Buffalo** *R* South Africa
58C1 **Buffalo Hump** *Mt* USA
54G3 **Buffalo L** Canada
54H4 **Buffalo Narrows** Canada
67B2 **Buford** USA
17F2 **Buftea** Romania
19E2 **Bug** *R* Poland/Ukraine
72C3 **Buga** Colombia
41F2 **Bugdayli** Turkmenistan
20H2 **Bugrino** Russian Federation
20J5 **Bugulma** Russian Federation
20J5 **Buguruslan** Russian Federation
40C2 **Buḩayrat al Asad** *Res* Syria
58D2 **Buhl** Idaho, USA
61E1 **Buhl** Minnesota, USA
7C3 **Builth Wells** Wales
50C4 **Bujumbura** Burundi
33E1 **Buka** *I* Papua New Guinea
51C4 **Bukama** Zaïre
50C4 **Bukavu** Zaïre
38E2 **Bukhara** Uzbekistan
27D7 **Bukittinggi** Indonesia
50D4 **Bukoba** Tanzania
27G7 **Bula** Indonesia
27F5 **Bulan** Philippines
42D3 **Bulandshahr** India
51C6 **Bulawayo** Zimbabwe
17F3 **Buldan** Turkey
42D4 **Buldāna** India
26D2 **Bulgan** Mongolia
17E2 **Bulgaria** *Republic* Europe
35B2 **Buller** *R* New Zealand
34C3 **Buller,Mt** Australia
32A4 **Bullfinch** Australia
34B1 **Bulloo** *R* Australia
34B1 **Bulloo Downs** Australia
34B1 **Bulloo L** Australia
63D1 **Bull Shoals Res** USA
32D1 **Bulolo** Papua New Guinea
47D2 **Bultfontein** South Africa
27E6 **Bulu, Gunung** *Mt* Indonesia
50C3 **Bumba** Zaïre
21D8 **Bu Menderes** *R* Turkey
30B2 **Bumphal Dam** Thailand
50D3 **Buna** Kenya
32A4 **Bunbury** Australia
9C2 **Buncrana** Irish Republic
33E3 **Bundaberg** Australia
34D2 **Bundarra** Australia
13E1 **Bünde** Germany
42D3 **Bündi** India
7E3 **Bungay** England
34C1 **Bungil** *R* Australia
51B4 **Bungo** Angola
28B4 **Bungo-suidō** *Str* Japan
27D6 **Bunguran** *I* Indonesia
27D6 **Bunguran, Kepulauan** *I* Indonesia
50D3 **Bunia** Zaïre
63D1 **Bunker** USA
63D2 **Bunkie** USA
67B3 **Bunnell** USA
27E7 **Buntok** Indonesia
27F6 **Buol** Indonesia
50C2 **Buram** Sudan
43E2 **Burang** China
50E3 **Burao** Somalia
45D2 **Burāq** Syria
41D4 **Buraydah** Saudi Arabia
59C4 **Burbank** USA
34C2 **Burcher** Australia
21E8 **Burdur** Turkey
50D2 **Burē** Ethiopia
7E3 **Bure** *R* England
26G1 **Bureinskiy Khrebet** *Mts* Russian Federation
26F2 **Bureya** Russian Federation
45B3 **Bûr Fu'ad** Egypt
18C2 **Burg** Germany
17F2 **Burgas** Bulgaria
67C2 **Burgaw** USA
47D3 **Burgersdorp** South Africa
15B1 **Burgos** Spain
13D1 **Burgsteinfurt** Germany
19D1 **Burgsvik** Sweden
17F3 **Burhaniye** Turkey
42D4 **Burhānpur** India
30C2 **Buriram** Thailand
75C2 **Buritis** Brazil
32C2 **Burketown** Australia
48B3 **Burkina** *Republic* W Africa
65D1 **Burk's Falls** Canada
56B2 **Burley** USA
60C3 **Burlington** Colorado, USA
57D2 **Burlington** Iowa, USA
68C2 **Burlington** New Jersey, USA
67C1 **Burlington** North Carolina, USA
57F2 **Burlington** Vermont, USA
58B1 **Burlington** Washington, USA
39H3 **Burma** *Republic* Asia
62C2 **Burnet** USA
58B2 **Burney** USA
68B2 **Burnham** USA
7E4 **Burnham-on-Crouch** England
32D5 **Burnie** Australia
6C3 **Burnley** England
58C2 **Burns** USA
54F4 **Burns Lake** Canada
24K5 **Burqin** China
34A2 **Burra** Australia
34D2 **Burragorang,L** Australia
8D2 **Burray** *I* Scotland
34C2 **Burren Junction** Australia
34C2 **Burrinjuck Res** Australia
62B3 **Burro, Serranías del** *Mts* Mexico
8C4 **Burrow Head** *Pt* Scotland
27G8 **Burrundie** Australia
21D7 **Bursa** Turkey
40B4 **Bur Safâga** Egypt
Bûr Saïd = Port Said
45B4 **Bûr Taufiq** Egypt
64C2 **Burton** USA
7D3 **Burton upon Trent** England
12J6 **Burtrask** Sweden
34B2 **Burtundy** Australia
27F7 **Buru** *I* Indonesia
50C4 **Burundi** *Republic* Africa
60D2 **Burwell** USA
7C3 **Bury** England
25N4 **Buryat Republic** Russian Federation
21J6 **Burynshik** Kazakhstan
7E3 **Bury St Edmunds** England
28A3 **Bushan** China
41F4 **Būshehr** Iran
9C2 **Bushmills** Northern Ireland
50B4 **Busira** *R* Zaïre
19E2 **Busko Zdrój** Poland
45D2 **Buşrá ash Shām** Syria
13D4 **Bussang** France
32A4 **Busselton** Australia
16B1 **Busto Arsizio** Italy
50C3 **Buta** Zaïre
50C4 **Butare** Rwanda
8C4 **Bute** *I* Scotland
26F2 **Butha Qi** China
65D2 **Butler** USA
32B1 **Buton** *I* Indonesia
48C4 **Butta** Togo
56B2 **Butte** USA
30C4 **Butterworth** Malaysia
47D3 **Butterworth** South Africa
10B2 **Butt of Lewis** *C* Scotland
55M3 **Button Is** Canada
66C3 **Buttonwillow** USA
27F6 **Butuan** Philippines
21G5 **Buturlinovka** Russian Federation
43E3 **Butwal** Nepal
13E2 **Butzbach** Germany
50E3 **Buulobarde** Somalia
50E3 **Buurhakaba** Somalia
7D3 **Buxton** England
20G4 **Buy** Russian Federation
31B1 **Buyant Ovoo** Mongolia
21H7 **Buynaksk** Russian Federation
25N5 **Buyr Nuur** *L* Mongolia
21G8 **Büyük Ağrı Daği** *Mt* Turkey
40A2 **Büyük Menderes** *R* Turkey
17F1 **Buzău** Romania
17F1 **Buzău** *R* Romania
75D3 **Búzios, Ponta dos** *Pt* Brazil
20J5 **Buzuluk** Russian Federation
68E2 **Buzzards B** USA
17F2 **Byala** Bulgaria
17E2 **Byala Slatina** Bulgaria
54H2 **Byam Martin Channel** Canada
54H2 **Byam Martin I** Canada
45C1 **Byblos** *Hist site* Lebanon
19D2 **Bydgoszcz** Poland
60C3 **Byers** USA
12F7 **Bygland** Norway
19G2 **Bykhov** Belarus
55L2 **Bylot I** Canada
34C2 **Byrock** Australia
66B2 **Byron** USA
34D1 **Byron** *C* Australia
25P3 **Bytantay** *R* Russian Federation
19D2 **Bytom** Poland

C

74E3 **Caacupú** Paraguay
75A4 **Caaguazú** Paraguay
51B5 **Caála** Angola
75A4 **Caapucú** Paraguay
75B3 **Caarapó** Brazil
74E3 **Caazapá** Paraguay
15C1 **Caballería, Cabo de** *C* Spain
62A2 **Caballo Res** USA
27F5 **Cabanatuan** Philippines
65F1 **Cabano** Canada
73M5 **Cabedelo** Brazil
15A2 **Cabeza del Buey** Spain
72D1 **Cabimas** Venezuela
50B4 **Cabinda** Angola
50B4 **Cabinda** *Province* Angola
58C1 **Cabinet Mts** USA
75D3 **Cabo Frio** Brazil
55L5 **Cabonga,Réservoire** Canada
34D1 **Caboolture** Australia
51D5 **Cabora Bassa Dam** Mozambique
70A1 **Caborca** Mexico
55M5 **Cabot Str** Canada
15B2 **Cabra** Spain
75D2 **Cabral, Serra do** *Mts* Brazil
15A1 **Cabreira** *Mt* Portugal
15C2 **Cabrera** *I* Spain
15B2 **Cabriel** *R* Spain
17E2 **Čačak** Serbia, Yugoslavia
68A3 **Cacapon** *R* USA
73G7 **Cáceres** Brazil
15A2 **Cáceres** Spain
63D1 **Cache** *R* USA
66A1 **Cache Creek** *R* USA
58D2 **Cache Peak** *Mt* USA
74C3 **Cachi** Argentina
73G5 **Cachimbo** Brazil
73G5 **Cachimbo, Serra do** *Mts* Brazil
73L6 **Cachoeira** Brazil
75B2 **Cachoeira Alta** Brazil
73L5 **Cachoeira de Paulo Afonso** *Waterfall* Brazil
74F4 **Cachoeira do Sul** Brazil
73K8 **Cachoeiro de Itapemirim** Brazil
66C3 **Cachuma,L** USA
51B5 **Cacolo** Angola
51B5 **Caconda** Angola
62B1 **Cactus** USA
75B2 **Caçu** Brazil
75D1 **Caculé** Brazil
51B5 **Caculuvar** *R* Angola
19D3 **Čadca** Slovakia
7C3 **Cader Idris** *Mt* Wales
57E2 **Cadillac** USA
15A2 **Cádiz** Spain
15A2 **Cádiz, Golfo de** *G* Spain
14B2 **Caen** France
7B3 **Caernarfon** Wales
7B3 **Caernarfon B** Wales
7C4 **Caerphilly** Wales
45C2 **Caesarea** *Hist Site* Israel
75D1 **Caetité** Brazil
74C3 **Cafayate** Argentina
40B2 **Caga Tepe** *Mt* Turkey
27F6 **Cagayan de Oro** Philippines
16B3 **Cagliari** Sardinia, Italy
16B3 **Cagliari, G di** Sardinia, Italy
69D3 **Caguas** Puerto Rico
67A2 **Cahaba** *R* USA
9C3 **Cahir** Irish Republic
9C3 **Cahore Pt** Irish Republic
14C3 **Cahors** France
51D5 **Caia** Mozambique
73G6 **Caiabis, Serra dos** *Mts* Brazil
51C5 **Caianda** Angola
75B2 **Caiapó** *R* Brazil
75B2 **Caiapônia** Brazil
75B2 **Caiapó, Serra do** *Mts* Brazil
73L5 **Caicó** Brazil
69C2 **Caicos Is** Caribbean Sea
57F4 **Caicos Pass** The Bahamas
8D3 **Cairngorms** *Mts* Scotland
8C4 **Cairnryan** Scotland
32D2 **Cairns** Australia
40B3 **Cairo** Egypt
57E3 **Cairo** USA
8D2 **Caithness** Scotland
34B1 **Caiwarro** Australia
72C5 **Cajabamba** Peru
72C5 **Cajamarca** Peru
48C4 **Calabar** Nigeria
69D5 **Calabozo** Venezuela

Caxias **Chisasibi**

73K4 **Caxias** Brazil
74F3 **Caxias do Sul** Brazil
51B4 **Caxito** Angola
67B2 **Cayce** USA
40D1 **Çayeli** Turkey
73H3 **Cayenne** French Guiana
70E3 **Cayman Brac** *I* Cayman Is, Caribbean Sea
69A3 **Cayman Is** Caribbean Sea
69A3 **Cayman Trench** Caribbean Sea
50E3 **Caynabo** Somalia
70E2 **Cayo Romano** *I* Cuba
70D3 **Cayos Miskito** *Is* Nicaragua
69A2 **Cay Sal** *I* Caribbean Sea
66B3 **Cayucos** USA
68B1 **Cayuga L** USA
68C1 **Cazenovia** USA
51C5 **Cazombo** Angola
Ceará = Fortaleza
73K5 **Ceará** *State* Brazil
27F5 **Cebu** Philippines
27F5 **Cebu** *I* Philippines
68C3 **Cecilton** USA
16C2 **Cecina** Italy
61E2 **Cedar** *R* USA
56B3 **Cedar City** USA
63C2 **Cedar Creek Res** USA
61E2 **Cedar Falls** USA
54H4 **Cedar L** Canada
66D1 **Cedar Mts** USA
57D2 **Cedar Rapids** USA
67A2 **Cedartown** USA
70A2 **Cedros** *I* Mexico
56B4 **Cedros, Isla de** Mexico
32C4 **Ceduna** Australia
50E3 **Ceelbuur** Somalia
50E2 **Ceerigaabo** Somalia
16C3 **Cefalù** Sicily, Italy
19D3 **Cegléd** Hungary
51B5 **Cela** Angola
70B2 **Celaya** Mexico
Celebes = Sulawesi
27F6 **Celebes S** SE Asia
64C2 **Celina** USA
16D1 **Celje** Slovenia
18C2 **Celle** Germany
7A4 **Celtic S** British Islands
7B3 **Cemmaes Hd** *Pt* Wales
27G7 **Cendrawasih** *Pen* Indonesia
63D2 **Center** USA
67A1 **Center Hill L** USA
68D2 **Center Moriches** USA
67A2 **Center Point** USA
62A2 **Central** USA
8C3 **Central** *Region* Scotland
50B3 **Central African Republic** Africa
61D2 **Central City** Nebraska, USA
68A2 **Central City** Pennsylvania, USA
68E2 **Central Falls** USA
64B3 **Centralia** Illinois, USA
56A2 **Centralia** Washington, USA
47C1 **Central Kalahari Game Res** Botswana
42A3 **Central Makran Ra** *Mts* Pakistan
58B2 **Central Point** USA
27H7 **Central Range** *Mts* Papua New Guinea
68B1 **Central Square** USA
67A2 **Centreville** Alabama, USA
68B3 **Centreville** Maryland, USA
Ceram = Seram
Ceram Sea = Seram Sea
73J7 **Ceres** Brazil
47B3 **Ceres** South Africa
66B2 **Ceres** USA
14C2 **Cergy-Pontoise** France
16D2 **Cerignola** Italy
21D7 **Cernavodă** Romania
13D4 **Cernay** France
56C4 **Cerralvo** *I* Mexico
72C6 **Cerro de Pasco** Peru
69D3 **Cerro de Punta** *Mt* Puerto Rico
69C4 **Cerron** *Mt* Venezuela
74C5 **Cerros Colorados, Embalse** *Res* Argentina
16C2 **Cesena** Italy
20D4 **Cēsis** Latvia
18C3 **České Budějovice** Czech Republic
18D3 **Českomoravská Vyosina** *Region* Czech Republic
17F3 **Çeşme** Turkey
32E4 **Cessnock** Australia
16D2 **Cetina** *R* Croatia
15A2 **Ceuta** NW Africa
40C2 **Ceyhan** Turkey
40C2 **Ceyhan** *R* Turkey
40C2 **Ceylanpınar** Turkey
44C4 **Ceylon** *I* Indian Oc
Ceylon *Republic* **= Sri Lanka**
25L4 **Chaa-Khol** Russian Federation
14C2 **Chaâteaudun** France
13B4 **Chablis** France
72C5 **Chachapoyas** Peru
42C3 **Chachran** Pakistan
42C3 **Chachro** Pakistan
74D3 **Chaco** *State* Argentina
50B2 **Chad** *Republic* Africa
50B2 **Chad, L** C Africa
56C2 **Chadron** USA
28B3 **Chaeryŏng** N Korea
63E1 **Chaffee** USA
42A3 **Chagai** Pakistan
25P4 **Chagda** Russian Federation
42B2 **Chaghcharan** Afghanistan
36E5 **Chagos Arch** Indian Ocean
69L1 **Chaguanas** Trinidad
38E3 **Chāh Bahār** Iran
28A2 **Ch'aho** N Korea
30C2 **Chai Badan** Thailand
43F4 **Chāībāsa** India
30C2 **Chaiyaphum** Thailand
42C2 **Chakwal** Pakistan
72D7 **Chala** Peru
51D5 **Chalabesa** Zambia
42A2 **Chalap Dalam** *Mts* Afghanistan
57G2 **Chaleurs, B des** Canada
13C4 **Chalindrey** France
31C4 **Chaling** China
42D4 **Chālisgaon** India
27H5 **Challenger Deep** Pacific Ocean
13C3 **Challerange** France
58D2 **Challis** USA
13C3 **Châlons-sur-Marne** France
14C2 **Chalon sur Saône** France
28B2 **Chaluhe** China
18C3 **Cham** Germany
62A1 **Chama** USA
42B2 **Chaman** Pakistan
42D2 **Chamba** India
42D3 **Chambal** *R* India
60D2 **Chamberlain** USA
65D3 **Chambersburg** USA
14D2 **Chambéry** France
13B3 **Chambly** France
65E1 **Chambord** Canada
42A3 **Chambor Kalat** Pakistan
41F3 **Chamgordan** Iran
43E4 **Chāmpa** India
14C2 **Champagne** *Region* France
47D2 **Champagne Castle** *Mt* Lesotho
57E2 **Champaign** USA
43N2 **Champaran** *District* India
30D3 **Champassak** Laos
57F2 **Champlain,L** USA
44B3 **Chāmrājnagar** India
74B3 **Chañaral** Chile
54D3 **Chandalar** USA
54D3 **Chandalar** *R* USA
63E3 **Chandeleur Is** USA
42D2 **Chandīgarh** India
59D4 **Chandler** USA
43G4 **Chandpur** Bangladesh
42D5 **Chandrapur** India
47E1 **Changane** *R* Mozambique
51D5 **Changara** Mozambique
28B2 **Changbai** China
28B2 **Changbai Shan** *Mts* China
28B2 **Changchun** China
31C4 **Changde** China
28A3 **Changdo** N Korea
28A3 **Changhai** China
28A3 **Changhang** S Korea
28A3 **Changhowan** S Korea
26E4 **Changhua** Taiwan
28A4 **Changhŭng** S Korea
30D2 **Changjiang** China
31D3 **Chang Jiang** *R* China
28B2 **Changjin** N Korea
28A2 **Changjin** *R* N Korea
28A2 **Changjin Res** N Korea
28B3 **Changnyŏn** N Korea
31C4 **Changsha** China
31E3 **Changshu** China
31B2 **Changwu** China
28A3 **Changyŏn** N Korea
31C2 **Changzhi** China
31E3 **Changzhou** China
14B2 **Channel Is** British Isles
56B3 **Channel Is** USA
55N5 **Channel Port-aux-Basques** Canada
30C3 **Chanthaburi** Thailand
13B3 **Chantilly** France
55J3 **Chantrey Inlet** *B* Canada
63C1 **Chanute** USA
24J4 **Chany, Ozero** *L* Russian Federation
31D5 **Chao'an** China
31D3 **Chao Hu** *L* China
30C3 **Chao Phraya** *R* Thailand
15A2 **Chaouen** Morocco
31E1 **Chaoyang** China
73K6 **Chapada Diamantina** *Mts* Brazil
73K4 **Chapadinha** Brazil
70B2 **Chapala, L de** Mexico
21J5 **Chapayevo** Kazakhstan
74F3 **Chapecó** Brazil
7D3 **Chapel-en-le-Frith** England
67C1 **Chapel Hill** USA
69H1 **Chapeltown** Jamaica
55K5 **Chapleau** Canada
25U3 **Chaplino, Mys** *C* Russian Federation
20G5 **Chaplygin** Russian Federation
60C2 **Chappell** USA
76G3 **Charcot I** Antarctica
7C4 **Chard** England
38E2 **Chardzhou** Turkmenistan
14C2 **Charente** *R* France
50B2 **Chari** *R* Chad
50B2 **Chari Baguirmi** *Region* Chad
42B1 **Charikar** Afghanistan
61E2 **Chariton** *R* USA
73G2 **Charity** Guyana
42D3 **Charkhāri** India
13C2 **Charleroi** Belgium
57F3 **Charles,C** USA
64B3 **Charleston** Illinois, USA
63E1 **Charleston** Missouri, USA
57F3 **Charleston** S Carolina, USA
57E3 **Charleston** W Virginia, USA
59C3 **Charleston Peak** *Mt* USA
68B3 **Charles Town** USA
68D1 **Charlestown** USA
50C4 **Charlesville** Zaïre
32D3 **Charleville** Australia
14C2 **Charleville-Mézières** France
64B1 **Charlevoix** USA
64C2 **Charlotte** Michigan, USA
57E3 **Charlotte** N Carolina, USA
67B3 **Charlotte Harbor** *B* USA
57F3 **Charlottesville** USA
55M5 **Charlottetown** Canada
69K1 **Charlotteville** Tobago
34B3 **Charlton** Australia
57F1 **Charlton I** Canada
13D3 **Charmes** France
42C2 **Charsadda** Pakistan
32D3 **Charters Towers** Australia
14C2 **Chartres** France
74E5 **Chascomús** Argentina
28B2 **Chasong** N Korea
14B2 **Châteaubriant** France
14B2 **Châteaulin** France
13B4 **Châteauneuf-sur-Loire** France
14C2 **Châteauroux** France
13D3 **Château-Salins** France
14C2 **Château-Thierry** France
13C2 **Châtelet** Belgium
14C2 **Châtellerault** France
61E2 **Chatfield** USA
7F6 **Chatham** England
68E2 **Chatham** Massachusetts, USA
55M5 **Chatham** New Brunswick, Canada
68D1 **Chatham** New York, USA
64C2 **Chatham** Ontario, Canada
65D3 **Chatham** Virginia, USA
33H5 **Chatham Is** New Zealand
54E4 **Chatham Str** USA
14C2 **Châtillon** France
13B4 **Châtillon-Coligny** France
13C4 **Châtillon-sur-Seine** France
43E5 **Chatrapur** India
68C3 **Chatsworth** USA
67B2 **Chattahoochee** USA
67A2 **Chattahoochee** *R* USA
57E3 **Chattanooga** USA
30A1 **Chauk** Burma
43L2 **Chauka** *R* India
14D2 **Chaumont** France
13B3 **Chauny** France
30D3 **Chau Phu** Vietnam
44E4 **Chaura** *I* Nicobar Is, Indian Ocean
15A1 **Chaves** Portugal
20J4 **Chaykovskiy** Russian Federation
18C2 **Cheb** Czech Republic
20H4 **Cheboksary** Russian Federation
57E2 **Cheboygan** USA
19G2 **Chechersk** Belarus
28B3 **Chech'on** S Korea
63C1 **Checotah** USA
7C4 **Cheddar** England
30A2 **Cheduba I** Burma
34B1 **Cheepie** Australia
48B2 **Chegga** Mauritius
51D5 **Chegutu** Zimbabwe
58B1 **Chehalis** USA
28B4 **Cheju** S Korea
28B4 **Cheju Do** *I* S Korea
28B4 **Cheju Haehyŏp** *Str* S Korea
25P4 **Chekunda** Russian Federation
58B1 **Chelan,L** USA
21J8 **Cheleken** Turkmenistan
16B3 **Chélia, Dj** *Mt* Algeria
15C2 **Cheliff** *R* Algeria
38D1 **Chelkar** Kazakhstan
19E2 **Chełm** Poland
19D2 **Chełmno** Poland
7E4 **Chelmsford** England
7C4 **Cheltenham** England
20L4 **Chelyabinsk** Russian Federation
25M2 **Chelyuskin, Mys** *C* Russian Federation
51D5 **Chemba** Mozambique
18C2 **Chemnitz** Germ
68B1 **Chemung** *R* USA
42D2 **Chenab** *R* India/Pakistan
48B2 **Chenachen** Algeria
68C1 **Chenango** *R* USA
58C1 **Cheney** USA
63C1 **Cheney Res** USA
31D1 **Chengde** China
31A3 **Chengdu** China
31E2 **Chengshan Jiao** *Pt* China
28A3 **Chengzitan** China
31C4 **Chenxi** China
31C4 **Chen Xian** China
31D3 **Cheo Xian** China
72C5 **Chepén** Peru
7C4 **Chepstow** Wales
64A1 **Chequamegon B** USA
14C2 **Cher** *R* France
67C2 **Cheraw** USA
14B2 **Cherbourg** France
15C2 **Cherchell** Algeria
20K3 **Cherdyn** Russian Federation
25M4 **Cheremkhovo** Russian Federation
20F4 **Cherepovets** Russian Federation
21E6 **Cherkassy** Ukraine
21G7 **Cherkessk** Russian Federation
21E5 **Chernigov** Ukraine
19G2 **Chernobyl** Ukraine
21D6 **Chernovtsy** Ukraine
20K4 **Chernushka** Russian Federation
20C5 **Chernyakhovsk** Russian Federation
21H6 **Chernyye Zemli** *Region* Russian Federation
61D2 **Cherokee** Iowa, USA
62C1 **Cherokee** Oklahoma, USA
63D1 **Cherokees,L o'the** USA
43G3 **Cherrapunji** India
33F2 **Cherry** *I* Solomon Islands
25S3 **Cherskiy** Russian Federation
25Q3 **Cherskogo, Khrebet** *Mts* Russian Federation
20D5 **Cherven'** Belarus
19E2 **Chervonograd** Ukraine
65D3 **Chesapeake** USA
65D3 **Chesapeake B** USA
7D4 **Chesham** England
68D1 **Cheshire** USA
7C3 **Cheshire** *County* England
20H2 **Chëshskaya Guba** *B* Russian Federation
59B2 **Chester** California, USA
7C3 **Chester** England
64B3 **Chester** Illinois, USA
68D1 **Chester** Massachusets, USA
58D1 **Chester** Montana, USA
65D3 **Chester** Pennsylvania, USA
67B2 **Chester** S Carolina, USA
68D1 **Chester** Vermont, USA
68B3 **Chester** *R* USA
7D3 **Chesterfield** England
33E2 **Chesterfield, Îles** Nouvelle Calédonie
55J3 **Chesterfield Inlet** Canada
68B3 **Chestertown** USA
65F1 **Chesuncook L** USA
70D3 **Chetumal** Mexico
35B2 **Cheviot** New Zealand
10C2 **Cheviots** *Hills* England/ Scotland
60C2 **Cheyenne** USA
60C2 **Cheyenne** *R* USA
60C3 **Cheyenne Wells** USA
43E3 **Chhapra** India
43G3 **Chhātak** Bangladesh
42D4 **Chhatarpur** India
42D4 **Chhindwāra** India
43F3 **Chhukha** Bhutan
51B5 **Chiange** Angola
30C2 **Chiang Kham** Thailand
30B2 **Chiang Mai** Thailand
31E5 **Chiayi** Taiwan
29E3 **Chiba** Japan
51B5 **Chibia** Angola
55L4 **Chibougamau** Canada
28B3 **Chiburi-jima** *I* Japan
47E1 **Chibuto** Mozambique
57E2 **Chicago** USA
64B2 **Chicago Heights** USA
54E4 **Chichagof I** USA
7D4 **Chichester** England
29C3 **Chichibu** Japan
26H4 **Chichi-jima** *I* Japan
57E3 **Chickamauga L** USA
63E2 **Chickasawhay** *R* USA
56D3 **Chickasha** USA
54D3 **Chicken** USA
72B5 **Chiclayo** Peru
56A3 **Chico** USA
74C6 **Chico** *R* Argentina
51D5 **Chicoa** Mozambique
65E2 **Chicopee** USA
55L5 **Chicoutimi** Canada
51D6 **Chicualacuala** Mozambique
44B3 **Chidambaram** India
55M3 **Chidley,C** Canada
67B3 **Chiefland** USA
48B4 **Chiehn** Liberia
51C4 **Chiengi** Zambia
13C3 **Chiers** *R* France
16C2 **Chieti** Italy
31D1 **Chifeng** China
73K7 **Chifre, Serra do** *Mts* Brazil
54C3 **Chigmit Mts** USA
47E1 **Chigubo** Mozambique
70B2 **Chihuahua** Mexico
62A3 **Chihuahua** *State* Mexico
44B3 **Chik Ballāpur** India
44B3 **Chikmagalūr** India
51D5 **Chikwawa** Malawi
30A1 **Chi-kyaw** Burma
44C2 **Chilakalūrupet** India
44B4 **Chilaw** Sri Lanka
34D1 **Childers** Australia
62B2 **Childress** USA
71C6 **Chile** *Republic* S America
51C5 **Chililabombwe** Zambia
43F5 **Chilka L** India
54F4 **Chilko L** Canada
74B5 **Chillán** Chile
61E3 **Chillicothe** Missouri, USA
64C3 **Chillicothe** Ohio, USA
43G3 **Chilmari** India
74B6 **Chiloé, Isla de** Chile
51D5 **Chilongozi** Zambia
58B2 **Chiloquin** USA
70C3 **Chilpancingo** Mexico
7D4 **Chiltern Hills** *Upland* England
64B2 **Chilton** USA
51D5 **Chilumba** Malawi
Chi-lung = Keelung
51D5 **Chilwa, L** Malawi
51D5 **Chimanimani** Zimbabwe
13C2 **Chimay** Belgium
24G5 **Chimbay** Uzbekistan
72C4 **Chimborazo** *Mt* Ecuador
72C5 **Chimbote** Peru
24H5 **Chimkent** Kazakhstan
51D5 **Chimoio** Mozambique
22F4 **China** *Republic* Asia
66D3 **China L** USA
66D3 **China Lake** USA
China, National Republic of = Taiwan
70D3 **Chinandega** Nicaragua
62B3 **Chinati Peak** *Mt* USA
72C6 **Chincha Alta** Peru
34D1 **Chinchilla** Australia
51D5 **Chinde** Mozambique
28A4 **Chindo** S Korea
43G4 **Chindwin** *R* Burma
51C5 **Chingola** Zambia
51B5 **Chinguar** Angola
48A2 **Chinguetti** Mauritius
28B3 **Chinhae** S Korea
51D5 **Chinhoyi** Zimbabwe
42C2 **Chiniot** Pakistan
28B3 **Chinju** S Korea
50C3 **Chinko** *R* Central African Republic
29C3 **Chino** Japan
51D5 **Chinsali** Zambia
16C1 **Chioggia** Italy
51D5 **Chipata** Zambia
51D6 **Chipinge** Zimbabwe
44A2 **Chiplūn** India
7C4 **Chippenham** England
64A1 **Chippewa** *R* USA
57D2 **Chippewa Falls** USA
64A1 **Chippewa,L** USA
7D4 **Chipping Norton** England
7C4 **Chipping Sodbury** England
72B4 **Chira** *R* Peru
44C2 **Chīrāla** India
51D6 **Chiredzi** Zimbabwe
50B1 **Chirfa** Niger
59E4 **Chiricahua Peak** *Mt* USA
70D4 **Chiriquí, G de** Panama
72B2 **Chiriquí, Lago de** Panama
17F2 **Chirpan** Bulgaria
72B2 **Chirripó Grande** *Mt* Costa Rica
51C5 **Chirundu** Zimbabwe
51C5 **Chisamba** Zambia
55L4 **Chisasibi** Canada

Condamine **Dalton, Kap**

34D1 **Condamine** Australia
75D1 **Condeuba** Brazil
32D4 **Condobolin** Australia
58B1 **Condon** USA
13C2 **Condroz** *Mts* Belgium
67A2 **Conecuh** *R* USA
68B1 **Conesus L** USA
75A3 **Confuso** *R* Paraguay
7C3 **Congleton** England
46F8 **Congo** *R* W Africa
46F8 **Congo** *Republic* Africa
Congo,R = Zaire
64C1 **Coniston** Canada
64C2 **Conneaut** USA
65E2 **Connecticut** *R* USA
57F2 **Connecticut** *State* USA
65D2 **Connellsville** USA
64B3 **Connersville** USA
10B3 **Conn, Lough** *L* Irish Republic
34B2 **Conoble** Australia
58D1 **Conrad** USA
63C2 **Conroe** USA
75D3 **Conselheiro Lafaiete** Brazil
6D2 **Consett** England
30D4 **Con Son** *Is* Vietnam
21D7 **Constanţa** Romania
16B3 **Constantine** Algeria
74B5 **Constitución** Chile
58D2 **Contact** USA
73K6 **Contas** *R* Brazil
13C3 **Contrexéville** France
54H3 **Contwoyto L** Canada
57D3 **Conway** Arkansas, USA
65E2 **Conway** New Hampshire, USA
67C2 **Conway** South Carolina, USA
7C3 **Conwy** Wales
7C3 **Conwy** *R* Wales
32C3 **Coober Pedy** Australia
67A1 **Cookeville** USA
54C3 **Cook Inlet** *B* USA
37L5 **Cook Is** Pacific Ocean
35B2 **Cook,Mt** New Zealand
9C2 **Cookstown** Northern Ireland
33G5 **Cook Str** New Zealand
32D2 **Cooktown** Australia
34C2 **Coolabah** Australia
34C1 **Cooladdi** Australia
34C2 **Coolah** Australia
34C2 **Coolamon** Australia
32B4 **Coolgardie** Australia
59D4 **Coolidge** USA
34C3 **Cooma** Australia
34C2 **Coonabarabran** Australia
34C2 **Coonambie** Australia
34B2 **Coonbah** Australia
44A3 **Coondapoor** India
34C1 **Coongoola** Australia
44B3 **Coonoor** India
34B1 **Cooper Basin** Australia
32C3 **Cooper Creek** Australia
34B1 **Cooper Creek** *R* Australia
67C3 **Cooper's Town** Bahamas
68C1 **Cooperstown** New York, USA
61D1 **Cooperstown** North Dakota, USA
34A3 **Coorong,The** Australia
34D1 **Cooroy** Australia
58B2 **Coos B** USA
58B2 **Coos Bay** USA
32D4 **Cootamundra** Australia
9C2 **Cootehill** Irish Republic
60C3 **Cope** USA
18C1 **Copenhagen** Denmark
74B3 **Copiapó** Chile
54D3 **Copper Center** USA
64C1 **Copper Cliff** Canada
64B1 **Copper Harbor** USA
54G3 **Coppermine** Canada
54G3 **Coppermine** *R* Canada
64C1 **Coppermine Pt** Canada
Coquilhatville = Mbandaka
74B3 **Coquimbo** Chile
17E2 **Corabia** Romania
67B3 **Coral Gables** USA
55K3 **Coral Harbour** Canada
32E2 **Coral S** Australia/Papua New Guinea
36J5 **Coral Sea Basin** Pacific Ocean
32E2 **Coral Sea Island Territories** Australia
34B3 **Corangamite,L** Australia
73G3 **Corantijn** *R* Guyana/Surinam
13B3 **Corbeil-Essonnes** France
64C3 **Corbin** USA
6D2 **Corbridge** England
7D3 **Corby** England
66C2 **Corcoran** USA
74B6 **Corcovado, Golfo** *G* Chile
15A1 **Corcubion** Spain
57E3 **Cordele** USA
15A1 **Cordillera Cantabrica** *Mts* Spain
69C3 **Cordillera Central** *Mts* Dominican Republic/Haiti
75A4 **Cordillera de Caaguazú** Paraguay
70D3 **Cordillera Isabelia** *Mts* Nicaragua
72C2 **Cordillera Occidental** *Mts* Colombia
72C3 **Cordillera Oriental** *Mts* Colombia
34B1 **Cordillo Downs** Australia
74D4 **Córdoba** Argentina
70C3 **Córdoba** Mexico
15B2 **Córdoba** Spain
74D4 **Córdoba** *State* Argentina
54D3 **Cordova** USA
17D3 **Corfu** Greece
17D3 **Corfu** *I* Greece
75D1 **Coribe** Brazil
34D2 **Coricudgy,Mt** Australia
16D3 **Corigliano Calabro** Italy
32E2 **Coringa Is** Australia
17E3 **Corinth** Greece
57E3 **Corinth** Mississippi, USA
68D1 **Corinth** New York, USA
17E3 **Corinth, Gulf of** Greece
73K7 **Corinto** Brazil
10B3 **Cork** Irish Republic
40A1 **Çorlu** Turkey
73K7 **Cornel Fabriciano** Brazil
75B3 **Cornélio Procópio** Brazil
55N5 **Corner Brook** Canada
34C3 **Corner Inlet** *B* Australia
13D4 **Cornimont** France
65D2 **Corning** USA
16C2 **Corno, Monte** *Mt* Italy
55L5 **Cornwall** Canada
7B4 **Cornwall** *County* England
7B4 **Cornwall,C** England
54H2 **Cornwall I** Canada
55J2 **Cornwallis I** Canada
72E1 **Coro** Venezuela
73K4 **Coroatá** Brazil
72E7 **Coroico** Bolivia
75C2 **Coromandel** Brazil
44C3 **Coromandel Coast** India
35C1 **Coromandel Pen** New Zealand
35C1 **Coromandel Range** *Mts* New Zealand
66D4 **Corona** California, USA
62A2 **Corona** New Mexico, USA
72B2 **Coronado, B. de** Costa Rica
54G3 **Coronation G** Canada
74B5 **Coronel** Chile
75D2 **Coronel Fabriciano** Brazil
74E3 **Coronel Oviedo** Paraguay
74D5 **Coronel Pringles** Argentina
72D7 **Coropuna** *Mt* Peru
34C3 **Corowa** Australia
14D3 **Corps** France
56D4 **Corpus Christi** USA
63C3 **Corpus Christi,L** USA
9B3 **Corraun Pen** Irish Republic
27F5 **Corregidor** *I* Philippines
75D1 **Corrente** *R* Bahia, Brazil
75C1 **Corrente** *R* Goias, Brazil
75B2 **Corrente** *R* Mato Grosso, Brazil
75D1 **Correntina** Brazil
10B3 **Corrib, Lough** *L* Irish Republic
74E3 **Corrientes** Argentina
74E3 **Corrientes** *State* Argentina
72C2 **Corrientes, Cabo** *C* Colombia
70B2 **Corrientes, Cabo** *C* Mexico
63D2 **Corrigan** USA
32A4 **Corrigin** Australia
34C3 **Corryong** England
Corse = Corsica
8C4 **Corsewall Pt** Scotland
16B2 **Corsica** *I* Medit Sea
56D3 **Corsicana** USA
55O3 **Cort Adelaer, Kap** *C* Greenland
16B2 **Corte** Corsica, France
56C3 **Cortez** USA
16C1 **Cortina d'Ampezzo** Italy
65D2 **Cortland** USA
21G7 **Çoruh** *R* Turkey
21F7 **Çorum** Turkey
73G7 **Corumbá** Brazil
75C2 **Corumbá** *R* Brazil
75C2 **Corumbaiba** Brazil
58B2 **Corvallis** USA
48A1 **Corvo** *I* Azores
7C3 **Corwen** Wales
16D3 **Cosenza** Italy
51E5 **Cosmoledo Is** Seychelles
66D2 **Coso Junction** USA
15B2 **Costa Blanca** *Region* Spain
15C1 **Costa Brava** *Region* Spain
15B2 **Costa Calída** *Region* Spain
15B2 **Costa de Almería** *Region* Spain
15A2 **Costa de la Luz** *Region* Spain
15B2 **Costa del Sol** *Region* Spain
15C1 **Costa Dorada** *Region* Spain
66D4 **Costa Mesa** USA
70D3 **Costa Rica** *Republic* Central America
27F6 **Cotabato** Philippines
72E8 **Cotagaita** Bolivia
14D3 **Côte d'Azur** *Region* France
Côte D'Ivoire = Ivory Coast
13C4 **Côte-d'Or** *Department* France
13C3 **Côtes de Meuse** *Mts* France
7B4 **Cothi** *R* Wales
48C4 **Cotonou** Benin
72C4 **Cotopaxi** *Mt* Ecuador
7C4 **Cotswold Hills** *Upland* England
58B2 **Cottage Grove** USA
18C2 **Cottbus** Germany
59D4 **Cottonwood** USA
62C3 **Cotulla** USA
68A2 **Coudersport** USA
13B3 **Coulommiers** France
65D1 **Coulonge** *R* Canada
66B2 **Coulterville** USA
54B3 **Council** USA
56D2 **Council Bluffs** USA
8D3 **Coupar Angus** Scotland
19E1 **Courland Lagoon** *Lg* Lithuania/Russian Federation
Courtrai = Kortrijk
14B2 **Coutances** France
7D3 **Coventry** England
15A1 **Covilhã** Portugal
67B2 **Covington** Georgia, USA
64C3 **Covington** Kentucky, USA
63D2 **Covington** Louisiana, USA
65D3 **Covington** Virginia, USA
34C2 **Cowal,L** Australia
34B3 **Cowangie** Australia
65E1 **Cowansville** Canada
8D3 **Cowdenbeath** Scotland
34C3 **Cowes** Australia
7D4 **Cowes** England
58B1 **Cowichan L** Canada
58B1 **Cowlitz** *R* USA
34C2 **Cowra** Australia
73H7 **Coxim** Brazil
75B2 **Coxim** *R* Brazil
68D1 **Coxsackie** USA
43G4 **Cox's Bazar** Bangladesh
66B2 **Coyote** USA
60D2 **Cozad** USA
70D2 **Cozumel, Isla de** Mexico
34D1 **Cracow** Australia
19D2 **Cracow** Poland
47D3 **Cradock** South Africa
56C2 **Craig** USA
9C2 **Craigavon** Northern Ireland
18C3 **Crailsheim** Germany
17E2 **Craiova** Romania
65E2 **Cranberry L** USA
54G5 **Cranbrook** Canada
58C2 **Crane** Oregon, USA
62B2 **Crane** Texas, USA
68E2 **Cranston** USA
58B2 **Crater L** USA
58B2 **Crater Lake Nat Pk** USA
73K5 **Crateús** Brazil
73L5 **Crato** Brazil
60C2 **Crawford** USA
64B2 **Crawfordsville** USA
67B2 **Crawfordville** USA
7D4 **Crawley** England
58D1 **Crazy Mts** USA
7C4 **Crediton** England
54H4 **Cree L** Canada
13B3 **Creil** France
16C1 **Cremona** Italy
13B3 **Crépy-en-Valois** France
16C2 **Cres** *I* Croatia
58B2 **Crescent** USA
56A2 **Crescent City** USA
61E2 **Cresco** USA
61E2 **Creston** USA
67A2 **Crestview** USA
34B3 **Creswick** Australia
61D2 **Crete** USA
17E3 **Crete** *I* Greece
17E3 **Crete,S of** Greece
15C1 **Creus, Cabo de** *C* Spain
14C2 **Creuse** *R* France
7C3 **Crewe** England
8C3 **Crianlarich** Scotland
7B3 **Criccieth** Wales
74G3 **Criciuma** Brazil
8D3 **Crieff** Scotland
21E6 **Crimea** *Pen* Ukraine
75C2 **Cristalina** Brazil
75B1 **Cristalina** *R* Brazil
75C1 **Crixás** Brazil
75C1 **Crixás Acu** *R* Brazil
75B1 **Crixás Mirim** *R* Brazil
16D1 **Croatia** *Republic* Europe
63C2 **Crockett** USA
61D2 **Crofton** USA
32C2 **Croker I** Australia
8D3 **Cromarty** Scotland
7E3 **Cromer** England
35A3 **Cromwell** New Zealand
6D2 **Crook** England
57F4 **Crooked** *I* The Bahamas
56D2 **Crookston** USA
34C2 **Crookwell** Australia
34D1 **Croppa Creek** Australia
7C3 **Crosby** England
61E1 **Crosby** USA
47A1 **Cross,C** Namibia
57D3 **Crossett** USA
54E4 **Cross Sd** USA
67A1 **Crossville** USA
16D3 **Crotone** Italy
63D2 **Crowley** USA
66C2 **Crowley,L** USA
69K1 **Crown Pt** Tobago
34D1 **Crows Nest** Australia
32D2 **Croydon** Australia
7D4 **Croydon** England
36E6 **Crozet Basin** Indian Ocean
36D7 **Crozet, Îles** *Is* Indian Ocean
54F2 **Crozier Chan** Canada
74F3 **Cruz Alta** Brazil
69B3 **Cruz, Cabo** *C* Cuba
74D4 **Cruz del Eje** Argentina
75D3 **Cruzeiro** Brazil
72D5 **Cruzeiro do Sul** Brazil
34A2 **Crystal Brook** Australia
63D1 **Crystal City** Missouri, USA
62C3 **Crystal City** Texas, USA
64B1 **Crystal Falls** USA
51D5 **Cuamba** Mozambique
51C5 **Cuando** *R* Angola
51B5 **Cuangar** Angola
Cuango,R = Kwango,R
70B2 **Cuauhtémoc** Mexico
68A1 **Cuba** USA
70D2 **Cuba** *Republic* Caribbean Sea
51B5 **Cubango** *R* Angola
51B5 **Cuchi** Angola
51B5 **Cuchi** *R* Angola
7D4 **Cuckfield** England
72E3 **Cucuí** Brazil
72D2 **Cúcuta** Colombia
44B3 **Cuddalore** India
44B3 **Cuddapah** India
66D3 **Cuddeback L** USA
32A3 **Cue** Australia
72C4 **Cuenca** Ecuador
15B1 **Cuenca** Spain
70C3 **Cuernavaca** Mexico
63C3 **Cuero** USA
73G7 **Cuiabá** Brazil
75A1 **Cuiabá** *R* Brazil
75D2 **Cuieté** *R* Brazil
8B3 **Cuillin Hills** Scotland
51B4 **Cuilo** *R* Angola/Zaïre
51B5 **Cuito** *R* Angola
51B5 **Cuito Cuanavale** Angola
30D3 **Cu Lao Hon** *I* Vietnam
60C1 **Culbertson** Montana, USA
60C2 **Culbertson** Nebraska, USA
34C3 **Culcairn** Australia
34C1 **Culgoa** *R* Australia
70B2 **Culiacán** Mexico
67A2 **Cullman** USA
65D3 **Culpeper** USA
75B1 **Culuene** *R* Brazil
35B2 **Culverden** New Zealand
72F1 **Cumaná** Venezuela
57F3 **Cumberland** Maryland, USA
64A1 **Cumberland** Wisconsin, USA
57E3 **Cumberland** *R* USA
55M3 **Cumberland Pen** Canada
64C3 **Cumberland Plat** USA
55M3 **Cumberland Sd** Canada
8C4 **Cumbernauld** Scotland
6C2 **Cumbria** *County* England
59B3 **Cummings** USA
8C4 **Cumnock** Scotland
51B5 **Cunene** *R* Angola/Namibia
16B2 **Cuneo** Italy
32D3 **Cunnamulla** Australia
8D3 **Cupar** Scotland
17E2 **Ćuprija** Serbia, Yugoslavia
69D4 **Curaçao** *I* Caribbean Sea
74B4 **Curicó** Chile
75B1 **Curisevo** *R* Brazil
74G3 **Curitiba** Brazil
34A2 **Curnamona** Australia
51B5 **Curoca** *R* Angola
73K7 **Curvelo** Brazil
68A2 **Curwensville** USA
63C1 **Cushing** USA
58E1 **Custer** Montana, USA
60C2 **Custer** S Dakota, USA
58D1 **Cut Bank** USA
67B2 **Cuthbert** USA
67B3 **Cutler Ridge** USA
43F4 **Cuttack** India
51B5 **Cuvelai** Angola
18B2 **Cuxhaven** Germany
64C2 **Cuyahoga Falls** USA
66C3 **Cuyama** *R* USA
72D6 **Cuzco** Peru
7C4 **Cwmbran** Wales
50C4 **Cyangugu** Zaïre
17E3 **Cyclades** *Is* Greece
40B3 **Cyprus** *Republic* Medit Sea
55M3 **Cyrus Field B** Canada
19C3 **Czech Republic** Europe
19D2 **Częstochowa** Poland

D

30C1 **Da** *R* Vietnam
26F2 **Da'an** China
45D3 **Dab'a** Jordan
45C3 **Dabab, Jebel ed** *Mt* Jordan
69C4 **Dabajuro** Venezuela
48B4 **Dabakala** Ivory Coast
50E3 **Dabaro** Somalia
31B3 **Daba Shan** *Mts* China
50D2 **Dabat** Ethiopia
42C4 **Dabhoi** India
31C3 **Dabie Shan** *U* China
48A3 **Dabola** Guinea
48B4 **Dabou** Ivory Coast
19D2 **Dabrowa Górn** Poland
Dacca = Dhākā
18C3 **Dachau** Germany
16C1 **Dachstein** *Mt* Austria
31A3 **Dada He** *R* China
67B3 **Dade City** USA
42B3 **Dadhar** Pakistan
42B3 **Dadu** Pakistan
26D3 **Dadu He** *R* China
27F5 **Daet** Philippines
31B4 **Dafang** China
30B2 **Daga** *R* Burma
48A3 **Dagana** Senegal
21H7 **Daghestan Republic** Russian Federation
27F5 **Dagupan** Philippines
43G3 **Dagzê** China
40B4 **Dahab** Egypt
25O5 **Da Hinggan Ling** *Mts* China
67B2 **Dahlonega** USA
42C4 **Dāhod** India
28A2 **Dahongqi** China
15C2 **Dahra** *Region* Algeria
21G8 **Dahuk** Iraq
28A2 **Dahushan** China
43E3 **Dailekh** Nepal
Dairen = Lüda
40B4 **Dairût** Egypt
26G4 **Daitō Is** Pacific Ocean
32C3 **Dajarra** Australia
48A3 **Dakar** Senegal
48A2 **Dakhla** Morocco
49E2 **Dakhla Oasis** Egypt
48C3 **Dakoro** Niger
61D2 **Dakota City** USA
17E2 **Dakovica** Serbia, Yugoslavia
17D1 **Dakovo** Croatia
20B3 **Dal** *R* Sweden
51C5 **Dala** Angola
48A3 **Dalaba** Guinea
31D1 **Dalai Nur** *L* China
26D2 **Dalandzadgad** Mongolia
30D3 **Da Lat** Vietnam
31A1 **Dalay** Mongolia
8D4 **Dalbeattie** Scotland
32E3 **Dalby** Australia
67A1 **Dale Hollow L** USA
12F7 **Dalen** Norway
6C2 **Dales,The** *Upland* England
67A2 **Daleville** USA
56C3 **Dalhart** USA
65F1 **Dalhousie** Canada
54E2 **Dalhousie,C** Canada
26D4 **Dali** China
31E2 **Dalian** China
8D4 **Dalkeith** Scotland
56D3 **Dallas** USA
58B1 **Dalles,The** USA
54E4 **Dall I** USA
43E4 **Dalli Rajhara** India
48C3 **Dallol** *Watercourse* Niger
8C3 **Dalmally** Scotland
16D2 **Dalmatia** *Region* Croatia
8C4 **Dalmellington** Scotland
26G2 **Dal'nerechensk** Russian Federation
48B4 **Daloa** Ivory Coast
31B4 **Dalou Shan** *Mts* China
8C4 **Dalry** Scotland
43E4 **Dāltenganj** India
6C2 **Dalton** England
67B2 **Dalton** Georgia, USA
68D1 **Dalton** Massachusetts, USA
55Q3 **Dalton, Kap** *C* Greenland

Diyarbakır Ebinur

21G8 Diyarbakır Turkey
41E3 Diz R Iran
50B3 Dja R Cameroon
50B1 Djado,Plat du Niger
50B4 Djambala Congo
48C2 Djanet Algeria
48C1 Djedi Watercourse Algeria
48C1 Djelfa Algeria
50C3 Djéma Central African Republic
48B3 Djenné Mali
48B3 Djibo Burkina
50E2 Djibouti Djibouti
50E2 Djibouti Republic E Africa
50C3 Djolu Zaïre
48C4 Djougou Benin
50B2 Djourab, Erg du Desert Region Chad
50D3 Djugu Zaïre
12C2 Djúpivogur Iceland
15C2 Djurdjura Mts Algeria
25P2 Dmitriya Lapteva, Proliv Str Russian Federation
20F4 Dmitrov Russian Federation
Dnepr R Ukraine = Dnieper
21E6 Dneprodzerzhinsk Ukraine
21F6 Dnepropetrovsk Ukraine
20D5 Dneprovskaya Nizmennost' Region Belarus
21C6 Dnestr R Ukraine = Dniester
21E6 Dnieper R Ukraine
21C6 Dniester R Ukraine
20E4 Dno Russian Federation
50B3 Doba Chad
19E1 Dobele Latvia
32C1 Dobo Indonesia
17D2 Doboj Bosnia-Herzegovina
17F2 Dobrich Bulgaria
21E5 Dobrush Belarus
73K7 Doce R Brazil
74D2 Doctor P P Peña Paraguay
44B3 Dod India
44B3 Doda Betta Mt India
17F3 Dodecanese Is Greece
56C3 Dodge City USA
64A2 Dodgeville USA
50D4 Dodoma Tanzania
64B1 Dog L Canada
64C1 Dog L Canada
29B3 Dōgo I Japan
48C3 Dogondoutchi Niger
41D2 Doğubayazit Turkey
41F4 Doha Qatar
43G3 Doilungdêqên China
13D1 Dokkum Netherlands
29F2 Dokuchayevo, Mys C Russian Federation
32C1 Dolak I Indonesia
61D2 Doland USA
55L5 Dolbeau Canada
14D2 Dole France
7C3 Dolgellau Wales
68C1 Dolgeville USA
20K2 Dolgiy, Ostrov I Russian Federation
50E3 Dolo Odo Ethiopia
74E5 Dolores Argentina
60B3 Dolores R USA
54G3 Dolphin and Union Str Canada
74E8 Dolphin,C Falkland Islands
27G7 Dom Mt Indonesia
21K5 Dombarovskiy Russian Federation
12F6 Dombås Norway
13D3 Dombasle-sur-Meurthe France
17D1 Dombóvár Hungary
14B2 Domfront France
69E3 Dominica I Caribbean Sea
69C3 Dominican Republic Caribbean Sea
55L3 Dominion,C Canada
55N4 Domino Canada
26E1 Domna Russian Federation
16B1 Domodossola Italy
74B5 Domuyo, Vol Argentina
34D1 Domville,Mt Australia
8D3 Don R Scotland
21G6 Don R Russian Federation
9C2 Donaghadee Northern Ireland
Donau R Bulgaria = Danube
Donau R Austria/ Germany = Danube
13E4 Donaueschingen Germany
18C3 Donauwörth Germany
15A2 Don Benito Spain
7D3 Doncaster England
51B4 Dondo Angola
51D5 Dondo Mozambique
44C4 Dondra Head C Sri Lanka
10B3 Donegal Irish Republic
9C2 Donegal County Irish Republic
10B3 Donegal B Irish Republic
9C2 Donegal Mts Irish Republic
9B3 Donegal Pt Irish Republic
21F6 Donetsk Ukraine
31C4 Dong'an China
32A3 Dongara Australia
31A4 Dongchuan China
30D2 Dongfang China
28B2 Dongfeng China
32A1 Donggala Indonesia
26C3 Donggi Cona L China
28A3 Donggou China
31C5 Donghai Dao I China
31A1 Dong He R China
30D2 Dong Hoi Vietnam
31C5 Dong Jiang R China
28A2 Dongliao He R China
28C2 Dongning China
50D2 Dongola Sudan
31D5 Dongshan China
26E4 Dongsha Qundao I China
31C2 Dongsheng China
31E3 Dongtai China
31C4 Dongting Hu L China
31B5 Dongxing China
31D3 Dongzhi China
63D1 Doniphan USA
16D2 Donji Vakuf Bosnia-Herzegovina
12G5 Dönna I Norway
59B3 Donner P USA
13D3 Donnersberg Mt Germany
47D2 Donnybrook South Africa
Donostia = San Sebatián
66B2 Don Pedro Res USA
8C4 Doon, Loch L Scotland
31A3 Do Qu R China
14D2 Dorbirn Austria
7C4 Dorchester England
55L3 Dorchester,C Canada
14C2 Dordogne R France
18A2 Dordrecht Netherlands
47D3 Dordrecht South Africa
68D1 Dorest Peak Mt USA
48B3 Dori Burkina
47B3 Doring R South Africa
7D4 Dorking England
13B3 Dormans France
18B3 Dornbirn Austria
8C3 Dornoch Scotland
8D3 Dornoch Firth Estuary Scotland
12H6 Dorotea Sweden
34D2 Dorrigo Australia
58B2 Dorris USA
7C4 Dorset County England
55L3 Dorset, Cape Canada
13D2 Dorsten Germany
18B2 Dortmund Germany
50C3 Doruma Zaïre
25N4 Dosatuy Russian Federation
42B1 Doshi Afghanistan
66B2 Dos Palos USA
48C3 Dosso Niger
24G5 Dossor Kazakhstan
57E3 Dothan USA
14C1 Douai France
50A3 Douala Cameroon
34D1 Double Island Pt Australia
62B2 Double Mountain Fork R USA
66C3 Double Mt USA
14D2 Doubs R France
35A3 Doubtful Sd New Zealand
48B3 Douentza Mali
56C3 Douglas Arizona, USA
67B2 Douglas Georgia, USA
6B2 Douglas Isle of Man, British Islands
47C2 Douglas South Africa
56C2 Douglas Wyoming, USA
67B1 Douglas L USA
13C2 Doulevant-le-Château France
13B2 Doullens France
75B2 Dourada, Serra Mts Brazil
75C1 Dourada, Serra Mts Brazil
73H8 Dourados Brazil
75B3 Dourados R Brazil
75B3 Dourados, Serra dos Mts Brazil
13B3 Dourdan France
15A1 Douro R Portugal
7D3 Dove R England
62A1 Dove Creek USA
65D3 Dover Delaware, USA
7E4 Dover England
65E2 Dover New Hampshire, USA
68C2 Dover New Jersey, USA
64C2 Dover Ohio, USA
7E4 Dover,Str of England/ France
19G2 Dovsk Belarus
9C2 Down County Northern Ireland
68C3 Downingtown USA
9D2 Downpatrick Northern Ireland
68C1 Downsville USA
68C2 Doylestown USA
28B3 Dōzen I Japan
65D1 Dozois, Réservoir Canada
48A2 Dr'aa Watercourse Morocco
75B3 Dracena Brazil
13D1 Drachten Netherlands
68E1 Dracut USA
14D3 Draguignan France
60C1 Drake USA
51D6 Drakensberg Mts South Africa
47D2 Drakensberg Mt South Africa
52E7 Drake Passage Atlantic O/ Pacific Ocean
17E2 Dráma Greece
12G7 Drammen Norway
12A1 Drangajökull Ice cap Iceland
16D1 Drava R Slovenia
13D1 Drenthe Province Netherlands
18C2 Dresden Germany
14C2 Dreux France
58C2 Drewsey USA
68A2 Driftwood USA
17E2 Drin R Albania
17D2 Drina R Bosnia-Herzegovina/Serbia, Yugoslavia
19F1 Drissa R Belarus
9C3 Drogheda Irish Republic
19E3 Drogobych Ukraine
9C3 Droihead Nua Irish Republic
7C3 Droitwich England
9C2 Dromore Northern Ireland
76F12 Dronning Maud Land Region Antarctica
54G4 Drumheller Canada
58D1 Drummond USA
64C1 Drummond I USA
65E1 Drummondville Canada
8C3 Drumochter Pass Scotland
19E2 Druskininkai Lithuania
25Q3 Druzhina Russian Federation
61E1 Dryberry L Canada
55J5 Dryden Canada
68B1 Dryden USA
69H1 Dry Harbour Mts Jamaica
30B3 Duang I Burma
40C4 Dubā Saudi Arabia
41G4 Dubai UAE
54H3 Dubawnt R Canada
54H3 Dubawnt L Canada
32D4 Dubbo Australia
9C3 Dublin Irish Republic
67B2 Dublin USA
9C3 Dublin County Irish Republic
20F4 Dubna Russian Federation
21D5 Dubno Ukraine
58D2 Dubois Idaho, USA
65D2 Du Bois USA
58E2 Dubois Wyoming, USA
19F3 Dubossary Moldavia
19F2 Dubrovica Ukraine
17D2 Dubrovnik Croatia
57D2 Dubuque USA
59D2 Duchesne USA
67A1 Duck R USA
66C3 Ducor USA
13D3 Dudelange Luxembourg
24K3 Dudinka Russian Federation
7C3 Dudley England
25L2 Dudypta R Russian Federation
48B4 Duekoué Ivory Coast
15B1 Duero R Spain
33F1 Duff Is Solomon Islands
8D3 Dufftown Scotland
16C2 Dugi Otok I Croatia
18B2 Duisburg Germany
47E1 Duiwelskloof South Africa
41E3 Dūkan Iraq
50D3 Duk Faiwil Sudan
41F4 Dukhān Qatar
31A4 Dukou China
26C3 Dulan China
70D4 Dulce, Golfo Costa Rica
43G4 Dullabchara India
13D2 Dülmen Germany
57D2 Duluth USA
7C4 Dulverton England
45D2 Dūmā Syria
27D6 Dumai Indonesia
56C3 Dumas USA
45D2 Ḑumayr Syria
8C4 Dumbarton Scotland
48B1 Dumer Rbia Morocco
8D4 Dumfries Scotland
8C4 Dumfries and Galloway Region Scotland
43F4 Dumka India
65D1 Dumoine,L Canada
76G8 Dumont d'Urville Base Antarctica
49F1 Dumyat Egypt
Dunărea R Romania = Danube
9C3 Dunary Head Pt Irish Republic
Dunav R Bulgaria = Danube
Dunav R Croatia/Serbia = Danube
28C2 Dunay Russian Federation
19F3 Dunayevtsy Ukraine
8D4 Dunbar Scotland
63C2 Duncan USA
68B2 Duncannon USA
44E3 Duncan Pass Chan Andaman Islands
8D2 Duncansby Head Pt Scotland
9C2 Dundalk Irish Republic
68B3 Dundalk USA
9C3 Dundalk B Irish Republic
55M2 Dundas Greenland
54G2 Dundas Pen Canada
27G8 Dundas Str Australia
47E2 Dundee South Africa
8D3 Dundee Scotland
68B1 Dundee USA
34B1 Dundoo Australia
9D2 Dundrum B Northern Ireland
43M2 Dundwa Range Mts Nepal
33G5 Dunedin New Zealand
67B3 Dunedin USA
34C2 Dunedoo Australia
8D3 Dunfermline Scotland
9C2 Dungannon Northern Ireland
42C4 Dūngarpur India
9C3 Dungarvan Irish Republic
7E4 Dungeness Pen England
34D2 Dungog Australia
50C3 Dungu Zaïre
50D1 Dungunab Sudan
28B2 Dunhua China
26C2 Dunhuang China
8D3 Dunkeld Scotland
Dunkerque = Dunkirk
13B2 Dunkirk France
57F2 Dunkirk USA
50D2 Dunkur Ethiopia
48B4 Dunkwa Ghana
10B3 Dun Laoghaire Irish Republic
9B4 Dunmanus Irish Republic
68C2 Dunmore USA
69B1 Dunmore Town The Bahamas
67C1 Dunn USA
8D2 Dunnet Head Pt Scotland
60C2 Dunning USA
8C4 Dunoon Scotland
8D4 Duns Scotland
60C1 Dunseith USA
58B2 Dunsmuir USA
35A2 Dunstan Mts New Zealand
13C3 Dun-sur-Meuse France
31D1 Duolun China
60C1 Dupree USA
64B3 Du Quoin USA
45C3 Dura Israel
14D3 Durance R France
64A2 Durand USA
70B2 Durango Mexico
15B1 Durango Spain
56C3 Durango USA
56D3 Durant USA
45D1 Duraykīsh Syria
74E4 Durazno Uruguay
47E2 Durban South Africa
13D2 Duren Germany
43E4 Durg India
43F4 Durgapur India
6D2 Durham England
57F3 Durham N Carolina, USA
68E1 Durham New Hampshire, USA
6D2 Durham County England
34B1 Durham Downs Australia
17D2 Durmitor Mt Montenegro, Yugoslavia
8C2 Durness Scotland
17D2 Durrës Albania
34B1 Durrie Australia
17F3 Dursunbey Turkey
35B2 D'Urville I New Zealand
41H2 Dushak Turkmenistan
31B4 Dushan China
39E2 Dushanbe Tajikistan
68B2 Dushore USA
35A3 Dusky Sd New Zealand
18B2 Düsseldorf Germany
59D3 Dutton,Mt USA
31B4 Duyun China
40B1 Düzce Turkey
20F2 Dvinskaya Guba B Russian Federation
42B4 Dwārka India
58C1 Dworshak Res USA
57E3 Dyersburg USA
7B3 Dyfed County Wales
21G7 Dykh Tau Mt Russian Federation
34B1 Dynevor Downs Australia
26C2 Dzag Mongolia
26E2 Dzamīn Uūd Mongolia
51E5 Dzaoudzi Mayotte, Indian Ocean
26C2 Dzavhan Gol R Mongolia
20G4 Dzerzhinsk Russian Federation
25O4 Dzhalinda Russian Federation
24J5 Dzhambul Kazakhstan
21E6 Dzhankoy Ukraine
24H5 Dzhezkazgan Kazakhstan
42B1 Dzhilikul' Tajikistan
25P4 Dzhugdzhur, Khrebet Mts Russian Federation
24J5 Dzhungarskiy Alatau Mts Kazakhstan
18D2 Dzierzoniów Poland
39G1 Dzungaria Basin China
25L5 Dzüyl Mongolia

E

55K4 Eabamet L Canada
60B3 Eagle Colorado, USA
60C1 Eagle Butte USA
58B2 Eagle L California, USA
65F1 Eagle L Maine, USA
65F1 Eagle Lake USA
63C2 Eagle Mountain L USA
56C4 Eagle Pass USA
62A2 Eagle Peak Mt USA
54E3 Eagle Plain Canada
59C3 Earlimart USA
8D3 Earn R Scotland
8C3 Earn, Loch L Scotland
59D4 Earp USA
62B2 Earth USA
6D2 Easingwold England
67B2 Easley USA
65D2 East Aurora USA
63E2 East B USA
7E4 Eastbourne England
68C1 East Branch Delaware R USA
33G4 East C New Zealand
64B2 East Chicago USA
26F3 East China Sea China/ Japan
7E3 East Dereham England
37O6 Easter I Pacific Ocean
51C7 Eastern Cape Province South Africa
43E5 Eastern Ghats Mts India
51C6 Eastern Transvaal Province South Africa
74E8 East Falkland Is Falkland Islands
59C3 Eastgate USA
61D1 East Grand Forks USA
7D4 East Grinstead England
68D1 Easthampton USA
68D2 East Hampton USA
8C4 East Kilbride Scotland
64B2 East Lake USA
7D4 Eastleigh England
64C2 East Liverpool USA
47D3 East London South Africa
55L4 Eastmain Canada
55L4 Eastmain R Canada
67B2 Eastman USA
64A2 East Moline USA
65D3 Easton Maryland, USA
65D2 Easton Pennsylvania, USA
68C2 East Orange USA
37O5 East Pacific Ridge Pacific Ocean
37O4 East Pacific Rise Pacific Ocean
67B2 East Point USA
65F2 Eastport USA
7D3 East Retford England
67A1 East Ridge USA
57D3 East St Louis USA
25R2 East Siberian S Russian Federation
7E4 East Sussex County England
65D3 Eastville USA
66C1 East Walker R USA
67B2 Eatonton USA
61E2 Eau Claire USA
27H6 Eauripik I Pacific Ocean
7C4 Ebbw Vale Wales
50B3 Ebebiyin Equatorial Guinea
68A2 Ebensburg USA
13E3 Eberbach Germany
18C2 Eberswalde Germany
29D2 Ebetsu Japan
31A4 Ebian China
24K5 Ebinur L China

Eboli Essex

16D2 **Eboli** Italy
50B3 **Ebolowa** Cameroon
15B1 **Ebro** *R* Spain
40A1 **Eceabat** Turkey
15C2 **Ech Cheliff** Algeria
31D2 **Eching** China
58C1 **Echo** USA
54G3 **Echo Bay** Canada
13D3 **Echternach** Luxembourg
34B3 **Echuca** Australia
15A2 **Ecija** Spain
55K2 **Eclipse Sd** Canada
72C4 **Ecuador** *Republic* S America
50E2 **Ēd** Eritrea
8D2 **Eday** *I* Scotland
50C2 **Ed Da'ein** Sudan
50D2 **Ed Damer** Sudan
50D2 **Ed Debba** Sudan
8C2 **Eddrachillis B** Scotland
50D2 **Ed Dueim** Sudan
34C4 **Eddystone Pt** Australia
13C1 **Ede** Netherlands
50A3 **Edea** Cameroon
34C3 **Eden** Australia
62C2 **Eden** Texas, USA
58E2 **Eden** Wyoming, USA
6C2 **Eden** *R* England
47D2 **Edenburg** South Africa
35A3 **Edendale** New Zealand
9C3 **Edenderry** Irish Republic
13D3 **Edenkoben** Germany
13E2 **Eder** *R* Germany
60D1 **Edgeley** USA
55M3 **Edgell I** Canada
60C2 **Edgemont** USA
24D2 **Edgeøya** *I* Svalbard, Norway
68B3 **Edgewood** USA
45C3 **Edh Dhahiriya** Israel
17E2 **Edhessa** Greece
62C3 **Edinburg** USA
8D3 **Edinburgh** Scotland
21D7 **Edirne** Turkey
66C3 **Edison** USA
67B2 **Edisto** *R* USA
58B1 **Edmonds** USA
54G4 **Edmonton** Canada
60D1 **Edmore** USA
55M5 **Edmundston** Canada
63C3 **Edna** USA
16C1 **Edolo** Italy
45C3 **Edom** *Region* Jordan
21D8 **Edremit** Turkey
17F3 **Edremit Körfezi** *B* Turkey
26C2 **Edrengiyn Nuruu** *Mts* Mongolia
54G4 **Edson** Canada
34B3 **Edward** *R* Australia
50C4 **Edward,L** Uganda/Zaïre
66D3 **Edwards** USA
56C3 **Edwards Plat** USA
64B3 **Edwardsville** USA
13B2 **Eeklo** Belgium
33F2 **Efate** *I* Vanuatu
57E3 **Effingham** USA
16C3 **Egadi,I** Sicily, Italy
59D3 **Egan Range** *Mts* USA
55N3 **Egedesminde** Greenland
54C4 **Egegik** USA
19E3 **Eger** Hungary
12F7 **Egersund** Norway
13E2 **Eggegebirge** *Mts* Germany
68C3 **Egg Harbor City** USA
54G2 **Eglinton I** Canada
35B1 **Egmont,C** New Zealand
35B1 **Egmont,Mt** New Zealand
6C2 **Egremont** England
40B2 **Eğridir Gölü** *L* Turkey
6D2 **Egton** England
75C1 **Eguas** *R* Brazil
25U3 **Egvekinot** Russian Federation
49E2 **Egypt** *Republic* Africa
15B1 **Eibar** Spain
34D1 **Eidsvold** Australia
13D2 **Eifel** *Region* Germany
8B3 **Eigg** *I* Scotland
39F5 **Eight Degree Chan** Indian Ocean
32B2 **Eighty Mile Beach** Australia
34C3 **Eildon,L** Australia
18B2 **Eindhoven** Netherlands
45C3 **Ein Yahav** Israel
18C2 **Eisenach** Germany
18C3 **Eisenerz** Austria
13D2 **Eitorf** Germany
31A1 **Ejin qi** China
60C1 **Ekalaka** USA
35C2 **Eketahuna** New Zealand
24J4 **Ekibastuz** Kazakhstan
25P4 **Ekimchan** Russian Federation
12H7 **Eksjö** Sweden
57E1 **Ekwan** *R* Canada
45A3 **El Abbâsa** Egypt
40A3 **El'Alamein** Egypt
47D2 **Elands** *R* South Africa
47C3 **Elands Berg** *Mt* South Africa
40B3 **El'Arîsh** Egypt
40B4 **Elat** Israel
50C2 **El' Atrun Oasis** Sudan
21F8 **Elazığ** Turkey
40C3 **El Azraq** Jordan
16C2 **Elba** *I* Italy
49F2 **El Balyana** Egypt
72D2 **El Banco** Colombia
17E2 **Elbasan** Albania
69D5 **El Baúl** Venezuela
18C2 **Elbe** *R* Germany
45D1 **El Beqa'a** *R* Lebanon
64B2 **Elberta** USA
56C3 **Elbert,Mt** USA
67B2 **Elberton** USA
14C2 **Elbeuf** France
40C2 **Elbistan** Turkey
19D2 **Elblag** Poland
74B6 **El Bolsón** Argentina
61D1 **Elbow Lake** USA
21G7 **Elbrus** *Mt* Russian Federation
Elburz Mts = Reshteh-ye Alborz
59C4 **El Cajon** USA
63C3 **El Campo** USA
59C4 **El Centro** USA
15B2 **Elche** Spain
74C5 **El Chocón, Embalse** *Res* Argentina
15B2 **Elda** Spain
25P3 **El'dikan** Russian Federation
72C3 **El Diviso** Colombia
48B2 **El Djouf** *Desert Region* Mauritius
63D1 **Eldon** USA
75B4 **Eldorado** Argentina
57D3 **El Dorado** Arkansas, USA
75C3 **Eldorado** Brazil
56D3 **El Dorado** Kansas, USA
70B2 **El Dorado** Mexico
62B2 **Eldorado** Texas, USA
72F2 **El Dorado** Venezuela
50D3 **Eldoret** Kenya
68A2 **Eldred** USA
45C1 **Elea, C** Cyprus
66C1 **Eleanor,L** USA
58D2 **Electric Peak** *Mt* USA
48B2 **El Eglab** *Region* Algeria
62A2 **Elephant Butte Res** USA
40D2 **Eleşkirt** Turkey
16B3 **El Eulma** Algeria
57F4 **Eleuthera** *I* The Bahamas
40B4 **El Faiyûm** Egypt
48B2 **El Farsia** *Well* Morocco
50C2 **El Fasher** Sudan
40B4 **El Fashn** Egypt
15A1 **El Ferrol** Spain
45B3 **El Firdân** Egypt
50C2 **El Fula** Sudan
48C1 **El Gassi** Algeria
50D2 **El Geteina** Sudan
50D2 **El Gezīra** *Region* Sudan
45C3 **El Ghor** *V* Israel/Jordan
57E2 **Elgin** Illinois, USA
60C1 **Elgin** N Dakota, USA
8D3 **Elgin** Scotland
40B3 **El Gîza** Egypt
48C1 **El Golea** Algeria
59D4 **El Golfo de Santa Clara** Mexico
50D3 **Elgon,Mt** Kenya/Uganda
50E3 **El Goran** Ethiopia
48B2 **El Guettara** *Well* Mali
48B2 **El Hank** *Region* Mauritius
48B2 **El Haricha** *Desert Region* Mali
40A4 **El Harra** Egypt
15C2 **El Harrach** Algeria
50D2 **El Hawata** Sudan
40B4 **El'Igma** *Desert Region* Egypt
Elisabethville = Lubumbashi
12K6 **Elisenvaara** Russian Federation
El Iskandarîya = Alexandria
21G6 **Elista** Russian Federation
32C4 **Elizabeth** Australia
65E2 **Elizabeth** USA
47B2 **Elizabeth B** Namibia
57F3 **Elizabeth City** USA
68E2 **Elizabeth Is** USA
67B1 **Elizabethton** Tennessee, USA
64B3 **Elizabethtown** Kentucky, USA
67C2 **Elizabethtown** N Carolina, USA
68B2 **Elizabethtown** Pennsylvania, USA
48B1 **El Jadida** Morocco
40C3 **El Jafr** Jordan
45D3 **El Jafr** *L* Jordan
50D2 **El Jebelein** Sudan
48D1 **El Jem** Tunisia
19E2 **Ełk** Poland
68C3 **Elk** *R* Maryland/Penn, USA
64C3 **Elk** *R* W Virginia, USA
61E2 **Elkader** USA
16B3 **El Kala** Algeria
50D2 **El Kamlin** Sudan
48C1 **El Kef** Tunisia
66B1 **Elk Grove** USA
El Khalil = Hebron Israel
45A3 **El Khânka** Egypt
40B4 **El Khârga** Egypt
40B4 **El-Khârga Oasis** Egypt
64B2 **Elkhart** USA
48B2 **El Khenachich** *Desert Region* Mali
61D2 **Elkhorn** *R* USA
17F2 **Elkhovo** Bulgaria
65D3 **Elkins** USA
68B2 **Elkland** USA
60B2 **Elk Mt** USA
58C1 **Elko** Canada
56B2 **Elko** USA
16B3 **El Kroub** Algeria
68C3 **Elkton** USA
45B3 **El Kûbri** Egypt
40B3 **El Kuntilla** Egypt
50C2 **El Lagowa** Sudan
54H2 **Ellef Ringnes I** Canada
60D1 **Ellendale** USA
59D3 **Ellen,Mt** USA
56A2 **Ellensburg** USA
68C2 **Ellenville** USA
55K2 **Ellesmere I** Canada
35B2 **Ellesmere,L** New Zealand
7C3 **Ellesmere Port** England
68B3 **Ellicott City** USA
47D3 **Elliot** South Africa
55K5 **Elliot Lake** Canada
58D2 **Ellis** USA
45C3 **El Lisān** *Pen* Jordan
47D1 **Ellisras** South Africa
65F2 **Ellsworth** USA
76F3 **Ellsworth Land** *Region* Antarctica
45A4 **El Ma'âdi** Egypt
49E1 **El Maghra** *L* Egypt
40B3 **El Mahalla el Kubra** Egypt
40B3 **El Mansûra** Egypt
45A3 **El Manzala** Egypt
45B3 **El Matarîya** Egypt
68C3 **Elmer** USA
48B3 **El Merejé** *Desert Region* Mali/Mauritius
16B3 **El Milia** Algeria
45C1 **El Mīna** Lebanon
40B4 **El Minya** Egypt
66B1 **Elmira** California, USA
57F2 **Elmira** New York, USA
59D4 **El Mirage** USA
62B3 **El Moral** Mexico
48B2 **El Mreiti** *Well* Mauritius
18B2 **Elmshorn** Germany
50C2 **El Muglad** Sudan
48B2 **El Mzereb** *Well* Mali
50D2 **El Obeid** Sudan
48C1 **El Oued** Algeria
59D4 **Eloy** USA
56C3 **El Paso** USA
59B3 **El Portal** USA
62A2 **El Porvenir** Mexico
15A2 **El Puerto del Sta Maria** Spain
El Qâhira = Cairo
45B3 **El Qantara** Egypt
El Quds = Jerusalem
45C3 **El Quseima** Egypt
45C4 **El Quwetra** Jordan
56D3 **El Reno** USA
54E3 **Elsa** Canada
45A4 **El Saff** Egypt
45B3 **El Sâlhîya** Egypt
70D3 **El Salvador** *Republic* Central America
59C4 **El Sauzal** Mexico
45B3 **El Shallûfa** Egypt
45B4 **El Shatt** Egypt
45A3 **El Simbillâwein** Egypt
66D4 **Elsinore L** USA
18C2 **Elsterwerde** Germany
62A3 **El Sueco** Mexico
El Suweis = Suez
45A4 **El Tabbin** Egypt
15A1 **El Teleno** *Mt* Spain
35B1 **Eltham** New Zealand
45C4 **El Thamad** Egypt
72F2 **El Tigre** Venezuela
40B4 **El Tîh** *Desert Region* Egypt
45B3 **El Tîna** Egypt
58C1 **Eltopia** USA
40B4 **El Tûr** Egypt
44C2 **Elūru** India
15A2 **Elvas** Portugal
72D5 **Elvira** Brazil
54H2 **Elvira,C** Canada
64B2 **Elwood** USA
7E3 **Ely** England
57D2 **Ely** Minnesota, USA
56B3 **Ely** Nevada, USA
64C2 **Elyria** USA
45A3 **El Zarqa** Egypt
41G2 **Emāmrūd** Iran
42B1 **Emām Sāheb** Afghanistan
18D1 **Eman** *R* Sweden
21K6 **Emba** Kazakhstan
21K6 **Emba** *R* Kazakhstan
Embalse de Ricobayo = Esla, Embalse
74D2 **Embarcación** Argentina
54G4 **Embarras Portage** Canada
50D4 **Embu** Kenya
18B2 **Emden** Germany
31A4 **Emei** China
32D3 **Emerald** Australia
54J5 **Emerson** Canada
58C2 **Emigrant P** USA
50B1 **Emi Koussi** *Mt* Chad
40B2 **Emirdağ** Turkey
68C2 **Emmaus** USA
18B2 **Emmen** Netherlands
13D3 **Emmendingen** Germany
13D2 **Emmerich** Germany
58C2 **Emmett** USA
68B3 **Emmitsburg** USA
56C4 **Emory Peak** *Mt* USA
70A2 **Empalme** Mexico
47E2 **Empangeni** South Africa
74E3 **Empedrado** Argentina
37K2 **Emperor Seamount Chain** Pacific Ocean
63C1 **Emporia** Kansas, USA
65D3 **Emporia** Virginia, USA
68A2 **Emporium** USA
18B2 **Ems** *R* Germany
28B2 **Emu** China
8C2 **Enard B** Scotland
74E3 **Encarnación** Paraguay
48B4 **Enchi** Ghana
62C3 **Encinal** USA
66D4 **Encinitas** USA
75D2 **Encruzilhada** Brazil
32B1 **Endeh** Indonesia
76G11 **Enderby Land** *Region* Antarctica
61D1 **Enderlin** USA
65D2 **Endicott** USA
54C3 **Endicott Mts** USA
16C3 **Enfida** Tunisia
67C1 **Enfield** USA
27F5 **Engaño, C** Philippines
29D2 **Engaru** Japan
45C3 **En Gedi** Israel
21H5 **Engel's** Russian Federation
27D7 **Enggano** *I* Indonesia
10C3 **England** UK
55N4 **Englee** Canada
67C1 **Englehard** USA
65D1 **Englehart** Canada
60C3 **Englewood** USA
10C3 **English Channel** England/France
63C1 **Enid** USA
29D2 **Eniwa** Japan
48B3 **Enji** *Well* Mauritius
13C1 **Enkhuizen** Netherlands
12H7 **Enköping** Sweden
16C3 **Enna** Sicily, Italy
50C2 **En Nahud** Sudan
50C2 **Ennedi** *Desert Region* Chad
9C3 **Ennell, L** Irish Republic
34C1 **Enngonia** Australia
60C2 **Enning** USA
10B3 **Ennis** Irish Republic
58D1 **Ennis** Montana, USA
63C2 **Ennis** Texas, USA
9C3 **Enniscorthy** Irish Republic
9C2 **Enniskillen** Northern Ireland
45C2 **Enn Nâqoûra** Lebanon
18C3 **Enns** *R* Austria
12F8 **Enschede** Netherlands
70A1 **Ensenada** Mexico
31B3 **Enshi** China
13D4 **Ensisheim** France
50D4 **Entebbe** Uganda
67A2 **Enterprise** Alabama, USA
58C1 **Enterprise** Oregon, USA
74E4 **Entre Ríos** *State* Argentina
48C4 **Enugu** Nigeria
13E3 **Enz** *R* Germany
29C3 **Enzan** Japan
14C2 **Epernay** France
40A2 **Ephesus** Turkey
59D3 **Ephraim** USA
68B2 **Ephrata** Pennsylvania, USA
58C1 **Ephrata** Washington, USA
33F2 **Epi** *I* Vanuatu
14D2 **Epinal** France
45B1 **Episkopi** Cyprus
45B1 **Episkopi B** Cyprus
7E4 **Epping** England
13E3 **Eppingen** Germany
7D4 **Epsom** England
47B1 **Epukiro** Namibia
41F3 **Eqlid** Iran
46D7 **Equator**
48C4 **Equatorial Guinea** *Republic* W Africa
68D1 **Equinox Mt** USA
68C2 **Equinunk** USA
13E3 **Erbach** Germany
13D3 **Erbeskopf** *Mt* Germany
41D2 **Erciş** Turkey
21F8 **Erciyas Dağları** *Mt* Turkey
28B2 **Erdaobaihe** China
28B2 **Erdao Jiang** *R* China
31C1 **Erdene** Mongolia
26D2 **Erdenet** Mongolia
50C2 **Erdi** *Desert Region* Chad
74F3 **Erechim** Brazil
40B1 **Ereğli** Turkey
40B2 **Ereğli** Turkey
26E2 **Erenhot** China
15B1 **Eresma** *R* Spain
13D2 **Erft** *R* Germany
18C2 **Erfurt** Germany
40C2 **Ergani** Turkey
48B2 **Erg Chech** *Desert Region* Algeria/Mali
48D3 **Erg du Ténéré** *Desert Region* Niger
40A1 **Ergene** *R* Turkey
48B2 **Erg Iguidi** *Region* Algeria/Mauritania
19F1 **Ērgli** Latvia
50B2 **Erguig** *R* Chad
25N4 **Ergun'** *R* China/Russian Federation
26E1 **Ergun** *R* China/Russian Federation
25O4 **Ergun Zuoqi** China
50D2 **Eriba** Sudan
8C2 **Eriboll, Loch** *Inlet* Scotland
8C3 **Ericht, Loch** *L* Scotland
57F2 **Erie** USA
57E2 **Erie,L** Canada/USA
29D2 **Erimo-misaki** *C* Japan
8B3 **Eriskay** *I* Scotland
50D2 **Eritrea** *Republic* Africa
13D2 **Erkelenz** Germany
18C3 **Erlangen** Germany
63D2 **Erling,L** USA
47D2 **Ermelo** South Africa
44B4 **Ernākulam** India
9C2 **Erne, L** Northern Ireland
44B3 **Erode** India
34B1 **Eromanga** Australia
47B1 **Erongoberg** *Mt* Namibia
48B1 **Er Rachidia** Morocco
50D2 **Er Rahad** Sudan
51D5 **Errego** Mozambique
10B2 **Errigal** *Mt* Irish Republic
10A3 **Erris Head** *Pt* Irish Republic
33F2 **Erromanga** *I* Vanuatu
50D2 **Er Roseires** Sudan
45C2 **Er Rummān** Jordan
61D1 **Erskine** USA
13D3 **Erstein** France
18C2 **Erzgebirge** *Upland* Germany
21F8 **Erzincan** Turkey
21G8 **Erzurum** Turkey
29D2 **Esan-misaki** *C* Japan
29D2 **Esashi** Japan
18B1 **Esbjerg** Denmark
59D3 **Escalante** USA
56C4 **Escalón** Mexico
57E2 **Escanaba** USA
70C3 **Escárcega** Mexico
13C3 **Esch** Luxembourg
59C4 **Escondido** USA
70B2 **Escuinapa** Mexico
70C3 **Escuintla** Guatemala
50B3 **Eséka** Cameroon
13D1 **Esens** Germany
14C3 **Esera** *R* Spain
15C1 **Esera** *R* Spain
41F3 **Eşfahān** Iran
47E2 **Eshowe** South Africa
45C3 **Esh Sharā** *Upland* Jordan
8D4 **Esk** *R* Scotland
35C1 **Eskdale** New Zealand
12C1 **Eskifjörður** Iceland
12H7 **Eskilstuna** Sweden
54E3 **Eskimo Lakes** Canada
55J3 **Eskimo Point** Canada
21E8 **Eskişehir** Turkey
15A1 **Esla** *R* Spain
15A1 **Esla, Embalse del** *Res* Spain
69B2 **Esmeralda** Cuba
74A7 **Esmeralda** *I* Chile
72C3 **Esmeraldas** Ecuador
14C3 **Espalion** France
64C1 **Espanola** Canada
62A1 **Espanola** USA
32B4 **Esperance** Australia
76G2 **Esperanza** *Base* Antarctica
15A2 **Espichel, Cabo** *C* Portugal
75D2 **Espinhaço, Serra do** *Mts* Brazil
75D2 **Espírito Santo** *State* Brazil
33F2 **Espiritu Santo** *I* Vanuatu
51D6 **Espungabera** Mozambique
74B6 **Esquel** Argentina
58B1 **Esquimalt** Canada
45D2 **Es Samrā** Jordan
48B1 **Essaouira** Morocco
18B2 **Essen** Germany
73G3 **Essequibo** *R* Guyana
7E4 **Essex** *County* England

Fort Dodge — Gennargentu, Monti del

57D2 **Fort Dodge** USA
32A3 **Fortescue** *R* Australia
57D2 **Fort Frances** Canada
54F3 **Fort Franklin** Canada
54F3 **Fort Good Hope** Canada
34B1 **Fort Grey** Australia
8C3 **Forth** *R* Scotland
62A2 **Fort Hancock** USA
55K4 **Fort Hope** Canada
8F3 **Forties** *Oilfield* N Sea
65F1 **Fort Kent** USA
48C1 **Fort Lallemand** Algeria
Fort Lamy = Ndjamena
60C2 **Fort Laramie** USA
57E4 **Fort Lauderdale** USA
54F3 **Fort Liard** Canada
54G4 **Fort Mackay** Canada
54G5 **Fort Macleod** Canada
54G4 **Fort McMurray** Canada
54E3 **Fort McPherson** Canada
64A2 **Fort Madison** USA
56C2 **Fort Morgan** USA
57E4 **Fort Myers** USA
54F4 **Fort Nelson** Canada
54F3 **Fort Norman** Canada
67A2 **Fort Payne** USA
60B1 **Fort Peck** USA
56C2 **Fort Peck Res** USA
57E4 **Fort Pierce** USA
60C2 **Fort Pierre** USA
68C1 **Fort Plain** USA
54G3 **Fort Providence** Canada
54G3 **Fort Resolution** Canada
50B4 **Fort Rousset** Congo
54F4 **Fort St James** Canada
54F4 **Fort St John** Canada
63D1 **Fort Scott** USA
54E3 **Fort Selkirk** Canada
55K4 **Fort Severn** Canada
21J7 **Fort Shevchenko** Kazakhstan
54F3 **Fort Simpson** Canada
54G3 **Fort Smith** Canada
57D3 **Fort Smith** USA
54F3 **Fort Smith** *Region* Canada
56C3 **Fort Stockton** USA
62B2 **Fort Sumner** USA
62C1 **Fort Supply** USA
58B2 **Fortuna** California, USA
60C1 **Fortuna** N Dakota, USA
54G4 **Fort Vermilion** Canada
67A2 **Fort Walton Beach** USA
57E2 **Fort Wayne** USA
8C3 **Fort William** Scotland
62A1 **Fort Wingate** USA
56D3 **Fort Worth** USA
54D3 **Fort Yukon** USA
31C5 **Foshan** China
55K2 **Fosheim Pen** Canada
61D1 **Fosston** USA
50B4 **Fougamou** Gabon
14B2 **Fougères** France
8D1 **Foula** *I* Scotland
13E3 **Foulness I** England
35B2 **Foulwind,C** New Zealand
50B3 **Foumban** Cameroon
48B2 **Foum el Alba** *Region* Mali
14C1 **Fourmies** France
17F3 **Foúrnoi** *I* Greece
48A3 **Fouta Djallon** *Mts* Guinea
33F5 **Foveaux Str** New Zealand
7B4 **Fowey** England
62B1 **Fowler** USA
64B2 **Fox** *R* USA
55K3 **Foxe Basin** *G* Canada
55K3 **Foxe Chan** Canada
55L3 **Foxe Pen** Canada
60B2 **Foxpark** USA
35C2 **Foxton** New Zealand
10B2 **Foyle, Lough** *Estuary* Irish Republic/Northern Ireland
51B5 **Foz do Cuene** Angola
74F3 **Foz do Iguaçu** Brazil
68B2 **Frackville** USA
15C1 **Fraga** Spain
68E1 **Framingham** USA
73J8 **Franca** Brazil
14C2 **France** *Republic* Europe
14D2 **Franche Comté** *Region* France
47D1 **Francistown** Botswana
58E2 **Francs Peak** *Mt* USA
13E2 **Frankenberg** Germany
64B2 **Frankfort** Indiana, USA
57E3 **Frankfort** Kentucky, USA
68C1 **Frankfort** New York, USA
47D2 **Frankfort** South Africa
18B2 **Frankfurt am Main** Germany
18C2 **Frankfurt an-der-Oder** Germany
18C3 **Fränkischer Alb** *Upland* Germany
58D2 **Franklin** Idaho, USA
64B3 **Franklin** Indiana, USA
63D3 **Franklin** Louisiana, USA
68E1 **Franklin** Massachusetts, USA
67B1 **Franklin** N Carolina, USA
68E1 **Franklin** New Hampshire, USA
68C2 **Franklin** New Jersey, USA
65D2 **Franklin** Pennsylvania, USA
67A1 **Franklin** Tennessee, USA
65D3 **Franklin** Virginia, USA
54F2 **Franklin B** Canada
58C1 **Franklin D Roosevelt** *L* USA
54F3 **Franklin Mts** Canada
54J2 **Franklin Str** Canada
68A1 **Franklinville** USA
35B2 **Franz Josef Glacier** New Zealand
Franz-Josef-Land = Zemlya Frantsa Josifa
54F5 **Fraser** *R* Canada
47C3 **Fraserburg** South Africa
8D3 **Fraserburgh** Scotland
34D1 **Fraser I** Australia
68C3 **Frederica** USA
18B1 **Fredericia** Denmark
65D3 **Frederick** Maryland, USA
62C2 **Frederick** Oklahoma, USA
62C2 **Fredericksburg** Texas, USA
65D3 **Fredericksburg** Virginia, USA
64A3 **Fredericktown** USA
55M5 **Fredericton** Canada
55N3 **Frederikshåp** Greenland
12G7 **Frederikshavn** Denmark
65D2 **Fredonia** USA
12G7 **Fredrikstad** Norway
68C2 **Freehold** USA
66C1 **Freel Peak** *Mt* USA
61D2 **Freeman** USA
64B2 **Freeport** Illinois, USA
63C3 **Freeport** Texas, USA
69B1 **Freeport** The Bahamas
62C3 **Freer** USA
48A4 **Freetown** Sierra Leone
18B3 **Freiburg** Germany
13D3 **Freiburg im Breisgau** Germany
18C3 **Freistadt** Austria
32A4 **Fremantle** Australia
66B2 **Fremont** California, USA
61D2 **Fremont** Nebraska, USA
64C2 **Fremont** Ohio, USA
73H3 **French Guiana** *Dependency* S America
60B1 **Frenchman** *R* USA
34C4 **Frenchmans Cap** *Mt* Australia
37M5 **French Polynesia** *Is* Pacific Ocean
15C2 **Frenda** Algeria
70B2 **Fresnillo** Mexico
56B3 **Fresno** USA
66C2 **Fresno** *R* USA
58D1 **Fresno Res** USA
13E3 **Freudenstadt** Germany
13B2 **Frévent** France
34C4 **Freycinet Pen** Australia
48A3 **Fria** Guinea
66C2 **Friant** USA
66C2 **Friant Dam** USA
16B1 **Fribourg** Switzerland
13E2 **Friedberg** Germany
18B3 **Friedrichshafen** Germany
13C1 **Friesland** *Province* Netherlands
62C3 **Frio** *R* USA
75D3 **Frio, Cabo** *C* Brazil
62B2 **Friona** USA
55M3 **Frobisher B** Canada
55M3 **Frobisher Bay** Canada
54H4 **Frobisher L** Canada
21G6 **Frolovo** Russian Federation
7C4 **Frome** England
7C4 **Frome** *R* England
32C4 **Frome,L** Australia
63D1 **Frontenac** USA
70C3 **Frontera** Mexico
65D3 **Front Royal** USA
16C2 **Frosinone** Italy
60B3 **Fruita** USA
31C5 **Fuchuan** China
31E4 **Fuding** China
70B2 **Fuerte** *R* Mexico
75A3 **Fuerte Olimpo** Brazil
74E2 **Fuerte Olimpo** Paraguay
48A2 **Fuerteventura** *I* Canary Islands
31C2 **Fugu** China
26B2 **Fuhai** China
41G4 **Fujairah** UAE
29C3 **Fuji** Japan
31D4 **Fujian** *Province* China
26G2 **Fujin** China
29C3 **Fujinomiya** Japan
29D3 **Fuji-san** *Mt* Japan
29C3 **Fujisawa** Japan
29C3 **Fuji-Yoshida** Japan
29D2 **Fukagawa** Japan
24K5 **Fukang** China
29D3 **Fukuchiyama** Japan
28A4 **Fukue** Japan
28A4 **Fukue** *I* Japan
29D3 **Fukui** Japan
28C4 **Fukuoka** Japan
29E3 **Fukushima** Japan
29C4 **Fukuyama** Japan
61D2 **Fulda** USA
18B2 **Fulda** Germany
18B2 **Fulda** *R* Germany
31B4 **Fuling** China
69L1 **Fullarton** Trinidad
66D4 **Fullerton** USA
6F1 **Fulmar** *Oilfield* N Sea
64A2 **Fulton** Illinois, USA
64B3 **Fulton** Kentucky, USA
65D2 **Fulton** New York, USA
13C2 **Fumay** France
29D3 **Funabashi** Japan
33G1 **Funafuti** *I* Tuvalu
48A1 **Funchal** Madeira
75D2 **Fundão** Brazil
55M5 **Fundy,B of** Canada
51D6 **Funhalouro** Mozambique
31B5 **Funing** China
31D3 **Funing** China
48C3 **Funtua** Nigeria
31D4 **Fuqing** China
51D5 **Furancungo** Mozambique
29D2 **Furano** Japan
41G4 **Fūrg** Iran
75B2 **Furnas, Serra das** *Mts* Brazil
32D5 **Furneaux Group** *Is* Australia
13D1 **Furstenau** Germany
18C2 **Fürstenwalde** Germany
18C3 **Fürth** Germany
29D2 **Furubira** Japan
29E3 **Furukawa** Japan
55K3 **Fury and Hecla Str** Canada
28A2 **Fushun** China
31A4 **Fushun** Sichuan, China
28B2 **Fusong** China
18C3 **Füssen** Germany
31E2 **Fu Xian** China
31E1 **Fuxin** China
31D3 **Fuyang** China
31E1 **Fuyuan** Liaoning, China
31A4 **Fuyuan** Yunnan, China
26B2 **Fuyun** China
31D4 **Fuzhou** China
28A3 **Fuzhoucheng** China
18C1 **Fyn** *I* Denmark
8C3 **Fyne, Loch** *Inlet* Scotland

G

50E3 **Gaalkacyo** Somalia
59C3 **Gabbs** USA
66C1 **Gabbs Valley Range** *Mts* USA
51B5 **Gabela** Angola
48D1 **Gabès, G de** Tunisia
66B2 **Gabilan Range** *Mts* USA
50B4 **Gabon** *Republic* Africa
47D1 **Gaborone** Botswana
15A1 **Gabriel y Galán, Embalse** *Res* Spain
17F2 **Gabrovo** Bulgaria
41F3 **Gach Sārān** Iran
66C2 **Gadag** India
67A2 **Gadsden** Alabama, USA
59D4 **Gadsden** Arizona, USA
16C2 **Gaeta** Italy
27H6 **Gaferut** *I* Pacific Ocean
67B1 **Gaffney** USA
45A3 **Gafra, Wadi el** Egypt
48C1 **Gafsa** Tunisia
20E4 **Gagarin** Russian Federation
55M4 **Gagnon** Canada
21G7 **Gagra** Georgia
43F3 **Gaibanda** Bangladesh
74C6 **Gaimán** Argentina
67B3 **Gainesville** Florida, USA
67B2 **Gainesville** Georgia, USA
63C2 **Gainesville** Texas, USA
7D3 **Gainsborough** England
32C4 **Gairdner, L** Australia
8C3 **Gairloch** Scotland
68B3 **Gaithersburg** USA
28A2 **Gai Xian** China
44B2 **Gajendragarh** India
31D4 **Ga Jiang** *R* China
47C2 **Gakarosa** *Mt* South Africa
50D4 **Galana** *R* Kenya
72N **Galapagos Is** Pacific Ocean
Gálápagos, Islas = Galapagos Islands
8D4 **Galashiels** Scotland
17F1 **Galaţi** Romania
64C3 **Galax** USA
62A2 **Galeana** Mexico
54C3 **Galena** Alaska, USA
64A2 **Galena** Illinois, USA
63D1 **Galena** Kansas, USA
69L1 **Galeota Pt** Trinidad
69L1 **Galera Pt** Trinidad
64A2 **Galesburg** USA
68B2 **Galeton** USA
20G4 **Galich** Russian Federation
15A1 **Galicia** *Region* Spain
Galilee,S of = Tiberias,L
69J1 **Galina Pt** Jamaica
50D2 **Gallabat** Sudan
67A1 **Gallatin** USA
58D1 **Gallatin** *R* USA
44C4 **Galle** Sri Lanka
62A3 **Gallego** Mexico
15B1 **Gállego** *R* Spain
72D1 **Gallinas, Puerta** Colombia
Gallipolī = Gelibolu
17D2 **Gallipoli** Italy
20C2 **Gällivare** Sweden
8C4 **Galloway** *District* Scotland
8C4 **Galloway,Mull of** *C* Scotland
62A1 **Gallup** USA
66B1 **Galt** USA
9B3 **Galty Mts** Irish Republic
70C2 **Galveston** USA
57D4 **Galveston B** USA
10B3 **Galway** Irish Republic
10B3 **Galway B** Irish Republic
43F3 **Gamba** China
48B3 **Gambaga** Ghana
54A3 **Gambell** USA
48A3 **Gambia** *R* Senegal/The Gambia
48A3 **Gambia,The** *Republic* Africa
37N6 **Gambier, Îles** Pacific Ocean
50B4 **Gamboma** Congo
51B5 **Gambos** Angola
44C4 **Gampola** Sri Lanka
59E3 **Ganado** USA
50E3 **Ganale Dorya** *R* Ethiopia
65D2 **Gananoque** Canada
Gand = Gent
51B5 **Ganda** Angola
51C4 **Gandajika** Zaïre
43N2 **Gandak** *R* India/Nepal
43M2 **Gandak Dam** Nepal
42B3 **Gandava** Pakistan
55N5 **Gander** Canada
42B4 **Gāndhīdhām** India
42C4 **Gāndhīnagar** India
42D4 **Gāndhi Sāgar** *L* India
15B2 **Gandia** Spain
75E1 **Gandu** Brazil
Ganga *R* **=Ganges**
42C3 **Gangānagar** India
43G4 **Gangaw** Burma
31A2 **Gangca** China
39G2 **Gangdise Shan** *Mts* China
22F4 **Ganges** *R* India
43F4 **Ganges, Mouths of the** Bangladesh/India
28B2 **Gangou** China
43F3 **Gangtok** India
31B3 **Gangu** China
58E2 **Gannett Peak** *Mt* USA
31B2 **Ganquan** China
12K8 **Gantsevichi** Belarus
31D4 **Ganzhou** China
48C3 **Gao** Mali
31A2 **Gaolan** China
31C2 **Gaoping** China
48B3 **Gaoua** Burkina
48A3 **Gaoual** Guinea
31D3 **Gaoyou Hu** *L* China
31C5 **Gaozhou** China
14D3 **Gap** France
42D2 **Gar** China
9C3 **Gara,L** Irish Republic
34C1 **Garah** Australia
73L5 **Garanhuns** Brazil
58B2 **Garberville** USA
75C3 **Garça** Brazil
15A2 **Garcia de Sola, Embalse de** *Res* Spain
75B3 **Garcias** Brazil
16C1 **Garda, L di** Italy
62B1 **Garden City** USA
64B1 **Garden Pen** USA
42B2 **Gardez** Afghanistan
58D1 **Gardiner** USA
68D2 **Gardiners I** USA
68E1 **Gardner** USA
33H1 **Gardner** *I* Phoenix Islands
66C1 **Gardnerville** USA
16D2 **Gargano, Monte** *Mt* Italy
16D2 **Gargano, Prom. del** Italy
42D4 **Garhākota** India
43K1 **Garhmuktesar** India
20L4 **Gari** Russian Federation
47B3 **Garies** South Africa
50D4 **Garissa** Kenya
63C2 **Garland** USA
18C3 **Garmisch-Partenkirchen** Germany
41F2 **Garmsar** Iran
63C1 **Garnett** USA
56B2 **Garnett Peak** *Mt* USA
14C3 **Garonne** *R* France
49D4 **Garoua** Cameroon
49D4 **Garoua Boulai** Cameroon
60C1 **Garrison** USA
9D2 **Garron** *Pt* Northern Ireland
8C3 **Garry** *R* Scotland
54H3 **Garry L** Canada
43E4 **Garwa** India
64B2 **Gary** USA
39G2 **Garyarsa** China
63C2 **Garza-Little Elm** *Res* USA
41F2 **Gasan Kuli** Turkmenistan
14B3 **Gascogne** *Region* France
63D1 **Gasconade** *R* USA
32A3 **Gascoyne** *R* Australia
50B3 **Gashaka** Nigeria
48D3 **Gashua** Nigeria
57G2 **Gaspé** Canada
57G2 **Gaspé,C de** Canada
57G2 **Gaspé, Peninsule de** Canada
67B1 **Gastonia** USA
67C1 **Gaston,L** USA
45B1 **Gata, C** Cyprus
15B2 **Gata, Cabo de** *C* Spain
20D4 **Gatchina** Russian Federation
8C4 **Gatehouse of Fleet** Scotland
6D2 **Gateshead** England
63C2 **Gatesville** USA
13B3 **Gâtinais** *Region* France
65D1 **Gatineau** Canada
65D1 **Gatineau** *R* Canada
67B1 **Gatlinburg** USA
34D1 **Gatton** Australia
33F2 **Gaua** *I* Vanuatu
43G3 **Gauhāti** India
19E1 **Gauja** *R* Latvia
43E3 **Gauri Phanta** India
17E4 **Gávdhos** *I* Greece
75D1 **Gavião** *R* Brazil
66B3 **Gaviota** USA
12H6 **Gävle** Sweden
32C4 **Gawler Ranges** *Mts* Australia
31A1 **Gaxun Nur** *L* China
43E4 **Gaya** India
48C3 **Gaya** Niger
48C3 **Gaya** Nigeria
28B2 **Gaya He** *R* China
64C1 **Gaylord** USA
34D1 **Gayndah** Australia
20J3 **Gayny** Russian Federation
19F3 **Gaysin** Ukraine
40B3 **Gaza** Israel
40C2 **Gaziantep** Turkey
48B4 **Gbaringa** Liberia
48D1 **Gbbès** Tunisia
19D2 **Gdańsk** Poland
19D2 **Gdańsk,G of** Poland
12K7 **Gdov** Russian Federation
19D2 **Gdynia** Poland
45A4 **Gebel el Galâla el Baharîya** *Desert* Egypt
50D2 **Gedaref** Sudan
17F3 **Gediz** *R* Turkey
18C2 **Gedser** Denmark
13C2 **Geel** Belgium
34B3 **Geelong** Australia
34C4 **Geeveston** Australia
48D3 **Geidam** Nigeria
13D2 **Geilenkirchen** Germany
50D4 **Geita** Tanzania
31A5 **Gejiu** China
16C3 **Gela** Italy
50E3 **Geladī** Ethiopia
13D2 **Geldern** Germany
17F2 **Gelibolu** Turkey
40B2 **Gelidonya Burun** Turkey
13E2 **Gelnhausen** Germany
13D2 **Gelsenkirchen** Germany
12F8 **Gelting** Germany
30C5 **Gemas** Malaysia
13C2 **Gembloux** Belgium
50B3 **Gemena** Zaïre
40C2 **Gemerek** Turkey
40A1 **Gemlik** Turkey
16C1 **Gemona** Italy
47C2 **Gemsbok Nat Pk** Botswana
50C2 **Geneina** Sudan
74C5 **General Alvear** Argentina
76F2 **General Belgrano** *Base* Antarctica
76G2 **General Bernardo O'Higgins** *Base* Antarctica
74B7 **General Carrera, Lago** Chile
74D2 **General Eugenio A Garay** Paraguay
66C2 **General Grant Grove Section** *Region* USA
74C3 **General Manuel Belgrano** *Mt* Argentina
74D5 **General Pico** Argentina
74C5 **General Roca** Argentina
27F6 **General Santos** Philippines
65D2 **Genesee** *R* USA
65D2 **Geneseo** USA
61D2 **Geneva** Nebraska, USA
68B1 **Geneva** New York, USA
16B1 **Geneva** Switzerland
Geneva,L of = Léman, L
Genève = Geneva
15B2 **Genil** *R* Spain
16B2 **Gennargentu, Monti del** *Mt* Sardinia, Italy

Genoa Gravelbourg

34C3 **Genoa** Australia
16B2 **Genoa** Italy
Genova = Genoa
16B2 **Genova, G di** Italy
13B2 **Gent** Belgium
27D7 **Genteng** Indonesia
18C2 **Genthin** Germany
21H7 **Geokchay** Azerbaijan
47C3 **George** South Africa
55M4 **George** *R* Canada
34C2 **George,L** Australia
67B3 **George,L** Florida, USA
65E2 **George,L** New York, USA
35A2 **George Sd** New Zealand
34C4 **George Town** Australia
66B1 **Georgetown** California, USA
65D3 **Georgetown** Delaware, USA
73G2 **Georgetown** Guyana
64C3 **Georgetown** Kentucky, USA
30C4 **George Town** Malaysia
69N2 **Georgetown** St Vincent
67C2 **Georgetown** S Carolina, USA
63C2 **Georgetown** Texas, USA
48A3 **Georgetown** The Gambia
76G8 **George V Land** *Region* Antarctica
62C3 **George West** USA
21G7 **Georgia** *Republic* Europe
76F12 **Georg Forster** *Base* Antarctica
67B2 **Georgia** *State* USA
64C1 **Georgian B** Canada
54F5 **Georgia, Str of** Canada
32C3 **Georgina** *R* Australia
21F5 **Georgiu-Dezh** Russian Federation
21G7 **Georgiyevsk** Russian Federation
76F1 **Georg von Neumayer** *Base* Antarctica
18C2 **Gera** Germany
13B2 **Geraardsbergen** Belgium
75C1 **Geral de Goiás, Serra** *Mts* Brazil
35B2 **Geraldine** New Zealand
75C2 **Geral do Paraná, Serra** *Mts* Brazil
32A3 **Geraldton** Australia
57E2 **Geraldton** Canada
75D2 **Geral, Serra** *Mts* Bahia, Brazil
75B4 **Geral, Serra** *Mts* Paraná, Brazil
45C3 **Gerar** *R* Israel
13D3 **Gérardmer** France
54C3 **Gerdine,Mt** USA
30C4 **Gerik** Malaysia
60C2 **Gering** USA
21C6 **Gerlachovsky** *Mt* Poland
47D2 **Germiston** South Africa
13D2 **Gerolstein** Germany
15C1 **Gerona** Spain
13E2 **Geseke** Germany
50E3 **Gestro** *R* Ethiopia
15B1 **Getafe** Spain
68B3 **Gettysburg** Pennsylvania, USA
60D1 **Gettysburg** S Dakota, USA
41D2 **Gevaş** Turkey
17E2 **Gevgeliija** Macedonia, Yugoslavia
45D2 **Ghabāghib** Syria
45D3 **Ghadaf, Wadi el** Jordan
48C1 **Ghadamis** Libya
41F2 **Ghaem Shahr** Iran
43E3 **Ghāghara** *R* India
48B4 **Ghana** *Republic* Africa
47C1 **Ghanzi** Botswana
48C1 **Ghardaïa** Algeria
49D1 **Gharyān** Libya
49D2 **Ghāt** Libya
15B2 **Ghazaouet** Algeria
42D3 **Ghāziābād** India
42B2 **Ghazni** Afghanistan
17F1 **Gheorgheni** Romania
40D3 **Ghudāf, Wadi al** *Watercourse* Iraq
16D3 **Giarre** Sicily, Italy
60D2 **Gibbon** USA
47B2 **Gibeon** Namibia
15A2 **Gibraltar** *Colony* SW Europe
7E7 **Gibraltar** *Pt* England
15A2 **Gibraltar,Str of** Africa/ Spain
32B3 **Gibson Desert** Australia
58B1 **Gibsons** Canada
44B2 **Giddalūr** India
45B3 **Giddi, Gebel el** *Mt* Egypt
45B3 **Giddi Pass** Egypt
50D3 **Gīdolē** Ethiopia
13B4 **Gien** France
18B2 **Giessen** Germany
8D4 **Gifford** Scotland
67B3 **Gifford** USA
29D3 **Gifu** Japan
8C4 **Gigha** *I* Scotland
16C2 **Giglio** *I* Italy
15A1 **Gijón** Spain
59D4 **Gila** *R* USA
59D4 **Gila Bend** USA
59D4 **Gila Bend Mts** USA
32D2 **Gilbert** *R* Australia
33G1 **Gilbert Is** Pacific Ocean
58D1 **Gildford** USA
51D5 **Gilé** Mozambique
45C2 **Gilead** *Region* Jordan
49E2 **Gilf Kebir Plat** Egypt
34C2 **Gilgandra** Australia
42C1 **Gilgit** Pakistan
42C1 **Gilgit** *R* Pakistan
34C2 **Gilgunnia** Australia
55J4 **Gillam** Canada
60B2 **Gillette** USA
7E4 **Gillingham** England
64B1 **Gills Rock** USA
64B2 **Gilman** USA
66B2 **Gilroy** USA
69P2 **Gimie, Mont** St Lucia
45B3 **Gineifa** Egypt
47E2 **Gingindlovu** South Africa
50E3 **Gīnīr** Ethiopia
17E3 **Gióna** *Mt* Greece
34C3 **Gippsland** *Mts* Australia
64C2 **Girard** USA
72D3 **Girardot** Colombia
8D3 **Girdle Ness** *Pen* Scotland
40C1 **Giresun** Turkey
40B4 **Girga** Egypt
42C4 **Gīr Hills** India
50B3 **Giri** *R* Zaïre
43F4 **Girīdīh** India
42A2 **Girishk** Afghanistan
13D4 **Giromagny** France
Girona = Gerona
14B2 **Gironde** *R* France
8C4 **Girvan** Scotland
35C1 **Gisborne** New Zealand
50C4 **Gitega** Burundi
Giuba,R = Juba,R
17F2 **Giurgiu** Romania
13C2 **Givet** France
25S3 **Gizhiga** Russian Federation
19E2 **Gizycko** Poland
17E2 **Gjirokastër** Albania
54J3 **Gjoatlaven** Canada
12G6 **Gjøvik** Norway
55M5 **Glace Bay** Canada
58B1 **Glacier Peak** *Mt* USA
55K2 **Glacier Str** Canada
32E3 **Gladstone** Queensland, Australia
34A2 **Gladstone** S Aust, Australia
34C4 **Gladstone** Tasmania, Australia
64B1 **Gladstone** USA
12A1 **Gláma** *Mt* Iceland
12G6 **Glåma** *R* Norway
13D3 **Glan** *R* Germany
61D3 **Glasco** USA
64B3 **Glasgow** Kentucky, USA
60B1 **Glasgow** Montana, USA
8C4 **Glasgow** Scotland
68C3 **Glassboro** USA
66C2 **Glass Mt** USA
7C4 **Glastonbury** England
20J4 **Glazov** Russian Federation
18D3 **Gleisdorf** Austria
35C1 **Glen Afton** New Zealand
9D2 **Glenarm** Northern Ireland
68B3 **Glen Burnie** USA
47E2 **Glencoe** South Africa
59D4 **Glendale** Arizona, USA
66C3 **Glendale** California, USA
60C1 **Glendive** USA
60C2 **Glendo Res** USA
9C2 **Glengad Hd** *Pt* Irish Republic
34D1 **Glen Innes** Australia
8C4 **Glenluce** Scotland
34C1 **Glenmorgan** Australia
34D2 **Glenreagh** Australia
68B3 **Glen Rock** USA
63C2 **Glen Rose** USA
8D3 **Glenrothes** Scotland
68D1 **Glens Falls** USA
63D2 **Glenwood** Arkansas, USA
61D1 **Glenwood** Minnesota, USA
62A2 **Glenwood** New Mexico, USA
60B3 **Glenwood Springs** USA
64A1 **Glidden** USA
12F6 **Glittertind** *Mt* Norway
19D2 **Gliwice** Poland
59D4 **Globe** USA
18D2 **Głogów** Poland
12G5 **Glomfjord** Norway
51E5 **Glorieuses, Isles** Madagascar
7C3 **Glossop** England
34D2 **Gloucester** Australia
7C4 **Gloucester** England
68E1 **Gloucester** USA
7C4 **Gloucester** *County* England
68C1 **Gloversville** USA
19F1 **Glubokoye** Belarus
13E1 **Glückstadt** Germany
21E5 **Glukhov** Ukraine
18D3 **Gmünd** Austria
18C3 **Gmunden** Austria
19D2 **Gniezno** Poland
44A2 **Goa, Daman and Diu** *Union Territory* India
47B2 **Goageb** Namibia
43G3 **Goālpāra** India
50D3 **Goba** Ethiopia
47B1 **Gobabis** Namibia
31B1 **Gobi** *Desert* China/ Mongolia
29C4 **Gobo** Japan
19G1 **Gobza** *R* Russian Federation
47B1 **Gochas** Namibia
7D4 **Godalming** England
44C2 **Godāvari** *R* India
66C2 **Goddard,Mt** USA
64C2 **Goderich** Canada
55N3 **Godhavn** Greenland
42C4 **Godhra** India
57D1 **Gods L** Canada
55N3 **Godthåb** Greenland
Godwin Austen *Mt* **=K2**
68E1 **Goffstown** USA
64C1 **Gogama** Canada
13E1 **Gohfeld** Germany
75C2 **Goiandira** Brazil
75C2 **Goianésia** Brazil
75C2 **Goiânia** Brazil
75B2 **Goiás** Brazil
73J6 **Goiás** *State* Brazil
75B3 **Goio-Erê** Brazil
50D3 **Gojab** *R* Ethiopia
17F2 **Gökçeada** *I* Turkey
17F3 **Gökova Körfezi** *B* Turkey
21F8 **Goksu** *R* Turkey
40C2 **Göksun** Turkey
43G3 **Golāghāt** India
9B2 **Gola, I** Irish Republic
40C2 **Gölbaşı** Turkey
24K2 **Gol'chikha** Russian Federation
58C2 **Golconda** USA
68B2 **Gold** USA
58B2 **Gold Beach** USA
34D1 **Gold Coast** Australia
35B2 **Golden B** New Zealand
58B1 **Goldendale** USA
66A2 **Golden Gate** *Chan* USA
63D3 **Golden Meadow** USA
59C3 **Goldfield** USA
66D2 **Gold Point** USA
67C1 **Goldsboro** USA
62C2 **Goldthwaite** USA
18C2 **Goleniów** Poland
66C3 **Goleta** USA
26C3 **Golmud** China
50E3 **Gololcha** Ethiopia
29F2 **Golovnino** Russian Federation
50C4 **Goma** Zaïre
43L2 **Gomati** India
48D3 **Gombe** Nigeria
19G2 **Gomel** Belarus
48A2 **Gomera** *I* Canary Islands
70B2 **Gómez Palacio** Mexico
25O4 **Gonam** *R* Russian Federation
69C3 **Gonâve, Isla de la** Cuba
41G2 **Gonbad-e Kāvūs** Iran
43E3 **Gonda** India
42C4 **Gondal** India
50D2 **Gonder** Ethiopia
43E4 **Gondia** India
40A1 **Gönen** Turkey
17F3 **Gonen** *R* Turkey
31A4 **Gongga Shan** *Mt* China
31A2 **Gonghe** China
75D1 **Gongogi** *R* Brazil
48D3 **Gongola** *R* Nigeria
66B2 **Gonzales** California, USA
63C3 **Gonzales** Texas, USA
47B3 **Good Hope,C of** South Africa
58D2 **Gooding** USA
60C3 **Goodland** USA
34C1 **Goodooga** *R* Australia
7D3 **Goole** England
34C2 **Goolgowi** Australia
34A3 **Goolwa** Australia
32A4 **Goomalling** Australia
34C2 **Goombalie** Australia
34D1 **Goomeri** Australia
34D1 **Goondiwindi** Australia
55N4 **Goose Bay** Canada
67C2 **Goose Creek** USA
58B2 **Goose L** USA
44B2 **Gooty** India
32D1 **Goraka** Papua New Guinea
43E3 **Gorakhpur** India
20K3 **Gora Koyp** *Mt* Russian Federation
25M4 **Gora Munku Sardyk** *Mt* Mongolia/Russian Federation
20K3 **Gora Narodnaya** *Mt* Russian Federation
20L2 **Gora Pay-Yer** *Mt* Russian Federation
20K3 **Gora Telpos-Iz** *Mt*
17D2 **Goražde** Bosnia-Herzegovina
54D2 **Gordon** USA
65D3 **Gordonsville** USA
50B3 **Goré** Chad
50D3 **Gorē** Ethiopia
35A3 **Gore** New Zealand
25P4 **Gore Topko** *Mt* Russian Federation
9C3 **Gorey** Irish Republic
41F2 **Gorgān** Iran
13C2 **Gorinchem** Netherlands
41E2 **Goris** Armenia
16C1 **Gorizia** Italy
19G2 **Gorki** Belarus
20M2 **Gorki** Russian Federation
Gorki = Novgorod
20G4 **Gor'kovskoye Vodokhranilishche** *Res* Russian Federation
7E3 **Gorleston** England
18C2 **Görlitz** Germany
21F6 **Gorlovka** Ukraine
66C3 **Gorman** USA
17F2 **Gorna Orjahovica** Bulgaria
26B1 **Gorno-Altaysk** Russian Federation
26H2 **Gornozavodsk** Russian Federation
20K3 **Goro Denezhkin Kamen'** *Mt* Russian Federation
20G4 **Gorodets** Russian Federation
19G2 **Gorodnya** Ukraine
19F1 **Gorodok** Belarus
19E3 **Gorodok** Ukraine
19F3 **Gorodok** Ukraine
27H7 **Goroka** Papua New Guinea
51D5 **Gorongosa** Mozambique
27F6 **Gorontalo** Indonesia
20L4 **Goro Yurma** *Mt* Russian Federation
75D2 **Gorutuba** *R* Brazil
25M4 **Goryachinsk** Russian Federation
21J7 **Gory Akkyr** *Upland* Turkmenistan
25L2 **Gory Byrranga** *Mts* Russian Federation
19F3 **Goryn'** *R* Ukraine
25L3 **Gory Putorana** *Mts* Russian Federation
19E2 **Góry Świętokrzyskie** *Upland* Poland
12H8 **Gorzów Wielkopolski** Poland
66C2 **Goshen** USA
29E2 **Goshogawara** Japan
16D2 **Gospić** Croatia
7D4 **Gosport** England
17E2 **Gostivar** Macedonia, Yugoslavia
19D2 **Gostynin** Poland
12G7 **Göteborg** Sweden
50B3 **Gotel Mts** Nigeria
60C2 **Gothenburg** USA
12H7 **Gotland** *I* Sweden
28B4 **Gotō-rettō** *Is* Japan
12H7 **Gotska Sandön** *I* Sweden
28C4 **Gōtsu** Japan
18B2 **Göttingen** Germany
28A2 **Goubangzi** China
13C2 **Gouda** Netherlands
50B2 **Goudoumaria** Niger
52H7 **Gough I** Atlantic Ocean
55L5 **Gouin, Réservoire** Canada
34C2 **Goulburn** Australia
48B3 **Goumbou** Mali
48B3 **Goundam** Mali
50B2 **Gouré** Niger
48B3 **Gourma Rharous** Mali
50B2 **Gouro** Chad
58E1 **Govenlock** Canada
27G8 **Gove Pen** Australia
21C6 **Goverla** *Mt* Ukraine
75D2 **Governador Valadares** Brazil
43E4 **Govind Ballabh Paht Sāgar** *L* India
42B3 **Gowārān** Afghanistan
7B4 **Gower** Wales
74E3 **Goya** Argentina
50C2 **Goz-Beída** Chad
16C3 **Gozo** *I* Malta
50D2 **Goz Regeb** Sudan
47C3 **Graaff-Reinet** South Africa
65D1 **Gracefield** Canada
69A4 **Gracias à Dios, Cabo** Honduras
34D1 **Grafton** Australia
61D1 **Grafton** N Dakota, USA
64C3 **Grafton** W Virginia, USA
54E4 **Graham I** Canada
59E4 **Graham,Mt** USA
47D3 **Grahamstown** South Africa
73J5 **Grajaú** Brazil
19E2 **Grajewo** Poland
17E2 **Grámmos** *Mt* Albania/ Greece
8C3 **Grampian** *Mts* Scotland
8D3 **Grampian** *Region* Scotland
72D3 **Granada** Colombia
72A1 **Granada** Nicaragua
15B2 **Granada** Spain
65E1 **Granby** Canada
60B2 **Granby** USA
48A2 **Gran Canaria** *I* Canary Islands
74D3 **Gran Chaco** *Region* Argentina
64B2 **Grand** *R* Michigan, USA
61E2 **Grand** *R* Missouri, USA
69Q2 **Grand B** Dominica
57F4 **Grand Bahama** *I* The Bahamas
13D4 **Grand Ballon** *Mt* France
55N5 **Grand Bank** Canada
52F2 **Grand Banks** Atlantic Ocean
48B4 **Grand Bassam** Ivory Coast
59D3 **Grand Canyon** USA
59D3 **Grand Canyon Nat Pk** USA
69A3 **Grand Cayman** *I* Cayman Is, Caribbean Sea
58C1 **Grand Coulee** USA
73K6 **Grande** *R* Bahia, Brazil
75C2 **Grande** *R* Minas Gerais/ São Paulo, Brazil
55L4 **Grande 2, Rēservoir de la** Canada
55L4 **Grande 3, Rēservoir de la** Canada
55L4 **Grande 4, Rēservoir de la** Canada
74C8 **Grande, Bahía** *B* Argentina
51E5 **Grande Comore** *I* Comoros
75D3 **Grande, Ilha** Brazil
63C2 **Grande Prairie** USA
50B2 **Grand Erg de Bilma** *Desert Region* Niger
48C1 **Grand Erg Occidental** *Desert* Algeria
48C2 **Grand Erg Oriental** *Desert* Algeria
55L4 **Grande Rivière de la Baleine** *R* Canada
58C1 **Grande Ronde** *R* USA
59D4 **Gran Desierto** USA
55M5 **Grand Falls** New Brunswick, Canada
55N5 **Grand Falls** Newfoundland, Canada
58C1 **Grand Forks** Canada
61D1 **Grand Forks** USA
68C1 **Grand Gorge** USA
64B2 **Grand Haven** USA
60D2 **Grand Island** USA
63E2 **Grand Isle** USA
60B3 **Grand Junction** USA
63D3 **Grand L** USA
64A1 **Grand Marais** USA
65E1 **Grand Mère** Canada
15A2 **Grândola** Portugal
54G4 **Grand Prairie** Canada
54J4 **Grand Rapids** Canada
64B2 **Grand Rapids** Michigan, USA
64A1 **Grand Rapids** Minnesota, USA
16B1 **Grand St Bernard, Col du** *P* Italy/Switzerland
56B2 **Grand Teton** *Mt* USA
58D2 **Grand Teton Nat Pk** USA
60B3 **Grand Valley** USA
58C1 **Grangeville** USA
58E1 **Granite Peak** *Mt* Montana, USA
59D2 **Granite Peak** *Mt* Utah, USA
15C1 **Granollérs** Spain
16B1 **Gran Paradiso** *Mt* Italy
7D3 **Grantham** England
66C1 **Grant,Mt** USA
8D3 **Grantown-on-Spey** Scotland
62A1 **Grants** USA
58B2 **Grants Pass** USA
14B2 **Granville** France
68D1 **Granville** USA
54H4 **Granville L** Canada
75D2 **Grão Mogol** Brazil
66C3 **Grapevine** USA
66D2 **Grapevine Mts** USA
47E1 **Graskop** South Africa
54G3 **Gras, Lac de** Canada
14D3 **Grasse** France
6D2 **Grassington** England
58E1 **Grassrange** USA
59B3 **Grass Valley** USA
74F4 **Gravatai** Brazil
54H5 **Gravelbourg** Canada

Halifax **Hijaz**

55M5 **Halifax** Canada
6D3 **Halifax** England
65D3 **Halifax** USA
45D1 **Halīmah, Jabal** *Mt* Lebanon/Syria
8D2 **Halkirk** Scotland
28A4 **Halla-san** *Mt* S Korea
55M1 **Hall Basin** *Sd* Canada/Greenland
55K3 **Hall Beach** Canada
13C2 **Halle** Belgium
18C2 **Halle** Germany
76F1 **Halley** *Base* Antarctica
65D1 **Halleybury** Canada
60C1 **Halliday** USA
12F6 **Hallingdal** *R* Norway
61D1 **Hallock** USA
55M3 **Hall Pen** Canada
32B2 **Hall's Creek** Australia
68C2 **Hallstead** USA
27F6 **Halmahera** *Is* Indonesia
12G7 **Halmstad** Sweden
16C3 **Halq el Oued** Tunisia
18B2 **Haltern** Germany
20C2 **Halti** *Mt* Finland/Norway
8D4 **Haltwhistle** England
41F4 **Halul** *I* Qatar
45C3 **Haluza** *Hist Site* Israel
28B4 **Hamada** Japan
48C2 **Hamada de Tinrhert** *Desert Region* Algeria
48B2 **Hamada du Dra** *Upland* Algeria
41E3 **Hamadān** Iran
48B2 **Hamada Tounassine** *Region* Algeria
21F8 **Ḩamāh** Syria
29C4 **Hamamatsu** Japan
12G6 **Hamar** Norway
40C5 **Hamâta, Gebel** *Mt* Egypt
29D1 **Hama-Tombetsu** Japan
44C4 **Hambantota** Sri Lanka
63D2 **Hamburg** Arkansas, USA
61D2 **Hamburg** Iowa, USA
68A1 **Hamburg** New York, USA
68C2 **Hamburg** Pennsylvania, USA
18B2 **Hamburg** Germany
68D2 **Hamden** USA
12J6 **Hämeenlinna** Finland
13E1 **Hameln** Germany
32A3 **Hamersley Range** *Mts* Australia
28B2 **Hamgyong Sanmaek** *Mts* N Korea
28B3 **Hamhŭng** N Korea
26C2 **Hami** China
45C1 **Ḩamīdīyah** Syria
63E2 **Hamilton** Alabama, USA
34B3 **Hamilton** Australia
65D2 **Hamilton** Canada
58D1 **Hamilton** Montana, USA
68C1 **Hamilton** New York, USA
35C1 **Hamilton** New Zealand
64C3 **Hamilton** Ohio, USA
8C4 **Hamilton** Scotland
66B2 **Hamilton,Mt** USA
12K6 **Hamina** Finland
43E3 **Hamīrpur** India
28A3 **Hamju** N Korea
18B2 **Hamm** Germany
49D2 **Hammādāh al Hamrā** *Upland* Libya
16C3 **Hammamet** Tunisia
16C3 **Hammamet, Golfe de** Tunisia
12H6 **Hammerdal** Sweden
12J4 **Hammerfest** Norway
64B2 **Hammond** Illinois, USA
63D2 **Hammond** Louisiana, USA
60C1 **Hammond** Montana, USA
68C3 **Hammonton** USA
35B3 **Hampden** New Zealand
7D4 **Hampshire** *County* England
63D2 **Hampton** Arkansas, USA
61E2 **Hampton** Iowa, USA
68E1 **Hampton** New Hampshire, USA
65D3 **Hampton** Virginia, USA
38D3 **Hāmūn-e-Jāz-Mūriān** *L* Iran
42B3 **Hamun-i-Lora** *Salt L* Pakistan
28A3 **Han** *R* S Korea
66E5 **Hana** Hawaiian Islands
66E5 **Hanalei** Hawaiian Islands
29E3 **Hanamaki** Japan
13E2 **Hanau** Germany
31C2 **Hancheng** China
31C3 **Hanchuan** China
65D3 **Hancock** Maryland, USA
64B1 **Hancock** Michigan, USA
68C2 **Hancock** New York, USA
29C4 **Handa** Japan
8C2 **Handa, I** Scotland
31C2 **Handan** China
50D4 **Handeni** Tanzania
66C2 **Hanford** USA
31B2 **Hanggin Qi** China
12J7 **Hangö** Finland
31E3 **Hangzhou** China
31E3 **Hangzhou Wan** *B* China
61D1 **Hankinson** USA
59D3 **Hanksville** USA
35B2 **Hanmer Springs** New Zealand
54G4 **Hanna** Canada
61E3 **Hannibal** USA
18B2 **Hannover** Germany
12G7 **Hanöbukten** *B* Sweden
30D1 **Hanoi** Vietnam
47C3 **Hanover** South Africa
68B3 **Hanover** USA
74B8 **Hanover** *I* Chile
31C3 **Han Shui** *R* China
42D3 **Hānsi** India
26D2 **Hantay** Mongolia
31B3 **Hanzhong** China
43F4 **Hāora** India
12J5 **Haparanda** Sweden
28A3 **Hapch'on** S Korea
43G3 **Hāpoli** India
43J1 **Hapur** India
40C4 **Ḩaql** Saudi Arabia
41E5 **Ḩaradh** Saudi Arabia
45C4 **Harad, Jebel el** *Mt* Jordan
50E3 **Hara Fanna** Ethiopia
29D3 **Haramachi** Japan
51D5 **Harare** Zimbabwe
50C2 **Harazé** Chad
26F2 **Harbin** China
64C2 **Harbor Beach** USA
42D4 **Harda** India
12F6 **Hardangerfjord** *Inlet* Norway
13D1 **Härdenberg** Netherlands
13C1 **Harderwijk** Netherlands
60B1 **Hardin** USA
43L2 **Hardoi** India
13D3 **Hardt** *Region* Germany
63D1 **Hardy** USA
45C3 **Hareidin, Wadi** Egypt
50E3 **Harēr** Ethiopia
50E3 **Hargeysa** Somalia
45C3 **Har Hakippa** *Mt* Israel
26C3 **Harhu** *L* China
27D7 **Hari** *R* Indonesia
29B4 **Harima-nada** *B* Japan
64C3 **Harlan** USA
7B3 **Harlech** Wales
58E1 **Harlem** USA
7E3 **Harleston** England
18B2 **Harlingen** Netherlands
63C3 **Harlingen** USA
7E4 **Harlow** England
58E1 **Harlowtown** USA
45C2 **Har Meron** *Mt* Israel
58C2 **Harney Basin** USA
58C2 **Harney L** USA
12H6 **Härnösand** Sweden
48B4 **Harper** Liberia
66D3 **Harper L** USA
65D3 **Harpers Ferry** USA
13E1 **Harpstedt** Germany
45C3 **Har Ramon** *Mt* Israel
40C4 **Harrāt al 'Uwayrid** *Region* Saudi Arabia
40D5 **Ḩarrāt Kishb** *Region* Saudi Arabia
55L4 **Harricanaw** *R* Canada
67B1 **Harriman** USA
68D1 **Harriman Res** USA
68C3 **Harrington** USA
55N4 **Harrington Harbour** Canada
8B3 **Harris** *District* Scotland
64B3 **Harrisburg** Illinois, USA
68B2 **Harrisburg** Pennsylvania, USA
47D2 **Harrismith** South Africa
63D1 **Harrison** USA
65D3 **Harrisonburg** USA
55N4 **Harrison,C** Canada
61E3 **Harrisonville** USA
8B3 **Harris,Sound of** *Chan* Scotland
64C2 **Harrisville** USA
6D2 **Harrogate** England
45C3 **Har Saggi** *Mt* Israel
45D2 **Ḩarsīr, Wadi al** Syria
12H5 **Harstad** Norway
28A2 **Hartao** China
47C2 **Hartbees** *R* South Africa
12F6 **Hårteigen** *Mt* Norway
68D2 **Hartford** Connecticut, USA
64B2 **Hartford** Michigan, USA
61D2 **Hartford** S Dakota, USA
12G6 **Hartkjølen** *Mt* Norway
65F1 **Hartland** Canada
7B4 **Hartland** England
7B4 **Hartland Pt** England
6D2 **Hartlepool** England
62B1 **Hartley** USA
67A2 **Hartselle** USA
63C2 **Hartshorne** USA
67B2 **Hartwell Res** USA
47C2 **Hartz** *R* South Africa
45C3 **Hārūn, Jebel** *Mt* Jordan
25L5 **Har Us Nuur** *L* Mongolia
38E2 **Harut** *R* Afghanistan
60B3 **Harvard,Mt** USA
60C1 **Harvey** USA
7E4 **Harwich** England
42D3 **Haryāna** *State* India
45C3 **Hāsā** Jordan
45B3 **Hasana, Wadi** Egypt
45C3 **Hāsā, Wadi el** Jordan
45C2 **Hāsbaiya** Lebanon
13E1 **Hase** *R* Germany
13D1 **Haselünne** Germany
29C4 **Hashimoto** Japan
41E2 **Hashtpar** Iran
41E2 **Hashtrūd** Iran
62C2 **Haskell** USA
7D4 **Haslemere** England
44B3 **Hassan** India
18B2 **Hasselt** Belgium
48C2 **Hassi Inifel** Algeria
48B2 **Hassi Mdakane** *Well* Algeria
48C1 **Hassi Messaoud** Algeria
12G7 **Hässleholm** Sweden
34C3 **Hastings** Australia
7E4 **Hastings** England
61E2 **Hastings** Minnesota, USA
56D2 **Hastings** Nebraska, USA
35C1 **Hastings** New Zealand
63E1 **Hatchie** *R* USA
34B2 **Hatfield** Australia
42D3 **Hāthras** India
30D2 **Ha Tinh** Vietnam
34B2 **Hattah** Australia
57F3 **Hatteras,C** USA
63E2 **Hattiesburg** USA
19D3 **Hatvan** Hungary
30D3 **Hau Bon** Vietnam
50E3 **Haud** *Region* Ethiopia
12F7 **Haugesund** Norway
35C1 **Hauhungaroa Range** *Mts* New Zealand
35B1 **Hauraki G** New Zealand
35A3 **Hauroko,L** New Zealand
48B1 **Haut Atlas** *Mts* Morocco
50C3 **Haute Kotto** *Region* Central African Republic
13C3 **Haute-Marne** *Department* France
13D4 **Haute-Saône** *Department* France
13C2 **Hautes Fagnes** *Mts* Belgium/Germany
65F2 **Haut, Isle au** USA
13C2 **Hautmont** France
13D4 **Haut-Rhin** *Department* France
42A2 **Hauz Qala** Afghanistan
70D2 **Havana** Cuba
64A2 **Havana** USA
44B4 **Havankulam** Sri Lanka
59D4 **Havasu L** USA
67C2 **Havelock** USA
35C1 **Havelock North** New Zealand
7E3 **Haverhill** England
68E1 **Haverhill** USA
44B3 **Hāveri** India
68D2 **Haverstraw** USA
18D3 **Havlíčkův Brod** Czech Republic
58E1 **Havre** USA
68B3 **Havre de Grace** USA
55M4 **Havre-St-Pierre** Canada
17F2 **Havsa** Turkey
66E5 **Hawaii** *Is, State* Pacific Ocean
66E5 **Hawaii Volcanoes Nat Pk** Hawaiian Islands
35A2 **Hawea,L** New Zealand
35B1 **Hawera** New Zealand
66E5 **Hawi** Hawaiian Islands
8D4 **Hawick** Scotland
35A2 **Hawkdun Range** *Mts* New Zealand
35C1 **Hawke B** New Zealand
34D2 **Hawke,C** Australia
34A2 **Hawker** Australia
68C2 **Hawley** USA
30B1 **Hawng Luk** Burma
41D3 **Hawr al Habbaniyah** *L* Iraq
41E3 **Hawr al Hammár** *L* Iraq
40D3 **Ḩawrān, Wadi** *R* Iraq
66C1 **Hawthorne** USA
34B2 **Hay** Australia
7C3 **Hay** England
54G3 **Hay** *R* Canada
13C3 **Hayange** France
54B3 **Haycock** USA
59D4 **Hayden** Arizona, USA
60B2 **Hayden** Colorado, USA
55J4 **Hayes** *R* Canada
55M2 **Hayes Halvø** *Region* Greenland
54D3 **Hayes, Mt** USA
7B4 **Hayle** England
7D4 **Hayling** *I* England
68B3 **Haymarket** USA
54G3 **Hay River** Canada
60D3 **Hays** USA
63C1 **Haysville** USA
66A2 **Hayward** California, USA
64A1 **Hayward** Wisconsin, USA
7D4 **Haywards Heath** England
42A2 **Hazarajat** *Region* Afghanistan
64C3 **Hazard** USA
43F4 **Hazārībāg** India
13B2 **Hazebrouck** France
63D2 **Hazelhurst** USA
54F4 **Hazelton** Canada
54B3 **Hazen B** USA
55L1 **Hazen L** Canada
54G2 **Hazen Str** Canada
45C3 **Hazeva** Israel
68C2 **Hazleton** USA
66A1 **Healdsburg** USA
34C3 **Healesville** Australia
36E7 **Heard I** Indian Ocean
63C2 **Hearne** USA
57E2 **Hearst** Canada
60C1 **Heart** *R* USA
62C3 **Hebbronville** USA
31D2 **Hebei** *Province* China
34C1 **Hebel** Australia
58D2 **Heber City** USA
58D2 **Hebgen L** USA
31C2 **Hebi** China
31C2 **Hebian** China
55M4 **Hebron** Canada
45C3 **Hebron** Israel
60C1 **Hebron** N Dakota, USA
61D2 **Hebron** Nebraska, USA
54E4 **Hecate Str** Canada
31B5 **Hechi** China
13E3 **Hechingen** Germany
54G2 **Hecla and Griper B** Canada
35C2 **Hector,Mt** New Zealand
12G6 **Hede** Sweden
12H6 **Hedemora** Sweden
58C1 **He Devil Mt** USA
18B2 **Heerenveen** Netherlands
13C2 **Heerlen** Netherlands
Hefa = Haifa
31D3 **Hefei** China
31B4 **Hefeng** China
26G2 **Hegang** China
29C3 **Hegura-jima** *I* Japan
30B1 **Heho** Burma
45C3 **Heidan** *R* Jordan
18B2 **Heide** Germany
47C3 **Heidelberg** Cape Province, South Africa
47D2 **Heidelberg** Transvaal, South Africa
18B3 **Heidelberg** Germany
18C3 **Heidenheim** Germany
25O4 **Heihe** China
47D2 **Heilbron** South Africa
18B3 **Heilbronn** Germany
18C2 **Heiligenstadt** Germany
12K6 **Heinola** Finland
28A2 **Heishan** China
31B4 **Hejiang** China
55R3 **Hekla** *Mt* Iceland
30C1 **Hekou** Vietnam
31A5 **Hekou Yaozou Zizhixian** China
31B2 **Helan** China
31B2 **Helan Shan** *Mt* China
63D2 **Helena** Arkansas, USA
58D1 **Helena** Montana, USA
66D3 **Helendale** USA
27G6 **Helen Reef** Pacific Ocean
8C3 **Helensburgh** Scotland
45A3 **Heliopolis** Egypt
41F4 **Helleh** *R* Iran
15B2 **Hellín** Spain
58C1 **Hells Canyon** *R* USA
13D2 **Hellweg** *Region* Germany
66B2 **Helm** USA
38E2 **Helmand** *R* Afghanistan/Iran
47B2 **Helmeringhausen** Namibia
13C2 **Helmond** Netherlands
8D2 **Helmsdale** Scotland
51F5 **Helodrano Antongila** *B* Madagascar
28B2 **Helong** China
12G7 **Helsingborg** Sweden
Helsingfors = Helsinki
18C1 **Helsingør** Denmark
12J6 **Helsinki** Finland
7B4 **Helston** England
9C3 **Helvick Hd** *Pt* Irish Republic
40B4 **Helwân** Egypt
7D4 **Hemel Hempstead** England
63C2 **Hempstead** USA
12H7 **Hemse** Sweden
31A3 **Henan** China
31C3 **Henan** *Province* China
35B1 **Hen and Chickens Is** New Zealand
29C2 **Henashi-zaki** *C* Japan
64B3 **Henderson** Kentucky, USA
67C1 **Henderson** N Carolina, USA
59D3 **Henderson** Nevada, USA
63D2 **Henderson** Texas, USA
67B1 **Hendersonville** N Carolina, USA
67A1 **Hendersonville** Tennessee, USA
47D3 **Hendrik Verwoerd Dam** South Africa
31E5 **Hengchun** Taiwan
26C4 **Hengduan Shan** *Mts* China
18B2 **Hengelo** Netherlands
31B2 **Hengshan** China
31D2 **Hengshui** China
30D1 **Heng Xian** China
31C4 **Hengyang** China
30A4 **Henhoaha** Nicobar Is, India
7D4 **Henley-on-Thames** England
68C3 **Henlopen,C** USA
68E1 **Henniker** USA
62C2 **Henrietta** USA
55K4 **Henrietta Maria,C** Canada
59D3 **Henrieville** USA
63C1 **Henryetta** USA
55M3 **Henry Kater Pen** Canada
47A1 **Henties Bay** Namibia
26D2 **Hentiyn Nuruu** *Mts* Mongolia
30B2 **Henzada** Burma
31B5 **Hepu** China
38E2 **Herat** Afghanistan
54H4 **Herbert** Canada
35C2 **Herbertville** New Zealand
13E2 **Herborn** Germany
69A4 **Heredia** Costa Rica
7C3 **Hereford** England
62B2 **Hereford** USA
7C3 **Hereford & Worcester** *County* England
13C2 **Herentals** Belgium
13E1 **Herford** Germany
61D3 **Herington** USA
35A3 **Heriot** New Zealand
68C1 **Herkimer** USA
8E1 **Herma Ness** *Pen* Scotland
47B3 **Hermanus** South Africa
34C2 **Hermidale** Australia
35B2 **Hermitage** New Zealand
32D1 **Hermit Is** Papua New Guinea
45C2 **Hermon, Mt** Lebanon/Syria
70A2 **Hermosillo** Mexico
75B4 **Hernandarias** Paraguay
68B2 **Herndon** USA
66C2 **Herndon** USA
13D2 **Herne** Germany
7E4 **Herne Bay** England
18B1 **Herning** Denmark
41E2 **Herowābad** Iran
75A4 **Herradura** Argentina
15B2 **Herrera del Duque** Spain
68B2 **Hershey** USA
7D4 **Hertford** England
7D4 **Hertford** *County* England
45C2 **Herzliyya** Israel
13C2 **Hesbaye** Region, Belgium
13A2 **Hesdin** France
31B2 **Heshui** China
66D3 **Hesperia** USA
18B2 **Hessen** *State* Germany
66C2 **Hetch Hetchy Res** USA
60C1 **Hettinger** USA
48B1 **Heuts Plateaux** Algeria/Morocco
7E3 **Hewett** *Oilfield* N Sea
6C2 **Hexham** England
31C5 **He Xian** China
6C2 **Heysham** England
47D2 **Heystekrand** South Africa
31C5 **Heyuan** China
34B3 **Heywood** Australia
31D2 **Heze** China
67B3 **Hialeah** USA
61E1 **Hibbing** USA
67B1 **Hickory** USA
35C1 **Hicks Bay** New Zealand
34C3 **Hicks,Pt** Australia
63C2 **Hico** USA
29D2 **Hidaka-sammyaku** *Mts* Japan
70B2 **Hidalgo del Parral** Mexico
75C2 **Hidrolândia** Brazil
48A2 **Hierro** *I* Canary Islands
29D3 **Higashine** Japan
28B4 **Higashi-suidō** *Str* Japan
45B3 **Higâyib, Wadi el** Egypt
58B2 **High Desert** USA
63D3 **High Island** USA
66D3 **Highland** USA
8C3 **Highland** *Region* Scotland
8E2 **Highlander** *Oilfield* N Sea
66C1 **Highland Peak** *Mt* USA
68C2 **Highland Falls** USA
67B1 **High Point** USA
54G4 **High Prairie** Canada
54G4 **High River** Canada
67B3 **High Springs** USA
68C2 **Hightstown** USA
7D4 **High Wycombe** England
12J7 **Hiiumaa** *I* Estonia
40C4 **Hijaz** *Region* Saudi Arabia

Hikigawa **Igarapava**

29C4 **Hikigawa** Japan
59C3 **Hiko** USA
29C3 **Hikone** Japan
35B1 **Hikurangi** New Zealand
56C4 **Hildago del Parral** Mexico
18B2 **Hildesheim** Germany
69R2 **Hillaby,Mt** Barbados
60D3 **Hill City** USA
18C1 **Hillerød** Denmark
61D1 **Hillsboro** N Dakota, USA
68E1 **Hillsboro** New Hampshire, USA
62A2 **Hillsboro** New Mexico, USA
64C3 **Hillsboro** Ohio, USA
58B1 **Hillsboro** Oregon, USA
63C2 **Hillsboro** Texas, USA
34C2 **Hillston** Australia
64C3 **Hillsville** USA
8E1 **Hillswick** Scotland
66E5 **Hilo** Hawaiian Islands
6C2 **Hilpsford** *Pt* England
68B1 **Hilton** USA
40C2 **Hilvan** Turkey
18B2 **Hilversum** Netherlands
42D2 **Himāchal Pradesh** *State* India
Himalaya = Great Himalayan Range
39G3 **Himalaya** *Mts* Asia
43N1 **Himalchuli** *Mt* Nepal
42C4 **Himatnagar** India
29C4 **Himeji** Japan
29D3 **Himi** Japan
45D1 **Ḩimş** Syria
7D3 **Hinckley** England
61E1 **Hinckley** Minnesota, USA
68C1 **Hinckley Res** USA
42D3 **Hindaun** India
42B1 **Hindu Kush** *Mts* Afghanistan
44B3 **Hindupur** India
54G4 **Hines Creek** Canada
42D4 **Hinganghāt** India
42B3 **Hingol** *R* Pakistan
42D5 **Hingoli** India
66D3 **Hinkley** USA
12H5 **Hinnøya** *I* Norway
68D1 **Hinsdale** USA
62C1 **Hinton** USA
28A4 **Hirado** Japan
28A4 **Hirado-shima** *I* Japan
43E4 **Hirakud Res** India
40B2 **Hirfanli Baraji** *Res* Turkey
44B3 **Hirihar** India
29D2 **Hiroo** Japan
29E2 **Hirosaki** Japan
28C4 **Hiroshima** Japan
13C3 **Hirson** France
17F2 **Hîrşova** Romania
18B1 **Hirtshals** Denmark
42D3 **Hisār** India
69C3 **Hispaniola** *I* Caribbean Sea
45D1 **Ḩisyah** Syria
40D3 **Hīt** Iraq
29E3 **Hitachi** Japan
29D3 **Hitachi-Ota** Japan
7D4 **Hitchin** England
28C4 **Hitoyoshi** Japan
12F6 **Hitra** *I* Norway
29B4 **Hiuchi-nada** *B* Japan
29B4 **Hiwasa** Japan
45C3 **Hiyon** *R* Israel
18B1 **Hjørring** Denmark
30B1 **Hka** *R* Burma
48C4 **Ho** Ghana
30D1 **Hoa Binh** Vietnam
30D3 **Hoa Da** Vietnam
34C4 **Hobart** Australia
62C2 **Hobart** USA
62B2 **Hobbs** USA
18B1 **Hobro** Denmark
50E3 **Hobyo** Somalia
30D3 **Ho Chi Minh City** Vietnam
18C3 **Hochkonig** *Mt* Austria
28A2 **Hochon** N Korea
13E3 **Hockenheim** Germany
Hodeida = Al Ḩudaydah
17E1 **Hódmezö'hely** Hungary
15C2 **Hodna, Monts du** Algeria
18D3 **Hodonin** Czech Republic
13C2 **Hoek van Holland** Netherlands
28A3 **Hoengsŏng** S Korea
28B2 **Hoeryŏng** N Korea
28A3 **Hoeyang** N Korea
18C2 **Hof** Germany
55R3 **Höfn** Iceland
12B2 **Hofsjökull** *Mts* Iceland
28C4 **Hōfu** Japan
48C2 **Hoggar** *Upland* Algeria
13D2 **Hohe Acht** *Mt* Germany
13E2 **Hohes Gras** *Mts* Germany
31C1 **Hohhot** China
26C3 **Hoh Sai Hu** *L* China
39G2 **Hoh Xil Shan** *Mts* China
50D3 **Hoima** Uganda
43G3 **Hojāi** India
28B4 **Hojo** Japan
35B1 **Hokianga Harbour** *B* New Zealand
35B2 **Hokitika** New Zealand
26H2 **Hokkaidō** *I* Japan
41G2 **Hokmābād** Iran
29D3 **Hokota** Japan
7E3 **Holbeach** England
34C3 **Holbrook** Australia
59D4 **Holbrook** USA
59D3 **Holden** USA
63C1 **Holdenville** USA
60D2 **Holdrege** USA
44B3 **Hole Narsipur** India
69Q2 **Holetown** Barbados
69B2 **Holguín** Cuba
18D3 **Hollabrunn** Austria
64B2 **Holland** USA
68A2 **Hollidaysburg** USA
62C2 **Hollis** USA
66B2 **Hollister** USA
63E2 **Holly Springs** USA
66C3 **Hollywood** California, USA
67B3 **Hollywood** Florida, USA
54G2 **Holman Island** Canada
12J6 **Holmsund** Sweden
45C2 **Holon** Israel
18B1 **Holstebro** Denmark
61D2 **Holstein** USA
55N3 **Holsteinsborg** Greenland
67B1 **Holston** *R* USA
64C2 **Holt** USA
61D3 **Holton** USA
54C3 **Holy Cross** USA
7B3 **Holyhead** Wales
6D3 **Holy I** England
7B3 **Holy I** Wales
60C2 **Holyoke** Colorado, USA
68D1 **Holyoke** Massachusetts, USA
9D2 **Holywood** Northern Ireland
13E2 **Holzminden** Germany
43G4 **Homalin** Burma
13E2 **Homburg** Germany
55M3 **Home B** Canada
63D2 **Homer** Louisiana, USA
54C4 **Homer** USA
35A2 **Homer Tunnel** New Zealand
67B2 **Homerville** USA
67B3 **Homestead** USA
67A2 **Homewood** USA
44B2 **Homnābād** India
51D6 **Homoine** Mozambique
Homs = Al Khums
Homs = Ḩimş
47B3 **Hondeklip B** South Africa
62A2 **Hondo** New Mexico, USA
62C3 **Hondo** Texas, USA
70D3 **Hondo** *R* Mexico
70D3 **Honduras** *Republic* Central America
70D3 **Honduras,G of** Honduras
12G6 **Hønefoss** Norway
68C2 **Honesdale** USA
59B2 **Honey L** USA
Hong *R* **= Nui Con Voi**
30C1 **Hong** *R* Vietnam
30D1 **Hon Gai** Vietnam
28A3 **Hongchŏn** S Korea
31A4 **Hongguo** China
31C4 **Hong Hu** *L* China
31B2 **Honghui** China
31C4 **Hongjiang** China
31C5 **Hong Kong** *Colony* SE Asia
26E2 **Hongor** Mongolia
31B5 **Hongshui He** *R* China
28A3 **Hongsong** S Korea
28A3 **Hongwon** N Korea
31A3 **Hongyuan** China
31D3 **Hongze Hu** *L* China
33E1 **Honiara** Solomon Islands
7C4 **Honiton** England
29D3 **Honjō** Japan
30C4 **Hon Khoai** *I* Cambodia
30D3 **Hon Lan** *I* Vietnam
12K4 **Honnigsvåg** Norway
20D1 **Honningsvåg** Norway
66E5 **Honokaa** Hawaiian Islands
66E5 **Honolulu** Hawaiian Islands
30C4 **Hon Panjang** *I* Vietnam
26G3 **Honshū** *I* Japan
58B1 **Hood,Mt** USA
58B1 **Hood River** USA
13D1 **Hoogeveen** Netherlands
62B1 **Hooker** USA
9C3 **Hook Head** *C* Irish Republic
54E4 **Hoonah** USA
54B3 **Hooper Bay** USA
47D2 **Hoopstad** South Africa
18A2 **Hoorn** Netherlands
68D1 **Hoosick Falls** USA
56B3 **Hoover Dam** USA
63D2 **Hope** Arkansas, USA
55M4 **Hopedale** Canada
24D2 **Hopen** *I* Svalbard
55M3 **Hopes Advance,C** Canada
34B3 **Hopetoun** Australia
47C2 **Hopetown** South Africa
68A2 **Hopewell** Pennsylvania, USA
65D3 **Hopewell** Virginia, USA
64B3 **Hopkinsville** USA
58B1 **Hoquiam** USA
40D2 **Horasan** Turkey
13E3 **Horb** Germany
50E2 **Hordiyo** Somalia
31B1 **Hörh Uul** *Mt* Mongolia
37L6 **Horizon Depth** Pacific Ocean
41G4 **Hormuz,Str of** Oman/Iran
18D3 **Horn** Austria
55Q3 **Horn** *C* Iceland
12H5 **Hornavan** *L* Sweden
63D2 **Hornbeck** USA
58B2 **Hornbrook** USA
35B2 **Hornby** New Zealand
7D3 **Horncastle** England
68B1 **Hornell** USA
55K5 **Hornepayne** Canada
63E2 **Horn I** USA
33H2 **Horn, Îles de** Pacific Ocean
54F3 **Horn Mts** Canada
74C9 **Hornos, Cabo de** *C* Chile
6D3 **Hornsea** England
28A2 **Horqin Zuoyi Houqi** China
74E2 **Horqueta** Paraguay
68B1 **Horseheads** USA
18C1 **Horsens** Denmark
58B1 **Horseshoe Bay** Canada
58C2 **Horseshoe Bend** USA
34B3 **Horsham** Australia
7D4 **Horsham** England
12G7 **Horten** Norway
54F3 **Horton** *R* Canada
27E6 **Hose Mts** Borneo
42D4 **Hoshangābād** India
42D2 **Hoshiārpur** India
62C1 **Hosington** USA
44B2 **Hospet** India
74C9 **Hoste** *I* Chile
39F2 **Hotan** China
47C2 **Hotazel** South Africa
63D2 **Hot Springs** Arkansas, USA
60C2 **Hot Springs** S Dakota, USA
54G3 **Hottah L** Canada
69C3 **Hotte, Massif de la** *Mts* Haiti
47A2 **Hottentot Pt** Namibia
64B1 **Houghton** USA
65F1 **Houlton** USA
31C2 **Houma** China
63D3 **Houma** USA
8C3 **Hourn, Loch** *Inlet* Scotland
68D2 **Housatonic** *R* USA
63E2 **Houston** Mississippi, USA
63C3 **Houston** Texas, USA
32A3 **Houtman** *Is* Australia
68A2 **Houtzdale** USA
26C2 **Hovd** Mongolia
26D1 **Hövsgol Nuur** *L* Mongolia
34D1 **Howard** Australia
64B2 **Howard City** USA
50C2 **Howa, Wadi** *Watercourse* Chad/Sudan
34C3 **Howe,C** Australia
58B1 **Howe Sd** Canada
47E2 **Howick** South Africa
65F1 **Howland** USA
9C3 **Howth** Irish Republic
13E2 **Höxter** Germany
8D2 **Hoy** *I* Scotland
12F6 **Høyanger** Norway
61E1 **Hoyt Lakes** USA
18D2 **Hradec-Králové** Czech Republic
19D3 **Hranice** Czech Republic
19D3 **Hron** *R* Slovakia
31E5 **Hsinchu** Taiwan
30B1 **Hsipaw** Burma
31E5 **Hsüeh Shan** *Mt* Taiwan
47A1 **Huab** *R* Namibia
31B2 **Huachi** China
72C6 **Huacho** Peru
31C1 **Huade** China
28B2 **Huadian** China
31D3 **Huaibei** China
31D3 **Huaibin** China
28A2 **Huaide** China
28A2 **Huaidezhen** China
31D3 **Huai He** *R* China
31C4 **Huaihua** China
31C5 **Huaiji** China
31D3 **Huainan** China
59D3 **Hualapai Peak** *Mt* USA
26F4 **Hualien** Taiwan
72C5 **Huallaga** *R* Peru
72C5 **Huallanca** Peru
72C5 **Huamachuco** Peru
51B5 **Huambo** Angola
72E7 **Huanay** Bolivia
72C5 **Huancabamba** Peru
72C6 **Huancavelica** Peru
72C6 **Huancayo** Peru
31D3 **Huangchuan** China
Huang Hai = Yellow Sea
31D2 **Huang He** *R* China
31B2 **Huangling** China
30D2 **Huangliu** China
28B2 **Huangnihe** China
31C3 **Huangpi** China
31D3 **Huangshi** China
31D4 **Huangshan** China
31E4 **Huangyan** China
28B2 **Huanren** China
72C5 **Huānuco** Peru
74C1 **Huanuni** Bolivia
31B2 **Huan Xian** China
72C5 **Huaráz** Peru
72C6 **Huarmey** Peru
72C5 **Huascarán** *Mt* Peru
74B3 **Huasco** Chile
31C2 **Hua Xian** China
70B2 **Huayapan** *R* Mexico
31C3 **Hubei** *Province* China
44B2 **Hubli** India
28B2 **Huch'ang** N Korea
7D3 **Hucknell Torkard** England
7D3 **Huddersfield** England
13E1 **Hude** Germany
12H6 **Hudiksvall** Sweden
67B3 **Hudson** Florida, USA
64C2 **Hudson** Michigan, USA
68D1 **Hudson** New York, USA
68D1 **Hudson** *R* USA
55K4 **Hudson B** Canada
54H4 **Hudson Bay** Canada
68D1 **Hudson Falls** USA
55L3 **Hudson Str** Canada
30D2 **Hue** Vietnam
15A2 **Huelva** Spain
15B2 **Húercal Overa** Spain
15B1 **Huesca** Spain
32D3 **Hughenden** Australia
54C3 **Hughes** USA
43F4 **Hugli** *R* India
63C2 **Hugo** USA
62B1 **Hugoton** USA
31D4 **Hui'an** China
35C1 **Huiarau Range** *Mts* New Zealand
47B2 **Huib Hochplato** *Plat* Namibia
28B2 **Hŭich'ŏn** N Korea
72C3 **Huila** *Mt* Colombia
31D5 **Huilai** China
31A4 **Huili** China
28B2 **Huinan** China
70C3 **Huixtla** Mexico
31A4 **Huize** China
31C5 **Huizhou** China
40D4 **Ḩulayfah** Saudi Arabia
26G2 **Hulin** China
65D1 **Hull** Canada
6D3 **Hull** England
33H1 **Hull** *I* Phoenix Islands
18D1 **Hultsfred** Sweden
25N5 **Hulun Nur** *L* China
72F5 **Humaitá** Brazil
47C3 **Humansdorp** South Africa
7D3 **Humber** *R* England
6D3 **Humberside** *County* England
54H4 **Humboldt** Canada
61E2 **Humboldt** Iowa, USA
63E1 **Humboldt** Tennessee, USA
58C2 **Humboldt** *R* USA
58B2 **Humboldt B** USA
55M2 **Humboldt Gletscher** *Gl* Greenland
59C3 **Humboldt L** USA
34C1 **Humeburn** Australia
34C3 **Hume,L** Australia
13D1 **Hümmling** *Hill* Germany
51B5 **Humpata** Angola
66C2 **Humphreys** USA
66C2 **Humphreys,Mt** California, USA
59D3 **Humphreys Peak** *Mt* Arizona, USA
12A1 **Húnaflóri** *B* Iceland
31C4 **Hunan** *Province* China
28C2 **Hunchun** China
17E1 **Hunedoara** Romania
19D3 **Hungary** *Republic* Europe
34B1 **Hungerford** Australia
28B3 **Hŭngnam** N Korea
58D1 **Hungry Horse Res** USA
28B2 **Hunjiang** China
47B2 **Hunsberge** *Mts* Namibia
13D3 **Hunsrück** *Mts* Germany
7E3 **Hunstanton** England
13E1 **Hunte** *R* Germany
34D2 **Hunter** *R* Australia
34C4 **Hunter Is** Australia
64B3 **Huntingburg** USA
7D3 **Huntingdon** England
64B2 **Huntingdon** Indiana, USA
68A2 **Huntingdon** Pennsylvania, USA
64C3 **Huntington** USA
66C4 **Huntington Beach** USA
66C2 **Huntington L** USA
35C1 **Huntly** New Zealand
8D3 **Huntly** Scotland
54F3 **Hunt, Mt** Canada
67A2 **Huntsville** Alabama, USA
65D1 **Huntsville** Canada
63C2 **Huntsville** Texas, USA
30D2 **Huong Khe** Vietnam
27H7 **Huon Peninsula** Papua New Guinea
34C4 **Huonville** Australia
64C1 **Hurd,C** Canada
28A2 **Hure Qi** China
40B4 **Hurghada** Egypt
64A1 **Hurley** USA
66B2 **Huron** California, USA
61D2 **Huron** S Dakota, USA
64C1 **Huron,L** Canada/USA
35B2 **Hurunui** *R* New Zealand
12B1 **Húsavík** Iceland
17F1 **Huşi** Romania
12G7 **Huskvarna** Sweden
45C2 **Husn** Jordan
18B2 **Husum** Germany
56D3 **Hutchinson** USA
63C1 **Hutchinson** USA
34C1 **Hutton,Mt** Australia
31D2 **Hutuo He** *R* China
13C2 **Huy** Belgium
31A2 **Huzhu** China
16D2 **Hvar** *I* Croatia
28A2 **Hwadae** N Korea
51C5 **Hwange** Zimbabwe
51C5 **Hwange Nat Pk** Zimbabwe
28A2 **Hwapyong** N Korea
68E2 **Hyannis** Massachusetts, USA
60C2 **Hyannis** Nebraska, USA
26C2 **Hyargas Nuur** *L* Mongolia
54E4 **Hydaburg** USA
68D2 **Hyde Park** USA
44B2 **Hyderābād** India
42B3 **Hyderabad** Pakistan
14D3 **Hyères** France
14D3 **Hyères, Iles d'** *Is* France
28B2 **Hyesan** N Korea
68A3 **Hyndman** USA
56B2 **Hyndman Peak** *Mt* USA
20D3 **Hyrynsalmi** Finland
7E4 **Hythe** England
12J6 **Hyvinkää** Finland

I

73K6 **Iaçu** Brazil
17F2 **Ialomiţa** *R* Romania
17F1 **Iaşi** Romania
48C4 **Ibadan** Nigeria
72C3 **Ibagué** Colombia
17E2 **Ibar** *R* Montenegro/Serbia, Yugoslavia
72C3 **Ibarra** Ecuador
13D1 **Ibbenbüren** Germany
75C2 **Ibiá** Brazil
75E1 **Ibicaraí** Brazil
74E3 **Ibicuí** *R* Brazil
74E4 **Ibicuy** Argentina
15C2 **Ibiza** Spain
15C2 **Ibiza** *I* Spain
51E5 **Ibo** Mozambique
73K6 **Ibotirama** Brazil
50C2 **Ibra, Wadi** *Watercourse* Sudan
41G5 **'Ibrī** Oman
72C6 **Ica** Peru
72E4 **Içá** *R* Brazil
72E3 **Içana** Brazil
12A1 **Iceland** *Republic* N Atlantic Ocean
25R4 **Icha** Russian Federation
44A2 **Ichalkaranji** India
29C3 **Ichinomiya** Japan
29E3 **Ichinosek** Japan
54B2 **Icy C** USA
63D2 **Idabell** USA
61D2 **Ida Grove** USA
58D2 **Idaho** State, USA
58C2 **Idaho City** USA
58D2 **Idaho Falls** USA
60B3 **Idaho Springs** USA
45B1 **Idalion** *Hist Site* Cyprus
58B2 **Idanha** USA
13D3 **Idar Oberstein** Germany
49D2 **Idehan Marzūg** *Desert* Libya
49D2 **Idehan Ubari** *Desert* Libya
48C2 **Idelès** Algeria
26C2 **Ideriym Gol** *R* Mongolia
40B5 **Idfu** Egypt
17E3 **Ídhi Óros** *Mt* Greece
17E3 **Ídhra** *I* Greece
50B4 **Idiofa** Zaïre
40C2 **Idlib** Syria
12K7 **Idritsa** Russian Federation
47D3 **Idutywa** South Africa
13B2 **Ieper** Belgium
17F3 **Ierápetra** Greece
25N4 **Iet Oktyob'ya** Russian Federation
51D4 **Ifakara** Tanzania
27H6 **Ifalik** *I* Pacific Ocean
51E6 **Ifanadiana** Madagascar
48C4 **Ife** Nigeria
48C3 **Iférouane** Niger
27E6 **Igan** Malaysia
75C3 **Igarapava** Brazil

Kamen-na-Obi Ketchikan

24K4 **Kamen-na-Obi** Russian Federation
25S3 **Kamenskoya** Russian Federation
20L4 **Kamensk-Ural'skiy** Russian Federation
47B3 **Kamieskroon** South Africa
54H3 **Kamilukuak L** Canada
51C4 **Kamina** Zaïre
55J3 **Kaminak L** Canada
29D3 **Kaminoyama** Japan
54F4 **Kamloops** Canada
41E1 **Kamo** Armenia
29D3 **Kamogawa** Japan
50D3 **Kampala** Uganda
30C5 **Kampar** Malaysia
18B2 **Kampen** Netherlands
30B2 **Kamphaeng Phet** Thailand
30C3 **Kampot** Cambodia
20K4 **Kamskoye Vodokhranilishche** *Res* Russian Federation
42D4 **Kāmthi** India
21H5 **Kamyshin** Russian Federation
20L4 **Kamyshlov** Russian Federation
55L4 **Kanaaupscow** *R* Canada
59D3 **Kanab** USA
50C4 **Kananga** Zaïre
20H4 **Kanash** Russian Federation
29C3 **Kanayama** Japan
29D3 **Kanazawa** Japan
44B3 **Kānchipuram** India
20E2 **Kandagan** Indonesia
42B2 **Kandahar** Afghanistan
20E2 **Kandalaksha** Russian Federation
12L5 **Kandalakshskaya Guba** *B* Russian Federation
13D3 **Kandel** *Mt* Germany
48C3 **Kandi** Benin
34C2 **Kandos** Australia
44C4 **Kandy** Sri Lanka
65D2 **Kane** USA
55L1 **Kane Basin** *B* Canada
50B2 **Kanem** *Desert Region* Chad
66E5 **Kaneohe** Hawaiian Islands
20F2 **Kanevka** Russian Federation
47C1 **Kang** Botswana
48B3 **Kangaba** Mali
40C2 **Kangal** Turkey
55N3 **Kangâmiut** Greenland
41F4 **Kangān** Iran
30C4 **Kangar** Malaysia
32C4 **Kangaroo I** Australia
55N3 **Kangâtsiaq** Greenland
41E3 **Kangavar** Iran
31C1 **Kangbao** China
39G3 **Kangchenjunga** *Mt* China/Nepal
31A4 **Kangding** China
32A1 **Kangean** *Is* Indonesia
55P3 **Kangerdlugssuaq** *B* Greenland
55P3 **Kangerdlugssuatsaiq** *B* Greenland
50D3 **Kangetet** Kenya
28B2 **Kanggye** N Korea
28B3 **Kanghwa** S Korea
55M4 **Kangiqsualujjuaq** Canada
55L3 **Kangiqsujuak** Canada
55L3 **Kangirsuk** Canada
28B3 **Kangnŭng** S Korea
50B3 **Kango** Gabon
28A2 **Kangping** China
26C4 **Kanĝto** *Mt* China/India
31B3 **Kang Xian** China
51C4 **Kaniama** Zaïre
44B2 **Kani Giri** India
20G2 **Kanin, Poluostrov** *Pen* Russian Federation
12J6 **Kankaanpää** Finland
64B2 **Kankakee** USA
64B2 **Kankakee** *R* USA
48B3 **Kankan** Guinea
43E4 **Kānker** India
67B1 **Kannapolis** USA
44B4 **Kanniyākumari** India
48C3 **Kano** Nigeria
60C3 **Kanorado** USA
43E3 **Kānpur** India
61D3 **Kansas** *R* USA
56D3 **Kansas** *State* USA
57D3 **Kansas City** USA
31D5 **Kanshi** China
25L4 **Kansk** Russian Federation
28A3 **Kansŏng** S Korea
48C3 **Kantchari** Burkina
48C4 **Kanté** Togo
43F4 **Kanthi** India
54C3 **Kantishna** USA
9B3 **Kanturk** Irish Republic
47D1 **Kanye** Botswana
26E4 **Kaohsiung** Taiwan
51B5 **Kaoka Veld** *Plain* Namibia
48A3 **Kaolack** Senegal
51C5 **Kaoma** Zambia
66E5 **Kapaa** Hawaiian Islands
66E5 **Kapaau** Hawaiian Islands
51C4 **Kapanga** Zaïre
12H7 **Kapellskär** Sweden
Kap Farvel = Farewell, C
51C5 **Kapiri** Zambia
63D2 **Kaplan** USA
18C3 **Kaplice** Czech Republic
30B4 **Kapoe** Thailand
51C4 **Kapona** Zaïre
17D1 **Kaposvár** Hungary
55L2 **Kap Parry** *C* Greenland
28A2 **Kapsan** N Korea
27E6 **Kapuas** *R* Indonesia
34A2 **Kapunda** Australia
42D2 **Kapurthala** India
55K5 **Kapuskasing** Canada
64C1 **Kapuskasing** *R* Canada
34D2 **Kaputar** *Mt* Australia
21H8 **Kapydzhik** *Mt* Armenia
28A3 **Kapyŏng** S Korea
21G8 **Kara** *R* Turkey
40B1 **Karabük** Turkey
17F2 **Karacabey** Turkey
42B4 **Karachi** Pakistan
44A2 **Karād** India
21F7 **Kara Dağları** *Mt* Turkey
21D7 **Karadeniz Boğazi** *Str* Turkey
26E1 **Karaftit** Russian Federation
24J5 **Karaganda** Kazakhstan
24J5 **Karagayly** Kazakhstan
25S4 **Karaginskiy, Ostrov** *I* Russian Federation
44B3 **Kāraikāl** India
41F2 **Karaj** Iran
40C3 **Karak** Jordan
24G5 **Karakalpak Republic** Uzbekistan
42D1 **Karakax He** *R* China
27F6 **Karakelong** *I* Indonesia
42D1 **Karakoram** *Mts* India
42D1 **Karakoram P** China/India
48A3 **Karakoro** *Watercourse* Mali/Mauritius
24G6 **Karakumy** *Desert* Turkmenistan
45C3 **Karama** Jordan
21E8 **Karaman** Turkey
24K5 **Karamay** China
35B2 **Karamea** New Zealand
35B2 **Karamea Bight** *B* New Zealand
42D4 **Kāranja** India
21E8 **Karanlik** *R* Turkey
40B2 **Karapınar** Turkey
24J2 **Kara S** Russian Federation
47B2 **Karasburg** Namibia
12K5 **Karasjok** Norway
24J4 **Karasuk** Russian Federation
40C2 **Karataş** Turkey
24H5 **Kara Tau** *Mts* Kazakhstan
30B3 **Karathuri** Burma
28B4 **Karatsu** Japan
24K2 **Karaul** Russian Federation
45B1 **Karavostasi** Cyprus
41F4 **Karāz** Iran
41D3 **Karbalā'** Iraq
19E3 **Karcag** Hungary
17E3 **Kardhítsa** Greece
20E3 **Karelian Republic** Russian Federation
44E3 **Karen** Andaman Islands
20K3 **Karepino** Russian Federation
12J5 **Karesvando** Sweden
48B2 **Karet** *Desert Region* Mauritius
24K4 **Kargasok** Russian Federation
20F3 **Kargopol'** Russian Federation
48D3 **Kari** Nigeria
51C5 **Kariba** Zimbabwe
51C5 **Kariba Dam** Zambia/Zimbabwe
51C5 **Kariba, L** Zambia/Zimbabwe
47B1 **Karibib** Namibia
50D2 **Karima** Sudan
27D7 **Karimata** *I* Indonesia
43G4 **Karīmganj** India
44B2 **Karīmnagar** India
50E2 **Karin** Somalia
12J6 **Karis** Finland
50C4 **Karisimbe** *Mt* Zaïre
17E3 **Káristos** Greece
44A3 **Kārkal** India
27H7 **Karkar** *I* Papua New Guinea
41E3 **Karkheh** *R* Iran
21E6 **Karkinitskiy Zaliv** *B* Ukraine
25L5 **Karlik Shan** *Mt* China
18D2 **Karlino** Poland
16D2 **Karlobag** Croatia
16D1 **Karlovac** Croatia
17E2 **Karlovo** Bulgaria
18C2 **Karlovy Vary** Czech Republic
12G7 **Karlshamn** Sweden
12G7 **Karlskoga** Sweden
12H7 **Karlskrona** Sweden
18B3 **Karlsruhe** Germany
12G7 **Karlstad** Sweden
61D1 **Karlstad** USA
54C4 **Karluk** USA
43G4 **Karnafuli Res** Bangladesh
42D3 **Karnāl** India
44A2 **Karnātaka** *State* India
17F2 **Karnobat** Bulgaria
51C5 **Karoi** Zimbabwe
51D4 **Karonga** Malawi
50D2 **Karora** Sudan
17F3 **Kárpathos** *I* Greece
55N2 **Karrats Fjord** Greenland
47C3 **Karree Berge** *Mts* South Africa
21G7 **Kars** Turkey
24H5 **Karsakpay** Kazakhstan
19F1 **Kārsava** Latvia
38E2 **Karshi** Uzbekistan
24G2 **Karskiye Vorota, Proliv** *Str* Russian Federation
12J6 **Karstula** Finland
45C1 **Kartaba** Lebanon
17F2 **Kartal** Turkey
20L5 **Kartaly** Russian Federation
68A2 **Karthaus** USA
41E3 **Kārūn** *R* Iran
19D3 **Karviná** Czech Republic
43E3 **Karwa** India
44A3 **Kārwār** India
26E1 **Karymskoye** Russian Federation
50B4 **Kasai** *R* Zaïre
51C5 **Kasaji** Zaïre
51D5 **Kasama** Zambia
51D4 **Kasanga** Tanzania
44A3 **Kāsaragod** India
54H3 **Kasba L** Canada
51C5 **Kasempa** Zambia
51C5 **Kasenga** Zaïre
50D3 **Kasese** Uganda
43K2 **Kasganj** India
41F3 **Kāshān** Iran
39F2 **Kashi** China
28B4 **Kashima** Japan
42D3 **Kāshipur** India
29D3 **Kashiwazaki** Japan
41G2 **Kāshmar** Iran
22E4 **Kashmir** *State* India
20G5 **Kasimov** Russian Federation
64B3 **Kaskaskia** *R* USA
12J6 **Kaskinen** Finland
20L4 **Kasli** Russian Federation
54G5 **Kaslo** Canada
50C4 **Kasongo** Zaïre
51B4 **Kasongo-Lunda** Zaïre
17F3 **Kásos** *I* Greece
21H6 **Kaspiyskiy** Russian Federation
50D2 **Kassala** Sudan
18B2 **Kassel** Germany
48C1 **Kasserine** Tunisia
51B5 **Kassinga** Angola
40B1 **Kastamonu** Turkey
17E3 **Kastélli** Greece
40A2 **Kastellorizon** *I* Greece
17E2 **Kastoría** Greece
17F3 **Kástron** Greece
29D3 **Kasugai** Japan
29B3 **Kasumi** Japan
51D5 **Kasungu** Malawi
42C2 **Kasur** Pakistan
51C5 **Kataba** Zambia
65F1 **Katahdin,Mt** USA
50C4 **Katako-kombe** Zaïre
54D3 **Katalla** USA
25Q4 **Katangli** Russian Federation
32A4 **Katanning** Australia
44E4 **Katchall** *I* Nicobar Is, Indian Ocean
17E2 **Kateríni** Greece
54E4 **Kates Needle** *Mt* Canada/USA
40B4 **Katharîna, Gebel** *Mt* Egypt
32C2 **Katherine** Australia
42C4 **Kāthiāwār** *Pen* India
45B3 **Kathib el Henu** *Hill* Egypt
43F3 **Kathmandu** Nepal
42D2 **Kathua** India
43F3 **Katihār** India
51C5 **Katima Mulilo** Namibia
48B4 **Katiola** Ivory Coast
54C4 **Katmai,Mt** USA
43E4 **Katni** India
34D2 **Katoomba** Australia
19D2 **Katowice** Poland
12H7 **Katrineholm** Sweden
8C3 **Katrine, Loch** *L* Scotland
48C3 **Katsina** Nigeria
48C4 **Katsina** *R* Cameroon/Nigeria
48C4 **Katsina Ala** Nigeria
29D3 **Katsuta** Japan
29D3 **Katsuura** Japan
29C3 **Katsuyama** Japan
24H6 **Kattakurgan** Uzbekistan
12G7 **Kattegat** *Str* Denmark/Sweden
13E3 **Katzenbuckel** *Mt* Germany
66E5 **Kauai** *I* Hawaiian Islands
66E5 **Kauai Chan** Hawaiian Islands
66E5 **Kaulakahi Chan** Hawaiian Islands
66E5 **Kaunakakai** Hawaiian Islands
20C5 **Kaunas** Lithuania
48C3 **Kaura Namoda** Nigeria
12J5 **Kautokeino** Norway
17E2 **Kavadarci** Macedonia, Yugoslavia
17D2 **Kavajë** Albania
44B3 **Kavali** India
17E2 **Kavála** Greece
42B4 **Kāvda** India
32E1 **Kavieng** Papua New Guinea
29C3 **Kawagoe** Japan
29C3 **Kawaguchi** Japan
66E5 **Kawaihae** Hawaiian Islands
35B1 **Kawakawa** New Zealand
51C4 **Kawambwa** Zambia
43E4 **Kawardha** India
65D2 **Kawartha Lakes** Canada
29D3 **Kawasaki** Japan
66C2 **Kaweah** *R* USA
35C1 **Kawerau** New Zealand
35B1 **Kawhia** New Zealand
48B3 **Kaya** Burkina
27E6 **Kayan** *R* Indonesia
44B4 **Kāyankulam** India
60B2 **Kaycee** USA
59D3 **Kayenta** USA
48A3 **Kayes** Mali
21F8 **Kayseri** Turkey
25P2 **Kazach'ye** Russian Federation
41E1 **Kazakh** Azerbaijan
24G5 **Kazakhstan** *Republic* Asia
20H4 **Kazan'** Russian Federation
17F2 **Kazanlŭk** Bulgaria
26H4 **Kazan Retto** *Is* Japan
19F3 **Kazatin** Ukraine
21G7 **Kazbek** *Mt* Georgia
41F4 **Kāzerūn** Iran
20J3 **Kazhim** Russian Federation
41E1 **Kazi Magomed** Azerbaijan
19E3 **Kazincbarcika** Hungary
20M3 **Kazym** *R* Russian Federation
20M3 **Kazymskaya** Russian Federation
17E3 **Kéa** *I* Greece
9C2 **Keady** Northern Ireland
66E5 **Kealaikahiki Chan** Hawaiian Islands
56D2 **Kearney** USA
59D4 **Kearny** USA
40C2 **Keban Baraji** *Res* Turkey
48A3 **Kébémer** Senegal
48C1 **Kebili** Tunisia
45D1 **Kebīr** *R* Lebanon/Syria
12H5 **Kebnekaise** *Mt* Sweden
19D3 **Kecskemét** Hungary
19E1 **Kedainiai** Lithuania
65F1 **Kedgwick** Canada
27E7 **Kediri** Indonesia
48A3 **Kédougou** Senegal
20J3 **Kedva** Russian Federation
54E3 **Keele Pk** *Mt* Canada
59C3 **Keeler** USA
27C8 **Keeling Is** Indian Ocean
26F4 **Keelung** Taiwan
66C3 **Keene** California, USA
65E2 **Keene** New Hampshire, USA
47B2 **Keetmanshoop** Namibia
64B2 **Keewanee** USA
64A1 **Keewatin** USA
55J3 **Keewatin** *Region* Canada
17E3 **Kefallinía** *I* Greece
45C2 **Kefar Sava** Israel
48C4 **Keffi** Nigeria
12A2 **Keflavík** Iceland
54G4 **Keg River** Canada
30B1 **Kehsi Mansam** Burma
48C3 **Keita** Niger
34B3 **Keith** Australia
8D3 **Keith** Scotland
54F3 **Keith Arm** *B* Canada
6C3 **Keithley** England
55M3 **Kekertuk** Canada
42D3 **Kekri** India
30C5 **Kelang** Malaysia
30C4 **Kelantan** *R* Malaysia
16C3 **Kelibia** Tunisia
42B1 **Kelif** Turkmenistan
40C1 **Kelkit** *R* Turkey
50B4 **Kellé** Congo
54F2 **Kellett,C** Canada
58C1 **Kellogg** USA
24D3 **Kelloselka** Finland
33B9 **Kells** Irish Republic
8C4 **Kells Range** *Hills* Scotland
19E1 **Kelme** Lithuania
54G5 **Kelowna** Canada
54F4 **Kelsey Bay** Canada
8D4 **Kelso** Scotland
58B1 **Kelso** USA
20E3 **Kem'** Russian Federation
20E3 **Kem'** *R* Russian Federation
48B3 **Ke Macina** Mali
24K4 **Kemerovo** Russian Federation
12J5 **Kemi** Finland
12K5 **Kemi** *R* Finland
12K5 **Kemijärvi** Finland
58D2 **Kemmerer** USA
13C2 **Kempen** *Region* Belgium
62C2 **Kemp,L** USA
69B2 **Kemps Bay** The Bahamas
34D2 **Kempsey** Australia
18C3 **Kempten** Germany
65E1 **Kempt,L** Canada
54C3 **Kenai** USA
54C3 **Kenai Pen** USA
50D3 **Kenamuke Swamp** Sudan
6C2 **Kendal** England
34D2 **Kendall** Australia
32B1 **Kendari** Indonesia
27E7 **Kendawangan** Indonesia
43F4 **Kendrāpāra** India
58C1 **Kendrick** USA
63C3 **Kenedy** USA
48A4 **Kenema** Sierra Leone
50B4 **Kenge** Zaïre
30B1 **Kengtung** Burma
47C2 **Kenhardt** South Africa
48A3 **Kéniéba** Mali
48B1 **Kenitra** Morocco
60C1 **Kenmare** USA
62B2 **Kenna** USA
65F1 **Kennebec** *R* USA
68E1 **Kennebunk** USA
63D3 **Kenner** USA
63E1 **Kennett** USA
68C3 **Kennett Square** USA
58C1 **Kennewick** USA
54F4 **Kenny Dam** Canada
55J5 **Kenora** Canada
57E2 **Kenosha** USA
62B2 **Kent** Texas, USA
58B1 **Kent** Washington, USA
7E4 **Kent** *County* England
64B2 **Kentland** USA
64C2 **Kenton** USA
54H3 **Kent Pen** Canada
64C3 **Kentucky** *R* USA
57E3 **Kentucky** *State* USA
57E3 **Kentucky L** USA
63D2 **Kentwood** Louisiana, USA
64B2 **Kentwood** Michigan, USA
50D3 **Kenya** *Republic* Africa
Kenya,Mt = Kirinyaga
64A2 **Keokuk** USA
43E4 **Keonchi** India
43F4 **Keonjhargarh** India
19D2 **Kępno** Poland
44B3 **Kerala** *State* India
34B3 **Kerang** Australia
12K6 **Kerava** Finland
21F6 **Kerch'** Ukraine
20J3 **Kerchem'ya** Russian Federation
32D1 **Kerema** Papua New Guinea
58C1 **Keremeos** Canada
50D2 **Keren** Eritrea
36E7 **Kerguelen** *Is* Indian Ocean
36E7 **Kerguelen Ridge** Indian Ocean
50D4 **Kericho** Kenya
27D7 **Kerinci** *Mt* Indonesia
50D3 **Kerio** *R* Kenya
48D1 **Kerkenna, Îles** Tunisia
38E2 **Kerki** Turkmenistan
Kérkira = Corfu
33H3 **Kermadec Is** Pacific Ocean
33H4 **Kermadec Trench** Pacific Ocean
41G3 **Kermān** Iran
66B2 **Kerman** USA
41E3 **Kermānshāh** Iran
62B2 **Kermit** USA
59C3 **Kern** *R* USA
66C3 **Kernville** USA
20J3 **Keros** Russian Federation
62C2 **Kerrville** USA
9B3 **Kerry Hd** Irish Republic
67B2 **Kershaw** USA
25N5 **Kerulen** *R* Mongolia
48B2 **Kerzaz** Algeria
17F2 **Keşan** Turkey
43N2 **Kesariya** India
29E3 **Kesennuma** Japan
21G7 **Kesir Dağları** *Mt* Turkey
12L5 **Kesten'ga** Russian Federation
6C2 **Keswick** England
48C4 **Kéta** Ghana
27E7 **Ketapang** Indonesia
54E4 **Ketchikan** USA

Keti Bandar Koma

42B4 **Keti Bandar** Pakistan
19E2 **Kętrzyn** Poland
7D3 **Kettering** England
64C3 **Kettering** USA
58C1 **Kettle** *R* Canada
66C2 **Kettleman City** USA
58C1 **Kettle River Range** *Mts* USA
55L3 **Kettlestone B** Canada
68B1 **Keuka L** USA
41G3 **Kevir-i-Namak** *Salt Flat* Iran
64B2 **Kewaunee** USA
64B1 **Keweenaw B** USA
64B1 **Keweenaw Pen** USA
64C1 **Key Harbour** Canada
67B3 **Key Largo** USA
57E4 **Key West** USA
25M4 **Kezhma** Russian Federation
45D2 **Khabab** Syria
26G2 **Khabarovsk** Russian Federation
21G8 **Khabūr, al** *R* Syria
42B3 **Khairpur** Pakistan
42B3 **Khairpur** *Division* Pakistan
47C1 **Khakhea** Botswana
45B3 **Khalig el Tîna** *B* Egypt
38D4 **Khalīj Maşīrah** *G* Oman
17F3 **Khálki** *I* Greece
17E2 **Khalkidhíki** *Pen* Greece
17E3 **Khalkís** Greece
20L2 **Khal'mer-Yu** Russian Federation
20H4 **Khalturin** Russian Federation
42C4 **Khambhāt,G of** India
42D4 **Khāmgaon** India
30C2 **Kham Keut** Laos
44C2 **Khammam** India
45B3 **Khamsa** Egypt
41E2 **Khamseh** *Mts* Iran
30C2 **Khan** *R* Laos
42B1 **Khanabad** Afghanistan
41E3 **Khānaqīn** Iraq
42D4 **Khandwa** India
42C2 **Khanewal** Pakistan
45D3 **Khan ez Zabīb** Jordan
30D4 **Khanh Hung** Vietnam
17E3 **Khaniá** Greece
26G2 **Khanka, Ozero** *L* China/Russian Federation
Khankendy = Stepanakert
42C3 **Khanpur** Pakistan
45D1 **Khān Shaykhūn** Syria
24H3 **Khanty-Mansiysk** Russian Federation
45C3 **Khan Yunis** Israel
42D1 **Khapalu** India
26E2 **Khapcheranga** Russian Federation
21H6 **Kharabali** Russian Federation
43F4 **Kharagpur** India
42B3 **Kharan** Pakistan
41G4 **Khārān** *R* Iran
41F3 **Kharānaq** Iran
41F4 **Khārg** *I* Iran
49F2 **Khârga Oasis** Egypt
42D4 **Khargon** India
45B3 **Kharîm, Gebel** *Mt* Egypt
21F6 **Khar'kov** Ukraine
20F2 **Kharlovka** Russian Federation
17F2 **Kharmanli** Bulgaria
20G4 **Kharovsk** Russian Federation
50D2 **Khartoum** Sudan
50D2 **Khartoum North** Sudan
28C2 **Khasan** Russian Federation
50D2 **Khashm el Girba** Sudan
43G3 **Khasi-Jaintīa Hills** India
17F2 **Khaskovo** Bulgaria
25M2 **Khatanga** Russian Federation
25N2 **Khatangskiy Zaliv** *Estuary* Russian Federation
25T3 **Khatyrka** Russian Federation
30B3 **Khawsa** Burma
40C4 **Khaybar** Saudi Arabia
40B5 **Khazzan an-Nasr** *L* Egypt
30C2 **Khe Bo** Vietnam
42C4 **Khed Brahma** India
15C2 **Khemis** Algeria
16B3 **Khenchela** Algeria
48B1 **Khenifra** Morocco
43L1 **Kheri** *District* India
15D2 **Kherrata** Algeria
21E6 **Kherson** Ukraine
25N4 **Khilok** Russian Federation
17F3 **Khíos** Greece
17F3 **Khíos** *I* Greece
21D6 **Khmel'nitskiy** Ukraine
19E3 **Khodorov** Ukraine
42B1 **Kholm** Afghanistan
19G1 **Kholm** Russian Federation
47B1 **Khomas Hochland** *Mts* Namibia
30D3 **Khong** Laos
41F4 **Khonj** Iran
26G2 **Khor** Russian Federation
41F5 **Khōr Duwayhin** *B* UAE
42C1 **Khorog** Tajikistan
41E3 **Khorramābad** Iran
41E3 **Khorramshahr** Iran
41G3 **Khosf** Iran
42B2 **Khost** Pakistan
21D6 **Khotin** Ukraine
21D5 **Khoyniki** Belarus
41G2 **Khrebet Kopet Dag** *Mts* Iran/Turkmenistan
20L2 **Khrebet Pay-khoy** *Mts* Russian Federation
45B1 **Khrysokhou B** Cyprus
39E1 **Khudzhand** Tajikistan
20L3 **Khulga** *R* Russian Federation
43F4 **Khulna** Bangladesh
42D1 **Khunjerāb P** China/India
41F3 **Khunsar** Iran
41E4 **Khurays** Saudi Arabia
43F4 **Khurda** India
42D3 **Khurja** India
42C2 **Khushab** Pakistan
45C2 **Khushnīyah** Syria
45D4 **Khush Shah, Wadi el** Jordan
19E3 **Khust** Ukraine
50C2 **Khuwei** Sudan
42B3 **Khuzdar** Pakistan
21H5 **Khvalynsk** Russian Federation
41G3 **Khvor** Iran
41F4 **Khvormūj** Iran
21G8 **Khvoy** Iran
42C1 **Khwaja Muhammad Ra** *Mts* Afghanistan
42C2 **Khyber P** Afghanistan/Pakistan
51C4 **Kiambi** Zaïre
63C2 **Kiamichi** *R* USA
50B4 **Kibangou** Congo
50D4 **Kibaya** Tanzania
50C4 **Kibombo** Zaïre
50D4 **Kibondo** Tanzania
50D4 **Kibungu** Rwanda
17E2 **Kicevo** Macedonia, Yugoslavia
54G4 **Kicking Horse P** Canada
48C3 **Kidal** Mali
7C3 **Kidderminster** England
48A3 **Kidira** Senegal
35C1 **Kidnappers,C** New Zealand
18C2 **Kiel** Germany
19E2 **Kielce** Poland
6C2 **Kielder Res** England
18C2 **Kieler Bucht** *B* Germany
21E5 **Kiev** Ukraine
38E2 **Kifab** Uzbekistan
48A3 **Kiffa** Mauritius
50D4 **Kigali** Rwanda
50C4 **Kigoma** Tanzania
66E5 **Kiholo** Hawaiian Islands
29C4 **Kii-sanchi** *Mts* Japan
29C4 **Kii-suidō** *Str* Japan
25R4 **Kikhchik** Russian Federation
17E1 **Kikinda** Serbia, Yugoslavia
Kikládhes = Cyclades
32D1 **Kikon** Papua New Guinea
29D2 **Kikonai** Japan
27H7 **Kikori** Papua New Guinea
50B4 **Kikwit** Zaïre
66E5 **Kilauea Crater** *Vol* Hawaiian Islands
8C4 **Kilbrannan Sd** Scotland
54C3 **Kilbuck Mts** USA
28B2 **Kilchu** N Korea
34D1 **Kilcoy** Australia
9C3 **Kildare** Irish Republic
9C3 **Kildare** *County* Irish Republic
63D2 **Kilgore** USA
50E4 **Kilifi** Kenya
50D4 **Kilimanjaro** *Mt* Tanzania
51D4 **Kilindoni** Tanzania
40C2 **Kilis** Turkey
19F3 **Kiliya** Ukraine
9D2 **Kilkeel** Northern Ireland
9C3 **Kilkenny** Irish Republic
9C3 **Kilkenny** *County* Irish Republic
17E2 **Kilkís** Greece
34D1 **Killarney** Australia
10B3 **Killarney** Irish Republic
63C2 **Killeen** USA
8C3 **Killin** Scotland
17E3 **Killíni** *Mt* Greece
9B3 **Killorglin** Irish Republic
9D2 **Killyleagh** Northern Ireland
8C4 **Kilmarnock** Scotland
20J4 **Kil'mez** Russian Federation
9C3 **Kilmichael Pt** Irish Republic
51D4 **Kilosa** Tanzania
10B3 **Kilrush** Irish Republic
8C4 **Kilsyth** Scotland
51C4 **Kilwa** Zaïre
51D4 **Kilwa Kisiwani** Tanzania
51D4 **Kilwa Kivinje** Tanzania
60C2 **Kimball** USA
54G5 **Kimberley** Canada
47C2 **Kimberley** South Africa
32B2 **Kimberley Plat** Australia
28B2 **Kimch'aek** N Korea
28B3 **Kimch'ŏn** S Korea
28A3 **Kimhae** S Korea
17E3 **Kími** Greece
28A3 **Kimje** S Korea
20F4 **Kimry** Russian Federation
28A3 **Kimwha** N Korea
27E6 **Kinabalu** *Mt* Malaysia
8D2 **Kinbrace** Scotland
64C2 **Kincardine** Canada
63D2 **Kinder** USA
48A3 **Kindia** Guinea
50C4 **Kindu** Zaïre
20J5 **Kinel'** Russian Federation
20G4 **Kineshma** Russian Federation
34D1 **Kingaroy** Australia
59B3 **King City** USA
54F4 **Kingcome Inlet** Canada
63C1 **Kingfisher** USA
76H4 **King George I** Antarctica
55L4 **King George Is** Canada
32D5 **King I** Australia
32B2 **King Leopold Range** *Mts* Australia
56B3 **Kingman** USA
50C4 **Kingombe** Zaïre
66C2 **Kingsburg** USA
59C3 **Kings Canyon Nat Pk** USA
32B2 **King Sd** Australia
64B1 **Kingsford** USA
67B2 **Kingsland** USA
7E3 **King's Lynn** England
33G1 **Kingsmill Group** *Is* Kiribati
68D2 **Kings Park** USA
56B2 **Kings Peak** *Mt* USA
67B1 **Kingsport** USA
32C4 **Kingston** Australia
55L5 **Kingston** Canada
70E3 **Kingston** Jamaica
65E2 **Kingston** New York, USA
35A3 **Kingston** New Zealand
68C2 **Kingston** Pennsylvania, USA
69N2 **Kingstown** St Vincent
56D4 **Kingsville** USA
7C3 **Kington** England
8C3 **Kingussie** Scotland
54J3 **King William I** Canada
47D3 **King William's Town** South Africa
50B4 **Kinkala** Congo
12G7 **Kinna** Sweden
8D3 **Kinnairds Head** *Pt* Scotland
29C3 **Kinomoto** Japan
8D3 **Kinross** Scotland
50B4 **Kinshasa** Zaïre
62C1 **Kinsley** USA
67C1 **Kinston** USA
27E7 **Kintap** Indonesia
8C4 **Kintyre** *Pen* Scotland
50D3 **Kinyeti** *Mt* Sudan
17E3 **Kiparissía** Greece
17E3 **Kiparissiakós Kólpos** *G* Greece
65D1 **Kipawa,L** Canada
51D4 **Kipili** Tanzania
9C3 **Kippure** *Mt* Irish Republic
51C5 **Kipushi** Zaïre
25M4 **Kirensk** Russian Federation
24J5 **Kirghizia** *Republic* Asia
39F1 **Kirgizskiy Khrebet** *Mts* Kirgizia
50B4 **Kiri** Zaïre
33G1 **Kiribati** *Is, Republic* Pacific Ocean
40B2 **Kırıkkale** Turkey
50D4 **Kirinyaga, Mt** Kenya
20E4 **Kirishi** Russian Federation
42B3 **Kirithar Range** *Mts* Pakistan
17F3 **Kirkağaç** Turkey
21H8 **Kirk Bulāg Dāgh** *Mt* Iran
6C2 **Kirkby** England
8D3 **Kirkcaldy** Scotland
8C4 **Kirkcudbright** Scotland
12K5 **Kirkenes** Norway
6C3 **Kirkham** England
55K5 **Kirkland Lake** Canada
40A1 **Kırklareli** Turkey
6C2 **Kirkoswald** England
76E7 **Kirkpatrick,Mt** Antarctica
57D2 **Kirksville** USA
41D2 **Kirkūk** Iraq
8D2 **Kirkwall** Scotland
47D3 **Kirkwood** South Africa
61E3 **Kirkwood** USA
20E5 **Kirov** Russian Federation
20H4 **Kirov** Russian Federation
41D1 **Kirovakan** Armenia
20K4 **Kirovgrad** Russian Federation
21E6 **Kirovograd** Ukraine
20E2 **Kirovsk** Russian Federation
25R4 **Kirovskiy** Kamchatka, Russian Federation
8D3 **Kirriemuir** Scotland
20J4 **Kirs** Russian Federation
40B2 **Kırşehir** Turkey
18C2 **Kiruna** Sweden
29C3 **Kiryū** Japan
50C3 **Kisangani** Zaïre
29C3 **Kisarazu** Japan
43F3 **Kishanganj** India
42C3 **Kishangarh** India
19F3 **Kishinev** Moldavia
29C4 **Kishiwada** Japan
50D4 **Kisii** Kenya
51D4 **Kisiju** Tanzania
17D1 **Kiskunfélegyháza** Hungary
19D3 **Kiskunhalas** Hungary
21G7 **Kislovodsk** Russian Federation
50E4 **Kismaayo** Somalia
29C3 **Kiso-sammyaku** *Mts* Japan
48B4 **Kissidougou** Guinea
67B3 **Kissimmee,L** USA
50D4 **Kisumu** Kenya
19E3 **Kisvárda** Hungary
48B3 **Kita** Mali
24H6 **Kitab** Uzbekistan
29D3 **Kitakami** Japan
29D3 **Kitakami** *R* Japan
29D3 **Kitakata** Japan
28C4 **Kita-Kyūshū** Japan
50D3 **Kitale** Kenya
26H4 **Kitalo** *I* Japan
29E2 **Kitami** Japan
29D2 **Kitami-Esashi** Japan
60C3 **Kit Carson** USA
55K5 **Kitchener** Canada
50D3 **Kitgum** Uganda
17E3 **Kíthira** *I* Greece
17E3 **Kíthnos** *I* Greece
45B1 **Kiti, C** Cyprus
54G2 **Kitikmeot** *Region* Canada
54F4 **Kitimat** Canada
12K5 **Kitinen** *R* Finland
28B4 **Kitsuki** Japan
65D2 **Kittanning** USA
65E2 **Kittery** USA
12J5 **Kittilä** Finland
67C1 **Kitty Hawk** USA
51D4 **Kitunda** Tanzania
51C5 **Kitwe** Zambia
18C3 **Kitzbühel** Austria
18C3 **Kitzingen** Germany
50C4 **Kiumbi** Zaïre
54B3 **Kivalina** USA
19F2 **Kivercy** Ukraine
50C4 **Kivu,L** Rwanda/Zaïre
54B3 **Kiwalik** USA
Kiyev = Kiev
19G2 **Kiyevskoye Vodokhranilishche** *Res* Ukraine
20K4 **Kizel** Russian Federation
20G3 **Kizema** Russian Federation
40C2 **Kizil** *R* Turkey
38D2 **Kizyl'-Arvat** Turkmenistan
21J8 **Kizyl-Atrek** Turkmenistan
18C2 **Kladno** Czech Republic
18C3 **Klagenfurt** Austria
20C4 **Klaipēda** Lithuania
58B2 **Klamath** *R* USA
56A2 **Klamath Falls** USA
58B2 **Klamath Mts** USA
18C3 **Klatovy** Czech Republic
45C1 **Kleiat** Lebanon
47B2 **Kleinsee** South Africa
47D2 **Klerksdorp** South Africa
19G2 **Kletnya** Russian Federation
13D2 **Kleve** Germany
19G2 **Klimovichi** Belarus
20F4 **Klin** Russian Federation
19D1 **Klintehamn** Sweden
21E5 **Klintsy** Russian Federation
47C3 **Klipplaat** South Africa
16D2 **Ključ** Bosnia-Herzegovina
18D2 **Kłodzko** Poland
54D3 **Klondike Plat** Canada/USA
18D3 **Klosterneuburg** Austria
19D2 **Kluczbork** Poland
6D2 **Knaresborough** England
7C3 **Knighton** Wales
16D2 **Knin** Croatia
32A4 **Knob,C** Australia
9B3 **Knockmealdown Mts** Irish Republic
13B2 **Knokke-Heist** Belgium
76G9 **Knox Coast** Antarctica
61E2 **Knoxville** Iowa, USA
57E3 **Knoxville** Tennessee, USA
55Q3 **Knud Rasmussens Land** *Region* Greenland
7C3 **Knutsford** England
47C3 **Knysna** South Africa
55O3 **Kobberminebugt** *B* Greenland
29D4 **Kōbe** Japan
København = Copenhagen
18B2 **Koblenz** Germany
19E2 **Kobrin** Belarus
27G7 **Kobroör** *I* Indonesia
54B3 **Kobuk** *R* USA
17E2 **Kočani** Macedonia, Yugoslavia
28B3 **Kochang** S Korea
28B3 **Koch'ang** S Korea
30C3 **Ko Chang** *I* Thailand
43F3 **Koch Bihār** India
55L3 **Koch I** Canada
44B4 **Kochi** India
29C4 **Kōchi** Japan
54C4 **Kodiak** USA
54C4 **Kodiak I** USA
44B3 **Kodikkarai** India
50D3 **Kodok** Sudan
29D2 **Kodomari-misaki** *C* Japan
19F3 **Kodyma** Ukraine
66D3 **Koehn L** USA
47B2 **Koes** Namibia
47D2 **Koffiefontein** South Africa
48B4 **Koforidua** Ghana
29D3 **Kofu** Japan
29C3 **Koga** Japan
12G7 **Køge** Denmark
42C2 **Kohat** Pakistan
42B2 **Koh-i-Baba** *Mts* Afghanistan
42B1 **Koh-i-Hisar** *Mts* Afghanistan
42B2 **Koh-i-Khurd** *Mt* Afghanistan
43G3 **Kohima** India
42B2 **Koh-i-Mazar** *Mt* Afghanistan
42B3 **Kohlu** Pakistan
20D4 **Kohtla Järve** Estonia
28A4 **Kohung** S Korea
28A4 **Kohyon** S Korea
29C3 **Koide** Japan
30A4 **Koihoa** Nicobar Is, India
28A2 **Koin** N Korea
28B4 **Koje Dŏ** *I* S Korea
29C2 **Ko-jima** *I* Japan
24H4 **Kokchetav** Kazakhstan
12J6 **Kokemäki** *L* Finland
12J6 **Kokkola** Finland
32D1 **Kokoda** Papua New Guinea
64B2 **Kokomo** USA
27G7 **Kokonau** Indonesia
26B2 **Kokpekty** Kazakhstan
28A3 **Koksan** N Korea
55M4 **Koksoak** *R* Canada
28A3 **Koksŏng** S Korea
47D3 **Kokstad** South Africa
30C3 **Ko Kut** *I* Thailand
20E2 **Kola** Russian Federation
27F7 **Kolaka** Indonesia
30B4 **Ko Lanta** *I* Thailand
44B3 **Kolār** India
44B3 **Kolār Gold Fields** India
48A3 **Kolda** Senegal
12F7 **Kolding** Denmark
20H2 **Kolguyev, Ostrov** *I* Russian Federation
44A2 **Kolhāpur** India
18D2 **Kolín** Czech Republic
44B4 **Kollam** India
Köln = Cologne
19D2 **Koło** Poland
66E5 **Koloa** Hawaiian Islands
18D2 **Kołobrzeg** Poland
48B3 **Kolokani** Mali
20F4 **Kolomna** Russian Federation
21D6 **Kolomyya** Ukraine
25R4 **Kolpakovskiy** Russian Federation
24K4 **Kolpashevo** Russian Federation
17F3 **Kólpos Merabéllou** *B* Greece
17E2 **Kólpos Singitikós** *G* Greece
17E2 **Kólpos Strimonikós** *G* Greece
17E2 **Kólpos Toronaíos** *G* Greece
20F2 **Kol'skiy Poluostrov** *Pen* Russian Federation
20K2 **Kolva** *R* Russian Federation
12G6 **Kolvereid** Norway
51C5 **Kolwezi** Zaïre
25R3 **Kolyma** *R* Russian Federation
25R3 **Kolymskaya Nizmennost'** *Lowland* Russian Federation
25S3 **Kolymskoye Nagor'ye** *Mts* Russian Federation
17E2 **Kom** *Mt* Bulgaria/Serbia, Yugoslavia
50D3 **Koma** Ethiopia
29D3 **Koma** Japan

Komadugu Gana
Kythrea

48D3 **Komadugu Gana** *R* Nigeria
29D2 **Komaga take** *Mt* Japan
25S4 **Komandorskiye Ostrova** *Is* Russian Federation
19D3 **Komárno** Slovakia
47E2 **Komati** *R* South Africa/ Swaziland
47E2 **Komati Poort** South Africa
29D3 **Komatsu** Japan
29B4 **Komatsushima** Japan
20J3 **Komi Republic** Russian Federation
26B1 **Kommunar** Russian Federation
27E7 **Komodo** *I* Indonesia
27G7 **Komoran** *I* Indonesia
29C3 **Komoro** Japan
17F2 **Komotiní** Greece
47C3 **Kompasberg** *Mt* South Africa
30D3 **Kompong Cham** Cambodia
30C3 **Kompong Chhnang** Cambodia
30C3 **Kompong Som = Sihanoukville**
30D3 **Kompong Thom** Cambodia
30D3 **Kompong Trabek** Cambodia
19F3 **Komrat** Moldavia
47C3 **Komsberg** *Mts* South Africa
25L1 **Komsomolets, Ostrov** *I* Russian Federation
20L2 **Komsomol'skiy** Russian Federation
25P4 **Komsomol'sk na Amure** Russian Federation
24H4 **Konda** *R* Russian Federation
43E5 **Kondagaon** India
50D4 **Kondoa** Tanzania
20E3 **Kondopoga** Russian Federation
44B2 **Kondukūr** India
20F3 **Konevo** Russian Federation
55P3 **Kong Christian IX Land** *Region* Greenland
55O3 **Kong Frederik VI Kyst** *Region* Greenland
28A3 **Kongju** S Korea
24D2 **Kong Karls Land** *Is* Svalbard
50C4 **Kongolo** Zaïre
12F7 **Kongsberg** Norway
12G6 **Kongsvinger** Norway
Königsberg = Kaliningrad
19D2 **Konin** Poland
17D2 **Konjic** Bosnia-Herzegovina
20G3 **Konosha** Russian Federation
29C3 **Konosu** Japan
21E5 **Konotop** Ukraine
19E2 **Końskie** Poland
18B3 **Konstanz** Germany
48C3 **Kontagora** Nigeria
30D3 **Kontum** Vietnam
21E8 **Konya** Turkey
58C1 **Kootenay L** Canada
42C5 **Kopargaon** India
55R3 **Kópasker** Iceland
12A2 **Kópavogur** Iceland
16C1 **Koper** Slovenia
38D2 **Kopet Dag** *Mts* Iran/ Turkmenistan
20L4 **Kopeysk** Russian Federation
30C4 **Ko Phangan** *I* Thailand
30B4 **Ko Phuket** *I* Thailand
12H7 **Köping** Sweden
28A3 **Kopo-ri** S Korea
44B2 **Koppal** India
16D1 **Koprivnica** Croatia
42B4 **Korangi** Pakistan
44C2 **Koraput** India
43E4 **Korba** India
18B2 **Korbach** Germany
17E2 **Korçë** Albania
16D2 **Korčula** *I* Croatia
31E2 **Korea B** China/Korea
28B2 **Korea, North** *Republic* Asia
28B3 **Korea, South** *Republic* Asia
26F3 **Korea Strait** Japan/Korea
19F2 **Korec** Ukraine
25S3 **Korf** Russian Federation
40B1 **Körğlu Tepesi** *Mt* Turkey
48B4 **Korhogo** Ivory Coast
42B4 **Kori Creek** India
Kórinthos = Corinth
29E3 **Kōriyama** Japan
20L5 **Korkino** Russian Federation
25R3 **Korkodon** Russian Federation
25R3 **Korkodon** *R* Russian Federation
40B2 **Korkuteli** Turkey
39G1 **Korla** China
45B1 **Kormakiti, C** Cyprus
16D2 **Kornat** *I* Croatia
21E7 **Köroğlu Tepesi** *Mt* Turkey
50D4 **Korogwe** Tanzania
34B3 **Koroit** Australia
27G6 **Koror** Palau, Pacific Ocean
19E3 **Körös** *R* Hungary
21D5 **Korosten** Ukraine
19F2 **Korostyshev** Ukraine
50B2 **Koro Toro** Chad
26H2 **Korsakov** Russian Federation
12G7 **Korsør** Denmark
20J3 **Kortkeros** Russian Federation
18A2 **Kortrijk** Belgium
25S3 **Koryakskoye Nagor'ye** *Mts* Russian Federation
28A3 **Koryong** S Korea
17F3 **Kós** *I* Greece
30C4 **Ko Samui** *I* Thailand
28A3 **Kosan** N Korea
19D2 **Kościerzyna** Poland
63E2 **Kosciusko** USA
32D4 **Kosciusko** *Mt* Australia
43J2 **Kosi** India
43K1 **Kosi** *R* India
19E3 **Košice** Slovakia
20J2 **Kosma** *R* Russian Federation
28B3 **Kosŏng** N Korea
17E2 **Kosovo** *Region* Serbia, Yugoslavia
17E2 **Kosovska Mitrovica** Serbia, Yugoslavia
48B4 **Kossou** *L* Ivory Coast
47D2 **Koster** South Africa
50D2 **Kosti** Sudan
19F2 **Kostopol'** Ukraine
20G4 **Kostroma** Russian Federation
18C2 **Kostrzyn** Poland
20K2 **Kos'yu** *R* Russian Federation
12H8 **Koszalin** Poland
42D3 **Kota** India
30C4 **Kota Baharu** Malaysia
42C2 **Kot Addu** Pakistan
27E6 **Kota Kinabalu** Malaysia
44C2 **Kotapad** India
20H4 **Kotel'nich** Russian Federation
21G6 **Kotel'nikovo** Russian Federation
25P2 **Kotel'nyy, Ostrov** *I* Russian Federation
12K6 **Kotka** Finland
20H3 **Kotlas** Russian Federation
54B3 **Kotlik** USA
17D2 **Kotor** Montenegro, Yugoslavia
21D6 **Kotovsk** Ukraine
42B3 **Kotri** Pakistan
44C2 **Kottagūdem** India
44B4 **Kottayam** India
50C3 **Kotto** *R* Central African Republic
44B3 **Kottūru** India
25L3 **Kotuy** *R* Russian Federation
54B3 **Kotzebue** USA
54B3 **Kotzebue Sd** USA
48C3 **Kouandé** Benin
50C3 **Kouango** Central African Republic
48B3 **Koudougou** Burkina
47C3 **Kougaberge** *Mts* South Africa
50B4 **Koulamoutou** Gabon
48B3 **Koulikoro** Mali
48B3 **Koupéla** Burkina
73H2 **Kourou** French Guiana
48B3 **Kouroussa** Guinea
50B2 **Kousséri** Cameroon
12K6 **Kouvola** Finland
12L5 **Kovdor** Russian Federation
12L5 **Kovdozero, Ozero** *L* Russian Federation
19E2 **Kovel** Ukraine
Kovno = Kaunas
20G4 **Kovrov** Russian Federation
20G5 **Kovylkino** Russian Federation
20F3 **Kovzha** *R* Russian Federation
30C4 **Ko Way** *I* Thailand
31C5 **Kowloon** Hong Kong
28A3 **Kowŏn** N Korea
42B2 **Kowt-e-Ashrow** Afghanistan
40A2 **Köycegğiz** Turkey
20G2 **Koyda** Russian Federation
44A2 **Koyna Res** India
20H3 **Koynas** Russian Federation
54C3 **Koyukuk** USA
40C2 **Kozan** Turkey
17E2 **Kozańi** Greece
44B3 **Kozhikode** India
20K2 **Kozhim** Russian Federation
20H4 **Koz'modemyansk** Russian Federation
29C4 **Kōzu-shima** *I* Japan
48C4 **Kpalimé** Togo
47D3 **Kraai** *R* South Africa
12F7 **Kragerø** Norway
17E2 **Kragujevac** Serbia, Yugoslavia
30B3 **Kra,Isthmus of** Burma/ Malaysia
45D1 **Krak des Chevaliers** *Hist Site* Syria
Kraków = Cracow Poland
17E2 **Kraljevo** Serbia, Yugoslavia
21F6 **Kramatorsk** Ukraine
12H6 **Kramfors** Sweden
16C1 **Kranj** Slovenia
20H3 **Krasavino** Russian Federation
20J1 **Krasino** Russian Federation
28C2 **Kraskino** Russian Federation
19E2 **Kraśnik** Poland
21H5 **Krasnoarmeysk** Russian Federation
21F6 **Krasnodar** Russian Federation
20K4 **Krasnokamsk** Russian Federation
20L4 **Krasnotur'insk** Russian Federation
20K4 **Krasnoufimsk** Russian Federation
20K5 **Krasnousol'skiy** Russian Federation
20K3 **Krasnovishersk** Russian Federation
21J7 **Krasnovodsk** Turkmenistan
25L4 **Krasnoyarsk** Russian Federation
19E2 **Krasnystaw** Poland
21H5 **Krasnyy Kut** Russian Federation
21F6 **Krasnyy Luch** Ukraine
21H6 **Krasnyy Yar** Russian Federation
30D3 **Kratie** Cambodia
55N2 **Kraulshavn** Greenland
18B2 **Krefeld** Germany
21E6 **Kremenchug** Ukraine
21E6 **Kremenchugskoye Vodokhranilische** *Res* Ukraine
19F2 **Kremenets** Ukraine
60B2 **Kremming** USA
48C4 **Kribi** Cameroon
20E5 **Krichev** Belarus
44B2 **Krishna** *R* India
44B3 **Krishnagiri** India
43F4 **Krishnanagar** India
12F7 **Kristiansand** Norway
12G7 **Kristianstad** Sweden
24B3 **Kristiansund** Norway
12J6 **Kristiinankaupunki** Finland
12G7 **Kristinehamn** Sweden
Kríti = Crete
21E6 **Krivoy Rog** Ukraine
16C1 **Krk** *I* Croatia
47D1 **Krokodil** *R* South Africa
25S4 **Kronotskaya Sopka** *Mt* Russian Federation
25S4 **Kronotskiy, Mys** *C* Russian Federation
55P3 **Kronprins Frederik Bjerge** *Mts* Greenland
12K7 **Kronshtadt** Russian Federation
47D2 **Kroonstad** South Africa
21G6 **Kropotkin** Russian Federation
47E1 **Kruger Nat Pk** South Africa
47D2 **Krugersdorp** South Africa
17D2 **Kruje** Albania
Krung Thep = Bangkok
19F2 **Krupki** Belarus
17E2 **Kruševac** Serbia, Yugoslavia
12K7 **Krustpils** Latvia
Krym = Crimea
21F7 **Krymsk** Russian Federation
18D2 **Krzyz** Poland
15C2 **Ksar El Boukhari** Algeria
15A2 **Ksar-el-Kebir** Morocco
48C1 **Ksour, Mts des** Algeria
27C6 **Kuala** Indonesia
30C5 **Kuala Dungun** Malaysia
30C4 **Kuala Kerai** Malaysia
30C5 **Kuala Kubu Baharu** Malaysia
30C5 **Kuala Lipis** Malaysia
30C5 **Kuala Lumpur** Malaysia
30C4 **Kuala Trengganu** Malaysia
27F6 **Kuandang** Indonesia
28A2 **Kuandian** China
30C5 **Kuantan** Malaysia
21H7 **Kuba** Azerbaijan
27H7 **Kubor** *Mt* Papua New Guinea
27E6 **Kuching** Malaysia
27E6 **Kudat** Malaysia
20J4 **Kudymkar** Russian Federation
18C3 **Kufstein** Austria
41G3 **Kuh Duren** *Upland* Iran
41F3 **Kūh-e Dinar** *Mt* Iran
41G2 **Kūh-e-Hazār Masjed** *Mts* Iran
41G4 **Kūh-e Jebāl Barez** *Mts* Iran
41F3 **Kūh-e Karkas** *Mts* Iran
41G4 **Kūh-e Laleh Zar** *Mt* Iran
41E2 **Kūh-e Sahand** *Mt* Iran
38E3 **Kuh-e-Taftān** *Mt* Iran
21H9 **Kūhhaye Alvand** *Mts* Iran
21H8 **Kūhhaye Sabalan** *Mts* Iran
41E3 **Kūhhā-ye Zāgros** *Mts* Iran
12K6 **Kuhmo** Finland
41F3 **Kūhpāyeh** Iran
41G3 **Kūhpāyeh** *Mt* Iran
41G4 **Kūh-ye Bashākerd** *Mts* Iran
41E2 **Kūh-ye Sabalan** *Mt* Iran
47B2 **Kuibis** Namibia
47B1 **Kuiseb** *R* Namibia
51B5 **Kuito** Angola
28A3 **Kujang** N Korea
29E2 **Kuji** Japan
28B4 **Kuju-san** *Mt* Japan
17E2 **Kukës** Albania
30C5 **Kukup** Malaysia
41G4 **Kūl** *R* Iran
17F3 **Kula** Turkey
21K6 **Kulakshi** Kazakhstan
50D3 **Kulal,Mt** Kenya
17E2 **Kulata** Bulgaria
20C4 **Kuldīga** Latvia
20G2 **Kulov** *R* Russian Federation
21J6 **Kul'sary** Kazakhstan
42D2 **Kulu** India
40B2 **Kulu** Turkey
24J4 **Kulunda** Russian Federation
34B2 **Kulwin** Australia
21H7 **Kuma** *R* Russian Federation
29C3 **Kumagaya** Japan
27E7 **Kumai** Indonesia
21L5 **Kumak** Russian Federation
28C4 **Kumamoto** Japan
29C4 **Kumano** Japan
17E2 **Kumanovo** Macedonia, Yugoslavia
48B4 **Kumasi** Ghana
21G7 **Kumayri** Armenia
48C4 **Kumba** Cameroon
44B3 **Kumbakonam** India
28A3 **Kūmch'ŏn** N Korea
20K5 **Kumertau** Russian Federation
28A3 **Kumgang** N Korea
12H7 **Kumla** Sweden
28A4 **Kūmnyŏng** S Korea
28A4 **Kūmo-do** *I* S Korea
44A3 **Kumta** India
39G1 **Kumüx** China
28B3 **Kumwha** S Korea
42C2 **Kunar** *R* Afghanistan
29F2 **Kunashir, Ostrov** *I* Russian Federation
12K7 **Kunda** Estonia
42C4 **Kundla** India
42B1 **Kunduz** Afghanistan
Kunene *R* **= Cunene R**
12G7 **Kungsbacka** Sweden
20K4 **Kungur** Russian Federation
30B1 **Kunhing** Burma
39G2 **Kunlun Shan** *Mts* China
31A4 **Kunming** China
20M3 **Kunovat** *R* Russian Federation
28B3 **Kunsan** S Korea
12K6 **Kuopio** Finland
16D1 **Kupa** *R* Bosnia-Herzegovina/Croatia
32B2 **Kupang** Indonesia
32D2 **Kupiano** Papua New Guinea
54E4 **Kupreanof I** USA
21F6 **Kupyansk** Ukraine
39G1 **Kuqa** China
21H8 **Kura** *R* Azerbaijan
29C3 **Kurabe** Japan
29C4 **Kurashiki** Japan
29B3 **Kurayoshi** Japan
41E2 **Kurdistan** *Region* Iran
17F2 **Kŭrdzhali** Bulgaria
28C4 **Kure** Japan
20C4 **Kuressaare** Estonia
25L3 **Kureyka** *R* Russian Federation
24H4 **Kurgan** Russian Federation
12J6 **Kurikka** Finland
25Q5 **Kuril Is** Russian Federation
Kuril'skiye Ostrova *Is* **= Kuril Islands**
36J2 **Kuril Trench** Pacific Ocean
21H8 **Kurinskaya Kosa** *Sand Spit* Azerbaijan
44B2 **Kurnool** India
29D2 **Kuroishi** Japan
29D3 **Kuroiso** Japan
35B2 **Kurow** New Zealand
34D2 **Kurri Kurri** Australia
21F5 **Kursk** Russian Federation
26B2 **Kuruktag** *R* China
47C2 **Kuruman** South Africa
47C2 **Kuruman** *R* South Africa
28C4 **Kurume** Japan
44C3 **Kurunegala** Sri Lanka
24K5 **Kurunktag** *R* China
20K3 **Kur'ya** Russian Federation
20K4 **Kusa** Russian Federation
17F3 **Kuşadası Körfezi** *B* Turkey
17F2 **Kus Golü** *L* Turkey
29D4 **Kushimoto** Japan
29E2 **Kushiro** Japan
38E2 **Kushka** Afghanistan
43F4 **Kushtia** Bangladesh
21J5 **Kushum** *R* Kazakhstan
20K4 **Kushva** Russian Federation
54B3 **Kuskokwim** *R* USA
54C3 **Kuskokwim Mts** USA
43E3 **Kusma** Nepal
28B3 **Kusŏng** N Korea
24H4 **Kustanay** Kazakhstan
27E7 **Kuta** *R* Indonesia
21D8 **Kütahya** Turkey
21G7 **Kutaisi** Georgia
29D2 **Kutchan** Japan
29E2 **Kutcharo-ko** *L* Japan
18D3 **Kutná Hora** Czech Republic
19D2 **Kutno** Poland
50B4 **Kutu** Zaïre
43G4 **Kutubdia I** Bangladesh
50C2 **Kutum** Sudan
55M4 **Kuujjuaq** Canada
55L4 **Kuujjuarapik** Canada
12K5 **Kuusamo** Finland
21K5 **Kuvandyk** Russian Federation
41E4 **Kuwait** Kuwait
38C3 **Kuwait** *Sheikhdom* SW Asia
29C3 **Kuwana** Japan
24J4 **Kuybyshev** Russian Federation
Kuybyshev = Samara
20H5 **Kuybyshevskoye Vodokhranilishche** *Res* Russian Federation
20E2 **Kuyto, Ozero** *L* Russian Federation
25M4 **Kuytun** Russian Federation
21F7 **Kuzey Anadolu Dağları** *Mts* Turkey
20F2 **Kuzomen** Russian Federation
20C2 **Kvænangen** *Sd* Norway
12G5 **Kvigtind** *Mt* Norway
20B2 **Kvikkjokk** Sweden
50D4 **Kwale** Kenya
28B3 **Kwangju** S Korea
50B4 **Kwango** *R* Zaïre
28A3 **Kwangyang** S Korea
28A2 **Kwanmo-bong** *Mt* N Korea
51D6 **KwaZulu Natal** *Province* South Africa
51C5 **Kwekwe** Zimbabwe
19D2 **Kwidzyn** Poland
54B4 **Kwigillingok** USA
27G7 **Kwoka** *Mt* Indonesia
34C3 **Kyabram** Australia
30B2 **Kyaikkami** Burma
30B2 **Kyaikto** Burma
26D1 **Kyakhta** Russian Federation
30B1 **Kyaukme** Burma
30B1 **Kyauk-padaung** Burma
30A2 **Kyaukpyu** Burma
20G2 **Kychema** Russian Federation
10B2 **Kyle of Lochalsh** Scotland
13D2 **Kyll** *R* Germany
34B3 **Kyneton** Australia
50D3 **Kyoga, L** Uganda
34D1 **Kyogle** Australia
28B3 **Kyŏngju** S Korea
28A3 **Kyongsang Sanmaek** *Mts* S Korea
28A2 **Kyŏngsŏng** N Korea
29D3 **Kyōto** Japan
45B1 **Kyrenia** Cyprus
20K3 **Kyrta** Russian Federation
20L4 **Kyshtym** Russian Federation
45B1 **Kythrea** Cyprus

Kyūshū **Leonardville**

28B4 **Kyūshū** *I* Japan
36H4 **Kyushu-Palau Ridge** Pacific Ocean
17E2 **Kyustendil** Bulgaria
25O2 **Kyusyur** Russian Federation
26C1 **Kyzyl** Russian Federation
24H5 **Kyzylkum** *Desert* Uzbekistan
24H5 **Kzyl Orda** Kazakhstan

L

50E3 **Laascaanood** Somalia
50E2 **Laas Dawaco** Somalia
13E2 **Laasphe** Germany
50E2 **Laasqoray** Somalia
72F1 **La Asunción** Venezuela
48A2 **Laâyoune** Morocco
58D2 **La Barge** USA
48A3 **Labé** Guinea
18D2 **Labe** *R* Czech Republic
65E1 **Labelle** Canada
67B3 **La Belle** USA
21G7 **Labinsk** Russian Federation
45D1 **Laboué** Lebanon
55M4 **Labrador** *Region* Canada
55M4 **Labrador City** Canada
55N4 **Labrador S** Canada/Greenland
72F5 **Lábrea** Brazil
27E6 **Labuk B** Malaysia
30A2 **Labutta** Burma
20M2 **Labytnangi** Russian Federation
13B2 **La Capelle** France
Laccadive Is = Lakshadweep
39F4 **Laccadive Is** India
70D3 **La Ceiba** Honduras
34A3 **Lacepede B** Australia
14C2 **La Châtre** France
45C3 **Lachish** *Hist Site* Israel
32D4 **Lachlan** *R* Australia
72C2 **La Chorrera** Panama
65E1 **Lachute** Canada
65D2 **Lackawanna** USA
54G4 **Lac la Biche** Canada
55L4 **Lac L'eau Claire** Canada
65E1 **Lac Mégantic** Canada
54G4 **Lacombe** Canada
65E2 **Laconia** USA
15A1 **La Coruña** Spain
57D2 **La Crosse** USA
63D1 **La Cygne** USA
42D2 **Ladākh Range** *Mts* India
27E6 **Ladd Reef** S China Sea
42C3 **Lādnūn** India
20E3 **Ladoga, L** Russian Federation
31B5 **Ladong** China
Ladozhskoye Oz *L* = **Ladoga, L**
55K2 **Lady Ann Str** Canada
34C4 **Lady Barron** Australia
47D2 **Ladybrand** South Africa
47D2 **Ladysmith** South Africa
64A1 **Ladysmith** USA
32D1 **Lae** Papua New Guinea
30C3 **Laem Ngop** Thailand
18C1 **Laesø** *I* Denmark
60B3 **Lafayette** Colorado, USA
57E2 **Lafayette** Indiana, USA
57D3 **Lafayette** Louisiana, USA
13B3 **La Fère** France
13B3 **La-Ferté-sous-Jouarre** France
48C4 **Lafia** Nigeria
48C4 **Lafiagi** Nigeria
14B2 **La Flèche** France
16B3 **La Galite** *I* Tunisia
18C1 **Lagan** *R* Sweden
73L6 **Lagarto** Brazil
8C3 **Laggan, L** Scotland
48C1 **Laghouat** Algeria
72C4 **Lago Agrio** Ecuador
48C4 **Lagos** Nigeria
15A2 **Lagos** Portugal
70B2 **Lagos de Moreno** Mexico
56B2 **La Grande** USA
32B2 **Lagrange** Australia
57E3 **La Grange** Georgia, USA
64B3 **La Grange** Kentucky, USA
67C1 **La Grange** N Carolina, USA
63C3 **La Grange** Texas, USA
72F2 **La Gran Sabana** *Mts* Venezuela
62A2 **Laguna** USA
59C4 **Laguna Beach** USA
56C4 **Laguna Seca** Mexico
28B2 **Lagusha** N Korea
27E6 **Lahad Datu** Malaysia
41F2 **Lāhījān** Iran
13D2 **Lahn** *R* Germany
13D2 **Lahnstein** Germany
42C2 **Lahore** Pakistan
13D3 **Lahr** Germany
12K6 **Lahti** Finland
50B3 **Lai** Chad
31B5 **Laibin** China
30C1 **Lai Chau** Vietnam
13C4 **Laignes** France
12J6 **Laihia** Finland
47C3 **Laingsburg** South Africa
8C2 **Lairg** Scotland
31E2 **Laiyang** China
31D2 **Laizhou Wan** *B* China
74B5 **Laja, Lago de la** Chile
74F3 **Lajes** Brazil
66D4 **La Jolla** USA
56C3 **La Junta** USA
60D2 **Lake Andes** USA
34C2 **Lake Cargelligo** Australia
57D3 **Lake Charles** USA
67B2 **Lake City** Florida, USA
61E2 **Lake City** Minnesota, USA
67C2 **Lake City** S Carolina, USA
6C2 **Lake District** *Region* England
66D4 **Lake Elsinore** USA
32C3 **Lake Eyre Basin** Australia
65D2 **Lakefield** Canada
64B2 **Lake Geneva** USA
68D1 **Lake George** USA
55M3 **Lake Harbour** Canada
59D4 **Lake Havasu City** USA
66C3 **Lake Hughes** USA
68C2 **Lakehurst** USA
66C3 **Lake Isabella** USA
63C3 **Lake Jackson** USA
67B3 **Lakeland** USA
55J5 **Lake of the Woods** Canada
58B1 **Lake Oswego** USA
12K7 **Lake Peipus** Estonia/Russian Federation
59B3 **Lakeport** USA
63D2 **Lake Providence** USA
35B2 **Lake Pukaki** New Zealand
34C3 **Lakes Entrance** Australia
66C2 **Lakeshore** USA
34B1 **Lake Stewart** Australia
65D1 **Lake Traverse** Canada
56A2 **Lakeview** USA
58B1 **Lakeview Mt** Canada
63D2 **Lake Village** USA
67B3 **Lake Wales** USA
66C4 **Lakewood** California, USA
60B3 **Lakewood** Colorado, USA
68C2 **Lakewood** New Jersey, USA
64C2 **Lakewood** Ohio, USA
67B3 **Lake Worth** USA
43E3 **Lakhīmpur** India
42B4 **Lakhpat** India
62B1 **Lakin** USA
42C2 **Lakki** Pakistan
17E3 **Lakonikós Kólpos** *G* Greece
48B4 **Lakota** Ivory Coast
12K4 **Laksefjord** *Inlet* Norway
12K4 **Lakselv** Norway
44A3 **Lakshadweep** *Is, Union Territory* India
72B4 **La Libertad** Ecuador
15A2 **La Linea** Spain
42D4 **Lalitpur** India
54H4 **La Loche** Canada
13C2 **La Louvière** Belgium
69A4 **La Luz** Nicaragua
55L5 **La Malbaie** Canada
56C3 **Lamar** Colorado, USA
63D1 **Lamar** Missouri, USA
63C3 **La Marque** USA
50B4 **Lambaréné** Gabon
72B5 **Lambayeque** Peru
76F10 **Lambert Glacier** Antarctica
47B3 **Lamberts Bay** South Africa
68C2 **Lambertville** USA
54F2 **Lambton,C** Canada
30C2 **Lam Chi** *R* Thailand
15A1 **Lamego** Portugal
72C6 **La Merced** Peru
62B2 **Lamesa** USA
59C4 **La Mesa** USA
17E3 **Lamía** Greece
8D4 **Lammermuir Hills** Scotland
12G7 **Lammhult** Sweden
61E2 **Lamoni** USA
66C3 **Lamont** California, USA
60B2 **Lamont** Wyoming, USA
27H6 **Lamotrek** *I* Pacific Ocean
13B4 **Lamotte-Beuvron** France
60D1 **La Moure** USA
62C2 **Lampasas** USA
7B3 **Lampeter** Wales
50E4 **Lamu** Kenya
66E5 **Lanai** *I* Hawaiian Islands
66E5 **Lanai City** Hawaiian Islands
27F6 **Lanao, L** Philippines
8D4 **Lanark** Scotland
30B3 **Lanbi** *I* Burma
30C1 **Lancang** *R* China
6C3 **Lancashire** *County* England
59C4 **Lancaster** California, USA
6C2 **Lancaster** England
61E2 **Lancaster** Missouri, USA
65E2 **Lancaster** New Hampshire, USA
68A1 **Lancaster** New York, USA
64C3 **Lancaster** Ohio, USA
57F3 **Lancaster** Pennsylvania, USA
67B2 **Lancaster** S Carolina, USA
55K2 **Lancaster Sd** Canada
13E3 **Landan** Germany
18C3 **Landeck** Austria
56C2 **Lander** USA
14B3 **Landes, Les** *Region* France
67B1 **Landrum** USA
18C3 **Landsberg** Germany
54F2 **Lands End** *C* Canada
7B4 **Land's End** *Pt* England
18C3 **Landshut** Germany
12G7 **Làndskrona** Sweden
67A2 **Lanett** USA
43E2 **La'nga Co** *L* China
60D1 **Langdon** USA
47C2 **Langeberg** *Mts* South Africa
18B2 **Langenhagen** Germany
13D1 **Langeoog** *I* Germany
8D4 **Langholm** Scotland
12A2 **Langjökull** *Mts* Iceland
30B4 **Langkawi** *I* Malaysia
34C1 **Langlo** *R* Australia
6B2 **Langness** *Pt* England
14B3 **Langon** France
14D2 **Langres** France
13C4 **Langres, Plateau de** France
27C6 **Langsa** Indonesia
26D2 **Lang Shan** *Mts* China
30D1 **Lang Son** Vietnam
62B3 **Langtry** USA
14C3 **Languedoc** *Region* France
74B5 **Lanin, Vol** Argentina
68C2 **Lansdale** USA
55K4 **Lansdowne House** Canada
68C2 **Lansford** USA
57E2 **Lansing** USA
48A2 **Lanzarote** *I* Canary Islands
31A2 **Lanzhou** China
27F5 **Laoag** Philippines
30C1 **Lao Cai** Vietnam
31D1 **Laoha He** *R* China
9C3 **Laois** *County* Irish Republic
28A2 **Laoling** China
13B3 **Laon** France
72C6 **La Oroya** Peru
30C2 **Laos** *Republic* SE Asia
75C4 **Lapa** Brazil
14C2 **Lapalisse** France
72C2 **La Palma** Panama
48A2 **La Palma** *I* Canary Islands
74C5 **La Pampa** *State* Argentina
66B3 **La Panza Range** *Mts* USA
72F2 **La Paragua** Venezuela
74E4 **La Paz** Argentina
72E7 **La Paz** Bolivia
70A2 **La Paz** Mexico
26H2 **La Perouse Str** Japan/Russian Federation
58B2 **La Pine** USA
45B1 **Lapithos** Cyprus
63D2 **Laplace** USA
60C1 **La Plant** USA
74E4 **La Plata** Argentina
64B2 **La Porte** USA
68B2 **Laporte** USA
12K6 **Lappeenranta** Finland
12H5 **Lappland** *Region* Finland/Sweden
62C3 **La Pryor** USA
25O2 **Laptev S** Russian Federation
12J6 **Lapua** Finland
56B4 **La Purísima** Mexico
50C1 **Laqiya Arbain** *Well* Sudan
74C2 **La Quiaca** Argentina
16C2 **L'Aquila** Italy
41F4 **Lār** Iran
15A2 **Larache** Morocco
56C2 **Laramie** USA
60B2 **Laramie Mts** USA
56C2 **Laramie Range** *Mts* USA
75B4 **Laranjeiras do Sul** Brazil
56D4 **Laredo** USA
41F4 **Larestan** *Region* Iran
Largeau = Faya
67B3 **Largo** USA
8C4 **Largs** Scotland
41E2 **Lārī** Iran
74C3 **La Rioja** Argentina
15B1 **La Rioja** *Region* Spain
74C3 **La Rioja** *State* Argentina
17E3 **Lárisa** Greece
42B3 **Larkana** Pakistan
40B3 **Larnaca** Cyprus
45B1 **Larnaca B** Cyprus
9C2 **Larne** Northern Ireland
62C1 **Larned** USA
15A1 **La Robla** Spain
13C2 **La Roche-en-Ardenne** Belgium
14B2 **La Rochelle** France
14B2 **La Roche-sur-Yon** France
15B2 **La Roda** Spain
69D3 **La Romana** Dominican Republic
54H4 **La Ronge** Canada
12F7 **Larvik** Norway
24J3 **Laryak** Russian Federation
15B2 **La Sagra** *Mt* Spain
65E1 **La Salle** Canada
64B2 **La Salle** USA
62B1 **Las Animas** USA
55L5 **La Sarre** Canada
62A2 **Las Cruces** USA
69C3 **La Selle** *Mt* Haiti
31B2 **Lasengmiao** China
74B3 **La Serena** Chile
74E5 **Las Flores** Argentina
30B1 **Lashio** Burma
16D3 **La Sila** *Mts* Italy
41F2 **Lāsjerd** Iran
42A2 **Laskar Gāh** Afghanistan
15A2 **Las Marismas** *Marshland* Spain
48A2 **Las Palmas de Gran Canaria** Canary Islands
16B2 **La Spezia** Italy
74C6 **Las Plumas** Argentina
58B2 **Lassen Peak** *Mt* USA
58B2 **Lassen Volcanic Nat Pk** USA
50B4 **Lastoursville** Gabon
16D2 **Lastovo** *I* Croatia
70B2 **Las Tres Marias** *Is* Mexico
56B3 **Las Vegas** USA
40C2 **Latakia** Syria
16C2 **Latina** Italy
69D4 **La Tortuga, I** Venezuela
34C4 **Latrobe** Australia
45C3 **Latrun** Israel
55L5 **La Tuque** Canada
44B2 **Lātūr** India
20C4 **Latvia** *Republic* Europe
8D4 **Lauder** Scotland
18B2 **Lauenburg** Germany
33H2 **Lau Group** *Is* Fiji
32D5 **Launceston** Australia
7B4 **Launceston** England
74B6 **La Unión** Chile
70D3 **La Unión** El Salvador
72C5 **La Unión** Peru
32D2 **Laura** Australia
65D3 **Laurel** Delaware, USA
68B3 **Laurel** Maryland, USA
57E3 **Laurel** Mississippi, USA
58E1 **Laurel** Montana, USA
67B2 **Laurens** USA
67C2 **Laurinburg** USA
16B1 **Lausanne** Switzerland
27E7 **Laut** *I* Indonesia
74B7 **Lautaro** Chile
13E2 **Lauterbach** Germany
13D3 **Lauterecken** Germany
65E1 **Laval** Canada
14B2 **Laval** France
66B2 **Laveaga Peak** *Mt* USA
58E1 **Lavina** USA
13C3 **La Vôge** *Region* France
73K8 **Lavras** Brazil
54A3 **Lavrentiya** Russian Federation
47E2 **Lavumisa** Swaziland
30B1 **Lawksawk** Burma
61D3 **Lawrence** Kansas, USA
65E2 **Lawrence** Massachusetts, USA
35A3 **Lawrence** New Zealand
63E1 **Lawrenceburg** USA
64B3 **Lawrenceville** Illinois, USA
68B2 **Lawrenceville** Pennsylvania, USA
56D3 **Lawton** USA
40C4 **Lawz, Jebel al** *Mt* Saudi Arabia
6B2 **Laxey** England
38C3 **Layla'** Saudi Arabia
50D3 **Laylo** Sudan
70B3 **Lázaro Cardenas** Mexico
29C2 **Lazo** Russian Federation
56C2 **Lead** USA
60B3 **Leadville** USA
63E2 **Leaf** *R* USA
62C3 **Leakey** USA
7D5 **Leamington Spa, Royal** England
61E3 **Leavenworth** USA
19D2 **Łeba** Poland
60D3 **Lebanon** Kansas, USA
63D1 **Lebanon** Missouri, USA
58B2 **Lebanon** Oregon, USA
65D2 **Lebanon** Pennsylvania, USA
64B3 **Lebanon** Tennessee, USA
40C3 **Lebanon** *Republic* SW Asia
66C3 **Lebec** USA
51D6 **Lebombo Mts** Mozambique/South Africa/Swaziland
19D2 **Lębork** Poland
74B5 **Lebu** Chile
13B2 **Le Cateau** France
17D2 **Lecce** Italy
16B1 **Lecco** Italy
13D3 **Le Champ du Feu** *Mt* France
14C2 **Le Creusot** France
7C3 **Ledbury** England
43H3 **Ledo** India
68D1 **Lee** USA
61E1 **Leech L** USA
10C3 **Leeds** England
7C3 **Leek** England
18B2 **Leer** Germany
67B3 **Leesburg** Florida, USA
68B3 **Leesburg** Virginia, USA
63D2 **Leesville** USA
34C2 **Leeton** Australia
47C3 **Leeugamka** South Africa
18B2 **Leeuwarden** Netherlands
32A4 **Leeuwin,C** Australia
66C2 **Lee Vining** USA
69E3 **Leeward Is** Caribbean Sea
45B1 **Lefka** Cyprus
45B1 **Lefkara** Cyprus
45B1 **Lefkoniko** Cyprus
27F5 **Legazpi** Philippines
18D2 **Legnica** Poland
73G2 **Leguan Island** Guyana
72D4 **Leguizamo** Peru
42D2 **Leh** India
14C2 **Le Havre** France
59D2 **Lehi** USA
68C2 **Lehigh** *R* USA
68C2 **Lehighton** USA
13D3 **Le Hohneck** *Mt* France
42C2 **Leiah** Pakistan
18D3 **Leibnitz** Austria
7D3 **Leicester** England
7D3 **Leicester** *County* England
32C2 **Leichhardt** *R* Australia
18A2 **Leiden** Netherlands
13B2 **Leie** *R* Belgium
32C4 **Leigh Creek** Australia
7E4 **Leigh on Sea** England
7D4 **Leighton Buzzard** England
18B2 **Leine** *R* Germany
9C3 **Leinster** *Region* Irish Republic
18C2 **Leipzig** Germany
15A2 **Leiria** Portugal
12F7 **Leirvik** Norway
8D4 **Leith** Scotland
31C4 **Leiyang** China
31B5 **Leizhou Bandao** *Pen* China
31C5 **Leizhou Wan** *B* China
18A2 **Lek** *R* Netherlands
16B3 **Le Kef** Tunisia
63D2 **Leland** USA
17D2 **Lelija** *Mt* Bosnia-Herzegovina
16B1 **Léman, Lac** France/Switzerland
14C2 **Le Mans** France
61D2 **Le Mars** USA
13E1 **Lemgo** Germany
58D2 **Lemhi Range** *Mts* USA
55M3 **Lemieux Is** Canada
56C2 **Lemmon** USA
59D4 **Lemmon,Mt** USA
59C3 **Lemoore** USA
14C2 **Lempdes** France
43G4 **Lemro** *R* Burma
16D2 **Le Murge** *Region* Italy
25O3 **Lena** *R* Russian Federation
20E3 **Lendery** Russian Federation
13D1 **Lengerich** Germany
31C4 **Lengshuijiang** China
Leningrad = St Petersburg
76F7 **Leningradskaya** *Base* Antarctica
20J5 **Leninogorsk** Russian Federation
26B1 **Leninogorsk** Kazakhstan
24K4 **Leninsk-Kuznetskiy** Russian Federation
26G2 **Leninskoye** Russian Federation
21H8 **Lenkoran'** Azerbaijan
13E2 **Lenne** *R* Germany
67B1 **Lenoir** USA
68D1 **Lenox** USA
13B2 **Lens** France
25N3 **Lensk** Russian Federation
16C3 **Lentini** Sicily, Italy
30B3 **Lenya** *R* Burma
16C1 **Leoben** Austria
7C3 **Leominster** England
68E1 **Leominster** USA
70B2 **León** Mexico
72A1 **León** Nicaragua
15A1 **León** Spain
47B1 **Leonardville** Namibia

Leonarisso Lorient

45C1 **Leonarisso** Cyprus
32B3 **Leonora** Australia
75D3 **Leopoldina** Brazil
Léopoldville = Kinshasa
20D5 **Lepel** Belarus
31D4 **Leping** China
14C2 **Le Puy-en-Velay** France
50B3 **Léré** Chad
47D2 **Leribe** Lesotho
15C1 **Lérida** Spain
17F3 **Léros** *I* Greece
68B1 **Le Roy** USA
10C1 **Lerwick** Scotland
69C3 **Les Cayes** Haiti
65F1 **Les Escoumins** Canada
31A4 **Leshan** China
17E2 **Leskovac** Serbia, Yugoslavia
47D2 **Leslie** South Africa
20J4 **Lesnoy** Russian Federation
25L4 **Lesosibirsk** Russian Federation
47D2 **Lesotho** *Kingdom* South Africa
26G2 **Lesozavodsk** Russian Federation
14B2 **Les Sables-d'Olonne** France
76E4 **Lesser Antarctica** *Region* Antarctica
69E3 **Lesser Antilles** *Is* Caribbean Sea
21G7 **Lesser Caucasus** *Mts* Azerbaijan/Georgia
17F3 **Lésvos** *I* Greece
18D2 **Leszno** Poland
47E1 **Letaba** *R* South Africa
43G4 **Letha Range** *Mts* Burma
54G5 **Lethbridge** Canada
73G3 **Lethem** Guyana
19F3 **Letichev** Ukraine
72E4 **Letícia** Colombia
32B1 **Leti, Kepulauan** *I* Indonesia
47D1 **Letlhakeng** Botswana
7E4 **le Touquet-Paris-Plage** France
30B2 **Letpadan** Burma
25N4 **Let Oktyabr'ya** Russian Federation
14C1 **Le Tréport** France
9C2 **Letterkenny** Irish Republic
27C6 **Leuser** *Mt* Indonesia
18A2 **Leuven** Belgium
17E3 **Levádhia** Greece
12G6 **Levanger** Norway
62B2 **Levelland** USA
8D3 **Leven** Scotland
8D3 **Leven, Loch** *L* Scotland
27F8 **Lévèque,C** Australia
13D2 **Leverkusen** Germany
19D3 **Levice** Slovakia
35C2 **Levin** New Zealand
55L5 **Lévis** Canada
65E2 **Levittown** USA
17E3 **Lévka Óri** *Mt* Greece
17E3 **Levkás** Greece
17E3 **Levkás** *I* Greece
32B2 **Lévêque,C** Australia
17F2 **Levski** Bulgaria
7E4 **Lewes** England
62C1 **Lewis** USA
10B2 **Lewis** *I* Scotland
68B2 **Lewisburg** USA
35B2 **Lewis P** New Zealand
56B2 **Lewis Range** *Mts* USA
67A2 **Lewis Smith,L** USA
56B2 **Lewiston** Idaho, USA
57F2 **Lewiston** Maine, USA
56C2 **Lewistown** Montana, USA
65D2 **Lewistown** Pennsylvania, USA
63D2 **Lewisville** USA
57E3 **Lexington** Kentucky, USA
61E3 **Lexington** Missouri, USA
67B1 **Lexington** N Carolina, USA
60D2 **Lexington** Nebraska, USA
65D3 **Lexington** Virginia, USA
65D3 **Lexington Park** USA
6D2 **Leyburn** England
27F5 **Leyte** *I* Philippines
17D2 **Lezhe** Albania
39H3 **Lhasa** China
43F3 **Lhazê** China
27C6 **Lhokseumawe** Indonesia
43G3 **Lhozhag** China
26C4 **Lhunze** China
Liancourt Rocks = Tok-do
28B2 **Liangbingtai** China
31B3 **Liangdang** China
31C5 **Lianjiang** China
31C5 **Lianping** China
31C5 **Lian Xian** China
31D3 **Lianyungang** China
31E1 **Liaodong Bandao** *Pen* China
31E1 **Liaodong Wan** *B* China
31E1 **Liao He** *R* China
28A2 **Liaoning** *Province* China
31E1 **Liaoyang** China
28A2 **Liaoyangwopu** China
31E1 **Liaoyuan** China
28A2 **Liaozhong** China
54F3 **Liard** *R* Canada
54F4 **Liard River** Canada
13C3 **Liart** France
45C2 **Liban, Jebel** *Mts* Lebanon
58C1 **Libby** USA
50B3 **Libenge** Zaïre
56C3 **Liberal** USA
18C2 **Liberec** Czech Republic
48A4 **Liberia** *Republic* Africa
61E3 **Liberty** Missouri, USA
65E2 **Liberty** New York, USA
68B2 **Liberty** Pennsylvania, USA
63D2 **Liberty** Texas, USA
45B3 **Libni, Gebel** *Mt* Egypt
14B3 **Libourne** France
48C4 **Libreville** Equatorial Guinea
49D2 **Libya** *Republic* Africa
49E2 **Libyan Desert** Egypt/ Libya/Sudan
49E1 **Libyan Plat** Egypt
16C3 **Licata** Sicily, Italy
7D3 **Lichfield** England
51D5 **Lichinga** Mozambique
47D2 **Lichtenburg** South Africa
64C3 **Licking** *R* USA
66B2 **Lick Observatory** USA
16C2 **Licosa, Punta** *Pt* Italy
66D2 **Lida** USA
20D5 **Lida** Belarus
12G7 **Lidköping** Sweden
16C2 **Lido di Ostia** Italy
16B1 **Liechtenstein** *Principality* Europe
18B2 **Liège** Belgium
19E1 **Lielupe** *R* Latvia
50C3 **Lienart** Zaïre
18C3 **Lienz** Austria
12J7 **Liepāja** Latvia
13C2 **Lier** Belgium
65E1 **Lièvre** *R* Canada
18C3 **Liezen** Austria
9C3 **Liffey** *R* Irish Republic
9C2 **Lifford** Irish Republic
33F3 **Lifu** *I* Nouvelle Calédonie
34C1 **Lightning Ridge** Australia
13C3 **Ligny-en-Barrois** France
51D5 **Ligonha** *R* Mozambique
16B2 **Ligurian S** Italy
33E1 **Lihir Group** *Is* Papua New Guinea
66E5 **Lihue** Hawaiian Islands
51C5 **Likasi** Zaïre
14C1 **Lille** France
12G6 **Lillehammer** Norway
13B2 **Lillers** France
12G7 **Lillestrøm** Norway
51D5 **Lilongwe** Malawi
17D2 **Lim** *R* Montenegro/ Serbia, Yugoslavia
72C6 **Lima** Peru
57E2 **Lima** USA
15A1 **Lima** *R* Portugal
58D2 **Lima Res** USA
40B3 **Limassol** Cyprus
9C2 **Limavady** Northern Ireland
48C4 **Limbe** Cameroon
51D5 **Limbe** Malawi
18B2 **Limburg** Germany
73J8 **Limeira** Brazil
10B3 **Limerick** Irish Republic
18B1 **Limfjorden** *L* Denmark
32C2 **Limmen Bight** *B* Australia
17F3 **Límnos** *I* Greece
73L5 **Limoeiro** Brazil
14C2 **Limoges** France
70D4 **Limón** Costa Rica
56C3 **Limon** USA
14C2 **Limousin** *Region* France
14C2 **Limousin, Plateaux de** France
47E1 **Limpopo** *R* Mozambique
74B5 **Linares** Chile
56D4 **Linares** Mexico
15B2 **Linares** Spain
26C4 **Lincang** China
74D4 **Lincoln** Argentina
7D3 **Lincoln** England
64B2 **Lincoln** Illinois, USA
65F1 **Lincoln** Maine, USA
56D2 **Lincoln** Nebraska, USA
65E2 **Lincoln** New Hampshire, USA
35B2 **Lincoln** New Zealand
7D3 **Lincoln** *County* England
58B2 **Lincoln City** USA
64C2 **Lincoln Park** USA
76A2 **Lincoln Sea** Greenland
16B2 **L'Incudine** *Mt* Corsica, France
18B3 **Lindau** Germany
73G2 **Linden** Guyana
12F7 **Lindesnes** *C* Norway
51D4 **Lindi** Tanzania
50C3 **Lindi** *R* Zaïre
47D2 **Lindley** South Africa
17F3 **Lindos** Greece
66C2 **Lindsay** California, USA
65D2 **Lindsay** Canada
60B1 **Lindsay** Montana, USA
37M4 **Line Is** Pacific Ocean
31C2 **Linfen** China
30D2 **Lingao** China
27F5 **Lingayen** Philippines
18B2 **Lingen** Germany
27D7 **Lingga** *I* Indonesia
60C2 **Lingle** USA
31C4 **Lingling** China
31B5 **Lingshan** China
31C2 **Lingshi** China
48A3 **Linguère** Senegal
31E4 **Linhai** Zhejiang, China
73L7 **Linhares** Brazil
31B1 **Linhe** China
28B2 **Linjiang** China
28A2 **Linjiatai** China
12H7 **Linköping** Sweden
8C3 **Linnhe, Loch** *Inlet* Scotland
31D2 **Linqing** China
75C3 **Lins** Brazil
31A2 **Lintao** China
60C1 **Linton** USA
26E2 **Linxi** China
31A2 **Linxia** China
18C3 **Linz** Austria
14C3 **Lion, Golfe du** *G* France
16C3 **Lipari** *I* Italy
16C3 **Lipari, Isole** *Is* Italy
21F5 **Lipetsk** Russian Federation
17E1 **Lipova** Romania
18B2 **Lippe** *R* Germany
13E2 **Lippstadt** Germany
50D3 **Lira** Uganda
50B4 **Liranga** Congo
50C3 **Lisala** Zaïre
Lisboa = Lisbon
15A2 **Lisbon** Portugal
61D1 **Lisbon** USA
9C2 **Lisburn** Northern Ireland
31D4 **Lishui** China
31C4 **Li Shui** *R* China
21F6 **Lisichansk** Ukraine
14C2 **Lisieux** France
21F5 **Liski** Russian Federation
13B3 **L'Isle-Adam** France
33E3 **Lismore** Australia
9C3 **Lismore** Irish Republic
31B5 **Litang** China
45C2 **Lītāni** *R* Lebanon
73H3 **Litani** *R* Surinam
64B3 **Litchfield** Illinois, USA
61E1 **Litchfield** Minnesota, USA
32E4 **Lithgow** Australia
20C4 **Lithuania** *Republic* Europe
68B2 **Lititz** USA
26G2 **Litovko** Russian Federation
63C2 **Little** *R* USA
57F4 **Little Abaco** *I* The Bahamas
44E3 **Little Andaman** *I* Andaman Islands
67C3 **Little Bahama Bank** Bahamas
35C1 **Little Barrier I** New Zealand
58D1 **Little Belt Mts** USA
45B3 **Little Bitter L** Egypt
70D3 **Little Cayman** *I* Cayman Is, Caribbean Sea
68C3 **Little Egg Harbor** *B* USA
61E1 **Little Falls** Minnesota, USA
68C1 **Little Falls** New York, USA
62B2 **Littlefield** USA
61E1 **Littlefork** USA
61E1 **Little Fork** *R* USA
8E2 **Little Halibut Bank** *Sandbank* Scotland
7D4 **Littlehampton** England
69C2 **Little Inagua** *I* The Bahamas
47C3 **Little Karoo** *Mts* South Africa
66D3 **Little Lake** USA
60C1 **Little Missouri** *R* USA
30A4 **Little Nicobar** *I* Nicobar Is, India
57D3 **Little Rock** USA
66D3 **Littlerock** USA
68B3 **Littlestown** USA
60B3 **Littleton** Colorado, USA
65E2 **Littleton** New Hampshire, USA
28B2 **Liuhe** China
31B2 **Liupan Shan** *Upland* China
31B5 **Liuzhou** China
17E3 **Livanátais** Greece
19F1 **Līvāni** Latvia
67B2 **Live Oak** USA
59B3 **Livermore** USA
62B2 **Livermore,Mt** USA
55M5 **Liverpool** Canada
7C3 **Liverpool** England
54E2 **Liverpool B** Canada
7C3 **Liverpool B** England
55L2 **Liverpool,C** Canada
34D2 **Liverpool Range** *Mts* Australia
56B2 **Livingston** Montana, USA
67A1 **Livingston** Tennessee, USA
63D2 **Livingston** Texas, USA
8D4 **Livingstone** Scotland
51C5 **Livingstone** Zambia
63C2 **Livingston,L** USA
16D2 **Livno** Bosnia-Herzegovina
21F5 **Livny** Russian Federation
64C2 **Livonia** USA
16C2 **Livorno** Italy
75D1 **Livramento do Brumado** Brazil
51D4 **Liwale** Tanzania
7B5 **Lizard Pt** England
16C1 **Ljubljana** Slovenia
12G6 **Ljungan** *R* Sweden
12G7 **Ljungby** Sweden
12H6 **Ljusdal** Sweden
20B3 **Ljusnan** *R* Sweden
7C4 **Llandeilo** Wales
7C4 **Llandovery** Wales
7C3 **Llandrindod Wells** Wales
7C3 **Llandudno** Wales
7D4 **Llanelli** Wales
7C3 **Llangollen** Wales
62C2 **Llano** USA
62C2 **Llano** *R* USA
56C3 **Llano Estacado** *Plat* USA
72D2 **Llanos** *Region* Colombia/ Venezuela
72F7 **Llanos de Chiquitos** *Region* Bolivia
7C4 **Llantrisant** Wales
7C3 **Llanwrst** Wales
Lleida = Lérida
15A2 **Llerena** Spain
7B3 **Lleyn** *Pen* Wales
54F4 **Lloyd George,Mt** Canada
54H4 **Lloydminster** Canada
74C2 **Llullaillaco** *Mt* Argentina/ Chile
74C2 **Loa** *R* Chile
50B4 **Loange** *R* Zaïre
47D2 **Lobatse** Botswana
50B3 **Lobaye** *R* Central African Republic
51B5 **Lobito** Angola
8B3 **Lochboisdale** Scotland
8C3 **Lochearnhead** Scotland
14C2 **Loches** France
8C3 **Lochgoilhead** Scotland
8C2 **Lochinver** Scotland
8D4 **Lochmaben** Scotland
8B3 **Lochmaddy** Scotland
8D3 **Lochnagar** *Mt* Scotland
8C3 **Loch Ness** Scotland
58C1 **Lochsa** *R* USA
8C3 **Lochy, Loch** *L* Scotland
8D4 **Lockerbie** Scotland
65D2 **Lock Haven** USA
65D2 **Lockport** USA
30D3 **Loc Ninh** Vietnam
16D3 **Locri** Italy
45C3 **Lod** Israel
34B3 **Loddon** *R* Australia
20E3 **Lodeynoye Pole** Russian Federation
58E1 **Lodge Grass** USA
42C3 **Lodhran** Pakistan
16B1 **Lodi** Italy
59B3 **Lodi** USA
50C4 **Lodja** Zaïre
50D3 **Lodwar** Kenya
19D2 **Łódź** Poland
47B3 **Loeriesfontein** South Africa
12G5 **Lofoten** *Is* Norway
6D2 **Loftus** England
62B1 **Logan** New Mexico, USA
56B2 **Logan** Utah, USA
54D3 **Logan,Mt** Canada
64B2 **Logansport** Indiana, USA
15D3 **Logansport** Louisiana, USA
68B2 **Loganton** USA
50B2 **Logone** *R* Cameroon/ Chad
15B1 **Logroño** Spain
43E4 **Lohārdaga** India
12J6 **Lohja** Finland
30B2 **Loikaw** Burma
12J6 **Loimaa** Finland
13B3 **Loing** *R* France
14C2 **Loir** *R* France
14C2 **Loire** *R* France
13B4 **Loiret** *Department* France
72C4 **Loja** Ecuador
15B2 **Loja** Spain
12K5 **Lokan Tekojärvi** *Res* Finland
13B2 **Lokeren** Belgium
27F7 **Lokialaki, G** *Mt* Indonesia
50D3 **Lokitaung** Kenya
19F1 **Loknya** Russian Federation
50C4 **Lokolo** *R* Zaïre
50C4 **Lokoro** *R* Zaïre
55M3 **Loks Land** *I* Canada
18C2 **Lolland** *I* Denmark
58D1 **Lolo P** USA
17E2 **Lom** Bulgaria
51C4 **Lomami** *R* Zaïre
48A4 **Loma Mts** Guinea/Sierra Leone
27F7 **Lomblen** *I* Indonesia
27E7 **Lombok** *I* Indonesia
48C4 **Lomé** Togo
50C4 **Lomela** Zaïre
50C4 **Lomela** *R* Zaïre
8C3 **Lomond, Loch** *L* Scotland
20D4 **Lomonosov** Russian Federation
59B4 **Lompoc** USA
19E2 **Łomza** Poland
44A2 **Lonāvale** India
74B5 **Loncoche** Chile
55K5 **London** Canada
7D4 **London** England
64C3 **London** USA
9C2 **Londonderry** Northern Ireland
9C2 **Londonderry** *County* Northern Ireland
74B9 **Londonderry** *I* Chile
32B2 **Londonderry,C** Australia
74C3 **Londres** Argentina
74F2 **Londrina** Brazil
66D1 **Lone Mt** USA
66C2 **Lone Pine** USA
27H7 **Long** *I* Papua New Guinea
57F4 **Long** *I* The Bahamas
25T2 **Longa, Proliv** *Str* Russian Federation
69H2 **Long B** Jamaica
67C2 **Long B** USA
56B3 **Long Beach** California, USA
65E2 **Long Beach** New York, USA
65E2 **Long Branch** USA
31D5 **Longchuan** China
58C2 **Long Creek** USA
7D3 **Long Eaton** England
34C4 **Longford** Australia
9C3 **Longford** Irish Republic
9C3 **Longford** *County* Irish Republic
8E3 **Long Forties** *Region* N Sea
28B2 **Longgang Shan** *Mts* China
31D1 **Longhua** China
57F4 **Long I** Bahamas
55L4 **Long I** Canada
32D1 **Long I** Papua New Guinea
57F2 **Long I** USA
68D2 **Long Island Sd** USA
28B2 **Longjing** China
64B1 **Long L** Canada
60C1 **Long L** USA
55K4 **Longlac** Canada
31B5 **Longlin** China
8C3 **Long, Loch** *Inlet* Scotland
7E3 **Long Melford** England
56C2 **Longmont** USA
13C3 **Longny** France
61E1 **Long Prairie** USA
32D3 **Longreach** Australia
31A2 **Longshou Shan** *Upland* China
60B2 **Longs Peak** *Mt* USA
7E3 **Long Sutton** England
6C2 **Longtown** England
65E1 **Longueuil** Canada
13C3 **Longuyon** France
57D3 **Longview** Texas, USA
56A2 **Longview** Washington, USA
14D2 **Longwy** France
31A3 **Longxi** China
30D3 **Long Xuyen** Vietnam
31D4 **Longyan** China
31B5 **Longzhou** China
13D1 **Löningen** Germany
74B5 **Lonquimay** Chile
14D2 **Lons-le-Saunier** France
7B4 **Looe** England
57F3 **Lookout,C** USA
50D4 **Loolmalasin** *Mt* Tanzania
25R4 **Lopatka, Mys** *C* Russian Federation
30C3 **Lop Buri** Thailand
26C2 **Lop Nur** *L* China
15A2 **Lora del Rio** Spain
57E2 **Lorain** USA
42B2 **Loralai** Pakistan
15B2 **Lorca** Spain
41F3 **Lordegān** Iran
33E4 **Lord Howe** *I* Australia
37K6 **Lord Howe Rise** Pacific Ocean
55J3 **Lord Mayor B** Canada
56C3 **Lordsburg** USA
75C3 **Lorena** Brazil
14B2 **Lorient** France

Maintirano
Marshall

51E5 **Maintirano** Madagascar
18B2 **Mainz** Germany
48A4 **Maio** *I* Cape Verde
74C4 **Maipó, Vol** Argentina/ Chile
72E1 **Maiquetía** Venezuela
43G3 **Mairābāri** India
43G4 **Maiskhal I** Bangladesh
32E4 **Maitland** New South Wales, Australia
76F12 **Maitri** *Base* Antarctica
70D3 **Maíz, Isla del** Caribbean Sea
29D3 **Maizuru** Japan
32A1 **Majene** Indonesia
72D7 **Majes** *R* Peru
50D3 **Maji** Ethiopia
31D2 **Majia He** *R* China
15C2 **Majorca** *I* Balearic Is, Spain
Majunga = Mahajanga
27E7 **Makale** Indonesia
43F3 **Makalu** *Mt* China/Nepal
50B3 **Makanza** Zaïre
20K2 **Makarikha** Russian Federation
16D2 **Makarska** Croatia
20G4 **Makaryev** Russian Federation
Makassar = Ujung Pandang
27E7 **Makassar Str** Indonesia
21J6 **Makat** Kazakhstan
48A4 **Makeni** Sierra Leone
13C1 **Makerwaard** *Polder* Netherlands
21F6 **Makeyevka** Ukraine
51C6 **Makgadikgadi** *Salt Pan* Botswana
21H7 **Makhachkala** Russian Federation
50D4 **Makindu** Kenya
Makkah = Mecca Saudi Arabia
55N4 **Makkovik** Canada
19E3 **Makó** Hungary
50B3 **Makokou** Gabon
35C1 **Makorako,Mt** New Zealand
50B3 **Makoua** Congo
42C3 **Makrāna** India
42A3 **Makran Coast Range** *Mts* Pakistan
16B3 **Makthar** Tunisia
21G8 **Mākū** Iran
50C4 **Makumbi** Zaïre
48C4 **Makurdi** Nigeria
44B3 **Malabar Coast** India
48C4 **Malabo** Equatorial Guinea
Malacca = Melaka
30C5 **Malacca,Str of** SE Asia
58D2 **Malad City** USA
72D2 **Málaga** Colombia
15B2 **Málaga** Spain
62B2 **Malaga** USA
51E6 **Malaimbandy** Madagascar
33F1 **Malaita** *I* Solomon Islands
50D3 **Malakal** Sudan
42C2 **Malakand** Pakistan
27F6 **Malanbang** Philippines
27E7 **Malang** Indonesia
51B4 **Malanje** Angola
48C3 **Malanville** Benin
25S3 **Mal Anyuy** *R* Russian Federation
12H7 **Mälaren** *L* Sweden
65D1 **Malartic** Canada
21F8 **Malatya** Turkey
51D5 **Malawi** *Republic* Africa
Malawi,L = Nyasa,L
41E3 **Malāyer** Iran
27D6 **Malaysia** *Federation* SE Asia
40D2 **Malazgirt** Turkey
19D2 **Malbork** Poland
18C2 **Malchin** Germany
63E1 **Malden** USA
39F5 **Maldives** *Is* Indian Ocean
36E4 **Maldives Ridge** Indian Ocean
7E4 **Maldon** England
74F4 **Maldonado** Uruguay
42C4 **Malegaon** India
18D3 **Malé Karpaty** *Upland* Slovakia
33F2 **Malekula** *I* Vanuatu
51D5 **Malema** Mozambique
20F3 **Malen'ga** Russian Federation
13B3 **Malesherbes** France
42B2 **Mālestān** Afghanistan
12H5 **Malgomaj** *L* Sweden
20B3 **Malgomaj** *R* Sweden
50C2 **Malha** *Well* Sudan
58C2 **Malheur L** USA
48B3 **Mali** *Republic* Africa
30B3 **Mali Kyun** *I* Burma
19F2 **Malin** Ukraine
27E6 **Malinau** Indonesia
50E4 **Malindi** Kenya
Malines = Mechelen
10B2 **Malin Head** *Pt* Irish Republic
42D4 **Malkāpur** India
17F2 **Malkara** Turkey
17F2 **Malko Tŭrnovo** Bulgaria
8C3 **Mallaig** Scotland
49F2 **Mallawi** Egypt
Mallorca *I* **= Majorca**
12G6 **Malm** Norway
12J5 **Malmberget** Sweden
13D2 **Malmédy** Germany
7C4 **Malmesbury** England
47B3 **Malmesbury** South Africa
12G7 **Malmö** Sweden
20J4 **Malmyzh** Russian Federation
65E2 **Malone** USA
47D2 **Maloti Mts** Lesotho
12F6 **Måloy** Norway
20J2 **Malozemel'skaya Tundra** *Plain* Russian Federation
71B3 **Malpelo** *I* Colombia
42D3 **Mālpura** India
58D2 **Malta** Idaho, USA
56C2 **Malta** Montana, USA
16C3 **Malta** *I and Republic* Medit Sea
16C3 **Malta Chan** Italy/Malta
47B1 **Maltahöhe** Namibia
6D2 **Malton** England
45D2 **Ma'lūlā, Jabal** *Mt* Syria
12G6 **Malung** Sweden
44A2 **Mālvan** India
63D2 **Malvern** USA
47E1 **Malvérnia** Mozambique
Malvinas, Islas = Falkland Islands
42D4 **Malwa Plat** India
25Q2 **Malyy Lyakhovskiy, Ostrov** *I* Russian Federation
25M2 **Malyy Taymyr, Ostrov** *I* Russian Federation
21H6 **Malyy Uzen'** *R* Kazakhstan
25N4 **Mama** Russian Federation
20J4 **Mamadysh** Russian Federation
50C3 **Mambasa** Zaïre
32C1 **Mamberamo** *R* Australia
27G7 **Mamberamo** *R* Indonesia
50B3 **Mambéré** *R* Central African Republic
48C4 **Mamfé** Cameroon
59D4 **Mammoth** USA
64B3 **Mammoth Cave Nat Pk** USA
66C2 **Mammoth Pool Res** USA
72E6 **Mamoré** *R* Bolivia/Brazil
48A3 **Mamou** Guinea
51E5 **Mampikony** Madagascar
48B4 **Mampong** Ghana
45C3 **Mamshit** *Hist Site* Israel
27E7 **Mamuju** Indonesia
47C1 **Mamuno** Botswana
48B4 **Man** Ivory Coast
66E5 **Mana** Hawaiian Islands
51E6 **Manabo** Madagascar
72F4 **Manacapuru** Brazil
15C2 **Manacor** Spain
27F6 **Manado** Indonesia
72A1 **Managua** Nicaragua
70D3 **Managua, L de** Nicaragua
51E6 **Manakara** Madagascar
32D1 **Manam** *I* Papua New Guinea
51E5 **Mananara** Madagascar
51E6 **Mananjary** Madagascar
35A3 **Manapouri** New Zealand
35A3 **Manapouri,L** New Zealand
39G1 **Manas** China
43G3 **Manas** *R* Bhutan
24K5 **Manas Hu** *L* China
43E3 **Manaslu** *Mt* Nepal
68C2 **Manasquan** USA
73G4 **Manaus** Brazil
21E8 **Manavgat** Turkey
40C2 **Manbij** Syria
6B2 **Man,Calf of** *I* Isle of Man, British Islands
64B2 **Mancelona** USA
44B2 **Mancherāl** India
65E2 **Manchester** Connecticut, USA
7C3 **Manchester** England
64C3 **Manchester** Kentucky, USA
57F2 **Manchester** New Hampshire, USA
68B2 **Manchester** Pennsylvania, USA
67A1 **Manchester** Tennessee, USA
68D1 **Manchester** Vermont, USA
26F2 **Manchuria** *Division* China
41F4 **Mand** *R* Iran
51D5 **Manda** Tanzania
75B3 **Mandaguari** Brazil
12F7 **Mandal** Norway
27G7 **Mandala, Peak** *Mt* Indonesia
30B1 **Mandalay** Burma
26D2 **Mandalgovĭ** Mongolia
56C2 **Mandan** USA
50E3 **Mandera** Ethiopia
69H1 **Mandeville** Jamaica
42D2 **Mandi** India
51D5 **Mandimba** Mozambique
75A2 **Mandiore, Lagoa** Brazil
43E4 **Mandla** India
51E5 **Mandritsara** Madagascar
42D4 **Mandsaur** India
17D2 **Manduria** Italy
42B4 **Māndvi** India
44B3 **Mandya** India
43E4 **Manendragarh** India
19F2 **Manevichi** Ukraine
40B4 **Manfalût** Egypt
16D2 **Manfredonia** Italy
75D1 **Manga** Brazil
50B2 **Manga** *Desert Region* Niger
35C1 **Mangakino** New Zealand
17F2 **Mangalia** Romania
50C2 **Mangalmé** Chad
44A3 **Mangalore** India
43H4 **Mangin Range** *Mts* Burma
26C3 **Mangnai** China
48C3 **Mango** Togo
51D5 **Mangoche** Malawi
51E6 **Mangoky** *R* Madagascar
27F7 **Mangole** *I* Indonesia
42B4 **Māngral** India
75B4 **Mangueirinha** Brazil
25O4 **Mangui** China
62C2 **Mangum** USA
21J7 **Mangyshiak, Poluostrov** *Pen* Kazakhstan
56D3 **Manhattan** USA
47E2 **Manhica** Mozambique
73K8 **Manhuacu** Brazil
51E5 **Mania** *R* Madagascar
51D5 **Manica** Mozambique
55M5 **Manicouagan** *R* Canada
55M5 **Manicouagan, Réservoir** Canada
41E4 **Manifah** Saudi Arabia
27F5 **Manila** Philippines
58E2 **Manila** USA
34D2 **Manilla** Australia
48B3 **Maninian** Ivory Coast
43G4 **Manipur** *R* Burma/India
43G4 **Manipur** *State* India
21D8 **Manisa** Turkey
10C3 **Man,Isle of** Irish Sea
64B2 **Manistee** USA
64B2 **Manistee** *R* USA
64B1 **Manistique** USA
54J4 **Manitoba** *Province* Canada
54J4 **Manitoba,L** Canada
60D1 **Manitou** Canada
64B1 **Manitou Is** USA
55K5 **Manitoulin** *I* Canada
60C3 **Manitou Springs** USA
64C1 **Manitowik L** Canada
64B2 **Manitowoc** USA
65D1 **Maniwaki** Canada
72C2 **Manizales** Colombia
51E6 **Manja** Madagascar
32A4 **Manjimup** Australia
44B2 **Mānjra** *R* India
57D2 **Mankato** USA
48B4 **Mankono** Ivory Coast
35B1 **Manly** New Zealand
42C4 **Manmād** India
34A2 **Mannahill** Australia
44B4 **Mannar** Sri Lanka
44B4 **Mannār,G of** India
44B3 **Mannārgudi** India
18B3 **Mannheim** Germany
67B2 **Manning** USA
34A2 **Mannum** Australia
48A4 **Mano** Sierra Leone
32C1 **Manokwari** Indonesia
51C4 **Manono** Zaïre
30B3 **Manoron** Burma
55L4 **Manouane, Lac** Canada
29C3 **Mano-wan** *B* Japan
28B2 **Manp'o** N Korea
42D2 **Mānsa** India
51C5 **Mansa** Zambia
55K3 **Mansel I** Canada
63D1 **Mansfield** Arkansas, USA
34C3 **Mansfield** Australia
7D3 **Mansfield** England
63D2 **Mansfield** Louisiana, USA
68E1 **Mansfield** Massachusetts, USA
57E2 **Mansfield** Ohio, USA
65D2 **Mansfield** Pennsylvania, USA
75B2 **Manso** *R* Brazil
27H5 **Mansyu Deep** Pacific Ocean
72B4 **Manta** Ecuador
28A2 **Mantap-san** *Mt* N Korea
72C6 **Mantaro** *R* Peru
66B2 **Manteca** USA
67C1 **Manteo** USA
14C2 **Mantes** France
59D3 **Manti** USA
75C3 **Mantiqueira, Serra da** *Mts* Brazil
16C1 **Mantova** Italy
12J6 **Mäntta** Finland
Mantua = Mantova
20G4 **Manturovo** Russian Federation
62B3 **Manuel Benavides** Mexico
75B3 **Manuel Ribas** Brazil
27F6 **Manukan** Philippines
33G4 **Manukau** New Zealand
27H7 **Manus** *I* Pacific Ocean
15B2 **Manzanares** Spain
70E2 **Manzanillo** Cuba
70B3 **Manzanillo** Mexico
25N5 **Manzhouli** China
45D3 **Manzil** Jordan
51D6 **Manzini** Swaziland
50B2 **Mao** Chad
27G7 **Maoke, Pegunungan** *Mts* Indonesia
31A2 **Maomao Shan** *Mt* China
31C5 **Maoming** China
51D6 **Mapai** Mozambique
43E2 **Mapam Yumco** *L* China
27G6 **Mapia** *Is* Pacific Ocean
27E6 **Mapin** *I* Philippines
54H5 **Maple Creek** Canada
47E1 **Mapulanguene** Mozambique
47E2 **Maputo** Mozambique
47E2 **Maputo** *R* Mozambique
47E2 **Maputo, Baia de** *B* Mozambique
Ma Qu = Huang He
31A3 **Maqu** China
43F3 **Maquan He** *R* China
50B4 **Maquela do Zombo** Angola
74C6 **Maquinchao** Argentina
73J5 **Marabá** Brazil
72D1 **Maracaibo** Venezuela
72D2 **Maracaibo, Lago de** Venezuela
73H3 **Maracá, Ilha de** *I* Brazil
75A3 **Maracaju** Brazil
75A3 **Maracaju, Serra de** *Mts* Brazil
75D1 **Máracás** Brazil
72E1 **Maracay** Venezuela
49D2 **Marādah** Libya
48C3 **Maradi** Niger
21H8 **Marāgheh** Iran
73J4 **Marajó, Baia de** *B* Brazil
73H4 **Marajó, Ilha de** *I* Brazil
28E5 **Marakech** Morocco
50D3 **Maralal** Kenya
33F1 **Maramasike** *I* Solomon Islands
Maramba = Livingstone
59D4 **Marana** USA
21H8 **Marand** Iran
75C1 **Maranhão** *R* Brazil
73J4 **Maranhão** *State* Brazil
34C1 **Maranoa** *R* Australia
72C4 **Marañón** *R* Peru
21F8 **Maras** Turkey
55K5 **Marathon** Canada
67B4 **Marathon** Florida, USA
68B1 **Marathon** New York, USA
62B2 **Marathon** Texas, USA
75E1 **Maraú** Brazil
27F6 **Marawi** Philippines
15B2 **Marbella** Spain
32A3 **Marble Bar** Australia
59D3 **Marble Canyon** USA
47D2 **Marble Hall** South Africa
68E1 **Marblehead** USA
18B2 **Marburg** Germany
Mar Cantabrico = Biscay, B of
51B5 **Marca, Punta da** *Pt* Angola
18B2 **Marche** Belgium
13C2 **Marche-en-Famenne** Belgium
15A2 **Marchena** Spain
74D4 **Mar Chiquita, Lagoa** *L* Argentina
67B3 **Marco** USA
65E2 **Marcy,Mt** USA
42C2 **Mardan** Pakistan
74E5 **Mar del Plata** Argentina
21G8 **Mardin** Turkey
33F3 **Maré** *I* New Caledonia
50D2 **Mareb** *R* Eritrea/Ethiopia
27H8 **Mareeba** Australia
8C3 **Maree, Loch** *L* Scotland
50E3 **Mareeq** Somalia
62B2 **Marfa** USA
68C1 **Margaretville** USA
69E4 **Margarita, Isla** Venezuela
72F1 **Margarita, Islas de** Venezuela
29C2 **Margaritovo** Russian Federation
7E4 **Margate** England
17E1 **Marghita** Romania
34C4 **Maria I** Australia
27H5 **Marianas** *Is* Pacific Ocean
36J4 **Mariana Trench** Pacific Ocean
43G3 **Mariāni** India
63D2 **Marianna** Arkansas, USA
67A2 **Marianna** Florida, USA
72B2 **Mariato, Puerta** Panama
57G4 **Maria Van Diemen,C** New Zealand
18D3 **Mariazell** Austria
16D1 **Maribor** Slovenia
47D1 **Marico** *R* Botswana/ South Africa
66C3 **Maricopa** USA
50C3 **Maridi** Sudan
76F5 **Marie Byrd Land** *Region* Antarctica
69E3 **Marie Galante** *I* Caribbean Sea
12H6 **Mariehamn** Finland
13C2 **Mariembourg** Belgium
73H2 **Marienburg** Surinam
47B1 **Mariental** Namibia
12G7 **Mariestad** Sweden
67B2 **Marietta** Georgia, USA
64C3 **Marietta** Ohio, USA
63C2 **Marietta** Oklahoma, USA
69Q2 **Marigot** Dominica
74G2 **Marília** Brazil
20C5 **Marijampole** Lithuania
51B4 **Marimba** Angola
57E2 **Marinette** USA
74F2 **Maringá** Brazil
50C3 **Maringa** *R* Zaïre
63D1 **Marion** Arkansas, USA
64B3 **Marion** Illinois, USA
57E2 **Marion** Indiana, USA
57E2 **Marion** Ohio, USA
67C2 **Marion** S Carolina, USA
57E3 **Marion,L** USA
33E2 **Marion Reef** Australia
59C3 **Mariposa** USA
66B2 **Mariposa** *R* USA
66B2 **Mariposa Res** USA
20H4 **Mari Republic** Russian Federation
21D7 **Marista** *R* Bulgaria
21F6 **Mariupol'** Ukraine
45C2 **Marjayoun** Lebanon
19F2 **Marjina Gorki** Belarus
45C3 **Marka** Jordan
50E3 **Marka** Somalia
18C1 **Markaryd** Sweden
7C3 **Market Drayton** England
7D3 **Market Harborough** England
6D3 **Market Weighton** England
76E7 **Markham,Mt** Antarctica
66C1 **Markleeville** USA
25T3 **Markovo** Russian Federation
68E1 **Marlboro** Massachusetts, USA
68D1 **Marlboro** New Hampshire, USA
32D3 **Marlborough** Australia
7D4 **Marlborough** England
13B3 **Marle** France
63C2 **Marlin** USA
68D1 **Marlow** USA
14C3 **Marmande** France
17F2 **Marmara Adasi** *I* Turkey
40A1 **Marmara,S of** Turkey
17F3 **Marmaris** Turkey
60C1 **Marmarth** USA
64C3 **Marmet** USA
61E1 **Marmion L** Canada
16C1 **Marmolada** *Mt* Italy
13C3 **Marne** *Department* France
13B3 **Marne** *R* France
50B3 **Maro** Chad
51E5 **Maroantsetra** Madagascar
51D5 **Marondera** Zimbabwe
73H3 **Maroni** *R* French Guiana
34D1 **Maroochydore** Australia
50B2 **Maroua** Cameroon
51E5 **Marovoay** Madagascar
57E4 **Marquesas Keys** *Is* USA
57E2 **Marquette** USA
37N5 **Marquises, Îles** Pacific Ocean
34C2 **Marra** *R* Australia
47E2 **Marracuene** Mozambique
50C2 **Marra, Jebel** *Mt* Sudan
48B1 **Marrakech** Morocco
32C3 **Marree** Australia
63D3 **Marrero** USA
51D5 **Marromeu** Mozambique
51D5 **Marrupa** Mozambique
40B4 **Marsa Alam** Egypt
50D3 **Marsabit** Kenya
16C3 **Marsala** Sicily, Italy
13E2 **Marsberg** Germany
14D3 **Marseilles** France
75D3 **Mar, Serra do** *Mts* Brazil
64B3 **Marshall** Illinois, USA
64C2 **Marshall** Michigan, USA
61D2 **Marshall** Minnesota, USA
61E3 **Marshall** Missouri, USA

Mezen'

Montemor-o-Novo

20G2 **Mezen'** Russian Federation
20H3 **Mezen'** *R* Russian Federation
14C3 **Mézenc, Mount** France
19G1 **Mezha** *R* Russian Federation
20J1 **Mezhdusharskiy, Ostrov** *I* Russian Federation
42D4 **Mhow** India
59D4 **Miami** Arizona, USA
57E4 **Miami** Florida, USA
63D1 **Miami** Oklahoma, USA
57E4 **Miami Beach** USA
21H8 **Miandowāb** Iran
51E5 **Miandrivazo** Madagascar
21H8 **Mīāneh** Iran
42C2 **Mianwali** Pakistan
31A3 **Mianyang** China
31C3 **Mianyang** China
31A3 **Mianzhu** China
31E2 **Miaodao Qundao** *Arch* China
31B4 **Miao Ling** *Upland* China
20L5 **Miass** Russian Federation
19E3 **Michalovce** Slovakia
58D1 **Michel** Canada
69D3 **Miches** Dominican Republic
57E2 **Michigan** *State* USA
64B2 **Michigan City** USA
57E2 **Michigan,L** USA
64C1 **Michipicoten** Canada
55K5 **Michipicoten I** Canada
17F2 **Michurin** Bulgaria
21G5 **Michurinsk** Russian Federation
36J4 **Micronesia, Fed. States of** *Is* Pacific Ocean
36J4 **Micronesia** *Region* Pacific Ocean
52F4 **Mid Atlantic Ridge** Atlantic Ocean
47C3 **Middelburg** Cape Province, South Africa
13B2 **Middelburg** Netherlands
47D2 **Middelburg** Transvaal, South Africa
58B2 **Middle Alkali L** USA
37O4 **Middle America Trench** Pacific Ocean
44E3 **Middle Andaman** *I* Indian Ocean
68E2 **Middleboro** USA
68B2 **Middleburg** Pennsylvania, USA
68B3 **Middleburg** Virginia, USA
68C1 **Middleburgh** USA
65E2 **Middlebury** USA
57E3 **Middlesboro** USA
6D2 **Middlesbrough** England
68D2 **Middletown** Connecticut, USA
68C3 **Middletown** Delaware, USA
65E2 **Middletown** New York, USA
64C3 **Middletown** Ohio, USA
68B2 **Middletown** Pennsylvania, USA
68C1 **Middleville** USA
7C3 **Middlewich** England
48B1 **Midelt** Morocco
7C4 **Mid Glamorgan** *County* Wales
50E2 **Mīdī** Yemen
36E5 **Mid Indian Basin** Indian Ocean
36E5 **Mid Indian Ridge** Indian Ocean
55L5 **Midland** Canada
64C2 **Midland** Michigan, USA
56C3 **Midland** Texas, USA
9B4 **Midleton** Irish Republic
51E6 **Midongy Atsimo** Madagascar
37K4 **Mid Pacific Mts** Pacific Ocean
58C2 **Midvale** USA
37L3 **Midway Is** Pacific Ocean
60B2 **Midwest** USA
63C1 **Midwest City** USA
40D2 **Midyat** Turkey
17E2 **Midžor** *Mt* Serbia, Yugoslavia
19E2 **Mielec** Poland
17F1 **Miercurea-Ciuc** Romania
15A1 **Mieres** Spain
68B2 **Mifflintown** USA
13B4 **Migennes** France
28B4 **Mihara** Japan
17E2 **Mikhaylovgrad** Bulgaria
21G5 **Mikhaylovka** Russian Federation
28C2 **Mikhaylovka** Russian Federation
24J4 **Mikhaylovskiy** Russian Federation
45C4 **Mikhrot Timna** Israel
12K6 **Mikkeli** Finland
17F3 **Míkonos** *I* Greece
18D3 **Mikulov** Czech Republic
51D4 **Mikumi** Tanzania
20J3 **Mikun** Russian Federation
29D3 **Mikuni-sammyaku** *Mts* Japan
29C4 **Mikura-jima** *I* Japan
61E1 **Milaca** USA
72C4 **Milagro** Ecuador
16B1 **Milan** Italy
63E1 **Milan** USA
51D5 **Milange** Mozambique
Milano = Milan
21D8 **Milas** Turkey
61D1 **Milbank** USA
32D4 **Mildura** Australia
31A5 **Mile** China
41D3 **Mileh Tharthār** *L* Iraq
32E3 **Miles** Australia
56C2 **Miles City** USA
16C2 **Miletto, Monte** *Mt* Italy
68D2 **Milford** Connecticut, USA
65D3 **Milford** Delaware, USA
61D2 **Milford** Nebraska, USA
68E1 **Milford** New Hampshire, USA
68C2 **Milford** Pennsylvania, USA
59D3 **Milford** Utah, USA
7B4 **Milford Haven** Wales
7B4 **Milford Haven** *Sd* Wales
61D3 **Milford L** USA
35A2 **Milford Sd** New Zealand
15C2 **Miliana** Algeria
54G4 **Milk** *R* Canada/USA
60B1 **Milk** *R* USA
25R4 **Mil'kovo** Russian Federation
50C2 **Milk, Wadi el** *Watercourse* Sudan
14C3 **Millau** France
68D2 **Millbrook** USA
67B2 **Milledgeville** USA
61E1 **Mille Lacs L** USA
61E1 **Mille Lacs, Lac des** Canada
60D2 **Miller** USA
21G6 **Millerovo** Russian Federation
68B2 **Millersburg** USA
68D1 **Millers Falls** USA
68D2 **Millerton** USA
66C2 **Millerton L** USA
65E2 **Millford** Massachusetts, USA
34B3 **Millicent** Australia
63E1 **Millington** USA
65F1 **Millinocket** USA
34D1 **Millmerran** Australia
6C2 **Millom** England
8C4 **Millport** Scotland
9B3 **Millstreet** Irish Republic
65F1 **Milltown** Canada
58D1 **Milltown** USA
66A2 **Mill Valley** USA
65E3 **Millville** USA
55Q2 **Milne Land** *I* Greenland
66E5 **Milolii** Hawaiian Islands
17E3 **Mílos** *I* Greece
32D3 **Milparinka** Australia
68B2 **Milroy** USA
67A2 **Milton** Florida, USA
35A3 **Milton** New Zealand
68B2 **Milton** Pennsylvania, USA
7D3 **Milton Keynes** England
57E2 **Milwaukee** USA
29D2 **Mimmaya** Japan
66C1 **Mina** USA
15C2 **Mina** *R* Algeria
41E4 **Mīnā' al Aḩmadī** Kuwait
41G4 **Mīnāb** Iran
74E4 **Minas** Uruguay
73J7 **Minas Gerais** *State* Brazil
75D2 **Minas Novas** Brazil
70C3 **Minatitlán** Mexico
30A1 **Minbu** Burma
30A1 **Minbya** Burma
8B3 **Minch,Little** *Sd* Scotland
8B2 **Minch,North** *Sd* Scotland
10B2 **Minch,The** *Sd* Scotland
27F6 **Mindanao** *I* Philippines
63D2 **Minden** Louisiana, USA
66C1 **Minden** Nevada, USA
18B2 **Minden** Germany
34B2 **Mindona L** Australia
27F5 **Mindoro** *I* Philippines
27F5 **Mindoro Str** Philippines
7C4 **Minehead** England
73H7 **Mineiros** Brazil
63C2 **Mineola** USA
62C2 **Mineral Wells** USA
68B2 **Minersville** USA
34B2 **Mingary** Australia
21H7 **Mingechaurskoye Vodokhranilische** *Res* Azerbaijan
8B3 **Mingulay, I** Scotland
31A2 **Minhe** China
44A4 **Minicoy** *I* India
31D4 **Min Jiang** *R* Fujian, China
31A4 **Min Jiang** *R* Sichuan, China
66C2 **Minkler** USA
34A2 **Minlaton** Australia
31A2 **Minle** China
48C4 **Minna** Nigeria
57D2 **Minneapolis** USA
54J4 **Minnedosa** Canada
61D2 **Minnesota** *R* USA
57D2 **Minnesota** *State* USA
15A1 **Miño** *R* Spain
15C1 **Minorca** *I* Spain
56C2 **Minot** USA
31A2 **Minqin** China
31A3 **Min Shan** *Upland* China
20D5 **Minsk** Belarus
19E2 **Mińsk Mazowiecki** Poland
54G2 **Minto Inlet** *B* Canada
55L4 **Minto,L** Canada
60B3 **Minturn** USA
26C1 **Minusinsk** Russian Federation
31A3 **Min Xian** China
45A3 **Minya el Qamn** Egypt
55N5 **Miquelon** *I* France
66D3 **Mirage L** USA
40D3 **Mīrah, Wadi al** *Watercourse* Iraq/Saudi Arabia
44A2 **Miraj** India
74E5 **Miramar** Argentina
42B2 **Miram Shah** Pakistan
75A3 **Miranda** Brazil
75A2 **Miranda** *R* Brazil
15B1 **Miranda de Ebro** Spain
75B3 **Mirante, Serra do** *Mts* Brazil
42B2 **Mīr Bachchen Kūt** Afghanistan
13C3 **Mirecourt** France
27E6 **Miri** Malaysia
48A3 **Mirik,C** Mauritius
74F4 **Mirim, Lagoa** *L* Brazil/Uruguay
25K3 **Mirnoye** Russian Federation
25N3 **Mirnyy** Russian Federation
76G9 **Mirnyy** *Base* Antarctica
19G3 **Mironovka** Ukraine
42C2 **Mirpur** Pakistan
42B3 **Mirpur Khas** Pakistan
17E3 **Mirtoan S** Greece
28B3 **Miryang** S Korea
43E3 **Mirzāpur** India
42C1 **Misgar** Pakistan
64B2 **Mishawaka** USA
28B4 **Mi-shima** *I* Japan
43H3 **Mishmi Hills** India
33E2 **Misima** *I* Papua New Guinea
74F3 **Misiones** *State* Argentina
19E3 **Miskolc** Hungary
45D2 **Mismīyah** Syria
27G7 **Misoöl** *I* Indonesia
49D1 **Misrātah** Libya
55K5 **Missinaibi** *R* Canada
64C1 **Missinaibi L** Canada
60C2 **Mission** S Dakota, USA
62C3 **Mission** Texas, USA
58B1 **Mission City** Canada
65D2 **Mississauga** Canada
57D3 **Mississippi** *R* USA
57D3 **Mississippi** *State* USA
63E3 **Mississippi Delta** USA
56B2 **Missoula** USA
48B1 **Missour** Morocco
57D3 **Missouri** *R* USA
57D3 **Missouri** *State* USA
61D2 **Missouri Valley** USA
57F1 **Mistassini,Lac** Canada
72D7 **Misti** *Mt* Peru
34C1 **Mitchell** Australia
56D2 **Mitchell** USA
32D2 **Mitchell** *R* Australia
57E3 **Mitchell,Mt** USA
27H8 **Mitchell River** Australia
45A3 **Mit el Nasâra** Egypt
45A3 **Mit Ghamr** Egypt
42C3 **Mithankot** Pakistan
17F3 **Mitilíni** Greece
45B3 **Mitla Pass** Egypt
29E3 **Mito** Japan
33G2 **Mitre** *I* Solomon Islands
Mits'iwa = Massawa
13D1 **Mittel Land Kanal** Germany
72D3 **Mitú** Colombia
51C4 **Mitumba, Chaine des** *Mts* Zaïre
50C4 **Mitumbar Mts** Zaïre
51C4 **Mitwaba** Zaïre
50B3 **Mitzic** Gabon
29C3 **Miura** Japan
31C3 **Mi Xian** China
26G3 **Miyake** *I* Japan
29C4 **Miyake-jima** *I* Japan
29E3 **Miyako** Japan
26F4 **Miyako** *I* Ryukyu Is, Japan
29C3 **Miyazu** Japan
28C4 **Miyoshi** Japan
31D1 **Miyun** China
31D1 **Miyun Shuiku** *Res* China
29D2 **Mi-zaki** *Pt* Japan
50D3 **Mīzan Teferī** Ethiopia
49D1 **Mizdah** Libya
17F1 **Mizil** Romania
43G4 **Mizo Hills** India
43G4 **Mizoram** *Union Territory* India
45C3 **Mizpe Ramon** Israel
29E3 **Mizusawa** Japan
12H7 **Mjölby** Sweden
51C5 **Mkushi** Zambia
47E2 **Mkuzi** South Africa
18C2 **Mladá Boleslav** Czech Republic
19E2 **Mława** Poland
17D2 **Mljet** *I* Croatia
47D2 **Mmabatho** South Africa
48A4 **Moa** *R* Sierra Leone
56C3 **Moab** USA
45C3 **Moab** *Region* Jordan
47E2 **Moamba** Mozambique
50B4 **Moanda** Congo
50B4 **Moanda** Gabon
9C3 **Moate** Irish Republic
51C4 **Moba** Zaïre
29D3 **Mobara** Japan
50C3 **Mobaye** Central African Republic
50C3 **Mobayi** Zaïre
57D3 **Moberly** USA
57E3 **Mobile** USA
57E3 **Mobile B** USA
63E2 **Mobile Pt** USA
56C2 **Mobridge** USA
51E5 **Moçambique** Mozambique
Moçâmedes = Namibe
30C1 **Moc Chau** Vietnam
Mocha = Al Mukhā
47D1 **Mochudi** Botswana
51E5 **Mocimboa da Praia** Mozambique
72C3 **Mocoa** Colombia
75C3 **Mococa** Brazil
51D5 **Mocuba** Mozambique
47D2 **Modder** *R* South Africa
16C2 **Modena** Italy
13D3 **Moder** *R* France
56A3 **Modesto** USA
66B2 **Modesto Res** USA
16C3 **Modica** Sicily,
18D3 **Mödling** Austria
8D4 **Moffat** Scotland
42D2 **Moga** India
50E3 **Mogadishu** Somalia
75C3 **Mogi das Cruzes** Brazil
19G2 **Mogilev** Belarus
21D6 **Mogilev Podol'skiy** Ukraine
75C3 **Mogi-Mirim** Brazil
51E5 **Mogincual** Mozambique
26E1 **Mogocha** Russian Federation
24K4 **Mogochin** Russian Federation
47D1 **Mogol** *R* South Africa
15A2 **Moguer** Spain
35C1 **Mohaka** *R* New Zealand
47D3 **Mohale's Hoek** Lesotho
60C1 **Mohall** USA
15C2 **Mohammadia** Algeria
43G4 **Mohanganj** Bangladesh
59D3 **Mohave,L** USA
68C1 **Mohawk** USA
65E2 **Mohawk** *R* USA
51E5 **Mohéli** *I* Comoros
51D4 **Mohoro** Tanzania
24J5 **Mointy** Kazakhstan
12G5 **Mo i Rana** Norway
14C3 **Moissac** France
59C3 **Mojave** USA
66D3 **Mojave** *R* USA
56B3 **Mojave Desert** USA
43F3 **Mokama** India
35B1 **Mokau** *R* New Zealand
66B1 **Mokelumne** *R* USA
66B1 **Mokelumne Aqueduct** USA
66B1 **Mokelumne Hill** USA
47D2 **Mokhotlong** Lesotho
16C3 **Moknine** Tunisia
43G3 **Mokokchūng** India
50B2 **Mokolo** Cameroon
28B4 **Mokp'o** S Korea
20G5 **Moksha** *R* Russian Federation
17E3 **Moláoi** Greece
7C3 **Mold** Wales
Moldavia = Moldova
12F6 **Molde** Norway
21D6 **Moldova** *Republic* Europe
17E1 **Moldoveanu** *Mt* Romania
47D1 **Molepolole** Botswana
13D3 **Molesheim** France
16D2 **Molfetta** Italy
72D7 **Mollendo** Peru
20D5 **Molodechno** Belarus
76G11 **Molodezhnaya** *Base* Antarctica
66E5 **Molokai** *I* Hawaiian Islands
20H4 **Moloma** *R* Russian Federation
34C2 **Molong** Australia
47C2 **Molopo** *R* Botswana/South Africa
50B3 **Molounddu** Cameroon
56D1 **Molson L** Canada
32B1 **Molucca S** Indonesia
27F7 **Moluccas** *Is* Indonesia
51D5 **Moma** Mozambique
73K5 **Mombaça** Brazil
50D4 **Mombasa** Kenya
29D2 **Mombetsu** Japan
75B2 **Mombuca, Serra da** *Mts* Brazil
50C3 **Mompono** Zaïre
18C2 **Mon** *I* Denmark
8B3 **Monach Is** Scotland
14D3 **Monaco** *Principality* Europe
8C3 **Monadhliath Mts** Scotland
9C2 **Monaghan** Irish Republic
9C2 **Monaghan** *County* Irish Republic
62B2 **Monahans** USA
69D3 **Mona Pass** Caribbean Sea
60B3 **Monarch P** USA
54G4 **Monashee Mts** Canada
10B3 **Monastereven** Irish Republic
16C3 **Monastir** Tunisia
29D2 **Monbetsu** Japan
73J4 **Monção** Brazil
12L5 **Monchegorsk** Russian Federation
18B2 **Mönchen-gladbach** Germany
70B2 **Monclova** Mexico
55M5 **Moncton** Canada
15A1 **Mondego** *R* Portugal
16B2 **Mondovi** Italy
69H1 **Moneague** Jamaica
65D2 **Monessen** USA
63D1 **Monett** USA
16C1 **Monfalcone** Italy
15A1 **Monforte de Lemos** Spain
50C3 **Monga** Zaïre
50C3 **Mongala** *R* Zaïre
50D3 **Mongalla** Sudan
30D1 **Mong Cai** Vietnam
50B2 **Mongo** Chad
26C2 **Mongolia** *Republic* Asia
51C5 **Mongu** Zambia
8D4 **Moniaive** Scotland
59C3 **Monitor Range** *Mts* USA
50C4 **Monkoto** Zaïre
64A2 **Monmouth** USA
7C4 **Monmouth** Wales
48C4 **Mono** *R* Benin/Togo
59C3 **Mono L** USA
17D2 **Monopoli** Italy
15B1 **Monreal del Campo** Spain
63D2 **Monroe** Louisiana, USA
64C2 **Monroe** Michigan, USA
67B2 **Monroe** N Carolina, USA
58B1 **Monroe** Washington, USA
64B2 **Monroe** Wisconsin, USA
61E3 **Monroe City** USA
48A4 **Monrovia** Liberia
66D3 **Monrovia** USA
18A2 **Mons** Belgium
68D1 **Monson** USA
18D1 **Mönsterås** Sweden
47C3 **Montagu** South Africa
54D4 **Montague I** USA
14B2 **Montaigu** France
16D3 **Montallo** *Mt* Italy
56B2 **Montana** *State* USA
15A1 **Montañas de León** *Mts* Spain
14C2 **Montargis** France
14C3 **Montauban** France
65E2 **Montauk** USA
65E2 **Montauk Pt** USA
13C4 **Montbard** France
14D2 **Montbéliard** France
Montblanc = Montblanch
16B1 **Mont Blanc** France/Italy
15C1 **Montblanch** Spain
14C2 **Montceau-les-Mines** France
16B1 **Mont Cenis, Col du** *P* France/Italy
15C1 **Montceny** *Mt* Spain
13C3 **Montcornet** France
14B3 **Mont-de-Marsan** France
14C2 **Montdidier** France
72F7 **Monteagudo** Bolivia
73H4 **Monte Alegre** Brazil
75D2 **Monte Azul** Brazil
65D1 **Montebello** Canada
32A3 **Monte Bello Is** Australia
14D3 **Monte Carlo** Monaco
75C2 **Monte Carmelo** Brazil
69C3 **Montecristi** Dominican Republic
16C2 **Montecristo** *I* Italy
69H1 **Montego Bay** Jamaica
14C3 **Montélimar** France
75A3 **Montelindo** *R* Paraguay
70C2 **Montemorelos** Mexico
15A2 **Montemor-o-Novo** Portugal

Murray **Neufchâteau**

34B2 **Murray** *R* Australia
34A3 **Murray Bridge** Australia
27H7 **Murray,L** Papua New Guinea
67B2 **Murray,L** USA
47C3 **Murraysburg** South Africa
37M3 **Murray Seacarp** Pacific Ocean
34B2 **Murrumbidgee** *R* Australia
34C2 **Murrumburrah** Australia
34D2 **Murrurundi** Australia
34B3 **Murtoa** Australia
28A2 **Muruin Sum** *R* China
35C1 **Murupara** New Zealand
43E4 **Murwāra** India
34D1 **Murwillimbah** Australia
27E7 **Muryo** *Mt* Indonesia
40D2 **Muş** Turkey
17E2 **Musala** *Mt* Bulgaria
28B2 **Musan** N Korea
41G4 **Musandam Pen** Oman
38D3 **Muscat** Oman
61E2 **Muscatine** USA
32C3 **Musgrave Range** *Mts* Australia
50B4 **Mushie** Zaïre
68E2 **Muskeget Chan** USA
64B2 **Muskegon** USA
64B2 **Muskegon** *R* USA
63C1 **Muskogee** USA
65D2 **Muskoka,L** Canada
50D2 **Musmar** Sudan
50D4 **Musoma** Tanzania
32D1 **Mussau** *I* Papua New Guinea
58E1 **Musselshell** *R* USA
51B5 **Mussende** Angola
14C3 **Mussidan** France
17F2 **Mustafa-Kemalpasa** Turkey
43E3 **Mustang** Nepal
74C7 **Musters, Lago** Argentina
28A2 **Musu-dan** *C* N Korea
34D2 **Muswellbrook** Australia
49E2 **Mut** Egypt
75E1 **Mutá, Ponta do** *Pt* Brazil
51D5 **Mutarara** Mozambique
51D5 **Mutare** Zimbabwe
20K2 **Mutnyy Materik** Russian Federation
51D5 **Mutoko** Zimbabwe
51E5 **Mutsamudu** Comoros
51C5 **Mutshatsha** Zaïre
29E2 **Mutsu** Japan
29E2 **Mutsu-wan** *B* Japan
75C1 **Mutunópolis** Brazil
31B2 **Mu Us Shamo** *Desert* China
51B4 **Muxima** Angola
25N4 **Muya** Russian Federation
20E3 **Muyezerskiy** Russian Federation
50D4 **Muyinga** Burundi
51C4 **Muyumba** Zaïre
39E1 **Muyun Kum** *Desert* Kazakhstan
42C2 **Muzaffarābād** Pakistan
42C2 **Muzaffargarh** Pakistan
42D3 **Muzaffarnagar** India
43F3 **Muzaffarpur** India
24H3 **Muzhi** Russian Federation
39G2 **Muzlag** *Mt* China
39F2 **Muztagala** *Mt* China
51D5 **Mvuma** Zimbabwe
50D4 **Mwanza** Tanzania
51C4 **Mwanza** Zaïre
50C4 **Mweka** Zaïre
51C4 **Mwene Ditu** Zaïre
51D6 **Mwenezi** Zimbabwe
47E1 **Mwenezi** *R* Zimbabwe
50C4 **Mwenga** Zaïre
51C4 **Mweru, L** Zaïre/Zambia
51C5 **Mwinilunga** Zambia
30B2 **Myanaung** Burma
Myanmar = Burma
18D3 **M'yaróvár** Hungary
30B1 **Myingyan** Burma
30B3 **Myinmoletkat** *Mt* Burma
30B3 **Myitta** Burma
43G4 **Mymensingh** Bangladesh
7C3 **Mynydd Eppynt** Wales
26G3 **Myojin** *I* Japan
28A2 **Myongchon** N Korea
28A2 **Myonggan** N Korea
12F6 **Myrdal** Norway
12B2 **Myrdalsjökull** *Mts* Iceland
67C2 **Myrtle Beach** USA
58B2 **Myrtle Creek** USA
12G7 **Mysen** Norway
20G2 **Mys Kanin Nos** *C* Russian Federation
19D3 **Myślenice** Poland
18C2 **Myśliborz** Poland
44B3 **Mysore** India
21E7 **Mys Sarych** *C* Ukraine
25U3 **Mys Shmidta** Russian Federation
20F2 **Mys Svyatoy Nos** *C* Russian Federation
68E2 **Mystic** USA
21J7 **Mys Tyub-Karagan** *Pt* Kazakhstan
24H2 **Mys Zhelaniya** *C* Russian Federation
30D3 **My Tho** Vietnam
58B2 **Mytle Point** USA
51D5 **Mzimba** Malawi
51D5 **Mzuzú** Malawi

N

66E5 **Naalehu** Hawaiian Islands
12J6 **Naantali** Finland
9C3 **Naas** Irish Republic
29C4 **Nabari** Japan
20J4 **Naberezhnyye Chelny** Russian Federation
16C3 **Nabeul** Tunisia
75A3 **Nabileque** *R* Brazil
45C2 **Nablus** Israel
51E5 **Nacala** Mozambique
58B1 **Naches** USA
51D5 **Nachingwea** Tanzania
66B3 **Nacimiento** *R* USA
66B3 **Nacimiento Res** USA
63D2 **Nacogdoches** USA
70B1 **Nacozari** Mexico
13E2 **Nadel** *Mt* Germany
42C4 **Nadiād** India
15B2 **Nador** Morocco
41F3 **Nadūshan** Iran
20E3 **Nadvoitsy** Russian Federation
19E3 **Nadvornaya** Ukraine
18C1 **Naestved** Denmark
49E2 **Nafoora** Libya
27F5 **Naga** Philippines
28B4 **Nagahama** Japan
43H3 **Naga Hills** India
29C3 **Nagai** Japan
43G3 **Nāgāland** *State* India
29D3 **Nagano** Japan
29D3 **Nagaoka** Japan
44B3 **Nāgappattinam** India
42C4 **Nagar Parkar** Pakistan
28B4 **Nagasaki** Japan
29C4 **Nagashima** Japan
28B4 **Nagato** Japan
42C3 **Nāgaur** India
44B4 **Nāgercoil** India
42B3 **Nagha Kalat** Pakistan
42D3 **Nagīna** India
13E3 **Nagold** Germany
29D3 **Nagoya** Japan
42D4 **Nāgpur** India
39H2 **Nagqu** China
18D3 **Nagykanizsa** Hungary
19D3 **Nagykörös** Hungary
26F4 **Naha** Okinawa, Japan
42D2 **Nāhan** India
54F3 **Nahanni Butte** Canada
45C2 **Nahariya** Israel
41E3 **Nahāvand** Iran
13D3 **Nahe** *R* Germany
31D2 **Nahpu** China
74B6 **Nahuel Haupí, Lago** Argentina
31E1 **Naimen Qi** China
55M4 **Nain** Canada
41F3 **Nā'īn** Iran
42D3 **Naini Tal** India
43E4 **Nainpur** India
8D3 **Nairn** Scotland
50D4 **Nairobi** Kenya
41F3 **Najafābād** Iran
40C4 **Najd** *Region* Saudi Arabia
28C2 **Najin** N Korea
50E2 **Najrān** Saudi Arabia
28A3 **Naju** S Korea
28A4 **Nakadori-jima** Japan
28B4 **Nakama** Japan
29E3 **Nakaminato** Japan
28B4 **Nakamura** Japan
29C3 **Nakano** Japan
29B3 **Nakano-shima** *I* Japan
28C4 **Nakatsu** Japan
29C3 **Nakatsu-gawa** Japan
50D2 **Nak'fa** Eritrea
21H8 **Nakhichevan** Azerbaijan
45B4 **Nakhl** Egypt
28C2 **Nakhodka** Russian Federation
30C3 **Nakhon Pathom** Thailand
30C3 **Nakhon Ratchasima** Thailand
30C4 **Nakhon Si Thammarat** Thailand
55K4 **Nakina** Ontario, Canada
54C4 **Naknek** USA
12G8 **Nakskov** Denmark
28A3 **Naktong** *R* S Korea
50D4 **Nakuru** Kenya
21G7 **Nal'chik** Russian Federation
44B2 **Nalgonda** India
44B2 **Nallamala Range** *Mts* India
49D1 **Nālūt** Libya
47E2 **Namaacha** Mozambique
24G6 **Namak** *L* Iran
41G3 **Namakzar-e Shadad** *Salt Flat* Iran
24J5 **Namangan** Uzbekistan
51D5 **Namapa** Mozambique
51B7 **Namaqualand** *Region* South Africa
34D1 **Nambour** Australia
34D2 **Nambucca Heads** Australia
30D4 **Nam Can** Vietnam
39H2 **Nam Co** *L* China
30D1 **Nam Dinh** Vietnam
51D5 **Nametil** Mozambique
47A1 **Namib Desert** Namibia
51B5 **Namibe** Angola
51B6 **Namibia** *Republic* Africa
27F7 **Namlea** Indonesia
43F3 **Namling** China
34C2 **Namoi** *R* Australia
58C2 **Nampa** USA
48B3 **Nampala** Mali
30C2 **Nam Phong** Thailand
28B3 **Namp'o** N Korea
51D5 **Nampula** Mozambique
12G6 **Namsos** Norway
30B1 **Namton** Burma
25O3 **Namtsy** Russian Federation
51D5 **Namuno** Mozambique
13C2 **Namur** Belgium
51B5 **Namutoni** Namibia
56A2 **Nanaimo** Canada
28B2 **Nanam** N Korea
34D1 **Nanango** Australia
29D3 **Nanao** Japan
29C3 **Nanatsu-jima** *I* Japan
31B3 **Nanbu** China
31D4 **Nanchang** China
31B3 **Nanchong** China
44E4 **Nancowry** *I* Nicobar Is, Indian Ocean
14D2 **Nancy** France
43E2 **Nanda Devi** *Mt* India
44B2 **Nānded** India
34D2 **Nandewar Range** *Mts* Australia
42C4 **Nandurbār** India
44B2 **Nandyāl** India
50B3 **Nanga Eboko** Cameroon
42C1 **Nanga Parbat** *Mt* Pakistan
27E7 **Nangapinon** Indonesia
13B3 **Nangis** France
28A2 **Nangnim** N Korea
28B2 **Nangnim Sanmaek** *Mts* N Korea
43G3 **Nang Xian** China
44B3 **Nanjangūd** India
31D3 **Nanjing** China
Nanking = Nanjing
29B4 **Nankoku** Japan
31C4 **Nan Ling** *Region* China
30D1 **Nanliu** *R* China
31B5 **Nanning** China
55O3 **Nanortalik** Greenland
31A5 **Nanpan Jiang** *R* China
43E3 **Nānpāra** India
31D4 **Nanping** China
28B2 **Nanping** China
55J1 **Nansen Sd** Canada
27E5 **Nanshan** *I* S China Sea
50D4 **Nansio** Tanzania
14B2 **Nantes** France
68C2 **Nanticoke** USA
31E3 **Nantong** China
68E2 **Nantucket** USA
68E2 **Nantucket I** USA
68E2 **Nantucket Sd** USA
7C3 **Nantwich** England
33G1 **Nanumanga** *I* Tuvalu
33G1 **Nanumea** *I* Tuvalu
75D2 **Nanuque** Brazil
31C3 **Nanyang** China
31D2 **Nanyang Hu** *L* China
50D3 **Nanyuki** Kenya
28A2 **Nanzamu** China
15C2 **Nao, Cabo de la** *C* Spain
29D3 **Naoetsu** Japan
42B4 **Naokot** Pakistan
66A1 **Napa** USA
65D2 **Napanee** Canada
24K4 **Napas** Russian Federation
55N3 **Napassoq** Greenland
30D2 **Nape** Laos
35C1 **Napier** New Zealand
67B3 **Naples** Florida, USA
16C2 **Naples** Italy
68B1 **Naples** New York, USA
63D2 **Naples** Texas, USA
31B5 **Napo** China
72D4 **Napo** *R* Ecuador/Peru
60D1 **Napoleon** USA
Napoli = Naples
41E2 **Naqadeh** Iran
45C3 **Naqb Ishtar** Jordan
29C4 **Nara** Japan
48B3 **Nara** Mali
32D4 **Naracoorte** Australia
44B2 **Narasarāopet** India
30C4 **Narathiwat** Thailand
43G4 **Narayanganj** Bangladesh
44B2 **Nārāyenpet** India
14C3 **Narbonne** France
30A3 **Narcondam** *I* Indian Ocean
42D2 **Narendranagar** India
55L2 **Nares Str** Canada
19E2 **Narew** *R* Poland
28B2 **Narhong** China
29D3 **Narita** Japan
42C4 **Narmada** *R* India
42D3 **Nārnaul** India
20F4 **Naro Fominsk** Russian Federation
50D4 **Narok** Kenya
19F2 **Narovl'a** Belarus
42C2 **Narowal** Pakistan
32D4 **Narrabri** Australia
34C1 **Narran** *R* Australia
34C2 **Narrandera** Australia
34C1 **Narran L** Australia
32A4 **Narrogin** Australia
34C2 **Narromine** Australia
64C3 **Narrows** USA
68C2 **Narrowsburg** USA
42D4 **Narsimhapur** India
44C2 **Narsīpatnam** India
55O3 **Narssalik** Greenland
55O3 **Narssaq** Greenland
55O3 **Narssarssuaq** Greenland
47B2 **Narubis** Namibia
29D3 **Narugo** Japan
29B4 **Naruto** Japan
20D4 **Narva** Russian Federation
12H5 **Narvik** Norway
42D3 **Narwāna** India
20J2 **Nar'yan Mar** Russian Federation
34B1 **Narylico** Australia
24J5 **Naryn** Kirgizia
48C4 **Nasarawa** Nigeria
52D6 **Nasca Ridge** Pacific Ocean
68E1 **Nashua** USA
63D2 **Nashville** Arkansas, USA
67A1 **Nashville** Tennessee, USA
17D1 **Našice** Croatia
42C4 **Nāsik** India
50D3 **Nasir** Sudan
69B1 **Nassau** The Bahamas
68D1 **Nassau** USA
49F2 **Nasser,L** Egypt
12G7 **Nässjö** Sweden
55L4 **Nastapoka Is** Canada
51C6 **Nata** Botswana
73L5 **Natal** Brazil
27C6 **Natal** Indonesia
36C6 **Natal Basin** Indian Ocean
41F3 **Natanz** Iran
55M4 **Natashquan** Canada
55M4 **Natashquan** *R* Canada
63D2 **Natchez** USA
63D2 **Natchitoches** USA
34C3 **Nathalia** Australia
55Q2 **Nathorsts Land** *Region* Greenland
59C4 **National City** USA
29D3 **Natori** Japan
50D4 **Natron, L** Tanzania
40A3 **Natrun, Wadi el** *Watercourse* Egypt
32A4 **Naturaliste,C** Australia
18C2 **Nauen** Germany
68D2 **Naugatuck** USA
18C2 **Naumburg** Germany
45C3 **Naur** Jordan
33F1 **Nauru** *I, Republic* Pacific Ocean
25M4 **Naushki** Russian Federation
47B2 **Naute Dam** *Res* Namibia
56C3 **Navajo Res** USA
15A2 **Navalmoral de la Mata** Spain
25T3 **Navarin, Mys** *C* Russian Federation
74C9 **Navarino** *I* Chile
15B1 **Navarra** *Province* Spain
63C2 **Navasota** USA
63C2 **Navasota** *R* USA
8C2 **Naver, L** Scotland
15A1 **Navia** *R* Spain
42C4 **Navlakhi** India
21E5 **Navlya** Russian Federation
70B2 **Navojoa** Mexico
17E3 **Návpaktos** Greece
17E3 **Návplion** Greece
42C4 **Navsāri** India
45D2 **Nawá** Syria
42B3 **Nawabshah** Pakistan
43F4 **Nawāda** India
42B2 **Nawah** Afghanistan
31B4 **Naxi** China
17F3 **Náxos** *I* Greece
41F4 **Nāy Band** Iran
41G3 **Nāy Band** Iran
29E2 **Nayoro** Japan
75E1 **Nazaré** Brazil
45C2 **Nazareth** Israel
72D6 **Nazca** Peru
40A2 **Nazilli** Turkey
25L4 **Nazimovo** Russian Federation
50D3 **Nazrēt** Ethiopia
41G5 **Nazwa'** Oman
24J4 **Nazyvayevsk** Russian Federation
51B4 **Ndalatando** Angola
50C3 **Ndélé** Central African Republic
50B4 **Ndendé** Gabon
33F2 **Ndende** *I* Solomon Islands
50B2 **Ndjamena** Chad
50B4 **Ndjolé** Gabon
51C5 **Ndola** Zambia
34C1 **Neabul** Australia
10B3 **Neagh, Lough** *L* Northern Ireland
17E3 **Neápolis** Greece
7C4 **Neath** Wales
34C1 **Nebine** *R* Australia
24G6 **Nebit Dag** Turkmenistan
56C2 **Nebraska** *State* USA
61D2 **Nebraska City** USA
16C3 **Nebrodi, Monti** *Mts* Sicily, Italy
63C2 **Neches** *R* USA
74E5 **Necochea** Argentina
43G3 **Nêdong** China
7E3 **Needham Market** England
59D4 **Needles** USA
7D4 **Needles** *Pt* England
64B2 **Neenah** USA
54J4 **Neepawa** Canada
13C2 **Neerpelt** Belgium
25M4 **Neftelensk** Russian Federation
50D3 **Negelē** Ethiopia
45C3 **Negev** *Desert* Israel
75A3 **Negla** *R* Paraguay
21C6 **Negolu** *Mt* Romania
44B4 **Negombo** Sri Lanka
30A2 **Negrais,C** Burma
72B4 **Negritos** Peru
72F4 **Negro** *R* Amazonas, Brazil
74D5 **Negro** *R* Argentina
74F4 **Negro** *R* Brazil/Uruguay
75A2 **Negro** *R* Mato Grosso do Sul, Brazil
75A3 **Negro** *R* Paraguay
15A2 **Negro, Cap** *C* Morocco
27F6 **Negros** *I* Philippines
17F2 **Negru Vodă** Romania
31B4 **Neijiang** China
64A2 **Neillsville** USA
Nei Monggol Zizhiqu = Inner Mongolia Aut. Region
72C3 **Neiva** Colombia
50D3 **Nejo** Ethiopia
50D3 **Nek'emte** Ethiopia
20E4 **Nelidovo** Russian Federation
61D2 **Neligh** USA
44B3 **Nellore** India
26G2 **Nel'ma** Russian Federation
54G5 **Nelson** Canada
6C3 **Nelson** England
35B2 **Nelson** New Zealand
34B3 **Nelson,C** Australia
47E2 **Nelspruit** South Africa
48B3 **Néma** Mauritius
31A1 **Nemagt Uul** *Mt* Mongolia
16B3 **Nementcha, Mts Des** Algeria
17F1 **Nemira** *Mt* Romania
13B3 **Nemours** France
19E1 **Nemunas** *R* Lithuania
29F2 **Nemuro** Japan
29F2 **Nemuro-kaikyō** *Str* Japan/Russian Federation
25O5 **Nen** *R* China
10B3 **Nenagh** Irish Republic
54D3 **Nenana** USA
7D3 **Nene** *R* England
26F2 **Nenjiang** China
63C1 **Neodesha** USA
63D1 **Neosho** USA
25M4 **Nepa** Russian Federation
39G3 **Nepal** *Kingdom* Asia
43E3 **Nepalganj** Nepal
59D3 **Nephi** USA
45C3 **Neqarot** *R* Israel
26E1 **Nerchinsk** Russian Federation
17D2 **Neretva** *R* Bosnia-Herzegovina/Croatia
27H5 **Nero Deep** Pacific Ocean
20G2 **Nes'** Russian Federation
12C1 **Neskaupstaður** Iceland
13B3 **Nesle** France
62C1 **Ness City** USA
8C3 **Ness, Loch** *L* Scotland
17E2 **Néstos** *R* Greece
45C2 **Netanya** Israel
68C2 **Netcong** USA
18B2 **Netherlands** *Kingdom* Europe
53M7 **Netherlands Antilles** *Is* Caribbean Sea
43G4 **Netrakona** Bangladesh
55L3 **Nettilling L** Canada
18C2 **Neubrandenburg** Germany
16B1 **Neuchâtel** Switzerland
13C3 **Neufchâteau** Belgium

Olochi
Palestine

26E1 **Olochi** Russian Federation
12G7 **Olofström** Sweden
50B4 **Olombo** Congo
18D3 **Olomouc** Czech Republic
20E3 **Olonets** Russian Federation
14B3 **Oloron-Ste-Marie** France
26E1 **Olovyannaya** Russian Federation
13D2 **Olpe** Germany
19E2 **Olsztyn** Poland
16B1 **Olten** Switzerland
17E2 **Olt** *R* Romania
58B1 **Olympia** USA
58B1 **Olympic Nat Pk** USA
Olympus *Mt* = **Ólimbos**
45B1 **Olympus,Mt** Cyprus
58B1 **Olympus,Mt** USA
25T4 **Olyutorskiy, Mys** *C* Russian Federation
29C3 **Omachi** Japan
29C4 **Omae-zaki** *C* Japan
9C2 **Omagh** Northern Ireland
61D2 **Omaha** USA
58C1 **Omak** USA
38D4 **Oman** *Sultanate* Arabian Pen
38D3 **Oman,G of** UAE
47B1 **Omaruru** Namibia
47A1 **Omaruru** *R* Namibia
29D2 **Ōma-saki** *C* Japan
50A4 **Omboué** Gabon
50D2 **Omdurman** Sudan
50D2 **Om Häjer** Eritrea
29D2 **Ōminato** Japan
54F4 **Omineca Mts** Canada
29C3 **Omiya** Japan
54H2 **Ommanney B** Canada
50D3 **Omo** *R* Ethiopia
16B2 **Omodeo, L** Sardinia, Italy
25R3 **Omolon** *R* Russian Federation
25P3 **Omoloy** *R* Russian Federation
29D3 **Omono** *R* Japan
24J4 **Omsk** Russian Federation
29D2 **Ōmu** Japan
28C4 **Omura** Japan
47C1 **Omuramba Eiseb** *R* Botswana
28C4 **Ōmuta** Japan
20J4 **Omutninsk** Russian Federation
64A2 **Onalaska** USA
65D3 **Onancock** USA
43K1 **Onandausi** India
64C1 **Onaping L** Canada
61D2 **Onawa** USA
51B5 **Oncócua** Angola
51B5 **Ondangua** Namibia
19E3 **Ondava** *R* Slovakia
48C4 **Ondo** Nigeria
26E2 **Öndörhaan** Mongolia
39F5 **One and Half Degree Chan** Indian Ocean
42F3 **Onega** Russian Federation
20F3 **Onega** *R* Russian Federation
20F3 **Onega, L** Russian Federation
68C1 **Oneida** USA
68B1 **Oneida L** USA
60D2 **O'Neill** USA
26J2 **Onekotan** *I* Kuril Is, Russian Federation
50C4 **Onema** Zaïre
68C1 **Oneonta** USA
17F1 **Onești** Romania
20F3 **Onezhskaya Guba** *B* Russian Federation
Onezhskoye, Oz *L* = **Onega, L**
47C3 **Ongers** *R* South Africa
51B5 **Ongiva** Angola
28B3 **Ongjin** N Korea
31D1 **Ongniud Qi** China
44C2 **Ongole** India
51E6 **Onilahy** *R* Madagascar
48C4 **Onitsha** Nigeria
26D2 **Onjüül** Mongolia
29C3 **Ono** Japan
29C4 **Ōnohara-jima** *I* Japan
29C4 **Onomichi** Japan
33G1 **Onotoa** *I* Kiribati
32A3 **Onslow** Australia
67C2 **Onslow B** USA
29C3 **Ontake-san** *Mt* Japan
66D3 **Ontario** California, USA
58C2 **Ontario** Oregon, USA
55J4 **Ontario** *Province* Canada
65D2 **Ontario,L** Canada/USA
15B2 **Onteniente** Spain
33E1 **Ontong Java Atoll** Solomon Islands
28A3 **Onyang** S Korea
66C3 **Onyx** USA
32C3 **Oodnadatta** Australia
32C4 **Ooldea** Australia
63C1 **Oologah L** USA
13C1 **Oostelijk Flevoland** *Polder* Netherlands
13B2 **Oostende** Belgium
13B2 **Oosterschelde** *Estuary* Netherlands
44B3 **Ootacamund** India
25R4 **Opala** Russian Federation
50C4 **Opala** Zaïre
44C4 **Opanake** Sri Lanka
20H4 **Oparino** Russian Federation
19D3 **Opava** Czech Republic
67A2 **Opelika** USA
63D2 **Opelousas** USA
60B1 **Opheim** USA
19F1 **Opochka** Russian Federation
19D2 **Opole** Poland
15A1 **Oporto** Portugal
35C1 **Opotiki** New Zealand
67A2 **Opp** USA
12F6 **Oppdal** Norway
35B1 **Opunake** New Zealand
17E1 **Oradea** Romania
12B2 **Öræfajökull** *Mts* Iceland
42D3 **Orai** India
15B2 **Oran** Algeria
72F8 **Orán** Argentina
28A2 **Orang** N Korea
34C2 **Orange** Australia
66D4 **Orange** California, USA
14C3 **Orange** France
63D2 **Orange** Texas, USA
47B2 **Orange** *R* South Africa
67B2 **Orangeburg** USA
73H3 **Orange, Cabo** *C* Brazil
61D2 **Orange City** USA
47D2 **Orange Free State** *Province* South Africa
67B2 **Orange Park** USA
64C2 **Orangeville** Canada
18C2 **Oranienburg** Germany
47B2 **Oranjemund** Namibia
47D1 **Orapa** Botswana
27F5 **Oras** Philippines
17E1 **Orăştie** Romania
17E1 **Oraviţa** Romania
16C2 **Orbetello** Italy
68B2 **Orbisonia** USA
34C3 **Orbost** Australia
13B2 **Orchies** France
66B3 **Orcutt** USA
60D2 **Ord** USA
32B2 **Ord** *R* Australia
59D3 **Orderville** USA
32B2 **Ord,Mt** Australia
25M6 **Ordos** *Desert* China
40C1 **Ordu** Turkey
62B1 **Ordway** USA
12H7 **Örebro** Sweden
64C2 **Oregon** USA
56A2 **Oregon** *State* USA
58B1 **Oregon City** USA
12H6 **Öregrund** Sweden
20F4 **Orekhovo Zuyevo** Russian Federation
21F5 **Orel** Russian Federation
59D2 **Orem** USA
21J5 **Orenburg** Russian Federation
15A1 **Orense** Spain
18C1 **Oresund** *Str* Denmark/ Sweden
35A3 **Oreti** *R* New Zealand
19F3 **Orgeyev** Moldavia
17F3 **Orhaneli** *R* Turkey
26D2 **Orhon Gol** *R* Mongolia
34B1 **Orientos** Australia
15B2 **Orihuela** Spain
65D2 **Orillia** Canada
72F2 **Orinoco** *R* Venezuela
68C1 **Oriskany Falls** USA
43E4 **Orissa** *State* India
16B3 **Oristano** Sicily, Italy
16B3 **Oristano, G. di** Sardinia, Italy
12K6 **Orivesi** *L* Finland
73G4 **Oriximiná** Brazil
70C3 **Orizaba** Mexico
75C2 **Orizona** Brazil
8D2 **Orkney** *Is, Region* Scotland
75C3 **Orlândia** Brazil
67B3 **Orlando** USA
14C2 **Orléanais** *Region* France
14C2 **Orléans** France
68E2 **Orleans** USA
25L4 **Orlik** Russian Federation
67B3 **Ormond Beach** USA
7C3 **Ormskirk** England
13C3 **Ornain** *R* France
14B2 **Orne** *R* France
12H6 **Örnsköldsvik** Sweden
28A2 **Oro** N Korea
72D3 **Orocué** Colombia
58C1 **Orofino** USA
45C3 **Oron** Israel
8B3 **Oronsay, I** Scotland
Orontes = **Asi**
19E3 **Orosháza** Hungary
25R3 **Orotukan** Russian Federation
59B3 **Oroville** California, USA
58C1 **Oroville** Washington, USA
19G2 **Orsha** Belarus
21K5 **Orsk** Russian Federation
12F6 **Ørsta** Norway
14B3 **Orthez** France
15A1 **Ortigueira** Spain
14E2 **Ortles** *Mt* Italy
69L1 **Ortoire** *R* Trinidad
61D1 **Ortonville** USA
25O3 **Orulgan, Khrebet** *Mts* Russian Federation
72E7 **Oruro** Bolivia
7E3 **Orwell** *R* England
20K4 **Osa** Russian Federation
61E2 **Osage** Iowa, USA
60C2 **Osage** Wyoming, USA
63D1 **Osage** *R* USA
29D4 **Ōsaka** Japan
70D4 **Osa,Pen de** Costa Rica
63E1 **Osceola** Arkansas, USA
61E2 **Osceola** Iowa, USA
58C2 **Osgood Mts** USA
29D2 **Oshamambe** Japan
65D2 **Oshawa** Canada
29D4 **Ō-shima** *I* Japan
60C2 **Oshkosh** Nebraska, USA
55K5 **Oshkosh** USA
64B2 **Oshkosh** Wisconsin, USA
21H8 **Oshnovīyeh** Iran
48C4 **Oshogbo** Nigeria
50B4 **Oshwe** Zaïre
17D1 **Osijek** Croatia
24K4 **Osinniki** Russian Federation
19F2 **Osipovichi** Belarus
61E2 **Oskaloosa** USA
20B4 **Oskarshamn** Sweden
12G6 **Oslo** Norway
40C2 **Osmaniye** Turkey
18B2 **Osnabrück** Germany
74B6 **Osorno** Chile
15B1 **Osorno** Spain
58C1 **Osoyoos** Canada
32D5 **Ossa,Mt** Australia
64A2 **Osseo** USA
68D2 **Ossining** USA
25S4 **Ossora** Russian Federation
20E4 **Ostashkov** Russian Federation
13E1 **Oste** *R* Germany
Ostend = **Oostende**
12G6 **Østerdalen** *V* Norway
13E1 **Osterholz-Scharmbeck** Germany
12G6 **Östersund** Sweden
13D1 **Ostfriesland** *Region* Germany
12H6 **Östhammär** Sweden
16C2 **Ostia** Italy
19D3 **Ostrava** Czech Republic
19D2 **Ostróda** Poland
19E2 **Ostrołęka** Poland
20D4 **Ostrov** Russian Federation
19D2 **Ostrów Wlkp** Poland
19E2 **Ostrowiec** Poland
19E2 **Ostrów Mazowiecka** Poland
15A2 **Osuna** Spain
65D2 **Oswego** USA
68B1 **Oswego** *R* USA
7C3 **Oswestry** England
19D3 **Oświęcim** Poland
29C3 **Ota** Japan
35B3 **Otago Pen** New Zealand
35C2 **Otaki** New Zealand
29E2 **Otaru** Japan
72C3 **Otavalo** Ecuador
51B5 **Otavi** Namibia
29D3 **Otawara** Japan
68C1 **Otego** USA
58C1 **Othello** USA
17E3 **Óthris** *Mt* Greece
60C2 **Otis** Colorado, USA
68D1 **Otis** Massachusetts, USA
68C2 **Otisville** USA
47B1 **Otjimbingwe** Namibia
51B6 **Otjiwarongo** Namibia
6D3 **Otley** England
31B2 **Otog Qi** China
29D2 **Otoineppu** Japan
35C1 **Otorohanga** New Zealand
12F7 **Otra** *R* Norway
17D2 **Otranto** Italy
17D2 **Otranto,Str of** *Chan* Albania/Italy
64B2 **Otsego** USA
68C1 **Otsego L** USA
29C3 **Ōtsu** Japan
12F6 **Otta** Norway
65D1 **Ottawa** Canada
64B2 **Ottawa** Illinois, USA
63C1 **Ottawa** Kansas, USA
65D1 **Ottawa** *R* Canada
55K4 **Ottawa Is** Canada
13E1 **Otterndorf** Germany
55K4 **Otter Rapids** Canada
55K1 **Otto Fjord** Canada
47D2 **Ottosdal** South Africa
64A2 **Ottumwa** USA
13D3 **Ottweiler** Germany
48C4 **Oturkpo** Nigeria
72C5 **Otusco** Peru
34B3 **Otway,C** Australia
19E2 **Otwock** Poland
30C1 **Ou** *R* Laos
63D2 **Ouachita** *R* USA
63D2 **Ouachita,L** USA
63D2 **Ouachita Mts** USA
48A2 **Ouadane** Mauritius
50C3 **Ouadda** Central African Republic
50C2 **Ouaddai** *Desert Region* Chad
48B3 **Ouagadougou** Burkina
48B3 **Ouahigouya** Burkina
50C3 **Ouaka** *R* Central African Republic
48C3 **Oualam** Niger
48C2 **Ouallen** Algeria
50C3 **Ouanda Djallé** Central African Republic
13B4 **Ouanne** *R* France
48A2 **Ouarane** *Region* Mauritius
48C1 **Ouargla** Algeria
48B2 **Ouarkziz, Jbel** *Mts* Morocco
50C3 **Ouarra** *R* Central African Republic
15C2 **Ouarsenis, Massif de l'** *Mts* Algeria
48B1 **Ouarzazate** Morocco
15C2 **Ouassel** *R* Algeria
50B3 **Oubangui** *R* Central African Republic/Congo/ Zaïre
13B2 **Oudenaarde** Belgium
47C3 **Oudtshoorn** South Africa
15B2 **Oued Tlělat** Algeria
48B1 **Oued Zem** Morocco
40B4 **Ouena, Wadi** *Watercourse* Egypt
14A2 **Ouessant, Ile d'** *I* France
50B3 **Ouesso** Congo
48B1 **Ouezzane** Morocco
9C2 **Oughter, L** Irish Republic
50B3 **Ouham** *R* Chad
48C4 **Ouidah** Benin
48B1 **Oujda** Morocco
12J6 **Oulainen** Finland
15C3 **Ouled Nail, Monts des** Algeria
12K5 **Oulu** Finland
12K6 **Oulu** *R* Finland
12K6 **Oulujärvi** *L* Finland
50C2 **Oum Chalouba** Chad
16B3 **Oumel Bouaghi** Algeria
50B2 **Oum Hadjer** Chad
50C2 **Oum Haouach** *Watercourse* Chad
12K5 **Ounas** *R* Finland
20C2 **Ounastunturi** *Mt* Finland
50C2 **Ounianga Kebir** Chad
13D2 **Our** *R* Germany
62A1 **Ouray** USA
13C3 **Ource** *R* France
13B3 **Ourcq** *R* France
Ourense = **Orense**
73K5 **Ouricurí** Brazil
75C3 **Ourinhos** Brazil
75D3 **Ouro Prêto** Brazil
13C2 **Ourthe** *R* Belgium
7E3 **Ouse** *R* Norfolk, England
6D2 **Ouse** *R* N Yorks, England
10B2 **Outer Hebrides** *Is* Scotland
66C4 **Outer Santa Barbara** *Chan* USA
51B6 **Outjo** Namibia
12K6 **Outokumpu** Finland
34B3 **Ouyen** Australia
16B2 **Ovada** Italy
74B4 **Ovalle** Chile
51B5 **Ovamboland** *Region* Namibia
13D1 **Overijssel** *Province* Netherlands
59D3 **Overton** USA
12J5 **Övertorneå** Sweden
60C2 **Ovid** Colorado, USA
68B1 **Ovid** New York, USA
15A1 **Oviedo** Spain
12F6 **Øvre** Norway
21D5 **Ovruch** Ukraine
25O4 **Ovsyanka** Russian Federation
35A3 **Owaka** New Zealand
68B1 **Owasco L** USA
29C4 **Owase** Japan
61E2 **Owatonna** USA
68B1 **Owego** USA
66C2 **Owens** *R* USA
64B3 **Owensboro** USA
66D2 **Owens L** USA
64C2 **Owen Sound** Canada
32D1 **Owen Stanley Range** *Mts* Papua New Guinea
48C4 **Owerri** Nigeria
58E2 **Owl Creek Mts** USA
48C4 **Owo** Nigeria
64C2 **Owosso** USA
58C2 **Owyhee** USA
58C2 **Owyhee** *R* USA
58C2 **Owyhee Mts** USA
72C6 **Oxapampa** Peru
12H7 **Oxelösund** Sweden
7D3 **Oxford** England
68E1 **Oxford** Massachusetts, USA
63E2 **Oxford** Mississippi, USA
68C1 **Oxford** New York, USA
7D4 **Oxford** *County* England
66C3 **Oxnard** USA
29D3 **Oyama** Japan
50B3 **Oyen** Gabon
8C3 **Oykel** *R* Scotland
25Q3 **Oymyakon** Russian Federation
34C4 **Oyster B** Australia
27F6 **Ozamiz** Philippines
19F2 **Ozarichi** Belarus
67A2 **Ozark** USA
63D1 **Ozark Plat** USA
63D1 **Ozarks,L of the** USA
19E3 **Ózd** Hungary
62B2 **Ozona** USA
40D1 **Ozurgety** Georgia

P

47B3 **Paarl** South Africa
8B3 **Pabbay** *I* Scotland
19D2 **Pabianice** Poland
43F4 **Pabna** Bangladesh
19F1 **Pabrade** Lithuania
72F3 **Pacaraima, Serra** *Mts* Brazil/Venezuela
72C5 **Pacasmayo** Peru
70C2 **Pachuca** Mexico
66B1 **Pacific** USA
37N7 **Pacific-Antarctic Ridge** Pacific Ocean
66B2 **Pacific Grove** USA
37L4 **Pacific O**
75D2 **Pacuí** *R* Brazil
27D7 **Padang** Indonesia
20E3 **Padany** Russian Federation
18B2 **Paderborn** Germany
54J3 **Padlei** Canada
43G4 **Padma** *R* Bangladesh
16C1 **Padova** Italy
50B4 **Padrão, Ponta do** *Pt* Angola
56D4 **Padre I** USA
7B4 **Padstow** England
34B3 **Padthaway** Australia
Padua = **Padova**
64B3 **Paducah** Kentucky, USA
62B2 **Paducah** Texas, USA
12L5 **Padunskoye More** *L* Russian Federation
28A2 **Paegam** N Korea
35C1 **Paeroa** New Zealand
47E1 **Pafuri** Mozambique
16C2 **Pag** *I* Croatia
27D7 **Pagai Selatan** *I* Indonesia
27C7 **Pagai Utara** *I* Indonesia
27H5 **Pagan** *I* Pacific Ocean
59D3 **Page** USA
27F8 **Pago Mission** Australia
17F3 **Pagondhas** Greece
62A1 **Pagosa Springs** USA
66E5 **Pahala** Hawaiian Islands
35C2 **Pahiatua** New Zealand
66E5 **Pahoa** Hawaiian Islands
67B3 **Pahokee** USA
12K6 **Päijänne** *L* Finland
66E5 **Pailola Chan** Hawaiian Islands
64C2 **Painesville** USA
59D3 **Painted Desert** USA
64C3 **Paintsville** USA
8C4 **Paisley** Scotland
15B1 **País Vasco** *Region* Spain
72B5 **Paita** Peru
12J5 **Pajala** Sweden
38E3 **Pakistan** *Republic* Asia
30C2 **Pak Lay** Laos
43H4 **Pakokku** Burma
16D1 **Pakrac** Croatia
17D1 **Paks** Hungary
30C2 **Pak Sane** Laos
30D2 **Pakse** Laos
50D3 **Pakwach** Uganda
50B3 **Pala** Chad
16D2 **Palagruža** *I* Croatia
13B3 **Palaiseau** France
47D1 **Palala** *R* South Africa
44E3 **Palalankwe** Andaman Islands
25S4 **Palana** Russian Federation
27E7 **Palangkaraya** Indonesia
44B3 **Palani** India
42C4 **Pālanpur** India
47D1 **Palapye** Botswana
67B3 **Palatka** USA
36H4 **Palau** *USA Dependency* Pacific Ocean
30B3 **Palaw** Burma
27E6 **Palawan** *I* Philippines
44B4 **Palayankottai** India
12J7 **Paldiski** Estonia
27D7 **Palembang** Indonesia
15B1 **Palencia** Spain
45B1 **Paleokhorio** Cyprus
16C3 **Palermo** Sicily, Italy
63C2 **Palestine** USA

Port Austin **Pyasina**

64C2 **Port Austin** USA
44E3 **Port Blair** Andaman Islands
34B3 **Port Campbell** Australia
43F4 **Port Canning** India
55M5 **Port Cartier** Canada
35B3 **Port Chalmers** New Zealand
67B3 **Port Charlotte** USA
68D2 **Port Chester** USA
64C2 **Port Clinton** USA
65D2 **Port Colborne** Canada
34C4 **Port Davey** *B* Australia
69C3 **Port-de-Paix** Haiti
30C5 **Port Dickson** Malaysia
47E3 **Port Edward** South Africa
75D2 **Porteirinha** Brazil
64C2 **Port Elgin** Canada
47D3 **Port Elizabeth** South Africa
8B4 **Port Ellen** Scotland
6B2 **Port Erin** Isle of Man, British Islands
69N2 **Porter Pt** St Vincent
66C2 **Porterville** USA
32D4 **Port Fairy** Australia
50A4 **Port Gentil** Gabon
63D2 **Port Gibson** USA
58B1 **Port Hammond** Canada
48C4 **Port Harcourt** Nigeria
54F4 **Port Hardy** Canada
55M5 **Port Hawkesbury** Canada
7C4 **Porthcawl** Wales
32A3 **Port Hedland** Australia
7B3 **Porthmadog** Wales
55N4 **Port Hope Simpson** Canada
66C3 **Port Hueneme** USA
64C2 **Port Huron** USA
15A2 **Portimão** Portugal
34D2 **Port Jackson** *B* Australia
68D2 **Port Jefferson** USA
68C2 **Port Jervis** USA
34D2 **Port Kembla** Australia
7C4 **Portland** England
64C2 **Portland** Indiana, USA
65E2 **Portland** Maine, USA
34C2 **Portland** New South Wales, Australia
58B1 **Portland** Oregon, USA
34B3 **Portland** Victoria, Australia
69H2 **Portland Bight** *B* Jamaica
7C4 **Portland Bill** *Pt* England
34C4 **Portland,C** Australia
35C1 **Portland I** New Zealand
69H2 **Portland Pt** Jamaica
9C3 **Port Laoise** Irish Republic
63C3 **Port Lavaca** USA
32C4 **Port Lincoln** Australia
48A4 **Port Loko** Sierra Leone
51F6 **Port Louis** Mauritius
34B3 **Port MacDonnell** Australia
34D2 **Port Macquarie** Australia
68A2 **Port Matilda** USA
32D1 **Port Moresby** Papua New Guinea
47B2 **Port Nolloth** South Africa
68C3 **Port Norris** USA
Porto = Oporto
74F4 **Pôrto Alegre** Brazil
Porto Alexandre = Tombua
69A5 **Porto Armuelles** Panama
75A1 **Pôrto Artur** Brazil
75B3 **Pôrto 15 de Novembro** Brazil
75B1 **Pôrto dos Meinacos** Brazil
74F2 **Pôrto E Cunha** Brazil
75A2 **Pôrto Esperança** Brazil
16C2 **Portoferraio** Italy
69L1 **Port of Spain** Trinidad
75A2 **Pôrto Jofre** Brazil
75B3 **Pôrto Mendez** Brazil
75A3 **Pôrto Murtinho** Brazil
48C4 **Porto Novo** Benin
75B3 **Pôrto Primavera, Reprêsa** *Res* Brazil
58B1 **Port Orchard** USA
58B2 **Port Orford** USA
75B3 **Pôrto Santa Helena** Brazil
48A1 **Porto Santo** *I* Madeira
75B3 **Pôrto São José** Brazil
73L7 **Pôrto Seguro** Brazil
16B2 **Porto Torres** Sardinia, Italy
75B4 **Pôrto União** Brazil
16B2 **Porto Vecchio** Corsica, France
72F5 **Pôrto Velho** Brazil
8C4 **Portpatrick** Scotland
35A3 **Port Pegasus** *B* New Zealand
34B3 **Port Phillip B** Australia
34A2 **Port Pirie** Australia
8B3 **Portree** Scotland
58B1 **Port Renfrew** Canada
69J2 **Port Royal** Jamaica
67B2 **Port Royal Sd** USA
9C2 **Portrush** Northern Ireland
45B3 **Port Said** Egypt
67A3 **Port St Joe** USA
47D3 **Port St Johns** South Africa
55N4 **Port Saunders** Canada
47E3 **Port Shepstone** South Africa
69Q2 **Portsmouth** Dominica
7D4 **Portsmouth** England
68E1 **Portsmouth** New Hampshire, USA
64C3 **Portsmouth** Ohio, USA
65D3 **Portsmouth** Virginia, USA
34D2 **Port Stephens** *B* Australia
9C2 **Portstewart** Northern Ireland
50D2 **Port Sudan** Sudan
63E3 **Port Sulphur** USA
12K5 **Porttipahdan Tekojärvi** *Res* Finland
15A2 **Portugal** *Republic* Europe
9B3 **Portumna** Irish Republic
68A1 **Portville** USA
64B2 **Port Washington** USA
30C5 **Port Weld** Malaysia
72E6 **Porvenir** Bolivia
12K6 **Porvoo** Finland
74E3 **Posadas** Argentina
15A2 **Posadas** Spain
41G3 **Posht-e Badam** Iran
27F7 **Poso** Indonesia
28A4 **Posŏng** S Korea
20M2 **Pos Poluy** Russian Federation
75C1 **Posse** Brazil
62B2 **Post** USA
19F1 **Postavy** Belarus
47C2 **Postmasburg** South Africa
16C1 **Postojna** Slovenia
28C2 **Pos'yet** Russian Federation
47D2 **Potchefstroom** South Africa
63D1 **Poteau** USA
16D2 **Potenza** Italy
47D1 **Potgietersrus** South Africa
62C3 **Poth** USA
21G7 **Poti** Georgia
48D3 **Potiskum** Nigeria
58C1 **Potlatch** USA
47C3 **Potloer** *Mt* South Africa
58C1 **Pot Mt** USA
65D3 **Potomac** *R* USA
72E7 **Potosí** Bolivia
74C3 **Potrerillos** Chile
18C2 **Potsdam** Germany
60C2 **Potter** USA
68C2 **Pottstown** USA
68B2 **Pottsville** USA
68D2 **Poughkeepsie** USA
75C3 **Pouso Alegre** Brazil
35C1 **Poverty B** New Zealand
20F3 **Povonets** Russian Federation
21G5 **Povorino** Russian Federation
55L4 **Povungnituk** Canada
60B1 **Powder** *R* USA
60B2 **Powder River** USA
58E2 **Powell** USA
32C2 **Powell Creek** Australia
59D3 **Powell,L** USA
54F5 **Powell River** Canada
7C3 **Powys** *County* Wales
75B2 **Poxoréo** Brazil
31D4 **Poyang Hu** *L* China
40C2 **Pozantı** Turkey
70C2 **Poza Rica** Mexico
18D2 **Poznań** Poland
74E2 **Pozo Colorado** Paraguay
16C2 **Pozzuoli** Italy
48B4 **Pra** *R* Ghana
30C3 **Prachin Buri** Thailand
30B3 **Prachuap Khiri Khan** Thailand
18D2 **Praděd** *Mt* Czech Republic
14C3 **Pradelles** France
75E2 **Prado** Brazil
18C2 **Prague** Czech Republic
Praha = Prague
48A4 **Praia** Cape Verde
75A1 **Praia Rica** Brazil
72F5 **Prainha** Brazil
62B2 **Prairie Dog Town Fork** *R* USA
64A2 **Prairie du Chien** USA
61E3 **Prairie Village** USA
30C3 **Prakhon Chai** Thailand
75C2 **Prata** Brazil
75C2 **Prata** *R* Brazil
Prates *I* **= Dongsha Qundao**
16C2 **Prato** Italy
68C1 **Prattsville** USA
67A2 **Prattville** USA
14B1 **Prawle Pt** England
25L4 **Predivinsk** Russian Federation
25Q3 **Predporozhnyy** Russian Federation
19E2 **Pregolyu** *R* Russian Federation
30D3 **Prek Kak** Cambodia
64A1 **Prentice** USA
18C2 **Prenzlau** Germany
44E3 **Preparis I** Burma
18D3 **Přerov** Czech Republic
59D4 **Prescott** Arizona, USA
63D2 **Prescott** Arkansas, USA
65D2 **Prescott** Canada
60C2 **Presho** USA
74D3 **Presidencia Roque Sáenz Peña** Argentina
75B3 **Presidente Epitácio** Brazil
75B2 **Presidente Murtinho** Brazil
75B3 **Presidente Prudente** Brazil
75B3 **Presidente Venceslau** Brazil
62B3 **Presidio** USA
19E3 **Prešov** Slovakia
65F1 **Presque Isle** USA
6C3 **Preston** England
56B2 **Preston** Idaho, USA
61E2 **Preston** Minnesota, USA
63D1 **Preston** Missouri, USA
8C4 **Prestwick** Scotland
73J8 **Prêto** Brazil
75C2 **Prêto** *R* Brazil
47D2 **Pretoria** South Africa
17E3 **Préveza** Greece
30D3 **Prey Veng** Cambodia
59D3 **Price** USA
63E2 **Prichard** USA
21E6 **Prichernomorskaya Nizmennost'** *Lowland* Ukraine
69M2 **Prickly Pt** Grenada
19F3 **Pridneprovskaya Vozvyshennost'** *Upland* Ukraine
19E1 **Priekule** Lithuania
47C2 **Prieska** South Africa
58C1 **Priest L** USA
58C1 **Priest River** USA
17E2 **Prilep** Albania/Macedonia, Yugoslavia/Greece
21E5 **Priluki** Ukraine
76G3 **Primavera** *Base* Antarctica
12K6 **Primorsk** Russian Federation
21F6 **Primorsko-Akhtarsk** Russian Federation
54H4 **Prince Albert** Canada
47C3 **Prince Albert** South Africa
54F2 **Prince Albert,C** Canada
54G2 **Prince Albert Pen** Canada
54G2 **Prince Albert Sd** Canada
55L3 **Prince Charles I** Canada
76F10 **Prince Charles Mts** Antarctica
55M5 **Prince Edward I** *Province* Canada
36C7 **Prince Edward Is** Indian Ocean
54F4 **Prince George** Canada
54H2 **Prince Gustaf Adolf Sea** Canada
27H8 **Prince of Wales I** Australia
54H2 **Prince of Wales I** Canada
54E4 **Prince of Wales I** USA
54G2 **Prince of Wales Str** Canada
54G2 **Prince Patrick I** Canada
55J2 **Prince Regent Inlet** *Str* Canada
54E4 **Prince Rupert** Canada
32D2 **Princess Charlotte B** Australia
69L1 **Princes Town** Trinidad
54F5 **Princeton** Canada
64B2 **Princeton** Illinois, USA
64B3 **Princeton** Kentucky, USA
61E2 **Princeton** Missouri, USA
68C2 **Princeton** New Jersey, USA
64C3 **Princeton** W Virginia, USA
54D3 **Prince William Sd** USA
48C4 **Príncipe** *I* Sao Tome & Principe
58B2 **Prineville** USA
55O3 **Prins Christian Sund** Greenland
76F12 **Prinsesse Astrid Kyst** *Region* Antarctica
76F12 **Prinsesse Ragnhild Kyst** *Region* Antarctica
24C2 **Prins Karls Forland** *I* Svalbard, Norway
70D3 **Prinzapolca** Nicaragua
20E3 **Priozersk** Russian Federation
19F2 **Pripet** *R* Belarus
Pripyat' *R* Belarus **= Pripet**
17E2 **Prispansko Jezero** *L* Albania/Macedonia, Yugoslavia/Greece
17E2 **Priština** Serbia, Yugoslavia
18C2 **Pritzwalk** Germany
20G5 **Privolzhskaya Vozvyshennost'** *Upland* Russian Federation
17E2 **Prizren** Serbia, Yugoslavia
27E7 **Probolinggo** Indonesia
61E1 **Proctor** USA
44B3 **Proddatūr** India
70D2 **Progreso** Mexico
58B2 **Project City** USA
21G7 **Prokhladnyy** Russian Federation
24K4 **Prokop'yevsk** Russian Federation
21G6 **Proletarskaya** Russian Federation
Prome = Pyè
75A2 **Promissão** Brazil
19G2 **Pronya** *R* Belarus
73L6 **Propriá** Brazil
32D3 **Proserpine** Australia
68C1 **Prospect** New York, USA
58B2 **Prospect** Oregon, USA
18D3 **Prostějov** Czech Republic
55N2 **Prøven** Greenland
14D3 **Provence** *Region* France
68E2 **Providence** USA
69A4 **Providencia, Isla de** Caribbean Sea
25U3 **Provideniya** Russian Federation
68E1 **Provincetown** USA
13B3 **Provins** France
59D2 **Provo** USA
54G4 **Provost** Canada
75B4 **Prudentópolis** Brazil
54D2 **Prudhoe Bay** USA
55M2 **Prudhoe Land** *Region* Greenland
19E2 **Pruszkow** Poland
19F3 **Prut** *R* Moldavia/ Romania
21D6 **Prutul** *R* Romania
19E2 **Pruzhany** Belarus
63C1 **Pryor** USA
19E3 **Przemyśl** Poland
17F3 **Psará** *I* Greece
20D4 **Pskov** Russian Federation
19F2 **Ptich** *R* Belarus
17E2 **Ptolemaïs** Greece
28A3 **Puan** S Korea
72D5 **Pucallpa** Peru
31D4 **Pucheng** China
12K5 **Pudasjärvi** Finland
20F3 **Pudozh** Russian Federation
44B3 **Pudukkottai** India
70C3 **Puebla** Mexico
15A1 **Puebla de Sanabria** Spain
15A1 **Puebla de Trives** Spain
62B1 **Pueblo** USA
73L5 **Puerta do Calcanhar** *Pt* Brazil
47E2 **Puerta do Oro** *Pt* South Africa
75B3 **Puerto Adela** Brazil
74B7 **Puerto Aisén** Chile
70D4 **Puerto Armuelles** Panama
73G6 **Puerto Artur** Brazil
72C3 **Puerto Asis** Colombia
72E2 **Puerto Ayacucho** Venezuela
70D3 **Puerto Barrios** Guatemala
72D2 **Puerto Berrio** Colombia
72E1 **Puerto Cabello** Venezuela
70D3 **Puerto Cabezas** Nicaragua
72E2 **Puerto Carreńo** Colombia
75A3 **Puerto Casado** Brazil
75A3 **Puerto Cooper** Brazil
70D4 **Puerto Cortés** Costa Rica
70D3 **Puerto Cortés** Honduras
48A2 **Puerto del Rosario** Canary Islands
73H8 **Puerto E. Cunha** Brazil
72D1 **Puerto Fijo** Venezuela
73J5 **Puerto Franco** Brazil
75A3 **Puerto Guaraní** Brazil
72E6 **Puerto Heath** Bolivia
70D2 **Puerto Juárez** Mexico
72F1 **Puerto la Cruz** Venezuela
15B2 **Puertollano** Spain
69C4 **Puerto López** Colombia
74D6 **Puerto Madryn** Argentina
72E6 **Puerto Maldonado** Peru
74B6 **Puerto Montt** Chile
73G8 **Puerto Murtinho** Brazil
74B8 **Puerto Natales** Chile
70A1 **Puerto Peñasco** Mexico
75A3 **Puerto Pinasco** Brazil
74D6 **Puerto Pirámides** Argentina
69C3 **Puerto Plata** Dominican Republic
74F3 **Puerto Presidente Stroessner** Brazil
27E6 **Puerto Princesa** Philippines
72C3 **Puerto Rico** Colombia
69D3 **Puerto Rico** *I* Caribbean Sea
69D3 **Puerto Rico Trench** Caribbean Sea
73H4 **Puerto Santana** Brazil
75A3 **Puerto Sastre** Brazil
74E1 **Puerto Suárez** Bolivia
70B2 **Puerto Vallarta** Mexico
74B6 **Puerto Varas** Chile
72F7 **Puerto Villarroel** Bolivia
21H5 **Pugachev** Russian Federation
42C3 **Pūgal** India
15C1 **Puigcerdá** Spain
28A2 **Pujŏn** N Korea
28A2 **Pujŏn Res** N Korea
35B2 **Pukaki,L** *L* New Zealand
28A2 **Pukchin** N Korea
28B2 **Pukch'ŏng** N Korea
35B1 **Pukekohe** New Zealand
35B2 **Puketeraki Range** *Mts* New Zealand
20G3 **Puksoozero** Russian Federation
16C2 **Pula** Croatia
65D2 **Pulaski** New York, USA
67A1 **Pulaski** Tennessee, USA
64C3 **Pulaski** Virginia, USA
27G7 **Pulau Kolepom** *I* Indonesia
27C7 **Pulau Pulau Batu** *Is* Indonesia
Pulau Pulau Macan - Kepulauan = Takabonerate
19E2 **Puławy** Poland
44C3 **Pulicat L** India
42B1 **Pul-i-Khumri** Afghanistan
44B4 **Puliyangudi** India
58C1 **Pullman** USA
27G6 **Pulo Anna** *I* Pacific Ocean
12L5 **Pulozero** Russian Federation
19E2 **Pułtusk** Poland
74C3 **Puna de Atacama** Argentina
72B4 **Puná, Isla** Ecuador
43F3 **Punakha** Bhutan
42C2 **Pūnch** Pakistan
47E1 **Punda Milia** South Africa
44A2 **Pune** India
28A2 **Pungsan** N Korea
28A2 **Pungso** N Korea
50C4 **Punia** Zaïre
74B4 **Punitaqui** Chile
42C2 **Punjab** *Province* Pakistan
42D2 **Punjab** *State* India
72D7 **Puno** Peru
74D5 **Punta Alta** Argentina
74B8 **Punta Arenas** Chile
59C4 **Punta Banda, Cabo** *C* Mexico
74F4 **Punta del Este** Uruguay
70D3 **Punta Gorda** Belize
67B3 **Punta Gorda** USA
72B1 **Puntarenas** Costa Rica
31C4 **Puqi** China
24J3 **Pur** *R* Russian Federation
72C3 **Purace, Vol** Colombia
63C1 **Purcell** USA
62B1 **Purgatoire** *R* USA
43F5 **Puri** India
44B2 **Pūrna** India
43F3 **Pūrnia** India
30C3 **Pursat** Cambodia
72F4 **Purus** *R* Brazil
63E2 **Purvis** USA
27D7 **Purwokerto** Indonesia
28B2 **Puryŏng** N Korea
42D5 **Pusad** India
28B3 **Pusan** S Korea
20E4 **Pushkin** Russian Federation
20F3 **Pushlakhta** Russian Federation
19F1 **Pustoshka** Russian Federation
43H3 **Putao** Burma
35C1 **Putaruru** New Zealand
31D4 **Putian** China
27E7 **Puting, Tanjung** *C* Indonesia
68E1 **Putnam** USA
68D1 **Putney** USA
44B4 **Puttalam** Sri Lanka
18C2 **Puttgarden** Germany
72C4 **Putumayo** *R* Colombia/ Ecuador/Peru
27E6 **Putussiban** Indonesia
12K6 **Puulavesi** *L* Finland
58B1 **Puyallup** USA
35A3 **Puysegur Pt** New Zealand
51C4 **Pweto** Zaïre
7B3 **Pwllheli** Wales
51C6 **PWV** *Province* South Africa
20F3 **Pyal'ma** Russian Federation
20E2 **Pyaozero, Ozero** *L* Russian Federation
30B2 **Pyapon** Burma
25K2 **Pyasina** *R* Russian Federation

Reidsville

Rufunsa

67C1 **Reidsville** USA
7D4 **Reigate** England
14B2 **Ré, Ile de** *I* France
13B3 **Reims** France
74B8 **Reina Adelaida, Archipiélago de la** Chile
61E2 **Reinbeck** USA
54H4 **Reindeer L** Canada
15B1 **Reinosa** Spain
68B3 **Reisterstown** USA
47D2 **Reitz** South Africa
54H3 **Reliance** Canada
58E2 **Reliance** USA
15C2 **Relizane** Algeria
34A2 **Remarkable,Mt** Australia
27E7 **Rembang** Indonesia
13D3 **Remiremont** France
13D2 **Remscheid** Germany
68C1 **Remsen** USA
12G6 **Rena** Norway
64B3 **Rend L** USA
18B2 **Rendsburg** Germany
65D1 **Renfrew** Canada
8C4 **Renfrew** Scotland
27D7 **Rengat** Indonesia
19F3 **Reni** Ukraine
50D2 **Renk** Sudan
55Q2 **Renland** *Pen* Greenland
34B2 **Renmark** Australia
33F2 **Rennell** *I* Solomon Islands
14B2 **Rennes** France
59C3 **Reno** USA
16C2 **Reno** *R* Italy
68B2 **Renovo** USA
68D1 **Rensselaer** USA
58B1 **Renton** USA
27F7 **Reo** Indonesia
19G2 **Repki** Ukraine
75C3 **Represa de Furnas** *Dam* Brazil
75C2 **Represa Três Marias** *Dam* Brazil
58C1 **Republic** USA
60D2 **Republican** *R* USA
55K3 **Repulse Bay** Canada
41F2 **Reshteh-ye Alborz** *Mts* Iran
31A2 **Reshui** China
74E3 **Resistencia** Argentina
17E1 **Reşiţa** Romania
55J2 **Resolute** Canada
35A3 **Resolution I** New Zealand
55M3 **Resolution Island** Canada
47E2 **Ressano Garcia** Mozambique
13C3 **Rethel** France
17E3 **Réthimnon** Greece
36D6 **Réunion** *I* Indian Ocean
15C1 **Reus** Spain
18B3 **Reutlingen** Germany
20K4 **Revda** Russian Federation
54G4 **Revelstoke** Canada
13C3 **Revigny-sur-Ornain** France
70A3 **Revillagigedo** *Is* Mexico
37O4 **Revilla Gigedo, Islas** Pacific Ocean
13C3 **Revin** France
45C3 **Revivim** Israel
43E4 **Rewa** India
42D3 **Rewāri** India
58D2 **Rexburg** USA
12A2 **Reykjavik** Iceland
70C2 **Reynosa** Mexico
14B2 **Rezé** France
19F1 **Rezekne** Latvia
20L4 **Rezh** Russian Federation
7C3 **Rhayader** Wales
45C1 **Rhazīr** Lebanon
13E2 **Rheda Wiedenbrück** Germany
18B2 **Rhein** *R* W Europe
18B2 **Rheine** Germany
14D2 **Rheinland Pfalz** *Region* Germany
Rhine *R* **= Rhein**
68D2 **Rhinebeck** USA
64B1 **Rhinelander** USA
65E2 **Rhode Island** *State* USA
68E2 **Rhode Island Sd** USA
17F3 **Rhodes** Greece
17F3 **Rhodes** *I* Greece
47D1 **Rhodes Drift** *Ford* Botswana/South Africa
58D1 **Rhodes Peak** *Mt* USA
7C4 **Rhondda** Wales
14C3 **Rhône** *R* France
7C3 **Rhyl** Wales
73L6 **Riachão do Jacuipe** Brazil
75D1 **Riacho de Santana** Brazil
15A1 **Ria de Arosa** *B* Spain
15A1 **Ria de Betanzos** *B* Spain
15A1 **Ria de Corcubion** *B* Spain
15A1 **Ria de Lage** *B* Spain
15A1 **Ria de Sta Marta** *B* Spain
15A1 **Ria de Vigo** *B* Spain
42C2 **Riāsi** Pakistan
27D6 **Riau, Kepulauan** *Is* Indonesia
15A1 **Ribadeo** Spain
75B3 **Ribas do Rio Pardo** Brazil
51D5 **Ribauè** Mozambique
6C3 **Ribble** *R* England
75C3 **Ribeira** Brazil
75C3 **Ribeirão Prêto** Brazil
72E6 **Riberalta** Bolivia
65D2 **Rice L** Canada
64A1 **Rice Lake** USA
47E2 **Richard's Bay** South Africa
63C2 **Richardson** USA
54E3 **Richardson Mts** Canada
59D3 **Richfield** USA
68C1 **Richfield Springs** USA
66C3 **Richgrove** USA
58C1 **Richland** USA
64C3 **Richlands** USA
66A2 **Richmond** California, USA
47C3 **Richmond** Cape Province, South Africa
6D2 **Richmond** England
64C3 **Richmond** Kentucky, USA
47E2 **Richmond** Natal, South Africa
34D2 **Richmond** New South Wales, Australia
35B2 **Richmond** New Zealand
32D3 **Richmond** Queensland, Australia
65D3 **Richmond** Virginia, USA
35B2 **Richmond Range** *Mts* New Zealand
68C1 **Richmondville** USA
7D4 **Rickmansworth** England
65D2 **Rideau Lakes** Canada
67B2 **Ridgeland** USA
68A2 **Ridgway** USA
69D4 **Riecito** Venezuela
18C2 **Riesa** Germany
74B8 **Riesco** *I* Chile
47C2 **Riet** *R* South Africa
16C2 **Rieti** Italy
15B2 **Rif** *Mts* Morocco
48B1 **Rif** *R* Morocco
60B3 **Rifle** USA
19E1 **Riga** Latvia
11H2 **Riga,G of** Estonia/Latvia
Rīgas Jūrās Līcis = Gulf of Riga
58D2 **Rigby** USA
58C1 **Riggins** USA
55N4 **Rigolet** Canada
Riia Laht = Gulf of Riga
12J6 **Riihimaki** Finland
16C1 **Rijeka** Croatia
29D3 **Rikuzen-Tanaka** Japan
12H7 **Rimbo** Sweden
16C2 **Rimini** Italy
17F1 **Rîmnicu Sărat** Romania
17E1 **Rîmnicu Vîlcea** Romania
57G2 **Rimouski** Canada
12F7 **Ringkøbing** Denmark
27E7 **Rinjani** *Mt* Indonesia
8B4 **Rinns Point** Scotland
13E1 **Rinteln** Germany
72C4 **Riobamba** Ecuador
48C4 **Rio Benito** Equatorial Guinea
72E5 **Rio Branco** Brazil
75C4 **Rio Branco do Sul** Brazil
62C3 **Rio Bravo** Mexico
70B1 **Rio Bravo del Norte** *R* Mexico/USA
75B3 **Rio Brilhante** Brazil
75C3 **Rio Claro** Brazil
69L1 **Rio Claro** Trinidad
74D4 **Ríocuarto** Argentina
75D3 **Rio de Janeiro** Brazil
75D3 **Rio de Janeiro** *State* Brazil
48A2 **Rio de Oro, Bahia de** *B* Morocco
74C8 **Río Gallegos** Argentina
74C8 **Río Grande** Argentina
74F4 **Rio Grande** Brazil
69A4 **Rio Grande** Nicaragua
70B2 **Rio Grande** *R* Mexico/USA
70D3 **Rio Grande** *R* Nicaragua
62C3 **Rio Grande City** USA
70B2 **Rio Grande de Santiago** *R* Mexico
73L5 **Rio Grande do Norte** *State* Brazil
74F3 **Rio Grande Do Sul** *State* Brazil
52G6 **Rio Grande Rise** Atlantic Ocean
69C4 **Ríohacha** Colombia
14C2 **Riom** France
72E7 **Rio Mulatos** Bolivia
75C4 **Rio Negro** Brazil
74C5 **Río Negro** *State* Argentina
74E4 **Rio Negro, Embalse de** *Res* Uruguay
74F3 **Rio Pardo** Brazil
74B8 **Rio Turbio** Argentina
75B2 **Rio Verde** Brazil
75B2 **Rio Verde de Mato Grosso** Brazil
7D3 **Ripley** England
64C3 **Ripley** Ohio, USA
63E1 **Ripley** Tennessee, USA
64C3 **Ripley** West Virginia, USA
6D2 **Ripon** England
66B2 **Ripon** USA
29E1 **Rishiri-tō** *I* Japan
45C3 **Rishon le Zion** Israel
68B3 **Rising Sun** USA
12F7 **Risør** Norway
44E3 **Ritchie's Arch** *Is* Andaman Islands
55N2 **Ritenbenk** Greenland
66C2 **Ritter,Mt** USA
58C1 **Ritzville** USA
74B3 **Rivadavia** Chile
72A1 **Rivas** Nicaragua
74E4 **Rivera** Uruguay
66B2 **Riverbank** USA
48B4 **River Cess** Liberia
66C2 **Riverdale** USA
68D2 **Riverhead** USA
34B3 **Riverina** *Region* Australia
35A3 **Riversdale** New Zealand
47C3 **Riversdale** South Africa
66D4 **Riverside** USA
35A3 **Riverton** New Zealand
58E2 **Riverton** USA
67B3 **Riviera Beach** USA
65F1 **Riviére-du-Loup** Canada
28A2 **Riwon** N Korea
41E5 **Rīyadh** Saudi Arabia
40D1 **Rize** Turkey
31D2 **Rizhao** China
45C1 **Rizokaipaso** Cyprus
16D3 **Rizzuto, C** Italy
12F7 **Rjukan** Norway
8B2 **Roag, Loch** *Inlet* Scotland
55K2 **Roanes Pen** Canada
14C2 **Roanne** France
67A2 **Roanoke** Alabama, USA
65D3 **Roanoke** Virginia, USA
65D3 **Roanoke** *R* USA
67C1 **Roanoke Rapids** USA
59D3 **Roan Plat** USA
58D2 **Roberts** USA
59C3 **Roberts Creek Mt** USA
12J6 **Robertsfors** Sweden
63D1 **Robert S Kerr Res** USA
47B3 **Robertson** South Africa
48A4 **Robertsport** Liberia
55L5 **Roberval** Canada
6D2 **Robin Hood's Bay** England
34B2 **Robinvale** Australia
63C3 **Robstown** USA
15A2 **Roca, Cabo de** *C* Portugal
70A3 **Roca Partida** *I* Mexico
73M4 **Rocas** *I* Brazil
74F4 **Rocha** Uruguay
7C3 **Rochdale** England
75B2 **Rochedo** Brazil
14B2 **Rochefort** France
64B2 **Rochelle** USA
54G3 **Rocher River** Canada
34B3 **Rochester** Australia
55L5 **Rochester** Canada
7E4 **Rochester** England
61E2 **Rochester** Minnesota, USA
68E1 **Rochester** New Hampshire, USA
68B1 **Rochester** New York, USA
64B2 **Rock** *R* USA
52H2 **Rockall** *I* UK
64B2 **Rockford** USA
67B2 **Rock Hill** USA
67C2 **Rockingham** USA
64A2 **Rock Island** USA
64B1 **Rockland** Michigan, USA
34B3 **Rocklands Res** Australia
67B3 **Rockledge** USA
63C3 **Rockport** USA
61D2 **Rock Rapids** USA
60B2 **Rock River** USA
60B1 **Rock Springs** Montana, USA
62B2 **Rocksprings** Texas, USA
58E2 **Rock Springs** Wyoming, USA
35B2 **Rocks Pt** New Zealand
34C3 **Rock,The** Australia
68D2 **Rockville** Connecticut, USA
64B3 **Rockville** Indiana, USA
68B3 **Rockville** Maryland, USA
65F1 **Rockwood** USA
62B1 **Rocky Ford** USA
64C1 **Rocky Island L** Canada
67C1 **Rocky Mount** USA
60B2 **Rocky Mountain Nat Pk** USA
56B1 **Rocky Mts** Canada/USA
18C2 **Rødbyhavn** Denmark
14C3 **Rodez** France
Ródhos = Rhodes
16D2 **Rodi Garganico** Italy
17E2 **Rodopi Planina** *Mts* Bulgaria
32A3 **Roebourne** Australia
47D1 **Roedtan** South Africa
13D2 **Roer** *R* Netherlands
13C2 **Roermond** Netherlands
13B2 **Roeselare** Belgium
55K3 **Roes Welcome Sd** Canada
19F2 **Rogachev** Belarus
72E6 **Rogaguado, Lago** Bolivia
63D1 **Rogers** USA
64C1 **Rogers City** USA
66D3 **Rogers L** USA
64C3 **Rogers,Mt** USA
58D2 **Rogerson** USA
47B3 **Roggeveldberge** *Mts* South Africa
58B2 **Rogue** *R* USA
42B3 **Rohri** Pakistan
42D3 **Rohtak** India
19E1 **Roja** Latvia
70C2 **Rojo, Cabo** *C* Mexico
75B3 **Rolândia** Brazil
63D1 **Rolla** USA
58D1 **Rollins** USA
Roma = Rome
34C1 **Roma** Australia
67C2 **Romain,C** USA
17F1 **Roman** Romania
52H5 **Romanche Gap** Atlantic Ocean
27F7 **Romang** *I* Indonesia
21C6 **Romania** *Republic* E Europe
67B3 **Romano,C** USA
14D2 **Romans-sur-Isère** France
27F5 **Romblon** Philippines
67A2 **Rome** Georgia, USA
16C2 **Rome** Italy
68C1 **Rome** New York, USA
65D2 **Rome** USA
14C2 **Romilly-sur-Seine** France
65D3 **Romney** USA
21E5 **Romny** Ukraine
18B1 **Rømø** *I* Denmark
14C2 **Romorantin** France
8C3 **Rona, I** Scotland
8B3 **Ronay, I** Scotland
75B1 **Roncador, Serra do** *Mts* Brazil
15A2 **Ronda** Spain
15A2 **Ronda, Sierra de** *Mts* Spain
72F6 **Rondônia** Brazil
72F6 **Rondônia** *State* Brazil
75B2 **Rondonópolis** Brazil
31B4 **Rong'an** China
31B4 **Rongchang** China
31E2 **Rongcheng** China
54H4 **Ronge, Lac la** Canada
31B4 **Rongjiang** China
31B4 **Rong Jiang** *R* China
30A1 **Rongklang Range** *Mts* Burma
12G7 **Rønne** Denmark
12H7 **Ronneby** Sweden
76F2 **Ronne Ice Shelf** Antarctica
13B2 **Ronse** Belgium
13D1 **Roodeschool** Netherlands
56C3 **Roof Butte** *Mt* USA
42D3 **Roorkee** India
13C2 **Roosendaal** Netherlands
59D2 **Roosevelt** USA
76E6 **Roosevelt I** Antarctica
61E2 **Root** *R* USA
32C2 **Roper** *R* Australia
8D2 **Rora Head** *Pt* Scotland
72F2 **Roraima** *Mt* Brazil/Guyana/Venezuela
72F3 **Roraima** *State* Brazil
12G6 **Røros** Norway
12G6 **Rorvik** Norway
19G3 **Ros'** *R* Ukraine
69Q2 **Rosalie** Dominica
66C3 **Rosamond** USA
66C3 **Rosamond L** USA
74D4 **Rosario** Argentina
73K4 **Rosário** Brazil
75A3 **Rosario** Paraguay
75A1 **Rosário Oeste** Brazil
68C2 **Roscoe** USA
14B2 **Roscoff** France
10B3 **Roscommon** Irish Republic
9C3 **Roscrea** Irish Republic
69Q2 **Roseau** Dominica
34C4 **Rosebery** Australia
60B1 **Rosebud** USA
58B2 **Roseburg** USA
63C3 **Rosenberg** USA
18C3 **Rosenheim** Germany
54H4 **Rosetown** Canada
66B1 **Roseville** USA
12G7 **Roskilde** Denmark
20E5 **Roslavl'** Russian Federation
20G4 **Roslyatino** Russian Federation
17E2 **Roşorii de Vede** Romania
35B2 **Ross** New Zealand
16D3 **Rossano** Italy
10B3 **Rossan Pt** Irish Republic
63E2 **Ross Barnett Res** USA
65D1 **Rosseau L** Canada
33E2 **Rossel** *I* Papua New Guinea
76E6 **Ross Ice Shelf** Antarctica
58B1 **Ross L** USA
9C3 **Rosslare** Irish Republic
35C2 **Ross,Mt** New Zealand
48A3 **Rosso** Mauritius
16B2 **Rosso, C** Corsica, France
7C4 **Ross-on-Wye** England
21F5 **Rossosh** Russian Federation
54E3 **Ross River** Canada
76F6 **Ross S** Antarctica
41F4 **Rostāq** Iran
18C2 **Rostock** Germany
20F4 **Rostov** Russian Federation
21F6 **Rostov-na-Donu** Russian Federation
67B2 **Roswell** Georgia, USA
62B2 **Roswell** New Mexico, USA
27H5 **Rota** *I* Pacific Ocean
27F8 **Rote** *I* Indonesia
18B2 **Rotenburg** Niedersachsen, Germany
13E2 **Rothaar-Geb** *Region* Germany
6D2 **Rothbury** England
76G3 **Rothera** *Base* Antarctica
7D3 **Rotherham** England
8C4 **Rothesay** Scotland
8D3 **Rothes-on-Spey** Scotland
34C2 **Roto** Australia
35B2 **Rotoiti,L** New Zealand
35B2 **Rotoroa,L** New Zealand
35C1 **Rotorua** New Zealand
35C1 **Rotorua,L** New Zealand
13E3 **Rottenburg** Germany
18A2 **Rotterdam** Netherlands
13E3 **Rottweil** Germany
33G2 **Rotuma** *I* Fiji
13B2 **Roubaix** France
14C2 **Rouen** France
6E3 **Rough** *Oilfield* N Sea
Roulers = Roeselare
51F6 **Round I** Mauritius
66D1 **Round Mountain** USA
34D2 **Round Mt** Australia
58E1 **Roundup** USA
8D2 **Rousay** *I* Scotland
14C3 **Roussillon** *Region* France
47D3 **Rouxville** South Africa
65D1 **Rouyn** Canada
12K5 **Rovaniemi** Finland
16C1 **Rovereto** Italy
16C1 **Rovigo** Italy
16C1 **Rovinj** Croatia
19F2 **Rovno** Ukraine
41E2 **Row'ān** Iran
34C1 **Rowena** Australia
55L3 **Rowley I** Canada
32A2 **Rowley Shoals** Australia
27F5 **Roxas** Philippines
67C1 **Roxboro** USA
35A3 **Roxburgh** New Zealand
58E1 **Roy** USA
9C3 **Royal Canal** Irish Republic
64B1 **Royale, Isle** USA
7D3 **Royal Leamington Spa** England
64C2 **Royal Oak** USA
7E4 **Royal Tunbridge Wells** England
14B2 **Royan** France
13B3 **Roye** France
7D3 **Royston** England
19E3 **Rožňava** Slovakia
13B3 **Rozoy** France
21G5 **Rtishchevo** Russian Federation
7C3 **Ruabon** Wales
51D4 **Ruaha Nat Pk** Tanzania
35C1 **Ruahine Range** *Mts* New Zealand
35C1 **Ruapehu,Mt** New Zealand
38C4 **Rub' al Khālī** *Desert* Saudi Arabia
8B3 **Rubha Hunish** *C* Scotland
8C3 **Rubha Réidh** *Pt* Scotland
75B3 **Rubinéia** Brazil
24K4 **Rubtsovsk** Russian Federation
54C3 **Ruby** USA
59C2 **Ruby Mts** USA
41G4 **Rudan** Iran
43L2 **Rudanli** India
41E2 **Rūdbār** Iran
29F2 **Rudnaya** Russian Federation
26G2 **Rudnaya Pristan'** Russian Federation
19G2 **Rudnya** Russian Federation
17E2 **Rudoka Planina** *Mt* Macedonia, Yugoslavia
24G1 **Rudol'fa, Ostrov** *I* Russian Federation
31E3 **Rudong** China
64C1 **Rudyard** USA
14C2 **Ruffec** France
51D4 **Rufiji** *R* Tanzania
74D4 **Rufino** Argentina
48A3 **Rufisque** Senegal
51C5 **Rufunsa** Zambia

Saratov

Shashe

21H5 **Saratov** Russian Federation
21H5 **Saratovskoye Vodokhranilishche** *Res* Russian Federation
30D2 **Saravane** Laos
27E6 **Sarawak** *State* Malaysia
40A2 **Saraykoy** Turkey
49D2 **Sardalas** Libya
41E2 **Sar Dasht** Iran
Sardegna = Sardinia
16B2 **Sardinia** *I* Medit Sea
12H5 **Sarektjåkkå** *Mt* Sweden
42C2 **Sargodha** Pakistan
50B3 **Sarh** Chad
48B1 **Sarhro, Jbel** *Mt* Morocco
41F2 **Sārī** Iran
45C2 **Sarida** *R* Israel
27H5 **Sarigan** *I* Pacific Ocean
40D1 **Sarıkamış** Turkey
32D3 **Sarina** Australia
42B1 **Sar-i-Pul** Afghanistan
49E2 **Sarīr** Libya
49D2 **Sarir Tibesti** *Desert* Libya
28B3 **Sariwŏn** N Korea
14B2 **Sark** *I* Channel Islands
40C2 **Şarkışla** Turkey
27G7 **Sarmi** Indonesia
74C7 **Sarmiento** Argentina
12G6 **Särna** Sweden
64C2 **Sarnia** Canada
19F2 **Sarny** Ukraine
42B2 **Sarobi** Afghanistan
17E3 **Saronikós Kólpos** *G* Greece
17F2 **Saros Körfezi** *B* Turkey
20M2 **Saroto** Russian Federation
12G7 **Sarpsborg** Norway
55N2 **Sarqaq** Greenland
13D3 **Sarralbe** France
13D3 **Sarrebourg** France
13D3 **Sarreguemines** France
13D3 **Sarre-Union** France
15B1 **Sarrion** Spain
42B3 **Sartanahu** Pakistan
16B2 **Sartène** Corsica, France
14B2 **Sarthe** *R* France
45D1 **Sārūt** *R* Syria
21J6 **Sarykamys** Kazakhstan
24H5 **Sarysu** *R* Kazakhstan
43E4 **Sasarām** India
28B4 **Sasebo** Japan
54H4 **Saskatchewan** *Province* Canada
54H4 **Saskatchewan** *R* Canada
54H4 **Saskatoon** Canada
25N2 **Saskylakh** Russian Federation
47D2 **Sasolburg** South Africa
20G5 **Sasovo** Russian Federation
48B4 **Sassandra** Ivory Coast
48B4 **Sassandra** *R* Ivory Coast
16B2 **Sassari** Sardinia, Italy
18C2 **Sassnitz** Germany
28A4 **Sasuna** Japan
44A2 **Sātāra** India
54G2 **Satellite B** Canada
12H6 **Säter** Sweden
67B2 **Satilla** *R* USA
20K4 **Satka** Russian Federation
42D2 **Satluj** *R* India
43E4 **Satna** India
42C4 **Sātpura Range** *Mts* India
17E1 **Satu Mare** Romania
12B1 **Sauðárkrókur** Iceland
12F7 **Sauda** Norway
38C3 **Saudi Arabia** *Kingdom* Arabian Pen
13D3 **Sauer** *R* Germany/ Luxembourg
13D2 **Sauerland** *Region* Germany
64B2 **Saugatuck** USA
68D1 **Saugerties** USA
61E1 **Sauk Center** USA
64B2 **Sauk City** USA
64C1 **Sault Ste Marie** Canada
64C1 **Sault Ste Marie** USA
27G7 **Saumlaki** Indonesia
14B2 **Saumur** France
51C4 **Saurimo** Angola
69M2 **Sauteurs** Grenada
17D2 **Sava** *R* Serbia, Yugoslavia
33H2 **Savai'i** *I* Western Samoa
48C4 **Savalou** Benin
67B2 **Savannah** Georgia, USA
63E1 **Savannah** Tennessee, USA
67B2 **Savannah** *R* USA
30C2 **Savannakhet** Laos
69G1 **Savanna la Mar** Jamaica
55J4 **Savant Lake** Canada
48C4 **Savé** Benin
51D6 **Save** *R* Mozambique
41F3 **Sāveh** Iran
13D3 **Saverne** France
13B3 **Savigny** France
20G3 **Savinskiy** Russian Federation
14D2 **Savoie** *Region* France
16B2 **Savona** Italy
12K6 **Savonlinna** Finland
54A3 **Savoonga** USA
32B2 **Savu** *I* Indonesia
12K5 **Savukoski** Finland
27F7 **Savu S** Indonesia
30A1 **Saw** Burma
42D3 **Sawai Mādhopur** India
30C2 **Sawankhalok** Thailand
29D3 **Sawara** Japan
60B3 **Sawatch Mts** USA
49D2 **Sawdā', Jabal as** *Mts* Libya
58C2 **Sawtooth Range** *Mts* USA
27F8 **Sawu** *I* Indonesia
7E3 **Saxmundham** England
68A2 **Saxton** USA
48C3 **Say** Niger
42B1 **Sayghan** Afghanistan
38D4 **Sayḩūt** Yemen
21H6 **Saykhin** Kazakhstan
26D2 **Saynshand** Mongolia
62C1 **Sayre** Oklahoma, USA
68B2 **Sayre** Pennsylvania, USA
21J7 **Say-Utes** Kazakhstan
68D2 **Sayville** USA
18C3 **Sázava** *R* Czech Republic
15C2 **Sbisseb** *R* Algeria
6C2 **Scafell Pike** *Mt* England
8E1 **Scalloway** Scotland
8C3 **Scalpay, I** Scotland
8D2 **Scapa Flow** *Sd* Scotland
65D2 **Scarborough** Canada
6D2 **Scarborough** England
69K1 **Scarborough** Tobago
8B2 **Scarp** *I* Scotland
16B1 **Schaffhausen** Switzerland
18C3 **Schärding** Austria
13E1 **Scharhörn** *I* Germany
13D2 **Scharteberg** *Mt* Germany
55M4 **Schefferville** Canada
13B2 **Schelde** *R* Belgium
59D3 **Schell Creek Range** *Mts* USA
68D1 **Schenectady** USA
62C3 **Schertz** USA
13C2 **Schiedam** Netherlands
13D1 **Schiermonnikoog** *I* Netherlands
13D2 **Schleiden** Germany
18B2 **Schleswig** Germany
18B2 **Schleswig Holstein** *State* Germany
68C1 **Schoharie** USA
32D1 **Schouten Is** Papua New Guinea
13E3 **Schramberg** Germany
55K5 **Schreiber** Canada
9B4 **Schull** Irish Republic
59C3 **Schurz** USA
68C2 **Schuylkill** *R* USA
68B2 **Schuylkill Haven** USA
18B3 **Schwabische Alb** *Upland* Germany
27E7 **Schwaner, Pegunungan** *Mts* Indonesia
47B2 **Schwarzrand** *Mts* Namibia
13E3 **Schwarzwald** *Mts* Germany
18C2 **Schweinfurt** Germany
47D2 **Schweizer Reneke** South Africa
18C2 **Schwerin** Germany
16B1 **Schwyz** Switzerland
16C3 **Sciacca** Italy
7A5 **Scilly, Isles of** England
64C3 **Scioto** *R* USA
60B1 **Scobey** USA
34D2 **Scone** Australia
55Q2 **Scoresby Sd** Greenland
52F7 **Scotia Sea** Atlantic Ocean
8C3 **Scotland** U K
76F7 **Scott** *Base* Antarctica
47E3 **Scottburgh** South Africa
62B1 **Scott City** USA
76G6 **Scott I** Antarctica
55L2 **Scott Inlet** *B* Canada
58B2 **Scott,Mt** USA
32B2 **Scott Reef** Timor Sea
60C2 **Scottsbluff** USA
67A2 **Scottsboro** USA
34C4 **Scottsdale** Australia
59D4 **Scottsdale** USA
68C2 **Scranton** USA
61D2 **Scribner** USA
7D3 **Scunthorpe** England
Scutari = Shkodër
47C3 **Seacow** *R* South Africa
7E4 **Seaford** England
54J4 **Seal** *R* Canada
34B3 **Sea Lake** Australia
59D3 **Searchlight** USA
63D1 **Searcy** USA
66D3 **Searles** USA
66B2 **Seaside** California, USA
58B1 **Seaside** Oregon, USA
68C3 **Seaside Park** USA
58B1 **Seattle** USA
65E2 **Sebago L** USA
70A2 **Sebastian Vizcaino, B** Mexico
66A1 **Sebastopol** USA
50D2 **Sebderat** Eritrea
19F1 **Sebez** Russian Federation
65F1 **Seboomook L** USA
67B3 **Sebring** USA
35A3 **Secretary I** New Zealand
61E3 **Sedalia** USA
13C3 **Sedan** France
6C2 **Sedbergh** England
35B2 **Seddonville** New Zealand
45C3 **Sede Boqer** Israel
45C3 **Sederot** Israel
48A3 **Sédhiou** Senegal
45C3 **Sedom** Israel
59D4 **Sedona** USA
47B2 **Seeheim** Namibia
76E4 **Seelig,Mt** Antarctica
35B2 **Sefton,Mt** New Zealand
30C5 **Segamat** Malaysia
20E3 **Segezha** Russian Federation
15B2 **Segorbe** Spain
48B3 **Ségou** Mali
Segovia = Coco
15B1 **Segovia** Spain
15C1 **Segre** *R* Spain
48B4 **Séguéla** Ivory Coast
63C3 **Seguin** USA
15B2 **Segura** *R* Spain
15B2 **Segura, Sierra de** *Mts* Spain
42B3 **Sehwan** Pakistan
62C1 **Seiling** USA
13D3 **Seille** *R* France
12J6 **Seinäjoki** Finland
61E1 **Seine** *R* Canada
14C2 **Seine** *R* France
13B3 **Seine-et-Marne** *Department* France
50D4 **Sekenke** Tanzania
48B4 **Sekondi** Ghana
50D2 **Sek'ot'a** Ethiopia
58B1 **Selah** USA
27G7 **Selaru** *I* Indonesia
27D6 **Selatan** *I* Indonesia
27G7 **Selat Dampier** *Str* Indonesia
27E7 **Selat Lombok** *Chan* Indonesia
27D7 **Selat Sunda** *Str* Indonesia
27F7 **Selat Wetar** *Chan* Indonesia
54C3 **Selawik** USA
32B1 **Selayar** *I* Indonesia
6D3 **Selby** England
60C1 **Selby** USA
17F3 **Selçuk** Turkey
47D1 **Selebi Pikwe** Botswana
25Q3 **Selennyakh** *R* Russian Federation
13D3 **Selestat** France
55Q3 **Selfoss** Iceland
60C1 **Selfridge** USA
50C1 **Selima Oasis** Sudan
19G1 **Selizharovo** Russian Federation
54J4 **Selkirk** Canada
8D4 **Selkirk** Scotland
54G4 **Selkirk Mts** Canada/USA
67A2 **Selma** Alabama, USA
66C2 **Selma** California, USA
63E1 **Selmer** USA
15B2 **Selouane** Morocco
72D5 **Selvas** *Region* Brazil
48A2 **Selvegens, Ilhas** *Is* Atlantic Ocean
58C1 **Selway** *R* USA
32D3 **Selwyn** Australia
54E3 **Selwyn Mts** Canada
27E7 **Semarang** Indonesia
20G4 **Semenov** Russian Federation
21F5 **Semiluki** Russian Federation
60B2 **Seminoe Res** USA
63C1 **Seminole** Oklahoma, USA
62B2 **Seminole** Texas, USA
67B2 **Seminole,L** USA
24K4 **Semipalatinsk** Kazakhstan
41F3 **Semirom** Iran
41F2 **Semnān** Iran
13C3 **Semois** *R* Belgium
72E5 **Sena Madureira** Brazil
51C5 **Senanga** Zambia
63E2 **Senatobia** USA
29E3 **Sendai** Japan
42D4 **Sendwha** India
68B1 **Seneca Falls** USA
68B1 **Seneca L** USA
62A2 **Senecu** Mexico
48A3 **Sénégal** *R* Mauritius/ Senegal
48A3 **Senegal** *Republic* Africa
47D2 **Senekal** South Africa
73L6 **Senhor do Bonfim** Brazil
16C2 **Senigallia** Italy
16D2 **Senj** Croatia
26F4 **Senkaku Gunto** *Is* Japan
13B3 **Senlis** France
50D2 **Sennar** Sudan
55L5 **Senneterre** Canada
13D3 **Senones** France
13B3 **Sens** France
17D1 **Senta** Serbia, Yugoslavia
50C4 **Sentery** Zaïre
42D4 **Seoni** India
28B3 **Seoul** S Korea
35B2 **Separation Pt** New Zealand
75D3 **Sepetiba, B de** Brazil
27H7 **Sepik** *R* Papua New Guinea
28A3 **Sep'o** N Korea
30D2 **Sepone** Laos
75A2 **Sepotuba** *R* Brazil
55M4 **Sept-Iles** Canada
50B1 **Séquédine** Niger
66C2 **Sequoia Nat Pk** USA
45C1 **Serai** Syria
27F7 **Seram** *I* Indonesia
27F7 **Seram Sea** Indonesia
17D2 **Serbia** *Republic* Yugoslavia
21G5 **Serdobsk** Russian Federation
13B4 **Serein** *R* France
30C5 **Seremban** Malaysia
50D4 **Serengeti Nat Pk** Tanzania
51D5 **Serenje** Zambia
19F3 **Seret** *R* Ukraine
20H4 **Sergach** Russian Federation
28C2 **Sergeyevka** Russian Federation
24H3 **Sergino** Russian Federation
73L6 **Sergipe** *State* Brazil
20F4 **Sergiyev Posad** Georgia
27E6 **Seria** Brunei
27E6 **Serian** Malaysia
17E3 **Sérifos** *I* Greece
49E2 **Serir Calanscio** *Desert* Libya
13C3 **Sermaize-les-Bains** France
32B1 **Sermata** *I* Indonesia
55P3 **Sermilik** *Fjord* Greenland
20J5 **Sernovodsk** Russian Federation
20L4 **Serov** Russian Federation
47D1 **Serowe** Botswana
15A2 **Serpa** Portugal
20F5 **Serpukhov** Russian Federation
15A1 **Serra da Estrela** *Mts* Portugal
73H3 **Serra do Navio** Brazil
17E2 **Sérrai** Greece
70D3 **Serrana Bank** *Is* Caribbean Sea
15B1 **Serraná de Cuenca** *Mts* Spain
75B2 **Serranópolis** Brazil
16B3 **Serrat, C** Tunisia
13B3 **Serre** *R* France
73L6 **Serrinha** Brazil
75D2 **Serro** Brazil
15C2 **Sersou, Plateau du** Algeria
75B3 **Sertanópolis** Brazil
31A3 **Sêrtar** China
47D1 **Serule** Botswana
51B5 **Sesfontein** Namibia
51C5 **Sesheke** Zambia
29D2 **Setana** Japan
14C3 **Sète** France
75D2 **Sete Lagoas** Brazil
15C2 **Sétif** Algeria
29C3 **Seto** Japan
28B4 **Seto Naikai** *S* Japan
48B1 **Settat** Morocco
6C2 **Settle** England
15A2 **Setúbal** Portugal
55J4 **Seul, Lac** Canada
21H7 **Sevan, Ozero** *L* Armenia
21E7 **Sevastopol'** Ukraine
7E4 **Sevenoaks** England
55K4 **Severn** *R* Canada
7C3 **Severn** *R* England
20G3 **Severnaya Dvina** *R* Russian Federation
25L1 **Severnaya Zemlya** *I* Russian Federation
20L3 **Severnyy Sos'va** *R* Russian Federation
20K3 **Severnyy Ural** *Mts* Russian Federation
25M4 **Severo Baykal'skoye Nagor'ye** *Mts* Russian Federation
21F6 **Severo Donets** *R* Ukraine
20F3 **Severodvinsk** Russian Federation
24H3 **Severo Sos'va** *R* Russian Federation
20L3 **Severoural'sk** Russian Federation
59D3 **Sevier** *R* USA
59D3 **Sevier Desert** USA
59D3 **Sevier L** USA
Sevilla = Seville
15A2 **Seville** Spain
17F2 **Sevlievo** Bulgaria
48A4 **Sewa** *R* Sierra Leone
61D2 **Seward** Nebraska, USA
54D3 **Seward** USA
54B3 **Seward Pen** USA
46K8 **Seychelles** *Is, Republic* Indian Ocean
40C2 **Seyhan** *R* Turkey
12C1 **Seyðisfjörður** Iceland
21F5 **Seym** *R* Russian Federation
25R3 **Seymchan** Russian Federation
34C3 **Seymour** Australia
68D2 **Seymour** Connecticut, USA
64B3 **Seymour** Indiana, USA
62C2 **Seymour** Texas, USA
13B3 **Sézanne** France
48D1 **Sfax** Tunisia
17F1 **Sfîntu Gheorghe** Romania
's-Gravenhage = The Hague
8C3 **Sgúrr na Lapaich,** *Mt* Scotland
31B3 **Shaanxi** *Province* China
50E3 **Shabeelle** *R* Ethiopia/ Somalia
50C4 **Shabunda** Zaïre
39F2 **Shache** China
76G9 **Shackleton Ice Shelf** Antarctica
42B3 **Shadadkot** Pakistan
41F3 **Shādhām** *R* Iran
66C3 **Shafter** USA
7C4 **Shaftesbury** England
28A2 **Shagang** China
74J8 **Shag Rocks** *Is* South Georgia
44B2 **Shāhābād** India
41E3 **Shāhābād** Iran
45D2 **Shahbā** Syria
41G3 **Shahdāb** Iran
43E4 **Shahdol** India
41E2 **Shāhīn Dezh** Iran
41G3 **Shāh Kūh** *Mt* Iran
41G3 **Shahr-e Bābak** Iran
Shahresa = Qomisheh
41F3 **Shahr Kord** Iran
21J8 **Shahsavār** Iran
20L3 **Shaim** Russian Federation
45C4 **Sha'īra, Gebel** *Mt* Egypt
40B5 **Sha'it, Wadi** *Watercourse* Egypt
42D3 **Shājahānpur** India
42D4 **Shājāpur** India
21G6 **Shakhty** Russian Federation
20H4 **Shakhun'ya** Russian Federation
48C4 **Shaki** Nigeria
61E2 **Shakopee** USA
29D2 **Shakotan-misaki** *C* Japan
20K4 **Shamary** Russian Federation
50D3 **Shambe** Sudan
68B2 **Shamokin** USA
62B1 **Shamrock** USA
68C1 **Shandaken** USA
66B3 **Shandon** USA
31D2 **Shandong** *Province* China
31C5 **Shangchuan Dao** *I* China
31C1 **Shangdu** China
31E3 **Shanghai** China
31C3 **Shangnan** China
51C5 **Shangombo** Zambia
31D3 **Shangqiu** China
31D4 **Shangrao** China
31B5 **Shangsi** China
31C3 **Shang Xian** China
7D4 **Shanklin** England
9B3 **Shannon** *R* Irish Republic
28B2 **Shansonggang** China
26G1 **Shantarskiye Ostrova** *I* Russian Federation
31D5 **Shantou** China
31C2 **Shanxi** *Province* China
31D3 **Shan Xian** China
31C5 **Shaoguan** China
31E4 **Shaoxing** China
31C4 **Shaoyang** China
8D2 **Shapinsay** *I* Scotland
45D2 **Shaqqā** Syria
41E4 **Shaqra'** Saudi Arabia
31A1 **Sharhulsan** Mongolia
29D2 **Shari** Japan
41G2 **Sharifābād** Iran
41G4 **Sharjah** UAE
32A3 **Shark B** Australia
41G2 **Sharlauk** Turkmenistan
45C2 **Sharon,Plain of** Israel
68B3 **Sharpsburg** USA
40C3 **Sharqi, Jebel esh** *Mts* Lebanon/Syria
20H4 **Sharya** Russian Federation
50D3 **Shashamenē** Ethiopia
47D1 **Shashani** *R* Zimbabwe
47D1 **Shashe** *R* Botswana

Shashi
Smolyan

31C3 **Shashi** China
58B2 **Shasta L** USA
58B2 **Shasta,Mt** USA
45D1 **Shaṭṭah at Taḥtā** Syria
41E3 **Shaṭṭ al Gharraf** *R* Iraq
45C3 **Shaubak** Jordan
66C2 **Shaver L** USA
68C2 **Shawangunk Mt** USA
64B2 **Shawano** USA
65E1 **Shawinigan** Canada
63C1 **Shawnee** Oklahoma, USA
60B2 **Shawnee** Wyoming, USA
31D4 **Sha Xian** China
32B3 **Shay Gap** Australia
45D2 **Shaykh Miskīn** Syria
50E2 **Shaykh 'Uthmān** Yemen
21F5 **Shchigry** Russian Federation
21E5 **Shchors** Ukraine
24J4 **Shchuchinsk** Kazakhstan
50E3 **Shebele** *R* Ethiopia
64B2 **Sheboygan** USA
50B3 **Shebshi Mts** Nigeia
9C3 **Sheelin, L** Irish Republic
9C2 **Sheep Haven** *Estuary* Irish Republic
7E4 **Sheerness** England
45C2 **Shefar'am** Israel
63E2 **Sheffield** Alabama, USA
7D3 **Sheffield** England
62B2 **Sheffield** Texas, USA
8C3 **Sheil, Loch** *L* Scotland
42C2 **Shekhupura** Pakistan
25T2 **Shelagskiy, Mys** *C* Russian Federation
68D1 **Shelburne Falls** USA
64B2 **Shelby** Michigan, USA
58D1 **Shelby** Montana, USA
67B1 **Shelby** N Carolina, USA
64B3 **Shelbyville** Indiana, USA
67A1 **Shelbyville** Tennessee, USA
61D2 **Sheldon** USA
54C4 **Shelikof Str** USA
58D2 **Shelley** USA
34D2 **Shellharbour** Australia
35A3 **Shelter Pt** New Zealand
58B1 **Shelton** USA
41E1 **Shemakha** Azerbaijan
61D2 **Shenandoah** USA
65D3 **Shenandoah** *R* USA
65D3 **Shenandoah Nat Pk** USA
48C4 **Shendam** Nigeria
50D2 **Shendi** Sudan
20G3 **Shenkursk** Russian Federation
31C2 **Shenmu** China
31E1 **Shenyang** China
31C5 **Shenzhen** China
42D3 **Sheopur** India
19F2 **Shepetovka** Ukraine
68B3 **Shepherdstown** USA
34C3 **Shepparton** Australia
7E4 **Sheppey** *I* England
55K2 **Sherard,C** Canada
7C4 **Sherborne** England
48A4 **Sherbro I** Sierra Leone
65E1 **Sherbrooke** Canada
68C1 **Sherburne** USA
42C3 **Shergarh** India
63D2 **Sheridan** Arkansas, USA
60B2 **Sheridan** Wyoming, USA
7E3 **Sheringham** England
63C2 **Sherman** USA
18B2 **'s-Hertogenbosch** Netherlands
10C1 **Shetland** *Is* Scotland
21J7 **Shevchenko** Kazakhstan
60D1 **Sheyenne** USA
60D1 **Sheyenne** *R* USA
41F4 **Sheyk Sho'eyb** *I* Iran
8B3 **Shiant, Sd of** Scotland
26J2 **Shiashkotan** *I* Kuril Is, Russian Federation
42B1 **Shibarghan** Afghanistan
29D3 **Shibata** Japan
29D2 **Shibetsu** Japan
49F1 **Shibîn el Kom** Egypt
45A3 **Shibîn el Qanâtir** Egypt
29C3 **Shibukawa** Japan
68B2 **Shickshinny** USA
28A3 **Shidao** China
31C2 **Shijiazhuang** China
42B3 **Shikarpur** Pakistan
26G3 **Shikoku** *I* Japan
29B4 **Shikoku-sanchi** *Mts* Japan
26H2 **Shikotan** *I* Russian Federation
29D2 **Shikotsu-ko** *L* Japan
20G3 **Shilega** Russian Federation
43F3 **Shiliguri** India
26E1 **Shilka** Russian Federation
26E1 **Shilka** *R* Russian Federation
68C2 **Shillington** USA
43G3 **Shillong** India
20G5 **Shilovo** Russian Federation
28B4 **Shimabara** Japan
29C4 **Shimada** Japan
26F1 **Shimanovsk** Russian Federation
29D3 **Shimizu** Japan
29C4 **Shimoda** Japan
44B3 **Shimoga** India
28C4 **Shimonoseki** Japan
29C3 **Shinano** *R* Japan
41G5 **Shināṣ** Oman
38E2 **Shindand** Afghanistan
68A2 **Shinglehouse** USA
29D4 **Shingū** Japan
29D3 **Shinjō** Japan
8C2 **Shin, Loch** *L* Scotland
29D3 **Shinminato** Japan
45D1 **Shinshār** Syria
50D4 **Shinyanga** Tanzania
29E3 **Shiogama** Japan
29C4 **Shiono-misaki** *C* Japan
31A5 **Shiping** China
68B2 **Shippensburg** USA
62A1 **Shiprock** USA
31B3 **Shiquan** China
29D3 **Shirakawa** Japan
29C3 **Shirane-san** *Mt* Japan
41F4 **Shīraz** Iran
45A3 **Shirbîn** Egypt
29F2 **Shiretoko-misaki** *C* Japan
29D2 **Shiriya-saki** *C* Japan
41F3 **Shīr Kūh** *Mt* Iran
29C3 **Shirotori** Japan
41G2 **Shirvān** Iran
54B3 **Shishmaref** USA
31B2 **Shitanjing** China
64B3 **Shively** USA
42D3 **Shivpuri** India
45C3 **Shivta** *Hist Site* Israel
59D3 **Shivwits Plat** USA
51D5 **Shiwa Ngandu** Zambia
31C3 **Shiyan** China
31B2 **Shizuishan** China
29C3 **Shizuoka** Japan
17D2 **Shkodër** Albania
19G2 **Shkov** Belarus
25L1 **Shmidta, Ostrov** *I* Russian Federation
34D2 **Shoalhaven** *R* Australia
28B4 **Shobara** Japan
44B3 **Shoranūr** India
44B2 **Shorāpur** India
59C3 **Shoshone** California, USA
58D2 **Shoshone** Idaho, USA
58E2 **Shoshone** *R* USA
58D2 **Shoshone L** USA
59C3 **Shoshone Mts** USA
58E2 **Shoshoni** USA
21E5 **Shostka** Ukraine
59D4 **Show Low** USA
63D2 **Shreveport** USA
7C3 **Shrewsbury** England
7C3 **Shropshire** *County* England
31E1 **Shuangliao** China
28B2 **Shuangyang** China
26G2 **Shuangyashan** China
21K6 **Shubar-Kuduk** Kazakhstan
20N2 **Shuga** Russian Federation
31D2 **Shu He** *R* China
31A4 **Shuicheng** China
42C3 **Shujaabad** Pakistan
42D4 **Shujālpur** India
26C2 **Shule He** *R* China
17F2 **Shumen** Bulgaria
20H4 **Shumerlya** Russian Federation
31D4 **Shuncheng** China
54C3 **Shungnak** USA
31C2 **Shuo Xian** China
38D3 **Shūr Gaz** Iran
51C5 **Shurugwi** Zimbabwe
20G4 **Shuya** Russian Federation
30B1 **Shwebo** Burma
30B2 **Shwegyin** Burma
42A2 **Siah Koh** *Mts* Afghanistan
42C2 **Sialkot** Pakistan
Sian = Xi'an
27F6 **Siargao** *I* Philippines
27F6 **Siaton** Philippines
19E1 **Šiauliai** Lithuania
20K5 **Sibay** Russian Federation
47E2 **Sibayi L** South Africa
16D2 **Šibenik** Croatia
25L5 **Siberia** Russian Federation
27C7 **Siberut** *I* Indonesia
42B3 **Sibi** Pakistan
50B4 **Sibiti** Congo
50D4 **Sibiti** *R* Tanzania
17E1 **Sibiu** Romania
61D2 **Sibley** USA
27C6 **Sibolga** Indonesia
43G3 **Sibsāgar** India
27E6 **Sibu** Malaysia
50B3 **Sibut** Central African Republic
31A3 **Sichuan** *Province* China
Sicilia = Sicily
16C3 **Sicilian Chan** Italy/Tunisia
16C3 **Sicily** *I* Medit Sea
72D6 **Sicuani** Peru
42C4 **Siddhapur** India
44B2 **Siddipet** India
43E4 **Sidhi** India
49E1 **Sidi Barrani** Egypt
15B2 **Sidi-bel-Abbès** Algeria
48B1 **Sidi Kacem** Morocco
8D3 **Sidlaw Hills** Scotland
76F5 **Sidley,Mt** Antarctica
7C4 **Sidmouth** England
58B1 **Sidney** Canada
60C1 **Sidney** Montana, USA
60C2 **Sidney** Nebraska, USA
68C1 **Sidney** New York, USA
64C2 **Sidney** Ohio, USA
67B2 **Sidney Lanier,L** USA
45C2 **Sidon** Lebanon
75B3 **Sidrolândia** Brazil
19E2 **Siedlce** Poland
13D2 **Sieg** *R* Germany
13D2 **Siegburg** Germany
13D2 **Siegen** Germany
30C3 **Siem Reap** Cambodia
16C2 **Siena** Italy
19D2 **Sierpc** Poland
62A2 **Sierra Blanca** USA
70B2 **Sierra de los Alamitos** *Mts* Mexico
48A4 **Sierra Leone** *Republic* Africa
48A4 **Sierra Leone,C** Sierra Leone
70B3 **Sierra Madre del Sur** Mexico
66B3 **Sierra Madre Mts** USA
70B2 **Sierra Madre Occidental** *Mts* Mexico
70B2 **Sierra Madre Oriental** *Mts* Mexico
56C4 **Sierra Mojada** Mexico
59B3 **Sierra Nevada** *Mts* USA
59D4 **Sierra Vista** USA
75A3 **Siete Puntas** *R* Paraguay
17E3 **Sífnos** *I* Greece
15B2 **Sig** Algeria
20E2 **Sig** Russian Federation
19E3 **Sighetu Marmaţiei** Romania
17E1 **Sighişoara** Romania
12B1 **Siglufjörður** Iceland
72A1 **Siguatepeque** Honduras
15B1 **Sigüenza** Spain
48B3 **Siguiri** Guinea
30C3 **Sihanoukville** Cambodia
42D4 **Sihora** India
40D2 **Siirt** Turkey
43J1 **Sikandarabad** India
42D3 **Sikar** India
42B2 **Sikaram** *Mt* Afghanistan
48B3 **Sikasso** Mali
63E1 **Sikeston** USA
26G2 **Sikhote-Alin'** *Mts* Russian Federation
17F3 **Síkinos** *I* Greece
17E3 **Sikionía** Greece
43F3 **Sikkim** *State* India
25O3 **Siktyakh** Russian Federation
15A1 **Sil** *R* Spain
43G4 **Silchar** India
48C2 **Silet** Algeria
43E3 **Silgarhi** Nepal
40B2 **Silifke** Turkey
45D1 **Şilinfah** Syria
39G2 **Siling Co** *L* China
17F2 **Silistra** Bulgaria
20A3 **Siljan** *L* Sweden
12F7 **Silkeborg** Denmark
6C2 **Silloth** England
63D1 **Siloam Springs** USA
63D2 **Silsbee** USA
50B2 **Siltou** *Well* Chad
19E1 **Šilute** Lithuania
40D2 **Silvan** Turkey
75C2 **Silvania** Brazil
42C4 **Silvassa** India
61E1 **Silver Bay** USA
59C3 **Silver City** Nevada, USA
62A2 **Silver City** New Mexico, USA
58B2 **Silver Lake** USA
66D2 **Silver Peak Range** *Mts* USA
68B3 **Silver Spring** USA
34B2 **Silverton** Australia
62A1 **Silverton** USA
27E6 **Simanggang** Malaysia
30C1 **Simao** China
65D1 **Simard,L** Canada
41E3 **Simareh** *R* Iran
17F3 **Simav** Turkey
17F3 **Simav** *R* Turkey
65D2 **Simcoe,L** Canada
27C6 **Simeulue** *I* Indonesia
21E7 **Simferopol'** Ukraine
17F3 **Sími** *I* Greece
43E3 **Simikot** Nepal
42D2 **Simla** India
60C3 **Simla** USA
13D2 **Simmern** Germany
66C3 **Simmler** USA
47B3 **Simonstown** South Africa
14D2 **Simplon** *Mt* Switzerland
16B1 **Simplon** *Pass* Italy/Switzerland
54C2 **Simpson,C** USA
32C3 **Simpson Desert** Australia
55K3 **Simpson Pen** Canada
12G7 **Simrishamn** Sweden
26J2 **Simushir** *I* Kuril Is, Russian Federation
50E3 **Sina Dhaga** Somalia
40B4 **Sinai** *Pen* Egypt
72C2 **Sincelejo** Colombia
67B2 **Sinclair,L** USA
75D1 **Sincora, Serra do** *Mts* Brazil
42D3 **Sind** *R* India
42B3 **Sindh** *Province* Pakistan
17F3 **Sindirği** Turkey
43F4 **Sindri** India
15A2 **Sines** Portugal
15A2 **Sines, Cabo de** *C* Portugal
50D2 **Singa** Sudan
30C5 **Singapore** *Republic* SE Asia
30C5 **Singapore,Str of** SE Asia
27E7 **Singaraja** Indonesia
13E4 **Singen** Germany
50D4 **Singida** Tanzania
43H3 **Singkaling Hkamti** Burma
27D6 **Singkawang** Indonesia
27D7 **Singkep** *I* Indonesia
34D2 **Singleton** Australia
30B1 **Singu** Burma
47E1 **Singuédeze** *R* Mozambique
28A3 **Sin'gye** N Korea
28A2 **Sinhŭng** N Korea
16B2 **Siniscola** Sardinia, Italy
40D2 **Sinjár** Iraq
42B2 **Sinkai Hills** *Mts* Afghanistan
50D2 **Sinkat** Sudan
39G1 **Sinkiang** *Autonomous Region* China
43K2 **Sinkobabad** India
73H2 **Sinnamary** French Guiana
45B4 **Sinn Bishr, Gebel** *Mt* Egypt
28A3 **Sinnyong** S Korea
40C1 **Sinop** Turkey
28A2 **Sinpa** N Korea
28A2 **Sinp'o** N Korea
28A3 **Sinp'yong** N Korea
17E1 **Sintana** Romania
27E6 **Sintang** Indonesia
63C3 **Sinton** USA
15A2 **Sintra** Portugal
72C2 **Sinú** *R* Colombia
28A2 **Sinŭiju** N Korea
19D3 **Siófok** Hungary
16B1 **Sion** Switzerland
61D2 **Sioux City** USA
61D2 **Sioux Falls** USA
69L1 **Siparia** Trinidad
28A2 **Siping** China
76F3 **Siple** *Base* Antarctica
76F5 **Siple I** Antarctica
27C7 **Sipora** *I* Indonesia
63E2 **Sipsey** *R* USA
45B4 **Sîq, Wadi el** Egypt
44B3 **Sira** India
Siracusa = Syracuse
43F4 **Sirajganj** Bangladesh
41F5 **Şīr Banī Yās** *I* UAE
32C2 **Sir Edward Pellew Group** *Is* Australia
17F1 **Siret** *R* Romania
40C3 **Sirhān, Wādi as** *V* Jordan/Saudi Arabia
40D2 **Şirnak** Turkey
42C4 **Sirohi** India
44C2 **Sironcha** India
42D4 **Sironj** India
17E3 **Síros** *I* Greece
66C3 **Sirretta Peak** *Mt* USA
41F4 **Sīrrī** *I* Iran
42C3 **Sirsa** India
44A3 **Sirsi** India
49D1 **Sirt** Libya
49D1 **Sirte Desert** Libya
49D1 **Sirte,G of** Libya
21H9 **Sirvan** *R* Iran
16D1 **Sisak** Croatia
30C2 **Sisaket** Thailand
30C3 **Sisophon** Cambodia
66B3 **Sisquoc** USA
66C3 **Sisquoc** *R* USA
61D1 **Sisseton** USA
13B3 **Sissonne** France
14D3 **Sisteron** France
25L4 **Sistig Khem** Russian Federation
43E3 **Sītāpur** India
17F3 **Sitía** Greece
75C1 **Sítio d'Abadia** Brazil
54E4 **Sitka** USA
30B2 **Sittang** *R* Burma
13C2 **Sittard** Netherlands
43G4 **Sittwe** Burma
40C2 **Sivas** Turkey
40C2 **Siverek** Turkey
40B2 **Sivrihisar** Turkey
25S4 **Sivuchiy, Mys** *C* Russian Federation
49E2 **Siwa** Egypt
42D2 **Siwalik Range** *Mts* India
43E3 **Siwalik Range** *Mts* Nepal
20G3 **Siya** Russian Federation
31D3 **Siyang** China
18C1 **Sjaelland** *I* Denmark
12G7 **Skagen** Denmark
12F7 **Skagerrak** *Str* Denmark/Norway
58B1 **Skagit** *R* USA
58B1 **Skagit Mt** Canada
54E4 **Skagway** USA
68B1 **Skaneateles** USA
68B1 **Skaneateles L** USA
12G7 **Skara** Sweden
19E2 **Skarzysko-Kamienna** Poland
54F4 **Skeena** *R* Canada
54F4 **Skeene Mts** Canada
54D3 **Skeenjek** *R* USA
7E3 **Skegness** England
20B2 **Skellefte** *R* Sweden
12J6 **Skellefteå** Sweden
9C3 **Skerries** Irish Republic
17E3 **Skíathos** *I* Greece
54E4 **Skidegate** Canada
19E2 **Skiemiewice** Poland
12F7 **Skien** Norway
16B3 **Skikda** Algeria
6D3 **Skipton** England
17E3 **Skíros** *I* Greece
12F7 **Skive** Denmark
18B1 **Skjern** Denmark
55O3 **Skjoldungen** Greenland
64B2 **Skokie** USA
17E3 **Skópelos** *I* Greece
17E2 **Skopje** Macedonia, Yugoslavia
12G7 **Skövde** Sweden
25O4 **Skovorodino** Russian Federation
65F2 **Skowhegan** USA
47E1 **Skukuza** South Africa
54C3 **Skwentna** USA
18D2 **Skwierzyna** Poland
10B2 **Skye** *I* Scotland
12G7 **Slagelse** Denmark
27D7 **Slamet** *Mt* Indonesia
9C3 **Slaney** *R* Irish Republic
17E2 **Slatina** Romania
54G3 **Slave** *R* Canada
19G2 **Slavgorod** Belarus
24J4 **Slavgorod** Russian Federation
19F2 **Slavuta** Ukraine
21F6 **Slavyansk** Ukraine
18D2 **Sławno** Poland
7D3 **Sleaford** England
8C3 **Sleat,Sound of** *Chan* Scotland
54C3 **Sleetmute** USA
63E2 **Slidell** USA
68C2 **Slide Mt** USA
9B3 **Slieve Aughty Mts** Irish Republic
9C3 **Slieve Bloom** *Mts* Irish Republic
10B3 **Sligo** Irish Republic
10B3 **Sligo B** Irish Republic
17F2 **Sliven** Bulgaria
59C3 **Sloan** USA
17F2 **Slobozia** Romania
19F2 **Slonim** Belarus
7D4 **Slough** England
66B2 **Slough** *R* USA
19D3 **Slovakia** *Republic* Europe
16C1 **Slovenia** *Republic* Europe
18C2 **Słubice** Poland
19F2 **Sluch'** *R* Ukraine
18D2 **Słupsk** Poland
19F2 **Slutsk** Belarus
19F2 **Slutsk** *R* Belarus
10A3 **Slyne Head** *Pt* Irish Republic
25M4 **Slyudyanka** Russian Federation
55M4 **Smallwood Res** Canada
48A2 **Smara** Morocco
17E2 **Smederevo** Serbia, Yugoslavia
17E2 **Smederevska Palanka** Serbia, Yugoslavia
21E6 **Smela** Ukraine
68A2 **Smethport** USA
66C1 **Smith** USA
54F3 **Smith Arm** *B* Canada
54F4 **Smithers** Canada
67C1 **Smithfield** N Carolina, USA
47D3 **Smithfield** South Africa
58D2 **Smithfield** Utah, USA
55L3 **Smith I** Canada
65D2 **Smiths Falls** Canada
34C4 **Smithton** Australia
60C3 **Smoky** *R* USA
34D2 **Smoky C** Australia
60D3 **Smoky Hills** USA
58D2 **Smoky Mts** USA
12F6 **Smøla** *I* Norway
20E5 **Smolensk** Russian Federation
17E2 **Smólikas** *Mt* Greece
17E2 **Smolyan** Bulgaria

Stikine
Tambacounda

54F4 **Stikine** *R* Canada
61E1 **Stillwater** Minnesota, USA
63C1 **Stillwater** Oklahoma, USA
59C3 **Stillwater Range** *Mts* USA
62B1 **Stinnett** USA
34A2 **Stirling** Australia
8D3 **Stirling** Scotland
12G6 **Stjørdal** Norway
13E4 **Stockach** Germany
68D1 **Stockbridge** USA
18D3 **Stockerau** Austria
12H7 **Stockholm** Sweden
7C3 **Stockport** England
66B2 **Stockton** California, USA
6D2 **Stockton** England
63D3 **Stockton** Kansas, USA
63D1 **Stockton L** USA
7C3 **Stoke-on-Trent** England
12G5 **Stokmarknes** Norway
25P2 **Stolbovoy, Ostrov** *I* Russian Federation
12K8 **Stolbtsy** Russian Federation
19F2 **Stolin** Belarus
7C3 **Stone** England
68C3 **Stone Harbor** USA
8D3 **Stonehaven** Scotland
63C2 **Stonewall** USA
7D3 **Stony Stratford** England
12H5 **Storavan** *L* Sweden
12G6 **Støren** Norway
34C4 **Storm B** Australia
61D2 **Storm Lake** USA
8B2 **Stornoway** Scotland
19F3 **Storozhinets** Ukraine
68D2 **Storrs** USA
12G6 **Storsjön** *L* Sweden
12H5 **Storuman** Sweden
60B2 **Story** USA
68E1 **Stoughton** USA
7E4 **Stour** *R* England
7C3 **Stourbridge** England
7C3 **Stourport** England
7E3 **Stowmarket** England
9C2 **Strabane** Northern Ireland
34C4 **Strahan** Australia
18C2 **Stralsund** Germany
47B3 **Strand** South Africa
12F6 **Stranda** Norway
9D2 **Strangford Lough** *L* Irish Republic
12H7 **Strängnäs** Sweden
8C4 **Stranraer** Scotland
14D2 **Strasbourg** France
65D3 **Strasburg** USA
66C2 **Stratford** California, USA
64C2 **Stratford** Canada
68D2 **Stratford** Connecticut, USA
35B1 **Stratford** New Zealand
62B1 **Stratford** Texas, USA
7D3 **Stratford-on-Avon** England
34A3 **Strathalbyn** Australia
8C4 **Strathclyde** *Region* Scotland
65E1 **Stratton** USA
64B2 **Streator** USA
8D2 **Stroma, I** Scotland
16D3 **Stromboli** *I* Italy
8D2 **Stromness** Scotland
61D2 **Stromsburg** USA
12H6 **Stromsund** Sweden
12G6 **Ströms Vattudal** *L* Sweden
8D2 **Stronsay** *I* Scotland
7C4 **Stroud** England
68C2 **Stroudsburg** USA
17E2 **Struma** *R* Bulgaria
7B3 **Strumble Head** *Pt* Wales
17E2 **Strumica** Macedonia, Yugoslavia
19E3 **Stryy** Ukraine
19E3 **Stryy** *R* Ukraine
34B1 **Strzelecki Creek** *R* Australia
67B3 **Stuart** Florida, USA
60D2 **Stuart** Nebraska, USA
54F4 **Stuart L** Canada
12G8 **Stubice** Poland
30D3 **Stung Sen** *R* Cambodia
30D3 **Stung Treng** Cambodia
16B2 **Stura** *R* Italy
76G7 **Sturge I** Antarctica
64B2 **Sturgeon Bay** USA
65D1 **Sturgeon Falls** Canada
64B3 **Sturgis** Kentucky, USA
64B2 **Sturgis** Michigan, USA
60C2 **Sturgis** S Dakota, USA
32B2 **Sturt Creek** *R* Australia
34B1 **Sturt Desert** Australia
47D3 **Stutterheim** South Africa
63D2 **Stuttgart** USA
18B3 **Stuttgart** Germany
12A1 **Stykkishólmur** Iceland
19F2 **Styr'** *R* Ukraine
75D2 **Suaçuí Grande** *R* Brazil
50D2 **Suakin** Sudan
28A3 **Suan** N Korea
31E5 **Suao** Taiwan
17D1 **Subotica** Serbia, Yugoslavia
21D6 **Suceava** Romania
72E7 **Sucre** Bolivia
75B2 **Sucuriú** *R* Brazil
50C2 **Sudan** *Republic* Africa
64C1 **Sudbury** Canada
7E3 **Sudbury** England
50C3 **Sudd** *Swamp* Sudan
73G2 **Suddie** Guyana
45B4 **Sudr** Egypt
50C3 **Sue** *R* Sudan
40B4 **Suez** Egypt
40B3 **Suez Canal** Egypt
40B4 **Suez,G of** Egypt
68C2 **Suffern** USA
65D3 **Suffolk** USA
7E3 **Suffolk** *County* England
65E2 **Sugarloaf Mt** USA
34D2 **Sugarloaf Pt** Australia
25R3 **Sugoy** *R* Russian Federation
41G5 **Suḥār** Oman
26D1 **Sühbaatar** Mongolia
42B3 **Sui** Pakistan
31C2 **Suide** China
28C2 **Suifen He** *R* China
26F2 **Suihua** China
31B3 **Suining** China
13C3 **Suippes** France
10B3 **Suir** *R* Irish Republic
31C3 **Sui Xian** China
31E1 **Suizhong** China
42C3 **Sujāngarh** India
27D7 **Sukadana** Indonesia
29E3 **Sukagawa** Japan
26C3 **Sukai Hu** *L* China
28B3 **Sukch'ŏn** N Korea
20F5 **Sukhinichi** Russian Federation
20G4 **Sukhona** *R* Russian Federation
21G7 **Sukhumi** Georgia
55N3 **Sukkertoppen** Greenland
55N3 **Sukkertoppen Isflade** *Ice field* Greenland
12L6 **Sukkozero** Russian Federation
42B3 **Sukkur** Pakistan
44C2 **Sukma** India
51B6 **Sukses** Namibia
28B4 **Sukumo** Japan
21F5 **Sula** *R* Russian Federation
42B3 **Sulaiman Range** *Mts* Pakistan
32B1 **Sula, Kepulauan** *I* Indonesia
8B2 **Sula Sgeir** *I* Scotland
27E7 **Sulawesi** *Is* Indonesia
41E2 **Sulaymānīyah** Iraq
8C2 **Sule Skerry** *I* Scotland
17F1 **Sulina** Romania
13E1 **Sulingen** Germany
12H5 **Sulitjelma** Norway
72B4 **Sullana** Peru
63D1 **Sullivan** USA
13B4 **Sully-sur-Loire** France
16C2 **Sulmona** Italy
63D2 **Sulphur** Louisiana, USA
63C2 **Sulphur** Oklahoma, USA
63C2 **Sulphur Springs** USA
21E8 **Sultan Dağları** *Mts* Turkey
43E3 **Sultānpur** India
27F6 **Sulu Arch** *Is* Philippines
27E6 **Sulu S** Philippines
13E3 **Sulz** Germany
74D3 **Sumampa** Argentina
27C6 **Sumatera** *I* Indonesia
27E8 **Sumba** *I* Indonesia
27E7 **Sumbawa** *I* Indonesia
27E7 **Sumbawa Besar** Indonesia
51D4 **Sumbawanga** Tanzania
51B5 **Sumbe** Angola
8E2 **Sumburgh Head** *Pt* Scotland
43N2 **Sumesar Ra** *Mts* Nepal
21H7 **Sumgait** Azerbaijan
26H3 **Sumisu** *I* Japan
54F4 **Summit Lake** Canada
59C3 **Summit Mt** USA
35B2 **Sumner,L** New Zealand
29B4 **Sumoto** Japan
67B2 **Sumter** USA
21E5 **Sumy** Ukraine
58D1 **Sun** *R* USA
29D2 **Sunagawa** Japan
28A3 **Sunan** N Korea
8C3 **Sunart, Loch** *Inlet* Scotland
68B2 **Sunbury** USA
28B3 **Sunch'ŏn** N Korea
28B4 **Sunch'ŏn** S Korea
60C2 **Sundance** USA
43E4 **Sundargarh** India
43F4 **Sunderbans** *Swamp* Bangladesh/India
6D2 **Sunderland** England
65D1 **Sundridge** Canada
12H6 **Sundsvall** Sweden
58C1 **Sunnyside** USA
59B3 **Sunnyvale** USA
64B2 **Sun Prairie** USA
25N3 **Suntar** Russian Federation
58D2 **Sun Valley** USA
48B4 **Sunyani** Ghana
20E3 **Suojarvi** Russian Federation
28B4 **Suō-nada** *B* Japan
12K6 **Suonenjoki** Finland
43F3 **Supaul** India
59D4 **Superior** Arizona, USA
61D2 **Superior** Nebraska, USA
64A1 **Superior** Wisconsin, USA
64B1 **Superior,L** Canada/USA
30C3 **Suphan Buri** Thailand
40D2 **Süphan Dağ** *Mt* Turkey
27G7 **Supiori** *I* Indonesia
41E3 **Sūq ash Suyūkh** Iraq
45D1 **Şuqaylibīyah** Syria
31D3 **Suqian** China
Suqutra = Socotra
38D3 **Sūr** Oman
20H5 **Sura** *R* Russian Federation
27E7 **Surabaya** Indonesia
29C4 **Suraga-wan** *B* Japan
27E7 **Surakarta** Indonesia
45D1 **Şūrān** Syria
34C1 **Surat** Australia
42C4 **Sūrat** India
42C3 **Sūratgarh** India
30B4 **Surat Thani** Thailand
42C4 **Surendranagar** India
68C3 **Surf City** USA
24J3 **Surgut** Russian Federation
44B2 **Suriāpet** India
27F6 **Surigao** Philippines
30C3 **Surin** Thailand
73G3 **Surinam** *Republic* S America
66B2 **Sur,Pt** USA
7D4 **Surrey** *County* England
49D1 **Surt** Libya
12A2 **Surtsey** *I* Iceland
16B1 **Susa** Italy
28B4 **Susa** Japan
29B4 **Susaki** Japan
59B2 **Susanville** USA
68C2 **Susquehanna** USA
68B3 **Susquehanna** *R* USA
68C2 **Sussex** USA
7D4 **Sussex West** England
47C3 **Sutherland** South Africa
60C2 **Sutherland** USA
42C2 **Sutlej** *R* Pakistan
59B3 **Sutter Creek** USA
64C3 **Sutton** USA
29D2 **Suttsu** Japan
29D3 **Suwa** Japan
19E2 **Suwałki** Poland
67B3 **Suwannee** *R* USA
45C2 **Suweilih** Jordan
28B3 **Suwŏn** S Korea
31D3 **Su Xian** China
29C3 **Suzaka** Japan
31E3 **Suzhou** China
29D3 **Suzu** Japan
29C4 **Suzuka** Japan
29C3 **Suzu-misaki** *C* Japan
24C2 **Svalbard** *Is* Barents Sea
19E3 **Svalyava** Ukraine
55N2 **Svartenhuk Halvø** *Region* Greenland
12G5 **Svartisen** *Mt* Norway
30D3 **Svay Rieng** Cambodia
12G6 **Sveg** Sweden
12G7 **Svendborg** Denmark
Sverdlovsk = Yekaterinburg
55J1 **Sverdrup Chan** Canada
54H2 **Sverdrup Is** Canada
26G2 **Svetlaya** Russian Federation
19E2 **Svetlogorsk** Russian Federation
12K6 **Svetogorsk** Russian Federation
17E2 **Svetozarevo** Serbia, Yugoslavia
17F2 **Svilengrad** Bulgaria
19F2 **Svir'** Belarus
20E3 **Svir'** *R* Russian Federation
18D3 **Švitavy** Czech Republic
26F1 **Svobodnyy** Russian Federation
12G5 **Svolvær** Norway
7E3 **Swaffam** England
33E3 **Swain Reefs** Australia
67B2 **Swainsboro** USA
33H2 **Swains I** American Samoa
47B1 **Swakop** *R* Namibia
47A1 **Swakopmund** Namibia
6D2 **Swale** *R* England
27E6 **Swallow Reef** S China Sea
44B3 **Swāmihalli** India
70D3 **Swan** *I* Honduras
7D4 **Swanage** England
34B3 **Swan Hill** Australia
69A3 **Swan I** Caribbean Sea
54H4 **Swan River** Canada
7C4 **Swansea** Wales
7C4 **Swansea B** Wales
47C3 **Swartberge** *Mts* South Africa
47D2 **Swartruggens** South Africa
Swatow = Shantou
47E2 **Swaziland** *Kingdom* South Africa
12G7 **Sweden** *Kingdom* N Europe
58B2 **Sweet Home** USA
62B2 **Sweetwater** USA
60B2 **Sweetwater** *R* USA
47C3 **Swellendam** South Africa
18D2 **Świdnica** Poland
18D2 **Świdwin** Poland
18D2 **Świebodzin** Poland
19D2 **Świecie** Poland
54H4 **Swift Current** Canada
9C2 **Swilly, Lough** *Estuary* Irish Republic
7D4 **Swindon** England
18C2 **Świnoujście** Poland
14D2 **Switzerland** Europe
9C3 **Swords** Irish Republic
43M1 **Syang** Nepal
9A3 **Sybil Pt** Irish Republic
34D2 **Sydney** Australia
20H3 **Syktyvkar** Russian Federation
67A2 **Sylacauga** USA
12G6 **Sylarna** *Mt* Sweden
43G4 **Sylhet** Bangladesh
18B1 **Sylt** *I* Germany
64C2 **Sylvania** USA
76G11 **Syowa** *Base* Antarctica
16D3 **Syracuse** Italy
62B1 **Syracuse** Kansas, USA
68B1 **Syracuse** New York, USA
65D2 **Syracuse** USA
24H5 **Syr Darya** *R* Kazakhstan
40C2 **Syria** *Republic* SW Asia
20L4 **Sysert'** Russian Federation
20H5 **Syzran'** Russian Federation
18C2 **Szczecin** Poland
18D2 **Szczecinek** Poland
19E2 **Szczytno** Poland
19E3 **Szeged** Hungary
19D3 **Székesfehérvar** Hungary
19D3 **Szekszárd** Hungary
19D3 **Szolnok** Hungary
18D3 **Szombathely** Hungary
18D2 **Szprotawa** Poland

T

47D3 **Tabankulu** South Africa
32E1 **Tabar Is** Papua New Guinea
16B3 **Tabarka** Tunisia
41G3 **Tabas** Iran
72E4 **Tabatinga** Brazil
48B2 **Tabelbala** Algeria
30C3 **Tabeng** Cambodia
54G5 **Taber** Canada
47B3 **Table Mt** South Africa
63D1 **Table Rock Res** USA
18C3 **Tábor** Czech Republic
50D4 **Tabora** Tanzania
20L4 **Tabory** Russian Federation
48B4 **Tabou** Ivory Coast
41E2 **Tabrīz** Iran
40C4 **Tabūk** Saudi Arabia
39G1 **Tacheng** China
27F5 **Tacloban** Philippines
72D7 **Tacna** Peru
59D4 **Tacna** USA
56A2 **Tacoma** USA
68D1 **Taconic Range** USA
75A3 **Tacuatí** Paraguay
48C2 **Tademait, Plateau du** Algeria
50E2 **Tadjoura** Djibouti
65F1 **Tadoussac** Canada
44B3 **Tādpatri** India
28B3 **Taebaek Sanmaek** *Mts* N Korea/S Korea
28B3 **T'aech'ŏn** N Korea
28A3 **Taech'on** S Korea
28A3 **Taedasa-Do** N Korea
28A3 **Taedong** *R* N Korea
28A3 **Taegang-got** *Pen* N Korea
28B3 **Taegu** S Korea
28A2 **Taehung** N Korea
28B3 **Taejŏn** S Korea
15B1 **Tafalla** Spain
48C2 **Tafasaset** *Watercourse* Algeria
7C4 **Taff** *R* Wales
45C3 **Tafila** Jordan
66C3 **Taft** USA
21F6 **Taganrog** Russian Federation
48A3 **Tagant** *Region* Mauritius
48B2 **Taguenout Hagguerete** *Well* Mali
33E2 **Tagula** *I* Papua New Guinea
Tagus = Tejo
48C2 **Tahat** *Mt* Algeria
37M5 **Tahiti** *I* Pacific Ocean
63C1 **Tahlequah** USA
59B3 **Tahoe City** USA
59B3 **Tahoe,L** USA
62B2 **Tahoka** USA
48C3 **Tahoua** Niger
40B4 **Tahta** Egypt
27F6 **Tahuna** Indonesia
31D2 **Tai'an** China
28A2 **Tai'an** China
31B3 **Taibai Shan** *Mt* China
31D1 **Taibus Qi** China
31E5 **Taichung** Taiwan
35B3 **Taieri** *R* New Zealand
31C2 **Taihang Shan** *Upland* China
35C1 **Taihape** New Zealand
31E3 **Tai Hu** *L* China
29D2 **Taiki** Japan
34A3 **Tailem Bend** Australia
8C3 **Tain** Scotland
31E5 **Tainan** Taiwan
75D2 **Taiobeiras** Brazil
31E5 **Taipei** Taiwan
30C5 **Taiping** Malaysia
29D3 **Taira** Japan
28B3 **Taisha** Japan
74B7 **Taitao,Pen de** Chile
31E5 **Taitung** Taiwan
12K5 **Taivalkoski** Finland
26F4 **Taiwan** *Republic* China
31D5 **Taiwan Str** China/Taiwan
45C3 **Taiyiba** Jordan
31C2 **Taiyuan** China
31D3 **Taizhou** China
50E2 **Ta'izz** Yemen
39E2 **Tajikistan** *Republic* Asia
15B1 **Tajo** *R* Spain
30B2 **Tak** Thailand
32B1 **Takabonerate, Kepulauan** *Is* Indonesia
29D3 **Takada** Japan
29B4 **Takahashi** Japan
35B2 **Takaka** New Zealand
29C4 **Takamatsu** Japan
29D3 **Takaoka** Japan
35B1 **Takapuna** New Zealand
29D3 **Takasaki** Japan
29C3 **Takayama** Japan
29D3 **Takefu** Japan
27C6 **Takengon** Indonesia
30C3 **Takeo** Cambodia
28B4 **Takeo** Japan
Take-shima = Tok-do
41E2 **Takestān** Iran
28B4 **Taketa** Japan
29D2 **Takikawa** Japan
29D2 **Takinoue** Japan
54G3 **Takiyvak L** Canada
50D2 **Takkaze** *R* Eritrea/Ethiopia
48B4 **Takoradi** Ghana
42C2 **Talagang** Pakistan
44B4 **Talaimannar** Sri Lanka
48C3 **Talak** *Desert Region* Niger
72B4 **Talara** Peru
32E1 **Talasea** Papua New Guinea
45B3 **Talata** Egypt
27F6 **Talaud, Kepulauan** *Is* Indonesia
15B2 **Talavera de la Reina** Spain
74B5 **Talca** Chile
74B5 **Talcahuano** Chile
43F4 **Tālcher** India
39F1 **Taldy Kurgan** Kazakhstan
27F7 **Taliabu** *I* Indonesia
42B1 **Taligan** Afghanistan
50D3 **Tali Post** Sudan
27E7 **Taliwang** Indonesia
54D3 **Talkeetna** USA
45A3 **Talkha** Egypt
67A2 **Talladega** USA
40D2 **Tall 'Afar** Iraq
67B2 **Tallahassee** USA
45D1 **Tall Bīsah** Syria
20C4 **Tallinn** Estonia
40C3 **Tall Kalakh** Syria
63D2 **Tallulah** USA
26B1 **Tal'menka** Russian Federation
21E6 **Tal'noye** Ukraine
19E2 **Talpaki** Russian Federation
74B3 **Taltal** Chile
34C1 **Talwood** Australia
61E2 **Tama** USA
27E6 **Tamabo Ra** *Mts* Borneo
48B4 **Tamale** Ghana
29C4 **Tamano** Japan
48C2 **Tamanrasset** Algeria
48C2 **Tamanrasset** *Watercourse* Algeria
68C2 **Tamaqua** USA
7B4 **Tamar** *R* England
Tamatave = Toamasina
48A3 **Tambacounda** Senegal

Trikomo
Upper Lough Erne

45B1 **Trikomo** Cyprus
9C3 **Trim** Irish Republic
44C4 **Trincomalee** Sri Lanka
52G6 **Trindade** *I* Atlantic Ocean
72F6 **Trinidad** Bolivia
74E4 **Trinidad** Uruguay
62B1 **Trinidad** USA
69E4 **Trinidad** *I* Caribbean Sea
69E4 **Trinidad & Tobago** *Is Republic* Caribbean Sea
63C2 **Trinity** USA
56D3 **Trinity** *R* USA
55N5 **Trinity B** Canada
67A2 **Trion** USA
45C1 **Tripoli** Lebanon
49D1 **Tripoli** Libya
17E3 **Trípolis** Greece
43G4 **Tripura** *State* India
52H6 **Tristan da Cunha** *Is* Atlantic Ocean
19D3 **Trnava** Slovakia
32E1 **Trobriand Is** Papua New Guinea
65F1 **Trois Pistoles** Canada
65E1 **Trois-Riviéres** Canada
20L5 **Troitsk** Russian Federation
20K3 **Troitsko Pechorsk** Russian Federation
12G7 **Trollhättan** Sweden
12F6 **Trollheimen** *Mt* Norway
46K9 **Tromelin** *I* Indian Ocean
47D3 **Trompsburg** South Africa
12H5 **Tromsø** Norway
66D3 **Trona** USA
12G6 **Trondheim** Norway
12G6 **Trondheimfjord** *Inlet* Norway
45B1 **Troödos Range** *Mts* Cyprus
8C4 **Troon** Scotland
52J3 **Tropic of Cancer**
52K6 **Tropic of Capricorn**
48B2 **Troudenni** Mali
55J4 **Trout L** Ontario, Canada
58E2 **Trout Peak** *Mt* USA
68B2 **Trout Run** USA
7C4 **Trowbridge** England
67A2 **Troy** Alabama, USA
58C1 **Troy** Montana, USA
68D1 **Troy** New York, USA
64C2 **Troy** Ohio, USA
68B2 **Troy** Pennsylvania, USA
17E2 **Troyan** Bulgaria
13C3 **Troyes** France
59C3 **Troy Peak** *Mt* USA
41F5 **Trucial Coast** *Region* UAE
59B3 **Truckee** *R* USA
70D3 **Trujillo** Honduras
72C5 **Trujillo** Peru
15A2 **Trujillo** Spain
72D2 **Trujillo** Venezuela
59D3 **Trumbull,Mt** USA
34C2 **Trundle** Australia
55M5 **Truro** Canada
7B4 **Truro** England
62A2 **Truth or Consequences** USA
26C2 **Tsagaan Nuur** *L* Mongolia
26C1 **Tsagan-Tologoy** Russian Federation
51E5 **Tsaratanana** Madagascar
51C6 **Tsau** Botswana
50D4 **Tsavo** Kenya
50D4 **Tsavo Nat Pk** Kenya
60C1 **Tschida,L** USA
24J4 **Tselinograd** Kazakhstan
47B2 **Tses** Namibia
26D2 **Tsetserleg** Mongolia
48C4 **Tsévié** Togo
47C2 **Tshabong** Botswana
47C1 **Tshane** Botswana
21F6 **Tshchikskoye Vdkhr** *Res* Russian Federation
50B4 **Tshela** Zaïre
51C4 **Tshibala** Zaïre
50C4 **Tshikapa** Zaïre
50C4 **Tshuapa** *R* Zaïre
21G6 **Tsimlyanskoye Vodokhranilishche** *Res* Russian Federation
Tsinan = Jinan
Tsingtao = Qingdao
51E6 **Tsiombe** Madagascar
51E5 **Tsiroanomandidy** Madagascar
19F2 **Tsna** *R* Belarus
31B1 **Tsogt Ovoo** Mongolia
47D3 **Tsomo** South Africa
26D2 **Tsomog** Mongolia
29C4 **Tsu** Japan
29C3 **Tsubata** Japan
29E3 **Tsuchiura** Japan
29E2 **Tsugarū-kaikyō** *Str* Japan
51B5 **Tsumeb** Namibia
51B6 **Tsumis** Namibia
29D3 **Tsuruga** Japan
29C3 **Tsurugi** Japan
29D3 **Tsuruoka** Japan
29C3 **Tsushima** Japan
28B4 **Tsushima** *Is* Japan
Tsushima-Kaikyō = Korea Str
29C3 **Tsuyama** Japan
15A1 **Tua** *R* Portugal
37M5 **Tuamotu, Îles** Pacific Ocean
21F7 **Tuapse** Russian Federation
35A3 **Tuatapere** New Zealand
59D3 **Tuba City** USA
37M6 **Tubai, Îles** Pacific Ocean
74G3 **Tubarão** Brazil
45C2 **Tubas** Israel
18B3 **Tübingen** Germany
49E1 **Tubruq** Libya
68C3 **Tuckerton** USA
59D4 **Tucson** USA
74C3 **Tucumán** *State* Argentina
62B1 **Tucumcari** USA
72F2 **Tucupita** Venezuela
15B1 **Tudela** Spain
40C3 **Tudmur** Syria
47E2 **Tugela** *R* South Africa
34D2 **Tuggerah L** Australia
27F5 **Tuguegarao** Philippines
25P4 **Tugur** Russian Federation
31D2 **Tuhai He** *R* China
27F7 **Tukangbesi, Kepulauan** *Is* Indonesia
54E3 **Tuktoyaktuk** Canada
19E1 **Tukums** Latvia
25O4 **Tukuringra, Khrebet** *Mts* Russian Federation
51D4 **Tukuyu** Tanzania
42B1 **Tukzar** Afghanistan
20F5 **Tula** Russian Federation
66C2 **Tulare** USA
66C2 **Tulare Lake Bed** USA
62A2 **Tularosa** USA
72C3 **Tulcán** Ecuador
21D6 **Tulcea** Romania
19F3 **Tul'chin** Ukraine
66C2 **Tule** *R* USA
51C6 **Tuli** Zimbabwe
47D1 **Tuli** *R* Zimbabwe
62B2 **Tulia** USA
45C2 **Tulkarm** Israel
67A1 **Tullahoma** USA
9C3 **Tullarnore** Irish Republic
14C2 **Tulle** France
63D2 **Tullos** USA
9C3 **Tullow** Irish Republic
68B1 **Tully** USA
63C1 **Tulsa** USA
72C3 **Tuluá** Colombia
40C3 **Tulūl ash Shāmīyah** *Desert Region* Iran/Syria
25M4 **Tulun** Russian Federation
72C3 **Tumaco** Colombia
25R3 **Tumany** Russian Federation
34C3 **Tumbarumba** Australia
72B4 **Tumbes** Ecuador
28B2 **Tumen** China
28B2 **Tumen** *R* China/N Korea
44B3 **Tumkūr** India
30C4 **Tumpat** Malaysia
42D4 **Tumsar** India
48B3 **Tumu** Ghana
73H3 **Tumucumaque, Serra** *Mts* Brazil
34C3 **Tumut** Australia
34C3 **Tumut** *R* Australia
69L1 **Tunapuna** Trinidad
7E4 **Tunbridge Wells, Royal** England
40C2 **Tunceli** Turkey
51D4 **Tunduma** Zambia
51D5 **Tunduru** Tanzania
17F2 **Tundzha** *R* Bulgaria
44B2 **Tungabhadra** *R* India
26E4 **Tungkang** Taiwan
12B2 **Tungnafellsjökull** *Mts* Iceland
25M3 **Tunguska** *R* Russian Federation
44C2 **Tuni** India
16C3 **Tunis** Tunisia
16C3 **Tunis, G de** Tunisia
48C1 **Tunisia** *Republic* N Africa
72D2 **Tunja** Colombia
68C2 **Tunkhannock** USA
Tunxi = Huangshan
66C2 **Tuolumne Meadows** USA
75B3 **Tupā** Brazil
75C2 **Tupaciguara** Brazil
63E2 **Tupelo** USA
19G1 **Tupik** Russian Federation
72E8 **Tupiza** Bolivia
66C3 **Tupman** USA
65E2 **Tupper Lake** USA
74C4 **Tupungato** *Mt* Argentina
43L3 **Tura** India
25L3 **Tura** Russian Federation
20L4 **Tura** *R* Russian Federation
41G2 **Turān** Iran
25L4 **Turan** Russian Federation
40C3 **Turayf** Saudi Arabia
38E3 **Turbat** Pakistan
72C2 **Turbo** Colombia
17E1 **Turda** Romania
24K5 **Turfan Depression** China
24H5 **Turgay** Kazakhstan
25L5 **Turgen Uul** *Mt* Mongolia
40A2 **Turgutlu** Turkey
40C1 **Turhal** Turkey
12K7 **Türi** Estonia
15B2 **Turia** *R* Spain
16B1 **Turin** Italy
20L4 **Turinsk** Russian Federation
26G2 **Turiy Rog** Russian Federation
50D3 **Turkana, L** Ethiopia/Kenya
38E1 **Turkestan** *Region* C Asia
40C2 **Turkey** *Republic* W Asia
38D1 **Turkmenistan** *Republic* Asia
41F2 **Turkmenskiy Zaliv** *B* Turkmenistan
69C2 **Turks Is** Caribbean Sea
12J6 **Turku** Finland
50D3 **Turkwel** *R* Kenya
66B2 **Turlock** USA
66B2 **Turlock L** USA
35C2 **Turnagain,C** New Zealand
70D3 **Turneffe I** Belize
68D1 **Turners Falls** USA
13C2 **Turnhout** Belgium
17E2 **Turnu Măgurele** Romania
17E2 **Turnu-Severin** Romania
25K5 **Turpan** China
69B2 **Turquino** *Mt* Cuba
8D3 **Turriff** Scotland
38E1 **Turtkul'** Uzbekistan
61D3 **Turtle Creek Res** USA
25K3 **Turukhansk** Russian Federation
26D1 **Turuntayevo** Russian Federation
75B2 **Turvo** *R* Goias, Brazil
75C3 **Turvo** *R* São Paulo, Brazil
19E2 **Tur'ya** *R* Ukraine
63E2 **Tuscaloosa** USA
68B2 **Tuscarora Mt** USA
64B3 **Tuscola** Illinois, USA
62C2 **Tuscola** Texas, USA
63E2 **Tuscumbia** USA
41G3 **Tusharīk** Iran
68A2 **Tussey Mt** USA
Tutera = Tudela
44B4 **Tuticorin** India
17F2 **Tutrakan** Bulgaria
18B3 **Tuttlingen** Germany
33H2 **Tutuila** *I* American Samoa
26D2 **Tuul Gol** *R* Mongolia
25L4 **Tuva Republic** Russian Federation
33G1 **Tuvalu** *Is* Pacific Ocean
45C4 **Tuwayīlel Hāj** *Mt* Jordan
70B2 **Tuxpan** Mexico
70C2 **Tuxpan** Mexico
70C3 **Tuxtla Gutiérrez** Mexico
15A1 **Túy** Spain
30D3 **Tuy Hoa** Vietnam
40B2 **Tuz Gölü** *Salt L* Turkey
41D3 **Tuz Khurmātū** Iraq
17D2 **Tuzla** Bosnia-Herzegovina
20F4 **Tver'** Russian Federation
8D4 **Tweed** *R* England/Scotland
34D1 **Tweed Heads** Australia
8D4 **Tweedsmuir Hills** Scotland
59C4 **Twentynine Palms** USA
55N5 **Twillingate** Canada
58D1 **Twin Bridges** USA
62B2 **Twin Buttes Res** USA
58D2 **Twin Falls** USA
35B2 **Twins,The** *Mt* New Zealand
66B3 **Twitchell Res** USA
64A1 **Two Harbors** USA
58D1 **Two Medicine** *R* USA
64B2 **Two Rivers** USA
25O4 **Tygda** Russian Federation
63C2 **Tyler** USA
26H1 **Tymovskoye** Russian Federation
26F1 **Tynda** Russian Federation
6D2 **Tyne** *R* England
6D2 **Tyne and Wear** *Metropolitan County* England
6D2 **Tynemouth** England
12G6 **Tynset** Norway
Tyr = Tyre
45C2 **Tyre** Lebanon
62A2 **Tyrone** New Mexico, USA
68A2 **Tyrone** Pennsylvania, USA
9C2 **Tyrone** *County* Northern Ireland
34B3 **Tyrrell,L** Australia
16C2 **Tyrrhenian S** Italy
21J7 **Tyuleni, Ova** *Is* Kazakhstan
24H4 **Tyumen'** Russian Federation
25O3 **Tyung** *R* Russian Federation
7B3 **Tywyn** Wales
47E1 **Tzaneen** South Africa
17E3 **Tzoumérka** *Mt* Greece

U

75D3 **Ubá** Brazil
75D2 **Ubaí** Brazil
75E1 **Ubaitaba** Brazil
50B3 **Ubangi** *R* Central African Republic/Congo/Zaïre
40D3 **Ubayyid, Wadi al** *Watercourse* Iraq
28B4 **Ube** Japan
15B2 **Ubeda** Spain
55N2 **Ubekendt Ejland** *I* Greenland
75C2 **Uberaba** Brazil
75A2 **Uberaba, Lagoa** Brazil
75C2 **Uberlândia** Brazil
30D2 **Ubon Ratchathani** Thailand
19F2 **Ubort** *R* Belarus
50C4 **Ubundu** Zaïre
72D5 **Ucayali** *R* Peru
42C3 **Uch** Pakistan
25P4 **Uchar** *R* Russian Federation
29E2 **Uchiura-wan** *B* Japan
13E1 **Uchte** Germany
58A1 **Ucluelet** Canada
25L4 **Uda** *R* Russian Federation
42C4 **Udaipur** India
43F3 **Udaipur Garhi** Nepal
12G7 **Uddevalla** Sweden
12H5 **Uddjaur** *L* Sweden
44B2 **Udgir** India
42D2 **Udhampur** India
16C1 **Udine** Italy
20J4 **Udmurt Republic** Russian Federation
30C2 **Udon Thani** Thailand
25P4 **Udskaya Guba** *B* Russian Federation
44A3 **Udupi** India
25N2 **Udzha** Russian Federation
29C3 **Ueda** Japan
50C3 **Uele** *R* Zaïre
25U3 **Uelen** Russian Federation
18C2 **Uelzen** Germany
50C3 **Uere** *R* Zaïre
20K5 **Ufa** Russian Federation
20K4 **Ufa** *R* Russian Federation
51B6 **Ugab** *R* Namibia
50D4 **Ugaila** *R* Tanzania
50D3 **Uganda** *Republic* Africa
45C3 **'Ugeiqa, Wadi** Jordan
26H2 **Uglegorsk** Russian Federation
20F4 **Uglich** Russian Federation
28C2 **Uglovoye** Russian Federation
20F5 **Ugra** *R* Russian Federation
8B3 **Uig** Scotland
51B4 **Uige** Angola
28A3 **Ŭijŏngbu** S Korea
21J6 **Uil** Kazakhstan
58D2 **Uinta Mts** USA
28A3 **Ŭiryŏng** S Korea
28A3 **Uisŏng** S Korea
47D3 **Uitenhage** South Africa
19E3 **Újfehértó** Hungary
29C4 **Uji** Japan
50C4 **Ujiji** Tanzania
74C2 **Ujina** Chile
42D4 **Ujjain** India
32A1 **Ujung Pandang** Indonesia
50D4 **Ukerewe I** Tanzania
43G3 **Ukhrul** India
20J3 **Ukhta** Russian Federation
59B3 **Ukiah** California, USA
58C1 **Ukiah** Oregon, USA
56A3 **Ukiah** USA
19E1 **Ukmerge** Lithuania
21D6 **Ukraine** *Republic* Europe
28A4 **Uku-jima** *I* Japan
26D2 **Ulaanbaatar** Mongolia
26C2 **Ulaangom** Mongolia
31C1 **Ulaan Uul** Mongolia
Ulan Bator = Ulaanbaatar
39G1 **Ulangar Hu** *L* China
26F2 **Ulanhot** China
26D1 **Ulan Ude** Russian Federation
26C3 **Ulan Ul Hu** *L* China
25Q3 **Ul'beya** *R* Russian Federation
28B3 **Ulchin** S Korea
17D2 **Ulcinj** Montenegro, Yugoslavia
26E2 **Uldz** Mongolia
26C2 **Uliastay** Mongolia
27G5 **Ulithi** *I* Pacific Ocean
19F1 **Ulla** Belarus
34D3 **Ulladulla** Australia
8C3 **Ullapool** Scotland
12H5 **Ullsfjorden** *Inlet* Norway
6C2 **Ullswater** *L* England
28C3 **Ullung-do** *I* Japan
18C3 **Ulm** Germany
34A1 **Uloowaranie,L** Australia
28B3 **Ulsan** S Korea
9C2 **Ulster** *Region* Northern Ireland
24K5 **Ulungur He** *R* China
24K5 **Ulungur Hu** *L* China
8B3 **Ulva** *I* Scotland
6C2 **Ulverston** England
34C4 **Ulverstone** Australia
25Q4 **Ulya** *R* Russian Federation
19G3 **Ulyanovka** Ukraine
20H5 **Ul'yanovsk** Russian Federation
62B1 **Ulysses** USA
21E6 **Uman'** Ukraine
55N2 **Umanak** Greenland
43E4 **Umaria** India
42B3 **Umarkot** Pakistan
58C1 **Umatilla** USA
20E2 **Umba** Russian Federation
50D4 **Umba** *R* Kenya/Tanzania
32D1 **Umboi I** Papua New Guinea
12H6 **Ume** *R* Sweden
12J6 **Umea** Sweden
45C2 **Um ed Daraj, Jebel** *Mt* Jordan
45C4 **Um el Hashīm, Jebel** *Mt* Jordan
47E2 **Umfolozi** *R* South Africa
54C3 **Umiat** USA
45C4 **Um Ishrīn, Jebel** *Mt* Jordan
47E3 **Umkomaas** *R* South Africa
41G4 **Umm al Qaiwain** UAE
50C2 **Umm Bell** Sudan
50C2 **Umm Keddada** Sudan
40C4 **Umm Lajj** Saudi Arabia
50D2 **Umm Ruwaba** Sudan
41F5 **Umm Sa'id** Qatar
51C5 **Umniaiti** *R* Zimbabwe
58B2 **Umpqua** *R* USA
42D4 **Umred** India
Umtali = Mutare
47D3 **Umtata** South Africa
75B3 **Umuarama** Brazil
47D3 **Umzimkulu** South Africa
47E3 **Umzimkulu** *R* South Africa
47D3 **Umzimvubu** *R* South Africa
47D1 **Umzingwane** *R* Zimbabwe
75E2 **Una** Brazil
16D1 **Una** *R* Bosnia-Herzegovina/Croatia
68C1 **Unadilla** USA
68C1 **Unadilla** *R* USA
75C2 **Unaí** Brazil
54B3 **Unalakleet** USA
41D4 **Unayzah** Saudi Arabia
68D2 **Uncasville** USA
60B3 **Uncompahgre Plat** USA
47D2 **Underberg** South Africa
60C1 **Underwood** USA
20E5 **Unecha** Russian Federation
45C3 **Uneisa** Jordan
55M4 **Ungava B** Canada
28C2 **Unggi** N Korea
74F3 **União de Vitória** Brazil
63D1 **Union** Missouri, USA
67B2 **Union** S Carolina, USA
65D2 **Union City** Pennsylvania, USA
63E1 **Union City** Tennessee, USA
47C3 **Uniondale** South Africa
67A2 **Union Springs** USA
65D3 **Uniontown** USA
41F5 **United Arab Emirates** Arabian Pen
4E3 **United Kingdom of Gt Britain & N Ireland** NW Europe
53H4 **United States of America**
55K1 **United States Range** *Mts* Canada
58C2 **Unity** USA
62A2 **University Park** USA
13D2 **Unna** Germany
43E3 **Unnão** India
28A2 **Unsan** N Korea
8E1 **Unst** *I* Scotland
40C1 **Ünye** Turkey
20G4 **Unzha** *R* Russian Federation
72F2 **Upata** Venezuela
51C4 **Upemba Nat Pk** Zaïre
55N2 **Upernavik** Greenland
47C2 **Upington** South Africa
66D3 **Upland** USA
33H2 **Upolu** *I* Western Samoa
35C2 **Upper Hutt** New Zealand
58B2 **Upper Klamath L** USA
58B2 **Upper L** USA
9C2 **Upper Lough Erne** *L* Northern Ireland

Vileyka **Wāw an Nāmūs**

19F2 **Vileyka** Belarus
12H6 **Vilhelmina** Sweden
73G6 **Vilhena** Brazil
19F2 **Viliya** Belarus
20D4 **Viljandi** Estonia
47D2 **Viljoenskroon** South Africa
25L2 **Vilkitskogo, Proliv** *Str* Russian Federation
19F3 **Vilkovo** Ukraine
62A2 **Villa Ahumada** Mexico
15A1 **Villaba** Spain
16C1 **Villach** Austria
74C4 **Villa Dolores** Argentina
74E5 **Villa Gesell** Argentina
75A4 **Villa Hayes** Paraguay
70C3 **Villahermosa** Mexico
74D4 **Villa Huidobro** Argentina
74D4 **Villa María** Argentina
72F8 **Villa Montes** Bolivia
15A1 **Villa Nova de Gaia** Portugal
15A2 **Villanueva de la Serena** Spain
15C1 **Villanueva-y-Geltrú** Spain
15B2 **Villarreal** Spain
74E3 **Villarrica** Paraguay
15B2 **Villarrobledo** Spain
62B3 **Villa Unión** Coahuila, Mexico
72D3 **Villavicencio** Colombia
14C2 **Villefranche** France
55L5 **Ville-Marie** Canada
15B2 **Villena** Spain
13B3 **Villeneuve-St-Georges** France
14C3 **Villeneuve-sur-Lot** France
13B3 **Villeneuve-sur-Yonne** France
63D2 **Ville Platte** USA
13B3 **Villers-Cotterêts** France
14C2 **Villeurbanne** France
47D2 **Villiers** South Africa
13E3 **Villingen-Schwenningen** Germany
44B3 **Villupuram** India
19F2 **Vilnius** Lithuania
25N3 **Vilyuy** *R* Russian Federation
25O3 **Vilyuysk** Russian Federation
15C1 **Vinaroz** Spain
64B3 **Vincennes** USA
12H5 **Vindel** *R* Sweden
42D4 **Vindhya Range** *Mts* India
68C3 **Vineland** USA
68E2 **Vineyard Haven** USA
30D2 **Vinh** Vietnam
30D3 **Vinh Cam Ranh** *B* Vietnam
30D4 **Vinh Loi** Vietnam
30D3 **Vinh Long** Vietnam
63C1 **Vinita** USA
17D1 **Vinkovci** Croatia
19F3 **Vinnitsa** Ukraine
76F3 **Vinson Massif** *Upland* Antarctica
61E2 **Vinton** USA
74B4 **Viõna del Mar** Chile
51B5 **Virei** Angola
75D2 **Virgem da Lapa** Brazil
59D3 **Virgin** *R* USA
47D2 **Virginia** South Africa
61E1 **Virginia** USA
57F3 **Virginia** *State* USA
65D3 **Virginia Beach** USA
59C3 **Virginia City** USA
69E3 **Virgin Is** Caribbean Sea
64A2 **Viroqua** USA
16D1 **Virovitica** Croatia
13C3 **Virton** Belgium
44B4 **Virudunagar** India
16D2 **Vis** *I* Croatia
66C2 **Visalia** USA
12H7 **Visby** Sweden
54H2 **Viscount Melville Sd** Canada
17D2 **Višegrad** Bosnia-Herzegovina
15A1 **Viseu** Portugal
44C2 **Vishākhapatnam** India
20K3 **Vishera** *R* Russian Federation
16B2 **Viso, Monte** *Mt* Italy
59C4 **Vista** USA
Vistula *R* = **Wisła**
44A2 **Vite** India
19G1 **Vitebsk** Belarus
16C2 **Viterbo** Italy
15A1 **Vitigudino** Spain
25N4 **Vitim** *R* Russian Federation
73K8 **Vitória** Brazil
15B1 **Vitoria** Spain
73K6 **Vitória da Conquista** Brazil
14B2 **Vitré** France
13C3 **Vitry-le-François** France
12J5 **Vittangi** Sweden
13C3 **Vittel** France
16C3 **Vittoria** Sicily, Italy
26J2 **Vityaz Depth** Pacific Ocean
Viviero = **Vivero**
15A1 **Vivero** Spain
25L3 **Vivi** *R* Russian Federation
15B1 **Vizcaya, Golfo de** Spain
25M4 **Vizhne-Angarsk** Russian Federation
44C2 **Vizianagaram** India
20J3 **Vizinga** Russian Federation
17E1 **Vlădeasa** *Mt* Romania
21G7 **Vladikavkaz** Russian Federation
20G4 **Vladimir** Russian Federation
19E2 **Vladimir Volynskiy** Ukraine
28C2 **Vladivostok** Russian Federation
18A2 **Vlieland** *I* Netherlands
13B2 **Vlissingen** Netherlands
47B2 **Vloosdrift** South Africa
17D2 **Vlorë** Albania
18C3 **Vltara** *R* Czech Republic
18C3 **Vöcklabruck** Austria
30D3 **Voeune Sai** Cambodia
13E2 **Vogelsberg** *Region* Germany
Vohemar = **Vohimarina**
Vohibinany = **Ampasimanolotra**
51F5 **Vohimarina** Madagascar
50D4 **Voi** Kenya
48B4 **Voinjama** Liberia
14D2 **Voiron** France
17D1 **Vojvodina** *Region* Serbia, Yugoslavia
60B1 **Volborg** USA
69A5 **Volcán Barú** *Mt* Panama
Volcano Is = **Kazan Retto**
20K4 **Volchansk** Russian Federation
21H6 **Volga** *R* Russian Federation
21G6 **Volgodonsk** Russian Federation
21G6 **Volgograd** Russian Federation
21H5 **Volgogradskoye Vodokhranilishche** *Res* Russian Federation
20E4 **Volkhov** Russian Federation
20E4 **Volkhov** *R* Russian Federation
19E2 **Volkovysk** Belarus
47D2 **Volksrust** South Africa
25L2 **Volochanka** Russian Federation
20G4 **Vologda** Russian Federation
17E3 **Vólos** Greece
21H5 **Vol'sk** Russian Federation
66B2 **Volta** USA
48B3 **Volta Blanche** *R* Burkina/Ghana
48B4 **Volta, L** Ghana
48B3 **Volta Noire** *R* W Africa
75D3 **Volta Redonda** Brazil
48B3 **Volta Rouge** *R* Burkina/Ghana
21G6 **Volzhskiy** Russian Federation
20F3 **Vonguda** Russian Federation
55R3 **Vopnafjörður** Iceland
18C1 **Vordingborg** Denmark
21C8 **Voriái** *I* Greece
20L2 **Vorkuta** Russian Federation
12G6 **Vorma** *R* Norway
21F5 **Voronezh** Russian Federation
12M5 **Voron'ya** *R* Russian Federation
21F6 **Voroshilovgrad** Ukraine
12K7 **Võru** Estonia
13D3 **Vosges** *Department* France
14D2 **Vosges** *Mts* France
12F6 **Voss** Norway
25L4 **Vostochnyy Sayan** *Mts* Russian Federation
76F9 **Vostok** *Base* Antarctica
20J4 **Votkinsk** Russian Federation
13C3 **Vouziers** France
61E1 **Voyageurs Nat Pk** USA
20K3 **Voy Vozh** Russian Federation
21E6 **Voznesensk** Ukraine
17E2 **Vranje** Serbia, Yugoslavia
17E2 **Vratsa** Bulgaria
17D1 **Vrbas** Serbia, Yugoslavia
16D2 **Vrbas** *R* Bosnia-Herzegovina
16C1 **Vrbovsko** Croatia
47D2 **Vrede** South Africa
47B3 **Vredendal** South Africa
73G2 **Vreed en Hoop** Guyana
44B3 **Vriddhāchalam** India
17E1 **Vršac** Serbia, Yugoslavia
16D2 **Vrtoče** Bosnia-Herzegovina
47C2 **Vryburg** South Africa
47E2 **Vryheid** South Africa
17D1 **Vukovar** Croatia
20K3 **Vuktyl'** Russian Federation
7F3 **Vulcan** *Oilfield* N Sea
16C3 **Vulcano** *I* Italy
30D3 **Vung Tau** Vietnam
12J5 **Vuollerim** Sweden
20E3 **Vyartsilya** Russian Federation
20J4 **Vyatka** *R* Russian Federation
26G2 **Vyazemskiy** Russian Federation
20E4 **Vyaz'ma** Russian Federation
20G4 **Vyazniki** Russian Federation
20D3 **Vyborg** Russian Federation
20F3 **Vygozero, Ozero** *L* Russian Federation
20J3 **Vym** *R* Russian Federation
7C3 **Vyrnwy** *R* Wales
20E4 **Vyshniy-Volochek** Russian Federation
18D3 **Vyškov** Czech Republic
20F3 **Vytegra** Russian Federation

W

48B3 **Wa** Ghana
13C2 **Waal** *R* Netherlands
54G4 **Wabasca** *R* Canada
64B2 **Wabash** USA
64B3 **Wabash** *R* USA
64C1 **Wabatongushi L** Canada
54J4 **Wabowden** Canada
55M4 **Wabush** Canada
67B3 **Waccasassa B** USA
68E1 **Wachusett Res** USA
63C2 **Waco** USA
42B3 **Wad** Pakistan
49D2 **Waddān** Libya
13C1 **Waddenzee** *S* Netherlands
54F4 **Waddington,Mt** Canada
7B4 **Wadebridge** England
61D1 **Wadena** USA
45C3 **Wadi es Sir** Jordan
50D1 **Wadi Halfa** Sudan
45C3 **Wādi Mūsā** Jordan
50D2 **Wad Medani** Sudan
28A3 **Waegwan** S Korea
28A2 **Wafang** China
41E4 **Wafra** Kuwait
13C2 **Wageningen** Netherlands
55K3 **Wager B** Canada
55J3 **Wager Bay** Canada
34C3 **Wagga Wagga** Australia
32A4 **Wagin** Australia
61D2 **Wagner** USA
66E5 **Wahiawa** Hawaiian Islands
61D2 **Wahoo** USA
61D1 **Wahpeton** USA
44A2 **Wai** India
66E5 **Waialua** Hawaiian Islands
35B2 **Waiau** New Zealand
35B2 **Waiau** *R* New Zealand
27G6 **Waigeo** *I* Indonesia
35C1 **Waihi** New Zealand
35C1 **Waikaremoana,L** New Zealand
35C1 **Waikato** *R* New Zealand
34A2 **Waikerie** Australia
35B3 **Waikouaiti** New Zealand
66E5 **Wailuku** Hawaiian Islands
35B2 **Waimakariri** *R* New Zealand
35B2 **Waimate** New Zealand
66E5 **Waimea** Hawaiian Islands
32B1 **Waingapu** Indonesia
54G4 **Wainwright** Canada
54B2 **Wainwright** USA
35C1 **Waioura** New Zealand
35B2 **Waipara** New Zealand
35C2 **Waipukurau** New Zealand
35C2 **Wairarapa,L** New Zealand
35B2 **Wairau** *R* New Zealand
35C1 **Wairoa** New Zealand
35C1 **Wairoa** *R* New Zealand
35B2 **Waitaki** *R* New Zealand
35B1 **Waitara** New Zealand
35C1 **Waitomo** New Zealand
35B1 **Waiuku** New Zealand
29C3 **Wajima** Japan
50E3 **Wajir** Kenya
29C3 **Wakasa-wan** *B* Japan
35A3 **Wakatipu,L** New Zealand
29D4 **Wakayama** Japan
60D3 **Wa Keeney** USA
7D3 **Wakefield** England
69H1 **Wakefield** Jamaica
64B1 **Wakefield** Michigan, USA
68E2 **Wakefield** Rhode Island, USA
30B2 **Wakema** Burma
29E1 **Wakkanai** Japan
34B3 **Wakool** *R* Australia
18D2 **Wałbrzych** Poland
34D2 **Walcha** Australia
18D2 **Wałcz** Poland
13D2 **Waldbröl** Germany
68C2 **Walden** USA
13E4 **Waldshut** Germany
54B3 **Wales** USA
7C3 **Wales** *Principality* U K
55K3 **Wales I** Canada
34C2 **Walgett** Australia
76F4 **Walgreen Coast** *Region* Antarctica
50C4 **Walikale** Zaïre
61E1 **Walker** USA
66C1 **Walker L** USA
66C3 **Walker Pass** USA
64C2 **Walkerton** Canada
60C2 **Wall** USA
58C1 **Wallace** USA
32C4 **Wallaroo** Australia
34C3 **Walla Walla** Australia
58C1 **Walla Walla** USA
68D2 **Wallingford** USA
37K5 **Wallis and Futuna** *Is* Pacific Ocean
33H2 **Wallis, Îles** Pacific Ocean
58C1 **Wallowa** USA
58C1 **Wallowa Mts** USA
34C1 **Wallumbilla** Australia
6C2 **Walney** *I* England
63D1 **Walnut Ridge** USA
68D1 **Walpole** USA
7D3 **Walsall** England
62B1 **Walsenburg** USA
67B2 **Walterboro** USA
67A2 **Walter F George Res** USA
62C2 **Walters** USA
68E1 **Waltham** USA
68C1 **Walton** USA
7E4 **Walton-on-the Naze** England
47A1 **Walvis Bay** Namibia
52J6 **Walvis Ridge** Atlantic Ocean
48C4 **Wamba** Nigeria
50B4 **Wamba** *R* Zaïre
61D3 **Wamego** USA
58E2 **Wamsutter** USA
42B2 **Wana** Pakistan
34B1 **Wanaaring** Australia
35A2 **Wanaka** New Zealand
35A2 **Wanaka,L** New Zealand
64C1 **Wanapitei L** Canada
28A4 **Wando** S Korea
34C1 **Wandoan** Australia
34B3 **Wanganella** Australia
35B1 **Wanganui** New Zealand
35C1 **Wanganui** *R* New Zealand
34C3 **Wangaratta** Australia
13D1 **Wangerooge** *I* Germany
28B2 **Wangqing** China
28A3 **Wanjialing** China
Wankie = **Hwange**
50E3 **Wanleweyne** Somalia
30E2 **Wanning** China
44B2 **Wanparti** India
6D2 **Wansbeck, R** England
7D4 **Wantage** England
31B3 **Wanxian** China
31B3 **Wanyuan** China
63D1 **Wappapello,L** USA
68D2 **Wappingers Falls** USA
61E2 **Wapsipinicon** *R* USA
44B2 **Warangal** India
34C4 **Waratah** Australia
34C3 **Waratah B** Australia
13E2 **Warburg** Germany
34C3 **Warburton** Australia
34C1 **Ward** *R* Australia
47D2 **Warden** South Africa
42D4 **Wardha** India
35A3 **Ward,Mt** New Zealand
54F4 **Ware** Canada
68D1 **Ware** USA
7C4 **Wareham** England
68E2 **Wareham** USA
13D2 **Warendorf** Germany
34D1 **Warialda** Australia
30D2 **Warin Chamrap** Thailand
47B2 **Warmbad** Namibia
51C6 **Warmbad** South Africa
7C4 **Warminster** England
68C2 **Warminster** USA
59C3 **Warm Springs** USA
18C2 **Warnemünde** Germany
58B2 **Warner Mts** USA
67B2 **Warner Robins** USA
34B3 **Warracknabeal** Australia
32D3 **Warrego** *R* Australia
63D2 **Warren** Arkansas, USA
34C2 **Warren** Australia
61D1 **Warren** Minnesota, USA
64C2 **Warren** Ohio, USA
65D2 **Warren** Pennsylvania, USA
68E2 **Warren** Rhode Island, USA
9C2 **Warrenpoint** Northern Ireland
61E3 **Warrensburg** USA
47C2 **Warrenton** South Africa
65D3 **Warrenton** USA
48C4 **Warri** Nigeria
7C3 **Warrington** England
63E2 **Warrington** USA
34B3 **Warrnambool** Australia
61D1 **Warroad** USA
19E2 **Warsaw** Poland
68A1 **Warsaw** USA
50E3 **Warshiikh** Somalia
Warszawa = **Warsaw**
19D2 **Warta** *R* Poland
34D1 **Warwick** Australia
7D3 **Warwick** England
68C2 **Warwick** New York, USA
68E2 **Warwick** Rhode Island, USA
7D3 **Warwick** *County* England
59D3 **Wasatch Range** *Mts* USA
47E2 **Wasbank** South Africa
66C3 **Wasco** USA
61E2 **Waseca** USA
64A1 **Washburn** USA
54H2 **Washburn L** Canada
58D2 **Washburn,Mt** USA
42D4 **Wāshīm** India
57F3 **Washington** District of Columbia, USA
67B2 **Washington** Georgia, USA
64B3 **Washington** Indiana, USA
61E2 **Washington** Iowa, USA
61E3 **Washington** Missouri, USA
67C1 **Washington** N Carolina, USA
68C2 **Washington** New Jersey, USA
64C2 **Washington** Pennsylvania, USA
59D3 **Washington** Utah, USA
56A2 **Washington** *State* USA
64C3 **Washington Court House** USA
55M1 **Washington Land** *Region* Canada
65E2 **Washington,Mt** USA
62C1 **Washita** *R* USA
7E3 **Wash,The** *B* England
42A3 **Washuk** Pakistan
51L4 **Waskaganish** Canada
69A4 **Waspán** Nicaragua
66C1 **Wassuk Range** *Mts* USA
13C3 **Wassy** France
27F7 **Watampone** Indonesia
47D3 **Waterberge** *Mts* South Africa
68D2 **Waterbury** USA
10B3 **Waterford** Irish Republic
9C3 **Waterford** *County* Irish Republic
9C3 **Waterford Harbour** Irish Republic
13C2 **Waterloo** Belgium
61E2 **Waterloo** USA
64B1 **Watersmeet** USA
58D1 **Waterton-Glacier International Peace Park** USA
65D2 **Watertown** New York, USA
61D2 **Watertown** S Dakota, USA
64B2 **Watertown** Wisconsin, USA
47E2 **Waterval-Boven** South Africa
65F2 **Waterville** Maine, USA
68C1 **Waterville** New York, USA
68D1 **Watervliet** USA
54G4 **Waterways** Canada
7D4 **Watford** England
60C1 **Watford City** USA
68B1 **Watkins Glen** USA
62C1 **Watonga** USA
56C1 **Watrous** Canada
62B1 **Watrous** USA
50C3 **Watsa** Zaïre
54F3 **Watson Lake** Canada
66B2 **Watsonville** USA
27H7 **Wau** Papua New Guinea
50C3 **Wau** Sudan
34D2 **Wauchope** Australia
67B3 **Wauchula** USA
64B2 **Waukegan** USA
64B2 **Waukesha** USA
64B2 **Waupaca** USA
64B2 **Waupun** USA
63C2 **Waurika** USA
64B2 **Wausau** USA
64B2 **Wauwatosa** USA
32C2 **Wave Hill** Australia
7E3 **Waveney** *R* England
60E2 **Waverly** Iowa, USA
68B1 **Waverly** New York, USA
64C3 **Waverly** Ohio, USA
13C2 **Wavre** Belgium
64C1 **Wawa** Canada
49D2 **Wāw Al Kabīr** Libya
49D2 **Wāw an Nāmūs** *Well* Libya

ACKNOWLEDGEMENTS

PICTURE CREDITS
The sources for the photographs and illustrations appearing in the atlas are listed below.

page

48-61   Physical maps by Duncan Mackay, copyright © Times Books., London

62   *Mercury* NSSDC/NASA
Venus NASA/Science Photo Library
Mars NASA/Science Photo Library
Neptune NASA/Science Photo Library
Uranus Jet Propulsion Laboratory/NASA
Saturn NASA

63   *Rock and Hydrological Cycles* Encyclopaedia Universalis Editeur, Paris

90   *Manhattan* Adapted from map by Nicholson Publications Ltd.

94-99   Robert Harding Picture Library Ltd.

Rear Endpaper   G.L. Fitzpatrick and M.J. Modlin: *Direct Line Distances. International Edition* Metuchen N.J. and London, 1986

Cities (diagonal labels): ABU DHABI, AMSTERDAM, ATHENS, AUCKLAND, BANGKOK, BARCELONA, BEIJING, BERLIN, BOMBAY, BOSTON, BRUSSELS, BUENOS AIRES, CAIRO, CALCUTTA, CAPE TOWN, CHICAGO, COPENHAGEN, DELHI, GENEVA, HAMBURG, HONG KONG, HONOLULU, ISTANBUL, JERUSALEM, LONDON, LOS ANGELES

5167	3260	14244	4975	5142	5972	4637	2003	10735	5158	13534	2367	3471	7498	11688	4845	2317	4903	4892	6071	13865	2987	2043	5478		
	2164	18728	9185	1237	7841	577	6864	5575	174	11424	3282	7620	9647	6628	623	6368	690	367	9300	11676	2213	3350	359		
		16775	7933	1822	7633	1803	5179	7639	2092	11677	1120	6325	7979	8765	2136	5019	1710	2026	8560	13439	562	1256	2394		
			9566	19204	10388	17743	12294	14478	18279	10372	16573	11176	11796	13181	17525	12482	18609	17813	9121	7052	17042	16287	18330		
3211				9692	3291	8613	3010	13733	9263	16885	7279	1610	10144	13789	8628	2917	9249	8824	1723	10634	7477	6895	9544		
2026	1345				8822	1500	7044	5881	1063	10447	2897	8084	8502	7101	1760	6782	624	1473	10087	12766	2238	3122	1138		
8851	11637	10424				7375	4760	10860	7983	19265	7557	3271	12947	10626	7218	3788	8223	7492	1972	8171	7072	7135	8160		
3091	5707	4930	5944				6298	6098	654	11890	2891	7045	9588	7103	355	5791	876	255	8770	11782	1739	2903	934		
3195	769	1132	11933	6023				12275	6891	14937	4363	1664	8216	12976	6430	1156	6725	6544	4311	12928	4818	4017	7205		
3711	4872	4743	6455	2045	5482				5598	8619	8737	12517	12411	1369	5904	11504	5929	5843	12831	8191	7783	8884	5280		
2881	358	1120	11025	5352	932	4583				11282	3212	7689	9490	6679	769	6427	533	491	9416	11825	2185	3302	320		
1245	4265	3218	7639	1870	4377	2958	3914				11811	16535	6891	8978	12046	15800	11045	11773	18463	12160	12235	12236	11105		
6671	3464	4747	8996	8534	3654	6748	3789	7628				5708	7208	9881	3206	4436	2816	3125	8158	14239	1234	426	3513		
3205	108	1300	11358	5756	661	4961	406	4282	3479				9684	12861	7083	1307	7651	7264	2654	11357	5867	5314	7978		
8410	7099	7256	6445	10492	6492	11971	7388	9282	5356	7011				13658	9942	9284	8958	9725	11867	18562	8367	7481	9635		
1471	2039	696	10298	4523	1800	4696	1796	2711	5429	1996	7339				6860	12047	7069	6850	12560	6849	8834	9978	6371		
2157	4735	3930	6945	1000	5023	2033	4378	1034	7778	4778	10275	3547				5857	1145	289	8688	11428	2021	3191	958		
4659	5995	4958	7330	6303	5283	8045	5958	5105	7712	5897	4282	4479	6018				6363	6020	3770	11930	4560	4032	6724		
7263	4119	5447	8191	8568	4413	6603	4414	8063	851	4150	5579	6140	7992	8487				862	9544	12358	1921	2959	748		
3011	387	1327	10890	5361	1094	4485	221	3996	3669	478	7485	1992	4401	6178	4263				8934	11629	1988	3150	723		
1440	3957	3119	7756	1813	4214	2354	3599	718	7148	3994	9818	2757	812	5769	7486	3640				8945	8034	7740	9646		
3047	429	1063	11563	5747	388	5110	544	4179	3684	331	6863	1750	4754	5566	4393	712	3954				13068	13969	11653		
3040	228	1259	11069	5483	915	4655	159	4066	3631	305	7291	1942	4514	6043	4257	180	3741	536				1170	2504		
3772	5779	5319	5668	1071	6268	1225	5450	2679	7973	5851	11473	5069	1649	7374	7805	5399	2343	5931	5552				3615		
8616	7255	8351	4382	6608	7933	5077	7321	8033	5090	7348	7556	8848	7057	11534	4256	7101	7413	7679	7226	5558					
1856	1375	349	10590	4646	1391	4394	1081	2994	4836	1358	7603	767	3646	5199	5489	1256	2834	1194	1235	4992	8120				
1270	2082	781	10121	4285	1940	4434	1804	2496	5520	2052	7603	265	3302	4649	6200	1983	2505	1839	1957	4810	8680	727			
3404	223	1488	11390	5931	707	5071	580	4477	3281	199	6901	2183	4957	5987	3959	595	4178	465	449	5994	7241	1556	2246		
8377	5570	6909	6512	8276	6013	6265	5799	8713	2597	5627	6107	7595	8166	9976	1746	5609	8005	5915	5653	7254	2563	6862	7587	5455	
3500	921	1475	12174	6336	314	5744	1163	4688	3410	818	6229	2085	5337	5304	4191	1289	4529	637	1111	6562	7874	1705	2238	785	5833
7263	10280	9289	1634	4573	10458	5650	9924	6096	10521	10325	7226	8678	5547	6424	9673	9930	6333	10271	10057	4593	5507	9090	8521	10503	7930
8932	5739	7024	6802	9739	5909	7754	6056	9739	2279	5757	4577	7700	9504	8515	1691	5921	9121	5962	5898	8796	3789	7114	7800	5560	1549
2893	514	910	11482	5614	452	5031	523	4029	3838	434	6943	1599	4619	5493	4542	720	3816	155	560	5823	7764	1041	1685	597	6051
6616	3428	4737	8935	8337	3677	6518	3740	7522	251	3451	5593	5427	7615	7919	744	3606	7013	3677	3581	7744	4918	4803	5502	3256	2469
2321	1337	1386	10063	4393	1873	3610	1002	3129	4498	1404	8365	1801	3443	6277	4984	971	2702	1504	1109	4672	7048	1091	1660	1557	6085
2126	4133	2828	8678	4485	3652	5727	3948	2816	7190	4066	6472	2186	3839	2542	8010	4155	3373	3764	4080	5449	10741	2952	2276	4229	9664
6860	3654	4937	8816	8668	3842	6843	3979	7808	191	3669	5276	5618	7936	7799	713	3857	7319	3874	3820	8068	4969	5026	5711	3471	2451
4808	5742	5797	5532	2615	6421	1110	5494	3956	6871	5840	9786	5796	2955	8906	6500	5363	3415	6036	5541	1549	4104	5448	5535	5919	5724
6692	3512	4825	8835	8353	3772	6509	3820	7582	313	3536	5612	5516	7649	8010	645	3682	7061	3766	3661	7734	4819	4887	5588	3342	2366
3260	266	1306	11521	5877	517	5118	547	4365	3446	163	6853	1998	4892	5783	4143	639	4102	257	464	5996	7449	1405	2075	212	5658
5614	8779	7628	3312	3301	8788	4944	8427	4514	11621	8793	7839	6992	4163	5416	10979	8499	4877	8660	8579	3728	6777	7467	6850	8989	9337
7310	5937	6033	7636	9993	5294	10766	6207	8338	4829	5844	1223	6141	9372	3775	5284	6321	8749	5673	6147	11005	8291	6380	6405	5750	6294
2674	804	655	11433	5494	534	5061	735	3845	4102	729	6919	1327	4495	5230	4821	951	3684	433	813	5779	8038	857	1435	891	6346
8145	5468	6792	6517	7930	5963	5918	567	8405	2699	5532	6453	7466	7828	10245	1859	5474	7693	5833	5533	6910	4261	672	7436	5369	347
9097	7452	7797	6021	10968	6923	11842	7772	9984	5217	7375	705	7954	10961	4946	5294	7835	10518	7274	7677	11607	6861	8136	2005	7240	5578
7527	6077	6221	7483	10196	5452	10933	6356	8558	4795	5985	1044	6345	9592	3949	5209	6462	8967	5826	6290	11221	8090	6567	6610	5885	6149
4299	5332	5305	5963	2312	5982	595	5064	3488	6815	5425	12073	5284	2514	8519	6546	4948	2920	5601	5123	1303	4549	4956	5023	5519	5968
4068	5530	5318	5815	1784	6119	669	5233	3131	7314	5616	12190	5199	2113	8053	7081	5143	2640	5753	5310	755	4955	4973	4934	5731	6507
3669	6526	5629	5227	887	6767	2775	6169	2428	9410	6566	9873	5139	1794	6009	9375	6195	2574	6525	6306	1600	6726	5376	4924	6748	8784
2978	701	1497	10565	5143	1417	4179	505	3878	3753	799	7793	2115	4204	6421	4286	325	3467	1032	505	5122	6872	1352	2064	892	5531
6085	2875	9523	1343	4675	10677	5545	9998	6305	10092	10404	7345	8957	5668	6856	9242	9963	6472	10422	10111	4566	5065	9286	8778	10557	7497
5018	5788	5922	5475	2865	6487	1307	5556	4195	6718	5888	11412	5957	3200	9157	6311	5415	3640	6101	5594	1798	3858	5574	5699	5956	5486
6905	3728	5044	8624	8480	3989	6594	4035	7777	431	3754	5545	5734	7810	8134	437	3896	7243	3985	3877	7815	4659	5103	5806	3560	2176
2635	582	797	11094	5251	1026	4647	326	3721	4045	570	7328	1480	4262	5653	4698	541	3465	500	462	5437	7634	794	1504	769	6116
7063	3858	5141	8621	8806	4044	6941	4181	8002	395	3873	5194	5822	8102	7892	595	4058	7501	4075	4023	8163	4838	5231	5915	3676	2300

MILES